The University
of

14 Store St

WC1E 7D

Immigration A
Remedies Handbook

Immigration Appeals and Remedies Handbook

Mark Symes, BA (Hons) (Oxon)
of Lincoln's Inn, Barrister

Peter Jorro, LLB
of Lincoln's Inn, Barrister

Bloomsbury Professional

Bloomsbury Professional Limited, Maxwelton House, 41–43 Boltro Road, Haywards Heath, West Sussex, RH16 1BJ

© Bloomsbury Professional Ltd 2015

Reprinted 2016

A CIP Catalogue record for this book is available from the British Library.

ISBN 978 1 78043 656 2

Typeset by Phoenix Photosetting, Chatham, Kent
Printed and bound in Great Britain by CPI Group (UK) Ltd, Croydon, CR0 4YY

Foreword

It has been my great pleasure to peruse the text of this work. Its arrival will be welcomed by practitioners and judges alike. In the increasingly complex and voluminous world of immigration law, this will be an invaluable addition to the armoury of all. Its layout is logical, convenient and user friendly. It contains an enviable, but indispensable, mix of key provisions of immigration legislation, salient provisions of the Immigration Rules and relevant legal principles. It also rehearses, where appropriate, the occasionally neglected instruments which apply to the daily decision making of tribunals, namely their rules of procedure and Practice Directions. The breakdown of every chapter demonstrates that the authors have gone to great lengths in their endeavours to leave no stone unturned. Furthermore, the admirable layout, in particular the punchy and informative cross headings, ensures that sections dealing with discrete issues and their offshoots are readily identified, leading to speedy problem solving. The treatment of case law is appropriately sparing – a positive virtue nowadays – given the nature and purposes of the publication. The advent of this excellent text could not have been better timed, having regard to the significant constitutional changes in the Upper Tribunal (Immigration and Asylum Chamber) introduced in November 2013 and the major innovations and reforms effected by the Immigration Act 2014. This is, ultimately, a lawyer's handbook and a compulsory addition to the library of every immigration judge and practitioner.

Bernard McCloskey

President, Upper Tribunal,
Immigration and Asylum Chamber

Preface

This book has been written over the months from November 2014 into April 2015 during the transitional period in which the changes to the immigration appeals system wrought by the Immigration Act 2014 have come into effect. These amendments have brought about the most wide-ranging and fundamental changes to the statutory system of immigration appeals since their inception in the Immigration Appeals Act 1969. From a system that provided for a right of appeal, albeit with limitations and restrictions, against an immigration decision, the Immigration Act 2014 has radically changed matters to a system providing for a right of appeal, again with limitations and restrictions, against refusals of asylum or 'protection' and human rights claims.

In so doing the coalition government purported to be reducing the number of rights of appeal available to migrants, in particular to so-called 'foreign criminals', from 17 to just four. This is nonsense. As can be seen in Chapter 3, the reality is that albeit under the former system there were 17 different types of decisions against which an appeal could be lodged (whether from within or only from without the UK), any given individual, 'foreign criminal' or otherwise, could only ever appeal against the actual decision, or at most two decisions, taken in his own particular case. In terms of the number of 'rights of appeal' that a given individual has, this remains at best one – if at all, a right of appeal to the First-tier Tribunal, Immigration and Asylum Chamber. Further rights of appeal, onwards to the Upper Tribunal, Court of Appeal and Supreme Court (as to all of which, see Chapter 6) depend on grants of permission to appeal and are unaffected by the amendments brought by the Immigration Act 2014.

Subject to transitional cases, the judges of the First-tier Tribunal will now only deal with appeals in asylum or protection and human rights cases and in respect to EEA decisions (as to which see Chapters 1 and 4). Challenges against immigration decisions on non-protection and non-human rights grounds will have to be brought by way of administrative review (see Chapter 9) and then by judicial review in the Upper Tribunal (see Chapter 8). In cases where decisions are made against a person on national security related grounds, an appeal or review can be brought in the Special Immigration Appeals Commission (see Chapter 7).

The book is structured as follows. Chapter 1 introduces the kinds of immigration decisions against which an appeal or review can or could be brought. Chapters 2 and 3 explain the development of the right of appeal in immigration cases up to the system in place, and still with effect in transitional cases, immediately prior to the amendments brought about by the Immigration Act 2014. Chapter 4 addresses rights of appeal, and limitations thereon, to the

First-tier Tribunal and Chapter 5 deals with practice, procedure and evidence in appeals before that tribunal. Chapter 6 explains onward rights of appeal to the Upper Tribunal, Court of Appeal and Supreme Court and practice and procedures thereon. Chapter 7 is dedicated to the Special Immigration Appeals Commission. Chapter 8 addresses judicial review, both in the Upper Tribunal and the High Court. And finally Chapter 9 explains the novel provisions relating to 'administrative review'.

As mentioned above, the book has been written during the transitional period, and so certain re-writes have been required as we went along owing to the then government's rather piecemeal introduction of the new appeals provisions as broadly staged from 20 October 2014 to 6 April 2015. The reason, of course, as to why it has taken us quite so long to write this book is that we both have busy practices as barristers at Garden Court Chambers. The book is intended principally as a practitioners' and decision makers' guide.

The law is stated as at 6 April 2015, although some subsequent developments and case law from the latter part of April have been mentioned. However, with regard to the amendments brought about by the Criminal Justice and Courts Act 2015, ss 62–66, providing for 'leap-frog' appeals direct to the Supreme Court from *inter alia* judgments and determinations of the High Court, the Upper Tribunal and the Special Immigration Appeals Commission, these have only been addressed, at the end of Chapter 6, in respect to such appeals from the High Court as the provisions relating to such appeals from the Upper Tribunal and the Special Immigration Appeals Commission have yet to be brought into force.

A note on case law citation: in the text, in order to save space, we have just used the 'neutral citation' with which a case can be easily looked up on the free BAILII website. Where applicable, law reports' citations for cases are provided in the table of cases.

Mark Symes and Peter Jorro

Garden Court Chambers,

May 2015

Contents

Contents

Table of Statutes

Table of Statutory Instruments

[All references are to paragraph number]

Table of Cases

[All references are to paragraph number]

Table of Cases

Table of Cases

T

Abbreviations

the 2003 Rules	Special Immigration Appeals Commission (Procedure) Rules 2003, SI 2003/1034
the 2005 Rules	Asylum and Immigration Tribunal (Procedure) Rules 2005, SI 2005/230
the 2014 Rules	Tribunal Procedure (First-tier Tribunal) (Immigration and Asylum Chamber) Rules 2014, SI 2014/2604
AIA 1996	Asylum and Immigration Act 1996
AIAA 1993	Asylum and Immigration Appeals Act 1993
A&I(TC)A 2004	Asylum and Immigration (Treatment of Claimants) Act 2004
AIT	Asylum and Immigration Tribunal
BCIA 2009	Borders, Citizenship and Immigration Act 2009
BIA	Border and Immigration Agency
CEAS	Common European Asylum System
the Citizens Directive	European Union Council Directive of 29 April 2004 on the right of citizens of the Union and their family members to move and reside freely within the territory of the Member States (2004/38/EC)
CMR	Case Management Review
CPR	Civil Procedure Rules
CPR PD	Civil Procedure Rules Practice Direction
CRC	Convention on the Rights of the Child
DFT	Detained Fast Track
DPA 1998	Data Protection Act 1998
the Dublin III Regulation	Regulation (EU) No 604/2013 of 26 June 2013 establishing the criteria and mechanisms for determining the Member State responsible for examining an application for international protection lodged in one of the Member States by a third-country national or a stateless person (recast)
EC	European Community
ECHR	European Convention on Human Rights
ECJ	European Court of Justice

ECtHR	European Court of Human Rights
EEA Regs 2006	Immigration (European Economic Area) Regulations 2006, SI 2006/1003
EIG	Enforcement Instructions and Guidance
EU	European Union
FCO	Foreign and Commonwealth Office
FRS	Facilitated Return Scheme
FTRs	Fast Track Rules
FTT	First-tier Tribunal (Immigration and Asylum Chamber)
GCHQ	Government Communications Headquarters
HRA 1998	Human Rights Act 1998
IA 1971	Immigration Act 1971
IA 1988	Immigration Act 1988
IA 2014	Immigration Act 2014
IAA 1999	Immigration and Asylum Act 1999
IANA 2006	Immigration, Asylum and Nationality Act 2006
IAT	Immigration Appeal Tribunal
ILPA	Immigration Law Practitioners' Association
IND	Immigration and Nationality Department
MI5	the Security Service
MI6	the Secret Intelligence Service
NIAA 2002	Nationality, Immigration and Asylum Act 2002
the Notice Regulations	Immigration (Notices) Regulations 2003, SI 2003/658
OISC	Office of the Immigration Services Commissioner
the One-Stop Procedure Regulations	Immigration and Asylum Appeals (One-Stop Procedure) Regulations 2000, SI 2000/2244
OSCU	Operational Support and Certification Unit
PAT	Pensions Appeal Tribunal
PO	Home Office Presenting Officer
the Practice Directions	Practice Directions made by the Senior President of Tribunals for the Immigration and Asylum Chambers of the First-tier Tribunal and the Upper Tribunal

the Practice Statements	Practice Statements made by the Senior President of Tribunals for the Immigration and Asylum Chambers of the First-tier Tribunal and the Upper Tribunal
the Procedures Directive	Council Directive 2005/85/EC of 1 December 2005 on minimum standards on procedures in Member States for granting and withdrawing refugee status
the Qualification Directive	Council Directive 2004/83/EC of 29 April 2004 on minimum standards for the qualification and status of third country nationals or stateless persons as refugees or as persons who otherwise need international protection and the content of the protection granted
the Reception Directive	Council Directive 2003/9/EC of 27 January 2003 laying down minimum standards for the reception of asylum seekers
SASO	Special Advocates Support Office
SIAC	Special Immigration Appeals Commission
SIACA 1997	Special Immigration Appeals Commission Act 1997
SSHD	Secretary of State for the Home Department
TCEA 2007	Tribunals, Courts and Enforcement Act 2007
TEC	Treaty Establishing the European Economic Community
TEU	Treaty on European Union
TFEU	Treaty on the Functioning of the European Union
UKBA	UK Border Agency
UKBA 2007	UK Borders Act 2007
UKVI	UK Visas and Immigration
UNHCR	United Nations High Commissioner for Refugees
UNRWA	United Nations Relief and Works Agency
UT	Upper Tribunal (Immigration and Asylum Chamber)
UT JR Practice Directions	Practice Directions regarding Immigration Judicial Review in the Immigration and Asylum Chamber of the Upper Tribunal
UT JR Practice Statement	Practice Statement regarding Immigration Judicial Review in the Immigration and Asylum Chamber of the Upper Tribunal on or after 1 November 2013
VOLO	Immigration (Variation of Leave) Order 1976, SI 1976/1572

Chapter 1

Introduction: immigration control and immigration decisions

1.1   This book is about challenging decisions made in immigration cases, principally concerning whether a person, who is not a British citizen, is permitted to enter into or stay in the United Kingdom,[1] by way of statutory appeals or by way of administrative or judicial review. It is not our objective here to lay out a detailed explanation of the substantive law and practice relating to immigration and asylum, nor of nationality law, European Union law or immigration detention, bail considerations and human rights in the migration context: these matters are all treated expertly in specialist texts.[2] Nor do we address the myriad criminal offences (and liabilities for various civil penalties) relating to immigration control and to the trafficking of persons.[3] However by way of introduction, in this chapter we set out the basic structure of immigration control, consider who are the decision takers in the immigration context and note the types of immigration decisions, as above, that can be challenged.

1   We also address certain decisions that affect the type of leave, or permission, that a person is granted to enter or remain in the UK and decisions to issue certificates, under various statutory provisions, that have effects on appeal rights in respect to, and/or on challenges by way of judicial review of, substantive immigration decisions.
2   See especially *Jackson's Immigration Law and Practice* (5th edition, Bloomsbury Professional), *Asylum Law and Practice* (2nd edition, Bloomsbury Professional) and *Fransman's British Nationality Law* (3rd edition, Bloomsbury Professional). See also *Macdonald's Immigration Law & Practice* (9th edition, LexisNexis), *Free Movement of Persons in the Enlarged European Union* (2nd edition, Sweet & Maxwell), *Foreign National Prisoners: Law and Practice* (Legal Action Group), *Detention under the Immigration Acts: Law and Practice* (Oxford University Press), *Immigration, Nationality & Refugee Law Handbook* (2006 edition, Joint Council for the Welfare of Immigrants (JCWI)) and *The JCWI Guide to the Points Based System* (JCWI).
3   See *The International Law of Human Trafficking* (Cambridge University Press).

SOURCES OF IMMIGRATION LAW DECISION MAKING

The principal statutory provisions

1.2   Immigration control in the United Kingdom is still governed principally by the Immigration Act 1971 (IA 1971) that came into force on

1 January 1973.[1] Other principal statutes and statutory instruments of particular relevance to the making of, and or bringing challenges to, immigration decisions relating to entry and stay in the UK, are:

- Immigration Act 1988 (IA 1988): s 7 provides that citizens of fellow Member States of the European Union shall not require leave to enter or remain under IA 1971 in circumstances where they are entitled to enter or stay by virtue of an enforceable EU right or of any provision made under the European Communities Act 1972, s 2(2). See also the Immigration (European Economic Area) Regulations 2006 below and see **1.7** *et seq* below.

- Special Immigration Appeals Commission Act 1997 (SIACA 1997): providing for appeals to the Special Immigration Appeals Commission (SIAC) in cases where the Secretary of State for the Home Department (SSHD, see below) has certified that the substantive decision has been taken in the interests of national security or in the interests of the relationship between the UK and another country – see especially Chapter 7.

- Immigration and Asylum Act 1999 (IAA 1999): of particular importance is s 10 (as amended by IA 2014, s 1 from 20 October 2014, although subject to complex transitional provisions which are explained in Chapters 3 and 4) which provides for the making of decisions to remove certain persons who are unlawfully present in the UK.

- Nationality, Immigration and Asylum Act 2002 (NIAA 2002): Part 5 (ss 81–117), as from 20 October 2014 significantly amended, although again subject to transitional provisions, by IA 2014, ss 15, 17 and Sch 9, provides for the principal statutory appeal rights to the First-tier Tribunal (FTT) and for the various restrictions and limitations thereon: see Chapter 3 for the position as per the 'saved provisions' of NIAA 2002 (that is as they were prior to amendment by IA 2014 but which still have effect for some appeals as per the transitional provisions[2]) and see Chapter 4 for the position as per the amended provisions of NIAA 2002 (that is as they are as amended by IA 2014). Section 72 provides for a certificate to be issued in cases where a person is deemed to be a 'serious criminal' with effect on an appeal on refugee asylum grounds (again there is currently both a 'saved' version of s 72 and an amended one). Section 76 (also with a saved and an amended version) provides for the making of decisions to revoke a person's indefinite leave to remain in the UK. Sections 78 and 79 provide for protection from removal in certain circumstances when an appeal is pending.[3] Part 5A (ss 117A–177D) (as inserted from 28 July 2014 by IA 2014, s 19) provides, on a statutory basis, for certain considerations as regards what is in the 'public interest' that a court or tribunal must take into account when determining whether an immigration decision breaches a person's right to respect for private and family life under the Human Rights Convention, Art 8.

- Asylum and Immigration (Treatment of Claimants) Act 2004 (A&I (TC)A 2004): s 8 of which lays down statutory requirements for consideration, including on a statutory appeal, of an asylum or human rights claimant's credibility. Schedule 3 provides for the removal of certain asylum and human rights claimants to 'safe third countries', without making substantive decisions on their asylum or human rights claims, and for consequential certifications by the SSHD that deny or restrict challenges by way of appeal and judicial review in these cases.

- Immigration, Asylum and Nationality Act 2006 (IANA 2006): s 55 provides for the issue of a certificate in relation to exclusion from the Refugee Convention and from the benefits of non-refoulement under that Convention, on national security grounds, with effect on an appeal on refugee asylum grounds. Prior to its repeal by IA 2014, Sch 9, para 5, from 20 October 2014 (but again subject to transitional provisions such that the unappealed provision can still apply in practice), IANA 2006, s 47 (as amended by the Crime and Courts Act 2013, s 51(3) from 8 May 2013) provided for the SSHD to make removal decisions against persons with statutorily extended leave under IA 1971, ss 3C and 3D (see further below).

- Tribunals, Courts and Enforcement Act 2007 (TCEA 2007) provides for onward appeal rights from the FTT to the Upper Tribunal (UT) and then to the Court of Appeal or the Court of Session (see Chapter 6) and for judicial review challenges in immigration cases being mainly brought in the UT rather than in the Administrative Court of the High Court (see Chapter 8).

- UK Borders Act 2007 (UKBA 2007): ss 32–39 provide for decisions in relation to the 'automatic deportation' of 'foreign criminals', exceptions to the same and appeal rights.

- Borders, Citizenship and Immigration Act 2009 (BCIA 2009): s 55 requires decision takers to have regard to the welfare of children when making decisions in immigration cases. Note that it is specifically provided in IA 2014, s 71 that IA 2014 does not limit any duty imposed on the SSHD or any other person by BCIA 2009, s 55 (duty regarding the welfare of children).

- Immigration Act 2014 (IA 2014): extensively amends previous Acts, in particular by substituting entirely new provisions for statutory appeals in NIAA 2002, Pt 5 and inserting the new Pt 5A (see above). These amendments have been subject to important and wide ranging transitional provisions that have come into effect during the writing of this book: see Chapters 3 and 4.

- Immigration (European Economic Area) Regulations 2006, SI 2006/1003 (EEA Regs 2006): these are made by the SSHD under powers conferred by the European Communities Act 1972, s 2(2) and NIAA 2002, s 109 and they transpose into UK domestic law provisions of the European Union Council Directive of 29 April 2004 on the right of citizens of the Union and their family members to move and reside freely within the territory of the Member States (2004/38/EC: 'the Citizens Directive'). The EEA Regs 2006 provide *inter alia* for the making of decisions relating to the entry into, stay in and removal from the UK of EEA citizens and their family members and for the issuing of residence documentation to the same.

● Refugee or Person in Need of International Protection (Qualification) Regulations 2006, SI 2006/2525 (see **1.9** below).

1   See IA 1971, s 35 and Immigration Act 1971 (Commencement) Order 1972, SI 1972/1514, art 2. For a full list of the 'Immigration Acts' – including most, but not all, of the statutes listed in the text above, see UKBA 2007, s 61(2) (as amended by IA 2014, s 73(5) from 14 May 2014).
2   The amending provisions in IA 2014 with which we are concerned were brought into force on 20 October 2014 by the Immigration Act 2014 (Commencement No 3, Transitional and Saving Provisions) Order 2014, SI 2014/2771 (as amended by the Immigration Act 2014 (Commencement No 4, Transitional and Saving Provisions and Amendment) Order 2015, SI 2015/371;and see also the Immigration Act 2014 (Transitional and Saving Provisions) Order 2014, SI 2014/2928, revoked from 6 April 2015 by the Immigration Act 2014 (Commencement No 4, Transitional and Saving Provisions and Amendment) Order 2015, SI 2015/371) but subject to transitional provisions as explained in Chapters 3 and 4.
3   NIAA 2002, s 78A (as added by IA 2014, s 2 from 28 July 2014 as per SI 2014/1820) provides for a 28-day moratorium on the removal of children and their parents or carers from the date on which their appeal rights are exhausted.

1.3   Also of relevance to immigration decision making are statutory instruments that provide for such matters as entry into the UK from the Republic of Ireland[1] and for juxtaposed controls, in practice with France;[2] exemptions from immigration control for diplomats and certain other persons;[3] entry clearances to have effect as leave to enter (see **1.11** below), grant and refusal of leave to enter prior to a person's arrival in the UK and for leave to enter or remain not lapsing when a person leaves the 'common travel area';[4] for giving removal directions (see **1.11** below)[5] and for designating travel ban orders;[6] and for the SSHD to make certain decisions that would normally be made by immigration officers in certain circumstances (see below).[7] The Immigration (Notices) Regulations 2003[8] set out requirements on decision takers to give written notice of appealable decisions and as to the contents of such notice. Finally the courts and tribunals that determine challenges to immigration decisions are subject to their own procedure rules (as to which see Chapters 5 to 8).

1   Immigration (Control of Entry through Republic of Ireland) Order 1972, SI 1972/1610 (as amended from 12 October 2014 by the Immigration (Control of Entry through Republic of Ireland) (Amendment) Order 2014, SI 2014/2475).
2   Nationality, Immigration and Asylum Act 2002 (Juxtaposed Controls) Order 2003, SI 2003/2818 by which provision is made for empowering the UK immigration authorities to exercise immigration control in certain French sea ports (currently Calais, Boulogne and Dunkirk), and for the French authorities to exercise immigration control in certain UK sea

ports (currently Dover). See also the Channel Tunnel (International Arrangements) Order 1993, SI 1993/1813 (as amended).

3 Immigration (Exemption from Control) Order 1972, SI 1972/1613 (as amended).

4 Immigration (Leave to Enter and Remain) Order 2000, SI 2000/1161 (as amended). The 'common travel area' means the United Kingdom, the Islands (that is to say, the Channel Islands and Isle of Man) and the Republic of Ireland and arrivals and departures on local journeys within the 'common travel area' are generally not subject to control under the Act: IA 1971, s 1(3) (exclusions can apply).

5 Immigration (Removal Directions) Regulations 2000, SI 2000/2243.

6 Immigration (Designation of Travel Bans) Order 2000, SI 2000/2724.

7 Immigration (Leave to Enter) Order 2001, SI 2001/2590.

8 SI 2003/658. See also the Immigration (Claimant's Credibility) Regulations 2004, SI 2004/3263 which also provide for the manner of notifying immigration decisions.

The Immigration Rules

1.4   Also of great importance are the Immigration Rules,[1] which set out the practice to be followed in the administration of IA 1971 for regulating the entry into and stay in the UK of persons required by the Act to have leave to enter.[2] The modern rules are very detailed and prescriptive – setting out exhaustive requirements that must be met in order to obtain leave in a given category (eg as a visitor, under the 'points-based system',[3] as a family member, as a refugee or person in need of protection,[4] etc) with stipulation that leave be refused if any requirement is not met. The Immigration Rules have a unique legal status:[5] they are not delegated legislation[6] and they have been the subject of much judicial consideration and rather wide-ranging *dicta* over the years – from being considered as mere statements of administrative policy indicative of how at any particular time the SSHD would exercise his discretion (*Odelola*[7]), to having acquired, by a combination of legislative recognition and executive practice, a status akin to that of law (*Pankina*[8]). In any event, the SSHD may, and sometimes does, depart from the Immigration Rules and similarly can authorise an immigration officer to do so (see below). Previous judicial views that this power to depart from the Rules lay, at least partly, in a residual prerogative power[9] was disapproved in the Supreme Court in *Munir*[10] where it was held that IA 1971 was the source of the SSHD's power to grant leave to enter or remain outside of the Immigration Rules.

1 These are now contained in House of Commons Paper (HC) 395 as originally laid before Parliament, in accordance with IA 1971, s 3(2) (see fn 2 below) on 23 May 1994, since when they have been substantially amended and added to by numerous 'statements of changes' as contained in House of Commons Papers (when Parliament is sitting) or Command Papers (when it is not), which by now number well over 100.

2 IA 1971, s 3(1) states that subject to exceptions as provided for by or under the Act, persons who are not British citizens shall not enter the UK unless given leave to do so. Section 3(2) requires the SSHD to 'lay before Parliament statements of the rules, or of any changes in the rules, laid down by him as to the practice to be followed in the administration of this Act for regulating the entry into and stay in the United Kingdom of persons required by this Act to have leave to enter, including any rules as to the period for which leave is to be given and the conditions to be attached in different circumstances.' The rules are subject to a negative resolution procedure which provides that if either House of Parliament disapproves

the statement of changes paper within 40 days of its being laid, then the SSHD shall as soon as possible make changes as appears to him to be required.

3   Since 2008 a points-based system (following an Australian model – see *A Points-Based System: Making Migration Work for Britain* (Cm 6741) (2006)) has been incrementally introduced into the Immigration Rules relating to entry and stay in the UK for economic reasons, including for study. These rules are now contained in Pt 6A of the Rules and nominally comprise five tiers (not all of which are operational). Tier 1 accommodates exceptionally talented and highly skilled migrants, entrepreneurs and graduate entrepreneurs, and investors. Tier 2 accommodates skilled workers with a job offer and includes sub-categories for ministers of religion, sportspersons and intra-company transfers. Tier 3 has never been implemented, but was originally designed for low-skilled workers filling specific temporary labour shortages. Tier 4 accommodates students, including child students; and Tier 5 accommodates temporary worker migrants and the youth mobility scheme.

4   See also in this respect the Refugee or Person in Need of International Protection (Qualification) Regulations 2006, SI 2006/2525.

5   Their legal status 'is not merely unusual but unique': see per Sedley LJ in *Pankina v Secretary of State for the Home Department* [2010] EWCA Civ 719 at [13].

6   IA 1971 makes provision for what the Rules must contain (ss 1(4) and 3(2)) and as to how they are to be approved (s 3(2) – see fn 2 above) but neither section purports to be the source of the power to make them: see *Odelola v Secretary of State for the Home Department* [2009] UKHL 25, per Lord Neuberger at [45]. It is, however, statutorily provided that the Rules may not lay down any practice which would be contrary to the Refugee Convention: see the Asylum and Immigration Appeals Act 1993, s 2; and must be read and given effect in a way which is compatible with the European Convention on Human Rights: see the Human Rights Act 1998, ss 3, 6; though see *R (Syed) v Secretary of State for the Home Department* [2011] EWCA Civ 1059: whilst, in applying the Rules, the SSHD has to respect rights under the ECHR, there is no requirement that the wording of the Rules be modulated so as to be compliant with the Convention.

7   *Odelola v Secretary of State for the Home Department* [2009] UKHL 25. See also *YM (Uganda) v Secretary of State for the Home Department* [2014] EWCA Civ 1292 at [39], per Aikens LJ: the Rules apply to decisions taken by the SSHD until such time as he promulgates new rules and the same applies to decisions by tribunals and the courts.

8   *Pankina* (see fn 5 above).

9   See eg *R v Secretary of State for the Home Department, ex parte Kaur* [1987] Imm AR 278 where Glidewell LJ considered that although the SSHD was empowered by IA 1971, s 4(1) to grant leave to remain outside of the Rules (see **1.10** below), the exercise of discretion in relation to leave to enter outside the rules is an exercise of the remaining part of the prerogative power.

10   *R (Munir) v Secretary of State for the Home Department* [2012] UKSC 32: the SSHD was given a wide discretion under IA 1971, ss 3, 3A, 3B and 3C to control the grant and refusal of leave to enter or to remain; the language of these provisions provide clearly, and without qualification, that where a person was not a British citizen, he may be given leave to enter or leave to remain in the UK; they authorise the SSHD to grant leave even where it would not be given under the Immigration Rules.

Policy guidance and instructions

1.5   The SSHD publishes guidance and instructions relating to the making of immigration decisions on the UK Visas and Immigration (UKVI) website.[1] Such guidance and instructions cannot restrict the rights given under the legislation and the Immigration Rules and they cannot be relied on to interpret the Rules[2] unless the rule is genuinely ambiguous.[3] However, they do give rise to a legitimate expectation that any policy approach they contain will be followed[4] and the SSHD is obliged to place any relevant policy material before the tribunal in an appeal.[5] Attempts by the SSHD, in the earlier stages of the points-based system,[6] to stipulate requirements for entry and leave by way of guidance, outside of the Rules, were found to be unlawful by the courts: in *Alvi*[7] the Supreme Court held that any requirement in immigration guidance or codes of practice which, if not satisfied by the migrant, would lead to an application for leave to enter or remain being refused was a 'rule' within the meaning of IA 1971, s 3(2) and so should be laid before Parliament (see **1.4** above).

1   See   www.gov.uk/government/organisations/uk-visas-and-immigration.   Instructions   are issued pursuant to the power in IA 1971, Sch 2, para 1(3) which provides that in the exercise of their functions under that Act immigration officers must act in accordance with such instructions (not inconsistent with the Immigration Rules) as may be given them by the SSHD (see below).

2   See *Mahad (Ethiopia) v Entry Clearance Officer* [2009] UKSC 16.

3   See *Adedoyin v Secretary of State for the Home Department* [2010] EWCA Civ 773 where public statements made by the minister were used to interpret the meaning of 'false' – as requiring deliberate dishonesty – in rules relating to general grounds for refusal: see the Immigration Rules, HC 395, paras 320(7A) and 322(1A).

4   See *R v Secretary of State for the Home Department, ex parte Popatia and Chew* [2000] EWHC 556 (QB). See also *R (Rashid) v Secretary of State for the Home Department* [2005] EWCA Civ 744.

5   See *AA (Afghanistan) v Secretary of State for the Home Department* [2007] EWCA Civ 12.

6   See **1.4**, fn 3 above.

7   *R (Alvi) v Secretary of State for the Home Department* [2012] UKSC 33. However in *R (New London College Ltd) v Secretary of State for the Home Department* [2013] UKSC 51 the Supreme Court held that the Tier 4 Sponsor Guidance issued by the SSHD did not set out rules requiring compliance by a migrant as a condition of his obtaining leave to enter or remain, because the guidance was wholly concerned with and directed to the sponsoring colleges and, accordingly, IA 1971, s 3(2) did not require the guidance to have been laid before Parliament.

International obligations

1.6   Of greatest relevance to the immigration decision making with which we are concerned are the UK's obligations under the Refugee Convention[1] and the European Convention on Human Rights (ECHR).[2] This is particularly so now, and into the future, as it is only decision making in relation to rights under these Conventions, as applied in respect of the Refugee Convention via the European Union Refugee, etc Qualification Directive[3] – with its additional provision of subsidiary or humanitarian protection – that can be challenged by way of statutory appeals as per NIAA 2002, s 82 (as substituted from 20 October 2014 by IA 2014, although currently subject to transitional provisions as explained in Chapters 3 and 4). The ECHR is largely incorporated into UK law by way of the Human Rights Act 1998 (HRA 1998), s 6(1) of which makes it 'unlawful for a public authority to act in a way which is incompatible with a Convention right'. Although the Refugee Convention is not directly incorporated into UK law,[4] there is a requirement that 'nothing in the immigration rules (within the meaning of the Immigration Act 1971) shall lay down any practice which would be contrary to the Convention.'[5] Parts 11 to 12 of the Immigration Rules and the Refugee, etc Qualification Regulations 2006[6] provide for decision making in asylum and humanitarian protection cases. In the *European Roma Rights* case[7] Lord Bingham, whilst rejecting the submission that asylum seeking is a purpose covered by the Immigration Rules in the way that visits or studies are, considered that the Rules simply provide for what must be done when an asylum claim is made in the UK. In practical terms, the key issues for decision making are whether a person's removal from the UK would breach the UK's obligations under the Refugee Convention and/ or whether a person's removal from, or denial of entry to, the UK would be unlawful under HRA 1998, s 6(1) (see above).[8] The most important ECHR human rights, for these purposes, are those protected by Arts 3 (prohibition of torture, etc) and 8 (right to respect for private and family life); for removal to be incompatible with rights protected under other Articles there generally needs to be shown a real risk of a flagrant breach or denial of the right in question, with serious consequences for the applicant, on return to the country of origin or removal.[9]

1   The Convention relating to the Status of Refugees (Geneva, 28 July 1951, Treaty Series (TS) 39 (1954), Cmd 9171) and Protocol (New York, 31 January 1967, TS 15 (1969), Cmnd 3906). Note that the New York Protocol of 1967 applies the 1951 Convention as if the words in Art 1A(2) of the Convention, which impose a temporal limitation ('events occurring before 1 January 1951') on refugee claims are omitted: see Art I of the Protocol. Thus the Protocol does not strictly amend the Convention but rather applies it in such a way as to allow for persons to be refugees as a result of events that have occurred since 1951 (see *Minister for Immigration and Multicultural Affairs v Savvin* [2000] FCA 478, per Katz J in the Full Federal Court of Australia).

2   The European Convention for the Protection of Human Rights and Fundamental Freedoms (Council of Europe Treaty Series (CETS), No 5, Cmd 8969) was signed in Rome on 4 November 1950 by Member States of the Council of Europe and came into force on 3 September 1953. There are numerous additional and amending protocols, some, but not all, of which have been signed and ratified by the UK (see further in *Asylum Law and Practice*, Ch 11). The Council of Europe was founded, in the aftermath of the Second World War, with the signing in London of the Statute of the Council of Europe (CETS No 1, Cmd 7778) on 5 May 1949. The Statute (which entered into force on 3 August 1949), in Art 3, obliges Member States to accept the principles of the rule of law and the enjoyment by all people within their jurisdiction of human rights and fundamental freedoms. The UK was one of the ten founder-Member States and there are now 47 member states including all of the 28 Member States of the European Union. Indeed, the EU is in the process of acceding to the ECHR in accordance with the EU's Lisbon Treaty – Treaty on European Union, Art 6(2).

3   The Council Directive, 2004/83/EC, of 29 April 2004 on minimum standards for the qualification and status of third country nationals or stateless persons as refugees or as persons who otherwise need international protection and the content of the protection granted: see **1.8** below.

4   See *EN (Serbia) v Secretary of State for the Home Department* [2009] EWCA Civ 630, per Stanley Burnton LJ at [52]–[60] and per Laws LJ at [119].

5   The Asylum and Immigration Appeals Act 1993, s 2, under the heading 'Primacy of Convention'.

6   Refugee or Person in Need of International Protection (Qualification) Regulations 2006, SI 2006/2525.

7   *European Roma Rights Centre v Immigration Officer at Prague Airport and Secretary of State for the Home Department* [2004] UKHL 55 at [30].

8   See eg the meanings of 'protection', 'asylum' and 'human rights claims' in NIAA 2002, ss 82(2) and 113(1) (as amended by IA 2014).

9   See eg *Soering v United Kingdom* (1989) 11 EHRR 439 at [113]; *Mamatkulov and Askarov v Turkey* (2005) 41 EHRR 25 at [84]–[91]; *Devaseelan* [2002] UKIAT 702 at [110]–[111]; *R (Ullah) v Special Adjudicator; Do v Immigration Appeal Tribunal* [2004] UKHL 26, per Lord Bingham at [24], per Lord Steyn at [44], [50] and per Lord Carswell at [68]–[69]; *RB (Algeria) v Secretary of State for the Home Department* [2009] UKHL 10, per Lord Phillips at [130]–[132]; *Brown (aka Bajinja) v Government of Rwanda and Secretary of State for the Home Department* [2009] EWHC 770 (Admin) at [66]. Similarly, where Article 8 is relied upon solely on the basis of breach of rights in the country of return – a so called 'foreign case' (see *Ullah* at [9]) only a real risk of a 'flagrant breach' of the right to respect for family life, or for private life in the sense of the right to 'physical and moral integrity' (see *Pretty v United Kingdom* (2002) 35 EHRR 1 at [61] and *Bensaid v United Kingdom* (2001) 33 EHRR 205 at [46]), will suffice to render removal disproportionate to the otherwise legitimate interests of immigration control: see *EM (Lebanon) v Secretary of State for the Home Department* [2008] UKHL 64. As to 'health cases', with respect to Arts 3 and 8, see eg *D v United Kingdom* (1997) 24 EHRR 423 (re HIV AIDS); *Bensaid* (re mental illness and whether Art 8 can be engaged); *N v United Kingdom* (2008) 47 EHRR 39 and *N v Secretary of State for the Home Department* [2005] UKHL 31 (AIDS); *R (Razgar) v Secretary of State for the Home Department* [2004] UKHL 27 (re possible engagement of Art 8); *J v Secretary of State for the Home Department* [2005] EWCA Civ 629 (re suicide risk); *AJ (Liberia) v Secretary of State for the Home Department* [2006] EWCA Civ 1736 (re availability to the applicant of medical treatment); *Y (Sri Lanka) and Z (Sri Lanka) v Secretary of State for the Home Department* [2009] EWCA Civ 362 (re suicide risk); *R (SQ (Pakistan)) v Upper Tribunal Immigration and Asylum Chamber* [2013] EWCA Civ 1251 and *AE (Algeria) v Secretary of State for the Home Department* [2014] EWCA Civ 653 (both re health and children and engagement of Art 8); and most recently, *GS (India) v Secretary of State for the Home Department* [2015] EWCA Civ 40 (limited engagement of Arts 3 and 8 in health cases).

The European Union: the Citizens Directive and the Common European Asylum System

1.7   The UK joined what was then the European Economic Community (now the European Union) in 1973.[1] Under the European Communities Act 1972, the Treaties – now the Treaty on European Union (TEU) (as amended) and the Treaty on the Functioning of the European Union (TFEU)[2] – and the Directives and Regulations made under them, are binding in the UK.[3] Rights under the Treaties themselves and under Regulations can usually be relied on by individuals as directly binding provisions of law.[4] Of fundamental importance is the right of free movement within the European Union, in particular for economic purposes.[5] The Treaty rights in this regard are recognised by the provision in IA 1988, s 7 that citizens of fellow Member States of the EU shall not require leave to enter or remain under IA 1971 in circumstances where they are entitled to enter or stay by virtue of an enforceable EU right (see **1.2** above). These free movement rights are further provided for by:

●   Directive 2004/38/EC of the European Parliament and of the Council of 29 April 2004 on the right of citizens of the Union and their family members to move and reside freely within the territory of Member States:

this 'Citizens' Directive' is transposed[6] into UK domestic law by the EEA Regulations 2006 (see **1.2** above) which apply also to citizens (and their family members) of non-EU states that are parties to the Agreement on the Economic Area (Oporto, 2 May 1992), ie Norway, Iceland and Liechtenstein, as well as to citizens (and their family members) of Switzerland.

1   The Treaty Establishing the European Economic Community (TEC) was signed in Rome on 25 March 1957. The six founding members – Belgium, France, Germany, Italy, Luxembourg and Netherlands – were joined in 1973 by Denmark, Ireland and the UK; in 1981 by Greece; and in 1986 by Portugal and Spain. The European Union (EU) was founded by the Treaty on European Union (TEU), signed in Maastricht on 7 February 1992, and entered into force on 1 November 1993. Austria, Finland and Sweden joined in 1995. The Treaty of Amsterdam, signed on 10 November 1997 (in force 1 May 1999), amended both the TEU and the TEC, *inter alia* by changing the name of the European Economic Community to the European Community (EC). The EC and EU existed side by side and the TEC and the TEU were further amended by the Treaty of Nice 2001, which entered into force on 1 February 2003. Cyprus, Czech Republic, Estonia, Hungary, Latvia, Lithuania, Malta, Poland, Slovakia and Slovenia all joined in 2004; and Bulgaria and Romania joined in 2007. The 'Treaty of Lisbon amending the Treaty on European Union and the Treaty establishing the European Community' (replacing the rejected European Constitution) was signed by the political heads of the 27 Member States in Lisbon on 13 December 2007, with a view to its coming into force on 1 January 2009. However owing to its initial rejection by Irish voters in a referendum on 12 June 2008 (reversed in a second referendum on 2 October 2009), implementation was delayed until 1 December 2009. The TEC was replaced by the Treaty on the Functioning of the European Union (TFEU) and so the EC was subsumed within the EU (see TEU, Art 1). Croatia joined in 2013.
2   See fn 1 above.
3   European Communities Act 1972, s 2. According to TFEU, Art 288: 'A regulation shall have general application. It shall be binding in its entirety and directly applicable in all Member States. A directive shall be binding, as to the result to be achieved, upon each Member State to which it is addressed, but shall leave to the national authorities the choice of form and methods.'
4   Regulations are rules that are directly applicable by their nature and should not be transposed into national law so as to avoid the risk of altering or distorting their meaning: see *Reed v Netherlands* [1988] 3 CMLR 448. On the other hand, there is a duty on Member States to implement measures binding on them in Directives, by transposing them into national law and the Court of Justice of the European Union (formerly known as the European Court of Justice (ECJ)) may declare that a state has not complied with an obligation in this regard: see TFEU, Art 260.
5   See especially TEU, Art 3(2); and TFEU, Arts 20 and 21 and, under Title IV (re 'Free movement of persons, services and capital'), Arts 45 and 46 (re 'workers'), 49 and 50 (re 'right of establishment') and 56 and 57 (re 'services').
6   Transposition of the Directive (see fn 4 above) was required by Art 40 within two years from its entry into force.

1.8   Also of relevance to immigration decision making are the series of Regulations and Directives (see above) that form the Common European Asylum System (CEAS) as per what is now Title V (of Part Three) of the TFEU.[1] The UK has opted into the following:

●   Council Directive 2001/55/EC of 20 July 2001 on minimum standards for giving temporary protection in the event of a mass influx of displaced persons and on measures promoting a balance of efforts between Member States in receiving such persons and bearing the consequences thereof;[2]

● Council Directive 2003/9/EC of 27 January 2003 laying down minimum standards for the reception of asylum seekers ('the Reception Directive');[3]

● Council Directive 2004/83/EC of 29 April 2004 on minimum standards for the qualification and status of third country nationals or stateless persons as refugees or as persons who otherwise need international protection and the content of the protection granted ('the Qualification Directive');[4]

● Council Directive 2005/85/EC of 1 December 2005 on minimum standards on procedures in Member States for granting and withdrawing refugee status ('the Procedures Directive');[5]

● Regulation (EU) No 604/2013 of 26 June 2013 establishing the criteria and mechanisms for determining the Member State responsible for examining an application for international protection lodged in one of the Member States by a third-country national or a stateless person (recast) – known as 'the Dublin III Regulation'.[6]

1   At a special meeting in Tampere, Finland, in October 1999, the Council of Ministers of the EU agreed to work towards establishing 'a Common European Asylum System, based on the full and inclusive application of the Geneva Convention relating to the Status of Refugees of 28 July 1951, as supplemented by the New York Protocol of 31 January 1967, thus maintaining the principle of non-refoulement and ensuring that nobody is sent back to persecution.' The CEAS is a constituent part of the EU's objective 'to maintain and develop the Union as an area of freedom, security and justice, in which the free movement of persons is assured in conjunction with appropriate measures with respect to external border controls, asylum, immigration and the prevention and combating of crime.' The Tampere conclusions provided that a Common European Asylum System should include, in the short term, common standards for fair and efficient asylum procedures in the Member States and, in the longer term, Community rules leading to a common asylum procedure in the then European Community. See now TEU, Art 3(2); and see TFEU, Pt 3, Title V, Ch 2 (Arts 77–80) entitled 'Policies on border checks, asylum and immigration'.

2   This Directive was formulated in response to the mass migrations consequent to the wars of the 1990s in the former Yugoslavia and under its terms, the existence of a mass influx of displaced persons shall be established by a Council Decision adopted by a qualified majority on a proposal from the Commission, which shall also examine any request by a Member State that it submit such a proposal to the Council (Art 5(1)).

3   Note that the EU Parliament and Council have adopted, on 26 June 2013, a 'recast' Reception Directive, 2013/33/EU, with a transposition date of 20 July 2015. However, the UK, along with Denmark and Ireland, have opted out of this recast directive.

4   The EU Parliament and Council have adopted, on 13 December 2011, a 'recast' 'Qualification Directive', 2011/95/EU, with a transposition date of 21 December 2013. The UK, along with Denmark and Ireland have opted out of this recast directive.

5   The EU Parliament and Council have adopted, on 26 June 2013, a 'recast' Procedures Directive, 2013/32/EU, with a transposition date of 20 July 2015. The UK, along with Denmark and Ireland have also opted out of this recast directive.

6   Replacing the Dublin II Regulation (343/2003 of 18 February 2003) which in turn replaced the Dublin Convention of 1990.

1.9   The provisions of these Directives, and to an extent those of the Dublin III Regulation, have been transposed into UK domestic law by changes in the Immigration Rules[1] and by the Refugee, etc (Qualification) Regulations 2006 (see **1.2** above). Also of relevance, with potential to become more so in the immigration field, is:

- the Charter of Fundamental Rights of the European Union, originally signed at Nice on 7 December 2000, with non-legally binding effect, though following the coming into force of the Treaty of Lisbon on 1 December 2009, the Charter has been re-proclaimed and under TEU, Art 6(1): 'The Union recognises the rights, freedoms and principles set out in the Charter of Fundamental Rights of the European Union ... which shall have the same legal value as the Treaties.'[2]

1   See, the Immigration Rules, HC 395, Pts 11, 11A, 11B and 12.
2   Note however that TEU, Art 6(1) then continues by stating: 'The provisions of the Charter shall not extend in any way the competences of the Union as defined in the Treaties. The rights, freedoms and principles in the Charter shall be interpreted in accordance with the general provisions in Title VII of the Charter governing its interpretation and application and with due regard to the explanations referred to in the Charter, that set out the sources of those provisions.' Note also that Protocol No 30 to 'the Treaties' is entitled 'On the application of the Charter of Fundamental Rights of the European Union to Poland and the United Kingdom' and provides in Art 1(1) that: 'The Charter does not extend the ability of the Court of Justice of the European Union, or any court or tribunal of Poland or of the United Kingdom, to find that the laws, regulations or administrative provisions, practices or action of Poland or of the United Kingdom are inconsistent with the fundamental rights, freedoms and principles that it reaffirms.' Art 2 of the Protocol states: 'To the extent that a provision of the Charter refers to national laws and practices, it shall only apply to Poland or the United Kingdom to the extent that the rights or principles that it contains are recognised in the law or practices of Poland or of the United Kingdom.' In *R (NS) v Secretary of State for the Home Department* (Case No C-411/10) [2013] QB 102, however, the ECJ gave a preliminary ruling to the effect that Protocol No 30 did not call into question the applicability of the Charter in the UK (or in Poland) and that according to the third recital in the preamble to the Protocol, TEU, Art 6 required the Charter to be applied and interpreted by the UK and Polish courts strictly in accordance with the explanations referred to in that article. In addition, according to the sixth recital in the preamble to the Protocol, the Charter reaffirmed the rights, freedoms and principles recognised in the EU and made those rights more visible, but did not create new rights or principles. In those circumstances, Art 1(1) of the Protocol explained Art 51 of the Charter with regard to the scope thereof and did not intend to exempt Poland or the UK from the obligation to comply with the provisions of the Charter or to prevent a court of one of those Member States from ensuring compliance with those provisions. See also *R (MK (Iran)) v Secretary of State for the Home Department* [2010] EWCA Civ 115; and *R (AB) v Secretary of State for the Home Department* [2013] EWHC 3453 (Admin).

IMMIGRATION DECISIONS AND DECISION TAKERS

The decision takers

1.10   The immigration decisions with which we are concerned are taken by the Secretary of State for the Home Department, by Immigration Officers and by Entry Clearance Officers.

- The Secretary of State for the Home Department or Home Secretary: the SSHD is one of Her Majesty's principal Secretaries of State[1] and is responsible for functions relating to immigration and asylum. In practice decisions are, in the vast majority of cases, made by civil servants working in the Home Office; the principal department responsible for immigration decision making is currently known as 'UK Visas and Immigration'.[2] In accordance with the '*Carltona* principle'[3] there is no need for specific delegation of power, though note that certain decisions – for example relating to personal exclusion orders (where the SSHD personally directs that a person's exclusion from the UK is conducive to the public good) and to national security certifications under NIAA 2002, s 97 – have to be taken by the SSHD acting in person.[4] Under IA 1971, s 4(1) there is a broad division of responsibility between the SSHD, who is responsible for granting and varying leave to remain, as well as issuing EEA registration certificates, residence cards, etc, and Immigration Officers who are responsible for giving or refusing leave to enter. However, under the Immigration (Leave to Enter) Order 2001,[5] the SSHD may grant or refuse leave to enter to persons who claim asylum. The SSHD is also responsible for deportation decisions.

- Immigration Officers: unlike their colleagues in the UKVI, Immigration Officers are specifically appointed under IA 1971, Sch 2, para 1(1), and have specific statutory duties in relation to control of entry, illegal entrants and removal and detention of persons subject to immigration control.[6] They must act in accordance with instructions given to them by the SSHD.[7] However, Immigration Officers are still in effect civil servants within the Home Office and as such can be authorised to take decisions, like their UKVI colleagues, on behalf of the SSHD without need for specific delegation of power.[8]

- Entry Clearance and Visa Officers: visas, entry clearances and EEA family permits are issued on application by Entry Clearance Officers who work, under the aegis of the Foreign Office, from British diplomatic posts abroad. Broadly speaking, all non-EEA nationals who wish to enter the UK in an immigration category other than as a visitor and for more than six months require an entry clearance, whilst 'visa nationals' – citizens of those countries and territories listed in Appendix 1 to the Immigration Rules (or, from 24 April 2015, the Immigration Rules for Visitors, Appendix 2 to Appendix V) – require a visa to enter the UK as a visitor for up to six months and even in order to transit the UK.[9] Although Entry Clearance Offices can seek guidance from the SSHD in respect to specific applications, the actual decision on whether to grant or refuse entry clearance, etc is that of the Officer.[10]

---

1   See the Interpretation Act 1978 s 5, Sch 1. In constitutional law the office of Secretary of State is a unified office, and each Secretary of State is capable of performing the functions of all or any of them.

2 Previously there was the UK Border Agency (UKBA) (from which the Border Force split off in March 2012); before that, the Border and Immigration Agency (BIA); and before that, the Immigration and Nationality Department (IND). See the Home Office website at www.gov. uk/government/organisations/home-office for the divisions of responsibility between UKVI, the Border Force and Immigration Enforcement.
3 *Carltona Ltd v Commissioners of Works* [1943] 2 All ER 560, CA.
4 See the Immigration Rules, HC 395, paras 320(6) and 321A(4); and see NIAA 2002, s 97(4).
5 SI 2001/2590, art 2.
6 See IA 1971, s 4(1) and (2).
7 See IA 1971, Sch 2, para 1(3).
8 See *Oladehinde v Immigration Appeal Tribunal* [1991] 1 AC 254, HL and *Odishu v Secretary of State for the Home Department* [1994] Imm AR 475, CA.
9 See the Immigration Rules, HC 395, para 24 (from 24 April 2015, see Appendix V, para V 1.2).
10 See the Immigration Rules, HC 395, para 26; and see *R (NA (Iraq)) v Secretary of State for Foreign and Commonwealth Affairs* [2007] EWCA Civ 759 and *R (Ivlev) v Entry Clearance Officer, New York* [2013] EWHC 1162 (Admin).

Immigration decisions

1.11   The term 'immigration decision' had a specific legal meaning in NIAA 2002, s 82 prior to its substitution, with transitional effect, from 20 October 2014, by IA 2014, s 15. It meant (and in practice currently still means for all cases subject to the saved provisions in NIAA 2002: see Chapter 3) a decision that could be appealed to the FTT and such immigration decisions are then comprehensively listed in s 82(2) (as a saved provision: see further in Chapter 3). However, for present purposes, we set out some of the broad range of the immigration decisions with which we are concerned, as per **1.1** above, that can be challenged by way of statutory appeal or judicial review. Inherently these are listed as negative decisions.

- A decision, by the SSHD, that a person be excluded from the UK: There is no specific statutory basis for the SSHD ordering that a person be excluded from the UK for reasons that such exclusion is conducive to the public good, rather it is an inherent power of the SSHD by which he can exercise his general discretion under IA 1971 as to who can and who cannot enter the UK (for EEA exclusion orders, see **1.12** *et seq* below regarding EEA decisions). The effect of a personal exclusion order made by the SSHD is that the subject of the exclusion order is to be refused entry clearance and to be refused leave to enter under the mandatory 'general grounds' for such refusals in Immigration Rules, paras 320(6) and 321A(4). Personal exclusion orders are generally reviewed every three years and can be challenged by way of judicial review.[1]

- Refusal of entry clearance: Entry clearance is defined in IA 1971, s 33(1) as meaning 'a visa, entry certificate or other document which, in accordance with the immigration rules, is to be taken as evidence or the requisite evidence of a person's eligibility, though not a British citizen, for entry into the United Kingdom (but does not include a work permit)'. All 'visa nationals' (as now listed in the Immigration Rules for Visitors, Appendix 2 to Appendix V) require a visa to enter or transit the UK. All non-EEA nationals who wish to enter the UK other than as a visitor and for a period in excess of six months require an entry clearance (unless they are seeking entry to join or accompany an EEA family member, in which case they can apply for an EEA family permit: see below regarding EEA decisions). It is the responsibility of Entry Clearance Officers to issue entry clearances[2] and refusal do so can be challenged by way of statutory appeal in certain circumstances (as to which see Chapters 3 and 4) or, if not appealable, by way of judicial review (as to which see Chapter 8).

- Refusal of a certificate of entitlement of the right of abode in the UK under NIAA 2002, s 10: Under IA 1971, s 2 a person has the right of abode in the UK if:

(a)   he is a British citizen; or

(b)   he is a Commonwealth citizen who –

   (i)   immediately before the commencement of the British Nationality Act 1981 (on 1 January 1983) was a Commonwealth citizen having the right of abode in the UK by virtue of relevant provisions of IA 1971 as then in force; and

   (ii)   has not ceased to be a Commonwealth citizen in the meanwhile.

Under Regulations made under NIAA 2002, s 10,[3] a person can apply for a certificate of entitlement[4] and a refusal to issue one was an immigration decision under saved NIAA 2002, s 82(2)(c) and so a right of appeal arises under saved s 82(1) in respect of applications made prior to 6 April 2015 (see Chapter 3).

- Refusal of leave to enter, or cancellation of entry clearance or of entry clearance acting as leave to enter, in respect of a person seeking entry at a UK port or airport: It is generally for Immigration Officers to determine whether a person who is not an EEA national should be permitted to enter the UK (see IA 1971, ss 3(1) and 4(1) and Sch 2[5]); however where a person claims asylum on arrival, it is for the SSHD to determine the claim,[6] and if he refuses it, he can refuse the claimant leave to enter.[7] Refusal of leave to enter can be challenged by way of statutory appeal in certain circumstances (as to which see Chapters 3 and 4) or, if not appealable, by way of judicial review.

- Refusal of leave to remain to a person who is in the UK, who has either entered illegally (see below for illegal entrants) or has overstayed a previous grant of leave and in either case does not have leave: It is for the SSHD to decide whether or not to grant leave to remain to such an applicant: IA 1971, ss 3(1) and 4(1).[8] Under the saved provisions of NIAA 2002, s 82, a refusal of leave to a person who did not have valid leave at the date of application is not an immigration decision within the meaning of s 82(2) and so no right of appeal arose under s 82(1) (see Chapter 3). A refusal can be challenged instead by way of judicial review. Under the amended NIAA 2002, s 82 it is possible to appeal against a refusal of leave but only where the SSHD has decided to refuse a protection claim or a human rights claim as made by the person (see Chapter 4).

- Refusal to vary leave to enter or remain in response to an application made by a person who at the time of making the application had current leave to enter or remain: Again the decision is that of the SSHD as per IA 1971, ss 3(1) and 4(1). A refusal to vary leave if, but only if, the result of the refusal is that the person has no (remaining) leave to enter or remain, is an immigration decision under saved NIAA 2002, s 82(2)(d) and so a right of appeal arises under saved s 82(1) in respect of applications made, without reference to an asylum or human rights claim, prior to 6 April 2015 (see further in Chapters 3 and 4). A refusal to vary leave in circumstances where the person has valid leave remaining can only be challenged by way of judicial review unless the variation application was made on the basis of an asylum or human rights claim (again see further in Chapter 4).

- An unwanted variation or cancellation of leave to enter or remain: Where the SSHD varies or cancels a person's leave (again under IA 1971, ss 3(1) and 4(1)[9]) a right of appeal arose under the saved provisions of NIAA 2002, s 82 but only if, when the variation took effect, prior to 6 April 2015, the person had no leave to enter or remain: saved NIAA 2002, s 82(1) and (2)(e) (see Chapter 3). Where the SSHD revokes a person's protection status – that is leave granted to enter or remain in the UK as a refugee or as a person eligible for a grant of humanitarian protection[10] – a right of appeal arises under amended NIAA 2002, s 82(1)(c) (see Chapter 4). Otherwise the remedy for an unwanted variation of leave, as regards duration and or conditions,[11] is by way of judicial review.

- Revocation by the SSHD under NIAA 2002, s 76 of a person's indefinite leave to enter or remain in the UK: See **1.2** above. Broadly, NIAA 2002, s 76 provides that a person's indefinite leave to enter or remain in the UK can be revoked:

    (a) where the person is liable to deportation but cannot be deported for 'legal reasons', which in practice means for human rights reasons;

    (b) where the leave was obtained by deception; and

    (c) where the person, or someone of whom he is a dependant, ceases to be a refugee as a result of specified circumstances.[12]

Again this was an appealable decision under the saved provisions in NIAA 2002, s 82(1) and (2)(f) (see Chapter 3) and, where the person had indefinite leave in the form of 'protection status' (see above), is an appealable decision under NIAA 2002, s 82(1)(c) (as amended: see Chapter 4).

- Decisions to remove, by way of removal directions, an illegal entrant[13] or a person who has overstayed, or who has breached the conditions of, a grant of leave to enter or remain, and the family members of the same: Immigration Officers or the SSHD can give removal directions[14] for the removal of illegal entrants under IA 1971, Sch 2, paras 9 and 10 and for the removal of family members under para 10A. Seamen and the crew of aircraft who desert from their ship or aircraft may be treated in the same way as illegal entrants.[15] IAA 1999, s 10 provides for the same to apply to persons who are unlawfully present in the UK and their family members.[16] Under the saved provision in IANA 2006, s 47 (see **1.2** above) the SSHD could make a decision to remove a person in respect of whom he has refused variation of leave or has varied so as to curtail his leave (see above). See Chapters 3 and 4 as to appeal rights.

- A decision to deport a person in respect of whom the SSHD deems it conducive to the public good for him to be deported or the family members of such a person under IA 1971, s 3(5)(a) or (b) respectively:[17] In the case of such persons, the SSHD will make a formal decision to deport them before making a deportation order (as to which see below)[18] and this constituted an immigration decision under saved NIAA 2002, s 82(2)(j) and so a right of appeal arose under saved s 82(1) in respect of such decisions made prior to 6 April 2015 (see further in Chapters 3 and 4). From 1 August 2008, the SSHD is statutorily obliged to make a deportation order in respect of a 'foreign criminal',[19] effectively defined as a person who is not a British citizen, who has been convicted in the UK of an offence and has been sentenced to a period of imprisonment of at least 12 months,[20] and it is statutorily provided that for the purposes of IA 1971, s 3(5)(a) (above) the deportation of a foreign criminal is conducive to the public good.[21] However there are exceptions to so-called 'automatic deportation':[22] 'exception 1' is where removal of the foreign criminal in pursuance of the deportation order would breach a person's human rights as protected by the ECHR or the UK's obligations under the Refugee Convention; 'exception 2' is where the SSHD thinks that the foreign criminal was under the age of 18 on the date of conviction; 'exception 3' relates to breaches of rights of the foreign criminal under the EU treaties; 'exception 4' relates to extradition cases; and 'exception 5' relates to mental health issues. Family members of those subject to 'automatic deportation' can also be subject to deportation themselves.[23] For appeal rights, see Chapters 3 and 4 and note that 'foreign criminals'[24] and their family members were amongst the first persons subject to the new appeals provisions in NIAA 2002, Pt 5 from 20 October 2014 (see Chapters 3 and 4).

- Refusal to revoke a deportation order: A 'deportation order', in relation to a person, means an order requiring him to leave and prohibiting him from entering the UK; and a deportation order against a person shall invalidate any leave to enter or remain in the UK (including indefinite leave) given him before the order is made or while it is in force: see IA 1971, s 5(1). The SSHD can make a deportation order following on from a decision to deport (see above) and must make one in accordance with the 'automatic deportation' provisions set out above. Furthermore, where a person, who is not a British citizen and who, being 17 years or older, is convicted by a criminal court of an offence punishable by imprisonment, that court may make a recommendation, to the SSHD, that the person be deported: see IA 1971, s 3(6).[25] However, in *R v Kluxen*[26] the Court of Appeal held that with the coming into force of the 'automatic deportation' provisions (above), it was no longer appropriate for a court to recommend the deportation of a foreign criminal within the meaning of those provisions, because, basically, no useful purpose would be served by doing so.[27] Under IA 1971, s 5(2) the SSHD may, by further order, revoke a deportation order and his refusal to do so – on application by the person (whether or not the person has left the UK) – was an immigration decision under saved NIAA 2002, s 82(2)(k) and so a right of appeal arose under saved s 82(1) in respect of such decisions made prior to 6 April 2015 (see Chapter 3). However note again that most persons subject to deportation orders will be 'foreign criminals' (see above) and so would have been subject to the new appeals provisions in NIAA 2002, Pt 5 since 20 October 2014 (see Chapter 4).

- A decision to deprive a person of the right of abode in the UK: Under IA 1971, s 2A the SSHD may by order remove from a specified person a right of abode in the UK which he has as a non-British Commonwealth citizen (see above regarding a certificate of entitlement of the right of abode) if the SSHD thinks that it would be conducive to the public good for the person to be excluded or removed from the UK.[28] Such a decision is an immigration decision under saved NIAA 2002, s 82(2)(ia) and so a right of appeal arose under saved s 82(1) in respect to such decisions made prior to 6 April 2015 (see Chapter 3).

- A decision to remove an asylum/protection claimant to a 'safe third country' under the Dublin III Regulation (see **1.8** above) or otherwise under the provisions of A&I(TC)A 2004, Sch 3 (see **1.2** above): Such a decision can only be challenged by way of judicial review (see Chapter 8).

- Certifications under NIAA 2002, ss 94, 94B and 96 and under A&I(TC) A 2004, Sch 3, paras 5(1) and (4), 10(1) and (4), 15(1) and (4) and 17 and 19(c) that limit or prevent statutory appeals: The effect of a certificate being issued under NIAA 2002, s 94 (clearly unfounded asylum and or human rights claims) and under s 94B (certification of human rights claims made by persons liable to deportation) is to prevent an in-country suspensive right of appeal to the FTT[29] and the effect of a certificate being issued under NIAA 2002, s 96 (earlier right of appeal) is to prevent any right of appeal at all (see further in Chapters 3 and 4). The overall effect of the double certificates under A&I(TC)A 2004, Sch 3, is also to prevent an in-country suspensive right of appeal to the FTT. Accordingly the challenge to such certificates has to be by way of judicial review. Note that the SSHD can issue certificates under other provisions that either effect, for example by limiting the grounds, the appeal to the FTT (NIAA 2002, s 72(9)(b) ('serious criminal') and saved s 98 ('other ground of public good') and IANA 2006, s 55 ('refugee convention: certification')) or prevent an appeal to the FTT but enable instead an appeal to the SIAC (NIAA 2002, s 97(1) and (3) ('national security, etc.' and s 97A 'national security: deportation'; and see SIACA 1997, s 2 and Chapter 7).

1   In practice though it is very difficult to successfully challenge a personal exclusion order made by the SSHD, who is considered to be in a better position than the court to make the decision and who is democratically accountable for making it: see eg *R (Farrakhan) v Secretary of State for the Home Department* [2002] EWCA Civ 606; *R (Naik) v Secretary of State for the Home Department* [2011] EWCA Civ 1546; and *R (Uba) v Secretary of State for the Home Department* [2014] EWHC 1166 (Admin). See also *R (Lord Carlile of Berriew QC) v Secretary of State for the Home Department* [2014] UKSC 60. See further in Chapter 7 regarding the SIAC's judicial review jurisdiction under SIACA 1997, s 2C in respect of exclusion decisions made in the interests of national security, etc.

2   Immigration Rules, HC 395, para 320 sets out circumstances in which entry clearance and leave to enter must be refused and circumstances where entry clearance and leave to enter should normally be refused.

3   The Immigration (Certificate of Entitlement to Right of Abode in the United Kingdom) Regulations 2006, SI 2006/3145.

4   An application for a certificate of entitlement must be made to the SSHD if the applicant is in the UK; to the Lieutenant-Governor or the SSHD if the applicant is in any of the Channel Islands or the Isle of Man; to the Governor if the applicant is in a British overseas territory; to the High Commissioner, or to the SSHD, if the applicant is in a Commonwealth country; or to any consular officer, any established officer in the Diplomatic Service of Her Majesty's Government in the UK or any other person authorised by the SSHD if the applicant is elsewhere: SI 2006/3145, art 3.

5   Note that under the Immigration (Leave to Enter and Remain) Order 2000, SI 2000/1161 (as provided for by IA 1971, ss 3A and 3B) in specified circumstances, entry clearance can take effect as leave to enter granted prior to the person's arrival in the UK. Where this applies, an Immigration Officer can examine the person on arrival for the purpose of establishing *inter alia* whether there has been such a change of circumstances of his case, since the leave was given, that it should be cancelled or whether that leave was obtained as a result of false information given by him or his failure to disclose material facts or whether there are medical grounds on which that leave should be cancelled or whether the person's purpose in arriving in the UK is different from the purpose specified in the entry clearance or whether it would be conducive to the public good for that leave to be cancelled: IA 1971, Sch 2, para 2A(1),(2),(2A) and (3); and see the Immigration Rules, HC 395, paras 320 (as per fn 2 above), 321 and 321A. Where the Immigration Officer is satisfied that one of the above does apply, the Immigration Officer may cancel the person's leave to enter and such cancellation of a person's leave to enter is to be treated, *inter alia* for appeal right's purposes, as if he had been

refused leave to enter at a time when he had a current entry clearance: IA 1971, Sch 2, para 2A(8) and (9) (see further in Chapters 3 and 4).

6 Immigration Rules, HC 395, para 328.

7 Under the Immigration (Leave to Enter) Order 2001, SI 2001/2590, art 2.

8 Though note that the Immigration Rules, HC 395, para 322 sets out circumstances in which leave to remain is to be refused and circumstances where leave to remain will normally be refused.

9 See also the Immigration Rules, HC 395, para 323.

10 NIAA 2002, s 82(2)(c).

11 Under IA 1971, s 3(1)(c) a person's leave to enter or remain can be subject to conditions restricting his employment or occupation in the UK; restricting his studies in the UK; requiring him to maintain and accommodate himself, and any dependants of his, without recourse to public funds; requiring him to register with the police; requiring him to report to an immigration officer or the SSHD; and about his residence. For an example of a judicial review challenge to a condition restricting access to public funds, see *R (Fakih) v Secretary of State for the Home Department* (IJR) [2014] UKUT 00513 (IAC).

12 That is where the person, or someone of whom he is a dependant, ceases to be a refugee as a result of: (a) voluntarily availing himself of the protection of his country of nationality; (b) voluntarily re-acquiring a lost nationality; (c) acquiring the nationality of a country other than the UK and availing himself of its protection; or (d) voluntarily establishing himself in a country in respect of which he was a refugee: NIAA 2002, s 76(3) and see the cessation clause in the Refugee Convention, Art 1C(1)–(4), though as regards Art 1C(3) relating to acquiring a new nationality, this is only relevant domestically, for obvious reasons, where the new nationality is other than British.

13 An illegal entrant is defined in IA 1971, s 33(1) as 'a person (a) unlawfully entering or seeking to enter in breach of a deportation order or of the immigration laws, or (b) entering or seeking to enter by means which include deception by another person, and includes also a person who has entered as mentioned in paragraph (a) or (b) above'.

14 Removal directions can be given to the owners, agents or captains of ships and aircraft or, in respect to removal directions under (at least saved) IAA 1999, s 10, to persons operating an international service through the Channel Tunnel, requiring them to remove the applicant and, where appropriate his family members, to a country of which he is a national or citizen; a country or territory in which he has obtained a passport or other document of identity; a country or territory from which he embarked for the UK; or a country or territory to which there is reason to believe he will be admitted: see IA 1971, Sch 2, para 8(1) as applied by paras 9, 10 or 10A (see text above); and the Immigration (Removal Directions) Regulations 2000, SI 2000/2243 (which have not been amended, so far, in keeping with amended IA 1999, s 10). As regards 'a country or territory to which there is reason to believe he will be admitted', in *Alsawaf v Secretary of State for the Home Department* [1988] Imm AR 410 at 422 Staughton LJ stated: 'the requirement is not that there is certainty that the appellant would be admitted, but that there should be reason to believe he would; nor is it a requirement that he will be admitted for settlement, but merely that he will be admitted.' See also *MS (Palestinian Territories) v Secretary of State for the Home Department* [2010] UKSC 25.

15 See IA 1971, Sch 2, paras 12–15.

16 Note that there is a saved IAA 1999 Act, s 10 (see further in Chapter 3) and a new s 10 as amended by IA 2014, s 1 from 20 October 2014 subject to the transitional provisions in SI 2014/2771 (see **1.2**, fn 2 above). See Chapter 4.

17 'Family members' are defined in IA 1971, s 5(4) (as amended *inter alia* by the Civil Partnership Act 2004, s 261(1), Sch 27, para 37(b)) so as to include a woman's husband as well as a man's wife and a man's or a woman's civil partner, along with the children (including adopted children and a woman's illegitimate children), aged under 18, of either. But see also the Immigration Rules, HC 395, paras 365 and 366 regarding when the SSHD will not normally decide to deport family members.

18 Immigration Rules, HC 395, para 381.

19 UKBA 2007, s 32(5) (see **1.2** above). However this does not create a private right of action in respect of consequences of non-compliance by the SSHD: s 32(7). The automatic deportation

provision is subject to IA 1971, ss 7 and 8 (regarding certain Commonwealth and Irish citizens and other exemptions from deportation): UKBA 2007, s 33(1)(b).

20 UKBA 2007, s 32(1), (2) – such a sentence being 'condition 1'. This does not include, *inter alia*, a period of imprisonment of at least 12 months only by virtue of consecutive sentences amounting in aggregate to more than 12 months: s 38(1)(b). UKBA 2007, s 32(1)(c) and (3) also provide that a non-British citizen who has been convicted of an offence specified by order of the SSHD under NIAA 2002, s 72(4)(a) (re 'serious criminal') and sentenced to imprisonment (of whatever duration) – 'condition 2' – is also a foreign criminal subject to automatic deportation. However, the Nationality, Immigration and Asylum Act 2002 (Specification of Particularly Serious Crimes) Order 2004, SI 2004/1910 was held to be *ultra vires* and unlawful by the Court of Appeal in *EN (Serbia) v Secretary of State for the Home Department* [2009] EWCA Civ 630 at [81]–[83]. The UK Borders Act 2007 (Commencement No 3 and Transitional Provisions) Order 2008, SI 2008/1818, art 2 and Sch, provide that the relevant sections of UKBA 2007 relating to automatic deportation (ss 32–39) come into force on 1 August 2008 but only in relation to 'condition 1'. Under the transitional provisions, in SI 2008/1818, art 3(1), UKBA 2007, s 32 (in relation to 'condition 1' only) applies to persons convicted before the passing of the 2007 Act who are in custody at the time of commencement (1 August 2008) or whose sentences are suspended at the time of commencement. However under art 3(2), para (1) does not apply to a person who has been served with a notice of decision to make a deportation order before 1 August 2008.

21 UKBA 2007, s 32(4).

22 As stated in UKBA 2007, s 33 (see also fn 19 above).

23 UKBA 2007, s 37 (and see fn 17 above).

24 For this purpose a 'foreign criminal' is more widely defined in NIAA 2002, s 117D(2) as a person who is not a British citizen, who has been convicted in the UK of an offence, and who has been sentenced to a period of imprisonment of at least 12 months, has been convicted of an offence that has caused serious harm, or is a persistent offender: see SI 2014/2771 (see fn 16 above), arts 9 and 10, as originally enacted (see further in Chapters 3 and 4).

25 The recommendation is part of the criminal sentence and as such is appealable to the appropriate appeal court within the criminal justice system (IA 1971, s 6(5)) and a deportation order is not to be made while such an appeal is pending against the recommendation (IA 1971, s 6(6)). Where, on an appeal to it, a criminal court quashes the recommendation for deportation, the SSHD, although in no way bound by that decision, must explain his reasons for disagreeing with that court's reasoning if he nevertheless decides to make a deportation order against the person under IA 1971, s 3(5)(a) on conducive grounds (see above): see *M v Secretary of State for the Home Department* [2003] EWCA Civ 146 at [15]–[19], [26], per Laws LJ. See also *DA (Colombia) v Secretary of State for the Home Department* [2009] EWCA Civ 682.

26 *R v Patricia Kluxen; R v German Rostas and Superman Adam* [2010] EWCA Crim 1081.

27 As to cases to which automatic deportation does not apply – where the offender does not amount to a foreign criminal because he did not receive a single custodial sentence of 12 months or more, or because he only received a non-custodial sentence – it would rarely be appropriate for the court to recommend his deportation whether or not he was an EU citizen: *R v Kluxen* (above) at [11]–[28]. Note however that it is offences involving matters such as the use of a forged or false passport or other identity documents that will still tend to result in a recommendation for deportation albeit the sentence of imprisonment is for less than 12 months: see *R v Benabbas (Ahmed)* [2005] EWCA Crim 2113 and see *R v Kluxen* (above) at [27].

28 IA 1971, s 2A(1) and (2). The SSHD may revoke such an order: IA 1971, s 2A(3).

29 See also saved NIAA 2002, s 97B that provides that where the SSHD curtails a person's leave and personally certifies that the decision is or was taken wholly or partly on the ground that it is no longer conducive to the public good for the person to have leave to enter or remain in the UK and the person was outside of the UK when the decision was made, he can only appeal to the FTT from outside of the UK and cannot re-enter the UK in order to pursue the appeal (see Chapter 3).

EEA decisions

1.12   Under the EEA Regs 2006 a discrete set of 'EEA decisions' can be made in respect of EEA citizens and their non-EEA family members who are seeking to enter or remain in the UK. Under reg 2, 'EEA decision' means a decision under the Regulations that concerns:

(a)   a person's entitlement to be admitted to the UK;[1]

(b)   a person's entitlement to be issued with or have renewed, or not to have revoked, a registration certificate, residence card, derivative residence card, document certifying permanent residence or permanent residence card;[2]

(c)   a person's removal from the UK;[3] or

(d)   the cancellation, pursuant to reg 20A, of a person's right to reside in the UK.[4]

1   In particular a person may be excluded from the UK under EEA Regs 2006, reg 19 on grounds of public policy, public security or public health in accordance with reg 21. Under reg 19(1B) if the SSHD considers that the exclusion of an EEA national or the family member of an EEA national is justified on the grounds of public policy, public security or public health in accordance with reg 21, the SSHD may make an order for the purpose of the Regulations prohibiting that person from entering the UK. Further a family member of an EEA citizen can apply to an Entry Clearance Officer for an EEA family permit, defined in reg 2 as 'a document issued to a person, in accordance with regulation 12, in connection with his admission to the United Kingdom'. The Entry Clearance Officer must determine whether to issue the EEA family permit and such a permit must be refused in specified circumstances: see EEA Regs 2006, regs 12(5) and (6) and 19. An Entry Clearance Officer or an Immigration Officer can revoke a person's EEA family permit pursuant to reg 20(5).
2   See EEA Regs 2006, Part 3, regarding residence documentation. Broadly, 'registration certificates' are for EEA citizens who are exercising EU treaty rights and their EEA citizen family members (see regs 4–8 and 16) whilst 'residence cards' are for non-EEA family members of EEA citizens (see regs 7–9 and 17). Residence documents can be revoked by the SSHD pursuant to reg 20.
3   EEA citizens and their family members can be removed from the UK pursuant to EEA Regs 2006, reg 19(3) on the grounds that: (a) the person does not have, or ceases to have, a right to reside under the Regulations; (b) the SSHD has decided that the person's removal is justified on grounds of public policy, public security or public health in accordance with reg 21; or (c) the SSHD has decided that the person's removal is justified on grounds of abuse of rights in accordance with reg 21B(2). Note also that EEA nationals, and their family members, can be subject to deportation (see **1.11** above) – although considerations under reg 21 come into play – and where the SSHD decides to remove an EEA citizen, or family member, under reg 19(3)(b) (above) the person is to be treated as if he were a person to whom IA 1971, s 3(5)(a) (liability to deportation – see **1.11** above) applies: reg 24(3).
4   Under EEA Regs 2006, reg 20A the SSHD may cancel a person's right to reside in the UK where the person has a right to reside in the UK as per the Regulations; the SSHD has decided that the cancellation of that person's right to reside in the UK is justified on grounds of public policy, public security or public health in accordance with reg 21 or on grounds of abuse of rights in accordance with reg 21B(2); but the circumstances are such (eg for human rights reasons) that the SSHD cannot make a decision under reg 20(1) (to revoke, etc residence documents); and it is not possible for the SSHD to remove the person from the UK pursuant to reg 19(3)(b) or (c) (see fn 3 above).

1.13   A person may appeal to the FTT against an EEA decision under reg 26, subject to conditions and restrictions, including as to whether the person can only appeal from abroad, that are considered further in Chapter 4. An appeal lies to the SIAC, instead of to the FTT, against an EEA decision where conditions set out in reg 28 apply (see further in Chapter 7). Furthermore, where a person is liable to be removed, and in effect deported on public policy, etc grounds,[1] the SSHD may certify that, despite the appeals process not having been begun or not having been finally determined, removal of the person to the country or territory to which it is proposed he is to be removed, pending the outcome of his appeal, would not be unlawful under HRA 1998, s 6 (human rights: see **1.6** above), in particular on the ground that the person would not, before the appeal is finally determined, face a real risk of serious irreversible harm if removed to that country or territory.[2] The person can challenge the certification by way of judicial review and can apply for an interim order to suspend enforcement of the removal decision and may not be removed until such time as the decision on the interim order has been taken unless certain conditions apply.[3]

1   That is, where reg 24(3) applies (see **1.12**, fn 3 above).
2   EEA Regs 2006, reg 24AA(1)–(3). As to the meaning of 'a real risk of serious irreversible harm', see in Chapter 4 in relation to NIAA 2002, s 94B.
3   Reg 24AA(4): the conditions under which the person can be removed pending a decision on the interim order are where the expulsion decision is based on a previous judicial decision; where the person has had previous access to judicial review; or where the removal decision is based on imperative grounds of public security.

Chapter 2

Outline of the development of statutory appeal rights in immigration and asylum cases

RIGHTS OF APPEAL UNDER THE IMMIGRATION ACT 1971

2.1   The current system of immigration appeals, initially with a two-tier Immigration Appellate Authority, consisting of adjudicators[1] at the first level and the Immigration Appeal Tribunal (IAT)[2] at the second level, was first introduced by the Immigration Appeals Act 1969 and was then adopted in IA 1971.[3] The immigration appeal rights structure, as regards in what immigration circumstances a right of appeal arose and when that right of appeal had suspensive effect, as well as restrictions and limitations on rights of appeal, as set out in IA 1971, Pt II,[4] has been broadly followed in subsequent legislation up until the radical changes were introduced, in a piecemeal fashion, by IA 2014 from October 2014 (see Chapter 4). In short, applicants who had a suspensive right of appeal, that could be lodged, prepared and heard whilst the applicant remained in the UK, were:

- persons who had been refused leave to enter, and who at the time held a current entry clearance or were named in a current work permit.[5] However a person in respect of whom the SSHD, acting in person, had certified that directions had been given that the person not be given entry to the UK on the ground that his exclusion is conducive to the public good, was not entitled to appeal against refusal of leave to enter;[6]

- persons whose limited leave had been varied (whether as regards duration or conditions) or who had been refused an application to vary it;[7] note that a person must have limited leave in order for it to be varied or for there to be a refusal of its variation: see *Suthendran*[8] and *Subramaniam*,[9] such that an application for further leave, which is made once leave has expired, would not, if refused, attract a right of appeal under this provision.[10] Again there were some limitations on the right of appeal, including where the SSHD had certified that the person's departure from the UK would be conducive to the public good, as being in the interests of national security or of the relations between the UK and any other country or for other reasons of a political nature, or the decision questioned by the appeal was taken on that ground by the SSHD (and not by a person acting under his authority);[11]

• persons who were the subject of a decision to deport under IA 1971, s 3(5).[12] Note that until amended by IA 1999, persons who overstayed or breached conditions of their limited leave were subject to decisions to deport under IA 1971, s 3(5)(a).[13] A person was not entitled to appeal against a decision to make a deportation order against him if the ground of the decision was that his deportation is conducive to the public good as being in the interests of national security or of the relations between the UK and any other country or for other reasons of a political nature.[14] Furthermore provision was made that an appeal would lie directly to the IAT where the ground for the decision to deport was that deportation of the appellant is conducive to the public good.[15] However, under IA 1988, s 5 in respect of a person who was last granted leave to enter the UK less than seven years before the date of decision to deport was made, the right of appeal was limited to the ground that on the facts of his case there was no power in law to make the deportation order for the reasons stated in the notice of the decision.[16] This draconian provision, in effect denying a merits appeal to such persons, was subject to certain exceptions specified by order which, prior to the Asylum and Immigration Appeals Act 1993 (AIAA 1993) (see below), included refused asylum claimants appealing on asylum grounds,[17] and then included asylum claimants whose leave to enter or remain had been curtailed under AIAA 1993, s 7 (see below),[18] enabling a full merits appeal against the decision to deport on both asylum and non-asylum grounds.[19]

---

1   Adjudicators were provided for by the Immigration Appeals Act 1969 and were continued by IA 1971, s 12 and Sch 5, Pt I, for the purposes of appeals under that Act.
2   The IAT was provided for by the Immigration Appeals Act 1969 and was continued by IA 1971, s 12 and Sch 5, Pt II, for the purposes of appeals under that Act.
3   The Immigration Appeals Act 1969 was repealed by IA 1971, s 34(1), Sch 6.
4   IA 1971, Pt II constituted ss 12–23 and was repealed from 2 October 2000 by IAA 1999, Sch 16, para 1 and the Immigration and Asylum Act 1999 (Commencement No 6, Transitional and Consequential Provisions) Order 2000, SI 2000/2444 subject to savings specified in SI 2000/2444, Sch 1 (see **2.13** below re appeals under IAA 1999).
5   IA 1971, s 13(1), (3) and (3A).
6   IA 1971, s 13(5).
7   IA 1971, s 14(1).
8   *Suthendran v Immigration Appeal Tribunal* [1977] 1 AC 359, HL.
9   *R v Immigration Appeal Tribunal, ex parte Subramaniam* [1977] 1 QB 190, CA.
10   In order to avoid the unfairness that could arise under the wording of IA 1971, s 14(1) – 'a person *who has* a limited leave under this Act to enter or remain in the United Kingdom *may appeal* to an adjudicator against any variation of the leave (whether as regards duration or conditions), *or against any refusal to vary it*' – where a person did in fact apply for variation of leave before its expiry but the decision to refuse was made after its expiry such that no right of appeal would arise (because by the date of refusal the person no longer *had* a limited leave),

26

the Immigration (Variation of Leave) Order 1976, SI 1976/1572 (VOLO) was brought into force on 27 September 1976 with the effect that where a person had limited leave and applied to the SSHD before its expiration to vary it, the duration of the leave was automatically extended by art 3(1) (subject to some exceptions in art 3(2)) until the expiration of the 28th day after either the date of the decision on the application or the date of the withdrawal of the application. VOLO was superseded by IA 1971, s 3C from 2 October 2000 (when s 3C was inserted into IA 1971 by IAA 1999) initially by being amended so as to not apply to decisions made on or after 2 October 2000: VOLO, art 3(2)(e) as inserted by the Immigration (Variation of Leave) (Amendment) Order 2000, SI 2000/2445 on that date. VOLO was only finally formally revoked by the Immigration (Variation of Leave) (Revocation) Order 2015, SI 2015/863 on 20 April 2015.

11 IA 1971, s 14(3). See also s 14(2A) (inserted by Asylum and Immigration Appeals Act 1993, s 11(2) from 26 July 1993 and later substituted by the Asylum and Immigration Act 1996, Sch 2, para 3(2) from 1 September 1996) that denied the right of appeal where the refusal was on the ground that: (a) a relevant document which is required by the immigration rules has not been issued; (b) the person or a person whose dependant he is does not satisfy a requirement of the immigration rules as to age or nationality or citizenship; (c) the variation would result in the duration of the person's leave exceeding what is permitted by the immigration rules; or (d) any fee required by or under any enactment has not been paid. Relevant documents were entry clearances, passports or other identity documents and work permits, or equivalent documents issued after entry: IA 1971, s 14(2B) (inserted as above).

12 IA 1971, s 15(1)(a).

13 IA 1971 s 3(5)(a). Under s 3(5)(aa) persons who had obtained leave to remain by deception could also be subject to decisions to deport. Under s 3(5)(c) the family members of such persons (as well as of persons subject to decisions to deport on conducive grounds under s 3(5)(b)) could also be subject to decisions to deport; and IA 1971 s 15(6) provided, with exceptions, that a family member over the age of 18 facing deportation as such could not seek to go behind a grant of leave to enter or remain as the principal's family member. Note that IA 1971, s 3(5) was substituted by IAA 1999 from 2 October 2000 such that decisions to deport under it only applied to those persons – and their family members – whom the SSHD deemed it to be conducive to the public good to deport, whilst overstayers, etc became removable under IA 1999, s 10 (see **1.11**). See further below re IAA 1999.

14 IA 1971, s 15(3).

15 IA 1971, s 15(7).

16 IA 1988, s 5(1) and (2). Note that this restriction only applied to persons subject to decisions to deport as overstayers, etc and their family members under IA 1971, s 3(5)(a), (aa) and (c) (see fn 13 above). Persons – and their family members – whom the SSHD deemed it to be conducive to the public good to deport and against whom decisions to deport were made under (pre-IAA 1999 amended) IA 1971, s 3(5)(b) and (c) were not restricted in their right of appeal by this provision.

17 See IA 1988, s 5(3) and the Immigration (Restricted Right of Appeal against Deportation) (Exemption) (No 2) Order 1988, SI 1988/1203, art 2(a). Article 2(b) exempted a person who would have been last given leave to enter the UK seven years or more before the date of the decision to make a deportation order against him but for his having obtained a subsequent leave after an absence from the UK within the period limited for the duration of the earlier leave where, by virtue of IA 1971, s 3(3)(b), the limitation on and any conditions attached to the earlier leave applied to the subsequent leave.

18 See Immigration (Restricted Right of Appeal against Deportation) (Exemption) Order 1993, SI 1993/1656, art 2(b). For curtailment under AIAA 1993, s 7 see **2.4** below. Article 2(a) exempted any person who would have been last given leave to enter the UK seven years or more before the date of the decision to make a deportation order against him but for his having obtained a subsequent leave after any absence from the UK within the period limited for the duration of the earlier leave.

19 On such an appeal the appellant could raise issues relating, for example, to compassionate factors in connection with the country of proposed deportation: see IAT determinations in *Elizabeth Kamara* (20155), *Mohammed Kamara* (21814) and *Kapusnik* (00/TH/01897).

2.2 A non-suspensive, exercisable only from abroad, right of appeal was available to:

- persons who were refused an entry clearance or a certificate of entitlement as to the right of abode.[1] This right of appeal was denied (as above, in respect to leave to enter) where the reason for refusal was certified to be that directions had been given, by the SSHD (acting in person), that the person not be given entry to the UK on the ground that his exclusion is conducive to the public good.[2] No right of appeal arose where the applicant sought entry as a visitor, a short-term student (accepted on a course of not more than six months duration) or with the intention of studying but without having been accepted on a course;[3] and also where the refusal of entry clearance was on the ground that he or any person whose dependant he is does not hold a relevant document which is required by the immigration rules; or he or any person whose dependant he is does not satisfy a requirement of the immigration rules as to age or nationality or citizenship; or he or any person whose dependant he is seeks entry for a period exceeding that permitted by the immigration rules;[4]

- persons refused leave to enter who did not have a current entry clearance, etc at the time of refusal – subject to the same exclusions as per entry clearance refusals for visitors, short term students and intending students, as above;[5]

- persons whose application to revoke a deportation order was refused,[6] but with appeal right excluded if the SSHD certified that the person's exclusion from the UK is conducive to the public good or if revocation was refused on that ground by the SSHD (and not by a person acting under his authority).[7] It was specifically provided that a person could not appeal against a refusal to revoke a deportation order so long as he was in the UK, whether because he had not complied with the requirement to leave or because he had contravened the prohibition on entering;[8]

- persons subject to removal directions as illegal entrants or as the crew of ships or aircraft (as to which see **1.11**), limited to the ground that on the facts of the case there was no power to give them on the ground on which they were given[9] but with the caveat as regards crew of ships and aircraft that the appeal was to be dismissed in any event if the adjudicator was satisfied that the appellant was in fact an illegal entrant.[10] It was specifically provided that a person could not appeal against such directions so long as he was in the UK, unless appealing against directions given by virtue of a deportation order (whether on the ground specifically that he had returned in breach of that order or on the ground that he was an illegal entrant) and was appealing on the ground that he was not the person named in the order.[11]

1   IA 1971, s 13(2).
2   IA 1971, s 13(5).

3   IA 1971, s 13(3A) (inserted by the Asylum and Immigration Appeals Act 1993, s 10 from 26 July 1993).
4   IA 1971, s 13(3B) (inserted by the Asylum and Immigration Appeals Act 1993, s 11(1) from 26 July 1993). Relevant documents were entry clearances, passports or other identity documents and work permits: IA 1971, s 13(3C) (inserted as above).
5   IA 1971, s 13(1) and see **2.1**, fn 5 above.
6   IA 1971, s 15(1)(b) and (5).
7   IA 1971, s 15(4).
8   IA 1971, s 15(5).
9   IA 1971, s 16(1)(a) and (b).
10 IA 1971, s 16(4).
11 IA 1971, s 16(2). Where a person appealed under s 16 against directions given by virtue of a deportation order, he was not allowed to dispute the original validity of that order: s 16(3).

2.3   An additional right of appeal arose against removal on objection to destination, on the somewhat curiously worded 'formula' that where directions were given under IA 1971 for a person's removal from the UK (on refusal of leave to enter, pursuant to a deportation order or on his having entered in breach of a deportation order) the person could appeal against the directions on the ground that 'he ought to be removed (if at all) to a different country or territory specified by him'.[1] However in *Muruganandarajah*[2] the Court of Appeal confirmed that this appeal right was limited to choice of destination and, notwithstanding the words 'if at all', was without prejudice to the issue of whether there should be a deportation or removal at all.

1   IA 1971, s 17(1). Similarly a person appealing in-country under s 13 or 15 against refusal of leave to enter or a decision to make a deportation order (see above) could, on that appeal, object to the country or territory to which he would be removed, in pursuance of directions consequent to the decisions, and claim that he ought to be removed (if at all) to a different country or territory specified by him: see IA 1971, s 17(2) and (3).
2   *R v Immigration Appeal Tribunal, ex parte Muruganandarajah* [1986] Imm AR 382.

ASYLUM APPEALS UNDER THE ASYLUM AND IMMIGRATION APPEALS ACT 1993

2.4   The consequence of these limited appeal rights under IA 1971 was that asylum claimants whose claims were refused by the SSHD and who did not have a suspensive right of appeal against a consequent adverse immigration decision, had to resort to seeking a judicial review of the refusal of asylum.[1] However, in *Vilvarajah v United Kingdom*,[2] the European Commission of Human Rights held that judicial review of a refusal of asylum was an inadequate remedy for the purposes of Art 13 to prevent a breach of Art 3 following removal.[3] Accordingly, AIAA 1993 on 26 July 1993 introduced a suspensive right of appeal for nearly all rejected asylum claimants.[4] The right of appeal, under AIAA 1993, s 8(1)–(4), lay against the immigration decision on the grounds that removal in consequence of the decision would be contrary to the UK's obligations under the Refugee Convention – such grounds have become known as 'asylum grounds'.

2.4 Outline of the development of statutory appeal rights

- A person refused leave to enter the UK had a right of appeal, on asylum grounds, against the decision to refuse leave to enter under AIAA 1993, s 8(1) (meaning that an on-entry claimant who had been refused asylum as a refugee but who had been granted exceptional leave to enter had nothing to appeal against: though see below for the situation where a grant of exceptional leave to enter was made after an appeal under AIAA 1993, s 8(1) had been lodged against an initial refusal of leave to enter).

- A person who had been refused a variation of his leave to enter or remain to that of a refugee had a right of appeal on asylum grounds against this refusal under AIAA 1993, s 8(2). However, under AIAA 1993, s 7, a person's limited leave could be curtailed on refusal of asylum and where such curtailment took place no right of appeal under s 8(2) (nor under IA 1971, s 14) arose and instead the SSHD could make a decision to deport the person.[5]

- A person against whom a decision to deport had been made could appeal against it on asylum grounds under AIAA 1993, s 8(3)(a). This applied, for example, to persons whose leave had been curtailed under s 7 (above). The point was to prevent repeat rights of appeal – an appeal against the refusal to vary the leave under s 8(2) followed, if unsuccessful, with an appeal against the decision to deport as an overstayer (see **2.1** above).

- A person against whom a deportation order had been made and who had unsuccessfully applied for it be revoked could appeal, on asylum grounds, against the refusal to revoke it under AIAA 1993, s 8(3)(b) (originally this right of appeal was only denied to persons who had already appealed against a decision to deport under AIAA 1993, s 8(3) (a); however, by an amendment,[6] a new AIAA 1993, s 8(3A) provided that a person may not appeal under AIAA 1993, s 8(3)(b) if he had had the right of appeal under AIAA 1993, s 8(3)(a), whether or not he had exercised it – again so as to prevent repeat rights of appeal).

- A person against whom removal directions were set, in particular as an illegal entrant, could appeal against them on asylum grounds under s 8(4).

1   See eg *R v Secretary of State for the Home Department, ex parte Sivakumaran* [1988] AC 958, [1988] Imm AR 147: the issue on judicial review was the correctness or otherwise, in judicial review terms – but applying the 'most anxious scrutiny' appropriate in cases involving fundamental human rights (see *R v Secretary of State for the Home Department, ex parte Bugdaycay* [1987] 1 AC 514 at 531, per Lord Bridge; though also see now *R (YH) v Secretary of State for the Home Department* [2010] EWCA Civ 116 at [8], [22]–[24], per Carnwath LJ critiquing the 'anxious scrutiny' approach – the real point in asylum cases however is not just the need for 'anxious scrutiny' but the importance of 'bearing in mind the relative gravity of the consequences of the court's expectation being falsified either in one way or in the other': per Lord Keith in *Sivakumaran* (above) at 994H citing Lord Diplock in *R v Governor of Pentonville Prison, ex parte Fernandez* [1971] 1 WLR 987, 994) – of the underlying decision to refuse asylum, rather than of the consequential immigration decision.

2   *Vilvarajah v United Kingdom* (1991) 14 EHRR 248: Vilvarajah and others were Sri Lankan
    Tamils who had been applicants in *R v Secretary of State for the Home Department, ex parte
    Sivakumaran* [1988] AC 958 (see fn 1 above).
3   That is ECHR, Arts 3 and 13. In fact, after the 1993 Bill was published the European Court of
    Human Rights (ECtHR) reversed the Commission on this issue, holding that judicial review
    is an effective remedy for the purposes of Art 13 in order to prevent a breach of Art 3 in the
    immigration context.
4   AIAA 1993, s 8 (commenced on 26 July 1993: Asylum and Immigration Appeals Act 1993
    (Commencement and Transitional Provisions) Order 1993, SI 1993/1655, art 2; repealed, from
    2 October 2000, except for transitional purposes, see below, by IAA 1999, Sch 14, para 104
    and Sch 16 and the Immigration and Asylum Act 1999 (Commencement No 6, Transitional
    and Consequential Provisions) Order 2000, SI 2000/2444).The exceptions related to persons
    whose exclusion, removal or deportation was considered by the SSHD to be conducive to the
    public good as being in the interests of national security: AIAA 1993, Sch 2, para 6, applying
    provisions contained in IA 1971, ss 13(5), 14(3) and 15(3), (4) to appeals, on asylum grounds,
    under AIAA 1993, s 8. See further below. The right of appeal lay to a 'special adjudicator':
    see AIAA 1993, s 8(5). The suspensive effect of asylum appeals under AIAA 1993, s 8 was
    provided for by AIAA 1993, Sch 2, paras 7–9. The right of appeal under AIAA 1993, s 8
    only lay against immigration decisions taken on or after commencement on 26 July 1993: SI
    1993/1655, art 3. In respect of decisions taken before that date the right of appeal lay under
    IA 1971, Pt II (see **2.1** above).
5   AIAA 1993, s 7. The SSHD could also curtail the leave of any dependant of the refused
    asylum claimant: s 7(1A). A person's whose leave had been curtailed and in respect of whom
    the SSHD had gone on to make a decision to deport could be detained: s 7(4).
6   Brought by AIA 1996 (see below).

2.5   In all cases a person could only appeal under AIAA 1993, s 8 if, before
the time of the refusal, variation, decision or directions (ie the immigration
decision) he had made a claim for asylum.[1] The problem then arose in those
cases where an asylum claim was only made after an adverse immigration
decision had been taken because, where the asylum claim was then refused,
there would be no right of appeal. The problem was solved by the government
undertaking to make a fresh immigration decision following the refusal of
asylum in such cases.[2]

1   AIAA 1993, Sch 2, para 2. This provision was brought in by way of a very late amendment
    to the 1993 Bill, in the House of Lords, to deal with the problem caused by the wording of
    the appeal rights creating subsections of s 8 that on their face implied that an asylum claim
    could be made, for the first time, in an appeal to a special adjudicator against an immigration
    decision (whereas the system and immigration rules require that all initial decisions on
    asylum claims are made by the SSHD: see eg the Immigration Rules, HC 395, para 328).
2   See per Earl Ferrers, Hansard, HL, 11 March 1993, p 1186. See also *Badmus* [1994] Imm AR
    137 and *Mayele* (10621) and note that in the case of refusals of leave to enter this undertaking
    was incorporated into the immigration rules – first in HC 251, para 75B (as inserted by HC
    725 from 26 July 1993, being also the date on which AIAA 1993 came into force) and now in
    the Immigration Rules, HC 395, para 332.

2.6   The question for the appellate authority was whether removal as at
the date of the hearing would contravene the Refugee Convention.[1] This was
the sole ground upon which such an appeal could succeed[2] and the wording
relating to 'removal' being contrary to the UK's obligations under the Refugee
Convention led to serious problems of interpretation where an appellant was

granted exceptional leave to enter or remain for a number of years. However, in *Saad and Diriye*[3] the Court of Appeal held, in cases involving appeals on asylum grounds against refusals to vary leave to remain to that of refugees, but where exceptional leave to remain for a number of years had been granted,[4] that the tribunals had erred in law in dismissing the appeals on the basis that, as no one could predict the future, the appellants could not overcome the burden of proof on them to demonstrate that there would be a real risk of their being persecuted on return to their homelands in a few years' time. The Court of Appeal held that, where an appellant who has been granted exceptional leave to remain satisfies the tribunal that, as at the date of the hearing, he is entitled to refugee status:

> 'the IAT must allow the appeal, if it is to avoid permitting a breach of the Convention to continue. The IAT will allow the appeal by proceeding on the hypothesis that, where the appellant has refugee status at the time of the appeal, that state of affairs will subsist at the time that ELR comes to an end. We consider that this is the approach that the appellate tribunal should adopt. Thus, an appeal under s 8(2) will, just as in the case of appeals under the other three sub-sections, raise as the crucial issue the question of whether the appellant enjoys refugee status at the time of the hearing of the appeal.'[5]

This was in part because the wording of the statutory provisions were in any case hypothetical in the sense that the question posed is whether removal *would be* contrary to the UK's obligations under the Refugee Convention and not whether removal *will be* contrary to them, and in part for practical and policy reasons as otherwise persons granted 'exceptional leave' (now 'humanitarian protection' or 'discretionary leave') but who were dissatisfied with not being recognised as refugees would have to resort to judicial review of the decision to refuse asylum (and this would have been contrary to part of the purpose in introducing the near universal appeal right in the first place – indeed the AIAA 1993 probably represented the high water mark of a comprehensive 'merits review' appeal system for asylum claimants in the UK and subsequently the approach has been towards again reducing the right of appeal in asylum cases with an apparent acceptance that this will be lead to more judicial reviews).

1   See *Sandralingham and Ravichandran v Secretary of State for the Home Department; R v Immigration Appeal Tribunal, ex parte Rajendrakumar* [1996] Imm AR 97 at 111–113, CA per Simon Brown LJ, distinguishing the situation in an asylum appeal under AIAA 1993, s 8 from that in a non-asylum appeal where the question posed by IA 1971, s 19 was whether the decision had been in accordance with the law and applicable immigration rules at the time that it was made (see *R v Immigration Appeal Tribunal, ex parte Weerasuriya* [1983] 1 All ER 195 and *R v Immigration Appeal Tribunal, ex parte Kotecha* [1983] 2 All ER 289), per Simon Brown LJ: 'the prospective nature of the question posed by section 8 of AIAA 1993 over-rides the retrospective approach ordinarily required (implicitly) on a section 19 appeal'. Furthermore, whether removal as at the date of the hearing would contravene the Refugee Convention was still the only relevant consideration on an appeal under AIAA 1993, s 8 even when the refusal of asylum was based on non-compliance grounds under the Immigration Rules, HC 395, para 340 (now deleted, but see para 339M): see *Ali Haddad* [2000] INLR 117 (IAT – starred).

2   Such that issues relating to Conventions other than the Refugee Convention or to matters of discretion were not relevant: see IA 1971, s 19(1) (as applied by AIAA 1993, Sch 2, para 4(2) (b) to appeals under AIAA 1993, s 8) re restrictions on the grounds of appeal and cf *R v A special adjudicator, ex parte Mehari* [1994] QB 474, per Laws J.
3   *Saad, Diriye and Osorio v Secretary of State for the Home Department* [2001] EWCA Civ 2008.
4   The appeals in *Saad* and *Diriye* were under AIAA 1993, s 8(2). The appeal in *Osorio* was against a refusal of leave to enter, under AIAA 1993, s 8(1) (see below).
5   *Saad, Diriye and Osorio* (above) at [68]. The Court of Appeal was impressed with the reasoning and determination of the IAT, on similar facts but in relation to an appeal under IA 1971, s 14, in *Laftaly* [1993] Imm AR 284. See also *Faraj* [2002] UKIAT 07376 at [18], holding that since the assessment of whether a person qualifies as a refugee is a hypothetical exercise which focuses on whether removal at the time of the hearing would be contrary to the Refugee Convention, purely practical difficulties in implementing removal to a safe part of the country of origin are irrelevant to that assessment. See also *GH (Iraq) v Secretary of State for the Home Department* [2005] EWCA Civ 1182; *Gedow v Secretary of State for the Home Department* [2006] EWCA Civ 1342.

2.7   A similar problem arose where, whilst an appeal on asylum grounds under AIAA 1993, s 8 was pending before the Appellate Authority, the original adverse immigration decision was withdrawn or reversed and the appellant was granted exceptional leave to enter or remain.[1] In *Massaquoi*[2] the Court of Appeal upheld the IAT's determination to the effect that where a decision to deport had been withdrawn and the appellant had been granted leave to remain following a hearing of her appeal by a special adjudicator, the IAT had to dismiss the appeal before it, against the decision to deport, because there was no decision left to appeal against. However, subsequently, in *Osorio*[3] the Court of Appeal, faced with an appeal, on asylum grounds, against a decision to refuse leave to enter, which had been dismissed by the tribunal due to a grant of exceptional leave to enter, held that although the wording of the statute directs attention to the consequences of removal of the appellant in terms of the UK's obligations under the Refugee Convention, the true position is that 'such an appeal provides a satisfactory vehicle for mounting a challenge to the Secretary of State's rejection of an asylum claim.'[4]

1   See **2.4** and **2.6** above for the situation where the initial decision was a grant of exceptional leave to enter. A person affected by such a decision and who was unhappy with the lack of refugee status would have to apply to vary his leave to remain to that of a refugee and if refused such variation would have the right of appeal under AIAA 1993, s 8(2) (subject, since the judgment of the Court of Appeal in *Onibiyo v Secretary of State for the Home Department* [1996] Imm AR 370, to the SSHD not holding that the variation application amounted only to further representations on the original on-entry asylum claim rather than to a fresh claim for asylum. However, in *Massaquoi* (19542) the IAT considered that it was unduly pessimistic to fear that the SSHD would take such an approach and that if he did, the courts would hold it to be irrational).
2   *Massaquoi v Secretary of State for the Home Department* [2000] All ER (D) 2375. See also *Dahmani* (21275) and *Unluyasar* (00525).
3   *Saad, Diriye and Osorio v Secretary of State for the Home Department* [2001] EWCA Civ 2008 (see **2.6**, fn 5 above).
4   *Saad, Diriye and Osorio* (above) at [56]. The Court of Appeal declined to extend *Massaquoi v Secretary of State for the Home Department* [2000] All ER (D) 2375 beyond appeals under AIAA 1993, s 8(3)(a): basically, it seems, because this Court of Appeal thought that the earlier court's decision was wrong and so they decided that it was only binding in terms of its narrow *ratio* which related specifically to appeals against decisions to deport.

CERTIFICATION UNDER AIAA 1993

2.8 The AIAA 1993, having provided a right of appeal on asylum grounds to refused asylum claimants regardless of the nature of the consequent immigration decision, also provided[1] that where the immigration decision was one of a kind that would not have attracted a suspensive right of appeal under IA 1971[2] and where the SSHD had certified that the refused asylum claim was without foundation,[3] then, if the special adjudicator on dismissing the appeal also agreed that the claim was without foundation, the claimant would have no right of appeal to the IAT.[4] This was the genesis of the subsequently much developed 'certification' procedure, the main effect of which, up until the changes in April 2003, was to deny a second-tier right of appeal to the IAT where the adjudicator agreed with the certificate on dismissing the appeal.[5] Under the originally enacted provision (in AIAA 1993, Sch 2, para 5) a claim could only be certified as being without foundation on two grounds:

(a) if (and only if) it did not raise any issue as to the UK's obligations under the Refugee Convention; or

(b) it was otherwise frivolous or vexatious.[6]

1 AIAA 1993, Sch 2, para 5 (as originally enacted).
2 AIAA 1993, Sch 2, para 5(1) stated that the provision for certification only applied to appeals under AIAA 1993, s 8(1), (3)(b) and (4) (ie to appeals against refusals of leave to enter, refusals to revoke deportation orders and removal directions: see **2.2** above). Furthermore, AIAA 1993, Sch 2, para 5(2) provided that the provision could not apply to appeals under AIAA 1993, s 8(1), against refusals of leave to enter, where the appellant could and did also appeal against the refusal under IA 1971, s 13, whilst being allowed to remain in the UK by virtue of IA 1971, s 13(3) (ie because at the time of the refusal he held a current entry clearance or was named in a current work permit: see **2.1** above).
3 AIAA 1993, Sch 2, para 5(1): for the certification to be valid, the SSHD had to certify the claim as being without foundation on its refusal and before any appeal was lodged: see *Mustafaraj* [1994] Imm AR 78 at 87. There did not have to be a piece of paper described as a 'certificate'; it was sufficient in practice that in his reasons for refusal letter, the SSHD stated or declared that in his opinion the claim was without foundation: *Mustafaraj* [1994] Imm AR 78. Certification could be done by an official acting under the authority of the SSHD: see *R v Secretary of State for the Home Department, ex parte Oladehinde* [1991] 1 AC 254, HL.
4 AIAA 1993, Sch 2, para 5(5). The remedy instead was judicial review, often concentrating on the special adjudicator's agreement with the certificate, rather than the determination of the substantive appeal, and often resulting in a quashing of the adjudicator's agreement with the certificate followed by a re-promulgation of the adjudicator's determination, *sans* certificate, such that the appellant could then apply for leave to appeal against it to the IAT. However, in eg *R v Immigration Adjudicator and Secretary of State for the Home Department, ex parte Gopalakrishnan* [2003] EWHC 6 (Admin), Richards J held that an adjudicator's agreement with a certificate should not be quashed unless there was a real prospect of a successful appeal to the IAT.
5 Although not relevant to the original, limited, form of certification, it is important to note that where, as was possible under the more developed forms of certification under the Asylum and Immigration Act 1996 and then IAA 1999 (see further below), an adjudicator allowed an appeal whilst agreeing with the certificate, there was no bar on the SSHD applying for leave to appeal to the IAT: see *Secretary of State for the Home Department v Abdul (Ghafoor) Khan* [1999] INLR 309, IAT.
6 AIAA 1993, Sch 2, para 5(3) (as originally enacted).

2.9   In *Mehari*[1] Laws J held that the first of these two grounds could only apply in third country cases, so that a claim to asylum could only fail to raise any issue as to the UK's obligations under the Refugee Convention if there was a safe third country that ought to be responsible for determining the claim. As to a claim being frivolous or vexatious, see further below as these are grounds upon which claims could still be certified under IAA 1999.[2] Under the original provision, where the claim was certified, a special adjudicator had an extra option for disposing of the appeal; if he did not agree that the claim was without foundation he could (as an alternative to allowing or dismissing the appeal) refer the case to the SSHD for reconsideration.[3] In practice, this third alternative only applied in relation to certifications under AIAA 1993, Sch 2, para 5(3)(a), on safe third country grounds.[4] In *Mehari*[5] Laws J envisaged three possible ways in which a special adjudicator could deal with an AIAA 1993, Sch 2, para 5(3)(a) case:

(i)   he could agree with the certificate, to the effect that he agreed that the appellant could properly be removed to a third safe country, and dismiss the appeal;

(ii)   he could disagree with the certificate, meaning that he did not agree that the appellant could properly be returned to a third country, and could either allow the appeal (against, for example, refusal of leave to enter) or refer the case back to the SSHD for reconsideration, under AIAA 1993, Sch 2, para 5(6) – effectively for substantive consideration of the asylum claim; or

(iii)   he could disagree with the certificate because he was in doubt as to whether the appellant could properly be removed to a third country and refer the matter back to the SSHD for further consideration as to whether the third country was in fact 'safe'.

1   *R v Special Adjudicator, ex parte Mehari* [1994] QB 474.
2   IAA 1999, Sch 4, para 9(6)(c).
3   AIAA 1993, Sch 2, para 5(6): this third alternative was unique to the period between the coming into force of AIAA 1993 in July 1993 and its amendment by the Asylum and Immigration Act 1996, three years later in October 1996.
4   In respect of certification under AIAA 1993, Sch 2, para 5(3)(b), 'frivolous or vexatious', the special adjudicator could allow the appeal and inherently therefore disagree with the certificate; dismiss the appeal but disagree that the claim was frivolous or vexatious (thereby allowing the appellant to apply for leave to appeal to the IAT); or dismiss the appeal and agree with the certificate (in which case AIAA 1993, Sch 2, para 5(5) barred an application for leave to appeal to the IAT).
5   See fn 1 above. The other leading case on appeals against third country certifications under the original AIAA 1993, Sch 2, para 5 was *Abdi and Gawe v Secretary of State for the Home Department* [1996] 1 All ER 641, HL.

THE EFFECT OF THE ASYLUM AND IMMIGRATION ACT 1996 ON APPEAL RIGHTS IN ASYLUM CASES

2.10   The Asylum and Immigration Act 1996 (AIA 1996) had two major effects on asylum appeals. First, third country cases were taken out of the general system of appeals on asylum grounds, against immigration decisions, under AIAA 1993, s 8[1] and were discretely dealt with under completely new provisions in AIA 1996 itself[2] and secondly a much more complicated certification regime was introduced.[3] In respect of third country cases, a suspensive right of appeal to a special adjudicator lay[4] only against a safe third country certificate[5] (rather than against a normal immigration decision[6]) and only where the third country in question was not a Member State of the European Union or a designated country.[7] There was no right of appeal, for either side, to the IAT against an adjudicator's determination of such an appeal.[8] It appears, unsurprisingly, that there were no appeals under this provision still pending as of 1 April 2003 and the commencement of the new appeals provisions in NIAA 2002.[9]

1   See above.
2   AIA 1996, ss 2 and 3.
3   AIAA 1993, Sch 2, para 5 was substituted by a completely new para 5 by AIA 1996, s 1.
4   Under AIA 1996, s 3(1). The sole ground of appeal was that any of the conditions for certifying, as listed in AIA 1996, s 2(2) (broadly to the effect that the asylum claimant was not a national or citizen of the country to which he was to be sent and that the country was safe and would not *refoul* him in breach of the Refugee Convention), was not fulfilled when the certificate was issued or had since ceased to be fulfilled.
5   As made under AIA 1996, s 2(1)(a).
6   See **2.1** *et seq* and **2.4** *et seq* above. Unless and until a certificate was set aside on an AIA 1996, s 3(1)(a) appeal, the appellant had no right of appeal under IA 1971, Pt II, or AIAA 1993, s 8: AIA 1996, s 3(1)(b).
7   AIA 1996, ss 2(3) and 3(2). The designated countries were Canada, Norway, Switzerland and the USA: see the Asylum (Designated Countries of Destination and Designated Safe Third Countries) Order 1996, SI 1996/2671, art 3. There was a right of appeal against certificates issued in relation to removals to Member States and designated countries, but only from abroad: AIA 1996, s 3(2). The CA held that such an appeal right was not an effective alternative remedy such as to prevent a judicial review of the certificate being sought: see *R v Secretary of State for the Home Department and Immigration Officer, Waterloo International Station, ex parte Canbolat* [1997] 1 WLR 1569, CA; *R v Secretary of State for the Home Department, ex parte Iyadurai* [1998] Imm AR 470, CA.
8   This was because IA 1971, s 20 (appeals to the IAT) was not included in the provisions of IA 1971 that were applied to these appeals by AIA 1996, s 3(4).
9   On 2 October 2000, when IAA 1999, Pt IV came into force (see **2.13** below), AIA 1996, s 3(1) and (2) remained in force in respect of third country certificates issued before that date: see the Immigration and Asylum Act 1999 (Commencement No 6, Transitional and Consequential Provisions) Order 2000, SI 2000/2444, arts 3(1)(a) and 4(1)(b)(iii). However, by 1 April 2003, when NIAA 2002, Pt 5 came into force (see Chapter 3), there was, apparently, no need to refer to old appeals provisions under AIA 1996 in the NIAA 2002 (Commencement No 4) Order 2003, SI 2003/754, art 3 or 4, for transitional purposes.

CERTIFICATION FOLLOWING AIA 1996

2.11   The new certification regime introduced by AIA 1996[1] was far more complex than before and allowed for certification on a number of bases, most of which were carried on into IAA 1999.[2] The first of these[3] was that the appellant was to be sent to a country or territory designated, in an order made by the SSHD by statutory instrument, as a country or territory in which it appeared to him that there was in general no serious risk of persecution.[4] The second was that the appellant, on arrival in the UK, had either failed to produce a passport without giving a reasonable explanation for his failure to do so or had produced an invalid passport without informing the immigration officer of that fact.[5] The third was that the appellant's asylum claim did not show a fear of persecution for a Refugee Convention reason.[6] The fourth was that the claimed fear of persecution was manifestly unfounded or that the circumstances giving rise to the fear had ceased to exist.[7] The fifth was that the asylum claim had been made after an adverse immigration decision had been taken against the appellant.[8] The sixth was that the claim was manifestly fraudulent or that any of the evidence adduced in its support was manifestly false.[9] The seventh and last was that the claim was frivolous or vexatious.[10] There was a caveat, however: the claim could not be certified if the evidence adduced in its support established a reasonable likelihood that the appellant had been tortured in the country or territory to which he was to be sent.[11]

---

1   By substituting a new para 5 in AIAA 1993, Sch 2.

2   IAA 1999, Sch 4, para 9 (see **2.26** below).

3   Which was not repeated in IAA 1999.

4   AIAA 1993, Sch 2, para 5(2) as substituted. The designated countries, on the so-called 'white list', were Bulgaria, Cyprus, Ghana, India, Pakistan, Poland and Romania: see the Asylum (Designated Countries of Destination and Designated Safe Third Countries) Order 1996, SI 1996/2671, art 2. However, in *R v Secretary of State for the Home Department, ex parte Javed* [2001] EWCA Civ 789, the Court of Appeal held that the inclusion of Pakistan in the countries designated in the order was unlawful due to the evidence of persecution of Ahmadis and women (following the House of Lords decision in *Islam v Secretary of State; R v IAT and Secretary of State, ex parte Shah* [1999] 2 AC 629) in that country. On the other hand, in *R (Balwinder Singh) v Secretary of State for the Home Department* [2001] EWHC Admin 925, Burton J held that the inclusion of India in the white list was lawful, partly because the particular problems for Sikhs in the Punjab affected only 0.76% of the total population of India.

5   AIAA 1993, Sch 2, para 5(3) as substituted. Repeated in IAA 1999, Sch 4, para 9(3), see below.

6   AIAA 1993, Sch 2, para 5(4)(a) as substituted. Repeated in IAA 1999, Sch 4, para 9(4)(a), see below.

7   AIAA 1993, Sch 2, para 5(4)(b) as substituted. Repeated in IAA 1999, Sch 4, para 9(4)(b), see below.

8   AIAA 1993, Sch 2, para 5(4)(c) as substituted. Repeated in IAA 1999, Sch 4, para 9(6)(a), see below.

9   AIAA 1993, Sch 2, para 5(4)(d) as substituted. Repeated in IAA 1999, Sch 4, para 9(6)(b), see below.

10   AIAA 1993, Sch 2, para 5(4)(e) as substituted. Repeated in IAA 1999, Sch 4, para 9(6)(c), see below.

11 AIAA 1993, Sch 2, para 5(5) as substituted. Repeated in IAA 1999, Sch 4, para 9(7) (see **2.26** and **2.30** below). This positive provision resulted from a late amendment to the 1996 Bill in the House of Lords. Incidentally, its use of the 'reasonable likelihood' test in relation to evidence of past events persuaded the IAT in *Horvath* [1999] INLR 7 at 23 that *Kaja* [1995] Imm AR 1 had been correctly decided by its majority (though see the somewhat more detailed and sophisticated approval of *Kaja* by the Court of Appeal in *Karanakaran v Secretary of State for the Home Department* [2000] 3 All ER 449).

2.12 The main consequence for appeal purposes of a claim being certified on its refusal by the SSHD was that if the adjudicator dismissed the appeal and agreed with the SSHD's opinion, as stated in the certificate,[1] that one of the positive certification criteria applied and that the negative criteria, relating to a reasonable likelihood of past torture in the country of proposed return, did not apply, the appellant would have no right of appeal to the IAT.[2] The other consequence was that the appeal before the adjudicator was processed more quickly than was the case with a non-certified refused claim.[3] Due to the requirement[4] that the provision applied to an appeal only if the SSHD had certified the claim on its refusal on the bases that:

(a) one of the positive grounds for certification applied, and

(b) the negative ground did not apply,

a certificate that did not state the latter was invalid and could not be amended once an appeal had been lodged against the consequent immigration decision.[5] Certificates and whether to agree with them or not came exclusively within the jurisdiction of special adjudicators. The IAT had no jurisdiction to consider certificates.[6] Accordingly, where the IAT remitted an appeal back to an adjudicator for a fresh hearing in respect of a claim that had been certified on its refusal, it was open to the second adjudicator to agree with the certificate notwithstanding that the first adjudicator had disagreed with it (thereby opening the route to the tribunal which had then led to the remittal).[7]

1 See AIAA 1993, Sch 2, para 5(1) as substituted. Again, the certification could simply be added to the refusal letter by the Home Office official responsible for the refusal (see **2.8** above).
2 AIAA 1993, Sch 2, para 5(7), as substituted.
3 AIAA 1993, Sch 2, para 5(6) allowed for special provisions in the then Procedure Rules to be applied to appeals in relation to certified claims: see Asylum Appeals (Procedure) Rules 1996, SI 1996/2070, rr 5(2) (two-day time limit for lodging appeal against refusal of leave to enter where claim certified on refusal and personal service effected on appellant, rather than normal seven days), 9(2) (special adjudicator to determine appeal within ten days of receiving papers from Home Office, rather than 42 days) and 11(2) (special adjudicator supposed to announce his decision orally at the hearing when agreeing with certificate).
4 In AIAA 1993, Sch 2, para 5(1) as substituted.
5 See *Salah Ziar* [1997] Imm AR 456: even if the appellant had never raised the issue of torture, the certification was invalid *ab initio* so that the defect could not be cured by amendment and so none of the consequences of certification could apply to the appeal. This meant, *inter alia*, that if a special adjudicator had erroneously agreed with such a defective certificate and dismissed the appeal with the result that the determination had then been promulgated declaring (erroneously) that there was no right of appeal against it, the time-limit for applying for leave to appeal to the IAT did not run and so an application for leave to appeal against

the determination had to be entertained, as in time, whenever subsequently made: see *Zolele* [1999] INLR 422; *Akhuemonkhan* [1998] INLR 265; and *Bequeen* (15586). The decision in *Ziar* was purportedly distinguished, but in reality disagreed with, by a differently constituted IAT in *Abdul (Ghafoor) Khan* [1999] INLR 309 and was criticised by another IAT in *Bajwa* (L00007) for being overly concerned with the nature of a 'certificate' when, in that IAT's view, the real question was whether on the facts as presented, one of the 'positive' sub-paras applied and sub-para (5) did not apply to the claim. However, the decision in *Ziar* was approved by the IAT in *Zolele* [1999] INLR 422.

6   See *Liu Dao Shiu* (01/TH/00103).

7   See *R (Rajah Vairavanathan) v Secretary of State for the Home Department* [2002] EWCA Civ 1310 in which Schiemann LJ emphasised the point that the SSHD certifies the claim, not the appeal. The adjudicator's jurisdiction in hearing an appeal emanating from that claim is different from that of the IAT's. For one thing the adjudicator, but not the IAT, has jurisdiction to consider the issue of the certificate. An appeal remitted to an adjudicator by the IAT was still an appeal, under the appropriate subsection of AIAA 1993, s 8 (or IAA 1999, s 69), arising out of the original claim that had been certified. Accordingly, the second adjudicator, on the remitted appeal, did have jurisdiction to consider the certificate.

RIGHTS OF APPEAL UNDER IAA 1999

2.13   In relation to immigration decisions taken on or after 2 October 2000 rights of appeal lay under IAA 1999, Pt IV[1] to an adjudicator[2] with a further right of appeal, with permission and subject to certification in asylum cases, to the IAT.[3] On this date, 2 October 2000, IA 1971, Pt II (see **2.1** *et seq* above) and AIAA 1993, s 8 (see **2.4** *et seq* above) were repealed.[4] However, in accordance with transitional provisions,[5] in respect of immigration decisions made before 2 October 2000, the right of appeal, whether pending on that date or even lodged on or after that date in respect of a decision made shortly before it, remained under IA 1971, Pt II, in respect of non-asylum appeals and under AIAA 1993, s 8, in respect of asylum appeals.[6] The most important innovation in IAA 1999, coinciding with the coming into general force of the Human Rights Act 1998 on that same date, 2 October 2000,[7] was the right of appeal, with suspensive effect, on human right grounds (see **2.21** *et seq* below).

1   See IAA 1999 (Commencement No 6 and Transitional and Consequential Provisions) Order 2000, SI 2000/2444, art 2 and Sch 1.

2   IAA 1999, s 57 (and ss 58–70) and Sch 3. Special adjudicators (see above) became adjudicators: IAA 1999, Sch 15, para 3(2).

3   IAA 1999, Sch 4, para 22 (note that this procedural provision also applied to the transitional appeals under IA 1971 and AIAA 1993, s 8 – see fn 6 below). See also in relation to the IAT, IAA 1999, s 56 and Sch 2. Regarding certification under IAA 1999, see **2.26** *et seq* below.

4   Repealed by IAA 1999, s 169(1) and (3), Sch 14, paras 49 and 104 and Sch 16 and SI 2000/2444, art 2 and Sch 1.

5   Transitional provisions provided for by SI 2000/2444, arts 3(1)(a) and 4 and Sch 2.

6   Procedural provisions in IAA 1999 (such as those relating to the definition of a pending appeal under IAA 1999, s 58(5)–(10) and those relating to the determination of appeals by adjudicators and appeals to and from the IAT under IAA 1999, Sch 4, paras 21–23) applied to these continuing appeals under IA 1971, Pt II and AIAA 1993, s 8 as they did to appeals under IAA 1999, Pt IV: SI 2000/2444, arts 3(1)(b), (c) and 4 and Sch 2.

7   The Human Rights Act 1998 (Commencement No 2) Order 2000, SI 2000/1851, brought all those provisions of HRA 1998 that were not already in force, into force on 2 October 2000.

NON-ASYLUM APPEALS UNDER IAA 1999

2.14   IAA 1999 followed the same approach as IA 1971 in providing for separate rights of appeal, with specified limitations and restrictions, against the main immigration decisions.

- Under IAA 1999, s 59(1) a person could appeal against a decision to refuse leave to enter[1] and under s 59(2) a person could appeal against a refusal of a certificate of entitlement or an entry clearance. Under s 59(3) and (4) a person appealing against a refusal of leave to enter could object to the country of destination, as set in consequent removal directions, and claim that he ought to be removed (if at all) to a different country specified by him.[2] IAA 1999, s 60 provided for limitations on the right of appeal under s 59. These included the stipulation in s 60(3) that s 59 did not entitle a person to appeal against refusal of leave to enter whilst he was in the UK unless at the time of the refusal he held a current entry clearance or was named in a current work permit. Intending visitors, other than 'family visitors',[3] short-term students and prospective students and dependants of the same were denied a right of appeal under s 59 by s 60(4) and (5); and persons refused entry clearance or leave to enter on the ground that they, or a person to whom they were dependant, did not hold a relevant document[4] or did not satisfy a requirement in immigration rules as to age or nationality or citizenship or sought entry for a period exceeding that permitted by the rules (eg seeking more than six months' leave as a visitor), were denied a right of appeal by s 60(7). A person could not appeal under s 59 against a refusal of leave to enter, or against a refusal of an entry clearance, if the SSHD certified that directions had been given by the SSHD, acting in person, for the appellant not to be given entry to the UK on the ground that his exclusion is conducive to the public good or if the leave to enter, or entry clearance, was refused in compliance with any such directions: s 60(9).

- Under IAA 1999, s 61 a person could appeal against a decision to vary, or to refuse to vary, his limited leave to enter or remain in the UK if, as a result of that decision, he may be required to leave the UK within 28 days of being notified of the decision.[5] IAA 1999, s 62 provided for limitations on the right of appeal under s 61. No right of appeal arose under s 61 where the refusal to vary leave was on the ground that a relevant document had not been issued,[6] the relevant person did not satisfy a requirement in immigration rules as to age or nationality or citizenship or the requested variation would have resulted in the duration of a person's leave exceeding that permitted by the rules: s 62(1). A person could not appeal under s 61 against a refusal to vary leave if the SSHD certified that the appellant's departure from the UK would be conducive to the public good as being in the interests of national security, the relations between the UK and any other country or for other reasons of a political nature, or the decision questioned by the appeal was taken on that ground by the SSHD (and not by a person acting under his authority): s 62(3) and (4). No right of appeal arose against a variation made by statutory instrument nor could a person appeal against a refusal of the SSHD to make a statutory instrument: s 62(5).

- Under IAA 1999, s 63(1)(a) a person could appeal against a decision by the SSHD to make a deportation order against him[7] and under s 63(1)(b) a person could appeal against a refusal by the SSHD to revoke a deportation order made against him. Under s 63(3) and (4) a person appealing under s 63(1) could object to the country of destination, as set in consequent removal directions, and claim that he ought to be removed (if at all) to a different country specified by him.[8] IAA 1999, s 64 provided for limitations on the right of appeal under s 63. These included the stipulation in s 64(3) that s 63 did not entitle a person to appeal against a refusal to revoke a deportation order whilst he was in the UK, whether because he had not complied with the requirement to leave or because he had contravened the prohibition on entering. A person could not appeal under s 63 against a decision to make a deportation order against him if the ground of the decision was that his deportation is conducive to the public good as being in the interests of national security or of the relations between the UK and any other country or for other reasons of a political nature: s 64(1). Nor could a person appeal against a refusal to revoke a deportation order if the SSHD certified that the appellant's exclusion from the UK would be conducive to the public good or if revocation was refused on that ground by the SSHD (and not by a person acting under his authority): s 64(2). A family member over the age of 18 facing deportation as such[9] could not, on an appeal under s 63, seek to go behind a statement made with a view to obtaining leave to enter or remain as the principal's family member unless he did not make or did not know that such a statement had been made: s 64(4)–(6).

- Under IAA, s 66 a person subject to removal directions as an illegal entrant, under IAA 1999, s 10 (see **1.11**) or as the crew of ships or aircraft (see **1.11**), could appeal on the sole ground that on the facts of his case there was in law no power to give them on the ground on which they were given.[10] IAA 1999, s 66(3) specifically provided that a person could not appeal against such directions so long as he was in the UK, unless he was also appealing on human rights or asylum grounds under s 65 or 69(5) (see below).

- Under IAA, s 67 a person could appeal against removal directions as given on refusal of leave to enter, pursuant to a deportation order or on his having entered in breach of a deportation order, on the ground that he ought to be removed (if at all) to a different country or territory specified by him.[11] IAA 1999, s 68 provided for the following limitations on the right of appeal under s 67: no right of appeal against directions given on refusal of leave to enter the UK unless the person was also appealing under s 59(1) against the decision that he requires leave to enter or he was refused leave at a time when he held a current entry clearance or was a person named in a current work permit: s 68(1); a person who had been entitled to object to a destination on an appeal under s 59 or 63 (above) but did not do so or his objection was not sustained, could not appeal against any directions subsequently given to the same country: s 68(2); and a person who claimed that he ought to be removed to a country other than one he had objected to on an appeal under s 59, 63 or 67 had to produce evidence, if he was not a national or citizen of that other country, that that country would admit him: s 68(3).

1   A person could appeal against: (a) the decision that he requires leave; or (b) the refusal: IAA 1999, s 59(1)(a) and (b).
2   As to 'if at all' see **2.3** above and *R v Immigration Appeal Tribunal, ex parte Muruganandarajah* [1986] Imm AR 382.
3   As regards 'family visitors', who could appeal under s 59, see the Immigration Appeals (Family Visitor) (No 2) Regulations 2000, SI 2000/2446 and the Immigration Appeals (Family Visitor) Regulations 2002, SI 2002/1147.
4   Namely entry clearances, passports or other ID documents and work permits: s 60(8).
5   The 28 days is linked to the old approach in VOLO 1976, SI 1976/1572 (see **2.1**, fn 10 above).
6   Namely entry clearances, passports or other ID documents and work permits or equivalent documents issued after entry: s 62(2).
7   As a result of his liability to deportation under IA 1971, s 3(5) (see **2.1** above). A deportation order under IA 1971, s 5(1) could not be made while an appeal could be brought against the decision to make it: IAA 1999, s 63(2).
8   See fn 2 above.
9   Under IA 1971, s 3(5)(c) (see **2.1**, fn 13 above).
10 IAA 1999, s 66(1) and (2). A person appealing under s 66 against directions given by virtue of a deportation order, could not dispute the original validity of that order: s 66(4).
11 See fn 2 above.

APPEALS AGAINST EEA DECISIONS

2.15   IAA 1999, s 80 provided that the SSHD may by regulations make provision for appeals against any immigration decision in relation to:

(a)   an EEA national;

(b)   a member of the family of an EEA national;

(c)   a member of the family of a UK national who is neither such a national nor an EEA national.[1]

In this context 'immigration decision' meant a decision concerning a person's removal from the UK or his entitlement to be admitted to the UK; to reside, or to continue to reside, in the UK; or to be issued with, or not to have withdrawn, a residence permit.[2] It was specifically provided that appeals under the regulation would lie to an adjudicator or, in such circumstances as may be prescribed, to the SIAC (as to which, see Chapter 7).[3] Pursuant to this provision, the Immigration (European Economic Area) Regulations 2000[4] were made. For appeals now under the EEA Regs 2006, see Chapter 4.

1   IAA 1999, s 80(1). Regarding family members of UK nationals who are not EEA nationals themselves, see *R v Immigration Appeal Tribunal, ex parte Secretary of State for the Home Department* (C370/90) [1992] 3 All ER 798, ECJ and see now EEA Regs 2006, reg 9.
2   IAA 1999, s 80(2).
3   IAA 1999, s 80(4).
4   SI 2000/2326: these regulations were revoked by EEA Regs 2006, Sch 3, Pt 1, para 1 from 30 April 2006.

ASYLUM APPEALS UNDER IAA 1999

2.16   Rights of appeal on refugee asylum grounds were provided for by IAA 1999, s 69 which also maintained the structure of the appeal being against the immigration decision on the ground that removal – as at the date of the hearing before the appellate authority[1] – in consequence of the decision would be contrary to the Refugee Convention. IAA 1999, s 69 nearly mirrored AIAA 1993, s 8 (see **2.4** *et seq* above) such that a right of appeal lay:

- under s 69(1), against a refusal of leave to enter on the ground that removal in consequence of the refusal would be 'contrary to the Convention';[2]

- under s 69(2), against a decision to vary, or to refuse to vary, limited leave to enter or remain in the UK, if as result the person may be required to leave the UK within 28 days of being notified of the decision;[3]

- under s 69(4)(a) against a decision to deport;

- under s 69(4)(b) against a refusal to revoke a deportation order;

- and under s 69(5) against removal directions as per s 66 for non-asylum appeals (see **2.14** above).

1   IAA 1999, s 77(3)(a) gave statutory effect to the judgment of the Court of Appeal in *Sandralingham and Ravichandran v Secretary of State for the Home Department; R v Immigration Appeal Tribunal, ex parte Rajendrakumar* [1996] Imm AR 97 (see **2.6**, fn 1 above).
2   Defined in IAA 1999, s 69(6) as meaning contrary to the UK's obligations under the Refugee Convention.
3   As to 28 days, see **2.14**, fn 5 above.

2.17   The 'distortion' in this mirror was caused by the new appeal right in IAA 1999, s 69(3) as to which see below. The sole issue on an appeal under IAA 1999, s 69, remained whether or not removal would be contrary to the UK's obligations under the Refugee Convention.[1] Asylum appeals under IAA 1999 had suspensive effect.[2] An important innovation was a new right of appeal, in IAA 1999, s 69(3), which provided that a person, who had been refused leave to enter or remain in the UK on the basis of a claim for asylum made by him, but who had been granted (whether before or after the decision to refuse leave as a refugee) limited leave to enter or remain in excess of 28 days, could appeal to an adjudicator against the refusal on the ground that requiring him to leave the UK after the time limited by that leave would be contrary to the Refugee Convention.[3] The statutory wording still therefore related to the consequences of removal, but the Tribunal in *Abdillahi*[4] held that the approach laid down by the Court of Appeal in *Saad and Diriye*[5] – that the appellate authority must consider whether the appellant is a refugee at the time of the appeal hearing and if so must allow the appeal 'on the premise that that would remain the situation when his leave expired'[6] – was the correct approach to be taken to appeals under IAA 1999, s 69(3).

1   See *Ali Haddad* [2000] INLR 117 (IAT – starred) and **2.6**, fn 1 above; see also *R (Zaier) v Immigration Appeal Tribunal and Secretary of State for the Home Department* [2003] EWCA Civ 937 at [31] and [37] and *Sheikh Mohamed* [2002] UKIAT 00075.
2   IAA 1999, Sch 4, paras 10–18.
3   IAA 1999, s 69(3). A person who had 28 days or less leave to enter or remain, as at the date of his being notified of the decision, had the right of appeal under IAA 1999, s 69(2). A person granted indefinite leave to enter or remain has never had any right of appeal under any of the Immigration Acts (as now listed in UKBA 2007, s 61(2): see **1.2**) and this remained the case with IAA 1999, s 69(3).
4   *Abdillahi* [2002] UKIAT 00266 (starred); see also *Andrabi* [2002] UKIAT 02884 at [16]–[18].
5   *Saad, Diriye and Osorio v Secretary of State for the Home Department* [2001] EWCA Civ 2008 (see **2.6** above).
6   *Saad, Diriye and Osorio* (above) at [75].

2.18   On the other hand, however, another new provision in IAA 1999 effectively reversed the Court of Appeal judgment in *Osorio*[1] (see **2.7** above). Under IAA 1999, s 58(9) a pending appeal under *any* provision of Part IV of the Act, other than under IAA 1999, s 69(3), was to be treated as abandoned if the appellant was granted leave to enter or remain in the UK.[2] In *Kanyenkiko*[3] the Court of Appeal held that the terms of IAA 1999, s 58(9) were unequivocal and that its application was triggered by the conditions contained in it, which, if met, meant that the appeal was to be treated as abandoned such that once (exceptional) leave to enter or remain was granted any pending appeal, other than one under IAA 1999, s 69(3), immediately ceased to be pending and therefore could not be varied or purportedly varied into an appeal under IAA 1999, s 69(3).[4] A pending appeal under IAA 1999, Pt IV was also to be treated as abandoned if the appellant left the UK.[5] Obviously this provision only applied to appeals with suspensive effect such that the appellant was in the UK in the first place when lodging the appeal. Leaving the UK means physically leaving UK territory or territorial waters, regardless of any intention to return; a day-trip to France will suffice to cause a pending appeal to be treated as abandoned.[6]

1   *Saad, Diriye and Osorio v Secretary of State for the Home Department* [2001] EWCA Civ 2008.
2   IAA 1999, s 58(9). As was pointed out by the IAT in *Abdillahi* [2002] UKIAT 00266 (starred) this provision was a procedural provision applicable to continuing appeals under AIAA 1993, s 8 (see **2.13**, fn 6 above) and so arguably the Court of Appeal should have dismissed the appeal in Osorio's case on this basis: see IAA 1999, s 58(5)–(7), (9).

3   *Kanyenkiko v Secretary of State for the Home Department* [2003] EWCA Civ 542.
4   The appeal in *Kanyenkiko* had been under IAA 1999, s 69(5) (against removal directions);
    after the adjudicator had dismissed the appeal the SSHD granted the appellant exceptional
    leave to remain. The IAT granted leave to appeal and the appellant, by notice, had sought to
    vary the grounds of the appeal to rely on IAA 1999, s 69(3) rather than IAA 1999, s 69(5) so
    as to avoid the effect of IAA 1999, s 58(9). The IAT dismissed the appeal on the basis that it
    had been abandoned and the Court of Appeal held that once the limited leave to remain had
    been granted the appeal fell to be treated as abandoned and thus there was nothing to vary
    or amend before the IAT. Arguably, a person unhappy with the grant of exceptional leave to
    enter or remain in this situation could have immediately lodged an appeal, to an adjudicator,
    under IAA 1999, s 69(3), against the decision to refuse leave to enter or remain as a refugee,
    as this was the very basis of the right of appeal under that provision (see above): see *Suleykha
    Abdi Ali v Secretary of State for the Home Department* [2003] EWCA Civ 1295 (grant of
    permission to appeal). Also, see now NIAA 2002, s 104(4A) and (4B) and the Tribunal
    Procedure (First-tier Tribunal) (Immigration and Asylum Chamber) Rules 2014, r 16(3); and
    see Chapters 3 and 4.
5   IAA 1999, s 58(8).
6   See *Dupovac v Secretary of State for the Home Department* [2000] Imm AR 265, CA; and see
    now saved NIAA 2002, s 104(4) (as to which see Chapter 3) and s 92(8) (as a new 'relevant
    provision' as per IA 2014 amendments: see Chapter 4) and *R (MM (Ghana)) v Secretary of
    State for the Home Department* [2012] EWCA Civ 827; *AS (Afghanistan) v Secretary of State
    for the Home Department* [2009] EWCA Civ 1076 at [61] and [93]. However, in *Shirazi v
    Secretary of State for the Home Department* [2003] EWCA Civ 1562 at [11]–[18], Sedley
    LJ, in interpreting the abandonment provision in IAA 1999, s 58(8), held that there was a
    distinction to be made between an appeal to an adjudicator or the IAT being abandoned by
    reason of the appellant leaving the UK on the one hand and a further appeal to the Court of
    Appeal being abandoned for that reason on the other (see also per Munby LJ at [35]–[39] and
    Mummery LJ at [41]).

LIMITATIONS ON APPEAL RIGHTS ON ASYLUM GROUNDS

2.19   In keeping with the theme of the Act in respect to appeal rights (see
2.14 above), IAA 1999, s 70 provided for limitations on the rights of appeal
under s 69. There was no right of appeal to an adjudicator on asylum grounds
under IAA 1999, s 69 where the SSHD, acting in person, either made the
immigration decision, or certified that the immigration decision was made,
on the grounds that the person's exclusion or removal from the UK was in the
interests of national security. In particular:

- IAA 1999, s 70(1) prevented an appeal to an adjudicator, under IAA
  1999, s 69(1), against a refusal of leave to enter where the SSHD
  certified that the appellant's exclusion from the UK was in the interests
  of national security;

- IAA 1999, s 70(2)–(3) prevented an appeal to an adjudicator, under IAA
  1999, s 69(2), against a variation or a refusal to vary leave to remain,
  where the SSHD had certified that the appellant's departure from the UK
  was in the interests of national security or where the decision was taken
  on that ground by the SSHD in person;

- IAA 1999, s 70(5) prevented an appeal to an adjudicator, under IAA 1999, s 69(4)(a), against a decision to make a deportation order if the ground of the decision was that the person's deportation was in the interests of national security;

- IAA 1999, s 70(6) prevented an appeal to an adjudicator, under IAA 1999, s 69(4)(b), against a refusal to revoke a deportation order where the SSHD had certified that the appellant's exclusion from the UK was in the interests of national security or where the revocation was refused on that ground by the SSHD in person.[1]

In such cases a right of appeal lay instead to the SIAC.[2] Similarly, where an asylum claimant was refused recognition as a refugee due to the application of the exclusion provisions in the Refugee Convention, Art 1F,[3] but was nonetheless granted limited (exceptional) leave to enter or remain, his right of appeal to an adjudicator under IAA 1999, s 69(3) could be precluded where the SSHD certified that the disclosure of material on which the refusal was based was not in the interests of national security.[4] In such a case a right of appeal lay instead to the SIAC.[5] A person could not bring an appeal on asylum grounds at all under s 69 of the Act unless, before the time of the immigration decision in question, he had made a claim for asylum.[6] A person could not appeal on refugee asylum grounds against a refusal to revoke a deportation order if he had had a right of appeal on such grounds against a decision to deport (whether or not he had exercised this right of appeal).[7] See further below regarding other limitations on or exclusions of the right of appeal under IAA 1999, s 69.

---

1   There was no need to prevent an appeal, under IAA 1999, s 69(5), against removal directions for an illegal entrant, etc on national security grounds as in such a case the SSHD would instead make a decision to deport, under IA 1971, s 3(5)(a) (as amended by IAA 1999, s 169(1) and Sch 14, para 44(2)). As for appeals under IAA 1999, s 69(3) see text and fn 4 below.

2   Under SIACA 1997, s 2(1) and (1B) (as amended by the Immigration (European Economic Area) Regulations 2000, SI 2000/2326, reg 32, but prior to its substitution by NIAA 2002, s 114(3) and Sch 7, para 20: see Chapter 7).

3   The Refugee Convention, Art 1F provides for exclusion from the benefits of the Refugee Convention where there are serious reasons for considering that the claimant has committed serious non-political crimes or variously defined heinous acts: see *Asylum Law and Practice* (2nd edition, Bloomsbury Professional), Ch 8, section 4.

4   IAA 1999, s 70(4).

5   Under SIACA 1997, s 2(1) and (1B) (as amended by SI 2000/2326, reg 32, but prior to its substitution by NIAA 2002, s 114(3) and Sch 7, para 20). On such an appeal the SIAC could, instead of determining the appeal itself, quash the certificate and remit the appeal to an adjudicator: SIACA 1997, s 4(1A) (as inserted by IAA 1999, s 169(1) and Sch 14, paras 118 and 122; but SIACA 1997, s 4 as a whole was repealed by NIAA 2002, ss 114(3) and 161, Sch 7, para 22 and Sch 9).

6   IAA 1999, s 70(7)(a). See below regarding certification in those cases where a claim for asylum was made after the initial immigration decision had been taken such that, on refusal of the asylum claim, a new immigration decision, with right of appeal under IAA 1999, s 69, had to be taken. Refugee asylum grounds (see **2.4** *et seq* above) could only be raised in an appeal under IAA 1999, s 69: IAA 1999, s 70(7)(b) (ie asylum grounds could not be raised in, for example, a human rights appeal).

7   IAA 1999, s 70(8).

THIRD COUNTRY APPEAL RIGHTS UNDER IAA 1999

2.20   As was the position under AIA 1996,[1] a discreet right of appeal lay, under IAA 1999, s 71, in third country cases, against the certificate itself[2] on the ground that any of the conditions applicable to that certificate was not satisfied when it was issued or had since ceased to be satisfied.[3] The right of appeal under IAA 1999, s 71 was, however, only suspensive in respect of third country certificates relating to removal to countries other than Member States of the European Union and designated countries.[4] As stated above, a non-suspensive right of appeal in these circumstances is of no real value[5] and in practice, appeals under IAA 1999, s 71 were rare. There was no right of appeal, for either side, to the IAT against an adjudicator's determination of such an appeal.[6]

1   See **2.10** above. AIA 1996, ss 2 and 3 were repealed as of 2 October 2000 by IAA 1999, s 169(3) and Sch 16. However, they remained in force in respect of certificates issued before that date and IAA 1999, s 71 did not apply in respect of such certificates: IAA 1999 (Commencement No 6 and Transitional and Consequential Provisions) Order 2000, SI 2000/2444, art 2 and Sch 1 and arts 3(1)(a) and 4(1)(b)(iii) and Sch 2, para 4.
2   Third country certificates could be issued under IAA 1999, ss 11(2)(a), 12(2)(a) and 12(5)(a) – see *Asylum Law and Practice* (2nd edition, Bloomsbury Professional), paras 14.5–14.12.
3   IAA 1999, s 71(2): see further in *Asylum Law and Practice* as above. Until and unless a certificate was set aside on an appeal under IAA 1999, s 71 or 65 (on human rights grounds, see below) or otherwise ceased to have effect, the person in respect of whom the certificate was issued was not entitled to appeal under IAA 1999 in respect of any immigration decision taken against him: IAA 1999, s 72(1).
4   IAA 1999, s 72(2)(b). The designated third countries were Canada, Norway, Switzerland and the USA: Asylum (Designated Safe Third Countries) Order 2000, SI 2000/ 2245. See further in *Asylum Law and Practice* as above.
5   See **2.10**, fn 7 above.
6   IAA 1999, Sch 4, para 22(1).

HUMAN RIGHTS APPEALS UNDER IAA 1999

2.21   As noted above, the enactment of IAA 1999, Pt IV coincided with that of the bulk of HRA 1998 and a novel provision in IAA 1999 was the right of appeal, with suspensive effect,[1] under IAA 1999, s 65, to an adjudicator,[2] for a person who alleged that an authority,[3] in taking any decision under the Immigration Acts[4] relating to his entitlement to enter or remain in the UK, acted in breach of his human rights[5] or racially discriminated against him.[6] The right of appeal under IAA 1999, s 65 only applied in relation to immigration decisions taken on or after 2 October 2000.[7] However, the SSHD accepted that where an appeal, under the previous legislation,[8] was pending at that date against an immigration decision and where that appeal was finally unsuccessful, he would reconsider the decision in light of representations made as to its compatibility with the Human Rights Convention and take a new decision (which could of course still be adverse to the applicant) accordingly.[9] Where the new decision was, for example, to (again) refuse leave to enter there was clearly then a right of appeal, under IAA 1999, s 65, on human rights grounds against it.[10] A problem arose, however, in respect of the setting of removal directions for illegal entrants.[11] The matter was settled by the Court of Appeal in *Kariharan*[12] in effect holding that if, as a result of HRA 1998, a person has a right not to be removed from the UK,[13] then any decision taken under the Immigration Acts, whether a refusal of leave to enter, a decision to deport, the making of a deportation order or the setting of removal directions, that will result in his removal, was a decision relating to his entitlement to remain and was appealable under IAA 1999, s 65.[14] Furthermore, third country certificates could be appealed against, on human rights grounds, under IAA 1999, s 65.[15] However, where a person was granted a limited period of (exceptional) leave to enter or remain but appealed against the decision not to recognise him as a refugee,[16] there could be no meaningful additional right of appeal under s 65, on human rights grounds, against the decision to grant leave to enter or remain for only a limited period.[17]

1   IAA 1999, Sch 4, para 20(1). However, removal directions or a deportation order could be made whilst a human rights appeal was pending: IAA 1999, Sch 4, para 20(2); but no such directions or order were to have effect during this period: IAA 1999, Sch 4, para 20(3) (now see NIAA 2002, ss 78 and 79).
2   IAA 1999, s 65(1). Where, however, the immigration decision was one that was made by, or having been made, was certified by, the SSHD as being in the interests of national security, the right of appeal lay instead to the SIAC under SIACA 1997, s 2A (as inserted by IAA 1999, s 169(1) and Sch 14, paras 118 and 121 (as amended by the Immigration (European Economic Area) Regulations 2000, SI 2000/2326, reg 32(4)(b)); repealed by NIAA 2002, ss 114(3) and 161 and Sch 7, para 21 and Sch 9). Where an appeal lay to the SIAC and had not been determined by it, no right of appeal lay under IAA 1999, s 65: IAA 1999, s 65(6).
3   Meaning, here, the SSHD, an immigration officer or a person responsible for the grant or refusal of entry clearance: IAA 1999, s 65(7).
4   As originally listed in IAA 1999, s 167(1) (but now see UKBA 2007, s 61(2) (as amended by IA 2014, s 73(5) from 14 May 2014)).
5   An immigration authority acts in breach of a person's human rights if he acts, or fails to act, in relation to that person in a way which is made unlawful by HRA 1998, s 6(1): IAA 1999, s 65(2)(b) (as amended by the Race Relations (Amendment) Act 2000, Sch 2, paras 32–34).
6   An immigration authority racially discriminates against a person if he acts, or fails to act, in relation to that person in a way which is unlawful by virtue of the Race Relations Act 1976, s 19B: IAA 1999, s 65(2)(a) (as amended by the Race Relations (Amendment) Act 2000, Sch 2, paras 32–34).
7   IAA 1999 (Commencement No 6 and Transitional and Consequential Provisions) Order 2000, SI 2000/2444, art 2 and Sch 1 and arts 3(1)(a) and 4(1)(a) and see *Pardeepan* [2000] INLR 447. Similarly, the right of appeal on human rights grounds to the SIAC under SIACA 1997, s 2A (see fn 2 above) only applied in respect of immigration decisions taken on or after 2 October 2000: SI 2000/2444, art 3(2) and Sch 2, para 5(2).
8   i.e. under IA 1971, Pt II and/or AIAA 1993, s 8: see above.
9   The SSHD accepted this as a concession made to the IAT in *Pardeepan* [2000] INLR 447 in October 2000 and subsequently announced it as a policy in Parliament on 19 July 2001: see *R (Kariharan) v Secretary of State for the Home Department* [2001] EWHC Admin 1004 at [7] for the policy.
10 A refusal of leave to enter is clearly a decision taken under the Immigration Acts relating to the person's entitlement to enter the UK for the purposes of IAA 1999, s 65(1).
11 It was in the context of removal directions set since 2 October 2000 against persons declared to be illegal entrants before that date that the controversy had arisen, with Stanley Burnton J

in *R (Kariharan) v Secretary of State for the Home Department* [2001] EWHC Admin 1004 holding that such directions did not give rise to a right of appeal on human rights grounds under IAA 1999, s 65(1), because they are purely administrative decisions (made consequent to an earlier substantive decision) and were not therefore decisions under the Immigration Acts relating to a person's entitlement to enter or remain in the UK for the purposes of being appealed against under IAA 1999, s 65(1). However, in *R (Kumarakuruparan) v Secretary of State for the Home Department* [2002] EWHC Admin 112 Newman J concluded (at [18]–[22]) that Stanley Burnton J was wrong on this issue and that a right of appeal under IAA 1999, s 65(1) was available against removal directions set against both illegal entrants and under IAA 1999, s 10 (see **1.11**). The Court of Appeal upheld Newman J's conclusion (see fn 12 below).

12   *R (Kariharan and Koneswaran) v Secretary of State for the Home Department; Secretary of State for the Home Department v Kumarakuruparan* [2002] EWCA Civ 1102. The SSHD's petition to appeal to the House of Lords was refused: [2003] 1 WLR 1386.

13   Because the removal would result in a breach of his human rights, as protected by the ECHR, such that the decision of the authority (see fn 3, above) that would lead to such removal would be rendered unlawful by HRA 1998, s 6(1).

14   See also, prior to the Court of Appeal's judgment in *R (Kariharan)*, but to the same effect, the IAT determinations in *Kehinde* (01/TH/2668, starred) and *Devaseelan* [2002] UKIAT 00702 (starred).

15   IAA 1999, s 11(2)(b) (prior to amendment by NIAA 2002, s 80) and IAA 1999, s 12(2)(b) and (5)(b) (prior to amendment by the Nationality, Immigration and Asylum Act 2002 (Consequential and Incidental Provisions) Order 2003, SI 2003/1016) all referred to the certificate (rather than any other immigration decision) being set aside on an appeal under IAA 1999, s 65. Note that a suspensive appeal under IAA 1999, s 65(1) could be prevented in respect of third country certificates issued under IAA 1999, ss 11(2)(a) and 12(2)(a), by the SSHD certifying that the person's human rights allegation (or claim) was manifestly unfounded: see IAA 1999, s 72(2)(a) and see *Asylum Law and Practice* (2nd edition, Bloomsbury Professional) at para 14.6.

16   Under IAA 1999, s 69(3) (see **2.17** above).

17   See eg *Kislizki* [2002] UKIAT 07097. Furthermore, a pending appeal under IAA 1999, s 65, was to be treated as abandoned if the appellant was granted leave to enter or remain: IAA 1999, s 58(9) (see **2.18** above).

2.22   Aside from lodging an appeal specifically on human rights grounds under IAA 1999, s 65(1), a person appealing against an immigration decision on any other ground or grounds could raise human rights issues in the proceedings before an adjudicator or the IAT and if the appellate authority decided that the immigration decision was incompatible with the appellant's human rights it could allow his appeal on that ground, notwithstanding that the SSHD had never considered nor formally refused any human rights claim made to him by the appellant.[1] Indeed, the appellant did not necessarily have to raise the issue himself; rather if a question arose, as to the compatibility of the appealed against decision with the appellant's human rights, in the course of the proceedings before the appellate authority,[2] the authority had jurisdiction to consider the question[3] and to allow the appeal on human rights grounds if appropriate to do so, notwithstanding that the SSHD had never considered the relevant 'question' beforehand.[4] In an appeal on human rights grounds under IAA 1999, s 65, there appeared to be a somewhat artificial distinction between ECHR, Art 3 and all other Articles, in that in respect of Art 3 the appellate authority, just as with refugee asylum grounds,[5] had to consider all relevant matters as at the date of the hearing before it,[6] whereas in respect of 'any other ground' the appellate authority was limited to considering only evidence that was available to the SSHD at the time the decision was made or that related to relevant facts as at that date.[7] However, the IAT, chaired by the then President, in *SK*[8] sought to limit the practical effect of this distinction by holding that the appellate authority, in dealing with any appeal concerned with potential removals from the UK, could consider any question relating to an appellant's rights under any Article of the ECHR as at the date of hearing, on the basis that 'such a question' was not 'a ground' within the meaning of the limiting provision.[9] The question as to what, if any, degree the rights of non-dependent (to the appeal) family members could and should be taken account of in human rights appeals involving Art 8 family life issues, troubled the tribunal and the courts until the matter was settled – positively in that the Art 8 rights of family members must be taken proper account of – by the House of Lords in *Beoku-Betts*.[10]

1   IAA 1999, s 65(3)–(5). See eg *Shamim Box* [2002] UKIAT 02212. Note the contrast with the right of appeal on refugee asylum grounds under IAA 1999, s 69, where an appeal on that ground could not be brought against an immigration decision unless before the decision in question the appellant had made a claim (to the SSHD) for asylum: IAA 1999, s 70(7)(a) (see **2.19** above). For the possible adverse consequences of failing to raise an issue relating to human rights during proceedings before the appellate authority, see below.

2   See IAA 1999, s 65(3).

3   IAA 1999, s 65(4).

4   IAA 1999, s 65(5). This could work to an appellant's disadvantage in that an adjudicator or the IAT could consider a human rights issue, not specifically raised by the appellant nor previously considered by the SSHD, in the course of an appeal and dismiss the appeal overall, in part on the basis that the decision was not incompatible with the appellant's human rights given that issue: see *R (Nyakonya) v Immigration Appeal Tribunal and Secretary of State for the Home Department* [2002] EWHC 1544 (Admin), per Ouseley J. The reason why this was disadvantageous to an appellant is that if later, after the appeal was finally determined, he made a human rights allegation or claim to the SSHD based on the same matter or matters (as rejected on the appeal) and if the SSHD rejected that allegation or claim, the SSHD could issue a certificate under IAA 1999, s 73 (now see NIAA 2002, s 96) effectively either preventing the appellant from appealing at all or from relying on that ground in any further appeal he may have: see further below and Chapters 3 and 4.

5   See **2.16**, fn 1 above.

6   IAA 1999, s 77(3)(b).

7   IAA 1999, s 77(4).

8   *SK* [2002] UKIAT 05613 (starred) at [19]–[22] and [46].

9   *SK* (above) at [22]. The IAT's reasoning was that Art 3 had been singled out for specific reference in IAA 1999, s 77(3) (alongside refugee asylum grounds) because of its prime importance in any removal case (see also *R (Ullah) v Special Adjudicator; Do v Immigration Appeal Tribunal* [2004] UKHL 26). See now NIAA 2002, ss 85(4)–(6).

10   *Beoku-Betts v Secretary of State for the Home Department* [2008] UKHL 39. Previously, in *Kehinde* (01/TH/02668, starred, 19 December 2001) at [9], the IAT held that the human rights of the non-immigrant family members of an appellant appealing under IAA 1999, s 65, do not need to be taken account of in the appeal. None the less, and despite the starring of *Kehinde*, the IAT chaired by the then President, in *Alban Krasniqi* [2002] UKIAT 00231 (4 February 2002) upheld the determination of an adjudicator allowing the appeal under IAA 1999, s 65, on ECHR, Art 8 grounds, on the basis that the Kosovan appellant's British baby daughter's situation was determinative. Following this, in *Baah* [2002] UKIAT 05998 at [42], the IAT, with reference to *Kehinde*, accepted that when considering an appellant's private or family life it may not be possible to separate that completely from the lives of other close

50

family members and that the degree to which the rights of other family members will enter into consideration will vary in every case. In *R (AC) v Immigration Appeal Tribunal and Secretary of State for the Home Department* [2003] EWHC 389 (Admin), Jack J held, at [38], that, although on an appeal on human rights grounds the appellate authority is primarily concerned with the human rights of the appellant, where Art 8 family life rights are in issue, 'the adjudicator and the Tribunal should take account of the impact of the proposed deportation on the family life of any person with whom the appellant has established a family life'. See also *AB (Jamaica) v Secretary of State for the Home Department* [2007] EWCA Civ 1302, per Sedley LJ at [20].

MIXED APPEALS

2.23   Under AIAA 1993 provision was made[1] for special adjudicators, when dealing with an appeal on asylum grounds under AIAA 1993, s 8,[2] to also deal, in the same proceedings, with any appeal against the same immigration decision which the appellant was entitled to bring under IA 1971, Pt II[3] on any other, non-asylum, ground[4] and with any appeal brought by the appellant under that Part against any other immigration decision or action.[5] The wording of the provision was mandatory[6] and this led the IAT in *Adeite*[7] to hold that failure by a special adjudicator to deal with all outstanding appeals on all permissible grounds in the same proceedings vitiated any, partial, determination that had been made. The IAT decided that it had no alternative but to remit the asylum appeal for a fresh hearing to be dealt with by a different special adjudicator along with the marriage appeal.[8] However, in *Gelo Dragica*[9] – where a special adjudicator had dismissed an appeal on asylum grounds under AIAA 1993, s 8(3)(a) against a decision to deport but had failed to explicitly deal with an appeal, against the same decision, under IA 1971, s 15(1)(a) (as restricted by IA 1988, s 5) – another division of the IAT distinguished the decision in *Adeite* on the grounds that the special adjudicator had implicitly dismissed the appeal under IA 1971, s 15(1)(a) because that, restricted, appeal could not possibly have succeeded as there clearly was on the facts of the case a power in law to deport the appellant.[10]

1   Under AIAA 1993, Sch 2, para 3.
2   See **2.4** *et seq* above.
3   See **2.1** above.
4   AIAA 1993, Sch 2, para 3(a). Note that, following enactment of AIAA 1993, no appeal could be brought on asylum grounds under IA 1971, Part II: AIAA 1993, Sch 2, para 1.
5   AIAA 1993, Sch 2, para 3(b).
6   'the special adjudicator shall in the same proceedings deal with ...'
7   *Adeite* (10874) in which the appellant was appealing under AIAA 1993, s 8(1) on asylum grounds against a refusal of leave to enter the UK while at the same time having an outstanding appeal under IA 1971, s 14 against a refusal to vary his leave to remain on the basis of his marriage to a British citizen (he had left the country while that appeal remained outstanding – under the subsequent wording of IA 1971, s 33(4), as amended by AIA 1996, Sch 2, para 4(2), that appeal would have been treated as abandoned by reason of his leaving the UK (and now see NIAA 2002, ss 104(4) (as a saved provision: see Chapter 3) and 92(8) (as a new 'relevant provision' as per IA 2014 amendments: see Chapter 4)), but at the time it was not – and on return had been refused leave to enter at which stage he claimed asylum).

The special adjudicator had noted that the IA 1971 appeal was pending, but then had gone on to consider the 'asylum appeal' without further reference to the 'marriage appeal'. The IAT held that AIAA 1993, Sch 2, para 3(b) required the special adjudicator to deal with both appeals – against different immigration decisions – in the same proceedings.

8   The marriage appeal was still outstanding but was not before the IAT (it not having been determined by an adjudicator yet) and so any attempt by the IAT to deal with the asylum appeal on its own would itself have offended against the requirements of AIAA 1993, Sch 2, para 3(b).

9   *Gelo Dragica* (13288).

10   See **2.1** above regarding IA 1988, s 5 and the restriction on the right of appeal under IA 1971, s 15(1)(a).

'ONE-STOP' APPEALS

2.24   Under IAA 1999, where a person who was an illegal entrant, liable to be removed under s 10,[1] or who had arrived in the UK without leave to enter, an entry clearance, or a current work permit in which he was named, made a claim for asylum under the Refugee Convention or a claim that it would be contrary to the UK's obligations under the Human Rights Convention for him to be removed from, or required to leave, the UK, he was also required to state any additional grounds which he had or may have had for wishing to enter or remain in the UK.[2] At this stage, if he had made his claim under one of the above Conventions and wished also to make a claim under the other, he had to do so in writing and serve it on the person responsible for the determination of the claim within a prescribed period.[3] Similarly, a person who had been refused leave to enter, or who had been refused a variation of leave to remain as a consequence of which he may have been required to leave the UK within 28 days, or against whom the SSHD had decided to make a deportation order and who, in each case, had a right of appeal against the relevant immigration decision while remaining in the UK, was required, at the same time as, or in the alternative to, lodging his appeal, to state any additional grounds he had or may have had for wishing to remain in the UK.[4] At this stage such a person who had not already made a claim for protection under either or both the Refugee Convention and the ECHR and who wished to do so, had to make his claim under either or both Conventions in writing and serve it on the SSHD before the end of the prescribed period.[5] In this way all the grounds upon which a person wished to enter or remain in the UK could be taken account of in one decision and if necessary could then be considered on one appeal against that immigration decision.[6] Where an appellant before an adjudicator was appealing on refugee asylum grounds[7] or, on non-asylum grounds, against a decision to refuse leave to enter or remain or to vary or refuse to vary limited leave to remain (where the result of the decision was that the appellant would have to leave the UK within 28 days) or to make a decision to deport,[8] the appellant was to be treated as also appealing on any additional grounds which he may have had for appealing against the immigration decision and which he was not prevented from relying on.[9] 'Additional grounds' meant any grounds specified in a statement made to the SSHD[10] other than those on which the appeal was brought.[11] The real purpose of the rather convoluted statutory wording was to prevent an appellant relying on a ground or grounds which he had not stated in a statement of additional grounds and of which he had been aware at the material time.[12] However, an appellant could not be prevented from raising human rights grounds on an appeal even if he had not raised such grounds in a statement of additional grounds[13] and could only be prevented from raising refugee asylum grounds on an appeal if he had applied for asylum[14] after the end of the prescribed period for serving a statement of additional grounds[15] and, on refusing the claim, the SSHD also certified that:

(a)   one purpose of making the claim was to delay the removal from the UK of the applicant or of any other member of his family, and

(b)   the applicant had no other legitimate purpose for making the application.[16]

1   IAA 1999, s 10 provides for the removal of persons who are unlawfully in the UK.
2   IAA 1999, s 75(1). Under s 75(2) the person responsible for the determination of the claim had to serve on the claimant and on any relevant member of his family (as defined in the Immigration and Asylum Appeals (One-Stop Procedure) Regulations 2000, SI 2000/2244 ('One-Stop Procedure Regulations'), r 7) a notice requiring the recipient to state any additional grounds which he had or may have had for wishing to enter or remain in the UK.
3   IAA 1999, s 75(3). The prescribed period for serving the statement was ten working days if the person was entitled to appeal under IAA 1999 and five working days if he was entitled to appeal under SIACA 1997: One-Stop Procedure Regulations, r 4.
4   IAA 1999, s 74(1)–(5). Under IAA 1999, s 74(4) the decision maker (meaning the SSHD or as the case may be an immigration officer: IAA 1999, s 74(5)) had to serve on the applicant and on any relevant member of his family (as defined in the One-Stop Procedure Regulations, r 6) a notice requiring the recipient to state any additional grounds which he had or may have had for wishing to enter or remain in the UK.
5   IAA 1999, s 74(6), (7). The prescribed period for serving the statement was the same as for serving a statement under IAA 1999, s 75 (fn 3 above).
6   IAA 1999, s 77.
7   IAA 1999, s 77(1)(a).
8   IAA 1999, s 77(1)(b).
9   IAA 1999, s 77(2). See below regarding grounds which the appellant was prevented from relying on by virtue of IAA 1999, s 76.
10   Under IAA 1999, ss 74 and 75 as above.
11   IAA 1999, s 77(5). The subsection only referred to a statement made under IAA 1999, s 74 but by virtue of the One-Stop Procedure Regulations, r 5(6)(b)(ii) it was to be read as including a reference to a statement made under IAA 1999, s 75.
12   IAA 1999, s 76(1), (2). An appellant could still raise an additional ground on an appeal if the SSHD considered that he had a reasonable excuse for omitting to do so in a statement of additional grounds: IAA 1999, s 76(3)(b).
13   IAA 1999, s 76(3)(a) and see IAA 1999, s 65(3)–(5) (see **2.22** above).
14   No appeal could be brought on asylum grounds in any case unless an application for asylum had previously been made to the SSHD: IAA 1999, s 70(7)(a) (see **2.19** above).
15   See fnn 3 and 5 above. Obviously this provision only applied where the appellant had not raised refugee asylum in his statement of additional grounds: IAA 1999, s 76(4).
16   IAA 1999, s 76(5). 'Member of the family' had such meaning as prescribed: IAA 1999, s 76(6) and One-Stop Procedure Regulations, r 8.

2.25   In *Balamurali*[1] the Court of Appeal considered the meaning of these conditions and held that the SSHD had to first form an opinion as to whether one purpose, not necessarily the only purpose, of the application having been made was to delay removal from the UK; if he did not conclude that a purpose of the application was to delay removal there could be no certification, but where the opposite conclusion was reached, the SSHD would go on to consider whether the applicant had any other legitimate purpose for making the application such as a desire to bring attention to a significant change in the law or in the circumstances relevant to the case.[2]

1   *Balamurali and Sandhu v Secretary of State for the Home Department* [2003] EWCA Civ 1806. Previously, in *R (Vemenac) v Secretary of State for the Home Department* [2002] EWHC 1636 (Admin), Burton J considered that it was inherent that any asylum claim always has as part of its purpose a desire to delay removal and so the real issue was always condition (b) which he equated with an application being manifestly unfounded (see also *R (Ngamguem) v Secretary of State for the Home Department* [2002] EWHC 1550 (Admin)). This was followed, though with some reservation, by Davis J in *R (Soylemez) v Secretary of State for the Home Department* [2003] EWHC 1056 (Admin) at [13]–[15] – the SSHD in *Soylemez* accepted (at [14]), for the purposes of the case, that *Vemenac* was correctly decided on this issue whilst reserving his position to argue otherwise in some other case. However, in *R (Balamurali) v Secretary of State for the Home Department* [2003] EWHC 1183 (Admin), Mitting J, and in *R (Duka) v Secretary of State for the Home Department* [2003] EWHC 1262 (Admin) Collins J, expressly disagreed with Burton J's interpretation of 'no other legitimate purpose' in IAA 1999, s 73 (see fn 2 below) and in *Balamurali* Mitting J granted permission to appeal to the Court of Appeal for the matter to be decided upon there.
2   Both *Balamurali* and *Vemenac* (above) dealt with certificates issued under IAA 1999, s 73(8) (as to which see **2.32** below) but the wording of both conditions (a) and (b) was, in all material respects, the same as between IAA 1999, ss 73(8) and 76(5). See now NIAA 2002, s 96 (see Chapters 3 and 4).

CERTIFICATION UNDER IAA 1999

2.26   The complex certification regime as introduced by AIA 1996[1] was continued with in IAA 1999[2] with some modifications. The first of these was that there was no longer provision for certification on the basis of proposed return to a designated safe country of origin.[3] The second was that separate provision was made for certification of claims under the ECHR.[4] The third was practical in that the only effect of certification, under IAA 1999, was that if the adjudicator agreed with the opinion expressed in the certificate, there was no right of appeal to the IAT in relation to the certified claim or claims;[5] unlike under the previous regime, there was no speeding-up of the appeal process before the adjudicator as a consequence of certification.[6] Thus, under IAA 1999 the bases for certification were as follows:

(a)   if on arrival in the UK the applicant was required by an immigration officer to produce a valid passport and either–

    (i)   failed to do so without a reasonable explanation, or

    (ii)   produced an invalid passport without informing the officer that it was not valid;[7]

(b)   with respect to a claim under the Refugee Convention, the claim–

    (i)   did not show a fear of persecution for a Refugee Convention reason, or

    (ii)   it showed such a fear but the fear was manifestly unfounded or the circumstances which gave rise to the fear no longer subsisted;[8]

(c)   with respect to a claim under the ECHR, the claim–

    (i)   did not disclose a right under the Convention, or

    (ii)   it did disclose such a right, but the claim was manifestly unfounded;[9]

(d)   the claim was made at any time after the claimant had–

    (i)   been refused leave to enter;

    (ii)   been recommended for deportation by a criminal court;

    (iii)   been notified of a decision to deport;

    (iv)   been notified of liability to removal as an illegal entrant;[10]

(e)   the claim was manifestly fraudulent or any of the evidence adduced in its support was manifestly false;[11]

(f)   the claim was frivolous or vexatious.[12]

However, as before,[13] regardless of all the above, if the applicant had adduced evidence which established a reasonable likelihood that he had been tortured in the country to which it was proposed he be sent, there could be no, valid, certification.[14]

---

1   See **2.11** above.
2   IAA 1999, Sch 4, para 9. The paragraph applied to an appeal under IAA 1999, Part IV by a person who claimed that it would be contrary to the Convention for him to be removed from, or required to leave, the UK, if the SSHD had certified that, in his opinion, that claim was one to which: (a) sub-paras (3), (4), (5) or (6) applied; and (b) sub-para (7) did not apply: IAA 1999, Sch 4, para 9(1) (as for sub-paras (3), etc, see below). 'Contrary to the Convention' meant contrary to the UK's obligations under the Refugee Convention or the ECHR: IAA 1999, Sch 4, para 9(8). IAA 1999, Sch 4, para 9A (as inserted by the Race Relations (Amendment) Act 2000, Sch 2, para 40 as from 2 April 2001: Race Relations (Amendment) Act 2000 (Commencement) Order 2001, SI 2001/566) provided separately for appeals under IAA 1999, s 65(1) on race discrimination grounds where the SSHD certified that, in his opinion, the race discrimination claim was manifestly unfounded.
3   See **2.11**, fnn 3 and 4 above.
4   IAA 1999, Sch 4, para 9(5) and see *Zenovics v Secretary of State for the Home Department* [2002] EWCA Civ 273 – see below.
5   IAA 1999, Sch 4, para 9(2). As to claim or claims, see *Zenovics* (above) and **2.27** below.
6   See **2.12**, fn 3 above. Unlike its predecessor, the Immigration and Asylum Appeals (Procedure) Rules 2000, SI 2000/2333 contained no provisions for the more rapid processing of certified appeals.
7   IAA 1999, Sch 4, para 9(3).

8   IAA 1999, Sch 4, para 9(4). Repealed by NIAA 2002, Sch 7, para 29(1) as of 7 November
     2002 (on commencement of NIAA 2002: see NIAA 2002, s 162(2)(w)) but without prejudice
     to: (a) the continuing effect of a certificate issued before commencement of NIAA 2002;
     or (b) the power of the SSHD after commencement of NIAA 2002 to issue a certificate in
     respect of a claim made before commencement: NIAA 2002, Sch 7, para 29(2). The reason
     for the repealing of this provision was in no way beneficial to asylum claimants; rather it
     was because it, and para 9(5) (see fn 9 below), were replaced by the far more draconian
     transitional provisions in NIAA 2002, s 115 (as repeated for NIAA 2002 appeals, in s 94:
     see Chapters 3 and 4) applying to appeals under IAA 1999 and denying a suspensive right of
     appeal on refugee asylum and/or human rights grounds all together where the SSHD certified
     that the claim was, or claims were, 'clearly unfounded' (see Chapters 3 and 4 for NIAA 2002
     appeals).
9   IAA 1999, Sch 4, para 9(5). This provision was also repealed as of 7 November 2002, in the
     same manner, with the same caveats and for the same reasons as described in fn 8 above.
10   IAA 1999, Sch 4, para 9(6)(a).
11   IAA 1999, Sch 4, para 9(6)(b).
12   IAA 1999, Sch 4, para 9(6)(c).
13   See **2.11**, fn 11 above.
14   IAA 1999, Sch 4, para 9(7).

2.27   As previously, there did not have to be any actual certificate, a
paragraph in the reasons for refusal letter sufficed.[1] For a certificate to be valid
it had to expressly state that not only one of the positive bases for certification
applied but also that the negative basis did not apply.[2] A certificate that did
not state this was invalid and could not be amended once an appeal had been
lodged against the consequent immigration decision.[3] However, the certifier
did not need to spell out the reasons why one of the positive bases applied and
why the negative basis did not apply: it was sufficient for him to simply state
that the relevant sub-paragraph applied and that IAA 1999, Sch 4, para 9(7)
did not apply.[4] Where a claim involved both Refugee Convention and ECHR
issues, it had to be certified in respect of each Convention-based claim[5] and the
adjudicator had to agree with the opinion expressed in respect of each claim
for there to be no right of appeal to the IAT at all: if the certificate only applied,
for example, to the Refugee Convention claim or if the adjudicator only
agreed with the opinion expressed in the certificate in relation to the Refugee
Convention claim, then it was still open to the appellant to apply for leave
to appeal to the IAT in respect of his claim under the ECHR (and his appeal
under IAA 1999, s 65) if the adjudicator had dismissed the appeal on both
its Convention grounds.[6] Certificates and whether to agree with them or not
still came exclusively within the jurisdiction of adjudicators such that the IAT
had no jurisdiction to consider certificates.[7] Furthermore, once an adjudicator
had agreed with a certificate (strictly, had agreed with the SSHD's opinion
as expressed in a certificate[8]) there was no power in the SSHD to withdraw
the certificate so as to allow for a right of appeal to the IAT.[9] The statutory
duty of an adjudicator in considering a certificate was to independently decide
whether or not he agreed with the opinion of the SSHD expressed in it, on the
basis of the evidence that was before him, the adjudicator, at the hearing and
not simply on the basis of the evidence that was before the SSHD at the time
of certifying.[10]

1   See *Mustafaraj* [1994] Imm AR 78 and see **2.8**, fn 3 above.
2   IAA 1999, Sch 4, para 9(1) – the SSHD had to expressly state that, in his opinion, a positive
     sub-paragraph applied and that IAA 1999, Sch 4, para 9(7) did not apply (see **2.26**, fn 14
     above): see *Salah Ziar* [1997] Imm AR 456 and see **2.12**, fn 5 above.
3   *Salah Ziar* (above) and *R (Gopalakrishnan) v Immigration Adjudicator* [2003] EWHC 6
     (Admin).
4   See *R (Farkondeh) v Special Adjudicator* [2002] EWHC 384 (Admin) and *Gopalakrishnan*
     (above). The rationale behind this was that the reasons for certification would in any case be
     clear from the reasons for refusing the substantive claim as contained in the refusal letter of
     which the certification formed a part.
5   See *Zenovics v Secretary of State for the Home Department* [2002] EWCA Civ 273. In
     practical terms this only applied specifically to certifications as per (b) and (c) in **2.26** above.
     The bases for certification as per (a) and (d) in **2.26** above inherently applied to claims under
     either or both Conventions and it was on this basis that the IAT in *Maria Mendes* [2002]
     UKIAT 03922 sought to distinguish the Court of Appeal judgment in *Zenovics* in relation
     to a certification under IAA 1999, Sch 4, para 9(3)(b) (ie as per (a) in **2.26** above). As to
     certifications as per (e) and (f) above, these were more ambiguous and no doubt best practice
     would have been to certify the claim under each Convention separately as being manifestly
     fraudulent, false, frivolous or vexatious.
6   *Zenovics* (above).
7   See *R (Rajah Vairavanathan) v Secretary of State for the Home Department* [2002] EWCA
     Civ 1310 and see **2.12** above, especially fnn 6 and 7.
8   See IAA 1999, Sch 4, para 9(1) and (2) and see **2.26**, fnn 2 and 5 above.
9   See *Dube v Secretary of State for the Home Department* [2003] EWCA Civ 114, reversing
     Keith J's judgment ([2002] EWHC 2032, Admin) on this issue.
10   *Gopalakrishnan* (above).

2.28   With regards (a) in **2.26** above, a passport or travel document meant
a document satisfactorily establishing identity and nationality or citizenship.[1]
A passport with pages missing was not valid for these purposes.[2] The fact that
a person simply did not have a passport amounted to a reasonable explanation
for not producing one so long as the immigration officer was informed of this
on arrival.[3] Certification on this basis was clearly inappropriate in the case of
clandestine illegal entrants.[4] It was in fact very hard to see the justification, as
distinct from legality, for certification of an asylum claim on this basis at all.
With respect to (b) and (c) in **2.26** above, it was important for the decision
maker not to certify, or for an adjudicator not to agree with such a certificate,
under IAA 1999, Sch 4, para 9(4)(a), for supposed failure of the claim to show
a fear of persecution for a Convention reason, if the real reason for rejection
was a supposed lack of credibility and where, if the account was believed, it
would show a fear for a Convention reason.[5] However, this was subject to the
caveat that certification (and agreement with certification) under that provision
would not be inhibited 'by a mere assertion of the relevant fear or fear for a
relevant reason if the material provided to support it could not conceivably do
so.'[6] As to a claim being 'manifestly unfounded', Latham LJ stated in *Atabaky*[7]
that such certification had 'to be based on the certainty that the claim could not
possibly succeed.' With regards (d) in **2.26** above, this was simply a matter of
fact; if a person claimed asylum for the first time after an adverse immigration
decision had been made against him, the SSHD would have to consider the
claim[8] and if he refused it he would:

(a)   also certify it under this provision (subject to the torture caveat), and

(b)   make a new immigration decision with a right of appeal on asylum (and human rights) grounds.[9]

1   See IA 1971, Sch 2, para 4(2).
2   See *R v Secretary of State for the Home Department, ex parte Karafu* [2001] Imm AR 26, QBD.
3   See *R v Naillie* [1993] AC 674, HL.
4   See *Hua* (G0077).
5   See *R (Gavira) v Secretary of State for the Home Department* [2001] EWHC Admin 250, per Stanley Burnton J at [10]–[13]; approved in *R (Atabaky) v Secretary of State for the Home Department* [2002] EWCA Civ 234, per Latham LJ at [18].
6   *Atabaky* (above) at [20]–[21]: an asylum claim could only mean the sum total of the material put forward by the applicant for asylum to substantiate his claim and the SSHD (and by agreeing, the adjudicator) were only entitled to certify under IAA 1999, Sch 4, para 9(4)(a) (or, as in that case, the equivalent provision in AIAA 1993, Sch 2, para 5(4)(a) (as substituted by AIA 1996, s 1) – see **2.11** above) if that information on its face failed to show a relevant fear or a fear for a relevant reason but in coming to that decision neither the SSHD nor the adjudicator would be inhibited from such certification by a mere assertion of the relevant fear or fear for a relevant reason if the material provided to support it could not conceivably do so.
7   *Atabaky* (above) at [22]. This same requirement for certainty should logically have also applied to certification based on the claim being manifestly fraudulent or any of the evidence adduced in its support being manifestly false (see (e) in **2.26** above). With regards claims being manifestly, or now, clearly, unfounded, see also *R (Yogathas and Thangarasa) v Secretary of State for the Home Department* [2002] UKHL 36; *ZT (Kosovo) v Secretary of State for the Home Department* [2009] UKHL 6; *ZL and VL v Secretary of State for the Home Department* [2003] EWCA Civ 25; and *AK (Sri Lanka) v Secretary of State for the Home Department* [2009] EWCA Civ 447 at [34].
8   See the Immigration Rules, HC 395, para 328.
9   See IAA 1999, s 70(7)(a) (see **2.19** above) and compare *Badmus* [1994] Imm AR 137 and *Mayele* (10621) (see **2.5**, fn 2 above).

2.29   As to a claim being 'frivolous or vexatious' (see (f) in **2.26** above), the Divisional Court in *Paulino and Edoukou*[1] held that a claim could be frivolous or vexatious either because it did not on its face engage the Refugee Convention at all or because the claimant's account was completely incredible or because, with respect to 'vexatious', the claim amounted to an attempt to re-litigate decided issues. Similarly, in *Farkondeh*,[2] the Court of Appeal held that a claim could be properly certified as 'frivolous' on the grounds that it was incredible.

1   *R v Special Adjudicator, ex parte Paulino and Edoukou* [1996] Imm AR 122. Mildly entertainingly, during the debate on the Bill that became AIAA 1993, in which the 'frivolous or vexatious' grounds for certification were first introduced, the government minister in the Lords, Earl Ferrers, gave examples of being bored of one's country or having argued with one's mother-in-law: cited in *Paulino and Edoukou* at [128].
2   *Farkondeh v Secretary of State for the Home Department* [2002] EWCA Civ 1535.

2.30   As to the meaning of 'torture' in IAA 1999, Sch 4, para 9(7) (see **2.26** above) there was no definition of the term in IAA 1999[1] and in *Sarbjit Singh*[2] Moses J warned against the dangers of attempting to define torture ('A definition may have the danger of impeding or inhibiting the very protection that it is designed to afford.') Moses J also rejected any notion that whether mistreatment could amount to torture could be measured by judging the culpability of the perpetrators.[3] However, in *Okonkwo*,[4] Collins J, in holding that rape *per se* did not amount to torture for certification purposes,[5] stated that:

> 'It seems to me that when one is considering torture one inevitably must have regard to the motive. I do not say that it has to be a Convention reason, but the motive of the person who carries out the violence must be material in deciding whether the rape can properly be said to constitute "torture" within the context of the Schedule.'[6]

The torture suffered in the past had to relate to the asylum claim being made, though clearly the torture itself did not need to have been for any Refugee Convention reason.[7] The issue was whether the appellant had suffered torture in the past and not whether a dependant to the appeal had so suffered.[8] The applicant's evidence only needed to establish a reasonable likelihood that he had been tortured for certification to be improper.[9] However, there was some disagreement as to whether, in considering whether the evidence did establish this, the SSHD, and then the adjudicator, needed to focus upon the *prima facie* nature of the evidence put forward or only upon such evidence as they found to be credible.[10]

1 Note the definition in the United Nations Convention Against Torture and Other Cruel, Inhuman or Degrading Treatment or Punishment 1984, where torture is defined in Art 1(1) as: 'any act by which severe pain or suffering, whether physical or mental, is intentionally inflicted on a person for such purposes as obtaining from him or a third person information or a confession, punishing him for an act he or a third person has committed or is suspected of having committed, or intimidating or coercing him or a third person, or for any reason based on discrimination of any kind, when such pain or suffering is inflicted by or at the instigation of or with the consent or acquiescence of a public official or other person acting in an official capacity. It does not include pain or suffering arising only from, inherent in or incidental to lawful sanctions.' See further in *Asylum Law and Practice* (2nd edition, Bloomsbury Professional) at paras 11.35–11.37. In *R (Roszkowski) v Special Adjudicator* (CO/2609/1999, 31 October 2000) the SSHD accepted that for mistreatment to constitute torture for the purposes of IAA 1999, Sch 4, para 9(7), it does not necessarily need to be officially instigated or sanctioned.

2 *R v Secretary of State for the Home Department, ex parte Sarbjit Singh* [1999] Imm AR 445 at 450. See also *R v Secretary of State for the Home Department, ex parte Singh* (3 March 2000), QBD – torture can involve relatively little physical force if such was designed to put the victim in fear or was for the purposes of extracting information; and *Sukhdeep Singh* (G0081) – error by the SSHD to have certified in a case where the appellant had been severely beaten at a police station to extract information.

3 *Sarbjit Singh* [1999] Imm AR 445 at 448: 'Torture, in my judgment, is not to be assessed according to the degree with which one seeks to blame those who are meting out that particular treatment. Whatever the correct definition or identification of torture, I am clear that the extent to which the behaviour can be condemned is not an appropriate measure.'

4 *R v Secretary of State for the Home Department, ex parte Okonkwo* [1998] Imm AR 502. See also *R (B) v Secretary of State for the Home Department* [2001] EWHC Admin 1192. Though regarding 'rape as torture', see fn 6 below.

5 Note that in *Sarbjit Singh*, *Okonkwo* and *R (B)* (above), the courts were considering certification under AIAA 1993, Sch 2 para 5 (as amended by AIA 1996, s 1) – the provision relating to non-certification in cases of past evidence of torture in AIAA 1993, Sch 2, para 5(5) was basically identical to the one in IAA 1999, Sch 4, para 9(7).

6 *Okonkwo* (above) at 506. Contrast *R v Secretary of State for the Home Department, ex parte Muiriu* (CO/1533/99, 21 May 1999), in which Keene J held that it was arguable that the rape of a woman at a police station was something which could amount to persecution (and presumably torture) given her vulnerability as someone held at a police station, because of her opposition to the government, who could accordingly be treated with impunity. See generally in this respect *Aydin v Turkey* (1998) 25 EHRR 251 at [83]; and *Prosecutor v Anto Furundzija* [1998] ICTY 3 (10 December 1998) at [163]. See also per Baroness Hale in *R (Hoxha) v Special Adjudicator* [2005] UKHL 19 at [30]–[32]. But see also *R v Immigration Appeal Tribunal, ex parte Subramanian* [1999] Imm AR 359, affmd [2000] Imm AR 173, CA (Collins J considered that whether rape amounts to torture when committed by soldiers during a conflict depends on all the circumstances and the motivations of the rapists) and *R v Special Adjudicator, ex parte Roomy* [1999] Imm AR 483 (Ognall J held that the adjudicator had not erred in reasoning that the claimant's rape by Sri Lankan soldiers had been a criminal act and therefore could not be accepted as proof of torture).

7 See *Nanthakumar v Secretary of State for the Home Department* [2000] INLR 480, CA; *R (Roszkowski) v Special Adjudicator* (CO/2609/1999, 31 October 2000); *R v Immigration Appeal Tribunal, ex parte Brylewicz* (26 March 1999), QBD.

8 See *R (B)* (above), per Harrison J at [16].

9 See *R (Chohan) v Special Adjudicator* (CO/2042/1999, 10 October 2000) per Gibbs J.

10 In *R (Prabaharen) v Secretary of State for the Home Department* [2001] EWHC Admin 764, Collins J held that the former test was applicable in that the requirement of IAA 1999, Sch 4, para 9(7) was to look at the allegations on their face to see whether they amounted to allegations of torture. On the other hand, in *R (Gopalakrishnan) v Immigration Adjudicator* [2003] EWHC 6 (Admin), Richards J disagreed (*Prabaharen* had been a permission decision) and held that the provision required the certifier and then the adjudicator to consider the credibility of the evidence put forward in support of the allegation of past torture and not to just look at the evidence on its face. See also *R (Farkondeh) v Special Adjudicator* [2002] EWHC 384 (Admin), affmd [2002] EWCA Civ 1535; and *R (Yahia) v Immigration Appeal Tribunal* [2003] EWHC 483 (Admin).

2.31   Since the purpose of certification was to prevent an appeal to the IAT where the adjudicator agreed with the opinion expressed in the certificate,[1] the only remedy for a claimant whose appeal had been dismissed with the certificate agreed upon, was a judicial review of the adjudicator's determination. As Moses J pointed out in *Sarbjit Singh*,[2] the IAT, on an appeal with leave,

> 'would be able to look at matters on appeal as a hearing *de novo*; in other words, would be able to reach their own conclusions as to issues on which the applicant lost, such as credibility. Certification is important, because it may have the effect of depriving an applicant of the opportunity of a wider consideration of his submissions than is possible on judicial review.'

However, this was subject to the important caveat that, given the discretionary nature of judicial review as a remedy, where the adjudicator's overall determination of the appeal was unimpeachable, so that an application for leave to appeal to the IAT was doomed to fail, the court should refuse relief even where there had been an error of law by the adjudicator in agreeing with the opinion expressed in the certificate.[3] The subject matter of such a judicial review was the adjudicator's determination and the adjudicator's agreement with the opinion expressed in the certificate and not the SSHD's decisions to refuse the claim and to certify it.[4] In practice, where permission to apply for judicial review was granted in such cases, it became usual for the SSHD, as interested party to the judicial review proceedings[5] and with the agreement of the IAT, to propose a consent order by which the adjudicator's agreement with the certificate was quashed so that the adjudicator's substantive determination could then be re-promulgated with a right to apply for leave to appeal against it to the IAT.

1   IAA 1999, Sch 4, para 9(2) (see **2.26** above).
2   *R v Secretary of State for the Home Department, ex parte Sarbjit Singh* [1999] Imm AR 445 at 446.
3   See *R (Atabaky) v Secretary of State for the Home Department* [2002] EWCA Civ 234, per Latham LJ at [25]–[27] and *R (Gopalakrishnan) v Immigration Adjudicator* [2003] EWHC 6 (Admin).
4   See *Gopalakrishnan*.
5   See CPR, r 54.1(f): '"interested party" means any person (other than the claimant and defendant) who is directly affected by the claim'.

DENIAL OF FURTHER APPEAL RIGHTS UNDER IAA 1999

2.32   An important part of the philosophy behind IAA 1999 (as very much carried over into NIAA 2002 – see Chapters 3 and 4) was the desire to ensure that all possible bases for being allowed to enter or remain in the UK were put by the immigrant to the SSHD or immigration officer at the first opportunity and that if leave to enter or remain was refused, that all of these issues were put in one appeal to an adjudicator and that if that appeal was finally dismissed,[1] the person could be removed without further rights of appeal or argument. In respect of persons who had been previously refused asylum as refugees in the UK and who then claimed asylum as a refugee again during the same period of stay in the UK, the rules concerning fresh claims for asylum applied.[2] Moreover, where a person, whose appeal under IAA 1999 or under SIACA 1997[3] against an immigration decision had been finally determined, then applied for leave to enter or remain on the ground that his being removed from, or required to leave, the UK, would be in breach of his rights under the ECHR, the immigration officer or, as the case may be, the SSHD, could refuse that application and could certify that in his opinion one purpose of making the application was to delay the removal of the applicant or any other member of his family and that he had no other legitimate purpose for making the application.[4] In such a case the person could not bring any appeal against the decision on the application.[5] Where a person, whose appeal against an immigration decision had been finally determined, served a notice of appeal against a further immigration decision on the ground that the decision was in breach of his rights under the ECHR, the SSHD could certify that the ground was considered in the previous appeal.[6] Alternatively and as appropriate, the SSHD could certify that in his opinion the appellant's claim under the ECHR could reasonably have been included in his statement of additional grounds[7] prior to his original appeal but was not so included or could reasonably have been made in the original appeal but was not so made and that one purpose of the claim would be to delay the removal from the UK of the appellant or any member of his family and that the appellant had no other legitimate purpose for the making the claim.[8] In either case, on the issuing of such certificates by the SSHD, the appellant's appeal, as far as relating to his human rights grounds or claim, was to be treated as finally determined.[9] In *Balamurali*[10] the Court of Appeal considered the meaning of these dual certification conditions and held that the SSHD had to first form an opinion as to whether one purpose, not necessarily the only purpose, of the application having been made was to delay removal from the UK; if he did not conclude that a purpose of the application was to delay removal there could be no certification, but where the opposite conclusion was reached, the SSHD would go on to consider whether the applicant had any other legitimate purpose for making the application such as a desire to bring attention to a significant change in the law or in the circumstances relevant to the case. The SSHD had an inherent discretion, as governed by general administrative law principles, whether or not to actually issue the certificate where the dual conditions did apply.[11]

1   An appeal was only finally determined once all appeal rights to an adjudicator, the IAT and the Court of Appeal and beyond had been exhausted or the time limit for making an application for leave to appeal further had expired without an application having been made: IAA 1999, s 58(5)–(7).

2   See now the Immigration Rules, HC 395, para 353 (formerly para 346). Under para 346 a refusal by the SSHD to treat further representations as a fresh application for asylum specifically meant that he was not required to make a new immigration decision against which an appeal would lie on asylum grounds: see IAA 1999, s 70(7)(a) (see **2.19** above). As regards para 353 and the more complex situation arising from the NIAA 2002 appeal rights, see Chapters 3 and 4 and see further in *Asylum Law and Practice* (2nd edition, Bloomsbury Professional) at paras 12.55–12.57 and 15.10–15.12.

3   The provisions in IAA 1999, s 73, entitled 'limitation on further appeals', only applied where a person had appealed under SIACA 1997 (see Chapter 7) or IAA 1999 and that appeal had been finally determined (see fn 1 above): IAA 1999, s 73(1). This was logical as persons who had previously appealed under IA 1971 or AIAA 1993, s 8 would not have been able to raise human rights grounds on that appeal (see **2.21** above).

4   IAA 1999, s 73(1), (7) and (8). As to the conditions for certification, see *Balamurali* (text above and fn 10 below).

5   IAA 1999, s 73(9). As pointed out by Collins J in *R (Duka) v Secretary of State for the Home Department* [2003] EWHC 1262 (Admin), a certificate under IAA 1999, s 73(8) could not be lawfully made once an appeal had already been lodged; any advantage thus gained by a claimant, however, would usually be nugatory, as the SSHD could issue a certificate under IAA 1999, s 73(2) or (5) instead (see fnn 6 and 8 below). See also *R (Bekim Alia) v Secretary of State for the Home Department* [2003] EWHC 1881 (Admin), per Keith J holding at [20]–[21] that the certificate issued by the SSHD under IAA 1999 Act, s 73(8) must be quashed because the claimant clearly had a legitimate purpose in making the claim, on the basis of a relationship in the UK, but at [22] that this may turn out to be a pyrrhic victory for the claimant because it could then be open to the SSHD to re-certify, once an appeal had been lodged, under IAA 1999, s 73(2) or (5) (see fnn 6 and 8 below).

6   IAA 1999, s 73(1), (4) and (5). Note that here all that mattered for certification was the fact that the human rights claim had been considered previously on an appeal. However, where, by applying the same rules as for determining whether further representations amounted to a fresh claim for asylum (see fn 2 above), it was properly to be considered that there was a 'fresh human rights claim', then the SSHD was obliged to make a new immigration decision

with a right of appeal against it: see *R (Sivasorubaratnam Ratnum) v Secretary of State for the Home Department* [2003] EWHC 398 (Admin), per Jackson J.

7   See **2.24** above regarding statements of additional grounds.

8   IAA 1999, s 73(1) and (2). See *Balamurali* (text above and fn 10 below) regarding the certification conditions.

9   IAA 1999, s 73(3) and (6). In *R (Balamurali) v Secretary of State for the Home Department* [2003] EWHC 1183 (Admin); affmd [2003] EWCA Civ 1806, Mitting J held at [12] that for the purposes of IAA 1999, s 73(2)–(6), both 'claim' and 'grounds' comprise the factual and legal grounds for contending that the claimant should not be removed from the UK. See in relation to the 'replacement provision' in NIAA 2002, s 96, *Khan v Secretary of State for the Home Department* [2014] EWCA Civ 88, [2014] 2 All ER 973 – see further in Chapter 3.

10 *Balamurali and Sandhu v Secretary of State for the Home Department* [2003] EWCA Civ 1806. See **2.25**, fn 1 above.

11 See per Mitting J in *R (Balamurali) v Secretary of State for the Home Department* [2003] EWHC 1183 (Admin) at [19]. See now per Stadlen J in *R (J) v Secretary of State for the Home Department* [2009] EWHC 705 (Admin) regarding this exercise of discretion in whether or not to certify under NIAA 2002, s 96 (see Chapter 3).

Chapter 3

Rights of appeal to the First-tier Tribunal under the 'saved provisions' of the Nationality, Immigration and Asylum Act 2002

NIAA 2002 AND THE ASYLUM AND IMMIGRATION TRIBUNAL

3.1 Immigration and asylum appeals are now dealt with in NIAA 2002, Pt 5, which, in its original form, came fully into force on 1 April 2003,[1] as of which date IAA 1999, Pt IV (see Chapter 2) ceased to have effect except for transitional purposes in relation to decisions made prior to that date.[2] From 1 April 2003 until 3 April 2005 the right of appeal under NIAA 2002 lay to an adjudicator and the two-tier Immigration Appellate Authority continued in place.[3] From 4 April 2005, however, this was replaced by a single-tier Asylum and Immigration Tribunal (AIT)[4] with a new specialist immigration judiciary.[5] Instead of applying for permission to appeal to an upper tier,[6] a party to an appeal under NIAA 2002, s 82, 83 or 83A (see **3.7**, **3.40** and **3.41** below) could apply to the appropriate court, on the grounds that the tribunal made an error of law, for an order requiring the tribunal to reconsider its decision on the appeal.[7] The appropriate court meant, in relation to an appeal decided in England and Wales, the High Court, in Scotland, the Court of Session and in Northern Ireland, the High Court in Northern Ireland.[8] However, throughout the period of existence and jurisdiction of the AIT, an application for reconsideration had to be made to and be considered by a member of the tribunal itself at first instance under what was described as the 'filter provision'.[9] If the tribunal member refused to order reconsideration, the applicant (who could be the appellant or respondent to the original appeal) could renew the application for reconsideration in the appropriate court (as above).[10] A decision, whether to order or to refuse to order reconsideration, of the appropriate court was final.[11] The appropriate court, and the AIT itself under the filter provision, could only order reconsideration if it considered that the tribunal may have made an error of law and only once in relation to an appeal.[12] Where an appeal had been reconsidered by the AIT (see **3.2** below) a party could bring a further appeal on a point of law to the appropriate appellate court[13] but only with the permission of the AIT or, if the tribunal refused permission, of the appropriate appellate court.[14] The appropriate appellate court meant, in relation to an appeal decided in England and Wales, the Court of Appeal, in Scotland, the Court of Session and in Northern Ireland, the Court of Appeal in Northern Ireland.[15] There were two exceptions to the reconsideration process: first on an application for reconsideration, the appropriate court (though not the AIT itself under the 'filter provision'), if it thought that the appeal raised a question of law of such importance that it should be decided by the appropriate appellate court, could refer the appeal to that court.[16] Secondly, where the appeal was originally determined by a panel of three or more legally qualified members of the AIT, a party to the appeal could bring a further appeal, on a point of law and with permission (as above), to the appropriate appellate court.[17]

1   See the Nationality, Immigration and Asylum Act 2002 (Commencement No 4 Order) 2003, SI 2003/754, art 2(1) and Sch 1 bringing into force NIAA 2002, Pt 5, along with Schs 4 (which made further provision about adjudicators), 5 (which made provision about the IAT), 6 (which made transitional provision in connection with the repeal of IAA 1999, Pt IV and its replacement by NIAA 2002, Pt 5) and 7 (making consequential amendments to other statutes in relation to appeals: see NIAA 2002, s 114(3), itself brought into force on 10 February 2003 by the Nationality, Immigration and Asylum Act 2002 (Commencement No 2) Order 2003, SI 2003/1). NIAA 2002, s 115 and Sch 7, para 29 – which provided for transitional provisions in relation to asylum and human rights appeals under IAA 1999, Pt IV in cases where, after commencement, the SSHD had certified claims under either or both Conventions as being clearly unfounded – came into force on the enactment of NIAA 2002 on 7 November 2002: see NIAA 2002, s 162(2)(w) and see *R (L) v Secretary of State for the Home Department* [2003] EWCA Civ 25.
2   NIAA 2002, s 114(1) as brought into force on 1 April 2003 by SI 2003/754, art 2(1) and Sch 1. As to transitional provisions relating to decisions made before 1 April 2003, see SI 2003/754, art 3 and Sch 2.
3   See Chapter 2. NIAA 2002, s 81 and Sch 4 provided for adjudicators and s 100 and Sch 5 provided for the IAT.
4   NIAA 2002, s 81 as substituted by A&I(TC)Act 2004, s 26 from 4 April 2005: Asylum and Immigration (Treatment of Claimants, etc) Act 2004 (Commencement No 5 and Transitional Provisions) Order 2005, SI 2005/565. NIAA 2002, s 100 which had provided that 'there shall continue to be an Immigration Appeal Tribunal' ceased to have effect from 4 April 2005: A&I(TC)A 2004, s 26 and SI 2005/565. NIAA 2002, s 81 was further substituted from 15 February 2010 by the Transfer of Functions of the Asylum and Immigration Tribunal Order 2010, SI 2010/21, art 5(1) and Sch 1, para 22 (see **3.3** below).
5   NIAA 2002, Sch 4 as substituted by A&I(TC)A 2004, s 26 from 4 April 2005: SI 2005/565, provided for appointment of members of the AIT to include a President (in practice a judge of the High Court) and one or more (in practice two) Deputy Presidents: Sch 4, para 5. Legally qualified members of the tribunal were known as immigration judges, with those of 'higher rank', as specified by the Lord Chancellor, entitled designated immigration judges and senior immigration judges: see the Asylum and Immigration Tribunal (Judicial Titles) Order 2005, SI 2005/227 (revoked by SI 2010/21, art 5(3) and Sch 3, as from 15 February 2010).
6   NIAA 2002, s 101, which provided for an appeal on a point of law from an adjudicator's determination to the IAT with the tribunal's permission, ceased to have effect from 4 April 2005: A&I(TC)A 2004, s 26 and SI 2005/565.
7   NIAA 2002, s 103A(1) as inserted by A&I(TC)A 2004, s 26 from 4 April 2005: SI 2005/565.
8   NIAA 2002, s 103A(9) (see fn 7 above for commencement). Applications to the Court of Session were to the Outer House: s 103A(10).
9   A&I(TC)A 2004, s 26(7) and Sch 2, para 30 (commenced 4 April 2005: SI 2005/565). This

was a 'transitional provision' to commence and end at such dates as may be appointed by the Lord Chancellor: para 30(1). In practice it remained in force throughout the period of jurisdiction of the AIT. As to its being described as the 'filter provision': see CPR, r 54.28(2) (f) as at the relevant time.

10 A&I(TC)A 2004, s 26(7) and Sch 2, para 30(5) (see fn 9 above for commencement) and see CPR, Pt 54, section III (rr 54.28–54.35).

11 NIAA 2002, s 103A(6). Accordingly no appeal lay from the appropriate court's decision to refuse to order reconsideration and since the application had to be determined by reference only to written submissions (NIAA 2002, s 103A(5)) there was no possibility to renew the application for an oral hearing. Consequently a decision by the appropriate court to refuse to order reconsideration constituted an exhaustion of domestic remedies for the purposes of ECHR, Art 35 (see further in eg *Asylum Law and Practice* (2nd edition, Bloomsbury Professional), para 11.6).

12 NIAA 2002, s 103A(2). Accordingly where an appeal had already been remitted to the AIT by the appropriate appellate court (as to which see fn 13 below and text above) a party could not apply for reconsideration but could appeal, with permission, again to the appropriate appellate court on a point of law against the determination on remittal: NIAA 2002, s 103B(2) (b).

13 NIAA 2002, s 103B(1) as inserted by A&I(TC)A 2004, s 26 from 4 April 2005: SI 2005/565.

14 NIAA 2002, s 103B(3) (see fn 13 above for commencement).

15 NIAA 2002, s 103B(5). Appeals to the Court of Session were to the Inner House: s 103B(6). In *HT (Cameroon) v Secretary of State for the Home Department* [2008] EWCA Civ 1508, the English Court of Appeal held that it had jurisdiction under NIAA 2002, s 103B in a case where the appeal had originally been determined in Scotland but 'first stage reconsideration' (see **3.2** below), holding that there had been no material error of law, had taken place in England.

16 NIAA 2002, s 103C(1) as inserted by A&I(TC)A 2004, s 26 from 4 April 2005: SI 2005/565. The 'appropriate court' and 'appropriate appellate court' had the same meanings as in NIAA 2002, ss 103A and 103B respectively (see fnn 8 and 15 and text above): NIAA 2002, s 103C(3). A reference in Scotland would be to the Inner House of the Court of Session: NIAA 2002, s 103C(4). One of the options for disposal by the appropriate appellate court was to restore the application under s 103A to the appropriate court: NIAA 2002, s 103C(2)(g).

17 NIAA 2002, s 103E(1), (2) as inserted by A&I(TC)A 2004, s 26 from 4 April 2005: SI 2005/565. Such an appeal could only be brought with the permission of the AIT or, if the AIT refused permission, of the appropriate appellate court: NIAA 2002, s 103E(3). The 'appropriate appellate court' had the same meaning as in NIAA 2002, s 103B (see fn 15 and text above): NIAA 2002, s 103E(5). Appeals to the Court of Session were to the Inner House: s 103E(6).

THE AIT AND 'RECONSIDERATION'

3.2   The process of reconsideration by the AIT (see **3.1** above), was governed by the AIT (Procedure) Rules 2005,[1] r 31 as interpreted for practical purposes by a series of judgments, most importantly that in *DK (Serbia).*[2] In brief, it become the practice of the AIT to refer to a hearing, following an order for reconsideration, in which the issue was whether or not the tribunal had made a material error of law in its original decision on the appeal, as a 'first stage reconsideration hearing'. If, at such a hearing, it was determined that no material error of law had been made, the AIT would order that the original determination of the appeal would stand. If however, at such a hearing, it was determined that a material error of law had been made, the AIT would either then move directly to a 'second stage reconsideration hearing' and re-determine the appeal on the basis of the facts as originally found or would then adjourn for a 'second stage reconsideration hearing' at which further evidence could be taken and considered and, to the extent necessary, further findings of fact could be made and the appeal then be re-determined in light of those original factual findings made in the original determination that were untainted by error of law plus any relevant 'new' facts as found at the second stage reconsideration hearing.

1   SI 2005/230, being rules made under NIAA 2002 Act, s 106. Part 3, originally entitled 'reconsideration of appeals etc' and consisting originally of rr 24–36, was substituted from 15 February 2010 by the Transfer of Functions of the Asylum and Immigration Tribunal Order 2010, SI 2010/21, art 5(2) and Sch 2, para 18 and entitled 'appeals to the Upper Tribunal' (see now Chapter 5 for the Tribunal Procedure (First-tier Tribunal) (Immigration and Asylum Chamber) Rules 2014).
2   *DK (Serbia) v Secretary of State for the Home Department* [2006] EWCA Civ 1747. See also *JH (Zimbabwe) v Secretary of State for the Home Department* [2009] EWCA Civ 78; *HS (Afghanistan) v Secretary of State for the Home Department* [2009] EWCA Civ 771; *R (Wani) v Secretary of State for the Home Department* [2005] EWHC 2815 (Admin); and *AH (Scope of s 103A reconsideration) Sudan* [2006] UKAIT 00038.

REPLACEMENT OF THE AIT BY THE IMMIGRATION AND ASYLUM CHAMBERS OF THE FIRST-TIER TRIBUNAL AND THE UPPER TRIBUNAL

3.3   From 15 February 2010 the AIT was abolished[1] and its functions were transferred to the FTT set up under the Tribunals, Courts and Enforcement Act 2007,[2] which provides that: 'There is to be a tribunal, known as the First-tier Tribunal, for the purpose of exercising the functions conferred on it under or by virtue of this Act or any other Act.'[3] The jurisdiction of the FTT extends throughout the UK.[4] See further in Chapter 5 for the FTT. NIAA 2002, s 81 was substituted from 15 February 2010[5] so as to provide, as regards NIAA 2002, Pt 5, 'Immigration and Asylum Appeals', that: 'In this Part "the Tribunal" means the First-tier Tribunal'. The immigration judiciary were transferred in as judges of the UT (as to which, see Chapter 6) and or the FTT.[6] The FTT and UT are organised into chambers and provision is made for the allocation of those tribunals' functions between the chambers.[7] From 15 February 2010 the Immigration and Asylum Chamber (IAC) was added to the list of FTT chambers[8] and to the IAC of the FTT are assigned all functions relating to immigration and asylum matters with two exceptions:[9] first, appeals in cases regarding support for asylum seekers, failed asylum seekers and their dependants are assigned to the Social Entitlement Chamber;[10] secondly, proceedings in respect of the decisions and actions of regulatory bodies (in as far as they are relevant to immigration and asylum matters) are assigned to the General Regulatory Chamber.[11] Accordingly the functions of the IAC of the FTT were to be the same as those of the former AIT – principally to hear and determine appeals against immigration, asylum and EEA decisions and to consider applications for bail.[12] For appeals against EEA decisions, see Chapter 4. With the abolition of the AIT, all provisions in NIAA 2002, Pt 5, relating to reconsideration and appeals to the appropriate appellate court (see **3.1** above) were repealed.[13] Onward appeals from determinations of the FTT are now provided for in TCEA 2007, ss 11–14, as to which, see Chapter 6.

1   The Transfer of Functions of the Asylum and Immigration Tribunal Order 2010, SI 2010/21, arts 1 and 2(2). SI 2010/21 is made by the Lord Chancellor under powers conferred by TCEA 2007, ss 30(1) and (4), 31(1), (2), (7) and (9) and 38.
2   SI 2010/21, art 2(1).
3   TCEA 2007, s 3(1) (in force from 3 November 2008: SI 2008/2696, art 5(a)).
4   TCEA 2007, s 26 (in force as above).
5   By SI 2010/21, arts 1, 5(1) and Sch 1, para 22.
6   The Deputy Presidents and senior immigration judges of the AIT (see **3.1**, fn 5 above) were transferred in as judges of the UT; designated immigration judges were transferred in as deputy judges of the UT and judges of the FTT; immigration judges were transferred in as judges of the FTT; and non-legal members of the AIT were transferred in as other members of the UT: see SI 2010/21, art 3.
7   By TCEA 2007, s 7(1) and the First-tier Tribunal and Upper Tribunal (Chambers) Order 2008, SI 2008/2684.
8   SI 2008/2684 (see above), art 2(f) as inserted by the First-tier Tribunal and Upper Tribunal (Chambers) (Amendment) Order 2010, SI 2010/40, arts 6 and 7 from 15 February 2010. Similarly the Immigration and Asylum Chamber was added to the list of UT chambers: SI 2008/2684, art 6(d) as inserted by SI 2010/40, arts 6 and 12 from 15 February 2010.
9   SI 2008/2684, art 5C as inserted by SI 2010/40, arts 6 and 11 from 15 February 2010.
10   SI 2008/2684, art 3(a) (as substituted by SI 2009/196, arts 2 and 4(a) from 1 April 2009) and art 5C(a) (as inserted by SI 2010/40, arts 6 and 12 from 15 February 2010).
11   SI 2008/2684, art 5B(a) (as inserted by SI 2009/1590, arts 2 and 5 from 1 September 2009) and art 5C(b) (as inserted by SI 2010/40, arts 6 and 12 from 15 February 2010). The General Regulatory Chamber of the FTT hears appeals under IAA 1999, s 87(2) (as amended by the Transfer of Tribunal Functions Order 2010, SI 2010/22 from 18 January 2010) by persons aggrieved by relevant decisions of the Immigration Services Commissioner and hears disciplinary charges laid by the Commissioner against relevant persons providing immigration advice or immigration services: see IAA 1999, s 87(4) (as substituted by SI 2010/22 from 18 January 2010) and Sch 5, para 9(1)(e) and (4) (as amended by SI 2010/22 from 18 January 2010). See generally IAA 1999, Pt V and Sch 5.
12   Note that the British Nationality Act 1981, s 40A (as amended by the Transfer of Functions of the Asylum and Immigration Tribunal Order 2010, SI 2010/21, art 5(1) and Sch 1, para 7) provides for a right of appeal to the FTT (IAC) where a person is given notice of a decision to make an order to deprive him of citizenship under the British Nationality Act 1981, s 40.
13   NIAA 2002, ss 103A–103E omitted from 15 February 2010 by SI 2010/21, arts 1 and 5(1) and Sch 1, paras 20 and 25.

THE SUBSTITUTION OF NIAA 2002, PT 5 BY IA 2014 AND THE 'SAVED PROVISIONS'

3.4   As noted in Chapter 1, NIAA 2002, Pt 5 was significantly amended, and in effect substituted, from 20 October 2014 by IA 2014[1] but subject to transitional provisions, the practical effect of which has been to introduce the amended appeal rights provisions on a staged basis.[2] The Commencement Order does this by:

- providing in art 1 for there to be 'relevant provisions' of IA 2014 and 'saved provisions' of *inter alia* NIAA 2002;[3] the most relevant 'saved provisions' for present purposes are:[4]

    – IAA 1999, s 10 ('removal of persons unlawfully in the UK'),

    – NIAA 2002, s 72 ('serious criminal'),

    – NIAA 2002, s 76 ('revocation of leave to enter or remain'),

    – NIAA 2002, Pt 5 ('immigration and asylum appeals'[5]),

    – IANA 2006, s 47 ('removal: persons with statutorily extended leave');

- providing in art 2 that certain of the 'relevant provisions', with which we are mostly concerned, come into force on 20 October 2014 subject to saving provision;[6]

- providing in art 9 (in its original form[7]) that notwithstanding the commencement of the 'relevant provisions', the 'saved provisions' continue to have effect, and the 'relevant provisions' do not have effect, other than so far as they relate to the persons set out respectively in arts 10 and 11, unless art 11(2) or (3) applies;[8]

- then setting out in arts 10 and 11 (in its original form) the persons to whom the 'relevant provisions' do apply;[9]

- and then by setting out in amended form, from 6 April 2015, in art 9,[10] the persons to whom the saved provision continue to apply.

See Chapter 4 for the staged process by which the new or relevant provisions in respect to appeal rights apply. See also Chapter 4 regarding rights of appeal against EEA decisions under the EEA Regs 2006.[11]

1   IA 2014, ss 15 and 17 and Sch 9(4) were brought into force on 20 October 2014 by the Immigration Act 2014 (Commencement No 3, Transitional and Saving Provisions) Order 2014, SI 2014/2771.
2   IA 2014, s 73(1) provides that the SSHD 'may, by order, make such transitional, transitory or saving provision as the Secretary of State considers appropriate in connection with the coming into force of any provision of this Act.'
3   SI 2014/2771, art 1(2)(d) and (e) respectively.
4   SI 2014/2771, art 1(2)(e): the additional 'saved provisions' are NIAA 2002, s 62 (detention by SSHD), A&I(TC)A 2004, s 8(7) ('claimant's credibility': definitions) and Legal Aid, Sentencing and Punishment of Offenders Act 2012, Sch 1, para 19(10) ('civil legal services: judicial review': definitions).
5   Note that this is the 'saved', pre-2014 amendment, wording of the 'title' to Pt 5.
6   SI 2014/2771, art 2.
7   See fn 1 above and fnn 8 and 9 below regarding the amendments to SI 2014/2771 effected by the Immigration Act 2014 (Commencement No 4, Transitional and Saving Provisions and Amendment) Order 2015, SI 2015/371.
8   SI 2014/2771, art 9, as amended from 2 March 2015 by SI 2015/371, art 7 and then as substituted from 6 April 2015 by SI 2015/371, art 8(2).
9   SI 2014/2771, arts 10 and 11: note that art 10 is omitted and art 11 is amended from 6 April 2015 by SI 2015/371, art 8(3) and (4) respectively (see fn 8 above).

10   SI 2014/2771, art 9 as amended from 6 April 2015 by SI 2015/371, art 8(2).
11   See **1.12** above regarding 'EEA decisions'.

RIGHTS OF APPEAL TO THE FTT UNDER THE 'SAVED PROVISIONS' OF NIAA 2002

3.5   Under the 'saved' NIAA 2002, Pt 5, there are three provisions for appeals to the FTT: first, in respect of 'immigration decisions' relating to exclusion or imminent removal from the UK (saved NIAA s 82);[1] secondly, and specifically on refugee asylum grounds, against a decision to refuse a person asylum as a refugee whilst granting him leave to enter or remain, other than as a refugee, for a period exceeding one year (or for periods exceeding one year in aggregate) (saved NIAA, s 83);[2] and thirdly, and again specifically on refugee asylum grounds, for a person who had limited leave to enter or remain as a refugee, against a decision that he is not, or is no longer, a refugee, in circumstances where following that decision he still has limited leave to enter or remain, for whatever duration, otherwise than as a refugee (saved NIAA, s 83A).[3] Following the transitional implementation of IA 2014 (see **3.4** above and see Chapter 4) the saved provisions of NIAA 2002, Pt 5 now apply as follows:

- To a decision made on or after 6 April 2015 to refuse an application to vary leave to enter or remain made before 20 October 2014 where the person was seeking leave to remain as a Tier 4 migrant or as the family member of a Tier 4 migrant and where the result of that decision is that the applicant has no leave to enter or remain (see **3.7** below).[4]

- To a decision made on or after 6 April 2015 to refuse an application to vary leave to enter or remain made before 2 March 2015 where the person was seeking leave to remain as a Tier 1 migrant or (as the case may be), a Tier 2 migrant or a Tier 5 migrant or as the family member of a Tier 1 migrant, a Tier 2 migrant or a Tier 5 migrant and where the result of that decision is that the applicant has no leave to enter or remain.[5]

- To a decision made on or after 6 April 2015 (so far as that is not a decision mentioned in the two bullet points above) to refuse an application made before 6 April 2015, where that decision is–

  – to refuse leave to enter;

  – to refuse entry clearance;

  – to refuse a certificate of entitlement under NIAA 2002, s 10;

  – to refuse to vary a person's leave to enter or remain and where the result of that decision is that the person has no leave to enter or remain;

  unless that decision is also a refusal of an asylum, protection or human rights claim.[6]

3.6 *Rights of appeal to the First-tier Tribunal under the 'saved provisions'*

- To an 'immigration decision' (see **3.7** below) made prior to 6 April 2015 – other than in respect to a person who became a 'foreign criminal' on or after 20 October 2014 and to a person liable to deportation from the UK under IA 1971, s 3(5)(b) because he belongs to the family of such a foreign criminal (see below) and other than in respect of deportation decisions made on or after 10 November 2014 in respect of foreign criminals and their family members – subject to the three points above and subject to such an appeal now needing an extension of time (see Chapter 5).[7]

- To a pending appeal under saved NIAA 2002, ss 82, 83 or 83A.[8]

1 'Saved' NIAA 2002, s 82(1).
2 'Saved' NIAA 2002, s 83(2).
3 'Saved' NIAA 2002, s 83A(2) as inserted by IANA 2006, s 1, from 31 August 2006 in respect of decisions made on or after that date: Immigration, Asylum and Nationality Act 2006 (Commencement No 2) Order 2006, SI 2006/2226.
4 Immigration Act 2014 (Commencement No 3, Transitional and Saving Provisions) Order 2014, SI 2014/2771, art 9(1)(a) as substituted from 6 April 2015 by the Immigration Act 2014 (Commencement No 4, Transitional and Saving Provisions and Amendment) Order 2015, SI 2015/371, art 8(2). Previously, from 20 October 2014, see SI 2014/2771, arts 9 and 11(1) as originally enacted.
5 SI 2014/2771, art 9(1)(b) as substituted from 6 April 2015 by SI 2015/371, art 8(2). Previously, from 2 March 2015, see SI 2014/2771, arts 9 and 11(1A) as inserted by SI 2015/371, art 7(3).
6 SI 2014/2771, art 9(1)(c) as substituted from 6 April 2015 by SI 2015/371, art 8(2). In respect to refusals of asylum, protection or human rights claim where the refusal is on or after 6 April 2015, see Chapter 4.
7 SI 2014/2771, art 9(1)(d) as substituted from 6 April 2015 by SI 2015/371, art 8(2).
8 SI 2014/2771, art 9(1)(d) as substituted from 6 April 2015 by SI 2015/371, art 8(2).

3.6 Note that a person who became a 'foreign criminal' within the definition in NIAA 2002, s 117D(2)[1] on or after 20 October 2014 has been subject to the 'relevant provisions' of NIAA 2002, Pt 5 (as amended by IA 2014) since that date;[2] as has such a person's family member who is liable to deportation as such under IA 1971, s 3(5)(b) (see **1.11**).[3]

1 Under NIAA 2002, s 117D(2) a 'foreign criminal' is defined as a person who is not a British citizen, who has been convicted in the UK of an offence and who has been sentenced to a period of imprisonment of at least 12 months; has been convicted of an offence that has caused serious harm; or is a persistent offender.
2 Immigration Act 2014 (Commencement No 3, Transitional and Saving Provisions) Order 2014, SI 2014/2771, arts 9 and 10(a) as originally enacted.
3 SI 2014/2771, arts 9 and 10(b) as originally enacted. See also **3.5** above re deportation decisions made in respect of 'foreign criminals' and their family members from 10 November 2014; and see **4.3**.

RIGHTS OF APPEAL UNDER 'SAVED' NIAA 2002, S 82 AGAINST 'IMMIGRATION DECISIONS'

3.7 Saved NIAA 2002, s 82(1) provides that where an 'immigration decision' is made in respect of a person he may appeal to the tribunal, now meaning the FTT.[1] Saved NIAA 2002, s 82(2) then goes on to exhaustively, subject to saved s 82(3A) (see below), define immigration decisions against which a right of appeal lies. These consist of (and see **1.11** above for a fuller explanation of these decisions):

(a)   refusal of leave to enter the UK;

(b)   refusal of entry clearance;

(c)   refusal of a certificate of entitlement under NIAA 2002, s 10;

(d)   refusal to vary a person's leave to enter or remain in the UK if the result of the refusal is that the person has no leave to enter or remain. Note that the wording of saved NIAA, s 82(2)(d) and (e) (see below) restricts the right of appeal in variation cases to situations where the refusal to vary or variation results in the person being without any leave. The meaning of this was considered by the AIT in *SA (Pakistan)*.[2] A person must have limited leave in order for it to be varied or for there to be a refusal of its variation (see *Suthendran*[3] and *Subramaniam*[4] and see **2.1** above). Thus an application for further leave, which is made once leave has expired, will not, if refused, attract a right of appeal under these provisions. A refusal to vary before leave has expired (unless that leave is also thereby curtailed) will also not attract a right of appeal because the decision will not result in the person having no leave. Accordingly, these provisions only provide a right of appeal when leave is curtailed or when an application for further leave is made before expiry of leave and the refusal is made after expiry.[5] However, IA 1971, s 3C statutorily extends leave during any period in which an in-time appeal may be brought and through the course of that appeal.[6] On the face of it NIAA 2002, s 82(2)(d) and IA 1971, s 3C are thus in conflict, unless one reads into NIAA 2002, s 82(2)(d) at the end the words: 'other than under IA 1971, s 3C'. The AIT in *SA (Pakistan)* (above) resolved this conflict by ruling that IA 1971, s 3C has no effect for the purposes of NIAA 2002, s 82(2)(d) because any other reading would make nonsense of the statutory provisions;

(e)   variation of a person's leave to enter or remain in the UK if, when the variation takes effect, the person has no leave to enter or remain. Again, the right of appeal only lies where, as a result of the variation, the person has no remaining leave to enter or remain in the UK. Again, however, IA 1971, s 3D statutorily extends the varied leave during any period in which an in-time appeal may be brought and through the course of that appeal.[7] So again, in order to make sense of the statutory provisions, IA 1971, s 3D must be read as having no effect for the purposes of NIAA 2002, s 82(2)(e).[8] Note that where the SSHD makes a decision to remove a person under saved IAA 1999, s 10 (see below and **1.2** and **1.11** above) this does not curtail but rather invalidates the limited leave the person has (see saved IAA 1999 Act, s 10(8)). This is not a decision, therefore, in respect of which NIAA, s 82(2)(e) provides a right of appeal (see instead NIAA, s 82(2)(g), see below): see *RK (Nepal)*;[9]

(f) revocation under NIAA 2002, s 76 of indefinite leave to enter or remain in the UK. IA 1971, s 3D statutorily extends the revoked leave during any period in which an in–time appeal may be brought and through the course of that appeal.[10] Note that here there is no need to 'worry' about the effect of s 3D as the appeal right arises upon the revocation of the indefinite leave without further conditions as to the effect of that revocation;

(g) a decision that a person is to be removed from the UK by way of directions under saved IAA 1999, s 10(1)(a), (b), (ba) or (c). Under saved IAA 1999, s 10(1) a person who is not a British citizen may be removed from the UK, in accordance with directions given by an immigration officer, if–

- '(a) having only a limited leave to enter or remain, he does not observe a condition attached to the leave or remains beyond the time limited by the leave',

- '(b) he uses deception in seeking (whether successfully or not) leave to remain',

- '(ba) his indefinite leave to enter or remain has been revoked under section 76(3) of the Nationality, Immigration and Asylum Act 2002 (person ceasing to be refugee)',[11] or

- '(c) directions have been given for the removal, under this section, of a person to whose family he belongs';

(h) a decision that an illegal entrant is to be removed from the UK by way of directions under IA 1971, Sch 2, paras 8–10. The 'immigration decisions' as listed in (g) and (h) were an innovation of NIAA 2002 that made clear that there can be no right of appeal against the actual giving of removal directions at any stage, whether concurrently with the decision to remove or, more importantly, subsequently. The purpose of this innovation was to reverse the effect of the Court of Appeal judgment in *Kariharan*.[12] There is, however, a special transitional provision that provides that where a decision has been taken under the Immigration Acts relating to a person's entitlement to enter or remain in the UK before 1 April 2003, a right of appeal under IAA 1999, s 65(1) would still be available, against removal directions, where a human rights allegation was made before 1 July 2003.[13] Aside from such, now historic, transitional cases, it is always important to distinguish between a decision to remove someone by way of removal directions ('immigration decisions' as per (g), (h), (ha), (i) and (ia), above and below) and the making of the removal directions themselves. Removal directions in some cases may be given some time after the notice of a decision that a person is to be removed (in the event that the person has not voluntarily departed). The making, or giving, of removal directions[14] does not provide a right of appeal: see *GH (Iraq)*[15] and *MS (Palestinian Territories)*.[16] See also per Ouseley J in *Rrapaj*[17] regarding the need for care in distinguishing between decisions to remove someone by way of removal directions and the making of the removal directions when applying for legal aid;

(ha) a decision that a person, with statutorily extended leave, is to be removed from the UK by way of directions under saved IANA 2006, s 47.[18] Much controversy and some divergence of judicial opinions arose over the question as to whether the SSHD is obliged to consider making a removal decision when refusing an application for further leave to remain on a variation basis. Ultimately, in *Patel*[19] the Court of Appeal concluded that the SSHD is under no such obligation. In *Ahmadi*[20] the tribunal held that a removal decision under IANA 2006, s 47, as originally enacted, could not be lawfully made in respect of a person until written notice of the decision to refuse to vary that person's leave to remain had been given to that person and that the practice of the SSHD to incorporate both decisions in a single notice was accordingly incompatible with the relevant legislation. The Court of Appeal upheld the UT's determination in this respect.[21] However by the Crime and Courts Act 2013, s 51(3), IANA 2006, s 47(1) was amended from 8 May 2013[22] so as to seek to avoid the problem raised in *Ahmadi*;

(i) a decision that a person is to be removed from the UK by way of directions given by virtue of IA 1971, Sch 2, para 10A, relating to family members. IA 1971, Sch 2, para 10A[23] provides that where directions are given in respect of a person under any of IA 1971, Sch 2, paras 8–10 (see (h) above), directions to the same effect may be given in respect of a member of the person's family;

(ia) a decision that a person is to be removed from the UK by way of directions under IA 1971, Sch 2, para 12(2), relating to seamen and aircrews;[24]

(ib) a decision to make an order under IA 1971, s 2A depriving a person of the right of abode in the UK;[25]

(j) a decision to make a deportation order under IA 1971, s 5(1). In terms of the right of appeal against such an 'immigration decision', no distinction is made between a decision to deport on the bases of a person's liability to deportation under IA 1971, s 3(5) (deportation conducive to the public good and family members) and IA 1971, s 3(6) (deportation following criminal court recommendation). See further **1.11** and **2.1** above. However, as regards 'automatic deportation', see below;

(k) refusal to revoke a deportation order under IA 1971, s 5(2).

1   NIAA 2002, s 82(1) as amended by A&I(TC)A 2004, s 26 from 4 April 2005: Asylum and Immigration (Treatment of Claimants, etc) Act 2004 (Commencement No 5 and Transitional Provisions) Order 2005, SI 2005/565, so as to provide that the appeal is to the tribunal instead

of to an adjudicator (see **3.1** above). From 15 February 2010 'the Tribunal' means the FTT: NIAA 2002, s 81 as substituted by the Transfer of Functions of the Asylum and Immigration Tribunal Order 2010, SI 2010/21, art 5(1) and Sch 1, para 22. See **3.1** and **3.3** above.

2   *SA (Section 82(2)(d): Interpretation and Effect) Pakistan* [2007] UKAIT 00083.

3   *Suthendran v Immigration Appeal Tribunal* [1977] 1 AC 359, HL.

4   *R v Immigration Appeal Tribunal, ex parte Subramaniam* [1977] 1 QB 190, CA.

5   See also *SA (work permit refusal not appealable) Ghana* [2007] UKAIT 00006, which also notes that an application for a work permit does not constitute an application for further leave. Though for an anomalous decision, see *OA (Nigeria) v Secretary of State for the Home Department* [2008] EWCA Civ 82.

6   IA 1971, s 3C(1) and (2)(b) and (c) (see **2.1** above). IA 1971, s 3C is amended from 20 October 2014 by IA 2014, Sch 9(4), para 21 and the Immigration Act 2014 (Commencement No 3, Transitional and Saving Provisions) Order 2014, SI 2014/2771, arts 1 and 2, so as to provide for 'administrative review' of decisions (see Chapter 9). Note that, whereas when existing leave is extended by IA 1971, s 3C(1) and (2)(a), pending a decision from the SSHD on the variation application, that original application can itself be varied, but once a negative decision has been made and leave is extended pending an appeal under s 3C(1) and (2)(b) or (c), it is no longer possible to apply to the SSHD for a variation of the original application: see IA 1971, s 3C(4) and (5) as interpreted by the Court of Appeal in *JH (Zimbabwe) v Secretary of State for the Home Department* [2009] EWCA Civ 78. It may, however, be possible to raise the desired new application as an additional ground on the appeal itself: see *AS (Afghanistan) v Secretary of State for the Home Department* [2009] EWCA Civ 1076 and *Patel v Secretary of State for the Home Department* [2013] UKSC 72 and see further **3.18** below.

7   IA 1971, s 3D(1)(a) and (2)(a) and (b). IA 1971, s 3D is amended from 20 October 2014 by IA 2014, Sch 9(4), para 22 and SI 2014/2771, arts 1 and 2, so as to provide for 'administrative review' of decisions (see Chapter 9).

8   Note that IA 1971, s 3D was inserted by IANA 2006, s 11 from 31 August 2006 in relation only to decisions made on or after that date: Immigration, Asylum and Nationality Act 2006 (Commencement No 2) Order 2006, SI 2006/2226. In respect to decisions to vary leave made prior to that date, a variation shall not have effect while an appeal under s 82(1) against that variation (a) could be brought (ignoring the possibility of an appeal out of time with permission), or (b) is pending: NIAA 2002, s 82(3), which ceased to have effect from 31 August 2006 except in relation to decisions made before that date: IANA 2006, s 11 and SI 2006/2226.

9   *R (RK (Nepal)) v Secretary of State for the Home Department* [2009] EWCA Civ 359. The Court of Appeal held that *CD (India)* [2008] UKAIT 00055 was wrongly decided on this issue.

10   IA 1971, s 3D(1)(b) and (2)(a) and (b). IA 1971, s 3D was inserted by IANA 2006, s 11 from 31 August 2006 in relation only to decisions made on or after that date: SI 2006/2226. In respect to decisions to revoke indefinite leave made prior to that date, the revocation shall not have effect while an appeal under s 82(1) against that revocation (a) could be brought (ignoring the possibility of an appeal out of time with permission), or (b) is pending: NIAA 2002, s 82(3), which ceased to have effect from 31 August 2006 except in relation to decisions made before that date: IANA 2006, s 11 and SI 2006/2226.

11   NIAA 2002, s 82(2)(g) was amended by IANA 2006, s 2 from 31 August 2006 (in relation to a decision made on or after that date): SI 2006/2226, so as to include a right of appeal against directions set under saved IAA 1999, s 10(1)(ba) where a person's indefinite leave to remain has been revoked under NIAA 2002, s 76(3) in relation to refugee cessation (see further *Asylum Law and Practice* (2nd edition, Bloomsbury Professional), paras 8.2–8.6 and 12.65).

12   *R (Kariharan and Koneswaran) v Secretary of State for the Home Department; Secretary of State for the Home Department v Kumarakuruparan* [2002] EWCA Civ 1102 (see **2.21** above).

13   See the Nationality, Immigration and Asylum Act 2002 (Commencement No 4 Order) 2003, SI 2003/754 (see **3.1**, fn 1 above), art 3(2) and Sch 2, para 6(5). For a full list of the 'Immigration Acts', see UKBA 2007, s 61(2) (as amended by IA 2014, s 73(5) from 14 May 2014).

14   Note that removal directions are given to the owners, agents or captains of ships and aircraft, etc (see **1.11**, fn 14 above).

15   *GH (Iraq) v Secretary of State for the Home Department* [2005] EWCA Civ 1182.

16 *MS (Palestinian Territories) v Secretary of State for the Home Department* [2009] EWCA Civ 17; aff'd [2010] UKSC 25.

17 *R (Rrapaj) v Director of Legal Aid Casework* [2013] EWHC 1837 (Admin).

18 NIAA 2002, s 82(2)(ha) inserted by IANA 2006, s 47(6) from 1 April 2008: Immigration, Asylum and Nationality Act 2006 (Commencement No 8 and Transitional and Saving Provisions) Order, SI 2008/310, art 3(c).

19 *Patel v Secretary of State for the Home Department* [2012] EWCA Civ 741; aff'd [2013] UKSC 72. Faced with the irreconcilable Court of Appeal authorities of *Lamichhane v Secretary of State for the Home Department* [2012] EWCA Civ 260 on the one hand and *R (Mirza) v Secretary of State for the Home Department* [2011] EWCA Civ 159 and *Sapkota v Secretary of State for the Home Department* [2011] EWCA Civ 1320 on the other, the Court of Appeal in *Patel* preferred the conclusion in *Lamichhane* that the SSHD was not obliged to make a removal decision at the same time or shortly after refusing variation of leave to remain.

20 *Ahmadi (s 47 decision: validity; Sapkota) Afghanistan* [2012] UKUT 147 (IAC).

21 *Secretary of State for the Home Department v Ahmadi* [2013] EWCA Civ 512.

22 See the Crime and Courts Act 2013 (Commencement No 1 and Transitional and Saving Provision) Order 2013, SI 2013/1042, art 2. The amended version of IANA 2006, s 47 was itself repealed by IA 2014, Sch 9, Pt 1, para 5 from 20 October 2014 subject to the savings and transitional provisions in SI 2014/2771 that make it a saved provision as explained above.

23 As inserted by NIAA 2002, s 73(1) from 10 February 2003.

24 NIAA 2002, s 82(2)(ia) inserted by A&I(TC)A 2004, s 31 from 1 October 2004: Asylum and Immigration (Treatment of Claimants, etc) Act 2004 (Commencement No 1) Order 2004, SI 2004/2523, art 2.

25 NIAA 2002, s 82(2)(ib) inserted by IANA 2006, s 57(2) from 16 June 2006: Immigration, Asylum and Nationality Act 2006 (Commencement No 1) Order 2006, SI 2006/1497, art 3.

3.8   However where a decision to make a deportation order is made in accordance with the 'automatic deportation' provisions in UKBA 2007, s 32 (see **1.11** above) this is not an immigration decision as listed in (j) above, but is a discrete immigration decision against which an appeal lies under NIAA 2002, s 82(1) by virtue of s 82(3A).[1] The reason for this distinction is that whereas a suspensive right of appeal lies in respect of a decision to make a deportation order as per saved NIAA 2002, ss 82(2)(j) and 92(1) and (2), this benefit does not apply to an appeal against a decision that automatic deportation provision applies: see further **3.25** below.

1 NIAA 2002, s 82(3A) as inserted by UKBA 2007, s 35(1) and (3), from 1 August 2008 (for certain purposes): UK Borders Act 2007 (Commencement No 3 and Transitional Provisions) Order 2008, SI 2008/1818, art 2(a).

3.9   Accordingly saved NIAA 2002, s 82(1) provides, or provided, for a right of appeal against a decision that either provides directly for the appellant's removal from, or non-admittance to, the UK or a decision that results in the appellant having no leave to enter or remain in the UK and thus facing the prospect of imminent removal from the UK. A person may have a right of appeal against two immigration decisions, as listed in NIAA 2002, s 82(2), in particular in the following combinations: (d) and (ha); (e) and (ha); and (f) and (g).[1] Where this is the case the FTT must treat an appeal against the one decision as including an appeal against the other decision.[2] Note particularly, however, that there is no right of appeal under 'saved' NIAA 2002, s 82(1) against a decision to refuse a person leave to remain in the UK in circumstances where such a decision does not constitute a decision to vary or to refuse to vary pre-existing leave to enter or remain. In *Daley-Murdock*[3] the Court of Appeal held, in the case of an overstayer who had been refused leave to remain, that there was no obligation on the SSHD to make a simultaneous decision to remove (as per NIAA 2002, s 82(2)(g) above) against which she (the overstayer) could appeal on Art 8 human rights grounds; and that even in such cases where children were involved there was no general obligation but rather each case would be fact sensitive. The SSHD subsequently issued policy guidance as to circumstances where he will, and where he generally will not, make a removal decision, with right of appeal (see especially (g) and (h) at **3.7** above), when refusing leave to remain to an overstayer or illegal entrant. The guidance entitled 'Requests for removal decisions'[4] provided, broadly, that the SSHD would normally only make a removal decision when requested in the following cases:

- the refused application for leave to remain included a dependent child under 18 resident in the UK for three years or more;

- the applicant has a dependent child under the age of 18 who is a British citizen;

- the applicant is being supported by the Home Office or has provided evidence of being supported by a local authority (under the National Assistance Act 1948, s 21 or the Children Act 1989, s 17);

- there are other exceptional and compelling reasons to make a removal decision at this time; or

- where it is operationally expedient or appropriate to make a removal decision.

The guidance was withdrawn on 13 April 2015 as being no longer necessary in view of the amended appeal rights (see Chapter 4). It was upheld as being lawful by the Court of Appeal in *Oboh*.[5]

1   Note that even here a person has the one right of appeal to the FTT against the two types of decision. In total, saved NIAA 2002, s 82(2) lists 14 types of immigration decisions with a further one in s 82(3A) against which a single right of appeal arises under saved s 82(1) (see **3.7** above). That makes 15 types of decision. Combined with the rights of appeal on asylum grounds in the circumstances set out in saved NIAA 2002, ss 83 and 83A, that makes 17 'types of decision' against which a single right of appeal to the FTT arises. Compare the muddled thinking (deliberate or ignorant) on the UKVI website where the government minister talks of IA 2014 having 'slashed the *number of appeals* [sic] available to foreign criminals from 17 to just four.'
2   NIAA 2002, s 85(1).
3   *R (Daley-Murdock) v Secretary of State for the Home Department* [2011] EWCA Civ 161.
4   See the UKVI website at www.gov.uk/government/publications/requests-for-removal-decisions.
5   *R (on the application of Oboh) v Secretary of State for the Home Department* [2015] EWCA Civ 514.

3.10   Where no appealable removal decision was made, the decision to refuse leave could only be challenged by way of judicial review (see further in Chapter 8). Note that when IA 2014 amended provisions of NIAA 2002, Pt 5 are brought fully into force for all possible appellants, a right of appeal will arise on refusal of an application for leave to remain on asylum and/or human rights grounds regardless of whether or not the applicant had current valid leave at the date of making the application. See further in Chapter 4.

RESTRICTIONS AND LIMITATIONS ON RIGHTS OF APPEAL UNDER SAVED NIAA 2002, S 82: SUMMARY OF THE PROVISIONS

3.11   Notwithstanding the ostensibly long list of decisions against which a right of appeal may arise (**3.7** and **3.9**, fn 1 above), in reality appeal rights are in many circumstances restricted to the extent of being effectively denied and in others are significantly limited. As saved NIAA 2002, s 82(4) stipulates, 'The right of appeal under subsection (1) is subject to the exceptions and limitations specified in this Part.' In summary the restrictions and limitations are as follows:

- Denial of a right of appeal – other than on asylum, human rights or race discrimination grounds – where an immigration decision relating to refusal of leave to enter, refusal of entry clearance and variation cases is taken on certain specified grounds: saved NIAA 2002, s 88 (see **3.19** below).

- Denial of a right of appeal – other than on human rights or race discrimination grounds – in respect of refusal of entry clearance in points-based system and visit categories: saved NIAA 2002, s 88A (see **3.21** below).

- Denial of a right of appeal – other than on asylum, human rights or race discrimination grounds – in respect of refusal of leave to enter unless the applicant had an entry clearance and is seeking entry for the same purpose as specified on his entry clearance document: saved NIAA 2002, s 89 (see **3.23** below).

- Denial of a right of appeal – other than on asylum (in respect of leave to enter only), human rights or race discrimination grounds – in respect of refusals of entry clearance and leave to enter where the decision is taken personally by the SSHD, or on his personal direction, on the grounds that the person's exclusion or removal from the UK is conducive to the public good: saved NIAA 2002, s 98 (see **3.24** below).

- Provisions that determine whether or not a person has an 'in-country' suspensive right of appeal against an immigration decision, or whether he can continue with the appeal whilst remaining in the UK, or whether he can only appeal from abroad, or continue the appeal from abroad, against the decision: saved NIAA 2002, ss 92, 94, 94A and 97B and NIAA 2002, s 94B[1] (see **3.25–3.30** below and see further Chapter 4).[2]

3.12 *Rights of appeal to the First-tier Tribunal under the 'saved provisions'*

- Denial of a right of appeal (on any grounds) against any immigration decision where a person had an earlier right of appeal against a previous immigration decision: saved NIAA 2002, s 96 (see **3.34**–**3.39** below).

1 Note that NIAA 2002, s 94B was added into Pt 5 by IA 2014, s 17(3) from 28 July 2014 (Immigration Act 2014 (Commencement No 1, Transitory and Saving Provisions) Order 2014, SI 2014/1820, art 3(n) subject to transitory and savings provisions as specified in art 4) and so has effect as part of both saved NIAA 2002, Pt 5 as well as the amended Pt 5 (see Chapter 4).

2 These provisions are also of relevance to certifications that limit appeal rights in 'safe third country cases' as relevant to asylum claimants and as provided for in A&I(TC)A 2004, Sch 3. See further in Chapter 4 for limited rights of appeal in 'safe third country cases'.

3.12   As will be noted from the above, some of these provisions have the effect of restricting or limiting the grounds upon which an appeal can be brought and so it is first necessary to consider the full gamut of the potentially available grounds of appeal under saved NIAA 2002. It will be noted in Chapter 4 how far reduced these available grounds are under IA 2014, amended Pt 5. Finally in this summary, it is to be noted that a right of appeal to the FTT under saved NIAA 2002, s 82, 83 or 83A (as to ss 83 and 83A see **3.40** and **3.41** below) is denied where the SSHD personally certifies that the decision is taken on, or in relation to, national security grounds: saved NIAA 2002, ss 97 and 97A (see **3.42** below and see Chapter 7 regarding appeals to the SIAC under SIACA 1997).

GROUNDS OF APPEAL IN APPEALS UNDER SAVED NIAA 2002, S 82

3.13   The grounds upon which an appeal to the FTT[1] can be lodged under saved NIAA 2002, s 82(1) are exhaustively provided for by saved NIAA 2002, s 84(1).[2] They are as follows:

(a) Saved s 84(1)(a): that the decision is not in accordance with immigration rules. The tribunal has held that, at least where the immigration rule in question does not specifically provide for a given requirement to be in place as at the date on which the application was made to the immigration authority,[3] an appellant can succeed on this ground of appeal where, by the date of the hearing before the tribunal, all requirements of the rule are met even if they were not all met as at the date of the decision.[4] Furthermore, as held by the Court of Appeal in *AS (Afghanistan)*[5] and approved by the Supreme Court in *Patel*,[6] subject to the 'one-stop procedure' (see **3.16** and **3.18** below) it can be possible to succeed on an appeal on this ground in relation to a decision not being in accordance with an immigration rule other than the one under which the application was originally made to, and refused by, the SSHD.

(b)   Saved s 84(1)(b): that the decision is unlawful by virtue of the Race
        Relations (Northern Ireland) Order 1997, art 20A or by virtue of the
        Equality Act 2010, s 29 (discrimination in the exercise of public
        functions, etc) so far as relating to race as defined by s 9(1) of that
        Act.[7] This relatively little used ground of appeal, that the immigration
        decision discriminates on racial grounds against the appellant,[8] was
        originally worded so as to refer to the Race Relations Act 1976, s 19B
        (and then to the Race Relations (Northern Ireland) Order 1997 as well)
        but commencement of the Equality Act 2010 led to the loss of this
        specific race discriminatory ground of appeal save in Northern Ireland,
        until further amendment by the Crime and Courts Act 2013 from 8 May
        2013.[9]

(c)   Saved s 84(1)(c): that the decision is unlawful under HRA 1998, s 6
        (public authority not to act contrary to ECHR) as being incompatible
        with the appellant's human rights. This human rights ground of appeal,
        not being related to the consequences of the removal of the appellant
        from the UK (as to which see ground (g) below), is particularly
        relevant in appeals against refusals of entry clearance in respect to Art
        8 family life grounds. The degree to which other protected rights can
        be successfully relied upon on such an appeal is severely limited by
        the principle that the ECHR does not have extra-territorial effect. See
        especially *Moon*[10] holding that HRA 1998 could not be invoked by
        someone outside the normal territorial jurisdiction of the UK so as to
        gain entry; Art 8 could only be engaged by the existence of someone in
        the UK whose (family life) right would be breached if entry clearance
        were not granted to the applicant and such cases were exceptional. On
        the other hand, in *Naik*[11] the Court of Appeal considered that Art 10
        (freedom of expression) was engaged in respect of the claimant's UK-
        based supporters, but that it was not necessary in the case to reach a
        final decision upon whether the claimant himself also enjoyed Art 10
        rights.[12]

(d)   Saved s 84(1)(d): that the appellant is an EEA national or a member of
        the family of an EEA national and the decision breaches the appellant's
        rights under the Community Treaties in respect of entry to or residence
        in the UK. See Chapter 4 for appeals against EEA decisions. This ground
        of appeal may be of use to an appellant against an immigration decision
        (as per saved NIAA 2002, s 82(2): see **3.7** above) as an additional ground
        (see **3.16** *et seq* below).

(e)   Saved s 84(1)(e): that the decision is otherwise not in accordance with the
        law, 'otherwise' in the sense of 'otherwise than not in accordance with
        race discrimination or human rights law'. The jurisdiction of the tribunal
        to consider failures to follow principles of administrative law was long
        the subject of controversy. However in *AA (Pakistan)*[13] the AIT held
        that under this ground of appeal the tribunal's jurisdiction encompasses

81

challenges to immigration decisions on public law grounds such as legitimate expectation, fairness and irrationality. Since then the tribunal has developed jurisprudence on the public law duty of fairness and its application to administrative actions and decisions by the SSHD and his officers.[14] However, the Court of Appeal has made clear that insofar as a question arises as to the *vires* of subordinate legislation, the AIT was not empowered to declare that such legislation is *ultra vires*; where the matter arises and in order that a decision, that depends on questionable subordinate legislation, not erroneously be held to be 'in accordance with the law', the Court of Appeal stated that the AIT should consider adjournment for the question to be put before the Administrative Court by way of judicial review: see *EN (Serbia)*.[15] However, with the transfer of the AIT into the two-tier tribunal regime, this position has probably changed – but only as regards the jurisdiction of the UT, which Laws LJ in *Cart*[16] held to be the *alter ego* of the High Court.

(f)   Saved s 84(1)(f): that the person taking the decision should have exercised differently a discretion conferred by immigration rules. In *EO (Turkey)*[17] the AIT held that word 'conferred' has to be read in some sense such as 'confirmed' because it is difficult to see that any discretions are 'conferred' by immigration rules. Rather discretion is conferred on the SSHD by IA 1971 (see **1.4** above) and under this statutory ground an appeal can succeed on the basis that a discretion conferred by IA 1971, but whose existence is confirmed in specific immigration rules, which contain instructions for exercising it, should have been exercised differently. In *AG (Kosovo)*[18] the AIT held that:

●   in cases where human rights are argued, they should be determined in advance of any argument based on discretion, because, if the appellant's human rights entitle him to enter or remain in the UK, any discretionary power to allow him to do so is otiose;

●   a policy that in all the circumstances of the case would apparently be exercised in the appellant's favour and contains no elements that genuinely would leave the decision open is relevant in the assessment of proportionality because it goes to the issue of the importance of maintaining immigration control in similar cases;

●   if the appellant fails to establish that his human rights compel the remedy he seeks, but is able to show that there was at the date of the decision a policy in force that governed his case but was not taken into account, he may win an appeal on the ground that the decision, having been made not in accordance with published policy, was 'otherwise not in accordance with the law' within the meaning of s 84(1)(e) (above);

●   if the policy was taken into account and the appellant can show that the terms of the policy and the facts of his case are such that there was no option open to the decision-maker other than to grant him the remedy he seeks, his appeal should be allowed with a direction;

● but where within the terms of the policy the benefit to the appellant depends on the exercise of a discretion outside the immigration rules, the tribunal has no power to substitute its own decision for that of the decision maker (see saved NIAA 2002, s 86(6): see below).

However, where an immigration rule 'confers' or 'confirms' no discretion, saved NIAA 2002, s 86(6) specifically provides that refusal to depart from or to authorise departure from immigration rules is not an exercise of a discretion reviewable on appeal by the FTT.

(g) Saved s 84(1)(g): that removal of the appellant from the UK in consequence of the immigration decision would breach the UK's obligations under the Refugee Convention or would be unlawful under HRA 1998, s 6 as being incompatible with the appellant's human rights. Although the focus must be on the consequences of removal from the UK as at the date of the hearing before the tribunal (see *Ravichandran*[19]) this ground of appeal was equally available, on both refugee asylum and human rights grounds, to persons whose leave has been varied by being curtailed or whose indefinite leave has been revoked or who have been refused variation of leave, as it is to persons who have been refused leave to enter or against whom a removal or deportation decision has been made.[20] For example, in *MS (Ivory Coast)*,[21] the Court of Appeal held that where the AIT was hearing an appeal on s 84(1)(g) grounds involving human rights issues, it should decide whether removal on the facts as they were when it heard the appeal would violate the person's human rights and that the AIT had erred by instead determining the appeal on the basis of an undertaking by the SSHD not to remove the appellant pending the outcome of family law contact proceedings that she was pursuing.

1 Regarding the appeal being to the FTT, see **3.3** above.
2 For appeals against EEA decisions and available grounds of appeal, see Chapter 4.
3 Which is certainly the case with 'points-based system' applications under the immigration rules: see *AQ (Pakistan) v Secretary of State for the Home Department* [2011] EWCA Civ 833; and *Secretary of State for the Home Department v Raju* [2013] EWCA Civ 754.
4 See *LS (Gambia)* [2005] UKAIT 85 and *YZ and LX (China)* [2005] UKAIT 157. The tribunals reached this conclusion on interpreting saved NIAA 2002, ss 84(1)(a), 85(4) and 86(3) (see further below).
5 *AS (Afghanistan) v Secretary of State for the Home Department* [2009] EWCA Civ 1076.
6 *Patel v Secretary of State for the Home Department* [2013] UKSC 72, per Lord Carnwath at [34]–[44] and per Lord Mance at [62]–[71] approving the majority judgments in *AS (Afghanistan)* (Moore-Bick and Sullivan LJJ).
7 Saved NIAA 2002, s 84(1)(b) as amended by the Race Relations Order (Amendment) Regulations (Northern Ireland) 2003, SI 2003/341, reg 60 from 19 July 2003 and by the Crime and Courts Act 2013, s 51(1) from 8 May 2013: Crime and Courts Act 2013 (Commencement No 1 and Transitional and Saving Provision) Order 2013, SI 2013/1042.

8 For an example of a successful challenge to the process that led to refusals of entry clearance, though by way of judicial review rather than appeal under NIAA 2002, ss 82(1) and (2) (b) and 84(1)(b), on race discrimination grounds, see *R (European Roma Rights Centre) v Immigration Officer, Prague Airport* [2004] UKHL 55. The House of Lords held that the system operated by immigration officers at Prague Airport was inherently and systemically discriminatory against Roma on racial grounds contrary to the Race Relations Act 1976, s 1(1)(a), and the claimants were granted a declaration to that effect (they were not granted entry clearances).

9 Reference to the Race Relations Act 1976, s 19B repealed by the Equality Act 2010 (Public Authorities and Consequential and Supplementary Amendments) Order 2011, SI 2011/1060, art 4(b) from 4 April 2011. See fn 7 above regarding the further amendment from 8 May 2013.

10 *Sun Myung Moon (human rights, entry clearance, proportionality) USA* [2005] UKIAT 00112. See also *H (Somalia)* [2004] UKIAT 00027.

11 *R (Naik) v Secretary of State for the Home Department* [2011] EWCA Civ 1546.

12 The claimant was a leading Muslim writer and public speaker whom the SSHD had banned from the UK.

13 *AA (highly skilled migrants: legitimate expectation) Pakistan* [2008] UKAIT 00003: see especially at [35]–[56] and the authorities therein considered. See also *AG (Kosovo)* (fn 18 below).

14 See eg *Thakur (PBS decision – common law fairness) Bangladesh* [2011] UKUT 00151; *Kabaghe (appeal from outside UK – fairness) Malawi* [2011] UKUT 00473; *Naved (student – fairness – notice of points)* [2012] UKUT 14; *Fiaz (cancellation of leave to remain – fairness)* [2012] UKUT 00057; and *Basnet (validity of application – respondent)* [2012] UKUT 00113. However for limits on the SSHD's 'duty of fairness' see especially: *Secretary of State for the Home Department v Rodriguez* [2014] EWCA Civ 2 (permission granted to appeal to the SC); *EK (Ivory Coast) v Secretary of State for the Home Department* [2014] EWCA Civ 1517; and *Kaur v Secretary of State for the Home Department* [2015] EWCA Civ 13.

15 *EN (Serbia) v Secretary of State for the Home Department* [2009] EWCA Civ 630 at [84]– [87]. Previously, in *IH (Eritrea)* [2009] UKAIT 00012, the AIT had considered (at [82] *et seq*) whether it had jurisdiction to determine the *vires* of a statutory instrument – being the Particularly Serious Crimes Order 2004, SI 2004/1910 (as then declared *ultra vires* by the Court of Appeal in *EN (Serbia)* at [83]). The AIT expressed clear reservation in respect of the submission that it had such jurisdiction, but recognised that the caselaw had developed such that it was at least arguable that jurisdiction does both extend outside judicial review and to a tribunal such as the AIT. However, ultimately, the AIT had concluded that it did not need to reach a conclusion on the particular issue.

16 *Cart v Upper Tribunal; R (C) and (U) v Special Immigration Appeals Commission* [2009] EWHC 3052 (Admin) at [94] and [97].

17 *EO (deportation appeals: scope and process) Turkey* [2007] UKAIT 62 at [10]–[19]; the Court of Appeal confirmed the correctness of the AIT's reasoning in this respect: [2008] EWCA Civ 671.

18 *AG (policies, executive discretions, tribunal's powers) Kosovo* [2007] UKAIT 00082.

19 Note the prospective wording of saved NIAA 2002, s 84(1)(g) – whether removal *would* breach the UK's obligations under the Refugee Convention, etc and see *Sandralingham and Ravichandran v Secretary of State for the Home Department; R v Immigration Appeal Tribunal, ex parte Rajendrakumar* [1996] Imm AR 97 at 111–113, CA, per Simon Brown LJ; see also saved NIAA 2002, s 85(4) and Chapter 5.

20 In respect to asylum grounds, see *Saad, Diriye and Osorio v Secretary of State for the Home Department* [2001] EWCA Civ 2008; *Abdillahi* [2002] UKIAT 00266 (starred); and *Andrabi* [2002] UKIAT 02884. In respect to human rights grounds, see *JM (Liberia) v Secretary of State for the Home Department* [2006] EWCA Civ 1402.

21 *MS (Ivory Coast) v Secretary of State for the Home Department* [2007] EWCA Civ 133.

3.14 It will be noted that there is no specific ground of appeal in saved NIAA 2002, s 84 providing for a challenge to a refusal to grant humanitarian protection.[1] In practice the FTT, on an appeal under saved NIAA 2002, s 82(1), will generally consider humanitarian protection under the rubric of the human rights grounds of appeal. However, with specific reference to appeals under saved NIAA 2002, s 83 (see **3.40** below), the Court of Appeal in *FA (Iraq)*,[2] relying on the EU law principle of equivalence, held that that provision must entitle an appellant to include a claim that the removal would breach the right to subsidiary protection pursuant to the Qualification Directive.

1   Saved NIAA 2002, s 84 was not subject to any amendments when provisions in the Qualification Directive providing for subsidiary protection were transposed domestically in the UK with effect from 9 October 2006 (see Chapter 1). Note, however, that the Refugee or Person in Need of International Protection (Qualification) Regulations 2006, SI 2006/2525 specifically do apply to any immigration appeal which has not been finally determined by 9 October 2006: reg 1(2).
2   *FA (Iraq) v Secretary of State for the Home Department* [2010] EWCA Civ 696 (see **3.40**, fn 14 below).

3.15   A particular issue that has arisen in asylum cases is whether an appellant may challenge the safety or lawfulness of proposed removal directions, including challenges as to the lawfulness of the destination and the safety of the method and route of removal. In *MS (Palestinian Territories)*[1] the Court of Appeal and the Supreme Court held that it was not within the scope of saved NIAA 2002, s 84(1)(e) (above) to challenge the lawfulness of removal directions that have not yet been made. In *MA (Somalia)*[2] the Court of Appeal held that where the SSHD indicates a destination in, for example, a disputed nationality case, he is merely proposing a destination so as to facilitate the appeal. If the appeal is dismissed in circumstances showing that the person is not a national of the country to which the removal is proposed, this does not mean that the appeal should be allowed on human rights (or on not in accordance with law) grounds.[3]

1   *MS (Palestinian Territories) v Secretary of State for the Home Department* [2009] EWCA Civ 17: aff'd [2010] UKSC 25.
2   *MA (Somalia) v Secretary of State for the Home Department* [2009] EWCA Civ 4.
3   See also *GH (Iraq) v Secretary of State for the Home Department* [2005] EWCA Civ 1182 and *Gedow v Secretary of State for the Home Department* [2006] EWCA Civ 1342.

MATTERS TO BE CONSIDERED AND THE 'ONE-STOP PROCEDURE'

3.16   NIAA 2002, s 120[1] attempted to simplify the so-called one-stop procedure previously contained in IAA 1999.[2] As originally enacted,[3] it applied to every person who has made an application to enter or remain in the UK[4] or in respect of whom any immigration decision within the meaning of (saved) NIAA 2002, s 82 (see **3.7** above) has been taken or may be taken.[5] The SSHD or immigration officer may by notice in writing require that person to state any other reasons or grounds upon the basis of which he wishes, or believes he should be permitted, to enter or remain or not be removed from or required to leave the UK.[6] Such a statement by the person need not repeat reasons or grounds set out in the original application or in the application to which the immigration decision relates (as above).[7] Then, on an appeal under saved NIAA 2002, s 82(1), the FTT shall treat the appeal as being against any and all appealable decisions against which the appellant has a right of appeal under that provision[8] and shall deal, on the one appeal, with all permissible grounds (as per saved NIAA 2002, s 84(1): see **3.13** above) raised by the appellant either initially (ie as the basis of the original application) or in his statement of 'additional grounds' made in accordance with NIAA 2002, s 120.[9] Furthermore, this applies to such a statement whether the statement was made before or after the appeal was commenced.[10] For provisions relating to what matters and what evidence the FTT can take into account on appeals against different kinds of immigration decisions, and depending on whether or not the decision was made under the points-based system, see Chapter 5.[11]

1 NIAA 2002, s 120 was substituted by IA 2014, Sch 9(4), para 55 from 20 October 2014. It is in NIAA 2002, Pt 6, which is entitled 'Immigration procedure', and its pre-amendment version is not a 'saved provision' within the Immigration Act 2014 (Commencement No 3, Transitional and Saving Provisions) Order 2014, SI 2014/2771, art 1(2)(e) (see **3.4** above). In the text above it is the pre-amended version that is considered. See Chapter 4 for the current version.
2 IAA 1999, ss 74–77 (see Chapter 2).
3 See fn 1 above.
4 Original NIAA 2002, s 120(1)(a).
5 Original NIAA 2002, s 120(1)(b).
6 Original NIAA 2002, s 120(2).
7 Original NIAA 2002, s 120(3).
8 Saved NIAA 2002, s 85(1). For examples of where there may be more than one appealable immigration decision, within the meaning of saved NIAA 2002, s 82(2), made against the same person at the same time, see **3.9** above.
9 Saved NIAA 2002, s 85(2).
10 Saved NIAA 2002, s 85(3).
11 Saved NIAA 2002, ss 85(4) and (5) and 85A as amended and inserted by UKBA 2007, s 19 from 23 May 2011. See Chapter 5.

3.17   Accordingly, an appellant may raise refugee asylum and human rights issues in an appeal against an immigration decision, whether by way of assertion in the grounds of appeal or in a statement of additional grounds, even though a claim to asylum or a human rights claim had not been made to the SSHD prior to the making of the immigration decision.[1] The point being that, unlike with previous statutes providing for appeal rights, there is no specific provision in saved NIAA 2002 to prevent an appellant relying on asylum grounds where no prior asylum claim had been made to the SSHD.[2] However this is subject to two very important caveats: first, that in respect to many of the immigration decisions listed in saved NIAA 2002, s 82(2), a person will only have a suspensive right of appeal, whilst remaining in the UK, if he has made an asylum or human rights claim in the UK prior to the making of the immigration decision.[3] Secondly, where asylum or protection issues are raised for the first time in grounds of appeal or in a statement of additional grounds, on a suspensive appeal (see **3.25** below), the SSHD will likely withdraw the decision in order to consider the asylum/protection claim himself at first instance rather than allow it be considered and determined at first instance by the FTT on appeal.[4] However it has not been at all uncommon for the FTT to have considered and determined non-protection-based human rights claims at first instance on saved NIAA 2002, s 82 appeals.

1   In *AS (Afghanistan) v Secretary of State for the Home Department* [2009] EWCA Civ 1076, Arden LJ (who was in the minority on the immigration rules issue at hand: see below) at [2] noted that this appeared to be uncontroversial.
2   Contrast IAA 1999, s 70(7)(a) (see **2.19** above) and AIAA 1993, Sch 2, para 2 (see **2.5** above).
3   Saved NIAA 2002, s 92(1) and (4)(a) (see **3.25** and **3.30** below).
4   See eg *R (Chichvarkin) v Secretary of State for the Home Department* [2011] EWCA Civ 91 and see **3.31** below.

3.18   Furthermore, in *AS (Afghanistan)*[1] the majority in the Court of Appeal[2] held that it is open to an appellant to raise, on a statement of additional grounds served in accordance with a s 120 one-stop notice (see above), a new basis under the immigration rules – perhaps under an entirely different category of rules from that under which the refused application was based – upon which he claims that he should be permitted to remain in the UK; and that the FTT can allow the appeal if it finds, effectively as the primary decision maker, that the appellant's claim succeeds as being in accordance, as at the date of hearing of the appeal, with the requirements of the newly raised immigration rule.[3] In *Patel*[4] the Supreme Court confirmed the correctness of the majority's approach. However, in *Lamichhane*[5] the Court of Appeal held that the SSHD was not under a duty to serve a s 120 notice (rather he has discretion – he may serve such a notice),[6] that the refusal to vary leave was not rendered unlawful by the non-service of such a notice, and, importantly, that in the absence of a s 120 notice having been served by the SSHD, it was not open to an appellant to raise any new immigration rules based grounds for being allowed to remain in the UK on an appeal to the FTT, because the FTT has no jurisdiction to consider such new grounds. Furthermore, a person appealing against refusal of an entry clearance, where the refusal was due to an outstanding deportation order, cannot seek to make good his failure to apply for the order to be revoked in his grounds of appeal or in a s 120 statement in respect to the entry clearance appeal.[7]

1   *AS (Afghanistan) v Secretary of State for the Home Department* [2009] EWCA Civ 1076.
2   Moore-Bick and Sullivan LJJ. Arden LJ dissented.
3   Though see **3.13**, fn 3 above regarding the limited value of this in points-based system cases under the rules.
4   *Patel v Secretary of State for the Home Department* [2013] UKSC 72.
5   *Lamichhane v Secretary of State for the Home Department* [2012] EWCA Civ 260. See also *R (Weiss) v Secretary of State for the Home Department* [2010] EWCA Civ 803.
6   Distinguishing in this respect apparently contradictory *obiter* comments in *R (Mirza) v Secretary of State for the Home Department* [2011] EWCA Civ 159 and *Sapkota v Secretary of State for*

the Home Department [2011] EWCA Civ 1320 (see **3.7**, fn 19 above). However if the SSHD does not serve a s 120 notice, he may not be able to prevent a subsequent right of appeal against a subsequent immigration decision by way of an NIAA 2002, s 96 certificate: see **3.37** below and see *R (Khan) v Secretary of State for the Home Department* [2014] EWCA Civ 88.

7   See *Latif (s 120: revocation of deportation order: Pakistan)* [2012] UKUT 78 (IAC): a person subject to a deportation order had to successfully apply for the deportation order to be revoked before making an application for entry clearance; it was a distinct two-stage procedure and there was no scope for both applications to be considered on appeal at the same time.

RESTRICTIONS AND LIMITATIONS ON RIGHTS OF APPEAL: REFUSAL OF LEAVE TO ENTER, REFUSAL OF ENTRY CLEARANCE AND VARIATION CASES: 'INELIGIBILITY'

3.19   Turning back now to the restrictions and limitations on rights of appeal under saved NIAA 2002, the first set of restrictions are contained in saved NIAA 2002, s 88, entitled 'ineligibility' and applying to immigration decisions of a kind referred to in saved s 82(2)(a), (b), (d) or (e) (see **3.7** above).[1] A person may not appeal under s 82(1) against such an immigration decision which is taken on the grounds that he or a person of whom he is a dependant:[2]

- does not satisfy a requirement as to age, nationality or citizenship specified in immigration rules;[3]

- does not have an immigration document of a particular kind (or any immigration document).[4] An 'immigration document' means:[5]

  – entry clearance,

  – a passport,

  – a work permit or other immigration employment document within the meaning of s 122,[6] and

  – a document which relates to a national of a country other than the UK and which is designed to serve the same purpose as a passport;

- has failed to supply a medical report or a medical certificate in accordance with a requirement of immigration rules;[7]

- is seeking to be in the UK for a period greater than that permitted in his case by immigration rules;[8] or

- is seeking to enter or remain in the UK for a purpose other than one for which entry or remaining is permitted in accordance with immigration rules.[9]

1   Saved NIAA 2002, s 88(1).
2   Saved NIAA 2002, s 88(2).
3   Saved NIAA 2002, s 88(2)(a).

4   Saved NIAA 2002, s 88(2)(b).
5   Saved NIAA 2002, s 88(3).
6   Note however that NIAA 2002, s 122 was repealed from 2 April 2007 by IANA 2006, Sch 3, para 1: Immigration, Asylum and Nationality Act 2006 (Commencement No 6) Order 2007, SI 2007/1109.
7   Saved NIAA 2002, s 88(2)(ba): added by IANA 2006, s 5 from 31 August 2006.
8   Saved NIAA 2002, s 88(2)(c).
9   Saved NIAA 2002, s 88(2)(d).

3.20   For the purposes of these provisions a passport or work permit means such a document that is valid and current.[1] A document confirming a grant of asylum may be sufficient for the purposes of constituting an immigration document as above.[2] A decision that purports to be on the ground that a person is seeking to enter or remain in the UK for a purpose which is not permitted by the Rules will not preclude a right of appeal where it is apparent that the ground for the decision is itself not lawful in that it bears no relation to the actual application.[3] These restrictions do not prevent an appeal on refugee asylum, human rights or race discrimination grounds[4] (see **3.13** above regarding grounds of appeal) however this will not avail those would-be appellants who have no basis for an asylum or human rights claim and leads to further complications over the timing of such claims and whether or not a suspensive right of appeal arises (see **3.25–3.30** below).

1   See *MC (Gambia)* [2008] UKAIT 00030 and *DS (India)* [2008] UKAIT 00035. Though note that a genuine document may contain a false representation – leading to mandatory refusal under the immigration rules: see *KB (Albania)* [2009] UKAIT 00043: genuine British passport obtained by deception by way of a false asylum claim made by an Albanian national pretending to be from Kosovo and so with false information as to place of birth appearing in the passport.
2   See *AM (Somalia)* [2009] UKAIT 00008.
3   See *AM (Ghana)* [2009] UKAIT 00002.
4   Saved NIAA 2002, s 88(4) with reference to saved NIAA 2002, s 84(1)(b),(c) and (g) (see **3.13** above).

RESTRICTION ON RIGHT OF APPEAL IN POINTS-BASED SYSTEM AND VISITOR ENTRY CLEARANCE CASES

3.21   There are significant and rather complex further restrictions to the right of appeal against a refusal of entry clearance contained in saved NIAA 2002, ss 88A, 90 and 91.[1]

- There are two versions of saved s 88A: one that was introduced by A&I(TC)A 2004 (here referred to as 'old s 88A');[2] the other that was introduced by IANA 2006 (here referred to as 'new s 88A').[3] The second of these replaces the former, and replaces saved ss 90 and 91 (see below). However from 1 April 2008, it only came into effect for the purposes of the points-based system[4] and from 9 July 2012 it came into effect also for the purpose of visits.[5] As to the effect of new s 88A, see below. For non-points-based system purposes and for non-visitors, the old s 88A and saved ss 90 and 91 remain (technically) in force.[6] The purported effect of old s 88A is that a person may not appeal under saved s 82(1) – other than on human rights and race discrimination grounds[7] – against refusal of entry clearance if the decision to refuse is taken on grounds which relate to a provision of immigration rules, and are specified for the purpose of this section by order of the SSHD.[8] However the necessary regulations were never made.

- Section 90 precluded any right of appeal – other than on human rights and race discrimination grounds[9] – against a refusal of entry clearance in visitor cases, unless the application was to visit a family member.[10] NIAA 2002, s 90 and the (old) Immigration Appeals (Family Visitor) Regulations 2003[11] still continue to have effect in relation to an appeal brought in respect of an application for entry clearance in order to visit a family member made before 9 July 2012.[12] The permitted family members were:[13]

  - the applicant's spouse, father, mother, son, daughter, grandfather, grandmother, grandson, granddaughter, brother, sister, uncle, aunt, nephew, niece or first cousin;[14]

  - the father, mother, brother or sister of the applicant's spouse;

  - the spouse of the applicant's son or daughter;

  - the applicant's stepfather, stepmother, stepson, stepdaughter, stepbrother or stepsister; or

  - a person with whom the applicant has lived as a member of an unmarried couple for at least two of the three years before the day on which his application for entry clearance was made.

- Section 91 precludes any right of appeal – other than on human rights and race discrimination grounds[15] – against a refusal of entry clearance in respect of a student accepted on a course that will last no more than six months, a prospective student or, in either case, his dependant.[16] Note that the Immigration Rules, in HC 395, paras 82–84, relating to prospective students were deleted from 30 September 2013.

- As already noted, from 1 April 2008, new s 88A replaced old s 88A and ss 90 and 91[17] but owing to the transitional provisions it only did so initially in relation to points-based system cases,[18] thereby denying a right of appeal against a refusal of entry clearance in such cases, other than on human rights and race discrimination grounds.[19] It did this by providing that a person may not appeal under s 82(1) against refusal of an application for entry clearance unless the application was made for a specified purpose with reference to regulations.[20] No such regulations were made until 2012 (see below) but since the new s 88A only applied to points-based system cases between 1 April 2008 and 8 July 2012, it was only such cases that were affected by its 'default' denial of the right of appeal.

• From 9 July 2012, the transitional provisions were amended[21] such that new s 88A also applied to visitor applications and (new) Immigration Appeals (Family Visitor) Regulations 2012[22] came into effect limiting the right of appeal against refusal of entry clearance as a visitor to cases where the application for entry clearance was in order to visit a family member.[23] Under the 2012 Regulations the person being visited in the UK had to be here with settled status (including, obviously, British citizens), or as a refugee or with a grant of humanitarian protection.[24] The permitted family members were:[25]

– the applicant's spouse, civil partner, father, mother, son, daughter, grandfather, grandmother, grandson, granddaughter, brother or sister;

– the father, mother, brother or sister of the applicant's spouse or civil partner;

– the spouse of the applicant's son or daughter;

– the son or daughter of the applicant's civil partner;

– the applicant's stepfather, stepmother, stepson, stepdaughter, stepbrother or stepsister (including by reference to an applicant's civil partner);

– a person with whom the applicant has been in a relationship akin to a marriage or civil partnership for at least two years prior to the application for entry clearance so long as the relationship is genuine and subsisting.

Determining whether the purpose of the application is to visit a family member is primarily to be done by examination of the application itself.[26]

• However, from 25 June 2013, new s 88A was again amended, by Crime and Courts Act 2013, with the effect of denying a right of appeal (other than on human rights and race discrimination grounds[27]) against a refusal of entry clearance in all visitor cases, thus including for the purpose of a family visit.[28] However this only applies to applications for entry clearance made on or after 25 June 2013 and the Immigration Appeals (Family Visitor) Regulations 2012 (see above) continue to have effect in relation to an appeal brought in respect of an application for entry clearance made before 25 June 2013.[29]

• Accordingly the final saved version of NIAA 2002, s 88A[30] provides, on a default position basis, that there is no right of appeal (other than on human rights and race discrimination grounds) against a refusal of entry clearance. Provision is made for further regulations to be made so as to provide for appeal rights against refusals of entry clearance where the application is for the purpose of entering as the dependant of a person in the UK.[31] However because new s 88A only ever applied to applications for entry clearance under the points-based system and for the purpose of entering the UK as a visitor (see above)[32] there was no need to make such regulations.

1 Note that NIAA 2002, ss 90 and 91 were repealed (in that they were substituted by 'new s 88A' – see text above) from 1 April 2008 by IANA 2006, s 4(1): Immigration, Asylum and Nationality Act 2006 (Commencement No 8 and Transitional and Saving Provisions) Order 2008, SI 2008/310, but with transitional provisions as explained in the text above.
2 Old s 88A inserted by A&I(TC)A 2004, s 29(1) from 1 October 2004: Asylum and Immigration (Treatment of Claimants, etc) Act 2004 (Commencement No 1) Order 2004, SI 2004/2523.
3 New s 88A substituted for old s 88A and ss 90 and 91 from 1 April 2008 by IANA 2006, s 4(1): SI 2008/310, but with transitional provisions as explained in the text above.
4 See SI 2008/310, arts 3 and 4.
5 See Immigration, Asylum and Nationality Act 2006 (Commencement No 8 and Transitional and Saving Provisions) (Amendment) Order, SI 2012/1531 amending SI 2008/310, art 4.
6 See SI 2008/310, art 4.
7 Old s 88A(2)(a) with reference to saved NIAA 2002, s 84(1)(b) and (c) (see **3.13** above).
8 Old s 88A(1).
9 NIAA 2002, s 90(4) with reference to saved NIAA 2002, s 84(1)(b) and (c) (see **3.13** above).
10 NIAA 2002, s 90(1).
11 Immigration Appeals (Family Visitor) Regulations 2003, SI 2003/518 as made under NIAA 2002, s 90(2) and (3).
12 See SI 2012/1531, art 3.
13 SI 2003/518, art 2(1).
14 For this purpose 'first cousin' means, in relation to a person, the son or daughter of his uncle or aunt: SI 2003/518, art 2(2).
15 NIAA 2002, s 91(2) with reference to 'saved' NIAA 2002, s 84(1)(b) and (c) (see **3.13** above).
16 NIAA 2002, s 91(1).
17 New s 88A substituted for old s 88A and ss 90 and 91 from 1 April 2008 by IANA 2006, s 4(1): SI 2008/310, art 3.
18 SI 2008/310, art 4.
19 New s 88A(3).
20 New s 88A(1).
21 SI 2012/1531, art 2 amended SI 2008/310, art 4.
22 Immigration Appeals (Family Visitor) Regulations 2012, SI 2012/1532, as made under new s 88A(1)(a) and (2).
23 This only applied to applications for entry clearance made on or after 9 July 2012: SI 2012/1532, reg 4. See above regarding NIAA 2002, s 90 and the 2003 Family Visitor Regulations.
24 SI 2012/1532, reg 3.
25 SI 2012/1532, reg 2.
26 See *Ajakaiye* [2011] UKUT 00375 (IAC).
27 New s 88A(3). A human rights appeal on Art 8 grounds may have some value in a refusal of entry clearance as a family visitor.
28 Crime and Courts Act 2013, s 52 amends saved NIAA 2002, s 88A *inter alia* by omitting s 88A(1)(a), which had provided for the visitor class of exception (by regulations: see fn 22 above) to the general or 'default' denial of a right of appeal against refusal of entry clearance, with effect from 25 June 2013: Crime and Courts Act 2013 (Commencement No 1 and Transitional and Saving Provision) Order 2013, SI 2013/1042, art 4.

29 SI 2013/1042, art 5(1) provides that the amendments (as per fn 28 above) only apply to applications for entry clearance made or after 25 June 2013; and art 5(2) provides that NIAA 2002, s 88A(1)(a) and (2)(b) and the Immigration Appeals (Family Visitor) Regulations 2012 continue to have effect in relation to an appeal brought in respect of an application for entry clearance made before 25 June 2013.
30 Meaning the version that was in force prior to the amendment by IA 2014 on 20 October 2014 (see **3.4** above).
31 Saved NIAA 2002, s 88A(1)(b) and (2).
32 SI 2008/310, art 4, as amended by SI 2012/1531, art 2.

3.22   The overall effect of these grossly over-complicated set of provisions with all their amendments and transitional limitations is that, at least from 25 June 2013, persons who apply for entry clearance either under the points-based system or as visitors (for family visits or otherwise) will only have a right of appeal under saved NIAA 2002, s 82(1) against a refusal on human rights and race discrimination grounds. See in this regard *Abisoye*[1] and *Ivlev*,[2] holding that it matters not whether the refusal of entry clearance in a points-based case is under the general grounds of refusal rather than owing to insufficient points being awarded. However, a person who applies for entry clearance in order to join, or accompany, a family member in the UK on a long-term (non-visit) basis – including as the family member of a person who is already here, or who is applying for entry clearance, under the points-based system – does have an unrestricted right of appeal under saved NIAA 2002, s 82(1) against the refusal of an entry clearance.[3]

1   *Abisoye (entry clearance appeal – Tier 2) Nigeria* [2012] UKUT 82 (IAC).
2   *R (Ivlev) v Entry Clearance Officer, New York* [2013] EWHC 1162 (Admin).
3   Clearly there will be little utility in such an appeal on eg not in accordance with immigration rules grounds if the principal family member is refused entry clearance, whether under the points-based system or otherwise.

REFUSAL OF LEAVE TO ENTER AND RESTRICTIONS ON RIGHT OF APPEAL

3.23   Saved NIAA 2002, s 89 precludes a right of appeal – other than on race discrimination, human rights or refugee asylum grounds[1] – against a refusal of leave to enter unless, on arriving in the UK, the person has an entry clearance and is seeking leave to enter for the same purpose as specified on his entry clearance document.[2] This does not, however, apply where the refusal of leave to enter is made in circumstances where the grant of entry clearance itself takes effect as a grant of leave to enter.[3] Furthermore it is insufficient, in order to deny the right of appeal, for the immigration officer to conclude that the applicant is lying about the purpose for which he is seeking entry.[4] However see below in **3.27** *et seq* regarding when such an appeal has or does not have suspensive effect.

1   Saved NIAA 2002, s 89(2) (as substituted as per fn 2 below) with reference to saved NIAA 2002, s 84(1)(b), (c) and (g) (see **3.13** above).

2   Saved NIAA 2002, s 89(1). NIAA 2002, s 89 was substituted by IANA 2006, s 6 from 31
    August 2006: Immigration, Asylum and Nationality Act 2006 (Commencement No 2) Order
    2006, SI 2006/2226.
3   See *GO (right of appeal: ss 89 and 92) Nigeria* [2008] UKAIT 00025.
4   See *R (Aiyegbeni) v Secretary of State for the Home Department* [2009] EWHC 1241 (Admin).

RESTRICTION ON RIGHTS OF APPEAL AGAINST REFUSALS OF ENTRY CLEARANCE AND LEAVE TO ENTER WHERE REFUSAL IS ON PUBLIC GOOD GROUNDS

3.24   Saved NIAA 2002, s 98 precludes a right of appeal against a refusal
of leave to enter or entry clearance if the SSHD certifies that he has personally
made the decision on the ground (whether wholly or in part) that the person's
exclusion or removal is conducive to the public good;[1] or that the decision is
in accordance with a direction of the SSHD identifying the person to whom
the decision relates and the direction was given on that ground (whether
wholly or in part).[2] It is specified that the reference to the SSHD is to the
SSHD acting in person.[3] However, even where the SSHD has so certified, a
person may still appeal to the FTT against a refusal of entry clearance on race
discrimination and human rights grounds[4] and against a refusal of leave to
enter on those grounds and on refugee asylum grounds as well.[5] The SSHD
may issue a certificate at any time, including after the commencement of an
appeal, in which case the appeal will lapse on its non-permitted grounds.[6] In
practice, where the SSHD intends to exclude a person from entering the UK,
he will personally make an exclusion order – the effect of which, *inter alia*,
is to require an Entry Clearance Officer to refuse any application for entry
clearance during any period when the exclusion order is in place[7] (see further
1.11 above). Rather than then try to challenge the refusal of entry clearance
by way of an appeal to the FTT limited to human rights grounds (owing to the
likely certification under s 98), persons in this position more commonly seek to
challenge the underlying exclusion decision by way of judicial review.[8] For an
example of a case where notwithstanding the refusal of entry clearance being
on the mandatory ground of the SSHD's extant personal exclusion order, the
applicant did appeal, unsuccessfully, under NIAA 2002, s 82(1), see *Moon*.[9]

1   Saved NIAA 2002, s 98(1) and (2)(a).
2   Saved NIAA 2002, s 98(1) and (2)(b).
3   Saved NIAA 2002, s 98(3). Accordingly the power to certify cannot be delegated to a civil
    servant either directly or under the '*Carltona* principle' (see **1.10** above).
4   Saved NIAA 2002, s 98(4) with reference to saved NIAA 2002, s 84(1)(b) and (c) (see **3.13**
    above).
5   Saved NIAA 2002, s 98(4) and (5) with reference to saved NIAA 2002, ss 82(2)(a) and 84(1)
    (b), (c) and (g) (see **3.13** above).
6   Saved NIAA 2002, s 99 as amended by the Crime and Courts Act 2013, s 51(2) from 8
    May 2013: Crime and Courts Act 2013 (Commencement No 1 and Transitional and Saving
    Provision) Order 2013, SI 2013/1042.

7   Immigration Rules, HC 395, paras 320(6) and 321A(4).
8   See eg *R (Farrakhan) v Secretary of State for the Home Department* [2002] EWCA Civ
    606; *R (Naik) v Secretary of State for the Home Department* [2010] EWHC 2825 (Admin);
    aff'd [2011] EWCA Civ 1546; *R (Cakani) v Secretary of State for Home Department* [2013]
    EWHC 16 (Admin); and *R (Uba) v Secretary of State for the Home Department* [2014]
    EWHC 1166 (Admin).
9   *Sun Myung Moon (human rights, entry clearance, proportionality) USA* [2005] UKIAT
    00112.

SUSPENSIVE OR NON-SUSPENSIVE RIGHT OF APPEAL AGAINST IMMIGRATION DECISIONS UNDER SAVED NIAA 2002, S 82

3.25   Saved NIAA 2002, s 92(1) provides that a person may not appeal under saved NIAA 2002, s 82(1) while he is in the UK unless his appeal is of a kind to which NIAA 2002, s 92 applies.[1] Accordingly the 'default position' is that an appeal under saved s 82(1) against an immigration decision as listed in saved s 82(2) (see **3.7** above) can only be brought from abroad, for example after the would-be appellant has left the UK. Saved NIAA 2002, s 92 does apply (so *prima facie* a suspensive, in-country right of appeal arises) to appeals against the following kinds of immigration decisions:[2]

- refusal of a certificate of entitlement under NIAA 2002, s 10: saved NIAA 2002, s 82(2)(c);

- refusal to vary a person's leave to enter or remain in the UK if the result of the refusal is that the person has no leave to enter or remain: saved NIAA 2002, s 82(2)(d);

- variation of a person's leave to enter or remain in the UK if, when the variation takes effect, the person has no leave to enter or remain: saved NIAA 2002, s 82(2)(e) – however this is subject to saved NIAA 2002, s 97B (as to which see below);[3]

- revocation under NIAA 2002, s 76 of indefinite leave to enter or remain in the UK: saved NIAA 2002, s 82(2)(f);

- a decision that a person is to be removed from the UK by way of directions under saved IANA 2006, s 47 (removal: persons with statutorily extended leave): saved NIAA 2002, s 82(2)(ha);

- a decision to make a deportation order under IA 1971, s 5(1): saved NIAA s 82(2)(j).[4]

1   Saved NIAA 2002, s 92(1). Note that appeals under saved NIAA 2002, ss 83(2) and 83A(2)
    (see **3.40** and **3.41** below) can inherently be brought whilst the appellant remains in the UK
    pursuant to the leave to remain that is a condition precedent to the right of appeal.

2   Saved NIAA 2002, s 92(2).
3   Saved NIAA 2002, s 92(2A) as added by Crime and Courts Act 2013, s 53(2) from 25
     June 2013: Crime and Courts Act 2013 (Commencement No 1 and Transitional and Saving
     Provision) Order 2013, SI 2013/1042.
4   Note that this immigration decision does not include a decision that the automatic deportation
     provision in UKBA 2007, s 32(4) applies (see **3.8** above).

3.26   However, as regards immigration decision (e) above – variation of
leave, etc – under saved NIAA 2002, s 97B,[1] where the SSHD, acting in
person, certifies that the decision to curtail leave (ie to vary leave such that
no leave remains) is or was taken wholly or partly on the ground that it is
no longer conducive to the public good for the person to have leave to enter
or remain in the UK,[2] and the person is outside of the UK at the time the
decision is made, then an appeal can only be brought from outside the UK[3]
and the person may not enter the UK for the purposes of an appeal against
that decision and the person's appeal against that decision is not one of a kind
to which saved s 92 applies.[4] Saved NIAA 2002, s 97B was introduced in
2013[5] in order to 'solve the problem', from the SSHD's point of view, caused
by the judgments in *MK (Tunisia)*[6] and *E (Russia)*[7] in which the SSHD
had sought to deprive the claimants of an opportunity to appeal in-country
against decisions to curtail leave to enter or remain made at a time when they
were outside of the UK. The court held that IA 1971, s 3D[8] provided that a
person's leave continues such as to enable him to return to the UK within the
time period for lodging an in-time, in-country appeal against the curtailment/
variation decision and that the SSHD must permit the person to return in this
circumstance.

1   Saved NIAA 2002, s 97B as added by the Crime and Courts Act 2013, s 53(3) from 25
     June 2013: Crime and Courts Act 2013 (Commencement No 1 and Transitional and Saving
     Provision) Order 2013, SI 2013/1042.
2   Saved NIAA 2002, s 97B(1).
3   Saved NIAA 2002, s 97B(2).
4   Saved NIAA 2002, s 97B(3).
5   See fn 1 above.
6   *R (MK (Tunisia)) v Secretary of State for the Home Department* [2011] EWCA Civ 333.
7   *R (E (Russia)) v Secretary of State for the Home Department* [2012] EWCA Civ 357.
8   For IA 1971, s 3D, see **3.7**, fn 8 above.

3.27   Saved NIAA 2002, s 92 also applies (so allowing for an in-country
suspensive right of appeal) to an appeal against refusal of leave to enter the
UK[1] if:

(a)   at the time of the refusal the appellant is in the UK, and

(b)   on his arrival in the UK the appellant had entry clearance.[2]

1   Saved NIAA 2002, s 82(2)(a) (see **3.7** above).
2   Saved NIAA 2002, s 92(3). See also **3.23** regarding saved NIAA 2002, s 89. Saved NIAA
     2002, s 92(3)–(3D) substituted for original s 92(3) by A&I(TC)A 2004, s 28 from 1 October
     2004.

3.28   However even where a person seeking entry does have an entry clearance, no suspensive, in-country, right of appeal will arise in the following circumstances:[1]

- Where the refusal of leave to enter is a deemed refusal under IA 1971, Sch 2, para 2A(9) resulting from cancellation of leave to enter by an immigration officer under para 2A(8) and on the grounds specified in para 2A(2A).[2] In other words, where a person's leave to enter derives from an entry clearance,[3] and the immigration officer cancels his leave to enter on the grounds that the person's purpose in arriving in the UK is different from the purpose specified in the entry clearance, no suspensive right of appeal arises. Note that such a person will, at least, have an out-of-country right of appeal against the refusal of leave to enter as he will not be 'caught' by saved NIAA 2002, s 89.[4]

- Where the refusal of leave to enter specifies that the grounds for refusal are that the leave is sought for a purpose other than that specified in the entry clearance.[5] Such a person is also 'caught' by saved NIAA 2002, s 89.[6]

1   Saved NIAA 2002, s 92(3A) with reference to (3B) and (3C) (see **3.27**, fn 2 above).
2   Saved NIAA 2002, s 92(3B).
3   Under IA 1971, s 3A(3) (see **1.11**, fn 5 above).
4   See *GO (right of appeal: ss 89 and 92) Nigeria* [2008] UKAIT 00025 and see **3.23** above.
5   Saved NIAA 2002, s 92(3C).
6   See **3.23** above.

3.29   Note that saved NIAA 2002, s 92 also nominally applies (so allowing for an in-country suspensive right of appeal) to an appeal against refusal of leave to enter the UK if at the time of the refusal the appellant is in the UK, has a work permit, and is a British overseas territories citizen, a British Overseas citizen, a British National (Overseas), a British protected person or a British subject.[1] 'Nominal' because work permits have been effectively replaced by the points-based system.

1   Saved NIAA 2002, s 92(3D). See the British Nationality Act 1981 for the nationality statuses.

SUSPENSIVE RIGHT OF APPEAL AND ASYLUM AND HUMAN RIGHTS CLAIMS

3.30   However, regardless of the immigration decision in issue, saved NIAA 2002, s 92 also applies (so allowing for an in-country suspensive right of appeal) if the appellant:

(a)   has made an asylum claim, or a human rights claim, while in the UK;[1] or

(b)   is an EEA national or a member of the family of an EEA national and makes a claim to the SSHD that the decision breaches the appellant's rights under the Community Treaties in respect of entry to or residence in the UK.[2]

1   Saved NIAA 2002, s 92(4)(a).
2   Saved NIAA 2002, s 92(4)(b).

3.31   As regards (b), see Chapter 4 regarding appeals against EEA decisions. As regards (a), where the person makes an asylum or human rights claim while in the UK:

- In *Nirula*[1] the Court of Appeal held that in order to have an in-country right of appeal, against an immigration decision to remove an illegal entrant (and so where the default position is that only a non-suspensive, out of country right of appeal arises: see **3.25** above), by reliance on saved NIAA 2002, s 92(4)(a), it was insufficient, because in effect too late, to raise a human rights claim, or an asylum claim, for the first time in a notice of appeal. In *Alighanbari*[2] the court, noting that whether a person has advanced a claim falling within the relevant definition is a question of substance, and not form, held that the following elements must be present on the facts for a human rights claim (here on Art 8 grounds) to have been made–

  (a)   a claim not to be removed from the UK;

  (b)   an assertion of facts that could constitute an existing or prospective private and or family life, the interference with which ECHR, Art 8 protects; and

  (c)   an assertion that removal will interfere with that private and or family life.

- However where a person does make an asylum or human rights protection claim for the first time in grounds of appeal, etc, the SSHD is obliged to consider the claim[3] and if he refuses it he will in practice make a new immigration decision. Furthermore, where a person raises asylum in grounds of appeal (statement of additional grounds: see **3.16** above) against an immigration decision that allows for a suspensive appeal in any event, for example a refusal to vary leave (see **3.25** above), the SSHD will in practice determine the asylum claim at first instance rather than allow the issue to be determined for the first time on appeal. In *Chichvarkin*[4] the Court of Appeal held that in such circumstance it was lawful and consistent with the statutory scheme governing the one-stop procedure for appeals (see **3.16** and **3.17** above) for the SSHD to withdraw the original decision refusing to vary leave and to reconsider the new issues raised on appeal as the primary decision maker.

- Even if the SSHD has previously refused an asylum or human rights claim, if a further such claim is made in relation to the making of a subsequent immigration decision, the Supreme Court held in *BA*

(Nigeria)[5] that an asserted subsequent claim does not have to be accepted as a 'fresh claim' by the SSHD[6] for the person to rely on saved NIAA 2002, s 92(4)(a) in order to have an in-country right of appeal against a new kind of immigration decision – for example against a decision not to revoke a deportation order where the earlier right of appeal was against a decision to deport. However where there is no need for the SSHD to make a new kind of immigration decision, for example in a refusal of leave to enter case, then it will be necessary for the claimant to have made a 'fresh claim' as per the Immigration Rules, para 353 in order to be able to rely on s 92(4)(a) in order to appeal from within the UK.[7]

- In any event, the suspensive right to appeal from within the UK may be excluded if the SSHD certifies that the claim or claims are 'clearly unfounded' under NIAA 2002, s 94, as to which see Chapter 4. So where the SSHD refuses an asylum, protection or human rights claim or claims, made in relation to a new immigration decision, the option is there to also certify the claim or claims as clearly unfounded and by that alternative route to deny a suspensive right of appeal.[8] Note however that this does not apply to a decision to revoke indefinite leave or a decision to make a deportation order under IA 1971, s 5(1) (the immigration decisions listed in saved NIAA 2002, s 82(2)(f) and (j) – the latter as very much distinct from a decision made under the automatic deportation provisions in UKBA 2007, s 32: see **3.8** above). This is because saved NIAA 2002, s 94 applies to an appeal under saved s 82(1) where the appellant has made an asylum claim or a human rights claim (or both)[9] and–

  - a person may not bring an appeal against an immigration decision of a kind specified in saved s 82(2)(c), (d), (e) or (ha) in reliance on s 92(2) (see **3.25** above and note that this includes all of the immigration decisions there listed except for those under s 82(2) (f) and (j)) if the SSHD certifies that the claim or claims mentioned above is or are clearly unfounded;[10]

  - a person may not bring an appeal to which this section applies in reliance on s 92(4)(a) (above) if the SSHD certifies that the claim or claims mentioned above is or are clearly unfounded.[11]

- Note however that a clearly unfounded certificate under saved NIAA 2002, s 94 needs to be issued along with the refusal of the claim, or at least prior to any appeal being lodged, in order to prevent a suspensive right of appeal 'being brought': in *AM (Somalia)*[12] Sedley LJ held that to 'bring an appeal' is a single event (the appeal is 'brought' at the moment that it is lodged) and there is no provision in saved NIAA 2002, s 94 to say that a certificate under it can stifle an in-country appeal that has already been brought (contrast saved NIAA 2002, ss 97(1), (3), 98(2) and 99: see **3.42** below and **3.24** above respectively).

1   *R (Nirula) v First-tier Tribunal* [2012] EWCA Civ 1436.
2   *R (Alighanbari) v Secretary of State for the Home Department* [2013] EWHC 1818 (Admin).
3   See the Immigration Rules, HC 395, paras 327, 328, 329 and 332.
4   *R (Chichvarkin) v Secretary of State for the Home Department* [2011] EWCA Civ 91. Though note that this approach was not followed in the extradition case of *Kozlowski v Poland* [2012] EWHC 1706 (Admin).
5   *R (BA (Nigeria) and PE (Cameroon)) v Secretary of State for the Home Department* [2009] UKSC 7.
6   As per the Immigration Rules, HC 395, para 353: see *Asylum Law and Practice* (2nd edition, Bloomsbury Professional), paras 12.56, 12.57.
7   See *R (ZA (Nigeria)) v Secretary of State for the Home Department* [2010] EWCA Civ 926.
8   See eg *R (YH (Iraq)) v Secretary of State for the Home Department* [2010] EWCA Civ 116.
9   Saved NIAA 2002, s 94(1).
10 Saved NIAA 2002, s 94(1A) as added by A&I(TC)A 2004, s 27(2) from 1 October 2004 and then amended by IANA 2006, s 47(8) from 1 April 2008: Immigration, Asylum and Nationality Act 2006 (Commencement No 8 and Transitional and Saving Provisions) Order 2008, SI 2008/310.
11 Saved NIAA 2002, s 94(2) as amended by A&I(TC)A 2004, s 27(3) from 1 October 2004.
12 *R (AM (Somalia)) v Secretary of State for the Home Department* [2009] EWCA Civ 114 at [13]–[17] – not directed at NIAA 2002, s 94 but the same reasoning must apply.

CONSEQUENCES OF HAVING A SUSPENSIVE RIGHT OF APPEAL

3.32   Where an appeal may be brought under saved NIAA 2002, s 82 from within the UK (with reference to s 92 above), the person may not be removed, or required to leave the UK while that appeal is pending.[1] However, this provision preventing removal whilst a suspensive appeal is pending does not prevent the giving of removal directions, or the making of a deportation order in respect of the appellant (subject to the provision below) or the taking of any other interim or preparatory action.[2] A deportation order cannot be made in respect of a person while an appeal under saved NIAA 2002, s 82(1) against a decision to deport could be brought (ignoring any possibility of an appeal out of time with permission) or is pending.[3] However this provision does not apply to 'automatic deportation' cases.[4]

1   NIAA 2002, s 78(1) and (4). An appeal is 'pending' in accordance with NIAA 2002, s 104 (see **3.43** *et seq* below): NIAA 2002, s 78(2).
2   NIAA 2002, s 78(3).
3   NIAA 2002, s 79(1). Again 'pending' has the meaning given by NIAA 2002, s 104: s 79(2).
4   NIAA 2002, s 79(3), as inserted by UKBA 2007, s 35 and the UK Borders Act 2007 (Commencement No 3 and Transitional Provisions) Order 2008, SI 2008/1818 from 1 August 2008. But a deportation order made in reliance on sub-s (3) does not invalidate leave to enter or remain, in accordance with IA 1971, s 5(1), if and for so long as NIAA 2002, s 78, above, applies: s 79(4).

APPEALS ONLY PERMITTED FROM WITHIN THE UK AND EFFECTIVENESS OF OUT-OF-COUNTRY APPEALS

3.33   A person may not appeal on the ground that his removal would be in breach of obligations under the Refugee Convention or HRA 1998 after he has left the UK unless his asylum or human rights claim(s) was certified under s 94: see saved NIAA 2002, s 95. However in *ZL*,[1] in the context of a clearly unfounded certificate, the Court of Appeal considered, in the context of asylum or protection claims, that such a right of appeal was effectively useless. Accordingly, the suspensive remedy in 'clearly unfounded certified cases' is a judicial review of the certification that the claim(s) is clearly unfounded. On the other hand, in an IAA 1999, s 10 removal case, where asylum or protection matters were not in issue, the Court of Appeal in *Lim*[2] held that an out-of-country appeal constituted an effective remedy, such that judicial review should be refused on discretionary grounds.[3] Similarly in *RK (Nepal)*,[4] where the SSHD had made an IAA 1999, s 10 decision to remove the applicants for breaches of the conditions of their leave to remain as students, the Court of Appeal rejected their submissions that they were entitled to a suspensive right of appeal, as per saved NIAA 2002, s 82(2)(e) (see **3.7** and **3.25** above), on the basis that the effect of the decision was to curtail their existing leave. Rather the effect of the s 10 removal decision was to invalidate their leave to remain and so they were only entitled to out-of-country appeals against the removal 'immigration decision' as per saved NIAA 2002, s 82(2)(g) (see **3.7** above). Where, however, the SSHD had sought wrongly to deny a suspensive right of appeal, by curtailing leave when the person was abroad, the Court of Appeal in *E (Russia)*,[5] whilst acknowledging that the fact that the appellant would not then have an in-country right of appeal did not entirely deprive him of an effective right of appeal, it did deprive him of a valuable right, namely, the right to pursue his appeal in-country (see further **3.26** above).

1   *ZL and VL v Secretary of State for the Home Department* [2003] 1 All ER 1062, sub nom *R (L) v Secretary of State for the Home Department* [2003] EWCA Civ 25.
2   *R (Lim) v Secretary of State for the Home Department* [2007] EWCA Civ 773. See also *R (CM (Jamaica)) v Secretary of State for the Home Department* [2010] EWCA Civ 160; *R (YZ (China)) v Secretary of State for the Home Department* [2012] EWCA Civ 1022; *R (Lewis) v Secretary of State for the Home Department* [2010] EWHC 1749 (Admin); *R (Zahid) v Secretary of State for the Home Department* [2013] EWHC 4290 (Admin); *R (Benjamin) v Secretary of State for the Home Department* [2014] EWHC 1396 (Admin); and *R (Ali) v Secretary of State for the Home Department* [2014] EWHC 3967 (Admin).
3   Following *R v Secretary of State for the Home Department, ex parte Swati* [1986] 1 WLR 477. See further Chapter 8.
4   *R (RK (Nepal)) v Secretary of State for the Home Department* [2009] EWCA Civ 359.
5   *R (E (Russia)) v Secretary of State for the Home Department* [2012] EWCA Civ 357. See also *R (MK (Tunisia)) v Secretary of State for the Home Department* [2011] EWCA Civ 333.

DENIAL OF A RIGHT OF APPEAL (ON ANY GROUNDS) AGAINST ANY IMMIGRATION DECISION WHERE A PERSON HAD AN EARLIER RIGHT OF APPEAL AGAINST A PREVIOUS IMMIGRATION DECISION

3.34   The most draconian provision affecting rights of appeal under saved NIAA 2002, s 82(1) is that contained in saved NIAA 2002, s 96 entitled 'earlier right of appeal'.[1] This represents the continuation of the approach as based on the provision in IAA 1999, s 73 (as to which see **2.32** above). First, an appeal under 'saved' NIAA 2002, s 82(1) against an immigration decision ('the new decision') in respect of a person may not be brought if the SSHD or an immigration officer certifies:

(a)   that the person was notified of a right of appeal under that section against another immigration decision ('the old decision') (whether or not an appeal was brought and whether or not any appeal brought has been determined);

(b)   that the claim or application to which the new decision relates relies on a matter that could have been raised in an appeal against the old decision; and

(c)   that, in the opinion of the SSHD or the immigration officer, there is no satisfactory reason for that matter not having been raised in an appeal against the 'old decision'.[2]

---

1   Saved NIAA 2002, s 96 as amended by A&I(TC)A 2004, s 30(1), (2) from 1 October 2004: Asylum and Immigration (Treatment of Claimants, etc) Act 2004 (Commencement No 1) Order 2004, SI 2004/2523 (original sub-ss (1)–(3) substituted for amended sub-ss (1) and (2)). Note that NIAA 2002, s 96 certificates can only apply to appeals under NIAA 2002, s 82(1) against immigration decisions (see **3.7** above) and could not be applied to prevent appeals under saved NIAA 2002, ss 83(2) or 83A(2) (see **3.40** and **3.41** below) being brought and this is logical as it may well be the case that a grant of humanitarian protection or discretionary leave (and thus the requisite leave to enter or remain in excess of one year for s 83 purposes) or the grant of leave as a refugee (relevant to appeals under s 83A) originally followed the lodging of an appeal under NIAA 2002, s 82(1) (see **3.45** below regarding appeals under NIAA 2002, s 82(1) being treated as abandoned under NIAA 2002, s 104(4A)). Note however also that a reference to an appeal under NIAA 2002, s 82(1) includes a reference to an appeal under SIACA 1997, s 2 which is or could be brought by reference to an appeal under NIAA 2002, s 82(1): see NIAA 2002, s 96(6). For appeals under SIACA 1997, s 2, see Chapter 7.

2   Saved NIAA 2002, s 96(1) (as substituted as per fn 1 above). The reference to an appeal under NIAA 2002, s 82(1), as well as including a reference to an appeal under SIACA 1997, s 2 which is or could be brought by reference to an appeal under NIAA 2002, s 82(1) (see fn 1 above), also includes a reference to an appeal or right of appeal under IAA 1999 (as to which see **2.13** *et seq*): NIAA 2002, s 114(2) and Sch 6, para 4(a). In other words, this limitation on further appeal rights under NIAA 2002, s 82(1) applies equally whether the initial right of appeal arose under NIAA 2002 itself or under the 1997 or 1999 Acts. It does not apply however to cases (which would be very rare by now) where an earlier right of appeal arose against an immigration decision made prior to 2 October 2000 under either IA 1971 or AIAA 1993 (see **2.1–2.12** above).

3.35   Secondly, an appeal under NIAA 2002, s 82(1) against an immigration decision ('the new decision') in respect of a person may not be brought if the SSHD or an immigration officer certifies:

(a)   that the person received a notice under NIAA 2002, s 120 by virtue of an application other than that to which the new decision relates or by virtue of a decision other than the new decision (see **3.16** above);

(b)   that the new decision relates to an application or claim that relies on a matter that should have been, but has not been, raised in a statement made in response to that notice, and

(c)   that, in the opinion of the SSHD or the immigration officer, there is no satisfactory reason for that matter not having been raised in a statement made in response to that notice.[1]

1   Saved NIAA 2002, s 96(2) (as substituted as per **3.34**, fn 1 above). For NIAA 2002, s 120, see **3.16** above. The reference to a statement made in response to a notice includes a reference to a statement made in response to a (one-stop) notice under IAA 1999: NIAA 2002, s 114(2) and Sch 6, para 4(c).

3.36   Both of these bases for preventing further appeal rights apply whether or not the affected person has been outside of the UK since an earlier right of appeal arose or a requirement to state additional grounds was imposed.[1]

1   Saved NIAA 2002, s 96(5). See also in this regard *R (YH) v Secretary of State for the Home Department* [2008] EWHC 2174 (Admin); aff'd [2010] EWCA Civ 116, as to the fresh claims procedure under the Immigration Rules, HC 395, para 353 also being potentially applicable where a person has returned to the UK from overseas.

3.37   As to condition (a), what matters is that the person was either notified of a right to appeal against the old decision,[1] regardless of whether or not he lodged such an appeal and whether or not he withdrew such an appeal (so that it was not determined), or that he received a notice under NIAA 2002, s 120 in relation to a previous application and or previous refusal. In *Lamichhane*[2] (see **3.18** above) the Court of Appeal considered that an adverse consequence from the SSHD's point of view of declining to serve a s 120 notice could be that he could not then later use s 96 to prevent a subsequent right of appeal. As to conditions (b) and (c), the first issue will be whether the new application or claim, in respect to which the new decision has been made, relies on matters and/or evidence that was not available when the previous decision or application was made and, secondly, if it was then available, whether the claimant will be able to satisfy the SSHD – or the court on judicial review – that there is a satisfactory reason for its not having been raised on the earlier appeal or in response to the earlier s 120 notice.[3] As Stadlen J explained in *R (J)*:[4]

'Under Section 96 (1) and (2) before the Secretary of State can lawfully decide to certify, she has to go through a four stage process. First she must be satisfied that the person was notified of a right of appeal under Section

82 against another immigration decision (Section 96(1)) or that the person received a notice under Section 120 by virtue of an application other than that to which the new decision relates or by virtue of a decision other than the new decision (Section 96(2)). Second she must conclude that the claim or application to which the new decision relates relies on a matter that could have been raised in an appeal against the old decision (Section 96(1)(b)) or that the new decision relates to an application or claim which relies on a matter that should have been but has not been raised in a statement made in response to that notice (Section 96(2)(b)). Third she must form the opinion that there is no satisfactory reason for that matter not having been raised in an appeal against the old decision (Section 96(1)(c)) or that there is no satisfactory reason for that matter not having been raised in a statement made in response to that notice (Section 96(2)(c)). Fourth she must address her mind to whether, having regard to all relevant factors, she should exercise her discretion to certify and conclude that it is appropriate to exercise the discretion in favour of certification.'

1   See the Immigration (Notices) Regulations 2003, SI 2003/658, reg 4(1): NIAA 2002, ss 96(4) and 105; but this includes a reference to notification in accordance with the previous Notices Regulations, SI 2000/2246: NIAA 2002, s 114(2) and Sch 6, para 4(d).

2   *Lamichhane v Secretary of State for the Home Department* [2012] EWCA Civ 260.

3   These conditions have similarity to the test for fresh asylum and human rights claims (see *Asylum Law and Practice* (2nd edition, Bloomsbury Professional), paras 12.55 *et seq*), in that the new claim will have to rely on some new material, such as a change of circumstances in the country in respect to which asylum is claimed, or the claimant will have to satisfy the SSHD that although there is no strictly new material there is a satisfactory reason for its not having been relied on in the earlier appeal: compare *Onibiyo v Secretary of State for the Home Department* [1996] QB 768 and the current Immigration Rules, HC 395, para 353 with deleted para 346 in relation to fresh claims (see *Asylum Law and Practice*, paras 12.55 and 12.56).

4   *R (J) v Secretary of State for the Home Department* [2009] EWHC 705 (Admin) at [106] in relation to an asylum case. See also *R (Mahmood) v Secretary of State for the Home Department* [2014] EWHC 259 (Admin) in which HHJ Pelling QC (sitting as a judge of the High Court) considered that Stadlen J's approach in *R (J)* should apply equally to Art 8 human rights cases.

3.38   In *Khan*[1] the Court of Appeal held that 'matter' (in (b) and (c)) was a broad word meaning little more than 'thing' and could include evidence as well as issues; and that the intention of s 96 was to prevent claimants from advancing on a new appeal new points and/or new material in aid of old points which might reasonably have been advanced in a previous appeal and that s 96(1) was properly directed to the advancing of new material as a whole, either in grounds of appeal or evidence in support.[2] As regards Stadlen J's fourth stage (above) and the exercise of discretion, the SSHD's Asylum Policy Instructions on Further Submissions notes the judgment in *R (J)* and states that caseworkers must consider whether, having regard to all relevant factors, it is still appropriate to certify the decision and that refusal letters must reflect that this consideration has taken place and that it has been decided that it is appropriate to certify. Factors to be considered include:

- the prospects of success at appeal for the underlying claim, particularly where asylum and Art 3 issues are raised;

- the reason why the claim was not advanced in the original appeal and the impact of that explanation on the credibility of the fresh claim;

- the fact that a claimant may have lied previously should be taken into account but is not necessarily determinative;

- if a claimant did appeal against the initial decision, raised the relevant matter in that appeal, but then abandoned the appeal, consideration should still be given to certifying under s 96 if further submissions made later rely on that matter.[3]

1   *R (Khan) v Secretary of State for the Home Department* [2014] EWCA Civ 88.
2   The appellant had unsuccessfully appealed against a decision to make a deportation order. By further submissions that included a social worker's report, relating to his contact with his children, he sought to revoke the deportation order. On refusing to revoke the order, the SSHD issued a certificate under s 96(1). The Court of Appeal held that the social worker's report fell within the definition in s 96(1) of a 'matter' that could have been raised in the earlier appeal such that the report could not be relied upon as grounds for a new appeal.
3   See API on 'Further submissions' (version 7.0, May 2014) at para 7.3.

3.39   Following the Supreme Court judgment in *BA (Nigeria)*,[1] certification under NIAA 2002, s 96 provides an alternative means for the SSHD to prevent a second appeal in cases where he has to make a 'new immigration decision' in response to a further asylum and or human rights claim which he considers to add nothing of substance to a previously refused claim in respect of which an appeal against an old immigration decision has been dismissed on asylum and or human rights grounds.[2] In practice, in such circumstances, the SSHD is likely to also certify the further asylum and or human rights claim or claims as being clearly unfounded under NIAA 2002, s 94 – because if the SSHD does not consider the further claim to be clearly unfounded then he must consider that there is something new in it with a realistic prospect of success on an appeal and so certification under NIAA 2002, s 96(1) or (2) would also be inappropriate[3] – and both certificates are likely to stand or fall together if challenged by way of judicial review.[4] Note that whereas a certificate under NIAA 2002, s 94 prevents a suspensive right of appeal being brought (see **3.31** above), a certificate under NIAA 2002, s 96 prevents any appeal being brought at all.[5] The remedy against both is by way of judicial review.[6] As with certificates under NIAA 2002, s 94,[7] either type of certificate under NIAA 2002, s 96 can only prevent an appeal being brought and it is explicitly provided that such a certificate shall have no effect in relation to an appeal instituted before the certificate is issued.[8]

1   *BA (Nigeria) and PE (Cameroon) v Secretary of State for the Home Department* [2009] UKSC 7 (see **3.31** above).
2   See eg *SB (Uganda) v Secretary of State for the Home Department* [2010] EWHC 338 (Admin).
3   See *ZT (Kosovo) v Secretary of State for the Home Department* [2009] UKHL 6 and *R (YH) v Secretary of State for the Home Department* [2010] EWCA Civ 116.

4   See eg *SB (Uganda)* (above), per Hickinbottom J at [58].
5   See *R (YZ (China)) v Secretary of State for the Home Department* [2012] EWCA Civ 1022 for
     a case where the claimant had been removed from the UK on the basis of an 'unlawful' (later
     withdrawn) s 96(2) certificate, but the Court of Appeal held that the judge had been correct, as
     an exercise of discretion, to decline to order the return of the claimant to the UK as he would
     have an effective out-of-country appeal.
6   As to which see Chapter 8.
7   See **3.31** above and *AM (Somalia) v Secretary of State for the Home Department* [2009]
     EWCA Civ 114 at [13]–[17].
8   Saved NIAA 2002, s 96(7) (as inserted by A&I(TC)A 2004, s 30(1) and (4) from 1 October
     2004: SI 2004/2523). This provision was inserted at the same time as current sub–ss (1) and
     (2) were substituted for original sub-ss (1)–(3) of s 96 (see **3.34**, fn 1 above). Sub-ss (1) and
     (2) originally provided that an appeal 'may not be brought or continued' if a certificate is
     issued and contrast the current wording in the para text above: an appeal 'may not be brought'
     and see *AM (Somalia)* (above). Unfortunately the Parliamentary draftsmen in 2004 failed to
     note the need to also amend NIAA 2002, s 99 which contradictorily still asserted, until it was
     finally amended by the Crime and Courts Act 2013, s 51(2) from 8 May 2013: Crime and
     Courts Act 2013 (Commencement No 1 and Transitional and Saving Provision) Order 2013,
     SI 2013/1042, that, where a certificate is issued under, *inter alia*, s 96(1) or (2), the appeal
     shall lapse. The current wording of saved s 99(1) now only refers to certificates under saved
     ss 97 and 98 causing an appeal to lapse.

APPEALS TO THE FTT ON REFUGEE ASYLUM GROUNDS UNDER SAVED NIAA 2002, SS 83 AND 83A

3.40   Prior to 6 April 2015 (see **3.4** and **3.5** above) where a person made an asylum claim[1] and:

(a)   the claim has been rejected by the SSHD, but

(b)   the person has been granted leave to enter or remain in the UK for a period exceeding one year (or for periods exceeding one year in aggregate),[2]

he may appeal to the FTT against the rejection of his asylum claim.[3] The decision maker must give written notice to the person of the relevant grant of leave to enter or remain where a right of appeal arose under NIAA 2002, s 83.[4] The right of appeal under s 83 arose only in circumstances where the grant of leave to remain post-dates the refusal of asylum, albeit that the grant of leave did not necessarily have to be a direct or immediate consequence of the refusal of asylum.[5] Note that the right of appeal only lay in respect of persons granted in excess of one year's limited leave to remain, whether at once or by extension – the right of appeal only accruing once the extension extended the total period of leave beyond a year, post the refusal of asylum.[6] Accordingly, for example where a person was refused asylum and on that same date was granted six month's discretionary or 'restricted' leave on exclusion grounds,[7] no right of appeal arose as at that date – that is no right of appeal under saved NIAA 2002, s 82 (see **3.7** above) because there was no removal decision and the result of the decision was that the person does have leave to enter or remain; and no right of appeal under saved NIAA 2002, s 83 because the condition as regards the necessary period of leave[8] had not been met. Furthermore, if the person was then granted a further six months of discretionary or restricted leave to follow immediately from the termination of the first grant of six months, such that the person would have been granted exactly 12 months of limited leave post the refusal of asylum, no right of appeal would have arisen as at the date of the second grant because again the condition as regards the necessary period of leave[9] would still not have been met. If and when the person was granted a further period of leave – so that the period of leave since the refusal of the asylum claim would now exceed one year – then the right of appeal under s 83(2) would have arisen. Accordingly, where on refusal of asylum a person was granted six months' discretionary or 'restricted' leave, any immediate challenge to the decision to refuse asylum would have to have been by way of judicial review.[10] Under saved NIAA 2002, s 84(3) the only stated permissible ground for such an appeal is that removal of the appellant from the UK would breach the UK's obligations under the Refugee Convention,[11] but, first, given the hypothetical use of 'would' the issue in practice is whether the appellant is currently, as at the date of the hearing, a refugee entitled to the protection from non-refoulment of the Refugee Convention, Art 33.[12] Secondly, this ground of appeal has been extended, relying on the EU law principle of equivalence, to include a claim that the removal would breach the right to subsidiary protection pursuant to the Qualification Directive:[13] see the decision of the Court of Appeal in *FA (Iraq)*.[14]

1   An 'asylum claim' means a claim made by a person to the SSHD at a place designated by the SSHD (eg a port or airport or UKVI headquarters in Croydon or a regional office) that to remove the person from or require him to leave the UK would breach the UK's obligations under the Refugee Convention: NIAA 2002, s 113(1).

2   Saved NIAA 2002, s 83(1).

3   Saved NIAA 2002, s 83(2).

4   Immigration (Notices) Regulations 2003, SI 2003/658, r 4(2) as revoked by Immigration (Notices) (Amendment) Regulations 2014, SI 2014/2768, reg 2(4)(b) from 6 November 2014 but subject to transitional provisions specified in SI 2014/2768, reg 3 which provide that the revoking provision in reg 2(4) only applies to a notice that is to be given in relation to a decision which is appealable under NIAA 2002, s 82(1) as amended by IA 2014, s 15(2) and thus the revocation does not apply to notices of decisions made prior to 6 April 2015 relevant to saved NIAA 2002, s 83. Where a person who was appealing on asylum grounds against an immigration decision (see **3.7** above) was, prior to 6 April 2015, granted leave to enter or remain other than as a refugee for a period exceeding 12 months, his appeal would not be treated as abandoned in so far as it is brought on asylum grounds if he gives notice, in accordance with the Procedure Rules (as to which see Chapter 5), that he wishes to pursue the appeal on that ground: see saved NIAA 2002, s 104(4B) (see **3.45** below).

5   See *Secretary of State for the Home Department v AS (Somalia)* [2011] EWCA Civ 1319 and *MS (Uganda) v Secretary of State for the Home Department* [2014] EWCA Civ 50.

6   See *MS (Uganda)* (above).

7   See fn 12 below and see UKVI Asylum Instruction on 'Restricted leave'.

8   In saved NIAA 2002, s 83(1)(b): see fn 2 and text above.

9   Ibid.

10 See eg *JS (Sri Lanka) v Secretary of State for the Home Department* [2010] UKSC 15 at [6].

11 Saved NIAA 2002, s 84(3). The tribunal has held that this meant it only had jurisdiction on such appeals to consider the refugee asylum ground: see *AN and NN (s 83 – asylum grounds only) Albania* [2007] UKAIT 00097.

12 See *Saad, Diriye and Osorio v Secretary of State for the Home Department* [2001] EWCA

Civ 2008; *Abdillahi* [2002] UKIAT 00266 (starred); *Andrabi* [2002] UKIAT 02884; and see **3.13** above regarding saved s 84(1)(g). The point made in the text above about the Refugee Convention, Art 33 is that in cases involving appeals under saved NIAA 2002, s 83, the appellant may have been refused asylum as a refugee for either Art 1F exclusion reasons or on the basis of being a person – eg a 'serious criminal' within the meaning of NIAA 2002, s 72 – who is considered by the SSHD not to benefit from the protection of Art 33 (see further in *Asylum Law and Practice* (2nd edition, Bloomsbury Professional), chs 8 and 9).

13   Council Directive 2004/83/EC of 29 April 2004 (see **1.8** above).
14   *FA (Iraq) v Secretary of State for the Home Department* [2010] EWCA Civ 696. The SSHD appealed to the Supreme Court against the Court of Appeal's judgment and the SC referred the questions to the European Court of Justice about whether the EU principle of equivalence required that there should be a right of appeal against the refusal of an application for humanitarian protection: see *FA (Iraq) v Secretary of State for the Home Department* [2011] UKSC 22. However, it is understood that the SSHD then conceded the issue.

3.41   Where a person who has had limited leave as a refugee, lost that status on or after 31 August 2006 (but prior to 6 April 2015: see **3.4** and **3.5** above), for example on a review or on an application for indefinite leave,[1] but was nonetheless granted limited leave in another capacity and for whatever duration (most likely in practice to be discretionary or restricted leave),[2] he may appeal to the FTT against the decision to curtail or to refuse to extend his refugee leave[3] on the ground that his removal from the UK would breach the UK's obligations under the Refugee Convention,[4] or, as per the principle of equivalence, on the ground that his removal would breach the right to subsidiary protection pursuant to the Qualification Directive.[5]

1   See the Immigration Rules, HC 395, paras 339A and 339R.
2   Saved NIAA 2002, s 83A(1) as inserted by IANA 2006, s 1 from 31 August 2006 in respect of decisions made on or after that date: Immigration, Asylum and Nationality Act 2006 (Commencement No 2) Order 2006, SI 2006/2226.
3   NIAA 2002, s 83A(2) as inserted as per fn 2 above.
4   NIAA 2002, s 84(4) as inserted by IANA 2006, s 3 from 31 August 2006 in respect of decisions made on or after that date: SI 2006/2226. See **3.40**, fn 12 above regarding the hypothetical use of the word 'would' – ie the issue is whether or not the appellant is, at the date of hearing, a refugee entitled to the protection from non-refoulment in the Refugee Convention, Art 33.
5   *FA (Iraq) v Secretary of State for the Home Department* [2010] EWCA Civ 696 (see **3.40**, fn 14 above).

DENIAL OF A RIGHT OF APPEAL TO THE FTT WHERE THE SSHD PERSONALLY CERTIFIES THAT THE DECISION IS TAKEN ON, OR IN RELATION TO, NATIONAL SECURITY GROUNDS

3.42   Under NIAA 2002, s 97, the SSHD may prevent a person from appealing against a decision, on any grounds, to the FTT under saved NIAA 2002, ss 82(1), 83(2) or 83A(2), by certifying that the decision was taken by himself or in accordance with his directions on the grounds that the person's exclusion or removal from the UK is in the interests of national security or in the interests of the relationship between the UK and another country.[1] Furthermore, the SSHD can also preclude an appeal to the FTT, under saved NIAA 2002, s 82(1), 83(2) or 83A(2), by certifying that the decision is or was taken wholly or partly in reliance on information which in his opinion should not be made public in the interests of national security, in the interests of the relationship between the UK and another country, or otherwise in the public interest.[2] In all cases, the reference to the SSHD certifying is to the SSHD acting in person.[3] An appeal will lie instead to the Special Immigration Appeals Commission (SIAC, as to which, see Chapter 7). Furthermore, the SSHD may certify that a decision to make a deportation order in respect of a person was taken on the grounds that his removal from the UK would be in the interests of national security,[4] or, in the case of a person subject to 'automatic deportation' under UKBA 2007, s 32(5), that the person's removal from the UK would be in the interests of national security,[5] and the consequence of such certifications is that no appeal lies to the FTT because the SSHD shall be taken to have certified the decision to make the deportation order under s 97.[6] The effect of a s 97 certificate is to prevent an appeal being 'brought or continued'[7] and NIAA 2002, s 99 provides that where a certificate is issued under NIAA 2002, s 97 in respect of a pending appeal,[8] that appeal shall lapse.[9] In these cases the person may appeal instead to the SIAC (see Chapter 7).

1   NIAA 2002, s 97(1) and (2) (as amended by IANA 2006, Sch 1 from 31 August 2006: Immigration, Asylum and Nationality Act 2006 (Commencement No 2) Order 2006, SI 2006/2226; and most recently by IA 2014, Sch 9(4) from 20 October 2014 to delete references to ss 83(2) and 83A(2): see **7.5** and **7.6**). Note that such a certificate prevents an appeal being 'brought or continued'. Clearly there is a logical problem with this provision in as far as it applied to appeals under saved ss 83(2) and 83A(2) where the person is inherently not in fact being excluded or removed from the UK due to having leave to enter or remain in the UK in another capacity.
2   NIAA 2002, s 97(3) (as amended as above). Again, such a certificate prevents an appeal being 'brought or continued' (see fn 1 above).
3   NIAA 2002, s 97(4).
4   NIAA 2002, s 97A(1). NIAA 2002, s 97A inserted by IANA 2006, s 7(1) from 31 August 2006: SI 2006/2226 and most recently amended by IA 2014, Sch 9(4) para 43 from 20 October 2014, subject to savings and transitional provisions as specified in the Immigration Act 2014 (Commencement No 3, Transitional and Saving Provisions) Order 2014, SI 2014/2771, arts 9–11 (as now amended). See further **7.7** below.
5   NIAA 2002, s 97A(1A) inserted by the Crime and Courts Act 2013, s 54(2) and the Crime and Courts Act 2013 (Commencement No 1 and Transitional and Saving Provision) Order 2013, SI 2013/1042 from 25 June 2013.
6   NIAA 2002, s 97A(2)(b).
7   NIAA 2002, s 97(1) and (3) and see fnn 1 and 2 above.
8   NIAA 2002, s 99(1).
9   NIAA 2002, s 99(2).

APPEALS TO THE TRIBUNAL UNDER SAVED NIAA 2002, SS 82, 83 AND 83A PENDING AND LAPSING

3.43   An appeal under saved NIAA 2002, s 82(1) is pending during the period beginning when it is instituted and ending when it is finally determined, withdrawn or abandoned or when it lapses under s 99.[1] An appeal under saved NIAA 2002, s 82(1) is not finally determined while:

(a)   an application for permission to appeal under TCEA 2007, ss 11 or 13[2] (as to which see Chapter 6) could be made or is awaiting determination;

(b)   permission to appeal under either of those sections has been granted and the appeal is awaiting determination; or

(c)   an appeal has been remitted under TCEA 2007, ss 12 or 14[3] (see Chapter 6) and is awaiting determination.[4]

1   Saved NIAA 2002, s 104(1). Under saved NIAA 2002, s 99 an appeal under saved NIAA 2002, s 82(1) will lapse when a certificate is issued under saved s 97 or 98 (see **3.42** and **3.24** above).
2   TCEA 2007, s 11 provides for an appeal on any point of law from the FTT to the UT; s 13 provides for an appeal on any point of law from the UT to the relevant appellate court (ie the Court of Appeal, the Court of Session or the Court of Appeal in Northern Ireland). See Chapter 6.
3   Under TCEA 2007, s 12 the UT may (but need not) remit an appeal to the FTT and under s 14 the relevant appellate court may (but need not) remit an appeal to the UT or to the FTT.
4   Saved NIAA 2002, s 104(2) (as substituted from 15 February 2010 by the Transfer of Functions of the Asylum and Immigration Tribunal Order 2010, SI 2010/21, arts 1 and 5(1), Sch 1, paras 20 and 26(a)).

3.44   In short this means that an appeal is not finally determined whilst an application for permission to appeal to the UT or to the Court of Appeal (etc) could be brought or is pending a decision, nor whilst an appeal is pending before the UT or the Court of Appeal nor whilst an appeal that has been remitted by the UT or by the Court of Appeal has not yet been determined. A pending appeal on asylum grounds, under saved NIAA 2002, s 83 or 83A, only lapses when a certificate is issued under NIAA 2002, s 97 (on national security grounds)[1] and, on the face of the statute, there is nothing to prevent such a certificate being issued at any stage in the proceedings before the tribunal.[2] An appeal under saved NIAA 2002, s 82(1) brought by a person while he is in the UK shall be treated as abandoned if the appellant leaves the UK.[3] 'Leaves the UK' has been held to mean physically leaving UK territory or territorial waters, regardless of any intention to return; a day trip to France will suffice to cause such a pending appeal to be treated as abandoned.[4] Clearly this provision does not apply to an appeal under saved NIAA 2002, s 82(1) brought by a person from outside the UK and it also does not apply to appeals to the FTT brought under saved NIAA 2002, s 83(2) or 83A(2) (see **3.40** and **3.41** above) where the appellant will have leave to enter or remain in the UK and can physically leave the UK without abandoning his appeal.[5]

1   Saved NIAA 2002, s 99. In such circumstance an appeal can be brought instead to the SIAC under SIACA 1997, s 2. See Chapter 7.
2   Saved NIAA 2002, s 97(1) and (3) (see **3.42** above).
3   Saved NIAA 2002, s 104(4).
4   See *Dupovac v Secretary of State for the Home Department* [2000] Imm AR 265, CA; and see *R (MM (Ghana)) v Secretary of State for the Home Department* [2012] EWCA Civ 827. Note that in *Shirazi v Secretary of State for the Home Department* [2003] EWCA Civ 1562 at [11]–[18], Sedley LJ, in interpreting abandonment provisions in IAA 1999, s 58, held that there was there a distinction to be made between an appeal to an adjudicator or the IAT being abandoned by reason of the appellant leaving the UK on the one hand and a further appeal to the Court of Appeal being abandoned for that reason on the other (see also per Munby LJ at [35]–[39] and Mummery LJ at [41]). Saved NIAA 2002, s 104(4) however clearly applies to an appeal under NIAA 2002, s 82(1) that has been brought by a person while he is in the UK at whatever stage in the appellate process it may be at; and see *AS (Afghanistan) v Secretary of State for the Home Department* [2009] EWCA Civ 1076 at [61] and [93].
5   Contrast the situation where the appeal is to the SIAC (see **7.6** and **7.40** below).

3.45   An appeal under saved NIAA 2002, s 82(1) brought by a person while he is in the UK shall be treated as abandoned if the appellant is granted leave to enter or remain in the UK, subject to two provisos:[1]

●   First, this provision shall not apply to an appeal, in so far as it is brought on asylum grounds, where the appellant is granted leave to enter or remain for a period exceeding 12 months and the appellant gives notice, in accordance with Tribunal Procedure Rules, that he wishes to pursue the appeal in so far as it is brought on that ground.[2] In effect the appeal under saved NIAA 2002, s 82(1) can be translated into an appeal under s 83(2) so long as the conditions for such an appeal are met (see **3.40** above) and so long as the appellant gives notice, in accordance with Tribunal Procedure Rules, that he wishes to pursue the appeal on refugee asylum grounds.[3]

●   Secondly, this provision shall not apply to an appeal in so far as it is brought on race discrimination grounds where the appellant gives notice, in accordance with Tribunal Procedure Rules, that he wishes to pursue the appeal in so far as it is brought on that ground.[4]

1   Saved NIAA 2002, s 104(4A) (as substituted by IANA 2006, s 9 from 13 November 2006: Immigration, Asylum and Nationality Act 2006 (Commencement No 3) Order 2006, SI 2006/2838).
2   Saved NIAA 2002, s 104(4B) (as substituted as above).
3   Contrast the position in *Kanyenkiko v Secretary of State for the Home Department* [2003] EWCA Civ 542 in relation to IAA 1999, ss 58 and 69 (see **2.18** above). The Tribunal Procedure Rules are: in respect of an appeal pending before the FTT when the appellant is granted the requisite period of leave to enter or remain – Tribunal Procedure (First-tier Tribunal) (Immigration and Asylum Chamber) Rules 2014, SI 2014/2604, r 16(2) and (3); and in respect of an appeal pending before the UT when the appellant is granted the requisite period of leave to enter or remain – Tribunal Procedure (Upper Tribunal) Rules 2008, SI 2008/2698, r 17A(3)–(5) (as inserted from 15 February 2010 by the Tribunal Procedure (Amendment No 2) Rules 2010, SI 2010/44, rr 1, 2 and 12).
4   Saved NIAA 2002, s 104(4C) (as substituted as per fn 1 above). For race discrimination grounds, see saved NIAA 2002, s 84(1)(b) (see **3.13** above). For the Tribunal Procedure Rules, see fn 3 above.

3.46 An appeal against an immigration decision refusing leave to enter, refusing a certificate of entitlement, varying or refusing to vary leave or revoking indefinite leave,[1] shall be treated as finally determined if a deportation order is made against the appellant.[2]

1 That is immigration decisions as listed in saved NIAA 2002, s 82(2)(a), (c), (d), (e) or (f) (see **3.7** above).

2 Saved NIAA 2002, s 104(5). Note that, at least prior to 6 April 2015, an asylum applicant could then apply, on the basis of an asylum claim, to have the deportation order revoked and refusal to revoke a deportation order was an appealable immigration decision for the purposes of saved NIAA 2002, s 82(1) and (2)(k) (see **3.7** above). Owing to the judgment in *BA (Nigeria) and PE (Cameroon) v Secretary of State for the Home Department* [2009] UKSC 7 (see **3.31** above) the SSHD could not prevent such a right of appeal by refusing to accept the new asylum claim as a 'fresh claim' and any certification of the new asylum claim, if refused, as clearly unfounded, under NIAA 2002, s 94 (see **3.31** above), would be highly vulnerable to judicial review, generally on grounds of gross unfairness and because the original asylum claim had not been so certified. Since in such a claim the person may well be relying exclusively on the same matters raised in his appeal against the previous immigration decision (see fn 1 above), the conditions for certification in saved NIAA 2002, s 96(1) or (2) would not be met either (see **3.34** above). See now the appeal rights under NIAA 2002, s 82(1)(a) (as amended by IA 2014: see Chapter 4) and the need for there to be a refusal of a protection claim which in turn depends on the acceptance of any further submissions constituting a 'fresh claim', as per Immigration Rules, HC 395, para 353; and see *R (Waqar) v Secretary of State for the Home Department (statutory appeals/paragraph 353)* (IJR) [2015] UKUT 169 (IAC).

Chapter 4

Current rights of appeal to the First-tier Tribunal

PART 1 – RIGHTS OF APPEAL TO THE FTT UNDER NIAA 2002 AS AMENDED BY IA 2014

AMENDMENTS TO NIAA 2002, PT 5 BY IA 2014

4.1   As noted in Chapters 1 and 3, NIAA 2002, Part 5 was significantly amended, and in effect substituted, from 20 October 2014 by IA 2014, ss 15 and 17 and Sch 9(4), paras 34–54.[1] The most significant amendments are as follows:

- NIAA 2002, ss 82 and 84, providing for right of appeal to the FTT and the grounds upon which such appeals can be brought, are fundamentally amended by IA 2014, s 15(2) and (4) as explained at **4.4–4.9** below.

- NIAA 2002, ss 83 and 83A (see **3.40** above) are repealed by IA 2014, s 15(3).

- NIAA 2002, s 85(5), 'matters to be considered', is substituted by IA 2014, s 15(5).

- NIAA 2002, s 92, providing for the place (ie from within the UK or from abroad) from which an appeal may brought or continued, is substituted by IA 2014, s 17(2) (see **4.15** and **4.16** below).

- In terms of consequential amendments as provided for by IA 2014, Sch 9(4):

    – the heading to NIAA 2002, Pt 5 is substituted so as to read 'Appeals in respect of protection and human rights claims';[2]

    – NIAA, 2002, ss 85(2) and (4) (matters to be considered), 86 (determination of appeal), 94 (appeal from within the UK: relating to clearly unfounded certifications), 94A (European Common List of Safe Countries of Origin), 96 (earlier right of appeal), 97 (national security, etc), 97A (national security: deportation), 99 (re appeals lapsing), 104 (pending appeal), 105 (notice of immigration decision), 106 (rules), 107 (practice directions), 108 (forged documents: proceedings in private), 112 (regulations) and 113 (interpretation) are all amended;

–   NIAA 2002, ss 85A (matters to be considered: new evidence: exceptions), 87 (successful appeal: direction), 88–91 (see **3.19– 3.23** above), 95 (appeal from outside the UK: removal), 97B (variation of leave on grounds of public good: rights of appeal), 98 (other grounds of public good) and 115 (a transitional provision relating to clearly unfounded human rights or asylum claim[3]) are repealed.

1   See the Immigration Act 2014 (Commencement No 3, Transitional and Saving Provisions) Order 2014, SI 2014/2771, art 2. For the saving provisions, see **3.4** and **3.5** above and see **4.3** below.
2   See **3.3** above regarding the previous title of Pt 5: 'Immigration and asylum appeals'.
3   See *ZL and VL v Secretary of State for the Home Department* [2003] 1 All ER 1062; *sub nom R (L) v Secretary of State for the Home Department* [2003] EWCA Civ 25.

OTHER RELEVANT AMENDMENTS BROUGHT BY IA 2014

4.2   Of further note for present purposes are the following amendments brought by IA 2014:

- IA 2014, s 1 substitutes IAA 1999, s 10 (removal of persons unlawfully in the UK) from 20 October 2014[1] so that s 10(1) now provides for the removal of a person from the UK under the authority of the SSHD or an immigration officer if the person requires leave to enter or remain in the UK but does not have it.[2] Clearly this continues to provide for the removal of persons who have overstayed their leave to enter or remain; and as regards persons who breach conditions of their leave or who obtained leave to remain by deception,[3] their leave can be curtailed or invalidated[4] and they can then be subject to removal under this provision, the point being that decisions to curtail leave and to remove under IAA 1999, s 10 are no longer separate 'immigration decisions' appealable as such under, pre-amended, NIAA 2002, s 82 (see **3.7** *et seq* above).

- IA 2014, s 2 inserts a new NIAA 2002, s 78A from 28 July 2014,[5] which provides for restrictions on the removal of children and their parents or carers for a period of 28 days following the exhaustion of appeals rights.

- IA 2014, s 17(3) inserts a new NIAA 2002, s 94B from 28 July 2014,[6] which provides for the SSHD to certify a human rights claim made by a person liable to deportation with the effect that the person can be removed from the UK pending the outcome of any appeal (see further **4.25** below).

- IA 2014, s 19 inserts a new Pt 5A into NIAA 2002, ss 117A–117D from 28 July 2014,[7] which provides for stipulated 'public interest considerations' to be taken account of by a court or tribunal, whether on appeal or judicial review, when determining whether a decision made under the Immigration Acts[8] breaches a person's ECHR, Art 8 rights so as to be rendered unlawful under HRA 1998, s 6.

- IA 2014, Sch 9(1), para 5 repeals IANA 2006, s 47 (removal of persons with statutorily extended leave: see **3.7** above) from 20 October 2014.[9]

- IA 2014, Sch 9(4), para 55 substitutes NIAA 2002, s 120 (requirement to state additional grounds for application, etc) from 20 October 2014.[10] See **3.16–3.18** above for pre-amendment NIAA 2002, s 120.

- IA 2014, Sch 9(4), para 56 amends A&I(TC)A 2004, Sch 3, in respect of appeal rights in safe third country cases, from 20 October 2014[11] (see further **4.46** below).

- IA 2014, Sch 9, also provides for consequential amendments to–

  - IA 1971, ss 3C and 3D (see **3.7** above) so as to provide for leave to be extended during any period when an 'administrative review' could be sought or is pending;[12]

  - NIAA 2002, ss 72 (serious criminal),[13] 76 (revocation of leave to enter or remain)[14] and 79 (deportation order: appeal);[15]

  - IANA 2006, s 55 (Refugee Convention: certification);[16]

  - IANA 2006, s 12 (relating to new definitions of asylum and human rights claim in NIAA 2002, s 113[17]) and repealing s 13 and Sch 1, para 11 (amending NIAA 2002, s 94, relating to clearly unfounded asylum and human rights claims, and consequentially, s 112) but which, in any event, have themselves either not been, or never were, brought into force.[18]

---

1   See the Immigration Act 2014 (Commencement No 3, Transitional and Saving Provisions) Order 2014, SI 2014/2771, art 2. Note though that the pre-amended version of IAA 1999, s 10 is a 'saved provision' as per SI 2014/2771, art 1(2)(e) (see para **3.4** above).
2   IAA 1999, s 10(2)–(5) (as amended) provide for the removal of such a person's family members.
3   See pre-amended IAA 1999, s 10(1).
4   Under IA 1971, s 3(3)(a) and Immigration Rules, HC 395, para 323.
5   Immigration Act 2014 (Commencement No 1, Transitory and Saving Provisions) Order 2014, SI 2014/1820, art 3(a).
6   SI 2014/1820, art 3(n).
7   SI 2014/1820, art 3(o).
8   For a full list of the 'Immigration Acts', see UKBA 2007, s 61(2) (as amended by IA 2014, s 73(5) from 14 May 2014).
9   SI 2014/2771, art 2 (see fn 1 above). Note though that IANA 2006, s 47 is a 'saved provision' as per SI 2014/2771, art 1(2)(e) (see **3.4** above).
10   SI 2014/2771, art 2.
11   Ibid.

12 IA 2014, Sch 9(4), paras 21 and 22, with effect from 20 October 2014: 2014/2771, art 2.
13 IA 2014, Sch 9(4), para 31, with effect from 20 October 2014: 2014/2771, art 2.
14 IA 2014, Sch 9(1), para 3(3), with effect from 20 October 2014: 2014/2771, art 2.
15 IA 2014, Sch 9(4), para 32, with effect from 20 October 2014: 2014/2771, art 2.
16 IA 2014, Sch 9(4), para 57(4), with effect from 20 October 2014: 2014/2771, art 2.
17 Basically, these amending provisions are designed to exclude from the definition of an 'asylum claim' and a 'human rights claim' any purported such 'fresh' claim that has not been accepted as such by the SSHD pursuant to Immigration Rules, para 353: see *R (BA (Nigeria)) v Secretary of State for the Home Department* [2009] UKSC 7, per Lord Hope at [12].
18 IA 2014, Sch 9(4), para 57(2),(3) and (5), with effect from 20 October 2014: 2014/2771, art 2.

COMMENCEMENT OF THE AMENDED PROVISIONS OF NIAA 2002, PT 5

4.3   As explained in **3.4** and **3.5** above, the substitution of the new, or 'relevant' (see **3.4** above), appeals provisions in NIAA 2002, Pt 5 for the old, or 'saved' provisions in the same, as effected by IA 2014 (as above) has been a staged process.[1] In practice the new provisions apply as follows:

- From 20 October 2014, the new NIAA 2002, Pt 5 provisions apply to–

  - a person who becomes a 'foreign criminal' within the definition in NIAA 2002, s 117D(2)[2] on or after 20 October 2014, and to a person liable to deportation from the UK under IA 1971, s 3(5)(b) because he belongs to the family of such a foreign criminal;[3]

  - a person who makes an application on or after 20 October 2014 for leave to remain as a Tier 4 (student) migrant, as the partner of a Tier 4 migrant or as the child of a Tier 4 migrant.[4]

- From 10 November 2014, the new NIAA 2002, Pt 5 provisions apply in relation to a deportation decision made by the SSHD on or after 10 November 2014 in respect of a person who is a foreign criminal within the definition in NIAA 2002, s 117D(2) (and thus to such a person regardless of when he became a foreign criminal) and to a person liable to deportation from the UK under IA 1971, s 3(5)(b) because he belongs to the family of such a foreign criminal.[5] A 'deportation decision' means a decision to make a deportation order, a refusal to revoke a deportation order or a decision made under UKBA 2007, s 32(5) (automatic deportation).[6]

- From 2 March 2015, the new NIAA 2002, Pt 5 provisions apply to a person who makes an application on or after 2 March 2015 for leave to remain as a Tier 1 migrant, a Tier 2 migrant or a Tier 5 migrant, as the partner of the same or as the child of the same.[7]

- From 6 April 2015, the new NIAA 2002, Pt 5 provisions apply to all cases unless the 'saved' provisions apply (as to which see **3.5** above).[8] In practical terms this means that the new rights of appeal under NIAA

2002, s 82 (see **4.4** *et seq* below) apply to all such appealable cases where the SSHD makes a decision to refuse a protection or human rights claim, or to revoke a person's protection status, on or after 6 April 2015. Furthermore, this means that in respect to all applications as made on non-protection and non-human rights grounds on or after 6 April 2015, no right of appeal will arise under NIAA 2002, s 82; and similarly, in respect to immigration decisions, eg to remove or to deport a person from the UK or to revoke indefinite leave to remain, where no protection or human rights issues are raised, made on or after 6 April 2015, no right of appeal will arise under NIAA 2002, s 82 (and see Chapters 8 and 9 for alternative remedies of judicial and administrative review).

1 As explained in **3.4** above, the Immigration Act 2014 (Commencement No 3, Transitional and Saving Provisions) Order 2014, SI 2014/2771, art 1(2)(d) and (e) provide respectively for the 'relevant provisions' of IA 2014 which effect the amendments to *inter alia* NIAA 2002, Pt 5 (see **4.1** above) and for the 'saved provisions' *inter alia* of NIAA 2002, Pt 5 (see **3.4** and **3.5** above).
2 Under NIAA 2002, s 117D(2) a 'foreign criminal' is defined as a person who is not a British citizen, who has been convicted in the UK of an offence, and who has been sentenced to a period of imprisonment of at least 12 months; has been convicted of an offence that has caused serious harm; or is a persistent offender.
3 SI 2014/2771, arts 2, 9 and 10 as originally enacted. In practical terms it would be in relation to deportation decisions made in respect to such persons that the new appeals provisions apply.
4 SI 2014/2771, arts 2, 9 and 11(1) as originally enacted. There were some further exceptions to this of potential relevance during the period between 20 October 2014 and 5 April 2015 in SI 2014/2771, art 11(2) and (3) as originally enacted. Now see SI 2014/2771, arts 2 and 9(1) (a) (as substituted from 6 April 2015 by the Immigration Act 2014 (Commencement No 4, Transitional and Saving Provisions and Amendment) Order 2015, SI 2015/371, arts 1(3) and 8(2): see **3.5** above).
5 The Immigration Act 2014 (Transitional and Saving Provisions) Order 2014, SI 2014/2928, art 2(1)(b). Note that SI 2014/2928 was revoked from 6 April 2015 by SI 2015/371, arts 1(3) and 9 (presumably as being no longer necessary).
6 SI 2014/2928, art 2(2).
7 SI 2014/2771, arts 2, 9 and 11(1A) (as inserted for the period between 2 March 2015 and 5 April 2015 by SI 2015/371, arts 1(2) and 7). Now see SI 2014/2771, arts 2 and 9(1)(b) (as substituted from 6 April 2015 by SI 2015/371, arts 1(3) and 8(2)).
8 SI 2014/2771, arts 2 and 9(1) (as substituted from 6 April 2015 by SI 2015/371, arts 1(3) and 8(2)).

RIGHT OF APPEAL TO THE FTT: NIAA 2002, S 82

4.4 Under NIAA 2002, s 82(1) a person, 'P', may appeal to the FTT[1] where:[2]

(a) the SSHD has decided to refuse a protection claim made by P,

(b) the SSHD has decided to refuse a human rights claim made by P, or

(c) the SSHD has decided to revoke P's protection status.

1 The 'tribunal' to which an appeal lies remains the FTT: NIAA 2002, s 81 (see **3.3** above).
2 NIAA 2002, s 82(1) as substituted by IA 2014, s 15(2) from 20 October 2014 (see above).

4.5 *Current rights of appeal to the First-tier Tribunal*

4.5 A 'protection claim' means a claim made by P that his removal from the UK (i) would breach the UK's obligations under the Refugee Convention, or (ii) would breach the UK's obligations in relation to persons eligible for a grant of humanitarian protection.[1] As can be seen, the Court of Appeal's judgment in *FA (Iraq)*[2] is given effect with full 'equivalence' given to refugee status[3] and humanitarian protection[4] for appeal rights purposes (see **3.14**, **3.40** and **3.41** above). P's protection claim is refused if the SSHD makes one or more of the following decisions:

(i)   that removal of P from the UK would not breach the UK's obligations under the Refugee Convention;

(ii)   that removal of P from the UK would not breach the UK's obligations in relation to persons eligible for a grant of humanitarian protection.[5]

1   NIAA 2002, s 82(2)(a) (substituted as per **4.4**, fn 2 above).
2   *FA (Iraq) v Secretary of State for the Home Department* [2010] EWCA Civ 696. See **3.40**, fn 14 above.
3   'Refugee' has the same meaning as in the Refugee Convention: NIAA 2002, s 82(2)(e) (substituted as per **4.4**, fn 2 above).
4   'Humanitarian protection' is to be construed in accordance with the Immigration Rules: NIAA 2002, s 82(2)(d) (substituted as per **4.4**, fn 2 above). See especially Immigration Rules, HC 395, paras 339C–339H.
5   NIAA 2002, s 82(2)(b) (substituted as per **4.4**, fn 2 above).

4.6   A person has 'protection status' if the person has been granted leave to enter or remain in the UK as a refugee or as a person eligible for a grant of humanitarian protection.[1] A 'human rights' claim means a claim made by a person to the SSHD at a place designated by the SSHD that to remove the person from or require him to leave the UK or to refuse him entry into the UK would be unlawful under HRA 1998, s 6 (public authority not to act contrary to the ECHR).[2] Accordingly a right of appeal will lie, on human rights grounds only (see **4.7** and **4.8** below), against a decision to refuse entry clearance. In all cases the right of appeal, as above, is subject to the exceptions and limitation specified in Pt 5.[3] Furthermore, in *Waqar*,[4] the tribunal held that in order for a right of appeal to arise under NIAA 2002, s 82(1)(a) or (b) (above), there has to have been an accepted protection or human rights 'claim' within the meaning *inter alia* (and if relevant) of the still applicable provisions in the Immigration Rules, para 353, in respect of when further representations constitute a 'fresh claim'.[5]

1   NIAA 2002, s 82(2)(c) (substituted as per **4.4**, fn 2 above).
2   NIAA 2002, s 113(1) as amended by IA 2014, Sch 9(4), para 53.
3   NIAA 2002, s 82(3) (substituted as per **4.4**, fn 2 above). See further below.
4   *R (Waqar) v Secretary of State for the Home Department (statutory appeals/paragraph 353)* (IJR) [2015] UKUT 169 (IAC).
5   Immigration Rules, HC 395, para 353. See *Asylum Law and Practice* (2nd edition, Bloomsbury Professional), paras 12.56 and 12.57.

GROUNDS OF APPEAL: NIAA 2002, S 84

4.7   The permitted grounds of appeal are provided for by NIAA 2002, s 84 as follows (with subsections and paragraphs):[1]

1   An appeal under s 82(1)(a) (refusal of protection claim: see **4.4** *et seq* above) must be brought on one or more of the following grounds–

   (a)   that removal of the appellant from the UK would breach the UK's obligations under the Refugee Convention;

   (b)   that removal of the appellant from the UK would breach the UK's obligations in relation to persons eligible for a grant of humanitarian protection;

   (c)   that removal of the appellant from the UK would be unlawful under HRA 1998, s 6 (public authority not to act contrary to Human Rights Convention).

2   An appeal under s 82(1)(b) (refusal of human rights claim: see **4.4** *et seq* above) must be brought on the ground that the decision is unlawful under HRA 1998, s 6.

3   An appeal under s 82(1)(c) (revocation of protection status: see **4.4** *et seq* above) must be brought on one or more of the following grounds–

   (a)   that the decision to revoke the appellant's protection status breaches the UK's obligations under the Refugee Convention;

   (b)   that the decision to revoke the appellant's protection status breaches the UK's obligations in relation to persons eligible for a grant of humanitarian protection.

1   NIAA 2002, s 84 as substituted by IA 2014, s 15(4) from 20 October 2014 (see above).

4.8   In line with existing case law, the appealable decision as per s 82(1) (a) and the permissible grounds of appeal in respect to it, as per s 84(1) (above), that removal *would* breach or *would* be unlawful, etc, should provide for the FTT to consider the position as at the date of hearing and without regard to whether, for example, the appellant had been granted a period of discretionary leave (at least as regards s 84(1)(a) and (b)) on refusal of the protection claim. See in this regard **3.13–3.15** and **3.40** above and see *Saad*.[1] Similarly, as regards the grounds of appeal as per s 84(3) (above), these effectively mirror the right of appeal on refugee asylum grounds, with an equivalent right as regards humanitarian protection, under saved ss 83A and 84(4) as interpreted in *FA (Iraq)*,[2] as to which see **3.41** *et seq* above. As noted in **4.4** *et seq* above, an appeal on human rights grounds only, as per s 84(2), will lie *inter alia* against a decision to refuse entry clearance. For the likely limited ambit to this ground of appeal against a refusal of entry clearance, see **3.13** above with regards to the ground of appeal in saved NIAA 2002,

4.9   *Current rights of appeal to the First-tier Tribunal*

s 84(1)(c).[3] However, in *Mostafa*[4] the tribunal allowed an appeal against refusal of entry clearance as a visitor on Art 8 grounds and further considered that where on such an appeal – limited to human rights grounds only under saved NIAA 2002, ss 82(1) and (2)(a) and 84(1)(c) (see **3.7**, **3.13** and **3.21** above) – it is established that the decision does interfere with family or private life rights to a sufficient degree so as to engage Art 8, the appellant's ability to satisfy the relevant immigration rules will be a weighty factor in the proportionality balancing exercise.[5]

1   *Saad, Diriye and Osorio v Secretary of State for the Home Department* [2001] EWCA Civ 2008. See also *JM (Liberia) v Secretary of State for the Home Department* [2006] EWCA Civ 1402; *MS (Ivory Coast) v Secretary of State for the Home Department* [2007] EWCA Civ 133; *FA (Iraq) v Secretary of State for the Home Department* [2010] EWCA Civ 696; *Abdillahi* [2002] UKIAT 00266 (starred); and *Andrabi* [2002] UKIAT 02884.
2   See fn 1 above.
3   See especially *Sun Myung Moon (human rights, entry clearance, proportionality) USA* [2005] UKIAT 00112.
4   *Mostafa (Art 8 in entry clearance)* [2015] UKUT 00112 (IAC).
5   See *R (Razgar) v Secretary of State for the Home Department* [2004] UKHL 27 at [17]–[20] concerning the series of questions to be considered in an Art 8 case, culminating, if reached, in the proportionality question.

4.9   Accordingly a right of appeal against a specified type of 'immigration decision' on a relatively wide gamut of permissible grounds (see especially **3.7** and **3.13** above) and on asylum grounds only against refusal of an asylum claim and, effectively, against revocation of refugee status (see especially **3.40** above) has been replaced by a right of appeal, limited to protection and human rights grounds, against refusals of protection and human rights claims and loss of 'protection status'. Putting aside the political propaganda nonsense of reducing 17 rights of appeal (sic) to just four (sic) (see **3.9** above), the effects of the amendments are *inter alia* that the FTT will, henceforth (once the new provisions come fully into effect and the backlog of saved appeals is cleared), deal only with 'protection', human rights and EEA appeals (see below); business people and others will no longer be able to appeal to the FTT on non-protection and non-human rights grounds against adverse, and all too often incorrect, decisions in their cases[1] (whilst 'foreign criminals' will retain their rights of appeal on *inter alia* human rights grounds); and, on the other hand, persons refused protection and human rights claims will be able to appeal to the FTT against the refusal, regardless of their immigration status, that is whether or not they have leave to enter or remain and if they have, regardless of the duration of such leave, if any, on refusal of the claim (see **3.9** above).

1   Though see the point made in *Mostafa (Art 8 in entry clearance)* [2015] UKUT 00112 (IAC) (see **4.8** above): if, but only if, an appellant can establish, by way of a human rights claim giving rise to an appeal on human rights grounds, that Art 8 is engaged on the facts of his case, such that the proportionality question is reached (see *Razgar* and **4.8**, fn 5 above), then if he can also demonstrate that the impugned decision is not in accordance with immigration rules, this could render the decision disproportionate and thus in breach of Art 8.

MATTERS TO BE CONSIDERED AND THE NEW 'ONE-STOP PROCEDURE': NIAA 2002, SS 85 AND 120

4.10   NIAA 2002, s 85(1) provides that an appeal under s 82(1) against a decision (see **4.4** *et seq* above) shall be treated by the FTT as including an appeal against any decision in respect of which the appellant has a right of appeal under s 82(1).[1] What this must now mean in practice is that where, for example, a person, 'P', makes a protection claim to the SSHD and also makes a human rights claim, in particular on Art 8 grounds, and both are refused, an appeal against the refusal of the protection claim, under s 82(1)(a) is to be treated by the FTT as also being an appeal against the refusal of the human rights claim, under s 82(1)(b) (see **4.4** *et seq* above). Similarly, where the SSHD has notified P that he is considering revoking P's protection status and P responds by *inter alia* making an Art 8 human rights claim and the SSHD goes on to both revoke P's protection status and to refuse the Art 8 human rights claim, P's appeal under s 82(1)(c) is to be treated by the FTT as including an appeal under s 82(1)(b). It is suggested that this interpretation is consistent with the unchanged wording of s 85(1) in light of the previous jurisprudence (see **3.16** above) and the new appeal rights provisions in s 82(1).

1   NIAA 2002, s 85(1): the wording is the same as per saved NIAA 2002, s 85(1) (see **3.9** and **3.16** above).

4.11   NIAA 2002, s 120 now applies to a person, 'P', if:

(a)   P has made a protection claim or a human rights claim,

(b)   P has made an application to enter or remain in the UK (on any basis), or

(c)   a decision to deport or remove P has been or may be taken.[1]

1   NIAA 2002, s 120(1) as substituted by IA 2014, Sch 9(4), para 55 from 20 October 2014 (see **4.2** above). Protection and human rights claims have the same meaning as in NIAA 2002, ss 82 and 113 as explained in **4.4** *et seq* above: NIAA 2002, s 120(6) (as so substituted).

4.12   The SSHD or an immigration officer may serve a notice on P, requiring P to provide a statement setting out his reasons for wishing to enter or remain in the UK, any *grounds* on which he should be permitted to enter or remain in the UK, and any *grounds* on which he should not be removed from or required to leave the UK.[1] Importantly here, 'grounds' means grounds under which an appeal may be brought as set out exhaustively in s 84 (see **4.7** and **4.8** above), ie relating only to protection and human rights issues.[2] Furthermore, where P has previously been served with such a notice and he requires leave to enter or remain in the UK but does not have it, or he has leave to enter or remain in the UK only by virtue of IA 1971, s 3C or 3D (continuation of leave pending decision or appeal),[3] and where his circumstances have changed since the SSHD or an immigration officer was last made aware of them (whether in the original application or claim or in a statement served in response to the notice) so that he has additional reasons for wishing to enter or remain in the UK, or additional grounds on which he should be permitted to enter or remain in the UK, or additional *grounds* on which he should not be removed from or required to leave the UK, he must, as soon as reasonably practicable, provide a supplementary statement to the SSHD or an immigration officer setting out the new circumstances and the additional reasons or *grounds*.[4] Again, note the specified and limited meaning here of 'grounds', as above.

1 NIAA 2002, s 120(2) (as substituted as above). A statement under sub-s (2) need not repeat reasons or grounds set out in P's protection or human rights claim, the application mentioned in (b) (in **4.11** above), or an application to which the decision mentioned in (c) (in **4.11** above) relates: s 102(3) (as so substituted).
2 NIAA 2002, s 120(6).
3 NIAA 2002, s 120(4) (as substituted above). For IA 1971, ss 3C and 3D, see **3.7** above.
4 NIAA 2002, s 120(5) (as substituted above).

4.13   NIAA 2002, s 85(2) provides that if an appellant makes a statement under s 120, the FTT shall consider any matter raised in the statement which constitutes a ground of appeal of a kind listed in s 84 against the decision appealed against,[1] and shall do so whether the statement was made before or after the appeal was commenced.[2] NIAA 2002, s 85(4) provides that on an appeal under s 82(1) against a decision the FTT may consider *any matter* which it thinks relevant to the substance of the decision, including a *matter* arising after the date of the decision.[3] (Prior to amendment by IA 2014,[4] this provision read: 'the FTT may consider *evidence about* any matter which it thinks relevant to the substance of the decision, including *evidence which concerns* a matter arising after the date of the decision.[5]) NIAA 2002, s 85(5) then goes on to provide: 'But the Tribunal must not consider a new matter unless the Secretary of State has given the Tribunal consent to do so.'[6] A matter is a 'new matter' if:

(a)   it constitutes a ground of appeal of a kind listed in s 84 (see **4.7** and **4.8** above); and

(b)   the SSHD has not previously considered the matter in the context of the decision mentioned in s 82(1) (see **4.4** above), or a statement made by the appellant under s 120 (see **4.12** above).[7]

1 NIAA 2002, s 85(2) as textually but inconsequentially amended by IA 2014, Sch 9(4), para 34(a) from 20 October 2014.
2 NIAA 2002, s 85(3): the provision is unaltered by IA 2014 (see **3.16** above).
3 NIAA 2002, s 85(4) as amended by IA 2014, Sch 9(4), para 34(b) from 20 October 2014 so as to delete references to ss 83(2) and 83A(2) and more significantly the words 'evidence about' and 'evidence which concerns'. See text above.
4 See fn 3 above.
5 Compare saved NIAA 2002, s 85(4): see further Chapter 5 concerning evidence.
6 NIAA 2002, s 85(5) as substituted by IA 2014, s 15(5) from 20 October 2014 (see **4.1** above).
7 NIAA 2002, s 85(6) as substituted as per fn 6 above.

4.14   On the one hand, the purpose behind the amendments to NIAA 2002, s 85 are clear: the SSHD expressly reserves the right to be the initial decision maker in respect to any protection or human rights claims that are made.[1] Accordingly, unless the SSHD has had the opportunity to consider such a claim, whether by way of the initial decision on the application or on consideration of a statement of additional grounds pre-appeal, the FTT can only consider an additional claim, as either made in a statement of additional grounds served after the appeal commenced (s 85(3)) or on the appeal itself (s 85(4)), if the SSHD consents to doing so (s 85(5)). On past practice the SSHD may well consent to Art 8 claims being considered in this way but is unlikely to do so in respect of a 'protection claim' raised for the first time on an appeal.[2] On the other hand, it is much less clear what affect the amendments to NIAA 2002, s 85 have on the question of what evidence, relating, that is, to the subject matter of the original decision, the FTT can consider on an appeal and in particular whether there is now any distinction between 'protection' appeals, where the jurisprudence has long held that the FTT can and indeed must consider the up-to-date evidential situation as at the date of hearing,[3] and appeals on human rights grounds against refusals of entry clearance, where previously the statutory provisions, as interpreted by the courts,[4] limited consideration of evidence to the circumstances appertaining as at the date of the Entry Clearance Officer's decision. See further Chapter 5.

1   Compare *R (Chichvarkin) v Secretary of State for the Home Department* [2011] EWCA Civ 91 and see **3.17** above.
2   See *Chichvarkin* (above).
3   See *Sandralingham and Ravichandran v Secretary of State for the Home Department; R v Immigration Appeal Tribunal, ex parte Rajendrakumar* [1996] Imm AR 97 at 111–113, CA, per Simon Brown LJ. See also the points made in **4.7** and **4.8** above regarding the prospective wording of 'removal *would* breach'.
4   See eg saved NIAA 2002, ss 85(4) and (5) and 85A(1) and (2) (and, prior to amendments brought by UKBA 2007, s 19 from 23 May 2011, NIAA 2002, s 85(4) and (5)) and see *AS (Somalia) v Entry Clearance Officer (Addis Ababa)* [2009] UKHL 32. See also *DR (ECO: post-decision evidence) Morocco* [2005] UKIAT 38.

SUSPENSIVE OR NON-SUSPENSIVE RIGHT OF APPEAL: PLACE FROM WHICH AN APPEAL MAY BE BROUGHT OR CONTINUED: NIAA 2002, S 92

4.15   NIAA 2002, s 92 provides for where an appeal can be brought and continued from, the UK or only from abroad, and thus whether an appeal has suspensive or non-suspensive effect:[1]

- In the case of an appeal under s 82(1)(a) (protection claim appeal), the appeal must be brought from within the UK (the 'default' position) unless–

> – the claim to which the appeal relates has been certified under
> s 94(1) or (7) (claim clearly unfounded or removal to safe third
> country); or
>
> – provisions in A&I(TC)A 2004, Sch 3, relating to removal of
> asylum seeker to safe third country, apply.[2]

- In the case of an appeal under s 82(1)(b) (human rights appeal) where
  the claim to which the appeal relates was made while the appellant was
  in the UK, the appeal must be brought from within the UK (the 'default'
  position) unless–

  > – the claim to which the appeal relates has been certified under
  > s 94(1) or (7) (claim clearly unfounded or removal to safe third
  > country) or s 94B (certification of human rights claims made by
  > persons liable to deportation); or
  >
  > – provisions in A&I(TC)A 2004, Sch 3, relating to removal of
  > asylum seeker to safe third country, apply.[3]

- In the case of an appeal under s 82(1)(b) (human rights appeal) where
  the claim to which the appeal relates was made while the appellant was
  outside the UK, in particular in an entry clearance case, the appeal must
  be brought from outside the UK.[4]

- In the case of an appeal under s 82(1)(c) (revocation of protection status)–

  > – the appeal must be brought from within the UK if the decision to
  > which the appeal relates was made while the appellant was in the
  > UK;[5]
  >
  > – the appeal must be brought from outside the United Kingdom if the
  > decision to which the appeal relates was made while the appellant
  > was outside the UK.[6]

1 NIAA 2002, s 92(1), as substituted by IA 2014, s 17(2) from 20 October 2014 (see **4.1** above).
2 NIAA 2002, s 92(2), as substituted as above. For clearly unfounded certifications see **4.17** *et
   seq* below and for appeals in safe third country cases, see **4.40** *et seq* below.
3 NIAA 2002, s 92(3), as substituted as above. For certification of human rights claims made
   by persons liable to deportation, see **4.25** below.
4 NIAA 2002, s 92(4), as substituted as above.
5 NIAA 2002, s 92(5)(a), as substituted as above.
6 NIAA 2002, s 92(5)(b), as substituted as above. Compare saved NIAA 2002, s 97B (repealed by
   IA 2014, Sch 9(4), para 44 from 20 October 2014) as added by the Crime and Courts Act 2013,
   s 53(3) from 25 June 2013: Crime and Courts Act 2013 (Commencement No 1 and Transitional
   and Saving Provision) Order 2013, SI 2013/1042, following the judgments in *R (MK (Tunisia))
   v Secretary of State for the Home Department* [2011] EWCA Civ 333 and *R (E (Russia)) v
   Secretary of State for the Home Department* [2012] EWCA Civ 357 (see **3.26** above).

4.16   However, if after an appeal under s 82(1)(a) or (b) has been brought
from within the UK, the SSHD certifies the claim to which the appeal relates
under s 94(1) or (7) or 94B (see all above), the appeal must be continued from

outside the UK.[1] This is a novel provision, which *inter alia* enables the SSHD to certify a protection and or human rights claim as clearly unfounded even after an in-country appeal has been brought, on a suspensive basis, against the earlier refusal and so reverses the effect of the judgment in *AM (Somalia)*[2] (see **3.31** above). It will be interesting to see whether, in such cases, the fact that the SSHD did not see fit to so certify the claim on initial refusal, will render such certificates in such circumstances more vulnerable to challenge by way of judicial review. In order to seek to avoid the inherent illogicality of a person appealing from outside the UK on the ground that his removal from the UK *would breach* the UK's obligations under *inter alia* the Refugee Convention, it is expressly provided that where a person brings or continues an appeal under s 82(1)(a) (refusal of protection claim) from outside the UK, for the purposes of considering whether the grounds of appeal are satisfied, the appeal is to be treated as if the person were not outside the UK.[3] Finally, it is provided that where an appellant brings an appeal from within the UK but leaves the UK before the appeal is finally determined, the appeal is to be treated as abandoned unless the claim to which the appeal relates has been certified under s 94(1) or (7) or 94B.[4] On the basis of previous case law, it is likely that 'leaves the UK' will be construed so as to include any departure from UK territory or territorial waters, however brief the departure was intended to be (see **3.44** above).[5]

1   NIAA 2002, s 92(6), as substituted as above.
2   *R (AM (Somalia)) v Secretary of State for the Home Department* [2009] EWCA Civ 114.
3   NIAA 2002, s 92(7), as substituted as above. Of course, if such an appeal is then finally allowed it must mean that the UK *has breached* its fundamental international obligations under the Refugee Convention.
4   NIAA 2002, s 92(8), as substituted as above. See further **4.35** below regarding appeals pending and NIAA 2002, s 104.
5   See *R (MM (Ghana)) v Secretary of State for the Home Department* [2012] EWCA Civ 827 and *Dupovac v Secretary of State for the Home Department* [2000] Imm AR 265, CA.

CLEARLY UNFOUNDED CERTIFICATIONS: NIAA 2002, S 94

4.17   Further to **2.11** and **2.26** above and the certification regime introduced by AIA 1996 and continued by IAA 1999, it was noted that whereas the IA 1999 system maintained certification of asylum claims, and as a novelty human rights claims also, on the ground *inter alia* of their being 'manifestly unfounded', there was no longer a 'white list' of supposedly safe countries of origin under the IA 1999 certification system. The use of the 'white list' however returned with a vengeance in NIAA 2002.[1] Under the current provisions of NIAA 2002, s 94, the SSHD may certify a protection claim (see **4.4** *et seq* above) or human rights claim as clearly unfounded[2] and, as has been seen above, can now do so even some time after its refusal and after an in-country appeal has been brought.[3] Furthermore, if the SSHD is satisfied that a claimant is entitled to reside in a State listed below, he shall certify the claim as clearly unfounded unless satisfied that it is not clearly unfounded.[4] The 26 currently 'white listed' States are:[5]

- Albania, Jamaica (but see below), Macedonia and Moldova (all added to the list from the commencement of NIAA 2002, s 94 on 1 April 2003: SI 2003/970);[6]

- Bolivia, Brazil, Ecuador, South Africa and Ukraine (all added to the list from 23 July 2003, save in relation to asylum or human rights claims made before that date: SI 2003/1919);[7]

- India (added to the list from 15 February 2005, save in relation to asylum or human rights claims made before that date: SI 2005/330);

- Mongolia, Ghana (in respect of men) and Nigeria (in respect of men) (all added to the list from 2 December 2005, except in relation to asylum or human rights claims made before that date: SI 2005/3306);

- Bosnia-Herzegovina, Gambia (in respect of men), Kenya (in respect of men), Liberia (in respect of men), Malawi (in respect of men), Mali (in respect of men), Mauritius, Montenegro, Peru, Serbia and Sierra Leone (in respect of men) (all added to the list from 27 July 2007 except in relation to claims made before that date: SI 2007/2221); and

- Kosovo and South Korea (both added to the list from 3 March 2010 except in relation to claims made before that date: SI 2010/561).

1   In NIAA 2002, ss 94 and 115 as originally enacted. NIAA 2002, s 94 did not come into force until 1 April 2003 (Nationality, Immigration and Asylum Act 2002 (Commencement No 4) Order 2003, SI 2003/754, art 2(1) and Sch 1), but transitional provisions under s 115, in identical terms, came into force on the passing of the Act on 7 November 2002: s 162(2) (w) (see **4.1** above for repeal of s 115). The originally enacted versions of ss 94(4) and 115(7) listed the Accession States (Cyprus, Czech Republic, Estonia, Hungary, Latvia, Lithuania, Malta, Poland, Slovak Republic and Slovenia) which joined the European Union on 1 May 2004. These States were removed from the list on 1 October 2004 by A&I(TC)A 2004, s 27(4): Asylum and Immigration (Treatment of Claimants, etc) Act 2004 (Commencement No 1) Order 2004, SI 2004/2523. From that date, the appeal rights of asylum claimants from one of those states are governed by the EEA Regs 2006 (see **4.57** *et seq* below).
2   NIAA 2002, s 94(1), as substituted for saved s 94(1),(1A) and (2) by IA 2014, Sch 9(4), para 38(3) from 20 October 2014.
3   NIAA 2002, 92(6) (see **4.16** above).
4   NIAA 2002, s 94(3) as textually amended by IA 2014, Sch 9(4), para 38(4) from 20 October 2014.
5   NIAA 2002, s 94(4) (with multiple amendments, but none brought by IA 2014).
6   These four States were also added to the list in NIAA 2002, s 115(7) from 1 April 2003. Also then added to both lists were Bulgaria, Serbia and Montenegro and Romania. Bulgaria and Romania were removed from the list by the Asylum (Designated States) (Amendment) Order 2006, SI 2006/3215 from 1 January 2007 when they also joined the EU (see fn 1 above). As for Serbia and Montenegro, these were added to the list as separate States by the Asylum (Designated States) Order 2007, SI 2007/2221 on 27 July 2007.
7   Also then added to the list were Bangladesh and Sri Lanka. Bangladesh was removed from the list by the Asylum (Designated States) (Amendment) Order 2005, SI 2005/1016 on 22 April 2005 and Sri Lanka by the Asylum (Designated States) (Amendment) (No 2) Order 2006, SI 2006/3275 on 13 December 2006 (see **4.20** below).

4.18   The criteria according to which the SSHD may by order add a State, or part of a State, to the 'white list' are that he must be satisfied that:

(a)   there is in general in that State or part no serious risk of persecution of persons entitled to reside in that State or part, and

(b)   removal to that State or part of persons entitled to reside there will not in general contravene the UK's obligations under the ECHR.[1]

1   NIAA 2002, s 94(5).

4.19   The range of States whose nationals may have their asylum or human rights claims certified as clearly unfounded was radically increased by A&I(TC)A 2004, s 27 which provided, by way of amendments to NIAA 2002, s 94, that a State or part of a State may be added to the list in respect of persons of a particular description (eg in relation to gender: see the list of States above where some apply in respect of men only) where in relation to persons of that description there is in general no serious risk of persecution in the State or part of the State and removal would not breach the UK's obligations under the ECHR.[1] The purpose of this provision was said to be 'to provide extra flexibility to identify groups of persons within a State or part for whom conditions are generally safe'.[2] By further amendment, intended to implement the Procedures Directive,[3] the SSHD is required, when deciding whether the statements in (a) and (b) above are true of a State or part of a State, to have regard to all the circumstances of the State or part (including its laws and how they are applied), and shall have regard to information from any appropriate source (including other Member States and international organisations).[4] The SSHD's policy is to consider including a State in the 'white list' if there are significant numbers of asylum claims made by nationals of the State and returns there can be enforced.[5] If a State is added to the list in respect of a particular description of people, such as 'men', a successful challenge to the inclusion (see further below) would have to show sufficiently systematic persecution of people of that description – so that evidence of children or women being persecuted would not suffice.[6] The 'white list' provision – requiring the SSHD to certify the claim as clearly unfounded unless satisfied that it is not clearly unfounded (see above) – shall not apply in relation to a claimant who, although entitled to reside in a listed State, is facing extradition proceedings.[7]

1   NIAA 2002, s 94(5A), (5B) and (5C) as added by A&I(TC)A 2004, s 27(5) from 1 October 2004: SI 2004/2523. The 'description of person' refers to Refugee Convention attributes and include additionally to gender: language, race, religion, nationality, membership of a social or other group, political opinion, or 'any other attribute or circumstance that the Secretary of State thinks appropriate': s 94(5C).
2   A&I(TC)A 2004 Explanatory Notes at para 129. This could apply to majority groups (defined by ethnicity, religion, etc) in countries where minorities are persecuted.
3   Council Directive 2005/85/EC of 1 December 2005 on minimum standards on procedures in Member States for granting and withdrawing refugee status (see **1.8** above).

4   NIAA 2002, s 94(5D) as added by the Asylum (Procedures) Regulations 2007, SI 2007/3187, reg 3 from 1 December 2007. See also regarding the European Common List of Safe Countries of Origin in NIAA 2002, s 94A as added by SI 2007/3187 reg 4 (see **4.24** below).
5   Evidence filed for the SSHD in *R (MD (Gambia)) v Secretary of State for the Home Department* [2011] EWCA Civ 121.
6   See *MD (Gambia)* above.
7   NIAA 2002, s 94(6A) as added by A&I(TC)A 2004, s 27(7) from 1 October 2004: SI 2004/2523.

4.20   Further to **2.11** above and the judgment in *Javed*[1] that the inclusion of Pakistan in the IAA 1996 'white list' was unlawful, it is to be noted that Pakistan has never been included on the NIAA 2002 'white list', and in *Husan*[2] the inclusion of Bangladesh on the 2002 'white list' of designated States was successfully challenged. In *Brown*[3] the Court of Appeal and then the Supreme Court have held that the inclusion of Jamaica on the list of designated States is unlawful owing to the serious risk of persecution faced there by the lesbian, gay, bisexual and transgender community. The SSHD may by order amend the 'white list' so as to omit a State or part added by previous order (see **4.17** above); and the omission may be general, or effected so that the State or part remains listed in respect of a description of person.[4] Note that all of the currently listed States have been added by order (see the list in **4.17** above).[5] Bangladesh and Sri Lanka have been removed from the 'white list' by orders[6] and presumably Jamaica will now also be.

1   *R v Secretary of State for the Home Department, ex parte Javed* [2001] EWCA Civ 789. Note, however, that India, whose inclusion on the 1996 'white list' was unsuccessfully challenged in *R (Balwinder Singh) v Secretary of State for the Home Department* [2001] EWHC Admin 925, has reappeared on the NIAA 2002, s 94(4) list, as above.
2   *R (Husan) v Secretary of State for the Home Department* [2005] EWHC 189 (Admin), per Wilson J, who held that no rational decision maker could have been satisfied that the statutory presumptions of safety were met. Following the judgment, Bangladesh was removed from the list of safe countries under s 94(6): see **4.17**, fn 7 above.
3   *R (Brown) v Secretary of State for the Home Department; aka R (JB (Jamaica)) v Secretary of State for the Home Department* [2013] EWCA Civ 666; aff'd [2015] UKSC 8.
4   NIAA 2002, s 94(6) as substituted by A&I(TC)A 2004, s 27(6) from 1 October 2004.
5   Note that the ten originally listed States were removed from the list by A&I(TC)A 2004, s 27(4) on 1 October 2004: Asylum and Immigration (Treatment of Claimants, etc) Act 2004 (Commencement No 1) Order 2004, SI 2004/2523. See **4.17**, fn 1 above.
6   See **4.17**, fn 7 above.

CLEARLY UNFOUNDED CERTIFICATION: PRACTICAL APPLICATION

4.21   In practical terms, the SSHD considers that persons 'entitled to reside' in a State include, as well as citizens, those who are:

'normally resident in the state and have a legal basis to reside there. This does not cover short stay residents such as visitors and students. Dual

nationals should be considered for certification if one of their nationalities is of a designated state.'[1]

If a person claims not to be entitled to reside in a listed State,

'the caseworker must consider whether there is evidence that they are entitled to reside there. For example, do they have a passport or travel document issued by the state or evidence that they had lived there for many years? If there is such evidence, then the claim should be considered on the basis that they are entitled to reside in a designated state.'[2]

1   See Asylum Decision Making Guidance, 'Non suspensive appeals (NSA) certification under
    section 94 of the NIA Act 2002', January 2015, section 3.5.4.
2   Ibid, section 3.5.5.

4.22   The test as to whether an individual claim is clearly unfounded is an objective one. Challenge to a clearly unfounded certification is by way of judicial review.[1] As explained in *ZT (Kosovo)*,[2] the test, being an objective one, does not depend on the SSHD's 'view' but upon a criterion which a court can readily re-apply once it has the materials which the SSHD had: 'A claim is either clearly unfounded or it is not'. Even if a person is entitled to reside in a 'white list' State, his protection claim is not to be certified if the SSHD is satisfied that the claim is not 'clearly unfounded'. If a person is not entitled to reside in a 'white list' State, his protection claim may nevertheless be certified if the SSHD is satisfied that it is 'clearly unfounded'.[3] If a person makes both a protection and a human rights claim and only one of them is considered clearly unfounded by the SSHD, it would not be correct to certify the 'clearly unfounded' claim.[4] The SSHD, in current (January 2015) guidance, envisages protection claims being certifiable as clearly unfounded in the following circumstances:[5]

●   where no fear of mistreatment is expressed;

●   where it is clear from the person's circumstances and the objective evidence that 'there is no arguable basis that the feared mistreatment will arise on return';

●   on the basis of the 'objective' or background evidence it is clear that the feared mistreatment, even if it were to occur, would not amount to persecution or 'treatment contrary to Article 3' (it is not clear here why other forms of 'serious harm' as per Immigration Rules, para 339C are not referenced);

●   the background evidence shows that where non-State agents are feared, it is clear that the State is providing sufficient protection;

●   internal relocation 'is available and it is reasonable to expect the claimant to relocate' which may be the case where the fear is of non-State agents or rogue State agents or the authorities do not control the entire country. However, for a claim to be certified on an internal relocation basis, the caseworker must have explored in interview, or by taking account of all available evidence, whether there were any factors which would make relocation unreasonable. More sensibly, given the issue, previous guidance provided that certification would only be appropriate where internal relocation is 'obviously available'. The current guidance does rather seem to conflate the reason for a claim being refused on internal relocation grounds with the supposed test for it being 'clearly unfounded';

• in respect of an asylum claim, where there is no 'refugee convention reason' for the fear.

1 See **3.33** above and Chapter 8.
2 *ZT (Kosovo) v Secretary of State for the Home Department* [2009] UKHL 6, per Lord Phillips at [23], per Lord Brown at [75]–[76] and per Lord Neuberger at [83]. See also *R (Yogathas and Thangarasa) v Secretary of State for the Home Department* [2002] UKHL 36; *ZL and VL v Secretary of State for the Home Department* [2003] EWCA Civ 25; *AK (Sri Lanka) v Secretary of State for the Home Department* [2009] EWCA Civ 447 at [34]; and *R (YH) v Secretary of State for the Home Department* [2010] EWCA Civ 116.
3 NIAA 2002, s 94(1) and (3).
4 See Asylum Decision Making Guidance, 'Non suspensive appeals (NSA) certification under section 94 of the NIA Act 2002', January 2015, section 3.9. Basically there would be no point because the person could appeal in-country on the basis of the non-clearly unfounded claim as per NIAA 2002, s 92(2) or (3) (see **4.15** and **4.16** above). Note, however, that different considerations can apply in criminal deportation case where the protection claim is considered clearly unfounded and the human rights claim could be certified under NIAA 2002, s 94B (see **4.25** below).
5 See Asylum Decision Making Guidance (above), section 3.7.

4.23 Guidance is also given as to when Art 8 human rights claims can be certified as clearly unfounded and it is stated in this regard that:

'The individual merits of the claim must be carefully considered when deciding whether or not it is clearly unfounded. It is only if the Article 8 claim is so clearly without substance that it is bound to fail that it should be treated as clearly unfounded.'

The guidance goes on to provide examples of when Art 8 claims are not likely to be suitable for certification:[1]

'• there is a child of the family who is a British Citizen;

• there is a child of the family who is not a British Citizen, but who has lived in the UK for seven years or longer;

• there are genuine obstacles to the applicant continuing family life outside the UK but we consider that these obstacles are not insurmountable;

• there is evidence of circumstances that are arguably exceptional, but we do not consider that the circumstances are exceptional.'

Note how this test is phrased and how the examples give clear indication of an appreciation of the difference between refusing a claim and certifying it as clearly unfounded. Compare with the 'test' for whether a protection claim can be certified as clearly unfounded on internal relocation grounds in **4.21** and **4.22** above.

1   See Asylum Decision Making Guidance, 'Non suspensive appeals (NSA) certification under section 94 of the NIA Act 2002', January 2015, section 3.8.4.

EUROPEAN COMMON LIST OF SAFE COUNTRIES OF ORIGIN: NIAA 2002, S 94A

4.24   In compliance with the Procedures Directive,[1] the SSHD shall by order prescribe a list of states to be known as the 'European Common List of Safe Countries of Origin'.[2] Where a person makes a protection claim or a human rights claim (or both) and that person is a national of a State which is listed in this European common list, or is a stateless person who was formerly habitually resident in such a State,[3] the SSHD shall consider the claim or claims to be unfounded unless satisfied that there are serious grounds for considering that the State in question is not safe in the particular circumstances of the relevant person[4] and the SSHD shall also certify the claim or claims under NIAA 2002, s 94(1) (see **4.17** above) unless satisfied that the claim or claims is or are not clearly unfounded.[5] However, in all the years since 2007, no such order has yet been made. This is because the Procedures Directive, Art 29(1), which provided for the EU Council, acting by qualified majority on a proposal from the Commission and after consultation with the European Parliament, to adopt a minimum common list of third countries which shall be regarded by Member States as safe countries of origin (as well as the provision for amending the common list in Art 29(2)), was annulled by the European Court of Justice in May 2008 in the case of *European Parliament v Council of the European Union*[6] because it purported to provide secondary legislative powers to the Council contrary to the primary legislation contained in former TEC, Art 67.[7] Consequently there is no EU common list of safe countries of origin.

1   Council Directive 2005/85/EC of 1 December 2005 on minimum standards on procedures in Member States for granting and withdrawing refugee status. See **1.8** above.
2   NIAA 2002, s 94A(1), as added by the Asylum (Procedures) Regulations 2007, SI 2007/3187, reg 4 from 1 December 2007 (SI 2007/3187, reg 1). An order under s 94A(1) may be made only if the SSHD thinks it necessary for the purpose of complying with the UK's obligations under EU law. It may include transitional, consequential or incidental provisions, shall be made by statutory instrument, and shall be subject to annulment in pursuance of a resolution of either House of Parliament: NIAA 2002, s 94A(5).
3   NIAA 2002, s 94A(2) as added as above and as textually amended by IA 2014, Sch 9(4) para 39(a) from 20 October 2014.
4   NIAA 2002, s 94A(3) as added as above.
5   NIAA 2002, s 94A(4) as added as above and as textually amended by IA 2014, Sch 9(4) para 39(b) from 20 October 2014.
6   *European Parliament v Council of the European Union* (Case C-133/06).
7   See **1.7**, fn 1 above.

CERTIFICATION OF HUMAN RIGHTS CLAIMS MADE BY PERSONS LIABLE TO DEPORTATION: NIAA 2002, S 94B

4.25   NIAA 2002, s 94B is a novel provision introduced by IA 2014 and inserted into NIAA 2002, Pt 5 from 28 July 2014, so prior to the general 'substitution' of Pt 5 on 20 October 2014 (see **4.1** above).[1] NIAA 2002, s 94B applies where a human rights claim has been made by a person ('P') who is liable to deportation under IA 1971, s 3(5)(a) (SSHD deeming deportation conducive to public good), or s 3(6) (court recommending deportation following conviction) (see **1.11** above).[2] The SSHD may certify the claim if he considers that, despite the appeals process not having been begun or not having been exhausted, removal of P to the country or territory to which P is proposed to be removed, pending the outcome of an appeal in relation to P's claim, would not be unlawful under HRA 1998, s 6 (public authority not to act contrary to ECHR).[3] The grounds upon which the SSHD may so certify a claim include (in particular) that P would not, before the appeals process is exhausted, face a real risk of serious irreversible harm if removed to the country or territory to which P is proposed to be removed.[4] The following points are to be noted:

- Protection claims cannot be certified under s 94B, as it applies only to human rights claims.[5]

- Only deportation cases can be certified under s 94B. Note that where a person is subject to 'automatic deportation' as a 'foreign criminal' under UKBA 2007, s 32 he is liable to deportation under IA 1971, s 3(5)(a).[6]

- A claim can be certified under s 94B on refusal so as to prevent a suspensive right of appeal; or can be certified after an in-country appeal has been lodged with the effect of preventing the appeal from proceeding until the appellant has left the UK and the appeal must then be continued from outside the UK (see **4.15** and **4.16** above).

- The real risk of serious irreversible harm test is derived from the ECtHR, which uses it to determine whether it should issue r 39 injunctions preventing removal.[7] It is accordingly a test that is far more likely to prevent removal in cases where Art 3 is in issue than in those where only Art 8 rights are asserted.

1   NIAA 2002, s 94B as added by IA 2014, s 17(3) from 28 July 2014 (Immigration Act 2014 (Commencement No 1, Transitory and Saving Provisions) Order 2014, SI 2014/1820, art 3(n)) subject to transitory and savings provisions, between that date and 14 October 2014, as specified in SI 2014/1820, art 4, so as, in effect, to provide for persons appealing against an 'immigration decision' as per saved NIAA 2002, s 82(2)(j), that is a decision to deport, not to have a suspensive right of appeal (as per saved NIAA 2002, s 92(2) and or (4): see **3.7**, **3.25** and **3.31** above) if the SSHD had certified the appellant's human rights claim under NIAA 2002, s 94B.
2   NIAA 2002, s 94B(1).
3   NIAA 2002, s 94B(2).

4   NIAA 2002, s 94B(3).
5   For the meaning of protection and human rights claims, see **4.4** *et seq* above.
6   UKBA 2007, s 32(4); the SSHD must make a deportation order in respect of foreign criminal: s 32(5), subject to, *inter alia*, the asylum and human rights exceptions in s 33. See **1.11** above.
7   See ECtHR, Rules of the Court (1 July 2014), r 39 entitled 'interim measures'.

GUIDANCE ON CERTIFICATION UNDER NIAA 2002, S 94B

4.26   The SSHD has issued guidance for Home Office caseworkers on s 94B certification.[1] It makes the following points, amongst others:

- From 28 July to 17 October 2014, s 94B certification was limited to cases where the deportee was aged 18 or over at the time of the deportation decision and did not have a genuine and subsisting parental relationship with a dependent child or children. Since 18 October 2014, s 94B certification must be considered in all deportation cases where a human rights claim has been made and falls for refusal, unless one of the provisions below applies.

- Clearly unfounded human rights claims that can be certified under NIAA 2002, s 94 (see **4.17** above) should not normally be certified under s 94B because s 94 'is a stronger power which will usually take precedence', and in any case will have the same effect as s 94B certification.

- Human rights claims (the text refers to 'protection claims' but this is to confuse the statutorily defined distinction between the two types of claim: see **4.4** *et seq* above) made wholly or in part under the ECHR, Arts 2 and/or 3 cannot be certified under s 94B, because they must be certified under s 94 if they are clearly unfounded, and if they are not clearly unfounded, then it will be arguable that there is a real risk of serious irreversible harm.

- For 'practical operational reasons' only, human rights claims from foreign criminals who are to be deported while they are minors will not normally be suitable for s 94B certification and nor will human rights claims from foreign criminals who are serving a determinate-length sentence where release is at the discretion of the Parole Board.

- As noted above, it is possible to certify under s 94B at any stage in the process as long as the person has not exhausted his appeal rights. In practice, this means that if a claim is not certified at the initial decision stage, and either party challenges the decision of the FTT, or that of the UT, the 'case owner' must consider whether it is appropriate to certify the claim before it is heard by the UT or the Court of Appeal.

- An example is then given that suggests that where the FTT has dismissed an appeal on protection grounds but has allowed it on Art 8 human rights grounds, and whereas the SSHD has appealed to the UT against the Art 8 decision but the appellant has not appealed the protection decision[2] and there is not a real risk of serious irreversible harm, 'it is likely that certification [under s 94B] will be appropriate particularly, as a matter of policy, if the person is otherwise removable (eg a travel document is now available)'.

- The relevant tribunal or court must be notified in writing if it is decided to certify at any stage after the person has lodged an appeal.

1 See 'Section 94B certification guidance for non-EEA deportation cases', version 3.0, 29 January 2015.

2 See *EG and NG (UT r 17: withdrawal; r 24: scope) Ethiopia* [2013] UKUT 143 (IAC) regarding the necessity of the appellant having applied for permission to appeal to the UT against the dismissal of his appeal by the FTT on its protection grounds.

4.27 Some consideration is then given to the consequences of an out-of-country appeal, in which the appellant was removed pursuant to a s 94B certification, being finally allowed:[1]

- The 'foreign criminal' is entitled to return to the UK and the deportation order must be revoked.

- Consideration must be given to whether the Home Office should pay for the foreign criminal's journey back to the UK if this is requested by the foreign criminal. In so considering, regard is to be had to the following factors–

  - (somewhat remarkably) the quality of the Home Office's decision to refuse the human rights claim;

  - whether the appeal was allowed on the basis of evidence or information that the foreign criminal failed to submit to the SSHD in advance of his deportation, despite a s 120 warning (see **4.11** and **4.12** above), and if so, whether there is any reasonable explanation for this;

  - whether there is evidence that, if the Home Office does not pay for the return journey, the foreign criminal will be unable to return to the UK, even though the human rights decision requires him to be able to return.

- However, where a person was accepted onto the Facilitated Return Scheme (FRS) and received financial assistance to leave the UK, but then appeals the refusal of a human rights claim abroad and wishes to return to the UK, the Home Office should not usually pay for his journey back to the UK.

1 'Section 94B certification guidance for non-EEA deportation cases', version 3.0, 29 January 2015, section 4.

'REAL RISK OF SERIOUS IRREVERSIBLE HARM' TEST

4.28   The SSHD's guidance[1] explains that the term 'real risk' is 'a relatively low threshold' and has the same meaning as when used to ascertain whether a person's removal would breach ECHR, Art 3.[2] (Indeed, the test is the same in effect for determining whether an asylum claimant's removal would breach the UK's obligations under the Refugee Convention.[3]) However, the terms 'serious' and 'irreversible' must be given their ordinary meanings. The guidance continues:

- 'Serious' indicates that the harm must meet a minimum level of severity, and 'irreversible' means that the harm would have a permanent or very long-lasting effect.

- If the human rights claim is based on Art 8, case owners must consider not only the impact on the foreign criminal's rights, but also those of any partner or child. The test relates only to the period of time between deportation and the conclusion of any appeal, and will not be met solely because the person will be separated from family members in the UK during that period.

- It will not normally be enough for a person to provide evidence that there is a real risk of harm which would be *either* serious *or* irreversible. In order for certification not to be possible, there must be a real risk of harm that would be *both* serious *and* irreversible.

- Examples are then given of scenarios in which a person could be deported before his appeal is determined and where it is considered to be unlikely, in the absence of additional factors, that there would be a 'real risk of serious irreversible harm' while an out-of-country appeal is pursued–[4]

  - a person will be separated from his child and/or partner for several months while he appeals against a human rights decision;

  - a family court case is in progress and there is no evidence that the case could not be pursued from abroad;

  - a child or partner is undergoing treatment for a temporary or chronic medical condition that is under control and can be satisfactorily managed through medication or other treatment and does not require the person liable to deportation to act as a full-time carer;

  - a person has a medical condition but removal would not breach Art 3;

  - a person has strong private life ties to a community that will be disrupted by deportation, eg he has a job, a mortgage, a prominent role in a community organisation, etc.

- The guidance then goes on to give examples of where the 'high threshold' for the test could be met[5] whilst asserting that 'such cases are likely to be rare, but case owners must consider every case on its individual merits to assess the likely effect of a non-suspensive right of appeal' –

  - the person has a genuine and subsisting parental relationship with a child who is seriously ill, requires full-time care, and there is no one else who can provide that care;

  - the person has a genuine and subsisting long-term relationship with a partner who is seriously ill and requires full-time care because he is unable to care for himself, and there is no one else, including medical professionals, who can provide that care.

1   See 'Section 94B certification guidance for non-EEA deportation cases', version 3.0, 29 January 2015.
2   For the 'real risk' test in this context, see *Soering v United Kingdom* (1989) 11 EHRR 439 at [86]. See also *Cruz Varas v Sweden* (1992) 14 EHRR 1; *Vilvarajah v United Kingdom* (1991) 14 EHRR 248; *Chahal v United Kingdom* (1997) 23 EHRR 413; *D v United Kingdom* (1997) 24 EHRR 423; *Saadi v Italy* (2009) 49 EHRR 30; and *R (Ullah) v Special Adjudicator; Do v Immigration Appeal Tribunal* [2004] UKHL 26.
3   See *Kacaj* [2001] INLR 354 (starred) at para [12], where the tribunal held that it would now be better in both refugee asylum and human rights cases, for the phrase, 'real risk', to be adopted in preference to those of a 'serious possibility' or a 'reasonable degree of likelihood' – all of which in any case seek to convey the same meaning. See also *PS (Sri Lanka) v Secretary of State for the Home Department* [2008] EWCA Civ 1213, per Sedley LJ at [11].
4   'Section 94B certification guidance for non-EEA deportation cases' (above), at section 3.6.
5   Note how the 'low threshold' of a 'real risk' has become a 'high threshold' for meeting the test, from the appellant's point of view, of there being a real risk of serious irreversible harm (albeit in an Art 8 context). See 'Section 94B certification guidance for non-EEA deportation cases' (above), at section 3.7.

4.29   The guidance acknowledges that the onus is on the SSHD to demonstrate that there is not a real risk of serious irreversible harm.

'However, if a person claims that a non-suspensive appeal would risk serious irreversible harm, the onus is on that person to substantiate the claim with documentary evidence, preferably from official sources, for example a signed letter on letter-headed paper from the GP responsible for treatment, a family court order, a marriage or civil partnership certificate, documentary evidence from official sources demonstrating long-term co-habitation, etc. Case owners should expect to see original documents rather than copies.'[1]

1   'Section 94B certification guidance for non-EEA deportation cases', version 3.0, 29 January 2015, section 3.8.

4.30   Any suspensive challenge to a s 94B certification must be by way of judicial review. It remains to be seen how the jurisprudence will develop on such challenges, but it is suggested that, as with 'clearly unfounded' certifications, the test must be an objective one, not dependent on the SSHD's 'view', but upon a criterion which a court can readily re-apply once it has the materials which the SSHD had (see **4.21** and **4.22** above).

DENIAL OF RIGHT OF APPEAL WHERE THERE WAS AN EARLIER RIGHT OF APPEAL: NIAA 2002, S 96

4.31   For the effect of, and the jurisprudence on, saved NIAA 2002, s 96, see **3.34–3.39** above. Following amendment by IA 2014 (see **4.1** above):

● NIAA 2002, s 96(1) now provides that a person may not bring an appeal under s 82 against a decision ('the new decision') if the SSHD or an immigration officer certifies–

   (a)   that the person was notified of a right of appeal under that section against another decision ('the old decision') (whether or not an appeal was brought and whether or not any appeal brought has been determined);

   (b)   that the claim or application to which the new decision relates relies on a ground (sic) that could have been raised in an appeal against the old decision; and

   (c)   that, in the opinion of the SSHD or the immigration officer, there is no satisfactory reason for that ground not having been raised in an appeal against the old decision.[1]

● NIAA 2002, s 96(2) now provides that a person may not bring an appeal under s 82 if the SSHD or an immigration officer certifies–

   (a)   that the person has received a notice under s 120(2) (see **4.11** and **4.12** above);

   (b)   that the appeal relies on a ground (sic) that should have been, but has not been, raised in a statement made under s 120(2) or (5); and

   (c)   that, in the opinion of the SSHD or the immigration officer, there is no satisfactory reason for that ground not having been raised in a statement under s 120(2) or (5).[2]

1   NIAA 2002, s 96(1) as most recently amended by IA 2014, Sch 9(4), para 41(2). Compare with the saved version in **3.34** above. Note that where the amended, or new, NIAA 2002, s 96(1) applies and an appeal has been previously brought under saved NIAA 2002, s 82(1) against an 'immigration decision', the reference to a 'decision' in new s 96(1)(a) (see text above) is to be read as a reference to an 'immigration decision' within the meaning of saved NIAA 2002, s 82(2) (see **3.7** above): Immigration Act 2014 (Commencement No 3, Transitional and Saving Provisions) Order 2014, SI 2014/2771, art 11(4) and (5)(b).
2   NIAA 2002, s 96(2) as substituted by IA 2014, Sch 9(4), para 41(3). Compare with the saved version in **3.35** above.

4.32   The remainder of sub-ss (4)–(7) remain the same.[1] In particular, as per s 96(7), a certificate under sub-ss (1) or (2) shall have no effect in relation to an appeal instituted before the certificate is issued.[2] Apart from, of obvious necessity, removing references to appeals being against 'immigration decisions' (as to which see **3.7** above and see **4.31**, fn 1 above), the most interesting and significant change is from the new claim relying on a 'matter' that could and should have been raised before, to its now relying on a 'ground' that could and should have been raised before. See especially in this respect **3.37** and **3.38** above and the judgment in *Khan*.[3] In practical terms the position is likely to be as follows. If a person makes a protection claim to the SSHD and that claim is refused and if the person does not then also raise, on an appeal against the refusal of the protection claim (see **4.7** and **4.8** above) or in a statement of additional grounds (see **4.11–4.13** above), a human rights claim, then the person may be prohibited, by way of a certificate under s 96(1) or (2), from appealing later on against the refusal of a later human rights claim, unless he can show a satisfactory reason for not having raised the human rights claim in the earlier appeal or in a statement of additional grounds.[4] If, on the other hand, the person seeks to rely upon new evidence in support of making a 'fresh' protection claim, that will be a matter for consideration of the 'fresh claim' provisions of the Immigration Rules, para 353.[5] Clearly, if it is accepted by the SSHD that a fresh protection claim has been made, as based on the new evidence, then a right of appeal will arise under s 82(1)(a) against its refusal (see **4.4** *et seq* above).

1   NIAA 2002, s 96(4): in sub-s (1) 'notified' means notified in accordance with regulations under s 105, ie the Immigration (Notices) Regulations 2003, SI 2003/658 (see **3.37** and **3.38** above and **4.34** below). NIAA 2002, s 96(5): sub-ss (1) and (2) apply to prevent a person's right of appeal whether or not he has been outside the UK since an earlier right of appeal arose or since a requirement under s 120 was imposed (see **3.36**, fn 1 above). NIAA 2002, s 96(6): in s 96 a reference to an appeal under s 82(1) also includes a reference to an appeal under SIACA 1997, s 2 (see **3.34**, fn 1 above).
2   NIAA 2002, s 96(7) as added by A&I(TC)A 2004, s 30(4) from 1 October 2004 (see **3.39**, fn 8 above).
3   *R (Khan) v Secretary of State for the Home Department* [2014] EWCA Civ 88.
4   See Stadlen J's analysis in *R (J) v Secretary of State for the Home Department* [2009] EWHC 705 (Admin) at [106] as cited in **3.37** above and note his fourth point regarding the SSHD's exercise of discretion in deciding to certify.
5   See **3.31** above.

NATIONAL SECURITY CERTIFICATIONS: NIAA 2002, SS 97 AND 97A

4.33   See **3.42** above. The only amendment to NIAA 2002, s 97 (national security, etc) brought by IA 2014 is to remove references to appeals to the FTT under NIAA 2002, ss 83(2) and 83A(2) (see **3.40** and **3.41** above). Accordingly, an appeal to the FTT under s 82(1) against a decision in respect of a person may not be brought or continued if the SSHD certifies that the decision is or was taken by the SSHD acting in person, or in accordance with a direction of the SSHD which identifies the person to whom the decision relates, wholly or partly on the grounds that the person's exclusion or removal from the UK is in the interests of national security or in the interests of the relationship between the UK and another country.[1] Furthermore, an appeal to the FTT under s 82(1) against a decision may not be brought or continued if the SSHD certifies that the decision is or was taken wholly or partly in reliance on information which in his opinion should not be made public in the interests of national security, in the interests of the relationship between the UK and another country or otherwise in the public interest.[2] In all cases, the reference to the SSHD certifying is to the SSHD acting in person.[3] An appeal will lie instead to the SIAC (as to which, see Chapter 7). Furthermore, the SSHD may certify that a decision to make a deportation order in respect of a person was taken on the grounds that his removal from the UK would be in the interests of national security,[4] or, in the case of a person subject to 'automatic deportation' under UKBA 2007, s 32(5), that the person's removal from the UK would be in the interests of national security,[5] and the consequence of such certifications is that no appeal lies to the FTT because the SSHD shall be taken to have certified the decision to make the deportation order under s 97.[6] The effect of a s 97 certificate is to prevent an appeal being 'brought or continued'[7] and NIAA 2002, s 99 provides that where a certificate is issued under NIAA 2002, s 97 in respect of a pending appeal,[8] that appeal shall lapse.[9] In these cases the person may appeal instead to the SIAC, and see Chapter 7.

1   NIAA 2002, s 97(1) (as amended by IA 2014, Sch 9(4), para 42(a)) and (2).
2   NIAA 2002, s 97(3) (as amended by IA 2014, Sch 9(4), para 42(b)).
3   NIAA 2002, s 97(4).
4   NIAA 2002, s 97A(1). NIAA 2002, s 97A inserted by IANA 2006, s 7(1), from 31 August 2006: Immigration, Asylum and Nationality Act 2006 (Commencement No 2) Order 2006, SI 2006/2226, and most recently amended by IA 2014, Sch 9, Pt 4, para 43 from 20 October 2014. See further **7.7** and **7.8** below.
5   NIAA 2002, s 97A(1A) inserted by the Crime and Courts Act 2013, s 54(2) and the Crime and Courts Act 2013 (Commencement No 1 and Transitional and Saving Provision) Order 2013, SI 2013/1042 from 25 June 2013.
6   NIAA 2002, s 97A(2)(b).
7   NIAA 2002, s 97(1) and (3) and see fnn 1 and 2 above.
8   NIAA 2002, s 99(1) as amended by IA 2014, Sch 9(4), para 46 from 20 October 2014. Note that an appeal under s 82(1) now only lapses, as per s 99, when a certificate under s 97 is issued. Compare saved NIAA 2002, s 99 (see **3.43**, fn 1 above).
9   NIAA 2002, s 99(2).

NOTICE OF AN APPEALABLE DECISION: NIAA 2002, S 105

4.34   Under NIAA 2002, s 105, the SSHD may make regulations requiring a person to be given written notice where an appealable decision is taken in respect of him.[1] An 'appealable decision' means a decision mentioned in s 82(1) (see **4.4** *et seq* above).[2] The regulations may, in particular, provide that notice of such a decision must state that there is a right of appeal under s 82 and how and when that right may be exercised[3] and the regulations may make provision (which may include presumptions) about service.[4] The SSHD has made the Immigration (Notices) Regulations 2003,[5] which provide that the decision maker must give written notice to a person of any decision taken in respect of him which is appealable under NIAA 2002, s 82(1) or any EEA decision taken in respect of him which is appealable.[6] The Notice Regulations also provide for the contents of such notices, to include *inter alia* information as to rights of appeal,[7] for how such notices may be served[8] and for certain notices under IA 1971 to be deemed to comply with the Regulations.[9] Note that under previous jurisprudence, failure by the SSHD to properly notify a person of an appealable decision, in particular failure to inform the person of rights of appeal and time limits for appealing, meant that the decision could be either treated as invalid[10] or the time limit for lodging an appeal could not start to run.[11] See further Chapter 5 concerning practice and procedure on appeals to the FTT; and see Chapter 6 concerning the FTT's and UT's jurisdiction to determine questions relating to their jurisdiction to consider *inter alia* the validity of an appeal.

1   NIAA 2002, s 105(1) as amended by IA 2014, Sch 9(4), para 48(2) from 20 October 2014.
2   NIAA 2002, s 105(4) as added by IA 2014, Sch 9(4), para 48(4) from 20 October 2014.
3   NIAA 2002, s 105(2) as amended by IA 2014, Sch 9(4), para 48(3) from 20 October 2014.
4   NIAA 2002, s 105(3).
5   SI 2003/658 ('the Notice Regulations') in force from 1 April 2003 and as most recently amended by the Immigration (Notices) (Amendment) Regulations 2014, SI 2014/2768.
6   SI 2003/658, reg 4(1) (as amended). For rights of appeal against EEA decisions, see **4.58** *et seq* below.
7   SI 2003/658, reg 5 (as amended).
8   SI 2003/658, reg 7 (as amended).
9   SI 2003/658, reg 6.
10   See eg *Akhuemonkhan* [1998] INLR 265, IAT; see also *Omar* [2002] UKIAT 04634; *ZA (Ethiopia)* [2004] UKIAT 00241; and *NM (no retrospective cancellation of leave) Zimbabwe* [2007] UKAIT 00002.
11   See eg *OI (notice of decision: time calculations) Nigeria* [2006] UKAIT 00042.

APPEAL PENDING: NIAA 2002, S 104

4.35   See **3.43** above. NIAA 2002, s 104 is amended and simplified by IA 2014.[1] It remains the case that an appeal under NIAA 2002, s 82(1) is pending during the period beginning when it is instituted and ending when it is finally determined, withdrawn or abandoned or when it lapses under s 99.[2] An appeal under NIAA 2002, s 82(1) is not finally determined while:

(a)   an application for permission to appeal under TCEA 2007, s 11 or 13 could be made or is awaiting determination;

(b)   permission to appeal under either of those sections has been granted and the appeal is awaiting determination; or

(c)   an appeal has been remitted under TCEA 2007, s 12 or 14 and is awaiting determination.[3]

1   Sub-ss (4), (4C) and (5) are repealed by IA 2014, Sch 9(4), para 47.
2   NIAA 2002, s 104(1). Under saved NIAA 2002, s 99 an appeal under NIAA 2002, s 82(1) will lapse when a certificate is issued under s 97 (see **4.33** above).
3   NIAA 2002, s 104(2) (see for further details **3.43** above).

4.36   An appeal under s 82(1) brought by a person while he is in the UK (see **4.15** and **4.16** above) shall be treated as abandoned if the appellant is granted leave to enter or remain in the UK[1] unless it has been brought on a ground specified in s 84(1)(a) or (b) or 84(3) (asylum or humanitarian protection grounds: see **4.7** and **4.8** above) and the appellant gives notice, in accordance with the Tribunal Procedure Rules, that he wishes to pursue the appeal in so far as it is brought on that ground.[2] The Tribunal Procedure Rules are:

- in respect of an appeal pending before the FTT when the appellant is granted the requisite period of leave to enter or remain – Tribunal Procedure (First-tier Tribunal) (Immigration and Asylum Chamber) Rules 2014,[3] r 16(2) and (3); and

- in respect of an appeal pending before the UT when the appellant is granted the requisite period of leave to enter or remain – Tribunal Procedure (Upper Tribunal) Rules 2008,[4] r 17A(3)–(5).[5]

1   NIAA 2002, s 104(4A) as substituted by IANA 2006, s 9, from 13 November 2006: Immigration, Asylum and Nationality Act 2006 (Commencement No 3) Order 2006, SI 2006/2838; and as amended by IA 2014, Sch 9(4), para 47.
2   NIAA 2002, s 104(4B) as substituted as above and as amended by IA 2014, Sch 9(4), para 47 so as *inter alia* to omit sub-s (4B)(a). See **3.45** above for saved s 104(4B).
3   SI 2014/2604. See further Chapter 5.
4   SI 2008/2698. See further Chapter 6.
5   As inserted from 15 February 2010 by the Tribunal Procedure (Amendment No 2) Rules 2010, SI 2010/44, rr 1, 2 and 12.

4.37   In practice this means that whilst an in-country appeal on human rights grounds (only) is always to be treated as abandoned if the appellant is granted leave to enter or remain, an in-country appeal on protection grounds can be 'kept alive' in such circumstance by the appellant giving the requisite notice, as above. See further **4.15** and **4.16** above, *inter alia* regarding an in-country appeal being treated as abandoned if the appellant leaves the UK.[1]

1   NIAA 2002, s 92(8).

STATUTORY DUTIES OF THE FTT ON APPEALS UNDER NIAA 2002, S 82(1)

4.38   The fundamental statutory duty of the FTT, in an appeal under NIAA 2002, s 82(1)[1] is to determine any matter raised as a ground of appeal and any matter which NIAA 2002, s 85 requires it to consider (see **4.10–4.13** above)[2] and accordingly to allow or dismiss the appeal. However, where in an asylum appeal,[3] the SSHD has issued a certificate under NIAA 2002, s 72, in relation to a 'serious criminal',[4] and/or under IANA 2006, s 55, stating that the appellant is not entitled to the protection of the Refugee Convention, Art 33(1) because Art 1F applies to him (whether or not he would otherwise be entitled to protection) or that Art 33(2) applies to him on grounds of national security (whether or not he would otherwise be entitled to protection),[5] the FTT must, in the former case, begin its substantive deliberation on the appeal by considering the certificate[6] and if in agreement that the presumptions, as to serious criminality and danger to the community, apply,[7] having given the appellant an opportunity for rebuttal, must dismiss the appeal in so far as it relies on refugee asylum grounds;[8] and, in the latter case, begin its substantive deliberations on the asylum appeal by considering the statements in the SSHD's certificate[9] and, if it agrees with those statements, it must dismiss the appeal on its asylum grounds before going on to consider any other aspect of the case.[10] In an appeal where the FTT is required to determine whether a decision breaches a person's right to respect for private or family life under ECHR, Art 8,[11] the FTT must have regard, in all cases, to the statutorily listed considerations in NIAA 2002, s 117B[12] and, in cases concerning the deportation of 'foreign criminals', also to the statutorily listed considerations in NIAA 2002, s 117C,[13] when considering the 'public interest question' relevant to the proportionality balancing exercise.[14] Note that NIAA 2002, s 87, under which the FTT could, on allowing an appeal under s 82, 83 or 83A, give a direction for the purpose of giving effect to its decision, was repealed by IA 2014.[15]

1   NIAA 2002, s 86(1) as amended by IA 2014, Sch 9(4), para 36(a) so as to omit references to NIAA 2002, ss 83 and 83A (see **3.40** above).
2   NIAA 2002, s 86(2), as most recently amended by IA 2014, Sch 9(4), para 36(b).
3   Meaning where a person appeals under NIAA 2002, s 82 wholly or partly on the ground mentioned in s 84(1)(a) or (3)(a) (breach of the UK's obligations under the Refugee Convention: see **4.7** and **4.8** above): see NIAA 2002, s 72(9)(a) and IANA 2006, s 55(2)(a).
4   NIAA 2002, s 72(9)(b). See further in *Asylum Law and Practice* (2nd edition, Bloomsbury Professional), para 12.52.
5   IANA 2006, s 55(1). See further in *Asylum Law and Practice* (above), para 12.53.
6   NIAA 2002, s 72(10)(a).
7   NIAA 2002, s 72(2)–(6) and see *EN (Serbia) v Secretary of State for the Home Department* [2009] EWCA Civ 630; and see fn 4 above.
8   NIAA 2002, s 72(10)(b).
9   IANA 2006, s 55(3).
10   IANA 2006, s 55(4).
11   NIAA 2002, s 117A(1). See **4.2** above regarding the insertion of Pt 5A, ss 117A–117D into NIAA 2002 by IA 2014, s 19 from 28 July 2014. See also *YM (Uganda) v Secretary of State for the Home Department* [2014] EWCA Civ 1292; *Dube (ss 117A–117D)* [2015] UKUT 90 (IAC); and *Chege (s 117D Art 8 approach)* [2015] UKUT 165 (IAC).
12   NIAA 2002, s 117A(2)(a).
13   NIAA 2002, s 117A(2)(b). A 'foreign criminal' for these purposes is defined in NIAA 2002, s 117D(2) as a person who is not a British citizen, who has been convicted in the UK of an offence, and who has been sentenced to a period of imprisonment of at least 12 months; has been convicted of an offence that has caused serious harm; or is a persistent offender.
14   NIAA 2002, s 117A(3). See per Lord Bingham in *R (Razgar) v Secretary of State for the Home Department* [2004] UKHL 27 at [17]–[20] concerning the series of questions to be considered in an Art 8 case, culminating, if reached, in the proportionality question.
15   NIAA 2002, s 87, repealed by IA 2014, Sch 9(4), para 37.

PART 2 – RIGHTS OF APPEAL TO THE FTT IN 'SAFE THIRD COUNTRY CASES'

4.39   Where a person makes a claim for protection in the UK, if the SSHD considers that the person can be sent to a 'safe third country' this can either provide a basis for refusing the claim, on the ground that the person's removal from the UK, to the safe third country, would not put the person at any real risk of being persecuted or seriously harmed,[1] or can provide a basis for the SSHD refusing to entertain and consider the claim substantively at all, on the ground that the claim can and will be properly considered in the safe third country.[2]

1   See Immigration Rules, HC 395, paras 334(v) and 336 regarding refusal of a claim for asylum on the ground that such a refusal would not result in the applicant being required to go (whether immediately or after the time limited by any existing leave to enter or remain) in breach of the Refugee Convention, to a country in which his life or freedom would be threatened on account of his race, religion, nationality, political opinion or membership of a particular social group. See paras 339C(iii) and 339F regarding refusal of a claim for humanitarian protection on the grounds that the person will not face a real risk of suffering serious harm in the country of return.
2   See Immigration Rules, HC 395, para 345 and A&I(TC)A 2004, Sch 3 (see **4.46** below).

SAFE THIRD COUNTRY CERTIFICATIONS ON REFUSAL OF A CLAIM: NIAA 2002, S 94(7) AND (8)

4.40   Under NIAA 2002, s 94(7), the SSHD may, on its refusal, certify a protection claim or human rights claim made by a person if:

(a)   it is proposed to remove the person to a country of which he is not a national or citizen; and

(b)   there is no reason to believe that the person's rights under the ECHR will be breached in that country.[1]

1   NIAA 2002, s 94(7) as amended by IA 2014, Sch 9(4), para 38(6) from 20 October 2014.

4.41   Under NIAA 2002, s 92 (see **4.15** and **4.16** above), where the SSHD has issued such a certificate on refusal of the claim, the person may only appeal against the refusal of the claim from abroad,[1] or, where the SSHD issues such a certificate after an appeal has been brought against the refusal of the claim, the appeal must be continued from abroad.[2] NIAA 2002, s 94(8) provides, in the form a 'deeming provision', that, in determining (on an appeal brought or continued from abroad,[3] or on a judicial review challenge to the certificate) whether a person in relation to whom a certificate has been issued under sub-s (7) may be removed from the UK, the country specified in the certificate is to be regarded as:

(a)   a place where a person's life and liberty is not threatened by reason of his race, religion, nationality, membership of a particular social group, or political opinion; and

(b)   a place from which a person will not be sent to another country otherwise than in accordance with the Refugee Convention or with the UK's obligations in relation to persons eligible for a grant of humanitarian protection.[4]

1   NIAA 2002, s 92(2)(a) and (3)(a) (see **4.15** and **4.16** above).
2   NIAA 2002, s 92(6) (see **4.15** and **4.16** above).
3   Note that under NIAA 2002, s 92(7), where a person brings or continues an appeal under s 82(1)(a) (refusal of protection claim) from outside the UK, for the purposes of considering whether the grounds of appeal are satisfied, the appeal is to be treated as if the person were not outside the UK (see **4.15** and **4.16** above).
4   NIAA 2002, s 94(8) as amended by IA 2014, Sch 9(4), para 38(6) from 20 October 2014.

4.42   See further below regarding the similar deeming provisions in relation to removals to safe third countries under the Dublin Regulations (see **4.47** below). In practice, up until now at least, it seems that certifications under NIAA 2002, s 94(7), following substantive consideration, have been few and far between.

RIGHTS OF APPEAL IN CASES OF REMOVAL TO A SAFE THIRD COUNTRY FOR THAT COUNTRY TO CONSIDER THE PROTECTION CLAIM

4.43   See **2.8–2.10** and **2.20** above for the rights of appeal, and the limitations thereon, under AIAA 1993, AIA 1996 and IAA 1999 in cases where the SSHD has declined to consider an asylum claim made by a person in the UK on the basis that there is a safe third country to which the claimant can be removed for his claim to be considered and determined there. Further to **2.20** above, IAA 1999, ss 71 and 72 were repealed from 1 April 2003.[1] Instead, from 1 April 2003 until 30 September 2004, NIAA 2002, s 93(1) provided that a person may not appeal under NIAA 2002, s 82(1) while he is in the UK if a certificate has been issued in relation to him under IAA 1999, s 11(2) or 12(2) (removal of asylum claimants to 'third country').[2] However, per s 93(2) this provision did not apply to prevent a suspensive right of appeal in such circumstance if:

(a)   the appellant had made a human rights claim, and

(b)   the SSHD had not certified that in his opinion the human rights claim is clearly unfounded.[3]

1   IAA 1999, ss 71 and 72 repealed by NIAA 2002, Sch 9 (repeals) on 1 April 2003: Nationality, Immigration and Asylum Act 2002 (Commencement No 4) Order 2003, SI 2003/754.
2   NIAA 2002, s 93(1), in force between 1 April 2003 and 30 September 2004 (see below re repeal).
3   NIAA 2002, s 93(2), in force as per fn 2 above.

4.44   To briefly summarise:

- IAA 1999, s 11[1] provided for 'third country' removal, without substantive consideration of an asylum claim, to a Member State of the EU under 'standing arrangements' and the SSHD could certify, under s 11(2), that the Member State has accepted that, under standing arrangements, it is the responsible State in relation to the claimant's claim for asylum, and in his opinion, the claimant is not a national or citizen of the Member State to which he is to be sent.[2]

- From 8 December 2002, a Member State was statutorily declared to be–[3]

  (a)   a place where a person's life and liberty is not threatened by reason of his race, religion, nationality, membership of a particular social group, or political opinion; and

  (b)   a place from which a person will not be sent to another country otherwise than in accordance with the Refugee Convention.

- 'Standing arrangements' meant arrangements in force as between Member States for determining which state is responsible for considering applications for asylum.[4] In practice these standing arrangements were the Dublin Convention as replaced by the Dublin II Regulation from 1 September 2003, or bilateral arrangements.[5]

- IAA 1999, s 12 provided for 'third country' removal, without substantive consideration of an asylum claim, in other circumstances. In particular, where removal was to either a Member State other than under 'standing arrangements' or to a non-Member State designated by order,[6] the SSHD could certify under s 12(2) that relevant conditions were met (see below).[7]

- The designated States were Canada, Norway, Switzerland and the United States of America.[8]

- Where removal was to a non-Member and non-designated State,[9] the SSHD could certify under s 12(5) that those same relevant conditions were met.[10]

- The conditions were that–[11]

  (a)   the claimant is not a national or citizen of the country to which he is to be sent;

  (b)   his life and liberty would not be threatened there by reason of his race, religion, nationality, membership of a particular social group, or political opinion; and

  (c)   the government of that country would not send him to another country otherwise than in accordance with the Refugee Convention.

---

1   IAA 1999, s 11 was substituted by NIAA 2002, s 80 with effect as regards substituted sub-ss (1), (3) and (5) from 8 December 2002: Nationality, Immigration and Asylum Act 2002

(Commencement No 1) Order 2002, SI 2002/2811; and with effect as regards substituted sub-ss (2) and (4) from 1 April 2003: SI 2003/754. See below regarding repeal of IAA 1999, s 11.

2   IAA 1999, s 11(2) as substituted (see fn 1 above). See further in *Asylum Law and Practice* (2nd edition, Bloomsbury Professional), paras 14.5–14.12.

3   IAA 1999, s 11(1) as substituted with effect from 8 December 2002 (see fn 1 above). For the history behind this 'deeming of safety' provision and the reason for its insertion, see *R v Secretary of State for the Home Department, ex parte Lul Adan, Subaskaran and Aitseguer* [1999] 3 WLR 1274, CA; subsequently (after IAA 1999, s 11 came into force on 2 October 2000) upheld by the House of Lords in *R v Secretary of State for the Home Department, ex parte Lul Adan and Aitsegeur* [2001] 2 AC 477. For the effect of this deeming provision, see per Simon Brown LJ in *R (Ibrahim) v Secretary of State for the Home Department* [2001] EWCA Civ 519 at [16]. See further in *Asylum Law and Practice* (above), paras 14.8–14.12.

4   IAA 1999, s 11(5) as substituted (see fn 1 above).

5   As to the Dublin Convention and the Dublin II Regulation (as now replaced in turn by the Dublin III Regulation) see **1.8** above and see *Asylum Law and Practice* (above), paras 10.9–10.12 and 10.15–10.18.

6   IAA 1999, s 12(1). See below regarding repeal of IAA 1999, s 12.

7   IAA 1999, s 12(2).

8   Asylum (Designated Safe Third Countries) Order 2000, SI 2000/2245, as made under IAA 1999, s 12(1)(b). SI 2000/2245 lapsed on the repeal of IAA 1999, s 12(1)(b) by A&I(TC)A 2004, Sch 4, para 1 on 1 October 2004 (see below).

9   IAA 1999, s 12(4).

10   IAA 1999, s 12(5).

11   IAA 1999, s 12(7).

4.45   It will be noted that NIAA 2002, s 93 only operated so as to prevent a suspensive right of appeal, where any human rights claim made by the person had been certified as clearly unfounded under s 93(2)(b) (above), in cases where the certificate was made under IAA 1999, ss 11(2) and 12(2). NIAA 2002, s 93 had no effect on cases where the certificate was made under IAA 1999, s 12(5). Accordingly a suspensive right of appeal, on human rights grounds, under (saved) NIAA 2002, ss 82(1) lay against any immigration decision (see **3.7** above) to remove the person to the third country (and see saved NIAA 2002, ss 84(1)(g) and 92(4)(a)) unless the SSHD also issued a certificate under NIAA 2002, s 94(7) (as to which, see **4.40** above).

ASYLUM AND IMMIGRATION (TREATMENT OF CLAIMANTS, ETC) ACT 2004, SCH 3

4.46   IAA 1999, ss 11 and 12 and NIAA 2002, s 93 were repealed, with effect from 1 October 2004,[1] and are replaced by new provisions contained in A&I(TC)A 2004, Sch 3, which is entitled 'Removal of asylum seeker to safe country'. Schedule 3 is divided into six parts. Part 1 is introductory and gives definitions and states that 'a reference to anything being done in accordance with the Refugee Convention is a reference to the thing being done in accordance with the principles of the Convention, whether or not by a signatory to it.'[2] A detailed analysis of the principles and jurisprudence relating to third country removals in asylum cases, whether or not under the provisions

146

of the Dublin III Regulation (see **1.8** above), is beyond the remit of this book.[3] For present purposes it is important to note that A&I(TC)A 2004, Sch 3 cross-refers to NIAA 2002, s 92 in respect to the place (meaning the UK or abroad) from which an appeal relating to an asylum or human rights claim may be brought or continued (see **4.15** and **4.16** above).[4] A&I(TC)A 2004, Sch 3, Pt 6, provides for amendments of the lists of countries in Pts 2, 3 and 4 (see below).[5]

1   IAA 1999, ss 11 and 12 repealed by A&I(TC)A 2004, s 33(2) and Sch 4 (repeals) from 1 October 2004: Asylum and Immigration (Treatment of Claimants, etc) Act 2004 (Commencement No 1) Order 2004, SI 2004/2523. NIAA 2002, ss 80 (see **4.44**, fn 1 above) and 93 also repealed by A&I(TC)A 2004, s 33(3) and Sch 4 (repeals) from 1 October 2004: SI 2004/2523. Note however that these provisions continued to have effect in relation to those already subject to certificates under IAA 1999, s 11(2) or 12(2) or (5) issued before 1 October 2004: SI 2004/2523, art 3.
2   A&I(TC)A 2004, Sch 3, para 1(2).
3   See instead *Asylum Law and Practice* (2nd edition, Bloomsbury Professional), Ch 14.
4   A&I(TC)A 2004, Sch 3, para 1(3), as added by IA 2014, Sch 9(4), para 56(2) from 20 October 2014.
5   A&I(TC)A 2004 Act, Sch 3, paras 20 and 21 – the provision and indeed the lack of provision to amend the lists in the relevant parts is dealt with below as regards each part and list.

FIRST LIST OF SAFE COUNTRIES (REFUGEE CONVENTION AND HUMAN RIGHTS (1))

4.47   A&I(TC)A 2004, Sch 3, Part 2 is titled as per the heading above and states that this part applies to a list of 29 States comprising 26 other EU Member States (UK excepted and Croatia not yet added) together with Iceland and Norway and Switzerland.[1] The point being that all of these other 29 States, along with the UK, are subject to, or have agreed to be bound by, the Dublin Regulations.[2] Additional countries joining the Dublin arrangements may be added by order.[3] Unlike the position with the Second and Third Lists in Sch 3 (see **4.51–4.54** below), there is no power to remove a State by order from the First List and nor is there any legal requirement on the SSHD to promote primary legislation to remove a State from the First List.[4] For the purposes of the determination, by any person, tribunal or court whether a person who has made an asylum claim or a human rights claim may be removed from the UK to a State of which he is not a national or citizen,[5] a First List State is to be treated as a place:[6]

(a)   where a person's life and liberty are not threatened by reason of his race, religion, nationality, membership of a particular social group or political opinion;

(b)   from which a person will not be sent to another State in contravention of his ECHR rights; and

(c)   from which a person will not be sent to another State otherwise than in accordance with the Refugee Convention.

4.48   *Current rights of appeal to the First-tier Tribunal*

1   A&I(TC)A 2004, Sch 3, para 2.
2   Regulation (EU) No 604/2013 of 26 June 2013 establishing the criteria and mechanisms for determining the Member State responsible for examining an application for international protection lodged in one of the Member States by a third country national or a stateless person (recast) – known as the Dublin III Regulation. This replaced the Dublin II Regulation (343/2003 of 18 February 2003) which in turn replaced the Dublin Convention of 1990.
3   A&I(TC)A 2004, Sch 3, Pt 6, para 20(1) provides that the SSHD may by order add a State to the list specified in para 2 (see fn 1 above). Bulgaria and Romania were added to the original list of 26 countries by Asylum (First List of Safe Countries) (Amendment) Order 2006, SI 2006/3393 with effect in relation to decisions refusing leave to enter or to remove made on or after 1 January 2007 in response to asylum and human rights claims even if made before 1 January 2007. Switzerland was added by Asylum (First List of Safe Countries) (Amendment) Order 2010, SI 2010/2802 with effect in relation to decisions refusing leave to enter or to remove made on or after 20 November 2010 in response to asylum and human rights claims even if made before 20 November 2010.
4   See *R (Nasseri) v Secretary of State for the Home Department* [2009] UKHL 23, per Lord Hoffmann at [21]–[22].
5   A&I(TC)A 2004, Sch 3, para 3(1).
6   A&I(TC)A 2004, Sch 3, para 3(2).

4.48   This deeming provision goes further than that contained in IAA 1999, s 11(1) (see **4.43** and **4.44** above) in that it additionally deems that the First List State will not 'refoule' an asylum applicant in contravention of the Human Rights Convention (as well as not doing so in contravention of the Refugee Convention). In *Nasseri*[1] the House of Lords held that this irrebutable presumption as to safety is not incompatible with ECHR, Art 3, first, because the presumption only applies for the purpose of determining whether a person may be removed lawfully from the UK to a listed country and does not preclude an inquiry into whether his Art 3 rights will be infringed for the different purpose of deciding whether a provision which makes such a removal lawful would be incompatible with ECHR rights – such a declaration of incompatibility has no effect on the lawfulness of the removal, which is the only purpose for which A&I(TC)A 2004 precludes an inquiry; secondly, because Art 3 does not create a procedural obligation to investigate whether there is a risk of a breach by the receiving state, independently of whether or not such a risk actually exists;[2] thirdly, because Members States of the EU were entitled to assume – not conclusively presume, but to start with the assumption – that other Member States would adhere to their treaty obligations, including those under the ECHR, unless the evidence demonstrated otherwise.

1   See **4.47**, fn 4 above.
2   The House of Lords dismissed the applicant's appeal from the judgment of the Court of Appeal ([2008] EWCA Civ 464) in turn reversing *R (Nasseri) v Secretary of State for the Home Department* [2007] EWHC 1548 (Admin), in which McCombe J had held that, in relation to Greece, the deeming provision in sub-para (b) (of A&I(TC)A 2004, Sch 3, para 3(2)) is incompatible with ECHR, Art 3 as it in effect directs the SSHD not to comply with the substantive obligation of investigation arising under Art 3.

4.49   NIAA 2002, s 77 (which normally prohibits removal of an asylum applicant whilst his claim for asylum is pending) shall not prevent a person who has made an asylum claim from being removed from the UK to a First

List State provided that the SSHD certifies that in his opinion the person is not a national or citizen of that State.[1] This is of course the key point – the SSHD will not substantively consider the asylum claim in the UK. If the SSHD does decide to remove the person to a First List State he will certify that it is proposed to remove the person to a First List State and that in his opinion the person is not a national or citizen of that State.[2] In which case:

- the person may not bring an immigration appeal from within the UK in reliance on–

  (a) an asylum claim which asserts that to remove the person to a First List State would breach the UK's obligations under the Refugee Convention, or

  (b) a human rights claim in so far as it asserts that to remove the person to a First List State would be unlawful under HRA 1998, s 6 because of the possibility of removal from that State to another State;[3]

- the person may not bring an immigration appeal from within the UK in reliance on a human rights claim, other than as per (b) above (re onward refoulment from the First List State) if the SSHD certifies that the claim is clearly unfounded; and the SSHD shall certify such a human rights claim unless satisfied that the claim is not clearly unfounded;[4]

- furthermore, and consistently with the deeming provision in A&I(TC)A 2004, Sch 3, para 3 (see **4.47** above), even from outside the UK a person may not bring an immigration appeal on any ground that is inconsistent with treating a First List State as a place–

  (a) where a person's life and liberty are not threatened by reason of his race, religion, nationality, membership of a particular social group or political opinion,

  (b) from which a person will not be sent to another State in contravention of his Convention rights, and

  (c) from which a person will not be sent to another State otherwise than in accordance with the Refugee Convention.[5]

1 A&I(TC)A 2004, Sch 3, para 4.
2 A&I(TC)A 2004, Sch 3, para 5(1).
3 A&I(TC)A 2004, Sch 3, para 5(3). Sub-para (2) deleted and sub-para (3) amended by IA 2014, Sch 9(4), para 56(3) from 20 October 2014. Sub-para (2) previously provided that a person could not bring an appeal by virtue of NIAA 2002, s 92(2) or (3) (appeal from within the UK: general); prior to amendment, sub-para (3) referred to the person not being entitled to bring an appeal by virtue of s 92(4)(a) (appeal from within UK: asylum or human rights). See saved NIAA 2002, s 92 and **3.25–3.31** above. In practical terms there is no substantive change as any appeal in such circumstances would inevitably be seeking to rely on asylum or human rights grounds.
4 A&I(TC)A 2004, Sch 3, para 5(4) and (5). Sub-para (4) amended by IA 2014, Sch 9(4), para 56(3). It previously referred to the person not being entitled to bring an appeal by virtue of s 92(4)(a) (see fn 3 above).

5   A&I(TC)A 2004, Sch 3, para 6. See for an example of such an out-of-country appeal, *VT (Dublin Regulation: post-removal appeal: Sri Lanka)* [2012] UKUT 308 (IAC).

4.50   Accordingly, where removal on safe third country grounds is to a First List State, effectively under the provisions of the Dublin III Regulation (see **4.46** and **4.47** above), the only possibility of a suspensive appeal to the FTT lies in a human rights claim, based either on Art 8 grounds or on grounds that assert a real risk of violation of rights in the First List State itself[1] (rather than on the basis of risk of *refoulment*), which although refused is not certified as clearly unfounded by the SSHD, notwithstanding the presumption that such a claim will be clearly unfounded (compare in this respect the difference between clearly unfounded certification in NIAA 2002, s 94(1) and (3) dependent on whether or not the claimant is entitled to reside in a s 94(4) listed State: see **4.17** above). Accordingly an in-country challenge to removal would most likely be by way of judicial review, but still subject to the statutory presumptions of safety as above.[2]

1   See in this regard the series of cases alleging, with varying degrees of success, that asylum claimants' human rights would be breached in Greece (see *R (Nasseri) v Secretary of State for the Home Department* [2009] UKHL 23; *MSS v Belgium* (2011) 53 EHRR 2; *R (NS) v Secretary of State for the Home Department (principles of Community law)* (ECJ: C-411/10) [2013] QB 102); in Cyprus (*R (Elayathamby) v Secretary of State for the Home Department* [2011] EWHC 2182 (Admin)); in Romania (*VT (Dublin Regulation: post-removal appeal: Sri Lanka)* [2012] UKUT 308 (IAC)); in Hungary (*R (HK (Sudan)) v Secretary of State for the Home Department* [2014] EWCA Civ 1481; *R (Simaei and Arap) v Secretary of State for the Home Department (Dublin returns – Hungary)* (IJR) [2015] UKUT 83 (IAC)); and in Italy (*R (EM (Eritrea)) v Secretary of State for the Home Department* [2014] UKSC 12; *R (Tabrizagh) v Secretary of State for the Home Department* [2014] EWHC 1914 (Admin); *Tarakhel v Switzerland* [2014] ECHR 1435 (4 November 2014)).
2   See *R (Ibrahim) v Secretary of State for the Home Department* [2001] EWCA Civ 519, per Simon Brown LJ at [16] and *Nasseri* (above).

SECOND LIST OF SAFE COUNTRIES (REFUGEE CONVENTION AND HUMAN RIGHTS (2))

4.51   A&I(TC)A 2004, Sch 3, Part 3 is titled as per the heading above and applies to such States as the SSHD may by order specify.[1] So far, no such order has ever been made and so there has never been a Second List of safe third countries. If there ever were to be such a list, the SSHD could both add and remove States to and from it (compare with the First List: **4.47** above).[2] If there were to be a Second List, then the listed States are to be deemed as places:

(a)   where a person's life and liberty are not threatened by reason of his race, religion, nationality, membership of a particular social group or political opinion; and

(b)   from which a person will not be sent to another State otherwise than in accordance with the Refugee Convention.[3]

1   A&I(TC)A 2004, Sch 3, para 7(1). Such an order shall be made by statutory instrument, and shall not be made unless a draft has been laid before and approved by resolution of each House of Parliament: para 7(2).
2   A&I(TC)A 2004, Sch 3, para 20(2).
3   A&I(TC)A 2004, Sch 3, para 8(2).

4.52   Note that there is no statutory presumption of non-refoulment contrary to ECHR. As with the First List countries in Sch 3, Pt 2, the presumption of safety precludes any appeal to the FTT (in or out of country) which is inconsistent with it.[1] NIAA 2002, s 77 (no removal while claim for asylum pending) will not prevent a person who has made a claim for asylum from being removed from the UK to a Second List State provided that the SSHD certifies that in his opinion the person is not a national or citizen of that State.[2] If the SSHD certifies that it is proposed to remove a person to a Second List State and that in his opinion the person is not a national or citizen of that State,[3] the person may not bring an immigration appeal from within the UK in reliance on an asylum claim which asserts that such removal would breach the UK's obligations under the Refugee Convention[4] and may not bring an immigration appeal from within the UK in reliance on a human rights claim if the SSHD certifies that the claim is clearly unfounded; and the SSHD shall certify a human rights claim in this circumstance unless satisfied that the claim is not clearly unfounded.[5] Note again the default position in favour of certification and note also that where the human rights claim alleges breach of human rights in the Second List State or on the basis of refoulment from that State in contravention of the ECHR, it is open to the SSHD to also certify such a claim, on refusal, as clearly unfounded under NIAA 2002, s 94(7), in which case the deeming provision as to that State not refouling in contravention of the UK's obligations in relation to persons entitled to a grant of humanitarian protection in s 94(8) will apply (see **4.40–4.42** above). The point here is that the UK is obliged to grant a non-excluded person humanitarian protection if at real risk of 'serious harm' in the form, inter alia, of breach of ECHR, Art 3 rights.[6]

1   A&I(TC)A 2004, Sch 3, paras 10(3) and 11.
2   A&I(TC)A 2004, Sch 3, para 9.
3   A&I(TC)A 2004, Sch 3, para 10(1).
4   A&I(TC)A 2004, Sch 3, para 10(3). Sub-para (2) deleted and sub-para (3) amended by IA 2014, Sch 9(4), para 56(4) from 20 October 2014 with the same effect as described in **4.49**, fn 3 above.
5   A&I(TC)A 2004, Sch 3, para 10(4), as amended by IA 2014, Sch 9(4), para 56(4) with the same effect as described in **4.49**, fn 4 above.
6   See Immigration Rules, HC 395, paras 339C and 339D.

THIRD LIST OF SAFE COUNTRIES (REFUGEE CONVENTION ONLY)

4.53   A&I(TC)A 2004, Sch 3, Part 4 is titled as per the heading above and applies to such States as the SSHD may by order specify.[1] Again, so far, no such order has ever been made and so there has never been a Third List of safe third countries. If there ever were to be such a list, the SSHD could both add and remove States to and from it.[2] If there were to be a Third List, then the listed States are to be deemed as places:

(a)   where a person's life and liberty are not threatened by reason of his race, religion, nationality, membership of a particular social group or political opinion; and

(b)   from which a person will not be sent to another State otherwise than in accordance with the Refugee Convention.[3]

1   A&I(TC)A 2004, Sch 3, para 12(1). Such an order shall be made by statutory instrument, and shall not be made unless a draft has been laid before and approved by resolution of each House of Parliament: para 12(2).
2   A&I(TC)A 2004, Sch 3, para 20(2).
3   A&I(TC)A 2004, Sch 3, para 13(2).

4.54   Again, the presumption of Refugee Convention safety precludes any appeal to the FTT (in or out of country) which is inconsistent with it.[1] NIAA 2002, s 77 (no removal while claim for asylum pending) will not prevent a person who has made a claim for asylum from being removed from the UK to a Third List State provided that the SSHD certifies that in his opinion the person is not a national or citizen of that State.[2] If the SSHD certifies that it is proposed to remove a person to a Third List State and that in his opinion the person is not a national or citizen of that State,[3] the person may not bring an immigration appeal from within the UK in reliance on an asylum claim which asserts that such removal would breach the UK's obligations under the Refugee Convention[4] and may not bring an immigration appeal from within the UK in reliance on a human rights claim if the SSHD certifies that the claim is clearly unfounded.[5] But such certification is not the default position.

1   A&I(TC)A 2004, Sch 3, paras 15(3) and 16.
2   A&I(TC)A 2004, Sch 3, para 14.
3   A&I(TC)A 2004, Sch 3, para 15(1).
4   A&I(TC)A 2004, Sch 3, para 15(3). Sub-para (2) deleted and sub-para (3) amended by IA 2014, Sch 9(4), para 56(5) from 20 October 2014 with the same effect as described in **4.49**, fn 3 above.
5   A&I(TC)A 2004, Sch 3, para 15(4), as amended by IA 2014, Sch 9(4), para 56(5) with the same effect as described in **4.49**, fn 4 above.

COUNTRIES CERTIFIED AS SAFE FOR INDIVIDUALS

4.55   A&I(TC)A 2004, Sch 3, Pt 5 is titled as per the heading above and applies to a person who has made an asylum claim if the SSHD certifies that:

(a)   it is proposed to remove the person to a specified (in the sense of named) State;

(b)   in the SSHD's opinion the person is not a national or citizen of that State; and

(c)   in the SSHD's opinion that State is a place–

(i)   where the person's life and liberty will not be threatened by reason of his race, religion, nationality, membership of a particular social group or political opinion, and

(ii)   from which the person will not be sent to another State otherwise than in accordance with the Refugee Convention.[1]

1   A&I(TC)A 2004, Sch 3, para 17.

4.56   In such case, NIAA 2002, s 77 (no removal while claim for asylum pending) shall not prevent the person's removal from the UK to that State[1] and:

● he may not bring an immigration appeal from within the UK in reliance on an asylum claim which asserts that to remove him to that State would breach the UK's obligations under the Refugee Convention;[2]

● he may not bring an immigration appeal from within the UK in reliance on a human rights claim if the SSHD certifies that the claim is clearly unfounded (but with no presumption);[3] and

● he may not while outside the UK bring an immigration appeal on any ground that is inconsistent with the opinion certified under (c) in **4.55** above.[4]

It is not clear how often, if ever, this certification provision has been used in practice.

1   A&I(TC)A 2004, Sch 3, para 18.
2   A&I(TC)A 2004, Sch 3, para 19(b). Sub-para (a) deleted and sub-para (b) amended by IA 2014, Sch 9(4), para 56(6) from 20 October 2014 with the same effect as described in **4.49**, fn 3 above.
3   A&I(TC)A 2004, Sch 3, para 19(c), as amended by IA 2014, Sch 9(4), para 56(6) with the same effect as described in **4.49**, fn 4 above.
4   A&I(TC)A 2004, Sch 3, para 19(d).

PART 3 – RIGHTS OF APPEAL TO THE FTT UNDER THE EEA REGS 2006

IMMIGRATION (EUROPEAN ECONOMIC AREA) REGULATIONS 2006, PT 6 AND SCHS 1 AND 2

4.57   The EEA Regs 2006[1] are made by the SSHD under powers conferred by the European Communities Act 1972, s 2(2) and NIAA 2002, s 109. EEA Regs 2006, Pt 6 provides for rights of appeal against EEA decisions (as to which, see **1.12** and **1.13** above). The regulations in Pt 6 are amended to an extent by the Immigration (European Economic Area) (Amendment) Regulations 2015,[2] so as to provide for the effect of the amendments to NIAA 2002, Pt 5, brought by IA 2014 (see **4.1** and **4.3** above). However, EEA (Amendment) Regs 2015, reg 6 provides that some of these amendments have no effect in relation to an appeal against an EEA decision where that decision was taken before 6 April 2015. EEA Regs 2006, Pt 6 provides for there to be a right of appeal against an EEA decision but this is then subject to various limitations and restrictions, including in relation to the need to produce certain evidence in order to be permitted to appeal (regs 26 and 29A). Provision is made for when an appeal can be in-country or only from abroad (reg 27) and for when a person may be temporarily admitted in order to be able to make submissions in person to the tribunal (reg 29AA). Provision is also made as to the effect of appeals to the FTT or UT (reg 29) and for when an appeal lies to the SIAC (as to which see Chapter 7) instead of to the FTT (regs 28 and 28A). EEA Regs 2006, Sch 1 provides for certain specified provisions of, or made under, NIAA 2002 to have effect in relation to an appeal under the EEA Regs 2006; and Sch 2, para 4 makes further provisions in terms of the application and the disapplication of provisions in NIAA 2002 to rights of appeal in EEA cases. Both Schs 1 and 2, para 4 are significantly amended, with effect from 6 April 2015, by the EEA (Amendment) Regs 2015.

1   Immigration (European Economic Area) Regulations 2006, SI 2006/1003 (see **1.2** above).
2   SI 2015/694: in force from 6 April 2015.

RIGHT OF APPEAL TO THE FTT AGAINST AN EEA DECISION AND LIMITATIONS AND RESTRICTIONS THEREON: EEA REGS 2006, REG 26

4.58   Under EEA Regs 2006, reg 26(1) a person may appeal under the Regulations against an EEA decision. Such an appeal lies to the FTT unless it lies to the SIAC in accordance with EEA Regs 2006, reg 28 (as to which see **7.9** below).[1] However this right of appeal is expressly subject to the following restrictions:[2]

●   If a person claims to be an EEA national, he may not appeal under the Regulations unless he produces a valid national identity card or passport issued by an EEA State.[3]

●   If a person claims to be in a durable relationship with an EEA national he may not appeal under the Regulations unless he produces a passport; and either–

   –   an EEA family permit; or

   –   sufficient evidence to satisfy the SSHD that he is in a relationship with that EEA national.[4]

- If a person claims to be a family member who has retained the right of residence or the family member or relative of an EEA national he may not appeal under the Regulations unless he produces a passport, and either–

    – an EEA family permit;

    – a qualifying EEA State residence card;

    – proof that he is the family member or relative of an EEA national; or

    – in the case of a person claiming to be a family member who has retained the right of residence, proof that he was a family member of the relevant person.[5]

- If a person claims to be a person with a derivative right of entry or residence he may not appeal under the Regulations unless he produces a valid national identity card issued by an EEA State or a passport, and either–

    – an EEA family permit; or

    – proof that he is related as claimed to an EEA national or British citizen upon the basis of which he claims to have the derivative right in question.[6]

- However, in all cases above in respect to the requirement to produce a valid identity card issued by an EEA State or a valid passport, the SSHD may accept alternative evidence of identity and nationality where the person is unable to obtain or produce the required document due to circumstances beyond his control.[7]

1   EEA Regs 2006, reg 26(6).
2   EEA Regs 2006, reg 26(1).
3   EEA Regs 2006, reg 26(2).
4   EEA Regs 2006, reg 26(2A), as added by the Immigration (European Economic Area) (Amendment) (No 2) Regulations 2012, SI 2012/2560, Sch 1, para 5(a) from 8 November 2012.
5   EEA Regs 2006, reg 26(3), as substituted by the Immigration (European Economic Area) (Amendment) Regulations 2012, SI 2012/1547, Sch 1, para 20(a) from 16 July 2012 and as subsequently amended by SI 2012/2560 from 8 November 2012 and by the Immigration (European Economic Area) (Amendment) (No 2) Regulations 2013, SI 2013/3032, Sch 1, para 22 from 7 April 2014.
6   EEA Regs 2006, reg 26(3A), as added by SI 2012/1547 from 16 July 2012 and as subsequently amended by SI 2012/2560 from 8 November 2012.
7   EEA Regs 2006, reg 29A, as added by SI 2012/2560, Sch 1, para 6 from 8 November 2012.

4.59   Accordingly, whether there is a right of appeal at all must be determined as a preliminary issue on the basis of the evidence presented in order to establish the right. In *Adetola*,[1] for example, the FTT dismissed the appeal for want of jurisdiction, over suspicion as to the validity of the appellant's marriage certificate as proof of relationship to an EEA national. On judicial review it was held that the Church of England marriage certificate was sufficient evidence of the marriage and, as a result, the decision that there was no right of appeal to the FTT, under reg 26(1), was flawed and could not stand.

1 *R (Adetola) v First-tier Tribunal (Immigration and Asylum Chamber)* [2010] EWHC 3197 (Admin). See also *R (AH (Iraq)) v Secretary of State for the Home Department* [2009] EWHC 1771 (Admin), in which the issue partly turned, prior to amendment of reg 26 so as to add reg 26(2A) (see **4.58**, fn 4 above), on whether a partner, in a 'durable relationship', needed to provide proof of the relationship in order to be permitted to appeal under reg 26(1) in light of reg 26(3) (see **4.58**, fn 5 above).

CERTIFICATION PREVENTING RELIANCE ON A GROUND OF APPEAL

4.60   The SSHD or an Immigration Officer may certify that a ground of appeal (as to which see **4.66**, **4.67** and **4.73** below) has been considered in a previous appeal brought under the EEA Regs 2006 or under NIAA 2002, s 82(1),[1] in which case the person may not bring an appeal under reg 26(1) (above) on that certified ground or rely on that ground in an appeal brought under reg 26(1).[2] However, in *BXS*[3] it was held, in the Administrative Court, that in the context of EEA cases the mere fact that a ground had previously been considered should not lead to the conclusion that that ground should be certified without adequate consideration of asserted material change of circumstances and that, as the SSHD's certification decision letter did not grapple with that change of circumstances, its reasoning was inadequate and flawed and fell to be quashed. See further in **4.68**, **4.74** and **4.75** below in respect of when the EEA decision was taken, as to the application of NIAA 2002, ss 85, 96 and 120 to appeals against EEA decisions.

1 EEA Regs 2006, reg 26(5).
2 EEA Regs 2006, reg 26(4).
3 *R (BXS) v Secretary of State for the Home Department* [2014] EWHC 737 (Admin) (appeal to CA pending).

SUSPENSIVE OR NON-SUSPENSIVE APPEALS AGAINST EEA DECISIONS: (1) GENERAL PROVISIONS APPLICABLE TO EEA DECISIONS WHENEVER TAKEN: EEA REGS 2006, REG 27

4.61   Subject to provisions that depend in part on whether the EEA decision was taken prior to 6 April 2015, or on or after that date, (as to which see below), a person may not appeal under reg 26 (above) whilst he is in the UK against an EEA decision:[1]

- to refuse to admit him to the UK;

- from 6 April 2015, to revoke his admission to the UK;[2]

- to make an exclusion order against him;

- to refuse to revoke a deportation or exclusion order made against him;

- to refuse to issue him with an EEA family permit;

- to revoke, or to refuse to issue or renew any document under the EAA Regs 2006 where that decision is taken at a time when he is outside the UK;

- to remove him from the UK after he has entered the UK in breach of a deportation or exclusion order; or

- from 6 April 2015, to remove him from the UK after he has entered the UK in circumstances where he is not entitled to be admitted pursuant to EEA Regs 2006, reg 19(1) (exclusion justified on grounds of public policy, public security or public health) or (1AB) (SSHD considers there to be reasonable grounds to suspect that his admission would lead to the abuse of a right to reside).[3]

1   EEA Regs 2006, reg 27(1) as amended by the Immigration (European Economic Area) (Amendment) Regulations 2009, SI 2009/1117 from 1 June 2009 and by the Immigration (European Economic Area) (Amendment) Regulations 2012, SI 2012/1547 from 16 July 2012.
2   EEA Regs 2006, reg 27(1)(zaa) as added by the Immigration (European Economic Area) (Amendment) Regulations 2015, SI 2015/694 (see **4.57** above), Sch 1, para 13(a) from 6 April 2015 (but without any transitional provision): SI 2015/694, reg 4.
3   EEA Regs 2006, reg 27(1)(d) as amended by SI 2015/694, Sch 1, para 13(b) from 6 April 2015 (but without any transitional provision): SI 2015/694, reg 4.

4.62   However in respect of EEA decisions to refuse admission, to revoke admission (from 6 April 2015) and to make an exclusion order, where the person is present in the UK he may appeal from within the UK if:[1]

(a)   he held a valid EEA family permit, registration certificate, residence card, derivative residence card, document certifying permanent residence, permanent residence card or qualifying EEA State residence card on his arrival in the UK or can otherwise prove that he is resident in the UK; or[2]

(b)   he is deemed not to have been admitted to the UK under reg 22(3)[3] but at the date on which notice of the decision to refuse to admit him is given he has been in the UK for at least three months.

1   EEA Regs 2006, reg 27(2) as amended by SI 2009/1117 from 1 June 2009, by SI 2012/1547 from 16 July 2012 and by the Immigration (European Economic Area) (Amendment) (No 2) Regulations 2013, SI 2013/3032 from 7 April 2014. Further amended by SI 2015/694, Sch 1, para 13(c)(i) from 6 April 2015 (but without any transitional provision): SI 2015/694, reg 4.
2   Amendment made by SI 2015/694, Sch 1, para 13(c)(ii) from 6 April 2015 (with transitional effect): SI 2015/694, reg 4 and 6. For reg 27(2)(c), as applicable only to EEA decisions taken prior to 6 April 2015, see **4.72** below.

3   EEA Regs 2006, reg 22(3) provides that for so long as a person to whom reg 22 applies
(that is to a person who claims a right of admission to the UK under reg 11) is detained, or
temporarily admitted or released while liable to detention, under the powers conferred by IA
1971, Sch 2, he is deemed not to have been admitted to the UK.

4.63   It will be noted that whereas refusal to revoke a deportation order
in respect to a non-EEA decision, can lead to a suspensive in-country right
of appeal under saved NIAA 2002, s 82(1) and (2)(k) (see **3.7** above), where
a person is an EEA national or a family member of an EEA national, in
accordance with saved NIAA 2002, s 92(4)(b) (see **3.30** above), where,
on the other hand, the SSHD makes an 'EEA decision' to refuse to revoke
a deportation order, no in-country right of appeal arises (see above).
Challenges, *inter alia*, to the justification of this distinction were rejected
in the Administrative Court in *BXS*[1] and in *Byczek*.[2] In *Nouazli*[3] the Court
of Appeal observed that EEA nationals are subject to an entirely different
deportation regime to 'aliens' with no EU law rights and that overall that
regime is more favourable to EEA nationals. See **4.72** and **4.76** below
regarding the effect of an asylum claim on whether a right of appeal against
an EEA decision, as listed above, has suspensive effect.

1   *R (BXS) v Secretary of State for the Home Department* [2014] EWHC 737 (Admin) (appeal
to CA pending).
2   *R (Byczek) v Secretary of State for the Home Department* [2014] EWHC 4298 (Admin).
3   *R (Nouazli) v Secretary of State for the Home Department* [2013] EWCA Civ 1608
(permission granted to appeal to the SC).

EFFECT OF APPEALS TO THE FTT AND UT IN EEA
CASES: EEA REGS 2006, REG 29

4.64   The following provisions apply where a person appeals to the FTT, or
onwards to the UT, under EEA Regs 2006, reg 26(1) (see **4.58** above):[1]

* If a person who is in the UK appeals to the FTT against an EEA decision
  to refuse to admit him to the UK – other than a decision under reg 19(1)
  (not admitted because exclusion justified on grounds of public policy,
  public security or public health), 19(1A) (person subject to a deportation
  or exclusion order) or 19(1B) (exclusion order made on grounds of
  public policy, public security or public health) – any directions for his
  removal from the UK previously given by virtue of the refusal cease to
  have effect, except in so far as they have already been carried out, and no
  directions may be so given while the appeal is pending.[2] In *AH (Iraq)*,[3]
  it was held that this provision did not render unlawful the removal of a
  person appealing against an EEA decision to refuse to issue him with a
  residence card (see **1.12** above).

- Similarly, if a person who is in the UK appeals to the FTT against an EEA decision to remove him from the UK – other than a decision under reg 19(3)(b) (SSHD has decided that the person's removal is justified on grounds of public policy, public security or public health) – any directions given under IAA 1999, s 10 (see **1.11** above) or IA 1971, Sch 3 (regarding deportation), for his removal from the UK are to have no effect, except in so far as they have already been carried out, while the appeal is pending.[4]

- However the provisions of IA 1971, Sch 2 or 3, with respect to detention and persons liable to detention, apply to a person appealing against a refusal to admit him, or from 6 April 2015, a decision to revoke his admission, or a decision to remove him, as if there were in force directions for his removal from the UK; except that he may not be detained on board a ship or aircraft so as to compel him to leave the UK while the appeal is pending,[5] unless the SSHD has certified, under reg 24AA, that despite the appeals process not having been begun or not having been finally determined, removal of the person to the country or territory to which it is proposed he is to be removed, pending the outcome of his appeal, would not be unlawful under HRA 1998, s 6 (see **1.13** above).[6]

- In calculating the period of two months limited by IA 1971, Sch 2, para 8(2) for giving directions, or notice of intention to give directions, for the removal of a person from the UK, any period during which there is a pending appeal under reg 26(1) is to be disregarded, except in cases where the EEA decision was taken pursuant to reg 19(1), (1A), (1B) or (3)(b) (as to each of which, see above).[7]

- If a person in the UK appeals against an EEA decision to remove him from the UK, a deportation order is not to be made against him under IA 1971, s 5 (see **1.11** above) while the appeal is pending.[8]

- A person who is detained under immigration powers whilst he is appealing to the FTT or UT against an EEA decision may be granted bail.[9]

---

1 EEA Regs 2006, reg 29(1).
2 EEA Regs 2006, reg 29(2), as amended by the Immigration (European Economic Area) (Amendment) (No 2) Regulations 2014, SI 2014/1976 from 28 July 2014.
3 *R (AH (Iraq)) v Secretary of State for the Home Department* [2009] EWHC 1771 (Admin).
4 EEA Regs 2006, reg 29(3), as amended by SI 2014/1976 from 28 July 2014.
5 EEA Regs 2006, reg 29(4), as amended by the Immigration (European Economic Area) (Amendment) Regulations 2015, SI 2015/694 (see **4.57** above), Sch 1, para 14 from 6 April 2015 (but without any transitional provision): SI 2015/694, reg 4.
6 EEA Regs 2006, reg 29(4A), as added by SI 2014/1976 from 28 July 2014.
7 EEA Regs 2006, reg 29(5), as amended by SI 2014/1976 from 28 July 2014.
8 EEA Regs 2006, reg 29(6).
9 EEA Regs 2006, reg 29(7) which applies IA 1971, Sch 2, para 29 to an appeal under reg 26(1) as it applies to a person appealing under NIAA 2002, s 82(1).

TEMPORARY ADMISSION IN ORDER TO SUBMIT CASE IN PERSON: EEA REGS 2006, REG 29AA

4.65   Uniquely applicable to appeals against EEA decisions, under EEA Regs 2006, reg 26(1) (see above), provision is made for a person who has been removed from the UK pursuant to reg 19(3)(b) – that is where the SSHD has decided that the person's removal is justified on grounds of public policy, public security or public health in accordance with reg 21 (which in turn makes provision for decisions taken on public policy, public security and public health grounds) – and who has appealed against this decision, to apply to the SSHD for permission to be temporarily admitted to the UK in order to make submissions in person before the FTT or the UT in circumstances where a date for the hearing has been set.[1] In such circumstance, the SSHD must grant the person temporary admission, except when his appearance may cause serious troubles to public policy or public security,[2] and in deciding the matter the SSHD must have regard to the dates upon which the person will be required to make submissions in person.[3] Once the hearing has taken place, the person may be removed from the UK to await the determination – with the possibility of returning on temporary admission if there is a further hearing listed, for example, before the UT on appeal from the FTT.[4] The person will be deemed not to have been admitted to the UK during any such period of temporary admission.[5]

1   EEA Regs 2006, reg 29AA(1) and (2). Reg 29AA added by the Immigration (European Economic Area) (Amendment) (No 2) Regulations 2014, SI 2014/1976 from 28 July 2014.
2   EEA Regs 2006, reg 29AA(3).
3   EEA Regs 2006, reg 29AA(4).
4   EEA Regs 2006, reg 29AA(5).
5   EEA Regs 2006, reg 29AA(8). Provision is made for a person temporarily admitted in these circumstances to be treated as a person refused leave to enter and then temporarily admitted under the provisions of IA 1971, Sch 2: reg 29AA(6) and (7).

(2) PROVISIONS ONLY APPLICABLE TO APPEALS TO THE FTT AGAINST EEA DECISIONS TAKEN BEFORE 6 APRIL 2015

Grounds of appeal: EEA decisions made prior to 6 April 2015

4.66   Prior to 6 April 2015, and in any event as applicable to EEA decisions taken prior to that date, EEA Regs 2006, Sch 1, para 1 provides that the grounds of appeal in saved NIAA 2002, s 84(1) (as to which, see **3.13** above), except paras (a) and (f), apply to an appeal under the Regulations as if it were an appeal against an 'immigration decision' under saved NIAA 2002, s 82(1) (see **3.7** above).[1] Accordingly, in respect to an EEA decision made before 6 April 2015, a person can appeal on the following grounds:

- that the decision is racially discriminatory and thereby unlawful by virtue of the Race Relations (Northern Ireland) Order 1997, art 20A or by virtue of the Equality Act 2010, s 29 (discrimination in the exercise of public functions, etc) so far as relating to race as defined by s 9(1) of that Act;[2]

- that the decision is unlawful under HRA 1998, s 6 (public authority not to act contrary to ECHR) as being incompatible with the appellant's human rights;[3]

- that the appellant is an EEA national or a member of the family of an EEA national and the decision breaches the appellant's rights under the Community Treaties in respect of entry to or residence in the UK;[4]

- that the decision is otherwise not in accordance with the law;[5]

- that removal of the appellant from the UK in consequence of the EEA decision would breach the UK's obligations under the Refugee Convention or would be unlawful under HRA 1998, s 6 as being incompatible with the appellant's human rights.[6]

1 EEA Regs 2006, reg 26(7) and Sch 1, para 1, pre-amendment on 6 April 2015, but with transitional effect so as to still apply to EEA decisions taken prior to that date: Immigration (European Economic Area) (Amendment) Regulations 2015, SI 2015/694 (see **4.57** above), regs 4 and 6 and Sch 1, para 15.
2 Saved NIAA 2002, s 84(1)(b) (see **3.13** above).
3 Saved NIAA 2002, s 84(1)(c) (see **3.13** above).
4 Saved NIAA 2002, s 84(1)(d) (see **3.13** above and **4.73** below).
5 Saved NIAA 2002, s 84(1)(e) (see **3.13** above).
6 Saved NIAA 2002, s 84(1)(g) as applied to an EEA decision. See **3.13** above, but see also **4.72** below regarding certification of asylum claims.

4.67   With respect to the ground of appeal that the appellant is an EEA national or a member of the family of an EEA national and that the decision breaches the appellant's rights under the Community Treaties in respect of entry to or residence in the UK, an 'EEA national' means a national of a State which is a contracting party to the Agreement on the European Economic Area signed at Oporto on 2 May 1992 (as it has effect from time to time)[1] or a Swiss national.[2]

1 Saved NIAA 2002, s 84(2) as applied by EEA Regs 2006, Sch 1, para 1 (see **4.66**, fn 1 above).
2 EEA Regs 2006, reg 30 and Sch 2, para 4(6), pre-deletion on 6 April 2015, but with transitional effect so as to still apply to an appeal against an EEA decision taken prior to that date: SI 2015/694, regs 4 and 6 and Sch 1, para 16(a).

Application of other saved provisions of NIAA 2002 to appeals against EEA decisions taken prior to 6 April 2015

4.68   In respect of EEA decisions taken prior to 6 April 2015, it is provided that saved NIAA 2002, ss 85 (matters to be considered), 86 (determination of appeal), 87 (successful appeal: directons), 105 and any regulations made under that section (see the Immigration (Notices) Regulations 2003: see **4.34** above) and 106 and any rules made under that section (Tribunal Procedure Rules: see Chapters 5 and 6) also apply to an appeal under the Regulations as if it were an appeal against an 'immigration decision' under saved NIAA 2002, s 82(1).[1] It is specifically provided that the Tribunal Procedure Rules have effect in relation to EEA appeals.[2] Furthermore, it is provided that an appeal under reg 26(1) (see **4.58** above) shall be treated as an appeal under saved NIAA 2002, s 82(1) against an immigration decision (see **3.7** above) for the purposes of saved NIAA 2002, s 96(1)(a) (see **3.34** above).[3] NIAA 2002, s 120 (meaning s 120 prior to amendment: see **3.16** above) shall apply to a person if an EEA decision has been taken or may be taken in respect of him and, accordingly, the SSHD or an immigration officer may by notice require a statement from that person under s 120(2) (see **3.16** above) and that notice shall have effect for the purpose of saved NIAA 2002, s 96(2) (see **3.35** above).[4]

1   EEA Regs 2006, reg 26(7) and Sch 1, para 1, pre-amendment on 6 April 2015, but with transitional effect so as to still apply to an appeal against an EEA decision taken prior to that date: Immigration (European Economic Area) (Amendment) Regulations 2015, SI 2015/694 (see **4.57** above), regs 4 and 6 and Sch 1, para 15.
2   EEA Regs 2006, Sch 1, para 2.
3   EEA Regs 2006, reg 30 and Sch 2, para 4(7), pre-deletion on 6 April 2015, but with transitional effect so as to still apply to an appeal against an EEA decision taken prior to that date: SI 2015/694, regs 4 and 6 and Sch 1, para 16(a).
4   EEA Regs 2006, reg 30 and Sch 2, para 4(8), pre-substitution on 6 April 2015, but with transitional effect so as to still apply to an appeal against an EEA decision taken prior to that date: SI 2015/694, regs 4 and 6 and Sch 1, para 16(b).

'Disapplication' of provisions of NIAA 2002 to appeals against EEA decisions taken prior to 6 April 2015

4.69   It is expressly provided that the following EEA decisions (see further **1.12** and **1.13** above) shall not be treated as immigration decisions for the purpose of saved NIAA 2002, s 82(2) (see **3.7** above):[1]

(a)   a decision that a person is to be removed under reg 19(3)(a) (person does not have or ceases to have a right to reside under the Regulations) or 19(3)(c) (SSHD has decided that the person's removal is justified on grounds of abuse of EEA rights) by way of a direction under saved IAA 1999, s 10(1)(a) (as provided for by reg 24(2));

(b)   a decision to remove a person under reg 19(3)(b) (SSHD has decided that the person's removal is justified on grounds of public policy, public security or public health) by making a deportation order under IA 1971, s 5(1) (as provided for by reg 24(3));

(c)   a decision to remove a person mentioned in reg 24(4) (a person who enters the UK in breach of a deportation or exclusion order shall be removable as an illegal entrant) by way of directions under IA 1971, Sch 2, paras 8–10.

1   EEA Regs 2006, reg 30 and Sch 2, para 4(1) (as amended by the Immigration (European Economic Area) (Amendment) (No 2) Regulations 2013, SI 2013/3032 from 1 January 2014), pre-deletion on 6 April 2015, but with transitional effect so as to still apply to an appeal against an EEA decision taken prior to that date: Immigration (European Economic Area) (Amendment) Regulations 2015, SI 2015/694 (see **4.57** above), regs 4 and 6 and Sch 1, para 16(a).

4.70   Furthermore, a person who has been issued with any of the following EEA documents, as well as a person whose passport has been stamped with a family member residence stamp, is not entitled to appeal under saved NIAA 2002, s 82(1) or under SIACA 1997, s 2 (see Chapter 7) against any decision and any existing appeal under those Acts (or under AIAA 1993, AIA 1996 or IAA 1999: as to which, see Chapter 2) shall be treated as abandoned if such a document or stamp is issued.[1] The documents are:

● a registration certificate;

● a residence card;

● a derivative residence card;

● a document certifying permanent residence or a permanent residence card under the EEA Regs 2006;

● a registration certificate under the EEA Regs 2006 as applied by the Accession of Croatia (Immigration and Worker Authorisation) Regulations 2013, reg 7;[2]

● a registration certificate under the Accession (Immigration and Worker Registration) Regulations 2004;[3]

● an accession worker card under the Accession (Immigration and Worker Authorisation) Regulations 2006;[4]

● a worker authorisation registration certificate under the Accession of Croatia (Immigration and Worker Authorisation) Regulations 2013.

1   EEA Regs 2006, reg 30 and Sch 2, para 4(2) (as amended inter alia to provide for further listed documents), pre-deletion as per **4.69**, fn 1 above.
2   SI 2013/1460.
3   SI 2004/1219.
4   SI 2006/3317.

4.71   Note however that a right of appeal as enjoyed by such a person under reg 26(1) (see **4.58** above) in respect to an EEA decision taken prior to 6 April 2015, can be brought on any of the grounds listed in **4.66** above, and these include asylum and human rights grounds. See below regarding asylum appeals.

Asylum appeals in relation to persons entitled to reside in the UK under the EEA Regs 2006: pre-6 April 2015

4.72   The first points to note are that an EEA national does not need to claim asylum in order to be entitled to reside in the UK because he has a right of residence in any event under EU law; and that by Protocol No 24 to the Treaty on European Union and to the Treaty on the Functioning of the European Union (see **1.7** above), it is provided that, save in the most exceptional circumstances, any asylum application made by a national of one Member State in another is to be treated by the receiving state as being manifestly unfounded.[1] Where an EEA national, or a family member, etc, does make an asylum claim and/or a human rights claim, whilst in the UK, in respect of an EEA decision, taken prior to 6 April 2015, to refuse to admit him to the UK, to make an exclusion order against him or to remove him from the UK after he has entered in breach of a deportation order, then he will have a suspensive right of appeal (contrary to the 'default' position in reg 27(1)(a), (aa) and (d): see **4.61** above), unless the SSHD certifies that the claim is, or the claims are, clearly unfounded.[2] As noted above the appeal, under reg 26(1), could be brought on asylum and or human rights grounds as per saved NIAA 2002, s 84(1)(g) as applied by EEA Regs, Sch 1, para 1 (see **4.66** above). Furthermore, a person may appeal to the FTT under NIAA 2002, s 83(2) (see **3.40** above) against the rejection of his asylum claim where that claim has been rejected, but he has a right to reside in the UK under the EEA Regs 2006;[3] however this right of appeal does not apply if the person is an EEA national and the SSHD certifies that the asylum claim is clearly unfounded[4] and the SSHD shall so certify the claim (and see regarding Protocol No 24 above) unless satisfied that it is not clearly unfounded.[5]

1   Protocol (No 24), on asylum for nationals of Member States of the EU (originally ECT, Protocol (No 29), adopted 1997). The most exceptional circumstances would be where the Member State from which the asylum seeker came was derogating from the ECHR (as to which, see TEU, Art 6(3)) or where that state is the subject of proceedings asserting a breach of the common fundamental principles of liberty, democracy, respect for human rights and the rule of law upon which the Union is founded: see TEU, Arts 6 and 7.
2   EEA Regs 2006, reg 27(2)(c) and (3), pre-deletion on 6 April 2015, but with transitional effect so as to still apply to an appeal against an EEA decision taken prior to that date: Immigration (European Economic Area) (Amendment) Regulations 2015, SI 2015/694 (see **4.57** above), regs 4 and 6 and Sch 1, para 13(d).
3   EEA Regs 2006, reg 30 and Sch 2, para 4(3), pre-deletion on 6 April 2015, but with transitional effect so as to still apply to an appeal against an EEA decision taken prior to that date: SI 2015/694, regs 4 and 6 and Sch 1, para 16(a).
4   EEA Regs 2006, reg 30 and Sch 2, para 4(4), pre-deletion on 6 April 2015 as per fn 3 above.
5   EEA Regs 2006, reg 30 and Sch 2, para 4(5), pre-deletion on 6 April 2015 as per fn 3 above.

(3) PROVISIONS ONLY APPLICABLE TO APPEALS TO THE FTT AGAINST EEA DECISIONS TAKEN ON OR AFTER 6 APRIL 2015

Grounds of appeal: EEA decisions made on or after 6 April 2015 and right of appeal under NIAA 2002, s 82(1)

4.73   In respect of an EEA decision made on or after 6 April 2015, EEA Regs 2006, Sch 1, para 1 (as amended) provides that the sole permitted ground of appeal is that the decision breaches the appellant's rights under the EU Treaties in respect of entry to or residence in the UK, to be known as 'an EU ground of appeal'.[1] Note, however, that in direct contrast to the position prior to 6 April 2015 (see **4.69** *et seq* above), from 6 April 2015 it is expressly provided, 'for the avoidance of doubt', that nothing in EEA Regs 2006, Pt 6 prevents a person who enjoys a right of appeal under reg 26 from appealing to the FTT under NIAA 2002, s 82(1) (see **4.4** *et seq* above), or, where relevant, to the SIAC pursuant to SIACA 1997, s 2 (see **7.5** and **7.6** below), provided the criteria for bringing such an appeal under those Acts are met.[2]

1   EEA Regs 2006, Sch 1, para 1, as substituted in part from 6 April 2015, but with transitional effect so as not to apply to an appeal against an EEA decision taken prior to that date, by the Immigration (European Economic Area) (Amendment) Regulations 2015, SI 2015/694 (see **4.57** above), regs 4 and 6 and Sch 1, para 15. As to the EU Treaties and the 'Citizens Directive', see **1.7** above. Discussion of substantive EU law and rights under the EU Treaties are outside the remit of this book: see **1.1** above.
2   EEA Regs 2006, reg 26(8), as added from 6 April 2015, but with transitional effect so as not to apply to an appeal against an EEA decision taken prior to that date, by SI 2015/694, regs 4 and 6 and Sch 1, para 12.

Application of other provisions of NIAA 2002 to appeals against EEA decisions taken on or after 6 April 2015

4.74   The following provisions of NIAA 2002 (as amended by IA 2014: see **4.1** above) apply to appeals against EEA decisions taken on or after 6 April 2015:

●   NIAA 2002, s 85 (matters to be considered: see **4.10–4.13** above) as though–[1]

  –   the references to a statement under NIAA 2002, s 120 (see **4.11** and **4.12** above) include, but are not limited to, a statement under that section as applied below; and

  –   a 'matter' in sub-s (2) and a 'new matter' in sub-s (6) (see **4.13** above) include a ground of appeal of a kind listed in NIAA 2002, s 84 (see **4.7** and **4.8** above) and an 'EU ground of appeal' (see **4.73** above).

- NIAA 2002, s 86 (determination of appeal: see **4.38** above).[2]

1   EEA Regs 2006, Sch 1, para 1, as substituted in part from 6 April 2015, but with transitional effect so as not to apply to an appeal against an EEA decision taken prior to that date, by the Immigration (European Economic Area) (Amendment) Regulations 2015, SI 2015/694 (see **4.57** above), regs 4 and 6 and Sch 1, para 15.
2   EEA Regs 2006, Sch 1, para 1, as substituted as per fn 1 above.

4.75   NIAA 2002, s 120 (see **4.11** and **4.12** above) applies to a person, 'P', if an EEA decision has been taken or may be taken in respect of P and, accordingly, the SSHD or an immigration officer may by notice require a statement from P under sub-s (2) and that notice has effect for the purpose of NIAA 2002, s 96(2) (see **4.31** above).[1] Where NIAA 2002, s 120 so applies, it has effect as though sub-s (3) also provides that a statement under sub-s (2) need not repeat reasons or grounds relating to the EEA decision under challenge previously advanced by P; and sub-s (5) also applies where P does not have a right to reside in the UK under the EEA Regs 2006, or only has such a right to reside by virtue of reg 15B (continuation of a right of residence).[2] For the purposes of an appeal brought pursuant to NIAA 2002, s 82(1), s 85(2) and (6)(a) (matters to be considered) have effect as though s 84 included a ground of appeal that the decision appealed against breaches the appellant's rights under the EU Treaties in respect of entry to or residence in the UK.[3]

1   EEA Regs 2006, Sch 2, para 4(8), as substituted from 6 April 2015, but with transitional effect so as not to apply to an appeal against an EEA decision taken prior to that date, by SI 2015/694, regs 4 and 6 and Sch 1, para 16(b).
2   EEA Regs 2006, Sch 2, para 4(9), as substituted as per fn 1 above.
3   EEA Regs 2006, Sch 2, para 4(10), as substituted as per fn 2 above.

Asylum appeals in relation to persons entitled to reside in the UK under the EEA Regs 2006: 6 April 2015 onwards

4.76   A person entitled to reside in the UK under the EEA Regs 2006 or being denied entry to or facing removal from the UK pursuant to an EEA decision, can make an asylum or a human rights claim and if such a claim is refused, a right of appeal will lie under NIAA 2002, s 82 (see **4.4** *et seq* and **4.73** above). It is likely that any asylum claim made by a person entitled to reside in an EEA State will be certified as clearly unfounded under NIAA 2002, s 94(1) (see **4.17** above and note Protocol No 24 as referred to in **4.72** above) with the consequence that he will not then have a suspensive right of appeal in accordance with NIAA 2002, s 92 (see **4.15** and **4.16** above).

Chapter 5

Procedure and evidence before the First-tier Tribunal

PART 1 – GENERAL PRINCIPLES

THE PROCEDURE RULES AND PRACTICE DIRECTIONS

5.1   Appeals are in general now governed by the Tribunal Procedure (First-tier Tribunal) (Immigration and Asylum Chamber) Rules 2014 ('the 2014 Rules'),[1] which replaced the Asylum and Immigration Tribunal (Procedure) Rules 2005[2] ('the 2005 Rules') and which regulate all immigration appeals, from their entry into force on 20 October 2014;[3] they apply to all appeals from that date, though there is discretion, in the interests of fairness, to apply provisions from the 2005 Rules or disapply elements of the 2014 Rules regarding appeals which were brought under the older regime.[4] Periods of time that have begun to run under the 2005 Rules before 20 October 2014 continue to apply until their expiry.[5] The 2014 Rules are made pursuant to the power conferred upon the Lord Chancellor under the Tribunal Courts and Enforcement Act 2007 and various other legislative instruments.[6] The Rules are supplemented by Practice Directions and Statements which became operative on 15 February 2010 and were revised to take account of the 2014 Rules on 13 November 2014;[7] the Directions and Statements may need to give way to the Rules should their provisions conflict.[8] There are also a series of Guidance Notes addressing particular aspects of procedure, addressed to adjudicators, but remaining current in the unified tribunal system.[9]

---

1   SI 2014/2604.
2   SI 2005/230.
3   SI 2014/2604, r 1(1).
4   SI 2014/2604, r 46(1). It would be wrong to penalise a party via retrospective application of the costs regime for unreasonable conduct to an appeal commenced before that regime entered force: *Cancino (costs – First-tier Tribunal – new powers)* [2015] UKFTT 59 (IAC).
5   SI 2014/2604, r 46(2).
6   See preamble to SI 2014/2604 referencing powers under TCEA 2007, ss 9, 22, 29(3) and (4)

and Sch 5, IA 1971, Sch 2, para 25, NIAA 2002, s 106(3), the British Nationality Act 1981, s 40A(3) and the EEA Regs 2006, SI 2006/1003, Sch 1.

7   Practice Directions made by the Senior President of Tribunals for the Immigration and Asylum Chambers of the First-tier Tribunal and the Upper Tribunal ('the Practice Directions'); Practice Statements made by the Senior President of Tribunals for the Immigration and Asylum Chambers of the First-tier Tribunal and the Upper Tribunal ('the Practice Statements').

8   *DM (Timing of Funding Application) Zimbabwe* [2006] UKAIT 00088 at [30].

9   They are presently styled 'Guidance notes for the former AIT that are now relevant to FTTIAC'.

5.2   Under the 2014 Rules, the written outcome of an appeal is given by way of decision and reasons:[1] thus judicial decisions are no longer styled 'determinations', and we seek to follow that description in this book. To summarise, the material legal framework governing procedure before the FTT comprises:

- the Tribunal Procedure (First-tier Tribunal) (Immigration and Asylum Chamber) Rules 2014;

- Senior President's Practice Directions addressing standard directions in fast track appeals, pursuing appeals after the grant of leave, notices of appeal, case management review hearings and directions, trial bundles, adjournments, expert evidence, citation of unreported determinations, starred and Country Guidance determinations, and bail applications;

- Senior President's Practice Statements addressing the composition of the FTT, acceptance of notices of appeal, review of FTT decisions, record of proceedings, transfer of proceedings, format and reporting of determinations;

- Presidential Guidance Note No 1 of 2014: The Tribunal Procedure (First-tier Tribunal) (Immigration and Asylum Chamber) Rules 2014;

- the First-tier Tribunal (Immigration and Asylum Chamber) Fees Order 2011;[2]

- Joint Presidential Guidance Note 2011 No 3: Judicial titles in UTIAC and FtTIAC (2011);

- FtTIAC Presidential Guidance Note No 2 (issued Feb 2011, revised July 2011): Anonymity directions in FT(IAC);

- Presidential Guidance Note No 1 (issued July 2011, amended June 2012): Bail guidance for immigration judges;

- Joint Presidential Guidance Note No 4 (2011): Fee awards in immigration appeals;

- Guidance Note No 1 (Nov 2001): Guidance on sitting for part time adjudicators;

- Guidance Note No 3 (May 2002): Pre-hearing introduction;

- Guidance Note No 4 (Feb 2003): Delayed promulgations;

- Guidance Note No 5 (Apr 2003): Unrepresented appellants;

- Guidance Note No 6 (Jun 2003): Guidance for adjudicators on deposit of recognizances;

- Guidance Note No 7 (Nov 2007): Guidance on withdrawals;

- Guidance Note No 8 (Apr 2004): Unaccompanied children;

- Guidance Note (Aug 2004): Unrepresented appellants who do not understand English;

- AIT Guidance Note and Checklist (Jul 2005): Case management review hearings.

1   Tribunal Procedure (First-tier Tribunal) (Immigration and Asylum Chamber) Rules 2014, SI 2014/2604, r 29.
2   SI 2011/2841.

OVERRIDING OBJECTIVE

5.3   The overriding objective of the Rules governing the FTT, which animates both its interpretation of the Rules and Practice Directions and any powers arising under them,[1] is to deal with cases 'fairly and justly',[2] rather than 'fairly, quickly and efficiently' (the overriding objective of its predecessor, the Asylum and Immigration Tribunal),[3] giving a clear steer that it is substantive justice rather than speed at which it aims. Rule 2(2) explains that:

'(2)   Dealing with a case fairly and justly includes–

(a)   dealing with the case in ways which are proportionate to the importance of the case, the complexity of the issues, the anticipated costs and the resources of the parties and of the Tribunal;

(b)   avoiding unnecessary formality and seeking flexibility in the proceedings;

(c)   ensuring, so far as practicable, that the parties are able to participate fully in the proceedings;

(d)   using any special expertise of the Upper Tribunal effectively; and

(e)   avoiding delay, so far as compatible with proper consideration of the issues.'

1   Tribunal Procedure (First-tier Tribunal) (Immigration and Asylum Chamber) Rules 2014, SI 2014/2604, r 2(3).
2   SI 2014/2604, r 2(1).
3   Asylum and Immigration Tribunal (Procedure) Rules 2005, SI 2005/230, r 4.

5.4   Additionally, the rule of law is a fundamental constitutional principle, as the Constitutional Reform Act 2005, s 1 reminds us, and fairness is at its core:[1] 'injustice is neither efficient nor fair.'[2] The parties are under a duty to help the FTT achieve its overriding objective, and to co-operate with it generally.[3] A number of the Rules require that the FTT is 'satisfied' of certain conditions: this term may imply some duty of further enquiry if the procedure is to secure justice.[4] As discussed in detail below, the FTT has powers to issue witness summonses and to order a party to produce documents,[5] and to provide further information, evidence or submissions about the case,[6] of its own motion where it thinks it necessary.[7] There may be occasions when the tribunal must assume an inquisitorial function;[8] as the Immigration Appeal Tribunal once put it in *Gimedhin*:[9]

> 'We would favour formulating any definition of the task facing the extent to which an adjudicator is required by the rules, the law and the nature of the issues he is called upon to resolve to be of an intrusive nature: the less the appellant has effective representation the more intrusive an adjudicator may have to be.'

1   Arden LJ in the Court of Appeal in *FP (Iran) v Secretary of State for the Home Department* [2007] EWCA Civ 13 at [59].
2   Sedley LJ in *FP (Iran)* (above) at [35]; see also Sedley LJ at [50] thereof; see also Roch LJ in the Court of Appeal in *Saleem v Home Secretary* [2000] Imm AR 529, citing Lord Wilberforce in *Raymond v Honey* [1983] AC 1; Hickinbottom J in the Administrative Court in *V, R (on the application of) v Asylum and Immigration Tribunal* [2009] EWHC 1902 (Admin) at [30].
3   Tribunal Procedure (First-tier Tribunal) (Immigration and Asylum Chamber) Rules 2014, SI 2014/2604, r 2(4)
4   Sedley LJ in the Court of Appeal in *FP (Iran)* (above) at [36].
5   See **5.73** below.
6   See **5.69** below.
7   SI 2014/2604, r 5(1).
8   Newman J in *R v Immigration Appeal Tribunal and a Special Adjudicator, ex parte Kumar* (CO/5073/98, 17 April 2000) spoke of a hearing which is 'more inquisitorial than adversarial'; see also Neuberger LJ in *HK v Secretary of State for the Home Department* [2006] EWCA Civ 1037 at [27]; Schiemann LJ in *Kesse v Secretary of State for the Home Department* [2001] EWCA Civ 177 at [37]; *RK (obligation to investigate) Democratic Republic of Congo* [2004] UKIAT 00129 at [46]; Sedley LJ in *AK (Iran) v Secretary of State for the Home Department* [2008] EWCA Civ 941 at [24]; Lord Carnwath in *Secretary of State for Home Department v MN and KY (Scotland)* [2014] UKSC 30 at [26].
9   *Gimedhin* (14019, 21 October 1996).

5.5   However, this role can only extend so far:[1]

> 'Courts and tribunals do not have evidence gathering functions or duties. While there is a power to direct a party or parties to produce evidence, enshrined in rule 45 Asylum and Immigration Tribunal (Procedure) Rules 2005 ("the Rules"), this neither requires nor empowers the Tribunal itself to engage in an evidence gathering exercise. Furthermore, and in any event, we consider that this power should be exercised sparingly, bearing in mind every tribunal's duty of impartial and independent adjudication.'

The Rules must not go beyond the statutory authority under which they are made (which mandates, in particular, that justice is done, that the system is accessible and fair, that proceedings are handled quickly and efficiently, and that the Rules are both simple and simply expressed)[2] or are 'productive of irremediable procedural unfairness.'[3]

1   *NA (UT rule 45: Singh v Belgium) Iran* [2014] UKUT 205 (IAC) at [14].
2   TCEA 2007, s 22(4).
3   Sedley LJ in *FP (Iran) v Secretary of State for the Home Department* [2007] EWCA Civ 13 at [48]; Laws J in *R v Secretary of State for Social Security, ex parte Sutherland* [1996] EWHC Admin 208 at [19]; *AM (Serbia) v Secretary of State for the Home Department* [2007] EWCA Civ 16 at [29], regarding Rules which go beyond the properly delegated authority; Sedley LJ in *FP (Iran)* (above) at [31] – see further **8.137**.

Fair trial

5.6   The right to fair trial in the determination of civil rights and obligations has so far been held by the ECtHR as inapplicable in immigration cases,[1] though the impact of this restrictive interpretation of the Convention is limited by the fact that ECHR, Art 8 includes a procedural dimension which ensures the effective protection of the right to family and private life,[2] and by the general application of the common law rules of fairness whether or not ECHR, Art 6 applies.[3] However, where European Union law is in play,[4] the Charter of Fundamental Rights provides protection, set out at Art 47:

'Everyone whose rights and freedoms guaranteed by the law of the Union are violated has the right to an effective remedy before a tribunal in compliance with the conditions laid down in this Article.

Everyone is entitled to a fair and public hearing within a reasonable time by an independent and impartial tribunal previously established by law. Everyone shall have the possibility of being advised, defended and represented.

Legal aid shall be made available to those who lack sufficient resources in so far as such aid is necessary to ensure effective access to justice.'

1   *Maaouia v France* (Grand Chamber), No 39652/98, ECHR 1999-II, at [37]–[38].
2   The Master of the Rolls for the Court of Appeal in *Gudanaviciene, R (on the application of) v Director of Legal Aid Casework* [2014] EWCA Civ 1622 at [70].
3   Hickinbottom J in *V, R (on the application of) v Asylum and Immigration Tribunal* [2009] EWHC 1902 (Admin) at [31].
4   ie most obviously in the context of international protection (refugee and Humanitarian Protection) which is part of the Common European Asylum System and is regulated by various Directives and Regulations, and free movement under the Treaty; *Bah (EO (Turkey) – liability to deport) Sierra Leone* [2012] UKUT 196 (IAC) at [54].

5.7   The ECtHR has not so far examined whether there is any need to change its traditional approach to immigration in the light of Art 47, and the domestic courts have not felt able to go further than Strasbourg, albeit that the impact of the Charter has not been examined in terms.[1] Nevertheless, 'everybody who comes before the courts and indeed the administrative authorities of this country is entitled at common law to be treated fairly'.[2] There will be a right to the public funding of immigration advice in some cases, notwithstanding the many limitations introduced in recent years, the key question being whether legal aid is necessary for 'effective access to the court'.[3]

> '72. Whether legal aid is required will depend on the particular facts and circumstances of each case, including (a) the importance of the issues at stake; (b) the complexity of the procedural, legal and evidential issues; and (c) the ability of the individual to represent himself without legal assistance, having regard to his age and mental capacity. The following features of immigration proceedings are relevant: (i) there are statutory restrictions on the supply of advice and assistance (see section 84 of the Immigration and Asylum Act 1999); (ii) individuals may well have language difficulties; and (iii) the law is complex and rapidly evolving'

The common law right to a fair hearing may be undermined if legal aid is not granted to a person unable to absorb complex materials disclosed by the SSHD.[4]

1   *MK (Iran), R (on the application of) v Secretary of State for the Home Department* [2010] EWCA Civ 115, see Sedley LJ at [70], Brooke LJ at [64].
2   Wall LJ in *FP (Iran) v Secretary of State for the Home Department* [2007] EWCA Civ 13 at [86]; Collins J in the Tribunal in *MNM* (00/TH/02258, 26 October 2000) at [16], making the point that it was only with regard to 'the requirement that the hearing be held within a reasonable time' that the common law's protection might be weaker.
3   The Master of the Rolls for the Court of Appeal in *Gudanaviciene, R (on the application of) v Director of Legal Aid Casework* [2014] EWCA Civ 1622 at [42], [72].
4   *Farquharson (removal – proof of conduct) Jamaica* [2013] UKUT 146 (IAC) at [93].

FIRST-TIER TRIBUNAL: CHARACTER

5.8   The tribunal is a guardian of the State's duties under HRA 1998;[1] and, as one UT President put it, 'respect for human dignity must be at the heart of our processes as Immigration Judges'.[2] Access to the tribunal is a fundamental right:

> 'In this day and age a right of access to a tribunal or other adjudicative mechanism established by the state is just as important and fundamental as a right of access to the ordinary courts.'[3]

1   Sedley LJ in *Sabiha Abdulrahman v Secretary of State for the Home Department* [2005] EWCA Civ 1620 at [27].
2   Speech by the Hon Mr Justice Blake, President of the UT to the Upper Tribunal Immigration Judiciary, 'The Arrival of the Upper Tribunal Immigration and Asylum Chamber' (11 February 2010): this will be all the truer in cases where European Union law is in play, *A v Staatssecretaris van Veiligheid en Justitie (United Nations High Commissioner for Refugees (UNHCR) intervening)* [2014] EUECJ C-148/13 at [53] and [65].

3   Hale LJ in *R v Secretary of State for the Home Department, ex parte Saleem* [2000] Imm AR
     529; see Sedley LJ in *FP (Iran) v Secretary of State for the Home Department* [2007] EWCA
     Civ 13 at [49]–[50]; Arden LJ in *FP (Iran)* (above) at [60] and [61]; cf Lord Phillips MR in *M,
     R (on the application of) v Immigration Appeal Tribunal* [2004] EWCA Civ 1731 at [33] and
     [35]; Lord Irvine of Lairg LC in the House of Lords in *Boddington v British Transport Police*
     [1999] 2 AC 143 at 161c; Collins J in the Administrative Court in *G, R (on the application of)
     v Immigration Appeal Tribunal* [2004] EWHC 588 (Admin) at [8]; Laws J in *R (John Witham)
     v Lord Chancellor* [1997] EWHC Admin 237.

5.9   No doubt decisions of the tribunal and courts made with reference
to predecessors of the 2005 Rules will have to be read in the light of changes
to their wording;[1] but they may very well retain a relevance in predicting the
response of the immigration judiciary to matters of practice and procedure
before them, and so we cite them in this chapter, though the impact of the
introduction of the unified tribunal, with its own overriding objectives, must be
taken into account (we also cite older tribunal decisions on general procedure
where these provide valuable insight on recurring issues).[2] Where the
substance of the rule is unchanged, decisions regarding their predecessors will
presumably remain authoritative.[3] It is the wording of the Rules which must
lie at the focus of decision making, not synonyms for them,[4] notwithstanding
the occasional imperfections identified in the drafting of their predecessors.[5]

1   See eg *Rajan* (01/TH/00244, 8 February 2001, starred), regarding the proper approach to
     Ognall J's decision in *Ex p Kimbesa* (29 January 1997, unreported); Kay J in *R v Immigration
     Appeal Tribunal, ex p Lou Bogou* [2000] Imm AR 494, regarding the failure of Tribunals to
     engage with changes in the Procedure Rules since those in force at time of the determination
     of the frequently cited case of *Ajeh* (13853; 30 August 1996); Carnwath LJ in *E v Secretary
     of State for the Home Department* [2004] EWCA Civ 49 at [17].
2   See by analogy Sedley LJ in *FP (Iran) v Secretary of State for the Home Department* [2007]
     EWCA Civ 13 at [19].
3   *Gyamfi* (14462; 10 January 1997).
4   See Munby J in the Administrative Court in *R v Immigration Appeal Tribunal, ex p Sarkisian*
     [2001] EWHC Admin 486.
5   *Brendan Colin Hughes* (01/TH/01147, 22 May 2001, starred) at [7].

Accessibility and fairness

5.10   In the asylum context, the Rules should be construed in a way which
gives life to appeal rights:[1] they should be 'clear, comprehensive and readily
accessible ... [and] applied with an acute sense of practicality',[2] and there may
be times where 'justice requires that the procedural hurdle should be knocked
down and the substance of the matter addressed'.[3] It is undesirable in asylum
cases to construe statutory provisions with excessive regard to the prospects of
abuse of the system;[4] principles imported from other areas of law may have to
be modified with this in mind.[5] In general the procedures of tribunals should be
less strict than those of the High Court, because it must be accessible by migrants
who lack a full understanding of the system:[6] the Court of Appeal in *Zenovics*
spoke of the undesirability, in an area where those drafting grounds of appeal
may lack familiarity with English law and language, of having disproportionate

consequences attend badly drafted grounds.[7] The FTT does not have an open-ended power to regulate its own procedure beyond those conferred by its Procedure Rules, though it may be assumed to hold such further 'powers that are necessary for the proper functioning of the tribunal'.[8] And:[9]

'it is well-established that when a statute has conferred on a body the power to make decisions affecting individuals, the courts will not only require the procedure prescribed by the statute to be followed, but will readily imply so much and no more to be introduced by way of additional procedural safeguards as will ensure the attainment of fairness.'

1   Ouseley J in *R v Immigration Appeal Tribunal, ex parte Nuredini* [2002] EWHC 1582 (Admin); *HH (sponsor as representative) Serbia* [2006] UKAIT 00063 at [15]; *AM (Serbia) v Secretary of State for the Home Department* [2007] EWCA Civ 16 at [16], citing *R (Quintavalle) v Human Fertilisation and Embryology Authority* [2005] UKHL 28; Sedley LJ in the Court of Appeal in *FP (Iran) v Secretary of State for the Home Department* [2007] EWCA Civ 13 at [53]; Latham LJ in the Court of Appeal in *R (Ahmed) v Immigration Appeal Tribunal* [2004] EWCA Civ 399 at [14]; the Lord Chief Justice in *P and M v Secretary of State for the Home Department* [2004] EWCA Civ 1640 at [27].
2   Blake J in the Administrative Court in *Semere, R (on the application of) v Asylum and Immigration Tribunal* [2009] EWHC 335 (Admin) at [53] and [59].
3   Schiemann LJ in *R (on the application of Tataw) v Immigration Appeal Tribunal* [2003] EWCA Civ 925 at [19]; Fox LJ in the Court of Appeal in *R v Diggines, ex parte Rahmani* [1985] QB 1109.
4   Collins J in the Administrative Court in *R (Secretary of State for the Home Department) v Immigration Appeal Tribunal* [2004] EWHC 3161 (Admin) at [31].
5   See eg Sedley LJ in the Court of Appeal in *FP (Iran)* (above) at [43].
6   Lord Woolf MR in *R v Secretary of State for the Home Department, ex parte Jeyeanthan* [1999] EWCA Civ 3010 at [32], Judge LJ at [44].
7   Schiemann LJ giving the judgment of the Court of Appeal in *Zenovics v Secretary of State for the Home Department* [2002] EWCA Civ 273.
8   Hickinbottom J in *V, R (on the application of) v Asylum and Immigration Tribunal* [2009] EWHC 1902 (Admin) at [26]–[28]; *Akewushola v Secretary of State for the Home Department* [2000] 1 WLR 2295 at 2301E–H, per Sedley LJ; *Secretary of State for Defence v President of the Pensions Appeal Tribunal* [2004] EWHC 141 (Admin).
9   Lord Bridge in *Lloyd v McMahon* [1987] AC 625, at 702–703, cited by Hickinbottom J in *V, R (on the application of) v Asylum and Immigration Tribunal* [2009] EWHC 1902 (Admin) at [17].

EXERCISE OF FUNCTIONS AND POWERS OF THE FTT

5.11   The Immigration and Asylum Chamber takes its place as part of the First-tier Tribunal over which the Senior President of Tribunals presides[1] (the dual roles of tribunal and High Court judge were held not to give rise to any legitimate apprehension of bias in the days when the President of the Immigration Appeal Tribunal sat in a judicial capacity reviewing decisions of the tribunal).[2] Its members will include those appointed to the Asylum and Immigration Tribunal under NIAA 2002;[3] permanent judges of the higher courts are members (as they are too of the Upper Tribunal).[4] Proceedings and procedural functions may be allocated to single First-tier judges, or to a panel of whom at least one must be an FTT judge and no more than one may be another member[5] (though a failure to adhere to a direction as to the panel before whom an appeal is listed needs to be the subject of timely objection if any procedural irregularity is to be made good).[6] Where a panel sits on an appeal, its decision is that of the majority, and so if a member dissents from the majority's ruling, he does so unbeknown to the parties.[7] Formal or administrative acts may be done by a member of the First-tier Tribunal's staff.[8] Staff appointed by the Lord Chancellor may, with the Senior President's approval, carry out functions of a judicial nature;[9] however parties have a right to apply for the reconsideration of such decisions by a judge.[10] The FTT, like its predecessors, will constitute a court or tribunal for the purposes of making a reference to the ECJ under the EC Treaty, Art 234.[11] For now, there is no requirement that consideration of such a reference be referred to the President or Deputy President.[12] Any member of the tribunal, when sitting, shall be addressed as 'Sir' or 'Madam' as the case may be, whatever their personal status; in correspondence, their address should be 'Immigration Judge [surname]' and 'Dear Judge'.[13] FTT judges sitting in that jurisdiction will be identified in their written decisions as 'Judge of the First-tier Tribunal X'.

1   Tribunals, Courts and Enforcement Act 2007, s 3(4). Blake J became President of the Immigration and Asylum Upper Chamber from 15 February 2010.
2   Thorpe LJ in the Court of Appeal dismissing a renewed application for permission for judicial review (against Collins J in *Spiro v Secretary of State* [2002] EWHC 1355 (Admin)) in *R v Immigration Appellate Authority, ex parte Spiro* [2001] EWCA Civ 2094.
3   Tribunals, Courts and Enforcement Act 2007, s 4(1)(d); the First-tier Tribunal and Upper Tribunal (Chambers) Order 2008, SI 2008/2684, art 3 gives the details by which the immigration judiciary were 'transferred-in' to the unified tribunal.
4   Tribunals, Courts and Enforcement Act 2007, s 6(1).
5   Practice Statement 2, para 2.1; First-tier Tribunal and Upper Tribunal (Composition of Tribunal) Order 2008, SI 2008/2835.
6   Richards LJ refusing permission to appeal to the Court of Appeal in *Luxmyranthan v Secretary of State for the Home Department* [2005] EWCA Civ 1481 at [9].
7   Practice Statements, para 10.2.
8   Tribunal Procedure (First-tier Tribunal) (Immigration and Asylum Chamber) Rules 2014, SI 2014/2604, r 3(1).
9   SI 2014/2604, r 3(2) and (3).
10   SI 2014/2604, r 3(4).
11   *El-Yassini v Secretary of State for the Home Department* (C416/96, 2 March 1999).
12   Formerly found in Consolidated Practice Directions as of April 2007, but unrepeated in the modern Rules: see Speech by the Hon Mr Justice Blake, President of the UT to the Upper Tribunal Immigration Judiciary, 'The Arrival of the Upper Tribunal Immigration and Asylum Chamber' (11 February 2010).
13   'What do I call a judge?' Judiciary of England and Wales website, www.judiciary.gov.uk/ you-and-the-judiciary/what-do-i-call-judge/ (accessed December 2014).

PART 2 – PRE-HEARING ISSUES

NOTICE OF APPEAL

5.12   Notice of appeal is given by sending the appeal forms (as found on the Ministry of Justice website),[1] (or completing them online, which is the recommended method),[2] to the tribunal[3] setting out:[4]

- the grounds of appeal therein including the reasons that support them;
- all the appellants;[5]
- their address and stating whether a representative has been appointed and his address;
- whether an interpreter is required, stating language and dialect;
- whether the appellant will be attending the hearing;
- whether the appellant will be represented at the hearing.

And additionally providing:[6]

- the notice of decision against which the appeal is brought, or an explanation as to why it is not practicable to do so;
- any statement of reasons for that decision;
- all documents not already supplied to the respondent;[7]
- an application to the Lord Chancellor to issue a certificate of fee satisfaction;
- any further documents or information required by any relevant practice direction.

The FTT has a jurisdiction to determine its own jurisdiction, and a dispute as to jurisdiction should normally be resolved via lodging an appeal to the First-tier Tribunal.[8] Whether a particular decision by a potential respondent amounts to the refusal of an asylum or human rights claim is fundamental to the FTT's jurisdiction: it may follow that a decision not to recognise further representations as a fresh claim under r 353 is to be litigated before the FTT rather than via judicial review proceedings.

1   Practice Directions, para 6.1(a).
2   First-tier Tribunal online guidance, www.justice.gov.uk/tribunals/immigration-asylum.
3   Tribunal Procedure (First-tier Tribunal) (Immigration and Asylum Chamber) Rules 2014, SI 2014/2604, r 19(1).
4   SI 2014/2604, r 19(4).
5   *AK (long-term third party support) Bangladesh* [2006] UKAIT 00069 at [15] is a salutary warning against failing to name all relevant appellants.
6   SI 2014/2604, r 19(5).
7   See Section 3, Boxes B and C of the application forms for documents being sent now and intended to be sent in the future.
8   See **6.8** and **8.90**, fn 5 below.

5.13   The relevant forms are:

- IAFT-1 for an 'in-country' appeal against an asylum or immigration decision;
- IAFT-2 for an 'out-of-country' appeal against a decision of an Entry Clearance Officer;

- IAFT-3 for an 'out-of-country' appeal against an asylum or immigration decision made by the Home Office, where the appellant has to leave the country before bringing his appeal.

The form should be signed and dated by the appellant or his representative, and if the latter alone, then the representative should certify that he has completed it in line with the appellant's instructions.[1] The forms include a section for explaining any lateness in bringing the appeal,[2] for making any statement of additional grounds,[3] and, in an asylum claim, for contending that the view of the Home Office as to credibility, country situation, internal relocation, convention reason, eligibility for Humanitarian Protection, or entitlement to remain on human rights grounds, is wrong.[4] Failure to use (or correctly complete) the appropriate form should not bar access to the FTT, and could be rectified via the power to condone irregularities.[5] Any procedural irregularity in the notice of appeal may be taken to have been waived by the respondent if no timely objection is raised to it when it is lodged.[6] An appeal that does not provide grounds of appeal might be dismissed without a hearing, absent a good reason being supplied for the failure.[7] The notice and grounds of appeal should be in English, as should any supporting documents; though in proceedings in Wales, or proceedings that have a connection there, translations may be in Welsh.[8] A person who has not heard from the FTT within three weeks (though not before) of seeking to lodge his appeal should contact the tribunal.[9] The FTT must send the notice of appeal and supporting documents to the respondent.[10] See generally **1.7** *et seq.*

1 Tribunal Procedure (First-tier Tribunal) (Immigration and Asylum Chamber) Rules 2014, SI 2014/2604, r 19(4)(b) and (c).
2 See Section 3, Box A of the application forms.
3 At the end of Section 3 (see **3.19** *et seq* above).
4 See Section 3, Box D of the application forms.
5 SI 2014/2604, r 6; Lord Woolf MR in *R v Secretary of State for the Home Department, ex parte Jeyanthan* [1999] EWCA Civ 3010*; Secretary of State for the Home Department v Ravichandran* [1999] INLR 241; Lloyd LJ also contemplated use of the slip rule to deal with deficiencies in a notice of appeal in *R v Immigration Appeal Tribunal, ex parte Secretary of State* [1990] Imm AR 166; *HH (sponsor as representative) Serbia* [2006] UKAIT 00063 at [14].
6 *HH* (above) at [16].
7 *RS and FD (appeals without grounds) Jamaica* [2006] UKAIT 00064 at [6].
8 SI 2014/2604, r 12(5) and (6).
9 First-tier Tribunal online guidance, www.justice.gov.uk/tribunals/immigration-asylum.
10 SI 2014/2604, r 19(6).

FEES

5.14   From 19 December 2011, it became necessary for appellants to the FTT to pay a fee.[1] The 2014 Rules make provision for appeals to proceed only where a fee is paid: the means by which this is assessed is by reference to a certificate of fee satisfaction issued by the Lord Chancellor.[2] At the time of writing it will cost, for each person appealing, either:

- £140 for an appeal to be determined at an oral hearing, or

- £80 for an appeal to be determined on the papers provided.[3]

1   First-tier Tribunal (Immigration and Asylum Chamber) Fees Order 2011, SI 2011/2841.
2   Tribunal Procedure (First-tier Tribunal) (Immigration and Asylum Chamber) Rules 2014, SI 2014/2604, r 1(4).
3   SI 2011/2841, r 3(3).

5.15   The following classes of appeal are exempt from fees[1] (this summary, addressed to appellants, is taken from HM Courts and Tribunals Service FTT Fees Guidance;[2] additionally no fee is payable where that is specified in arrangements between the United Kingdom and 'any foreign power'[3] and there is power to defer payment in cases arising from the Refugee Convention or Qualification Directive[4] (which are in any event very often likely to benefit from the exemption consequent to receipt of Asylum Support Funding)):

'1.   Your appeal is against a decision made under the following legislation. Please note – your Notice of Decision may contain more than one decision. If so, a fee may still be due if the decision is not one of those listed below. Please read your Notice of Decision carefully to check this:

- section 2A of the 1971 Act(1) (deprivation of right of abode);

- section 5(1) of the 1971 Act (a decision to make a deportation order);

- paragraphs 8, 9,10, 10A or 12(2) of Schedule 2 to the 1971 Act(1) (a decision that an illegal entrant, any family or seaman and aircrew is or are to be removed from the United Kingdom by way of directions);

- section 40 of the British Nationality Act 1981(1) (deprivation of citizenship);

- section 10(1) of the 1999 Act(1) (removal of certain persons unlawfully in the United Kingdom);

- section 76 of the 2002 Act (revocation of indefinite leave to enter or remain in the United Kingdom);

- section 47 of the Immigration, Asylum and Nationality Act 2006(1) (removal: persons with statutorily extended leave);

- regulation 19(3) of the Immigration (European Economic Area) Regulations 2006(1) (a decision to remove an EEA national or the family member of such a national); or

- having an appeal in the Detained Fast Track Process (see page 5 of your Notice of Decision to see if this applies to you)

2.   You are being provided with Asylum Support Funding by the UKBA under sections 95 or 98 under the Immigration and Asylum Act 1999;

3.   You are in receipt of Legal Aid (to note: from April 1st 2013 legal aid is no longer available in England and Wales for most non-asylum immigration cases); or

4.   You are the person for whose benefit services are provided by a local authority under section 17 of the Children Act 1989.'

1   First-tier Tribunal (Immigration and Asylum Chamber) Fees Order 2011, SI 2011/2841, r 5.
2   HM Courts and Tribunals Service Fees Guidance: First-tier Tribunal (Immigration and Appeals Chamber).
3   SI 2011/2841, r 5(5).
4   SI 2011/2841, r 6.

5.16   Additionally, a fee may be reduced or remitted where the Lord Chancellor is satisfied that there are exceptional circumstances which justify doing so.[1] In those classes of case where the Immigration Rules imply or require economic independence or self-sufficiency, it will be assumed that a person has the relevant means.[2] However, as the Guidance points out:

'Not all immigration appellants are subject to UKBA's requirements to maintain and accommodate themselves without recourse to public funds. The requirements do not apply, for example, to:

●   nationals of one of the countries in the European Economic Area (EEA): Austria, Belgium, Bulgaria, Cyprus, the Czech Republic, Denmark, Estonia, Finland, France, Germany, Greece, Hungary, Iceland, the Republic of Ireland, Italy, Latvia, Liechtenstein, Lithuania, Luxembourg, Malta, the Netherlands, Norway, Poland, Portugal, Romania, Slovakia, Slovenia, Spain, Sweden and the UK);

●   nationals of Switzerland;

●   members of the family of an EEA or Swiss national, whether or not the members are EEA or Swiss nationals themselves;

●   family members of those granted Refugee or Humanitarian Protection status; or

●   those making an application for discretionary leave to remain.'

In considering the necessity of exempting a fee in a case involving fundamental rights, regard should be had to the test of 'effective access to the court' set out above.[3]

1   First-tier Tribunal (Immigration and Asylum Chamber) Fees Order 2011, SI 2011/2841, r 7.
2   HM Courts and Tribunals Service Fees Guidance: First-tier Tribunal (Immigration and Appeals Chamber).
3   See **5.7**, fn 3 above; and see further the analogous fee exemption case law in relation to applications to the Home Office, eg *Carter, R (on the application of) v Secretary of State for the Home Department* [2014] EWHC 2603 (Admin); *SS, R (on the application of) v Secretary of State for the Home Department* [2011] EWHC 3390 (Admin).

Fee certificates and awards

5.17   An application for such a certificate is made with the notice of appeal,[1] and a notice of appeal may not be accepted absent its subsequent issue.[2] The fee can be paid using a payment card (credit or debit card), either when making an online appeal or by writing down the payment card details in the space provided on the appeal form.[3] Where the tribunal is notified by the Lord Chancellor that a certificate of fee satisfaction has been revoked, the appeal shall automatically be struck out, without the need for any further order, the FTT notifying the parties of this development.[4] An appeal may be reinstated on application by the appellant where the Lord Chancellor has issued a new certificate of fee satisfaction. Such application must be made in writing and received by the tribunal within 14 days, or if the appellant is outside the United Kingdom within 28 days, of the date on which the tribunal sent notification of the striking out to the appellant.[5] An appeal may be determined without a hearing where it otherwise comes to light that no certificate has been issued, regardless of the appellant's consent.[6] When allowing an appeal, the FTT may order that the respondent pays the appellant, by way of costs, an amount not greater than any fee payable under the First-tier Tribunal (Immigration and Asylum Chamber) Fees Order 2011 that has not been refunded or which the appellant is otherwise liable to pay.[7] In assessing whether a fee award is appropriate, a judge should consider:[8]

- that as a first principle, if an appellant has been obliged to appeal to establish a claim that could and should have been accepted by the decision maker, then he should be able to recover the whole fee;

- a different outcome may be appropriate if an appeal has been allowed principally because of evidence produced only at the appeal stage that could or should have been produced earlier, or if the appellant has otherwise contributed to the need for the appeal by his own action or inaction, or if he has contributed to adjournments or delayed in responding to submissions from the respondent or in responding to directions.

1   Tribunal Procedure (First-tier Tribunal) (Immigration and Asylum Chamber) Rules 2014, SI 2014/2604, r 19(5)(d).
2   SI 2014/2604, r 22(2)(b) (see **5.19**, fn 3 below).
3   HM Courts and Tribunals Service Fees Guidance: First-tier Tribunal (Immigration and Appeals Chamber), 'Method of payment'.
4   SI 2014/2604, r 7(1).
5   SI 2014/2604, r 7(2), (3).
6   SI 2014/2604, r 25(1)(b).
7   SI 2014/2604, r 9(1).
8   Joint Presidential Guidance: Fee awards in immigration appeals (December 2011), paras 5–8(a).

5.18   The judicial decision should be proportionate, taking into account all available information at the date of the hearing, and the parties should be prepared to make any submissions on fees at the hearing orally or in writing. In the absence of attendance at the hearing the parties cannot expect the judge to give a further opportunity to make submissions on fees.[1] Brief reasons should be given for a fee award decision.[2]

1   Joint Presidential Guidance: Fee awards in immigration appeals (December 2011), para 8.
2   Joint Presidential Guidance, para 9.

REJECTION OF INVALID NOTICE OF APPEAL

5.19   The FTT has specific powers to reject an invalid notice of appeal.[1] These operate where a person has given a notice of appeal to the tribunal and:

• there is no appealable decision (ie no 'decision from which there is a right of appeal to the Immigration and Asylum Chamber of the First-tier Tribunal');[2]

• the Lord Chancellor has not issued a certificate of fee satisfaction.

In these circumstances the tribunal shall decline to accept the notice of appeal, notify the person giving the notice of appeal and the respondent, and then take no further action.[3] The Practice Statements explain that in such a case the tribunal will scrutinise a notice of appeal as soon as practicable after it has been given, noting that 'First-tier rule 22 makes no provision for the issue of validity to be determined by means of a hearing or by reference to any representations of the parties';[4] where the matter reaches a hearing, validity still may be raised at that point.[5] The decision on validity, where determined without a hearing under the r 22 notice procedure, will be a procedural or preliminary decision[6] and thus any challenge by way of appeal to the Upper Tribunal will be forestalled, though where the matter is identified at a hearing, the tribunal will issue a decision to such effect (where this arises in circumstances other than under the preliminary notice procedure, a right of appeal will follow).[7]

1   Tribunal Procedure (First-tier Tribunal) (Immigration and Asylum Chamber) Rules 2014, SI 2014/2604, r 22.
2   SI 2014/2604, rr 22(2)(a) and 1(4).
3   SI 2014/2604, r 22(3).
4   Practice Statements, paras 3.1–3.2.
5   Practice Statements, para 3.4.
6   Practice Statements, para 3.3; *BO (extension of time for appealing) Nigeria* [2006] UKAIT 00035 at [7].
7   See **6.5** *et seq* below.

SERVICE OF NOTICE OF DECISIONS OF THE SSHD

5.20   Although (as the next paragraph discusses) the calculation of time for appealing runs from the date on which decisions are sent rather than from any deemed date of service, it is nevertheless relevant to be aware of the provisions as to service because sometimes the necessity for making an application for extension of time for appealing can only be determined by reference to when a document was deemed served. The Notice Regulations[1] (which apply only to appealable immigration decisions)[2] address out-of-country service, though do not address service within the United Kingdom. Where notice is sent by post to a place outside the United Kingdom to an address provided by its subject or his representative or, absent such address, his last-known or usual place of abode or place of business, it shall be deemed to have been received on the 28th day after it was posted (excluding the day of posting), unless the contrary is proved.[3] However there is no deeming provision for in-country cases under the Regulations since the repeal (on 5 November 2014)[4] of the provision, which, hitherto, deemed service on the second day after posting. Whilst it might be thought that the Interpretation Act 1978 would plug the gap as to provisions for service, it does so only with respect to statutes that authorise postal service, and the Immigration Act 1971 has so far been read as not doing so.[5]

1   Immigration (Notices) Regulations 2003, SI 2003/658.
2   *Syed (curtailment of leave – notice) India* [2013] UKUT 144 (IAC), headnote at (1).
3   SI 2003/658, reg 7(1)(c), (4) and (5).
4   Immigration (Notices) (Amendment) Regulations 2014, SI 2014/2768, reg 2(6)(a).
5   *Syed* (above) at [26] and [27].

5.21   The notice shall be deemed to have been given when the decision maker records the following circumstances and places the notice on the relevant file:[1]

- where a person's whereabouts are unknown, and no address has been provided for correspondence and the decision maker does not know the last-known or usual place of abode or place of business of the person; or

- the address provided to the decision maker is defective, false or no longer in use by the person; and

- no representative appears to be acting for the person.

1   Immigration (Notices) Regulations 2003, SI 2003/658, reg 7(2).

5.22   If the person is subsequently located, then he is to be given the notice of decision as soon as practicable, and the time limit for appeal is to be calculated from the deemed service on the file.[1] However, this provision of the Notice Regulations must be read alongside *Anufrijeva*, where Lord Steyn stated:[2]

'Notice of a decision is required before it can have the character of a determination with legal effect because the individual concerned must be in a position to challenge the decision in the courts if he or she wishes to do so. This is not a technical rule. It is simply an application of the right of access to justice.'

1   Immigration (Notices) Regulations 2003, SI 2003/658, reg 7(3).
2   *Anufrijeva, R (on the application of) v Secretary of State for the Home Department* [2003] UKHL 36.

5.23   Where a notice of decision does not comply with the Notices Regulations, time for appealing against the decision does not begin to run against its subject; but, if he does enter a notice of appeal, he may be taken to have waived any such procedural defect, and subsequently the notice of decision may be treated as a valid basis for appeal.[1] We address the relevant authorities on deemed service and the calculation of time further in Chapter 6, and below where we deal with service, notices and addresses.[2]

1   *LO (partner of EEA national) Nigeria* [2009] UKAIT 00034 at [12].
2   See **6.13** *et seq* and **5.36**.

5.24   This chapter addresses appealable immigration decisions, however in passing it is noteworthy that, regarding non-appealable decisions, the 1971 Act, s 4(1) provides that decision-making powers 'shall be exercised by notice in writing given to the person affected', and thus that the SSHD has to be able to prove that notice of such a decision was communicated to the person concerned, in order for it to be effective.[1]

1   *Syed (curtailment of leave – notice) India* [2013] UKUT 144 (IAC).

TIME LIMIT FOR GIVING NOTICE OF APPEAL

5.25   The time limit for lodging notice of appeal for 'in-country' appellants is calculated from the date that the notice of the decision against which the appeal is brought is sent (there are no deeming provisions as to its receipt):[1]

- 14 days (whether or not the person is detained, subject to being in the Detained Fast Track process).[2]

1   Presidential Guidance Note No 1 of 2014, para 4.
2   Tribunal Procedure (First-tier Tribunal) (Immigration and Asylum Chamber) Rules 2014, SI 2014/2604, r 19(2).

5.26   The time limit for 'out-of-country' appellants is calculated from specific events:

- for 'out-of-country' appellants who were in the United Kingdom when the decision was made and may not appeal because of the non-suspensive appeals provisions of NIAA 2002, 28 days from their departure from the United Kingdom;[1]

- for other 'out-of-country' appellants, not later than 28 days after they receive notice of the decision.[2]

1   Tribunal Procedure (First-tier Tribunal) (Immigration and Asylum Chamber) Rules 2014,
     SI 2014/2604, r 19(3)(a).
2   SI 2014/2604, r 19(3)(b).

5.27   There is no longer any specific provision governing the timing of an appeal for asylum seekers whose asylum claim is rejected but who receive a form of limited leave greater than one year: in a saved provisions case, it might be presumed that time will run from the receipt of the notice of the grant of leave that causes their leave to exceed a period of one year, alone or in aggregate;[1] in new-style appeals under the relevant provisions of NIAA 2002, time will run from notification of the decision rejecting the asylum claim. It is undesirable to require appellants to have to perform complex calculations as to the deadline by reference to the Notice Regulations and the 2014 Rules if they are not provided with copies of them.[2]

1   NIAA 2002, s 83 (see **3.40** above)
2   *OI (notice of decision: time calculations) Nigeria* [2006] UKAIT 00042 at [17].

EXTENSION OF TIME FOR LODGING NOTICE OF APPEAL

5.28   Late appeals are governed by a particular procedure, set out in r 20. If a notice of appeal is given outside the applicable time limit, it must include a reasoned application for an extension of time,[1] accompanied by supporting evidence:[2] absent some explanation, time is likely to be extended only if there are obvious and quite exceptional reasons for so doing.[3] If a notice of appeal appears to the tribunal to have been given outside the applicable time limit but does not include an extension application[4] (unless minded to extend time of its own initiative, as where a disruption of the postal services is known to have occurred)[5] it must notify the person giving notice of appeal in writing that it proposes to treat the notice of appeal as being out of time, and the appellant may file written evidence supporting a contention either that the notice of appeal was given in time, or that an extension of time is appropriate.[6] Such matters are to be determined as a preliminary issue, and the FTT may do so without a hearing.[7] Written notice with reasons must be given under this rule.[8] The FTT will need to consider the case for an extension of time against the overriding objective.[9] Assertions of fact by the appellant, including as to the date of service, made in the appeal form may well be unchallengeable if the respondent has failed to provide adequate information to the contrary.[10]

1   Tribunal Procedure (First-tier Tribunal) (Immigration and Asylum Chamber) Rules 2014,
     SI 2014/2604, r 20(1).
2   *BO (extension of time for appealing) Nigeria* [2006] UKAIT 00035 at [19].
3   *BO* (above) at [14].
4   SI 2014/2604, r 20(2).
5   As was formerly expressly mentioned as a possibility, in Consolidated Practice Direction 4.4.
6   SI 2014/2604, r 20(3).

7   SI 2014/2604, r 20(4).
8   SI 2014/2604, r 20(5).
9   See **5.3** *et seq* above.
10   *OI (notice of decision: time calculations) Nigeria* [2006] UKAIT 00042 at [17].

Relevant considerations in extending time

5.29   Relevant considerations in granting an extension include:

- error of a representative;[1]

- the merits of the grounds[2] albeit that this should not be determinative;[3]

- loss of an 'in-country' right of appeal;[4]

- the length of delay and the explanation for it: 'there is no difference in principle between a long delay and a short delay ... an explanation that is adequate cannot be rendered less so by the length of the delay';[5]

- an error by the respondent that has misled or disadvantaged the appellant[6] or conduct by the respondent such as a lengthy delay in himself sending papers to the tribunal;[7]

- the availability of legal representation where a person is detained.[8]

Lack of prejudice to the respondent is of no particular importance in an individual case.[9]

1   *BO (extension of time for appealing) Nigeria* [2006] UKAIT 00035 at [16]–[18].
2   The Court of Appeal in *Mehta* [1976] Imm AR 38; *BO* (above) at [21](i).
3   *SV (alleging misconduct and suppressing evidence) Iran* [2005] UKAIT 00160 at [10]; *BO* (above) at [13].
4   *BO* (above) at [21](ii).
5   *BO* (above) at [21](iii).
6   *BO* (above) at [21](v).
7   *BO* (above) at [42].
8   Brooke LJ in *ID* [2005] EWCA Civ 38 at [49]–[52].
9   *BO* (above) at [21](iv).

EXTENSION OF TIME IN 'IMMINENT REMOVAL' CASES

5.30   There is a special process for 'imminent removal' cases,[1] which applies in any case in which the respondent notifies the tribunal that removal directions have been issued against a person who has given notice of appeal, pursuant to which it is proposed to remove him from the United Kingdom within five calendar days of the date on which the notice of appeal was given.[2] In these cases the tribunal must, if reasonably practicable, make any preliminary decision as to extension of time under r 20 before the moment of removal.[3] Under this process the r 20 procedure (set out in **5.28** above) may be modified such that the tribunal may give notification orally, which may include notifying the appellant of an intention to treat it as out of time by telephone,[4] shortening the time for giving evidence and directing that any evidence showing the appeal was timely or that there are special circumstances justifying an extension of time be given orally, which may include requiring the evidence to be given by telephone, and holding a hearing or 'telephone hearing' for the purpose of receiving such evidence.[5] A decision may be made by one First-tier judge approved for such a role.[6]

1   Tribunal Procedure (First-tier Tribunal) (Immigration and Asylum Chamber) Rules 2014, SI 2014/2604, r 21.
2   SI 2014/2604, r 21(1).
3   SI 2014/2604, r 21(2).
4   SI 2014/2604, r 21(3)(a).
5   SI 2014/2604, r 21(3)(c).
6   Practice Statements, para 2.1(2).

VARIATION OF GROUNDS OF APPEAL

5.31   The grounds of appeal may be varied with the permission of the FTT.[1] The Case Management Review hearing provides an obvious opportunity for the grounds of appeal to be amended and indeed there is an obligation, where there is such a hearing, to particularise any application to amend the grounds or the reasons in support of the grounds.[2]

1   Tribunal Procedure (First-tier Tribunal) (Immigration and Asylum Chamber) Rules 2014, SI 2014/2604, r 19(1).
2   Practice Directions, para 7.3(a)–(b).

RESPONDENT'S DUTIES TO SEND DOCUMENTS TO THE TRIBUNAL; REFUSAL LETTERS AND THEIR VARIATION

5.32   When the respondent is served with a copy of a notice of appeal, he must file a response, which has differing requirements depending on whether or not the appeal is against refusal of entry clearance or family permit. In all cases, the respondent should provide:

- a copy of the notice of the decision to which the notice of appeal relates[1] and any other document served on the appellant giving reasons for that decision;

- any statement of evidence (for asylum cases) or application form completed by the appellant;[2]

- any record of an interview with the appellant, in relation to the decision being appealed;[3]

- any other unpublished document which is referred to in the notice of decision or its written reasons;[4] and

- notice of any other immigration decision made in relation to the appellant in respect of which he has a right of appeal.[5]

1 Tribunal Procedure (First-tier Tribunal) (Immigration and Asylum Chamber) Rules 2014, SI 2014/2604, rr 23(1)(a) and 24(1)(a).
2 SI 2014/2604, rr 23(1)(c) and 24(1)(b).
3 SI 2014/2604, rr 23(1)(d) and 24(1)(c).
4 SI 2014/2604, rr 23(1)(e) and 24(1)(d).
5 SI 2014/2604, rr 23(1)(f) and 24(1)(e).

5.33 A failure to provide such material should meet with a robust response from the immigration judiciary:[1]

'Where the Visa Officer has not provided the documents that he is required to provide, it is open to the First-tier Judge to issue directions that if such documents are not provided within a prompt timetable the appeal will be decided on the basis that the Visa Officer no longer opposes the appeal or supports any contention that he makes in the decision letter. The appeal can then be decided on the papers, and in the absence of evidence of some mandatory ground for refusal it is likely that the appeal will succeed.'

1 *Cvetkovs (visa – no file produced – directions) Latvia* [2011] UKUT 212 (IAC) at [10] and [11].

5.34 In entry clearance and family permit cases, additionally the respondent should provide:

- a statement of whether the respondent opposes the appellant's case, and the grounds for such opposition.[1]

In all other appeals, he should additionally provide:

- if he is intending to change or add to the grounds or reasons for refusal, a statement of whether he opposes the appellant's case and the grounds of such opposition.[2]

1 Tribunal Procedure (First-tier Tribunal) (Immigration and Asylum Chamber) Rules 2014, SI 2014/2604, r 23(1)(b).
2 SI 2014/2604, r 23(1)(c).

5.35 These documents and any statement of opposition to the appellant's case must be provided to the FTT and other parties within 28 days of receipt of the notice of appeal and supporting documents from the FTT.[1] It is important to appreciate that the power to vary the refusal letter is itself subject to the FTT's general case management powers 'to permit or require a party to amend a document'.[2] Aside from this procedural constraint, as a matter of natural justice any variation of the notice of decision must be given with sufficient notice to the appellant to avoid his being disadvantaged.[3]

1   Tribunal Procedure (First-tier Tribunal) (Immigration and Asylum Chamber) Rules 2014,
     SI 2014/2604, rr 23(3) and 24(3).
2   SI 2014/2604, r 4(3)(c).
3   See Woolf J (as he then was) in *R v Immigration Appeal Tribunal, ex parte Hubbard* [1985]
     Imm AR 110.

SERVICE, NOTICES AND ADDRESSES

5.36   Any document that is required or permitted under the Rules or the
tribunal's directions to be provided to the tribunal or any other person may be:

- delivered, or sent by post, to an address;

- sent via a document exchange to a document exchange number or
  address;

- sent by fax to a fax number;

- sent by e-mail to an e-mail address;

- sent or delivered by any other method identified for that purpose by the
  tribunal or recipient;[1]

- left with an individual, where a document is to be provided to him.[2]

1   Tribunal Procedure (First-tier Tribunal) (Immigration and Asylum Chamber) Rules 2014,
     SI 2014/2604, r 12(1).
2   SI 2014/2604, r 12(3).

5.37   If the respondent believes that an address specified for the provision
of documents to the appellant is not appropriate for that purpose, he must
notify the tribunal in writing of this and, if aware of it, provide an appropriate
address.[1] A document provided to a person who has notified the tribunal that he
is acting as a party's representative shall be deemed to have been provided to
that party[2] (and from the time he comes on the record, a copy of any document
provided to the appellant must be provided to him).[3] Service of notices of
immigration decisions is governed by the Notices Regulations (which we
address above)[4] with which the SSHD and Entry Clearance Officers must
comply: the requirements of service by post need to be followed for service
by post to be effective;[5] and the deemed times in those Regulations are of
importance in calculating the time for appealing.[6]

1   Tribunal Procedure (First-tier Tribunal) (Immigration and Asylum Chamber) Rules 2014,
     SI 2014/2604 r 12(3).
2   SI 2014/2604 r 12(4).
3   SI 2014/2604 r 10(6).
4   See **5.20** above.
5   Immigration (Notices) Regulations 2003, SI 2003/658 (see **5.20**, fn 3 above).
6   *OI (notice of decision: time calculations) Nigeria* [2006] UKAIT 00042, headnote.

PART 3 – THE HEARING

PREPARATION FOR THE HEARING

5.38   The standard judicial directions make it clear that cases should be properly prepared well in advance of the hearing. Care should be taken in the production of a witness statement, a prerequisite of proper presentation of an appeal in the modern era.[1] The tribunal has explained that the proper procedure when taking a statement in a language other than English is for a competent interpreter, in the correct language and dialect, to read back the statement and for the maker of the statement then to sign it, confirming that such a process has been undertaken. The interpreter should then add a paragraph confirming that he has read back the contents of the document to the witness in the witness's own language. That paragraph should then be signed and dated by the interpreter, whose name should be given.[2]

1   Practice Directions, para 7(5)(a)(1).
2   *Njehia* (16523, 14 May 1999).

NOTICE OF HEARING; APPEALS WITHOUT HEARINGS

5.39   When the tribunal fixes a hearing it must serve notice of the time and place of the hearing on every party, for both the original hearing and for any variation thereof.[1] A hearing is required before making a decision which disposes of proceedings, unless the appeal is being determined without a hearing as:

- in the cases of lapse, withdrawal, abandonment, or certification;[2]

- where the parties consent;[3]

- where the Lord Chancellor has refused to issue a certificate of fee satisfaction;[4]

- where the appellant is outside the United Kingdom and does not have a representative with an address for service in this country;[5]

- where it is impracticable to give the appellant notice of hearing;[6]

- where a party has failed to comply with the Rules, a Practice Direction or direction, and the FTT is satisfied in all the circumstances that, including the extent of the failure and the reasons for it, that this is appropriate;[7]

- where the tribunal considers that it is in the interests of justice.[8]

1   Tribunal Procedure (First-tier Tribunal) (Immigration and Asylum Chamber) Rules 2014, SI 2014/2604, r 26.

2   SI 2014/2604, rr 16(1) and (2), 18 and 25(1)(f).
3   SI 2014/2604, r 25(1)(a).
4   SI 2014/2604, r 25(1)(b).
5   SI 2014/2604, r 25(1)(c).
6   SI 2014/2604, r 25(1)(d).
7   SI 2014/2604, r 25(1)(e).
8   SI 2014/2604, r 25(1)(g).

5.40   The FTT must not decide an appeal without a hearing without first giving the parties notice of its intention to do so and an opportunity to make written representations as to whether there should be a hearing.[1] The decision to proceed without a hearing needs to be justified on a reasoned basis, and doubtless more reasoning will be required where there is a greater degree of judgment or assessment involved[2] (as was said of a predecessor rule, 'the decision-maker must first identify the procedural failures ... and form a view of their causes, their persistence and their gravity'[3] – bearing in mind that it is the date of consideration of the substance of the case which is the relevant one, by which time there may be more material available than that originally on file when the appeal was identified for determination without a hearing).[4] If the appeal cannot properly or justly be determined on the basis of the documents on file, no judge should regard themselves as forced to proceed without a hearing.[5] Liaison with the representatives is not a prerequisite of proper listing; indeed, the date of the hearing may be brought forward, so long as no lack of notice to the appellant results,[6] bearing in mind that justice demands that an opportunity to present one's case extends to preparing it, too.[7]

1   Tribunal Procedure (First-tier Tribunal) (Immigration and Asylum Chamber) Rules 2014, SI 2014/2604, r 25(2).
2   *OE and NK (no hearing, compliance with rules) Nigeria* [2006] UKAIT 00055 at [12]–[14].
3   Sedley LJ in *Benkaddouri v Secretary of State for the Home Department* [2003] EWCA Civ 1250 at [13].
4   *JZ (procedure – adjudicators – no hearing) Ivory Coast* [2004] 00102 at [14].
5   *OE and NK* (above) at [12].
6   Richards J in *R v Immigration Appeal Tribunal, ex parte Shandar* [2000] Imm AR 181.
7   Lord Widgery CJ in *R v Thames Magistrates' Court, ex parte Polemis* [1974] 2 All ER 1219 at 1223.

PARTIES TO THE APPEAL

5.41   The parties to an appeal will no doubt in most cases be the appellant and the respondent. The FTT may make a direction adding a person to the proceedings as respondent (or substituting a person, because of a change of circumstances or the naming of the wrong person as respondent).[1] The United Nations High Commissioner for Refugees (UNHCR) may give notice, in an asylum appeal, of its wish to be treated as a party and having done so it will duly become one.[2] Other agencies may apply to intervene:[3] whether an intervention should be countenanced is usually dependent upon the court's judgment as to whether the interests of justice will be promoted by allowing the intervention, the extent to which the court will be assisted in performing the role upon which it is engaged, balancing the benefits which are to be derived from the intervention as against the inconvenience, delay and expense which an intervention by a third person can cause to the existing parties.[4] The FTT may give consequential directions following the involvement of the UNHCR or a new respondent.[5] In the First-tier Tribunal, the appellant is the party who has given notice of appeal against an immigration decision, whereas the respondent is the administrative decision maker;[6] this is to be contrasted with the UT where the appellant is the person who has brought the application or appeal (unless the matter has been transferred or referred to it, in which case it is the person who initiated proceedings below).[7]

1 Tribunal Procedure (First-tier Tribunal) (Immigration and Asylum Chamber) Rules 2014, SI 2014/2604, r 8(2), (1).
2 SI 2014/2604, r 8(3).
3 Liberty made written submissions in the case of *Kacaj* (01/TH/00634, 19 July 2001). The Court of Appeal in *Krayem v Secretary of State for the Home Department* [2003] EWCA Civ 649 noted the possibility that the United Nations Relief and Works Agency for Palestinian refugees (UNRWA) *might* wish to give evidence.
4 Lord Woolf in *Northern Ireland Human Rights Commission, In Re* [2002] UKHL 25 at [32].
5 SI 2014/2604, r 8(4).
6 SI 2014/2604, r 1(4).
7 Tribunal Procedure (Upper Tribunal) Rules 2008, SI 2008/2698, r 1.

PRELIMINARY ISSUES

5.42   There is no distinct procedure set out in the Rules for the determination of issues on this basis, though it remains the case that one of the specific forms of directions that may be given in an appeal is to permit 'a particular matter to be dealt with as a preliminary issue';[1] issues of late notice of appeal are normally to be dealt with as a preliminary issue without a hearing.[2] Whether the substantive appeal will be determined immediately following resolution of the preliminary issue is a matter as to which the Rules are silent, although their general policy of avoiding delay where that is compatible with proper consideration of the issues may point to such a course;[3] then again, the expenditure of resources on all sides spent preparing the substance of a case in which the appellant fails, for example, to establish a right of appeal may be thought disproportionate,[4] suggesting that there may be occasional call for a two-stage process. A tribunal faced with a challenge to a 'preliminary issue' ruling made earlier in the case is not bound by the earlier decision, for all that public policy suggests matters should not be lightly reopened:[5]

'Essentially some deference is due to the decision reached by the previous adjudicator. The start-point should be that the decision reached by the previous adjudicator was based on the evidence and should not be re-opened unless there is cogent evidence – which will normally have to be served in accordance with IAA directions – pointing in a contrary direction.'

1   Tribunal Procedure (First-tier Tribunal) (Immigration and Asylum Chamber) Rules 2014,
    SI 2014/2604, r 4(3)(e).
2   SI 2014/2604, r 20(4); the Fast Track Rules, r 5(4) (see **5.3** *et seq* above and **5.162** below).
3   SI 2014/2604, r 2(e) (see **5.28** above).
4   SI 2014/2604, r 2(a).
5   *YL (nationality, statelessness, Eritrea, Ethiopia) Eritrea CG* [2003] UKIAT 16 at [27] *et seq*,
    cited passage at [29].

CASE MANAGEMENT REVIEW HEARINGS

5.43   Case Management Review (CMR) hearings are to be held where the
tribunal so directs where the appellant is present in the United Kingdom with
an 'in-country' right of appeal.[1] It is now standard for hearing notices to warn
of the possibility of substantive determination of the appeal in the appellant's
absence for want of diligence in prosecuting the appeal, as do the Practice
Directions:

> 'It is important that the parties and their representatives understand that a
> CMR hearing or similar first hearing is a hearing in the appeal and that the
> appeal may be determined under the relevant Procedure Rules if a party
> does not appear and is not represented at that hearing.'[2]

1   Practice Directions, para 7.
2   Practice Directions, para 7.2.

5.44   At these hearings appellants are to provide particulars of any
application for permission to vary the grounds of appeal, particulars of any
amendments to the reasons in support of the grounds of appeal, particulars of
any witnesses to be called or whose written statement or report is proposed
to be relied upon at the full hearing; and a draft of any directions that the
appellant is requesting the tribunal to make.[1] The respondent's duties are to
provide the tribunal and the appellant with any amendment that has been made
or that is proposed to be made to the notice of decision to which the appeal
relates or to any other document served on the appellant giving reasons for
that decision, and a draft of any directions that the respondent is requesting
the tribunal to make at the CMR hearing.[2] Some CMRs may be conducted by
telephone.[3] At the end of the CMR hearing the tribunal will give to the parties
any further written directions relating to the conduct of the appeal,[4] aside from
the standard ones, which are as follows:[5]

> '(a)   not later than 5 working days before the full hearing (or 10 days in
>   the case of an out-of-country appeal) the appellant shall serve on the
>   Tribunal and the respondent:
>
>   (i)   witness statements of the evidence to be called at the hearing,
>   such statements to stand as evidence in chief at the hearing;
>
>   (ii)   a paginated and indexed bundle of all the documents to be
>   relied on at the hearing with a schedule identifying the essential
>   passages;

(iii) a skeleton argument, identifying all relevant issues including human rights claims and citing all the authorities relied upon; and

(iv) a chronology of events;

(b) not later than 5 working days before the full hearing, the respondent shall serve on the Tribunal and the appellant a paginated and indexed bundle of all the documents to be relied upon at the hearing, with a schedule identifying the relevant passages, and a list of any authorities relied upon.'

1   Practice Directions, para 7.3.
2   Practice Directions, para 7.4.
3   See eg the material headed 'Case management review by telephone' in the Secretary of State's Guidance, 'Appeal hearings' (version 7.0, valid from 20 January 2014).
4   Practice Directions, para 7.6.
5   Practice Directions, para 7.5.

5.45 At the end of the CMR the tribunal will give to the parties written confirmation of any agreed issues or concessions.[1] CMRs offer constructive possibilities to representatives to agree facts prior to the substantive appeal, and are consistent with the tribunal's wish for early clarification of the SSHD's approach to the facts on an appeal:[2] the Home Office's representative should have the power to concede an issue, and indeed the old Consolidated Practice Directions for the Asylum and Immigration Tribunal proceeded on the understanding that 'the presenting officer should have the power to concede particular points where appropriate, such as age, nationality, or ethnicity'.[3] Other relevant considerations that may arise are:

● whether there is any relevant reported case law, particularly any relevant country guideline case, that should be drawn to the party's attention;

● whether any of the appellant's family members has an appeal hearing (in which case it is desirable to see a copy of the determination thereof so that the FTT is aware of the findings therein);

● whether there are any children that might be attending the full hearing for whom special arrangements need be made; and

● whether any issues arise regarding unaccompanied minors, vulnerable witnesses or the possible need for a male or female judge.

1   Practice Directions, para 7.8.
2   See *Carcabuk and Bla* (00/TH/01426, 18 May 2000) at [12](1).
3   Guidance Note 10, para 23: 'Be very aware of what you say and do not make any concessions or withdrawals without – where practical – prior permission from SCW or your TM.' See http://freemovement.files.wordpress.com/2008/12/presenting-officer-induction-course-day-one-v2.pdf.

ADJOURNMENT

5.46   The FTT has a power to adjourn proceedings, now found within the general case management powers rather than warranting an express rule in its own right:

'(3)   In particular, and without restricting the general powers in paragraphs (1) and (2), the Tribunal may–

...

(h)   adjourn or postpone a hearing;'[1]

---

1   Tribunal Procedure (First-tier Tribunal) (Immigration and Asylum Chamber) Rules 2014, SI 2014/2604, r 4(3)(h).

5.47   There is no longer a rule to the effect that that adjournment should be granted only where the tribunal is satisfied that 'the appeal or application cannot otherwise be justly determined',[1] and it remains to be seen whether the new overriding objective will modify the philosophy that has long animated the FTT, which is that 'adjournments should be sparingly granted'.[2] Whilst the rules no longer contain these express requirements,[3] it is nevertheless advisable to:

- if practicable, notify all other parties of the application;

- show good reason why an adjournment is necessary (the application 'must be supported by full reasons');[4]

- produce evidence of any fact or matter relied on in support of the application.

Following an adjournment, the tribunal will fix a new hearing date and notify the parties thereof.[5]

---

1   Asylum and Immigration Tribunal (Procedure) Rules 2005, SI 2005/230, r 21(2).
2   *Rajan* (01/TH/00244, 8 February 2001, starred). Or as Collins J put it in *Tatar* (00/TH/01914, 26 July 2000): 'The whole tenor of our rules is that we should get on with it'; see further Sir Christopher Staughton refusing permission on a renewed application for judicial review in *R v Secretary of State for the Home Department, ex parte Patel* (LTA 97/7243 CMS4, 19 February 1998), repeating his own words in *R v Immigration Appeal Tribunal, ex parte Adrees* (FC3 95/5564/D) – see Charles J in the Administrative Court in *R (Bosombanguwa) v Secretary of State for the Home Department and Immigration Appeal Tribunal* [2004] EWHC 1656 (Admin) at [50] for comment on the general public interest in the expeditious and fair disposal of applications for asylum and thus of appeals relating thereto, the overriding objective of the Rules aside; see further Latham J in *R v Secretary of State for the Home Department, ex parte Janneh* [1997] IAR 154.
3   Found within SI 2005/230, r 21(1).
4   Practice Directions, para 9.3 – see Moses J in the High Court in *R v Special Adjudicator, ex parte Demeter* (CO/3483/98, 20 March 2000) criticising an unreasoned grant of an adjournment, made in the absence of a Presenting Officer but absent any application from the Home Office.
5   Tribunal Procedure (First-tier Tribunal) (Immigration and Asylum Chamber) Rules 2014, SI 2014/2604, r 26.

Practicalities of adjournment applications

5.48 Applications for adjournment of appeals must be made not later than 4pm one clear working day before the date of hearing.[1] Late applications must be made at the hearing itself absent the most exceptional circumstances.[2] No assumption should be made that an application will be granted absent appropriate confirmation from the tribunal; a party who fails to attend a hearing always risks its determination in his absence.[3] Where an adjournment is granted at a hearing, the relevant adjournment forms will be filled out to ensure that appropriate notice of the next hearing is given,[4] consideration being given to any necessary further directions[5] An adjournment refusal should be addressed in the subsequent decision and reasons.[6] Adjournment decisions may be challenged on grounds of public law error or lack of fairness.[7]

1   Practice Directions, para 9.1 read with Presidential Guidance Note No 1 of 2014, para 11.
2   Practice Directions, paras 9.4 and 9.5.
3   Practice Directions, para 9.6.
4   Presidential Guidance Note No 1 of 2014, para 12.
5   Presidential Guidance Note No 1 of 2014, para 13.
6   Presidential Guidance Note No 1 of 2014, para 14.
7   *Nwaigwe (adjournment: fairness)* [2014] UKUT 00418 (IAC), headnote.

Adjournments: Presidential and other guidance

5.49 Presidential Guidance Note No 1 of 2014 addresses adjournments in some detail. Relevant considerations in favour of adjournment, even at a late stage in proceedings, include:

- sudden illness or other compelling reason preventing a party or a witness attending a hearing ('Somebody who is too sick to go to work is not likely to be fit enough to attend a judicial hearing at which he is expected to give a detailed account of himself'[1] though 'The court is not obliged to accept any excuse proffered, however unconvincing it may be.'[2]);

- late changes to the grounds of appeal or the reasons for refusal which change the nature of the case;

- where further time is needed because of a delay in obtaining evidence which is outside the party's control, for example where an expert witness fails to provide a report within the period expected.

1   Sedley J in *R v Secretary of State for the Home Department, ex parte Adumy* (CO/1241/97, 16 June 1998).
2   Henry LJ refusing permission on a renewed application for judicial review in *R v Secretary of State for the Home Department, ex parte Patel* (LTA 97/7243 CMS4, 19 February 1998), citing Bingham LJ in *R v Bolton Magistrates' Court, ex parte Merna* [1991] Crim LR 848.

5.50 The following factors, where relevant, may weigh against the granting of an adjournment, where:

- the application to adjourn is not made at the earliest opportunity;

- the application is speculative, such as, for example, a request for time for lodging further evidence where there is no reasonable basis to presume that such evidence exists or could be produced within a reasonable period;

- the application does not show that anything material would be achieved by the delay, for example where an appellant wants more time to instruct a legal representative but there is no evidence that funds or legal aid are available;

- the application does not explain how the reason for seeking an adjournment is material to the case, for example where there is a desire to seek further evidence but this evidence does not appear to be material to the issues to be decided;

- the application seeks more time to prepare the appeal when adequate time has already been given. In such circumstances, the tribunal may take into consideration a failure to comply with directions. However, a failure to comply with directions will not be sufficient of itself to refuse an adjournment.

5.51 In times past the tribunal has recommended the considerations raised in the *Martin* case as being relevant, so they bear repetition:[1]

'1.   The importance of the proceedings and their likely consequences to the party seeking the adjournment.[2]

2.   The risk of the party being prejudiced in the conduct of the proceedings if the application were refused.

3.   The risk of prejudice or other disadvantage to the other party if the adjournment were granted.

4.   The convenience of the court.

5.   The interests of justice generally in the efficient dispatch of court business.

6.   The desirability of not delaying future litigants by adjourning early and thus leaving the court empty.

7.   The extent to which the party applying for the adjournment had been responsible for creating the difficulty which had led to the application.'

1   Simon Brown LJ in the Divisional Court in *R v Kingston-upon-Thames Magistrates, ex parte Martin* [1994] Imm AR 172, cited eg in *Mulumba* (14760, 24 March 1997).
2   See eg Silber J in the Administrative Court in *R v Special Adjudicator, ex parte Fana* [2002] EWHC 777 (Admin) at [27], therein equating human rights appeals with asylum ones.

5.52 The FTT will have regard to its own expertise when considering whether an adjournment should be granted.[1] Where an application is refused, it would be prudent to improve upon the supporting material before renewing it.[2] An adjournment should not be granted merely because a representative threatens to withdraw from proceedings if it is refused.[3] Where a case is part-heard, any relisting should take account of the dangers in permitting the period that elapses between the original taking of oral evidence and the final decision to become so great as to raise doubts as to the judge's ability to recollect the hearing clearly.[4] Where an adjournment is refused because an expert report is not yet available, consideration should be given to whether that report should nevertheless be admitted if it is received after the hearing and before the decision is made.[5] It would be advisable to carefully consider whether an adjournment should be granted because the respondent has not complied with directions to complete verification enquiries.[6] An opportunity should be given for witnesses to support an appeal:[7]

'It is fundamental that the parties should be allowed to answer adverse material by evidence as well as argument'[8]

1   Presidential Guidance Note No 1 of 2014, para 7, citing Tribunal Procedure (First-tier Tribunal) (Immigration and Asylum Chamber) Rules 2014, SI 2014/2604, r 2(2)(d).
2   Sullivan J in *Ex parte Singh* (3 February 1998) (cited by the tribunal in *Nazir* (19753, 7 January 1999)).
3   *AD (fresh evidence) Algeria* [2004] UKIAT 00155.
4   See **6.113**.
5   Silber J in *R v Special Adjudicator, ex parte Fana* [2002] EWHC 777 (Admin) at [21].
6   Scott Baker LJ in the Court of Appeal in *Pant v Secretary of State for the Home Department* [2003] EWCA Civ 1964 at [29].
7   *AS (Pakistan) v Secretary of State for the Home Department* [2007] EWCA Civ 703.
8   Moses LJ in *SH (Afghanistan) v Secretary of State for the Home Department* [2011] EWCA Civ 1284 at [8], citing *In Re D* [1996] AC 593 at 603.

Adjournments for consolidation of the appeals of family members and for other reasons; stay of appeals

5.53   One of the more frequently encountered circumstances in which adjournments are sought is where there are outstanding applications for asylum involving family members. Adjournment for consolidation of proceedings may be appropriate, although it it is not always essential (*Rajan* shows that adjournments are not compelled by the fact that there were concurrent applications by relatives which were at different stages of the process[1] – the relevance of a relative's asylum claim is borne out by the fact that membership of a person's family is one of the grounds for citation of an unreported determination;[2] separate determination has been described as 'undesirable' by the Court of Appeal).[3] Under its case management powers,[4] the tribunal may–

'(b)   consolidate or hear together two or more sets of proceedings or parts of proceedings raising common issues;'

1   *Rajan* (01/TH/00244, 8 February 2001, starred), referencing Ognall J's decision in *Ex parte Kimbesa* (unreported, 29 January 1997).

2   Practice Directions, para 11.1(a).
3   Sedley LJ in *MJ (Iran) v Secretary of State for the Home Department* [2008] EWCA Civ 564 at [15].
4   Tribunal Procedure (First-tier Tribunal) (Immigration and Asylum Chamber) Rules 2014, SI 2014/2604, r 4(3)(b).

5.54   It will be relevant to consider whether the cases are so factually intertwined as to be best heard together, whether hearing the cases individually risks the chance of inconsistency in their determination that would be contrary to the interests of justice,[1] and whether it would be unfair to expect a person recently arrived in the United Kingdom to have 'his account tested in an appeal hearing before being interviewed on his claim or having an opportunity to present it in a non-adversarial and non-intimidatory setting'.[2] Where cases are legally aided:

'There is ... an obligation on solicitors whose clients have the benefit of Legal Aid to have due regard to economy ... where ... members of the same family arrive in the United Kingdom together, the representatives of such claimants should notify the Tribunal of their related outstanding appeals and request that they be heard together.'[3]

1   Forbes J in the Administrative Court in *R v Secretary of State for the Home Department, ex parte Kallova* [2001] EWHC Admin 1137 at [4].
2   Munby J in *Dirisu, R (on the application of) v Immigration Appeal Tribunal* [2001] EWHC Admin 970 at [34], citing *Kimbesa* (above).
3   Lord Hardie in *DBNBK (Ap) v Secretary of State for the Home Department* [2009] ScotCS CSIH_83 at [12].

5.55   Another scenario is where a relevant decision is anticipated from the higher courts or senior immigration judiciary. There is no general obligation to adjourn proceedings[1] (we address the relevant considerations in more detail in Chapter 6);[2] the essential test is that:

'It may be necessary to grant a stay if the impending appellate decision is likely to have a critical impact on the current litigation.'[3]

1   *BD (application of SK and DK) Croatia CG* [2004] UKIAT 00032.
2   See **6.101** *et seq* below.
3   Jackson LJ in *AB (Sudan) v Secretary of State for the Home Department* [2013] EWCA Civ 921 at [32].

FAMILY LAW PROCEEDINGS

5.56   Where there are parallel family and immigration law proceedings extant, it is necessary to consider whether one set would benefit from findings made in the other. As it was put in *RS India*:[1]

'The family court may well be assisted by knowing whether a person in the position of the appellant is likely to be able to remain in the United

Kingdom and be an active presence in the child's life. The immigration court would be informed by the family court's assessment of the child's welfare ... the Tribunal does not have any means of assessing [best interests] for itself, in particular: there is no local authority or children's guardian, no access to the service provided by CAFCAS, and no independent means of ascertaining the wishes, concerns and interests of the child'

And:[2]

'The Tribunal does not have the benefit of separate representation on behalf of the child. It does not have highly qualified and independent Guardians to represent the child's best interests and put forward their views and nor does it have the availability of social workers who alongside the Guardian interview all persons and professionals concerned in the child's life to come to a view as to where the child's best interests lie.'

1   *RS (immigration and family court proceedings) India* [2012] UKUT 218 (IAC) at [36]–[37].
2   *RS (immigration/family court liaison: outcome)* [2013] UKUT 82(IAC) at [25].

5.57   Although the two sets of proceedings have different focuses, family law making a child's best interests paramount where in immigration cases they are of primary importance and to be weighed in the balance together with other compelling rights-based factors, '[a]n informed decision of the family judge on the merits and, in some cases at least, the material underlying that decision, is likely to be of value to the immigration judge'.[1] The Presidents of the Family Division and the Senior President of Tribunals have produced a Protocol on Communications between judges of the Family Court and Immigration and Asylum Chambers of the First-tier Tribunal and Upper Tribunal which addresses case management in detail.[2] Where there is an opportunity to have the benefit of findings from the family jurisdiction (ie where the family court decision will be a 'weighty consideration' in the immigration proceedings, bearing in mind that it would be wrong for judges in either jurisdiction to predict the result in the other),[3] the immigration judge will need to determine these questions:[4]

'(i)   Does the claimant have at least an Article 8 right to remain until the conclusion of the family proceedings?

(ii)   If so should the appeal be allowed to a limited extent and a discretionary leave be directed?

(iii)   Alternatively, is it more appropriate for a short period of an adjournment to be granted to enable the core decision to be made in the family proceedings?

(iv)   Is it likely that the family court would be assisted by a view on the present state of knowledge of whether the appellant would be allowed to remain in the event that the outcome of the family proceedings is the maintenance of family contact between him or her and a child resident here?'

1   *Nimako-Boateng (residence orders – Anton considered)* [2012] UKUT 00216 (IAC) at [31]–[33], approved by Maurice Kay LJ in *Mohan v Secretary of State for the Home Department* [2012] EWCA Civ 1363 at [17].
2   Presidents' Protocol on Communications, para 6.
3   Available at www.judiciary.gov.uk.
4   *RS (immigration and family court proceedings) India* [2012] UKUT 218 (IAC) at [44], generally approved by Maurice Kay LJ in *Mohan* (above) at [18]–[20].

5.58   Where the appellant before them has a criminal record or an adverse immigration history, these further questions arise:[1]

'(i)   Is the outcome of the contemplated family proceedings likely to be material to the immigration decision?

(ii)   Are there compelling public interest reasons to exclude the claimant from the United Kingdom irrespective of the outcome of the family proceedings or the best interest of the child?

(iii)   In the case of contact proceedings initiated by an appellant in an immigration appeal, is there any reason to believe that the family proceedings have been instituted to delay or frustrate removal and not to promote the child's welfare?

(iv)   In assessing the above questions, the judge will normally want to consider: the degree of the claimant's previous interest in and contact with the child, the timing of contact proceedings and the commitment with which they have been progressed, when a decision is likely to be reached, what materials (if any) are already available or can be made available to identify pointers to where the child's welfare lies?'

1   *RS (immigration and family court proceedings) India* [2012] UKUT 218 (IAC) at [43].

5.59   When recognising that deferral of the immigration case is necessary, the immigration judge should consider whether this should be achieved by an adjournment, or whether it would be better that the appeal be allowed with a direction that leave to remain be granted consistent with the progress of the family case, bearing in mind that an irregular migrant will not have the ability to work or obtain social security, a factor which may itself be contrary to a child's interests or otherwise adversely impact on the family proceedings.[1] Documents in family proceedings cannot be disclosed to third parties including judges of the FTT without an order from the family court, though the tribunal system is not so circumscribed, and may order disclosure via a direction.[2]

1   *RS (immigration and family court proceedings) India* [2012] UKUT 218 (IAC) at [45]–[48].
2   Presidents' Protocol on Communications, para 7.

DIRECTIONS

5.60   The tribunal is free, within the confines of the Rules, to regulate procedure as it sees fit,[1] always bearing in mind the fundamental human rights which it has to determine.[2] This it may do both by the issue of directions in a particular case, and standard directions, the latter made by the President of the Tribunal.[3] Directions will be aimed at securing the overriding objective.[4] They may be made orally or in writing, following an application (giving reasons) by a party or on the FTT's own initiative.[5] The 2014 Rules particularise the matters upon which directions may be made, although the list is not exhaustive (the examples given are 'in particular, and without restricting the general powers').[6] Beyond powers that we deal with in other paragraphs, such as the consolidation/joining of proceedings, provision of documents, information, evidence or submissions, holding of case management hearings, making of decisions as to the form of hearings, and adjournments, the examples given by the Rules[7] are to:

'(a)   extend or shorten the time for complying with any rule, practice direction or direction;

...

(c)   permit or require a party to amend a document;

...

(i)   require a party to produce a bundle for a hearing;

(j)   stay (or, in Scotland, sist) proceedings;

(k)   transfer proceedings to another court or tribunal if that other court or tribunal has jurisdiction in relation to the proceedings and–

   (i)   because of a change of circumstances since the proceedings were started, the Tribunal no longer has jurisdiction in relation to the proceedings; or

   (ii)   the Tribunal considers that the other court or tribunal is a more appropriate forum for the determination of the case; or

(l)   suspend the effect of its own decision pending the determination by the Tribunal or the Upper Tribunal of an application for permission to appeal against, and any appeal or review of, that decision.'

1   Tribunal Procedure (First-tier Tribunal) (Immigration and Asylum Chamber) Rules 2014, SI 2014/2604, r 4(1).
2   See **5.8** *et seq* above.
3   SI 2014/2604, r 4(2)–(3) empowers the FTT to make specific directions; the President's generic Practice Directions are referred to throughout this text.
4   See **5.3** *et seq* above.
5   SI 2014/2604, r 5(1)–(3).
6   SI 2014/2604, r 4(3).
7   SI 2014/2604, r 4(3)(a)–(l).

5.61   There is no longer any express enjoinder to give only directions with which the FTT is satisfied that an unrepresented appellant is capable of compliance;[1] however, the need to ensure 'so far as practicable, that the parties are able to participate fully in the proceedings' may well have similar effect.[2] Whilst directions given earlier in the proceedings must deserve some respect, they do not irreversibly bind judges later seized of the appeal, who are masters of the proceedings before them,[3] and an application may be made for another direction which amends, suspends or sets aside an earlier one.[4] Unless there is good reason not to do so, the FTT must send written notice of a direction to every party and to any other person affected by it.[5]

1   Contrast Asylum and Immigration Tribunal (Procedure) Rules 2005, SI 2005/230, r 45(5).
2   Tribunal Procedure (First-tier Tribunal) (Immigration and Asylum Chamber) Rules 2014, SI 2014/2604, r 4(2)(c).
3   *TK (consideration of prior determination, directions) Georgia* [2004] UKIAT 00149 at [14]; see further *YL Ethiopia (nationality, statelessness, Eritrea, Ethiopia) Eritrea CG* [2003] UKIAT 16 (see **5.42**, fn 5 above).
4   SI 2014/2604, rr 4(2) and 5(5).
5   SI 2014/2604, r 5(6).

Scope of the power to give directions

5.62   There is no definition as to what constitutes a direction in the 2014 Rules. The tribunal has ruled that the essence of a direction is that it is something in the form of an order or an instruction by one person to another person, failure to observe which carries consequences; strongly worded exhortations to a party to conduct the appeal in a particular fashion will not necessarily constitute a direction absent these qualities.[1] The power to give directions is linked to the conduct or disposal of the appeal,[2] considerations which led the Court of Appeal in *Mwanza* to find that directions which trespassed onto substantive matters – such as a direction to a respondent to issue a fresh refusal letter – would be unlawful, falling outwith the powers of the then Appellate Authority[3] (although the situation would be different where the direction was aimed at seeking clarification of the Home Office approach, where for example country circumstances appeared to have changed in an asylum case,[4] or where the SSHD acknowledged the inadequacy of his original decision).[5] Collins J as President of the Tribunal suggested that directions which essentially sought to clarify whether removal would take place were essentially procedural rather than substantive:[6] and, indeed, clarification of the SSHD's position may be imperative in an asylum appeal where the details of removal are unclear but within the Home Office's knowledge.[7] However, whilst the SSHD may not be coerced into taking actions by the authority of formal directions, he may still be encouraged by other steps: thus, the tribunal has pointed out that where a person has been refused asylum on grounds of 'non-compliance', and the SSHD resists the issue of a further refusal letter, there will be a temptation to acquiesce to a request by the asylum seeker that the hearing proceed substantively there and then, the appellant being permitted to place any and all documents before the court that he wished, without the SSHD having a chance to consider their contents. This would, from the asylum seeker's perspective, achieve the tactical advantage of 'trial by ambush'.[8] Alternatively, where the Home Office perceived the wisdom of taking a further step in an asylum claim, such as conducting an interview, an immigration judge might adjourn a case whilst setting down a timetable for this to take place.[9] Where the SSHD has not clarified his stance on some material issue, he may find his conduct of an appeal prevents his case being taken as seriously as might otherwise be the case.[10] Directions should not be used so as to create an effect whereby the burden of proof is reversed, as would be the case if an immigration judge prevented a party who lacks the burden of proof from challenging the other party's account.[11]

1   *Ipek* (01/TH/01333, 19 July 2001); Tuckey LJ refusing permission in a reported decision, *Secretary of State for Home Department v Ipek* [2002] EWCA Civ 391 at [8].
2   Tribunal Procedure (First-tier Tribunal) (Immigration and Asylum Chamber) Rules 2014, SI 2014/2604, r 4(2).
3   Swinton Thomas LJ in *Mwanza v Secretary of State for the Home Department* (C/2000/0616, 3 November 2000) at [31]; Tuckey LJ refusing permission in a reported decision, *Secretary of State for Home Department v Ipek* [2002] EWCA Civ 391 at [16]; Auld LJ in *Zaier, R (on the application of) v Immigration Appeal Tribunal* [2003] EWCA Civ 937 at [32]–[36].
4   *Razi* (01/TH/01836, 29 September 2001) at [11]–[13]; Auld LJ in *Zaier* (above) at [30].
5   See **5.128** below.
6   *N'da* (01/TH/01769, 3 August 2001) at [13]; though difficulties with this approach, if it presupposed an ability to 'remit' an appeal to the SSHD, were identified by Auld LJ in *Zaier* (above).
7   Sedley LJ in *HH (Somalia) v Secretary of State for the Home Department* [2010] EWCA Civ 426 at [69]–[63] and [81].
8   *Ipek* (01/TH/01333, 19 July 2001). For modern appeals, cf the consent requirement and the general policy for the SSHD to be the primary decision maker, at **4.13** above.
9   Auld LJ in *Zaier* (above) at [46].
10 *C (Yugoslavia)* [2003] UKIAT 00007 at [11].
11 *Khalil* [2002] UKIAT 01742 (29 May 2002).

DIRECTIONS REGARDING ORAL EVIDENCE

5.63   The tribunal's standard directions contain a requirement for the filing of witness statements which shall, in normal circumstances, stand as evidence in chief at the hearing.[1] This is not intended to fetter the immigration judge's discretion 'to conduct the substantive appeal hearing in the most appropriate way depending upon the facts of the individual case. There may be cases where it will be appropriate for appellants or witnesses to have the opportunity of adding to or supplementing their witness statements.[2] It has been said that fundamental justice requires an oral hearing where credibility issues are involved[3] (and in some cases it may be thought that justice would be better done by the appellant benefitting from having an opportunity to acclimatise himself to the stresses of questioning at court prior to adversarial cross-examination). The President once issued a Memorandum stating that there are practical and procedural reasons militating against the feasibility of the giving of evidence and cross-examination via telephone conference calls, however the Court of Appeal has ruled that an application to call a witness from abroad in such fashion must be given the most careful attention.[4] It should always be recalled that giving evidence in an asylum appeal is a gruelling experience at the best of times.[5]

1   Practice Directions, para 7.5(a)(i).
2   *R v Secretary of State for the Home Department, ex parte Singh* [1998] INLR 608.
3   Bertha Wilson J in *Federation of Canadian Sikh Societies v Canadian Council of Churches* [1985] 1 SCR 178 at 213, cited by Sullivan J in *R v Immigration Appeal Tribunal, ex parte S* [1998] INLR 168 at 182; Sedley LJ thought this to be a principle of some importance, at least: *R v Secretary of State for the Home Department, ex parte Yousaf and Jamil* (C/1999/1004 and C/1999/1155, 21 June 2000) at [41]; Sedley LJ in the Court of Appeal in *FP (Iran) v Secretary of State for the Home Department* [2007] EWCA Civ 13 at [20].
4   Rix LJ giving permission to apply for judicial review in the Court of Appeal in *AM (Cameroon), R (on the application of) v Asylum and Immigration Tribunal* [2007] EWCA Civ 131: the appeal went on to become *AM (Cameroon) v Secretary of State for the Home Department* [2008] EWCA Civ 100.
5   Carnwath LJ in the Court of Appeal in *HF (Algeria) v Secretary of State for the Home Department* [2007] EWCA Civ 445 at [26].

OTHER STANDARD DIRECTIONS

5.64   The standard directions[1] require the provision of:

- paginated and indexed bundles of all the documents to be relied on at the hearing with a schedule identifying the essential passages;[2]

- a skeleton argument which briefly defines and confines the issues, identifying all relevant issues including human rights claims and citing all legal authorities to be relied on[3] (it is extremely useful if it is cross referenced to the relevant pages where the supporting evidence is found);[4]

- a chronology of events;[5]

- certified translations of documents.[6]

1   Practice Directions, para 7.5 onwards.
2   Practice Directions, para 7.5(a)(ii).
3   Practice Directions, para 7.5(a)(iii) and 8.2(e).
4   Practice Directions, para 8.2(e).
5   Practice Directions, para 7.5(a)(iv).
6   Practice Directions, para 8.2(b).

5.65   There is a direction setting out best practice, with which parties should aim to comply so far as is 'reasonably practicable'[1] in the preparation of bundles.[2] Its recommendations include:

- proper pagination and indexing;

- that all documents be relevant ('We deplore the practice of filing enormous bundles of irrelevant documents especially in publicly funded cases and there is no authority for requiring the Adjudicator to read the whole of such bundles unless his attention is drawn to them');[3]

- that the documents be presented in logical order and be legible;

● relevant passages of lengthy documents should be highlighted;

● large bundles should be contained in a ring binder or lever arch file, capable of lying flat when opened.[4]

1 Practice Directions, para 8.1.
2 Practice Directions, para 8.2.
3 *RB (credibility – objective evidence) Uganda* [2004] UKIAT 00339.
4 Practice Direction, para 8.2(g).

5.66 The parties should not assume that the judge has 'any prior familiarity with any country information or background reports in relation to the case in question', so should provide copies.[1] Nevertheless, in asylum cases, the Procedures Directive requires that Member States shall ensure that precise and up-to-date information is obtained from various sources, such as the UNHCR, as to the general situation prevailing in the countries of origin of applicants for asylum,[2] and the FTT should draw upon its own expertise when determining appeals.[3] As Sedley J once put it in an analogous context in the era of in-country appeal rights against return to third countries:[4]

'Adjudicators are not recruited from the Clapham omnibus. They are skilled and specialised office-holders carrying out an independent and, in many respects, judicial function of profound importance to the individuals who come before them ... From case to case they will build up a fund of information about different third countries. It would be wrong, of course, for them to decide cases upon the basis of private information of this kind; but it would also, in my judgment, be wrong for them to ignore such information and close their minds to everything except the evidence that the Home Office chose or the applicant was able to put before them.'

1 Practice Direction, para 8.6.
2 Council Directive 2005/85/EC (1 December 2005), Art 8(b), transposed by the Immigration Rules, HC 395, para 339JA.
3 See **5.78**, fn 2.
4 Sedley J in *Secretary of State for the Home Department v Abdi* [1994] Imm AR 402 at 412.

5.67 There is a duty to cite all relevant authorities: 'unqualified, but paid advocates of any kind have just the same duty as counsel or solicitors to draw the attention of tribunals before whom they appear to any relevant citable decisions, whether or not those go against them',[1] including those which are outside the immigration jurisdiction.[2] As the Immigration Rules have become more complex, it is very desirable indeed to provide copies of those in force at the relevant date of decision. It is surprising how often legal submissions are made without providing copies of the increasingly complex fabric of rules, leaving the immigration judges to find the relevant legal matrix for themselves.

1 *C (China)* [2003] UKIAT 00009 at [6]; *SD (treatment of post-hearing evidence) Russia* [2008] UKAIT 00037 at [8].
2 *KP (para 317: mothers-in-law) India* [2006] UKAIT 00093, headnote.

FAILURE TO COMPLY WITH DIRECTIONS OR THE 2014 RULES

5.68   Failure to comply either with the rules themselves or directions given pursuant to them may lead the tribunal to determine the appeal without a hearing,[1] notably the power to determine an appeal where the appellant was in default without consideration of its substance did not survive the repeal of the 2003 Procedure Rules.[2] Non-compliance is to be met by such action as the FTT considers just,[3] which may include:

- waiving the requirement;

- requiring the failure to be remedied; or

- referring the matter to the UT where the failing relates to a requirement to attend any place, be available, give evidence as a witness, or produce a document or facilitate its inspection.[4] The UT has powers to punish for contempt, having as it does the same powers, rights, privileges and authority as the High Court and Court of Session regarding functions including the attendance and examination of witnesses and the production and inspection of documents.[5]

Application of this rule must be considered in the context of the overriding objective.[6] Relevant considerations might include a lack of prejudice to the other party to the appeal.[7]

1   Tribunal Procedure (First-tier Tribunal) (Immigration and Asylum Chamber) Rules 2014, SI 2014/2604, rr 4(3)(g), 6(2), 25(1)(e).
2   Immigration and Asylum Appeals (Procedure) Rules 2003, SI 2003/652, r 45(2).
3   SI 2014/2604, r 6(2)(a)–(b).
4   SI 2014/2604, r 6(2)(c) and (3).
5   TCEA 2007 addressing 'Supplementary powers of Upper Tribunal' at s 25; Lord Glennie in *Eba, Re Judicial Review* [2010] ScotCS CSOH_45 at [23].
6   See **5.3** *et seq* above.
7   *BO (extension of time for appealing) Nigeria* [2006] UKAIT 00035 at [23](v).

DISCLOSURE

5.69   The FTT holds a power to 'permit or require a party or another person to provide documents, information, evidence or submissions to the Tribunal or a party';[1] additionally the respondent is under an obligation to provide to the FTT and other parties, within 28 days of receiving a copy of the notice of appeal from the tribunal, 'any other unpublished document which is referred to in [the notice of the decision to which the notice of appeal relates and any other document the respondent provided to the appellant giving reasons for that decision] or relied upon by the respondent'.[2] Where such an unpublished document is not provided, the tribunal may take the view that it is no longer relied upon by the respondent.[3] Interview records should be disclosed, as should any related comments, or opinions, of the interviewing officer adverse to the subject's case which are conveyed to the decision maker;[4] so too should any allegations made by a third party informant, subject to the requirement to anonymise him unless fairness requires the person to be identified because of the possibility that his evidence is unreliable or ill motivated.[5] There is also the power to require attendance by way of witness summons, addressed in the next paragraph. The immigration appellate authority found itself able to request the provision of further details regarding persons said to be the subject of interest by the authorities of the Ivory Coast, that had been filed and served in redacted form, as they were relevant to the then relevant scope of the Rules which fixed on materials relevant to 'the preparation for and the conduct of' an appeal.[6] The tribunal may wish to make such a direction at its own instance.[7] HRA 1998 has not so far been recognised as a strong source of additional disclosure obligations on the SSHD.[8] It is possible that the better remedy for an appellant whose case requires significant disclosure will be in the Administrative Court given the greater obligations of a defendant to disclose material in judicial review proceedings.[9] It should always be recalled that, notwithstanding any opportunities for disclosure that the FTT's procedures may provide, under the Data Protection Act 1998 (DPA 1998) individuals have a right of access to personal data held on them by organisations processing personal data such as government departments, subject to certain limited exemptions.[10] A request by an individual for access to his personal data is known as a 'subject access request', and for any case with a significant procedural history, it will be advisable for an appellant's representative to obtain this. Subject access requests should be made in writing, providing a fee of £10, to:[11]

The Data Protection Unit
Lunar House
40 Wellesley Rd
Croydon
CR9 2B

---

1 Tribunal Procedure (First-tier Tribunal) (Immigration and Asylum Chamber) Rules 2014, SI2014/2604, r 4(3)(d).
2 SI 2014/2604, rr 23(1)(e) and (a) and 24(1)(d) and (a).
3 *MH (respondent's bundle: documents not provided) Pakistan* [2010] UKUT 168 (IAC) at [13].
4 *Miah (interviewer's comments: disclosure: fairness)* [2014] UKUT 515 (IAC) at [2], [12]–[19], [22]–[23].
5 *Miah* (above) at [2] and [14].
6 Pearl J in in *A, B, C, and D* (R17367, R21180, R16463, R21181, 12 May 1999).
7 SI 2014/2604, rr 5(1), 2(1), 4(1)–(2); Burton J in *R v Immigration Appeal Tribunal, ex parte Agbenyenu* [1999] Imm AR 460.
8 *S (Serbia and Montenegro – Kosovo)* [2003] UKIAT 00031; for the more modern authorities see **6.49** below.
9 See eg Blake J in the Administrative Court in *Limbu, R (on the application of) v Secretary of State for the Home Department* [2008] EWHC 2261 (Admin); see further *CM (EM Country Guidance, disclosure) Zimbabwe CG* [2013] UKUT 59 (IAC) (see **6.49** below).
10 Data Protection Act 1998, s 7.
11 See the Home Office Immigration Directorates' Instructions, Ch 24, section 11 'Subject access requests' (November 2008).

5.70   The SSHD aims to comply with the 40-day deadline laid down by DPA 1998 and his policy is to provide all documents held on file including personal data, subject to certain exceptions going to national security, criminal offending and material that may be subject to legal professional privilege. There is a right of complaint to the Information Commissioner if the material provided is thought incomplete and then onwards to the Information Tribunal.[1]

1   The procedures for such remedies are beyond the scope of this book, but see generally the Home Office Immigration Directorates' Instructions above, the Information Commissioner's website, https://ico.org.uk/concerns/getting/, and the Tribunal Procedure (First-tier Tribunal) (General Regulatory Chamber) Rules 2009, SI 2009/1976.

INSPECTION OF DOCUMENTARY EVIDENCE

5.71   Whilst there is no longer any express rule to the effect that the FTT should only take evidence into account where it is available to all parties, it is a fundamental principle of open justice[1] that:

> 'A party has a right to know the case against him and the evidence on which it is based. He is entitled to have the opportunity to respond to any such evidence and to any submissions made by the other side.'

1   Lord Dyson in *Al Rawi v Security Service* [2011] UKSC 34 at [12].

5.72   Availability to all the parties may include the scenario where the evidence is available at a hearing at which one party has chosen not to be represented.[1] A judge should not obtain further evidence at his own motion following the hearing without informing the parties of an intention to do so, and without giving them an opportunity to be addressed upon it.[2] The SSHD was once found to be under no positive duty to disclose the material which founded his conclusions as to the safety of removal in the context of the expedited 'third country' cases said to be without foundation;[3] his responsibilities in this regard may be higher in full asylum appeals.[4] The provision of imperfect copies by one party to the other has been viewed as constituting a serious procedural error which casts a shadow over proceedings – the appropriate direction in such circumstances was that the respondent supply to the appellant forthwith a legible copy of the document in question together with a full translation of that document and that the original document be available at any further proceedings in respect of the appeal.[5]

1   *MA (Procedure Rules 45 and 46) Pakistan* [2004] UKIAT 00330 at [27].
2   See **5.88**, fn 2 below.
3   *R v Secretary of State for the Home Department, ex parte Abdi and Gawe* [1996] Imm AR 288.
4   Simon Brown LJ in the Court of Appeal in *Konan v Secretary of State for the Home Department* (IATRF 2000/0020/C, 20 March 2000).
5   *Abadi* (18078, 6 May 1999).

WITNESS SUMMONS

5.73   The tribunal may, by issuing a summons ('a witness summons'), require any person in the United Kingdom to attend as a witness at the hearing of an appeal[1] to answer any questions or produce any documents in his possession or under his control which relate to any matter in issue in the appeal.[2] He may not be compelled to give evidence which he could not be required to give in a civil trial.[3] Fourteen days' notice, or such shorter period as is directed, should be given, and where the person is not a party, provision for his payment should be stated (including who should pay).[4] A summons, citation or order under this rule must explain that its subject may apply to the FTT for it to be varied or set aside, if he has not had an opportunity to object to it, and state the consequences of non-compliance.[5] The FTT may make such orders of its own motion, as where it is necessary to make good some inadequacy of representation.[6] Failure to attend without reasonable excuse is an offence, the perpetrator being liable on summary conviction to a fine not exceeding level 3 on the standard scale.[7] The tribunal has declined to call a witness from the SSHD's Country Action Team regarding the practicality of return, in circumstances where such return was considered to fall outside the tribunal's remit.[8]

1   Tribunal Procedure (First-tier Tribunal) (Immigration and Asylum Chamber) Rules 2014, SI 2014/2604, r 15(1)(a).
2   SI 2014/2604, r 15(1)(b).
3   SI 2014/2604, r 15(3) (see **5.166**, fn 3 below).
4   SI 2014/2604, r 15(2).
5   SI 2014/2604, r 15(4). See **5.68** above for further information on the FTT's powers in relation to failure to comply with directions and orders.
6   SI 2014/2604, r 15(1); Schiemann LJ in *Kesse v Secretary of State for the Home Department* [2001] EWCA Civ 177 at [37].
7   NIAA 2002, s 106(4) and (5).
8   *GH (former Kaz – country conditions – effect) Iraq CG* [2004] UKIAT 00248 at [21].

CONCESSIONS AND AGREED FACTS

5.74   The parties may agree certain facts so narrowing the issues in dispute, and there is some encouragement to do so in the Practice Directions which require any concession made at a CMR hearing to be judicially recorded.[1] It has been said that the tribunal should go behind a concession on credibility in 'adversarial litigation ... only in plain and obvious cases,'[2] and always subject only to considerations of fairness.[3] In a determination intended to be followed in preference to any others on the issue, the tribunal in *Carcabuk and Bla*[4] authoritatively ruled that a judge should not go behind concessions of fact, 'for example that a particular document is genuine or that an event described by the appellant or a witness did occur'[5] (although he might wish to raise doubts as to the correctness of a concession).[6] A concession may be withdrawn, but such a retraction, if not made in good time (and bearing in mind that a CMR hearing should focus minds on this issue), may well require an adjournment to be offered to an appellant, risking undesirable delay, meaning that withdrawal should be permitted only where the SSHD's change of tack was down to good reason, such as the discovery of fresh evidence.[7]

'the Tribunal may in its discretion permit a concession to be withdrawn if in its view there is good reason in all the circumstances for that course to be taken. Its discretion is wide. Its exercise will depend on the particular circumstances of the case before it. Prejudice to the applicant is a significant feature. So is its absence. Its absence does not however mean that an application to withdraw a concession will invariably be granted. Bad faith will almost certainly be fatal to an application to withdraw a concession.'[8]

1   Practice Directions, para 7.8(b).
2   Keith J in the Administrative Court in *R (Bouttora) v Immigration Appeal Tribunal* [2004] EWHC 1873 (Admin); see further Schiemann LJ for the Court of Appeal in *Secretary of State for the Home Department v Maheshwaran* [2002] EWCA Civ 173 at [4]; *ST (child asylum seekers) Sri Lanka* [2013] UKUT 292(IAC), headnote at (6); Ouseley J in *WN (Surendran, credibility, new evidence) Democratic Republic of Congo* [2004] UKIAT 00213. See further the discussion in *Carcabuk and Bla* (00/TH/01426, 18 May 2000) at [10] of *R v Immigration Appeal Tribunal, ex parte Hubbard* [1985] Imm AR 110, and *Ex parte Kaur* (unreported, 15 March 1996), where Ward LJ giving the judgment of the Court of Appeal accepted that it would be wrong to go behind findings of fact which were favourable to an appellant.
3   *ST* (above), headnote at (6)
4   *Carcabuk and Bla* (above): Laws LJ in the Court of Appeal in *R v Immigration Appeal Tribunal, ex parte Davila-Puga* [2001] EWCA Civ 931 was content to accept *Carcabuk* as correctly decided, without going so far as to distinctly uphold its approach.
5   *Carcabuk and Bla* (above) at [11].
6   *Carcabuk and Bla* (above) at [12](4) and (5).
7   *Carcabuk and Bla* (above) at [12](3) and (6).
8   Goldring LJ in the Court of Appeal in *NR (Jamaica) v Secretary of State for the Home Department* [2009] EWCA Civ 856 at [12]; Moses LJ in *CD (Jamaica) v Secretary of State for the Home Department* [2010] EWCA Civ 768 at [18]–[32].

Concessions: general guidance

5.75   An intention to withdraw a concession between the first instance hearing and an appeal onwards should be communicated in good time, for the tribunal would not normally permit adjournments (and hence should not countenance an act by a party which made one inevitable) if this was not done with due despatch.[1] To this end, the Home Office should make it clear in the refusal letter which of the historical facts asserted by the claimant are accepted, and should avoid confusion by, for example, categorising material as 'not credible' when on analysis the true reasoning is based on an absence of risk rather than an allegation of falsehood.[2] If the refusal letter is unclear in this regard, then any preliminary hearing should be used to clarify matters.[3] Those representing the SSHD are free to make concessions even at the substantive hearing of the appeal.[4] It is vital that a distinction be made between concessions and failures to challenge evidence for whilst the former should not be revisited, the latter leaves the fact-finding powers of the tribunal unfettered.[5] Positions taken in the SSHD's Operational Guidance must be respected by his advocates in court,[6] albeit that subsequent country of origin information from other Home Office sources may have an impact on it.[7] Concessions made by representatives of immigrants will normally bind them,[8] although this is not an inflexible rule, particularly given the 'anxious scrutiny' that attends asylum claims.[9]

1   *Carcabuk and Bla* (00/TH/01426, 18 May 2000) at [12](7).
2   *Carcabuk and Bla* (above) at [12](1).
3   *Carcabuk and Bla* (above) at [12](2).
4   *Carcabuk and Bla* (above) at [12](3).
5   *Carcabuk and Bla* (above) at [12](5).
6   *MA (operational guidance – prison conditions – significance) Sudan* [2005] UKAIT 00149 at [22]; *FS (domestic violence, SN and HM, OGN) Pakistan CG* [2006] UKAIT 00023 at [50].
7   *FS* (above) at [50]; Potter LJ in *Krotov v Secretary of State for the Home Department* [2004] EWCA Civ 69 at [52].
8   *IS (concession made by representative) Sierra Leone* [2005] UKIAT 00009 at [13]–[18].
9   Sedley LJ in *AK (Iran) v Secretary of State for the Home Department* [2008] EWCA Civ 941 at [5] (see also **8.135**, fn 5).

5.76   Because of the possibility for confusion as to the scope of concessions, the tribunal in *Kalidas* made the following recommendations:[1]

'(1)   Parties should assist the First-tier Tribunal at Case Management Review hearings (CMRs) to produce written confirmation of issues agreed and concessions made.

(2)   If credibility is not in issue, it will often be unnecessary to submit a further statement by an appellant, or call her to give evidence. If this approach is taken, the judge should be told why.

(3)   Any further statement should not be a rehash of what has already been said. It should be directed to the remaining live issues.

(4)   Any skeleton argument should contain not just general law. It should be directed to the live issues.

(5)   A judge who accepts and records an agreement is best placed to understand its scope, and should consider reserving the case to herself.

(6)   Representatives are jointly responsible for drawing attention of the hearing judge to the agreement reached, and the nature of the decision still required.

(7)   Judges look behind factual concessions only in exceptional circumstances. If the scope of a concession is unclear, or if evidence develops in such a way that its extent and correctness need to be revisited, the judge must draw that to attention of representatives. Adjournment may become necessary.'

1   *Kalidas (agreed facts – best practice)* [2012] UKUT 00327(IAC).

QUESTIONS FROM THE IMMIGRATION JUDGE

5.77 Although, in the absence of a representative for the Home Office, the immigration judiciary is entitled to probe evidence where it contains apparent improbabilities in order to satisfy itself of the account's reliability,[1] it should do so less freely where both parties are represented,[2] and should certainly not 'set about "clarifying" evidence by taking positive action to explore contradictions in depth in the manner which a cross-examiner might choose to do'.[3] It is likely to find it better not to interrupt the flow of the evidence given, and so to reserve any questions until after examination in chief, cross-examination and re-examination,[4] unless the evidence is so unclear as to require it to be repeated.[5] In general it is for

> 'the parties to bring out evidence in the order they think appropriate and it is for the parties to put whatever contradictions in the evidence need to be put to the witness. If the Adjudicator does ask the witness any questions, he must then always give an opportunity to the parties to ask any further questions which arise from his. An Adjudicator who intervenes during the course of evidence is running the risk that he will be seen to be taking the side of one party or the other.'[6]

1   See **5.98** below.
2   *Oyono* [2002] UKIAT 2034 at [32], cited and approved in *SW (adjudicator's questions) Somalia* [2005] UKIAT 00037 at [21]; the Opinion of Lord Carloway in the Court of Session in *Mehmet Koca v SSHD* (22 November 2002), *Immigration Law Update*, Vol 7, No 4, [29]–[32], cited in *AA (credibility, totality of evidence, fair trial) Sudan* [2004] UKIAT 00152.
3   Lord Carloway in the Court of Session in *Mehmet Koca* (above) at [32]; Arden LJ in *JK (Democratic Republic of Congo) v Secretary of State for the Home Department* [2007] EWCA Civ 831 at [41].
4   *SW (adjudicator's questions) Somalia* [2005] UKIAT 00037 at [21].
5   *Oyono* [2002] UKIAT 2034 at [32].
6   Ibid.

THE IMMIGRATION JUDGE'S OWN KNOWLEDGE AND OPINIONS

5.78 From time to time the immigration judge will have accumulated knowledge of a particular country, and may have formed views upon the situation there. In such cases, it will be appropriate for him to indicate as much to the parties; such views in no way bar him from continuing to hear the case, so long as he maintains an open mind and considers any submissions that seek to dissuade him from a particular view: no complaint can be made subsequently if no objection is raised at the hearing.[1] Whereas the knowledge gained from previous experience of objective country evidence is part of the expertise on which a judge may draw,[2] beyond this (for example as to perceptions of particular ethnic groups),

'Reliance ... on ... personally acquired information gives rise to a significant risk about fairness to an Appellant who will be in no position to test the reliability of the matters being held against him. It should invariably ... be avoided'.[3]

1   *MM* (01/TH/00994, 4 June 2001).
2   Tribunal Procedure (First-tier Tribunal) (Immigration and Asylum Chamber) Rules 2014, SI 2014/2604, r 2(2)(d).
3   Newman J in the Administrative Court in *R v Immigration Appellate Authority, ex parte Mohammed* (CO/918/00); *AJ (assessment of medical evidence – examination of scars) Cameroon* [2005] UKIAT 00060 at [34].

EXAMINATION AND CROSS-EXAMINATION

5.79   The power to make directions extends to the form of evidence (and submissions) provided to the FTT. Under the 2014 Rules, r 14 it may make directions as to:

'(a)   issues on which it requires evidence or submissions;

(b)   the nature of the evidence or submissions it requires;

(d)   any limit on the number of witnesses whose evidence a party may put forward, whether in relation to a particular issue or generally;

(e)   the manner in which any evidence or submissions are to be provided, which may include a direction for them to be given–

     (i)   orally at a hearing; or

     (ii)   by witness statement or written submissions; and

(f)   the time at which any evidence or submissions are to be provided.'

5.80   A judge may need to take steps to ensure that the proceedings are appropriately directed, albeit that they should never give the impression that the length of the list requires the curtailment of the giving of evidence:[1]

'It is proper ... to intervene during examination-in-chief and cross-examination for the purposes of moving the proceedings along, so long as that is done in a fair manner. It is necessary and proper for an Adjudicator to point out that a line of questioning is irrelevant or valueless or repetitious or is going nowhere. It will, of course, be necessary to consider any response made by a representative to such an approach.'[2]

1   *SA (clarificatory questions from IJs – best practice) Iran* [2006] UKAIT 00017 at [27] – therein the tribunal noted that the then average length of an appeal was 80 minutes.
2   *K (Côte d'Ivoire)* [2004] UKIAT 00061 at [42].

5.81   By Practice Direction, it is now routinely ordered that witness statements stand as evidence in chief.[1] It would be very hard to justify a refusal to permit cross-examination when the witness had been called to give examination in chief.[2] A failure to cross-examine on a point does not compel belief of the evidence in question; however, it does greatly weaken any challenge subsequently made in submissions, as was well explained by the unreported determination of the tribunal in *Ezzi*:[3]

'Proceedings before the Tribunal are judicial in nature. The purpose of cross-examination in proceedings such as these is not only to seek clarification of matters which are unclear but to challenge assertions made by a witness or witnesses (in this case the appellant) with a view to testing the credibility of a witness's evidence in chief and putting to that witness the basis for the cross-examiner's case. If the cross-examiner does not accept the evidence given in chief, or considers that it is not truthful, any contrary proposition which the cross-examiner intends to make in submissions should be put to the witness in order to elicit his response thereto. If that is not done, the evidence in chief of the witness has not been challenged nor tested. The Tribunal is thereby denied the opportunity to have matters fully explored and the Tribunal may be left in some doubt as to where the truth may lie. Furthermore, while submissions made in respect of key matters which have not been raised or challenged in cross-examination may not be incompetent, they cannot have the forcefulness of submissions in respect of matters which have been addressed during the hearing of evidence. The proceedings must be conducted in a manner which is fair to both sides'

1   See **5.63** *et seq* above.
2   *GY (refusal to allow cross-examination) Iran* [2004] UKIAT 00264 at [10].
3   *Ezzi* (G0003A, 29 May 1997).

5.82   Where there is no cross-examination of a witness whatsoever, the respondent must be taken as not disputing the evidence that he tenders.[1] It is not appropriate for a judge to make good failures to cross-examine by inviting recall of a witness once submissions have been reached.[2] The judge should never address a witness in a hostile tone: he should pose 'open ended questions, neutrally phrased'.[3]

1   Maurice Kay LJ in *MS (Sri Lanka) v Secretary of State for the Home Department* [2012] EWCA Civ 1548 at [14].
2   Arden LJ in *JK (Democratic Republic of Congo) v Secretary of State for the Home Department* [2007] EWCA Civ 831 at [41].
3   Ouseley J in *WN (Surendran; credibility; new evidence) Democratic Republic of Congo* [2004] UKIAT 00213 at [38].

SUBMISSIONS

5.83   Oral argument is of central importance to the adversarial system.[1] Nevertheless immigration judges possess an express power to limit oral submissions made to them.[2] It would be wholly unacceptable for an immigration judge to limit a party making representations properly available to him on the evidence put forward, although if it becomes clear that the submissions sought to be made are of no relevance, they might properly be curtailed.[3] There is no obligation for a judge to keep silent during submissions:

'The degree of intervention will depend entirely upon the focus and relevance of the submissions made; their helpfulness and their succinctness. It is perfectly proper for an Adjudicator to move submissions on by indicating that she has understood the point or to prevent the irrelevant in order to try and obtain the relevant answers for the purposes of writing the decision. Much will depend upon the nature of the case and the style of the advocates and Adjudicator. It is important, however, that the Adjudicator does not intervene to such an extent that relevant submissions are disrupted and relevant points are prevented from being made. In that way, the Adjudicator would fail to understand the case and potentially would miss important points being made to her.'[4]

1   Laws LJ in *Sengupta v Holmes* [2002] EWCA Civ 1104 at [38].
2   See the Tribunal Procedure (First-tier Tribunal) (Immigration and Asylum Chamber) Rules 2014, SI 2014/2604, r 14 set out above.
3   Collins J in *Aftab Ahmed* (00/TH/00230, 1 March 2000, starred) at [5]–[6].
4   Ouseley J in *K (Côte d'Ivoire)* [2004] UKIAT 00061 at [45].

5.84   It may be appropriate to proceed to ask for one party's submissions without having those of the other, where the judge's provisional view has moved in a particular direction, so long as this represents the case theory of the respondent and is not a theory of the judge's own, a development which would risk the appearance of bias.[1] If there is not time to hear submissions, it may be expedient for them to be delivered in writing: but such a procedure must be rigorously administered to ensure that no want of natural justice or administrative error ensues, and is strongly discouraged because of the administrative challenges it presents.[2] It is not in the public interest that any tribunal should be left to decide a significant issue of law in the absence of argument on both sides.[3]

1   *XS (Kosovo – adjudicator's conduct – psychiatric report) Serbia and Montenegro* [2005] UKIAT 00093 at [35].
2   Adjudicator Guidance Note No 4 (February 2003).
3   *PG and VG (EEA, 'direct descendants' includes grandchildren) Portugal* [2007] UKAIT 00019.

INTERPRETATION

5.85   For those giving evidence of life and death affairs in a foreign language, the quality of interpretation takes on particular importance.[1] Whilst the judge should take action upon a concern as to interpretation being raised, the conduct of the hearing is ultimately a matter for them, subject to doing justice in the case:

> 'When a responsible legal representative expresses some dissatisfaction about the quality of the interpretation and the skills of the interpreter, that plainly gives rise to a concern which the court, or in this instance the adjudicator, should immediately address. That is what this adjudicator did. The responsibility for deciding whether or not the proceedings should continue with the existing interpreter, or whether the interpreter should be discharged and the proceedings restarted, falls not on the legal representatives, but on the adjudicator.'[2]

1   Judge LJ in *Perera v Secretary of State for the Home Department* [2004] EWCA Civ 1002 at [3]–[4].
2   Judge LJ in *Perera* (above) at [5].

5.86   However it will be difficult for an immigration judge to be satisfied himself, once an objection is made to interpretation, of the accuracy of translation absent some further level of interpreting: '*ex hypothesi* there [is] no way of checking as to whether what the appellant said was faithfully reflected in what the interpreter said without further interpretation'.[1] Whether evidence is given through the medium of an interpreter is a matter for the appellant and his advisors alone, subject only to evidence that the system is being abused.[2] Representatives often have interpreters present at the hearing who can offer some assistance in evaluating the reality of asserted problems, and it would be wrong to thwart their ability to do so.[3] The interpreter is not a witness and should not be called upon to assist on disputed issues, nor be invited to comment on the dialect being spoken, that role being reserved for an appropriate expert.[4]

1   *N'Cho* (11621, 9 December 1994).
2   The right to an interpreter is not necessarily an absolute one, however see Roger Haines QC in *Refugee Appeal No 72752/01* (15 November 2001), giving a thorough review of the international human rights authorities in the context of a situation where there seemed a clear attempt to abuse the process in New Zealand by seeking to give evidence in a language no longer spoken in the country of origin.
3   *SJ (hearing interpreters) Iran* [2004] UKIAT 00131.
4   *AA (language diagnosis: use of interpreters) Somalia* [2008] UKAIT 00029 at [7]–[11]; *Mohamed (role of interpreter) Somalia* [2011] UKUT 337 (IAC) at [7]–[11].

Role of the tribunal interpreter; translations

5.87   There is a Guidance Note which sets out an appropriate style of introduction between appellant and court interpreter ('It is bad practice to have no form of introduction of the appellant and the interpreter').[1] There is no objection to the court interpreter assisting legal representatives to communicate with their clients in uncontentious matters, so long as they do not become embroiled in complicated instruction-taking; additionally it may be appropriate for a willing interpreter to translate a short document for the court's benefit.[2] Any notice of appeal or application notice filed with the tribunal must be completed in English; and any other document filed with the tribunal must be in English, or accompanied by a translation signed by the translator to certify that the translation is accurate.[3]

1   Guidance Note No 3 (May 2002).
2   Guidance Note No 3 (May 2002) at [7].
3   Tribunal Procedure (First-tier Tribunal) (Immigration and Asylum Chamber) Rules 2014, SI 2014/2604, r 12(5); or alternatively, documents may be provided in Welsh where the case is being heard there, or has a Welsh connection.

NATURAL JUSTICE

5.88   Fairness lies at the centre of the tribunal's processes. This applies with particular force to asylum appeals, which must be afforded the most anxious scrutiny.[1] The case law shows that an effective opportunity should be afforded to the parties to comment on any matter upon which the immigration judge might take into account. Thus an immigration judge should give the parties a chance to make submissions on any researches they themselves might enter upon (save for 'evidence of an uncontroversial and objectively verifiable nature, eg ... geographical distance' and even then they should be circumspect, to avoid misunderstandings[2]), and upon their own accumulated specialist knowledge that they consider themselves to hold;[3] so too they should give an opportunity to be addressed upon decisions of factual relevance of which they are aware,[4] and, in general, upon legal authorities they consider relevant that come to their attention after a hearing,[5] including those decided post-hearing.[6] As ever in the common law, it is particularly important that an opportunity is given to address any material said to be adverse to a party's case:

> 'it is a first principle of fairness that each party to a judicial process shall have an opportunity to answer by evidence and argument any adverse material which the tribunal may take into account when forming its opinion.'[7]

The principle is at its highest in international protection cases:

> 'Asylum decisions are of such moment that only the highest standards of fairness will suffice'[8]

1   See **6.117**, fn 5 below.
2   *KC (adjudicator wrongly obtaining post-hearing evidence) Turkey* [2005] UKIAT 00010 at [10].
3   *MD (judge's knowledge; standard of English) Pakistan* [2009] UKAIT 00013 at [6].
4   Glidewell LJ in *Gnanavarathan and Norbert v Special Adjudicator* [1995] Imm AR 64 at 71–72.
5   *Rajan* (01/TH/00244, 8 February 2001, starred) at [12].
6   Schiemann LJ for the Court of Appeal in *Secretary of State for the Home Department v Maheshwaran* [2002] EWCA Civ 173 at [4].
7   Lord Mustill in the House of Lords in *Re D* [1995] UKHL 17.
8   *R v Secretary of State, ex parte Thirukumar* [1989] Imm AR 402 at 414, per Bingham LJ.

Natural justice: fairness at the hearing

5.89   Less straightforward is the case where the immigration judge relies upon issues not raised at the hearing to find against an appellant's credibility.

Judges and tribunals have expressed the view that specific challenge should be made to assertions by an appellant with respect to which concerns are held:[1]

> 'It is an elementary aspect of fairness that if a Court or Tribunal is to reject on the basis of lack of truth an allegation, then there should be specific challenge in the first place and secondly, on a reasons basis, adequate reasons should be given in the face of that forensic challenge why it has or has not succeeded'

even if such an approach requires further written or oral submissions,[2] albeit that such a step should be rare.[3] Matters raised in an asylum refusal letter need not be specifically addressed by the representative at the hearing: this is a tactical decision for the appellant.[4] Where a matter arises in the course of a hearing which has not been anticipated, it may be necessary for the immigration judge to offer an adjournment to ensure justice is done.[5] Whether fairness demands that a particular concern be put to a witness explicitly depends on the facts of the case:[6]

> 'It is not necessary for a fair hearing that every point of concern which an Adjudicator has, be put expressly to a party, where credibility is plainly at issue. As we have said elsewhere, it is a matter of judgment whether to omit to do so is unfair or whether to do so risks appearing to be unfair as a form of cross-examination. On balance, the Adjudicator's major points of concern are better put, especially if they are not obvious. The questions should be focussed but open, not leading, expressed in a neutral way and manner, and not at too great a length or in too great a number. But, whether or not that is done, it is for the Claimant to make his case.'

Thus, where an account contains patent discrepancies, it is not necessary for the immigration judge to draw them to the attention of the appellant,[7] unless they are matters which are peripheral or could not reasonably have been anticipated as being construed as adverse to him.[8]

---

1   Turner J in the High Court in *Gunn* (CO/4630/97; although cited with approval by the then President in *Sikyurek* (18778, 28 October 1998)); Lord Reed in *HA and TD v Secretary of State for the Home Department* [2010] CSIH 28, United Kingdom at [31], citing *HA v Secretary of State for the Home Department* 2008 SC 58; Schiemann LJ in *v Secretary of State for the Home Department* [2002] EWCA Civ1906 at [13]; Sedley LJ in *MJ (Iran) v Secretary of State for the Home Department* [2008] EWCA Civ 564 at [15]–[18].
2   *AJ (assessment of medical evidence – examination of scars) Cameroon* [2005] UKIAT 00060.
3   Schiemann LJ for the Court of Appeal in *Secretary of State for the Home Department v Maheshwaran* [2002] EWCA Civ 173 at [4].
4   *Devaseelan* (also known as *D (Tamils)*) [2002] UKIAT 00702 (starred) at [23].
5   *R v Immigration Appeal Tribunal, ex parte Hubbard* [1985] Imm AR 110 at 119; Burnton J in the Administrative Court in *R v Special Adjudicator and Secretary of State for the Home Department, ex parte Kolcak* [2001] EWHC Admin 532 at [30].
6   *WN (Surendran, credibility, new evidence) Democratic Republic of Congo* [2004] UKIAT 00213; Schiemann LJ for the Court of Appeal in *Maheshwaran* (above) at [6].
7   Schiemann LJ for the Court of Appeal in *Maheshwaran* (above) at [5].
8   *AA (credibility, totality of evidence, fair trial) Sudan* [2004] UKIAT 00152 at [11].

RE-OPENING THE HEARING AND RECEIVING EVIDENCE POST-HEARING

5.90 There will be occasions where it is thought proper to reopen a hearing; indeed, as discussed above, fairness may occasionally require this.[1] The tribunal remains seized of an appeal until it promulgates its decision;[2] and a delay in promulgating a decision may make it all the more necessary to contemplate updating the evidence.[3] Evidence can be received after a hearing albeit (absent cases where its reception is considered appropriate by the judge without objection by either party) only in 'very exceptional circumstances'. Where late evidence is sent after a hearing, then its admission is governed by *Ladd v Marshall* principles,[4] the relevant questions being whether it could not have been previously obtained with due diligence, whether it would have had an important influence on the result, and whether it is apparently credible. If application of that test suggests a risk of serious injustice, then it should be admitted, and it will then be necessary either to reconvene the hearing or to obtain the written submissions of the other side in relation to the matters included in the late submission, by way of formal direction.[5]

1   See **5.89**, fn 1 above.
2   Carnwath LJ giving judgment of the Court of Appeal in *E v Secretary of State for the Home Department* [2004] EWCA Civ 49 at [27].
3   Carnwath LJ giving judgment of the Court of Appeal in *E* (above) at [93]–[94].
4   *Ladd v Marshall* [1954] 1 WLR 1489.
5   *SD (treatment of post-hearing evidence) Russia* [2008] UKAIT 00037 at [9] and [16]–[17]; Adjudicator's Guidance Note No 4 (February 2003).

BIAS

5.91 Like any other judicial officer, an immigration judge must act without bias, the test for which is whether the circumstances would

> 'lead a fair-minded and informed observer to conclude that there was a real possibility, or a real danger, the two being the same, that the tribunal was biased.'[1]

That observer 'is neither complacent nor unduly sensitive or suspicious', and[2]

> 'is well informed and in possession of quite extensive knowledge ... the fund of knowledge held by the hypothetical observer will include the terms of the judicial oath of office, the pedigree, scale and longevity of the practice and the alertness of the Judges concerned to the constraints imposed by principle and the overarching duties of the appointed panel.'

1   Lord Hope in *Porter v Magill* [2001] UKHL 67 at [103].
2   *MOJ (return to Mogadishu) (CG)* [2014] UKUT 442 (IAC) at [13].

5.92 Bias may range from irrational prejudice to 'particular circumstances which, for logical reasons, predispose a judge towards a particular view of the evidence or issues before him'; and it may be actual, or apparent, in form, the latter found where circumstances exist which give rise to a reasonable apprehension that the judge may have been, or may be, biased.[1] Few things can be more important to the judicial decision maker than the ability to maintain an open mind, and it is important not to lose 'objectivity [so] as to become, subconsciously or otherwise, incapable of rendering an unbiased decision', as where a prior procedural decision is maintained notwithstanding a change of circumstances – it is critical that any submissions relating to a change of circumstances since an argument was rejected are entertained fairly.[2] A judge should be very wary of expressing a provisional view on an appeal, where credibility is in issue, prior to hearing evidence; although if he has doubts as to the prospects of a case succeeding even at its highest, he is entitled to raise them[3] (though he need not necessarily do so).[4] Even cases which at first sight seem to lack merit may well have hidden strengths:[5]

'As everybody who has anything to do with the law well knows, the path of the law is strewn with examples of open and shut cases which, somehow, were not; of unanswerable charges which, in the event, were completely answered; of inexplicable conduct which was fully explained; of fixed and unalterable determinations that, by discussion, suffered a change.'

1   The Master of the Rolls in *Re Medicaments and Related Classes of Goods (No 2)* [2001] 1 WLR 711.
2   Rix LJ in *AM (Cameroon) R (on the application of) v Asylum and Immigration Tribunal* [2007] EWCA Civ 131 at [131], and Waller LJ at [109]–[111].
3   The President in *XS (Kosovo – adjudicator's conduct – psychiatric report) Serbia and Montenegro* [2005] UKIAT 00093 at [29]; Kay J in the High Court in *R v Special Adjudicator of the Immigration Appellate Authority* (CO/1357/99, 11 February 2000).
4   *Makhan Singh* [1999] Imm AR 92.
5   Megarry J in *John v Rees* [1970] 1 Ch 345 at 347.

5.93 Once a bias challenge is raised, a judge cannot absolve himself by providing evidence of his state of mind, given the objective nature of the test.[1] A solicitor whose firm practises at the same centre as he appears as an immigration judge must recuse himself from sitting the moment that a person from his firm appears before him, for in such cases he has an actual interest in the proceedings, and his sittings should be administered to minimise the risk of that eventuality.[2] Judicial ethnicity or nationality is exceedingly unlikely to give rise to any well-founded allegation of bias;[3] a judge's rate of dismissing appeals might, depending on the evidence.[4] A system in which one party receives notification of a decision first, as was long the case in asylum appeals generally, though now prevails only with regard to those decisions that exhaust appeal rights, is not unfair such as to compromise the independence and impartiality of the appeals process or to otherwise establish bias.[5]

1   Peter Gibson LJ in the Court of Appeal in *BLP UK Ltd v Anthony Douglas Marsh* [2003] EWCA Civ 132 cited the Employment Appeal Tribunal, itself interpreting *Locabail UK v Bayfield Properties* [2000] QB 451, to such effect.
2   *Kaur* (01/TH/02438, 26 September 2001). Adjudicator's Guidance Note No 1 (November 2001) gives guidance on the administration of part-time adjudicators.
3   Richards J in the Administrative Court in *R v Immigration Appeal Tribunal, ex parte Krishnarajah* [2001] EWHC Admin 351, citing *Locabail UK v Bayfield Properties* [2000] QB 451.
4   *Bulut v Canada (Minister of Citizenship and Immigration)* 2005 FC 1627 (CanLII); *Nyembo v Refugee Appeals Tribunal* [2007] IESC 25 and [2006] IEHC 388.
5   *Bubaker v Lord Chancellor* [2002] EWCA Civ 1107.

AUTHORITY TO REPRESENT AND RECEIVE DOCUMENTS

5.94   At appeal, a party may be represented by any person authorised to act on his behalf who is not prohibited from representing by IAA 1999[1] (which generally requires regulation by the Office of the Immigration Services Commissioner (OISC), or the General Council of the Bar, the Law Society of England and Wales, the Chartered Institute of Legal Executives, the Faculty of Advocates, the Law Society of Scotland, the General Council of the Bar of Northern Ireland, or the Law Society of Northern Ireland).[2] A family friend or other individual may represent, so long as not acting 'in the course of a business carried on (whether or not for profit) by him or by another person', and his role should not be restricted to that of a McKenzie friend (and so he may make submissions on the appellant's behalf).[3] A sponsor may represent the appellant, though he should notify the tribunal that he intends to do so, and in such a case he would be permitted to give evidence as well as make submissions.[4] The fact that a person prohibited from providing legal services has represented the appellant does not render proceedings void.[5] Where a representative begins to act for a party, he must immediately notify the tribunal and the other party of that fact, providing his name and address (this may be done at a hearing);[6] and once acting for a party, he may do anything required by the Rules on the party's behalf, save for signing a witness statement.[7] A party should provide any documents to a person's representative upon learning that the representative is acting, and may assume that the representative remains instructed subject to receiving written notification to the contrary.[8] Once a representative is on the record, the FTT must provide him with a copy of any document that is given to the appellant.[9] There is no duty on the Home Office to investigate an appellant's address where there is no cause for suspicion about it, for example where the respondent has received a change of address or a document has been returned undelivered, or where the person is detained, or where there is something adverse known about his representative (particularly where a representative was on the record at the time the hearing notice was sent out).[10] However, if an appeal is determined without an appellant's attendance, the FTT may set aside its decision disposing of proceedings if procedural irregularity comes to light, as where 'a party, or a party's representative, was not present at a hearing related to the proceedings' or where 'a document relating to the proceedings was not provided to, or was not received at an appropriate time by, a party or a party's representative', where the interests of justice require this.[11] It can be anticipated that legal assistance for purposes such as the collation of evidence will concentrate on the key moments in the appeal process.[12]

1   Tribunal Procedure (First-tier Tribunal) (Immigration and Asylum Chamber) Rules 2014, SI 2014/2604, r 10(1); IAA 1999, s 84.
2   See eg the explanation in the Guidance issued by the Office of the Immigration Services Commissioner, 'How to become a regulated immigration adviser' (updated 1 December 2014), para 1.
3   IAA 1999, s 82(2); *RK (entitlement to represent: s 84) Bangladesh* [2011] UKUT 00409(IAC) at [2]; for more on the possible role of McKenzie friends, see Presidential Guidance Note 2013 No 3, 'Guidance for unrepresented claimants in the upper tribunal immigration and asylum chamber', Pt 7.
4   *HH (sponsor as representative) Serbia* [2006] UKAIT 00063.
5   SI 2014/2604, r 10(2).
6   SI 2014/2604, r 10(3).
7   SI 2014/2604, r 10(4).
8   SI 2014/2604, r 10(5).
9   SI 2014/2604, r 10(6).
10   *HC (2005 Procedure Rules ultra vires?) Iran* [2005] UKAIT 00139 at [17].
11   SI 2014/2604, r 32(1)(a), (2)(a) and (c).
12   Carnwath LJ giving judgment of the Court of Appeal in *E v Secretary of State for the Home Department* [2004] EWCA Civ 49 at [94].

LACK OF REPRESENTATION

5.95   Where an appellant expects representation but it does not materialise at a hearing, it would be advisable for an immigration judge to investigate the explanation before proceeding with the appeal.[1] An asylum seeker does not necessarily require representation where his case is straightforward and turns wholly on his credibility,[2] though it would be unduly prejudicial for a person 'to have their account tested in an appeal hearing before being interviewed on his claim or having an opportunity to present it in a non-adversarial and non-intimidatory setting.'[3] However,

> 'A court or tribunal must provide a party with a fair opportunity to prepare and this will usually involve allowing him sufficient time to secure representation ... If it is an asylum seeker who is moving for an adjournment in an immigration case and a refusal will leave him without representation, the court or tribunal must, of course, proceed with particular care and sensitivity given his potential vulnerability.'[4]

1   Charles J in the Administrative Court in *R (Bosombanguwa) v Secretary of State for the Home Department and Immigration Appeal Tribunal* [2004] EWHC 1656 [Admin] at [60]–[69]; Munby J in the Administrative Court in *Dirisu, R (on the application of) v Immigration Appeal Tribunal* [2001] EWHC Admin 970 at [20]; Sedley LJ in *AK (Iran) v Secretary of State for the Home Department* [2008] EWCA Civ 941 at [20]–[32].

2   Longmore LJ in *HH (Iran) v Secretary of State for the Home Department* [2008] EWCA Civ
     504 at [17]; cf Kay J in *R v Secretary of State for the Home Department and Immigration
     Appeal Tribunal, ex parte Bogou* (CO/2972/99, 15 February 2000).
3   Munby J in *Dirisu* (above) at [34].
4   Lord Carloway in *Khan, Re Application for Judicial Review* [2004] ScotCS 125 at [15]–[16];
     Munby J in the Administrative Court in *R v Immigration Appeal Tribunal, ex parte Sarkisian*
     [2001] EWHC Admin 486 at [7]–[8] considering that the line of authority that began with
     Ajeh (13853, 30 August 1996), which stated that the need for representation was axiomatic in
     asylum appeals, did not take account of the stringent requirements then (but no longer) in the
     governing Procedure Rules – the Asylum Appeals (Procedure) Rules 1996, SI 1996/2070, r
     10 provided that a special adjudicator 'shall not adjourn a hearing unless he is satisfied that an
     adjournment is necessary for the just disposal of the appeal' and further required the special
     adjudicator to have 'particular regard to the need to secure the just, timely and effective
     conduct of the proceedings'.

CONDUCT OF HEARING WITH AN UNREPRESENTED PARTY

5.96   Where proceeding with an appeal with a litigant in person, the FTT
must bear in mind the following considerations:[1]

'A litigant in person may pose particular problems for a court or tribunal.
Some litigants in person, often perhaps those who are litigants in person
through choice, will be confident, assertive, articulate and undaunted at
the prospect of appearing in a setting which may be far from unfamiliar to
them. Some litigants in person are able to display an enviable mastery of
the details of even the most complex and heavily documented case. Other
litigants in person may be lacking in confidence, unassertive, inarticulate
and daunted at the prospect of appearing for the first time in an unfamiliar
setting. The court or tribunal must be sensitive to the problems facing such
a litigant in person.'

1   Munby J in *Dirisu, R (on the application of) v Immigration Appeal Tribunal* [2001] EWHC
     Admin 970 at [20].

5.97   Where an asylum seeker is unrepresented, the immigration judge
may have to take a particularly intrusive role, giving him every assistance to
adequately present his case:[1]

'[where] the appellant is ... conducting his own appeal ... it is the duty of
the Special Adjudicator to give every assistance, which he can give, to the
appellant.'

1   *Surendran* (19197, 25 June 1999) at [6].

5.98   Where the respondent is unrepresented, the *Surendran* guidelines[1]
(which are voiced to deal with asylum claims, though may have application
beyond such cases; and which are, as their name suggests, only guidelines,
rather than a straitjacket)[2] are as follows:

'Where the Home Office is not represented, we do not consider that a special adjudicator is entitled to treat a decision appealed against as having been withdrawn. The withdrawal of a decision to refuse leave to enter and asylum requires a positive act on the part of the Home Office in the form of a statement in writing that the decision has been withdrawn. In the instant case, and in similar cases, this is not the position. The Home Office, on the contrary, requests that the special adjudicator deals with the appeal on the basis of the contents of the letter of refusal and any other written submissions which the Home Office makes when indicating that it would not be represented.

Nor do we consider that the appeal should be allowed simpliciter. The function of the adjudicator is to review the reasons given by the Home Office for refusing asylum within the context of the evidence before him and the submissions made on behalf of the appellant, and then come to his own conclusions as to whether or not the appeal should be allowed or dismissed. In doing so he must, of course, observe the correct burden and standard of proof.

Where an adjudicator is aware that the Home Office is not to be represented, he should take particular care to read all the papers in the bundle before him prior to the hearing and, if necessary, in particular in those cases where he has only been informed on the morning of the hearing that the Home Office will not appear, he should consider the advisability of adjourning for the purposes of reading the papers and therefore putting the case further back in his list for the same day.

Where matters of credibility are raised in the letter of refusal, the special adjudicator should request the representative to address these matters, particularly in his examination of the appellant or, if the appellant is not giving evidence, in his submissions. Whether or not these matters are addressed by the representative, and whether or not the special adjudicator has himself expressed any particular concern, he is entitled to form his own view as to credibility on the basis of the material before him.

Where no matters of credibility are raised in the letter of refusal but, from a reading of the papers, the special adjudicator himself considers that there are matters of credibility arising therefrom, he should similarly point these matters out to the representative and ask that they be dealt with, either in examination of the appellant or in submissions.

It is our view that it is not the function of a special adjudicator to adopt an inquisitorial role in cases of this nature. The system pertaining at present is essentially an adversarial system and the special adjudicator is an impartial judge and assessor of the evidence before him. Where the Home Office does not appear the Home Office's argument and basis of refusal, as contained in the letter of refusal, is the Home Office's case purely and simply, subject to any other representations which the Home Office may make to the special adjudicator. It is not the function of the special adjudicator to expand upon that document, nor is it his function to raise matters which are not raised in it, unless these are matters which are apparent to him from a reading of the papers, in which case these matters should be drawn to the attention of the appellant's representative who should then be invited to make submissions or call evidence in relation thereto. We would add that this is not necessarily the same function which has to be performed by a special adjudicator where he has refused to adjourn a case in the absence of a representative for the appellant, and the appellant is virtually conducting his own appeal. In such event, it is the duty of the special adjudicator to give every assistance, which he can give, to the appellant.

Where, having received the evidence or submissions in relation to matters which he has drawn to the attention of the representatives, the special adjudicator considers clarification is necessary, then he should be at liberty to ask questions for the purposes of seeking clarification. We would emphasise, however, that it is not his function to raise matters which a Presenting Officer might have raised in cross-examination had he been present.

There might well be matters which are not raised in the letter of refusal which the special adjudicator considers to be relevant and of importance. We have in mind, for example, the question of whether or not, in the event that the special adjudicator concludes that a Convention ground exists, internal flight is relevant, or perhaps, where, from the letter of refusal and the other documents in the file, it appears to the special adjudicator that the question of whether or not the appellant is entitled to Convention protection by reason of the existence of civil war (matters raised by the House of Lords in the case of *Adan*). Where these are matters which clearly the special adjudicator considers he may well wish to deal with in his determination, then he should raise these with the representative and invite submissions to be made in relation thereto.

There are documents which are now available on the Internet and which can be considered to be in the public domain, which may not be included in the bundle before the special adjudicator. We have in mind the US State Department Report, Amnesty Reports and Home Office Country Reports. If the special adjudicator considers that he might well wish to refer to these documents in his determination, then he should so indicate to the representative and invite submissions in relation thereto.

We do not consider that a special adjudicator should grant an adjournment except in the most exceptional circumstances and where, in the view of the special adjudicator, matters of concern in the evidence before him cannot be properly addressed by examination of the appellant by his representative or submissions made by that representative. If, during the course of a hearing, it becomes apparent to a special adjudicator that such circumstances have arisen, then he should adjourn the case part heard, require the Home Office to make available a Presenting Officer at the adjourned hearing, and prepare a record of proceedings of the case, which should be submitted to both parties up to the point of the adjournment, and such record to be submitted prior to the adjourned hearing.'

1   Annexed to *MNM (Surendran guidelines for adjudicators) (Kenya)* [2000] UKIAT 00005.
2   Ouseley J in *WN (Surendran; credibility; new evidence) Democratic Republic of Congo* [2004] UKIAT 00213 at [29].

5.99   It is not an error of law to fail to follow the Guidelines, though where they are overlooked, procedural error may be more easily established.[1] There is a Guidance Note that specifically addresses procedure where the SSHD is unrepresented.[2] It warns against presuming that the lack of representation is due to an adverse merits assessment by a solicitor which led to controlled legal representation being refused (it may equally be down to a breakdown in the relationship, a conflict of interest, or a misunderstanding as to the costs of representation). If an asylum seeker explains that he is seeking representation and can point to realistic endeavours to obtain the same, an adjournment may be desirable; the existence of supporting documents such as a witness statement will be relevant in assessing whether the case should proceed as listed.[3] The Guidance Note gives careful guidance as to the process to be adopted for oral evidence, and for the making of submissions, consistent with the *Surendran* guidelines. The obligation remains on the appellant to address obvious points regarding his credibility rather than await their being raised by the judge,[4] and there is a public interest in only well-founded asylum claims succeeding.[5] A judge should not let his own theory of a case develop and pursue questions based on it.[6] Where new material is submitted following a refusal letter that does not challenge credibility, and where the appellant is represented, it is not essential that self-evident concerns are put by the judge: in determining whether they should be put,

> 'Obvious points are: why the material had not been mentioned before; why there were contradictions between that and what had been said before; and how obvious implausibilities or improbabilities in it are to be answered. For an unrepresented Appellant, the Adjudicator is likely to have to draw his attention explicitly to the point, in order fairly to be able to rely on it.'[7]

There is a useful guide to general procedure on the www.justice.gov.uk website: Form T359 'Guide for unrepresented appellants First-tier Tribunal Immigration and Asylum Chamber'.

1   *WN (Surendran; credibility; new evidence) Democratic Republic of Congo* [2004] UKIAT 00213 at [30].
2   Guidance Note 5 (April 2003). There is also Presidential Guidance Note 2013 No 3, the 'Guide for unrepresented claimants in Upper Tribunal Immigration and Asylum Chamber', which is itself useful as to expectations of procedure at substantive hearings.
3   See generally Guidance Note 5.
4   *WN* (above) at [31].
5   *SH (subsequent decision: how far relevant?) Turkey* [2005] UKIAT 00068 at [36].

6   *WN* (above) at [33].
7   *WN* (above) at [34].

ERRORS BY LEGAL REPRESENTATIVES

5.100   Parties may find their cases affected by errors of their legal representatives, and given the pressures on publicly funded lawyers, occasional mishaps are entirely understandable:[1] 'Immigration judges will know of the great pressure that anyone working in the field of immigration and asylum is under with regard to case load and throughput.'[2] Thus, 'there is no general principle of law which fixes a party with the procedural errors of his or her representative' albeit that, outside of the asylum context with its necessity of anxious scrutiny, the acts of a representative may be imputed to his client depending on the circumstances,[3] as in the cases of students who are failed by their representatives[4] or their educational sponsors.[5] Serially offending representatives should not expect their recidivism to escape notice.[6] The Court of Appeal has referred to the need for a broad construction of powers as necessary to ameliorate inadequate representation.[7] Where negligence is alleged, the tribunal will generally expect the matter to be duly evidenced:[8]

> 'We wish to make it clear that, in general, we will not make a finding of fact based on an allegation against former representatives unless, first, it is clear that the former representatives have been given an opportunity to respond to the allegation which is being made expressly or implicitly against them, and secondly, we are either shown the response or shown correspondence which indicates that there has been no response.'

1   Sedley LJ in *FP (Iran) v Secretary of State for the Home Department* [2007] EWCA Civ 13 at [7].
2   Blake J in *Semere, R (on the application of) v Asylum and Immigration Tribunal* [2009] EWHC 335 (Admin) at [58].
3   *FP (Iran)* (above) at [42]–[46]; *R v Secretary of State for the Home Department, ex parte Al-Mehdawi* [1990] 1 AC 87; Collins J in *AFP Nori, R (on the application of) v Secretary of State for the Home Department* [2011] EWHC 1604 (Admin) at [48]; *MM (unfairness; E & R) Sudan* [2014] UKUT 105 (IAC) at [25]; Simon Brown LJ giving permission to appeal to the Court of Appeal in *Haile v Immigration Appeal Tribunal* [2001] EWCA Civ 663; Sullivan J in the High Court in *R v Immigration Appeal Tribunal, ex parte S* [1998] INLR 168; Wilson J in *R (Makke) v Immigration Appeal Tribunal* [2004] EWHC 1523 (Admin) at [25].
4   *Al-Mehdawi v Secretary of State for the Home Department* [1990] 1 AC 876, the effect of which was described by Dillon LJ in *Mohammed Hassan v Secretary of State for the Home Department* [1994] Imm AR 483.
5   Sales LJ for the majority in *EK (Ivory Coast) v Secretary of State for the Home Department* [2014] EWCA Civ 1517 at [34]–[36].
6   *BO (extension of time for appealing) Nigeria* [2006] UKAIT 00035 at [17].
7   Schiemann LJ for the Court in *Kesse v Secretary of State for the Home Department* [2001] EWCA Civ 177 at [37].
8   *BT (former solicitors' alleged misconduct) Nepal* [2004] UKIAT 00311 at [5]; *AG (Turkey – CA – fresh evidence)* [2005] UKIAT 00014 at [17].

5.101 This does not mean that only an admission of an error by the previous lawyers will suffice,[1] and nor should an application to the UT be further delayed whilst such evidence is sought.[2] The tribunal has indicated that representatives should expect repeated negligence leading to a material difference in the outcome of appeals to lead to referral to the Office for the Immigration Services Commissioner (or other relevant regulator).[3] Allegations of this nature must be clearly pleaded, and consideration given to the necessity of waiving legal professional privilege.[4] As appellants may be represented by whomever they choose, it is not incumbent upon an immigration judge to adjourn where the representation is incompetent, at least so long as the advocate does not stray beyond his brief,[5] though the tribunal should be alert to any suggestion by an appellant that a representative is not currently acting on his instructions.[6] It cannot be presumed that an ostensibly competent solicitor would deliberately lodge an unmeritorious appeal.[7] The presumption must be, subject to contrary evidence, that a person is properly advised and has made an informed decision.[8]

1   *SV (alleging misconduct and suppressing evidence) Iran* [2005] UKAIT 00160 at [28].
2   *BO (extension of time for appealing) Nigeria* [2006] UKAIT 00035 at [18].
3   *Abo-Dawoud* [2002] UKIAT 00327.
4   Andrew Nicol QC sitting as a Deputy Judge of the High Court in *R (Mamedov) v Secretary of State for the Home Department and Immigration Appeal Tribunal* [2003] EWHC 3174 (Admin).
5   *IS (concession made by representative) Sierra Leone* [2005] UKIAT 00009 at [17] and [18].
6   *HH (sponsor as representative) Serbia* [2006] UKAIT 00063 at [17].
7   HHJ Pelling QC in *B, R (on the application of) v Secretary of State for the Home Department* [2009] EWHC 2273 (Admin) at [13].
8   Hickinbottom J in *Hashemite, R (on the application of) v Upper Tribunal (Immigration and Asylum Chamber)* [2013] EWHC 2316 (Admin) at [57](i).

HOME OFFICE PRESENTING OFFICERS

5.102 The SSHD is represented by Home Office Presenting Officers (POs) or by counsel, either for operational reasons or because of the particular importance of the individual case. They are not subject to the general prohibition on providing immigration advice and services, as those employed by, or for the purposes of, a government department, when acting in that capacity, or under the control of a government department, or otherwise exercising functions or holding office on behalf of the Crown, are exempted from the prohibition under IAA 1999.[1] Nevertheless, they should be aware of their duties as advocates.[2] Thus, for example, a failure to challenge a judicial declaration of opinion regarding a particular country will prevent the matter being revisited on appeal.[3] There is no automatic barrier to a person who has taken some prior role in an asylum claim (eg as interviewer) from representing on appeal, subject to the interests of justice (it would not be appropriate for an interviewing officer to both give evidence and act as advocate).[4] The administration of the Home Office's side of litigation has from time to time been the subject of lament by the tribunal, with the late allocation of cases to POs and a lack of response to directions being prominent amongst the criticisms levelled.[5] The deficiencies, it should be made clear, are systemic rather than being the fault of the officers themselves, who often labour under heavy workloads.

1 IAA 1999, s 84(1) and (6).
2 *SD (treatment of post-hearing evidence) Russia* [2008] UKAIT 00037 at [8].
3 Collins J in *MM* (01/TH/00994, 4 June 2001) at [11].
4 *HK (interviewer as advocate: unfair?) Ethiopia* [2006] UKAIT 00081.
5 *Tatar* (00/TH/01914, 26 July 2000); *Razi* (01/TH/01836, 29 September 2001) at [16]; *Mefaja* [2002] UKIAT 01188; *Nori* [2002] UKIAT 01887; Sedley LJ in the Court of Appeal in *Benkaddouri v Secretary of State for the Home Department* [2003] EWCA Civ 1250.

Duties and conduct of POs

5.103   There is a duty on the Home Office to put forward policies relevant to the case in hand, even if they are not necessarily applicable if the respondent's preferred factual approach to a case prevails.[1] It is undesirable for the SSHD to submit generic lists of authorities and then to complain that points not raised therein have been overlooked.[2] The greater resources available to the SSHD militate against indulgences being granted to his representatives.[3] The failure to field a representative does not entitle a party to ventilate factual matters on appeal that were not raised at first instance.[4] The judge need not pursue aspects of a refusal letter that are not pressed by the respondent's advocate before them.[5] The absence of a PO should not put the SSHD in a better position regarding the non-admittance of evidence than if a PO was present.[6]

1 Keene LJ in *AA (Afghanistan) v Secretary of State for the Home Department* [2007] EWCA Civ 12 at [28]; see also Sedley LJ granting permission to appeal to the Court of Appeal in *SH (Afghanistan) v Secretary of State for the Home Department* [2007] EWCA Civ 1197.
2 *AM (s 88 (2): immigration document) Somalia* [2009] UKAIT 00008.
3 See *GH (Afghanistan) v Secretary of State for the Home Department* [2005] EWCA Civ 1603 at [17].
4 Laws LJ in *R (Kelangin) v Immigration Appeal Tribunal* [2004] EWCA Civ 323 at [9].
5 Toulson LJ in *JK (Democratic Republic of Congo) v Secretary of State for the Home Department* [2007] EWCA Civ 831 at [35].
6 *A (absence of party – late evidence) Sri Lanka* [2005] UKIAT 00028 at [21].

PART 4 – DECISIONS

DETERMINATION OF ISSUES

Issues to be determined and relevant rules

5.104   In new-style appeals under the relevant provisions introduced by IA 2014, the only question on appeal is compatibility with the ECHR.[1] This is likely to significantly narrow the scope for procedural failings and unfairness to lead to an appeal being allowed. It remains to be seen whether stage 3 of the *Razgar*[2] test, which investigates whether an interference with private and family life is in accordance with the law, might be interpreted more broadly than has so far been suggested by the tribunal: the 'law' for the purposes of the Strasbourg Court usually implies qualitative requirements, including those of accessibility and foreseeability, rather than necessarily embracing the full ambit of the domestic public law principles which over time have come to be recognised by the UT as potentially relevant in statutory appeals.[3] The tribunal must determine the issues raised by the grounds of appeal and other matters raised in a one-stop notice subject to those 'new matters' raised post-application where the consent of the SSHD is required.[4] In old-style appeals under the saved provisions of NIAA 2002, a refusal letter which misstates the law will make the decision it contains less defensible, but it will not necessarily be the case that the appeal must then be allowed, for the immigration judge's jurisdiction is to make a determination on the facts and law for himself.[5] The tribunal's focus will be upon the application made and the decision in response to it, bearing in mind that it may be unrealistic to expect the applicant to precisely identify the immigration rule that best suits his case, albeit that he should identify the relevant facts: then the decision maker should identify the relevant rule(s), and apply them to the facts of the case:[6]

'the duty to consider the applicable rules is not an all-embracing obligation to seek out and find any (or every) potentially applicable rule.'

1   See Chapter 3.
2   *Razgar, R (on the application of) v Secretary of State for the Home Department* [2004] UKHL 27 at [17].
3   *MA (seven-year child concession) Pakistan* [2005] UKIAT 00090 at [17]–[18]; see eg the European Court of Human Rights in *Kafkaris v Cyprus* (2008) 49 EHRR 877; Lady Hale at [323] of *Nicklinson, R (on the application of)* [2014] UKSC 38 indicated that 'in accordance with the law' entailed accessibility and foreseeability, as well as consistency and lack of arbitrariness.
4   See Chapter 3.
5   Woolf J (as he then was) in *R v Immigration Appeal Tribunal, ex parte Hubbard* [1985] Imm AR 110 at 118; Ralph Gibson LJ held in *Nadeem Tahir v Immigration Appeal Tribunal* [1989] Imm AR 98.
6   *SZ (applicable immigration rules) Bangladesh* [2007] UKAIT 00037 at [8]–[11]; *CP Dominica* [2006] UKAIT 00040); *IAT v Tohur Ali* [1988] Imm AR 237 (CA); *Mohammed Fazor Ali v SSHD* [1988] Imm AR 274 (CA).

5.105   Subject to considerations of natural justice, concessions and express agreement that the issues are limited ones (and bearing in mind that there is now a requirement for timely notification of any alteration to the reasons for refusal, see above),[1] on appeal the immigration judge must determine whether a case brought under the Rules satisfies each relevant part of them:[2]

'the notice of refusal is not equivalent to a pleading; if new elements of the Immigration Rules come into play they are to be dealt with on the appeal, and the parties must be allowed any appropriate adjournment in order to avoid the injustice of being taken by surprise.'[3]

1   See **5.32** *et seq* above.
2   *R v Immigration Appeal Tribunal, ex parte Kwok On Tong* [1981] Imm AR 214; *R v Immigration Appeal Tribunal, ex parte Hubbard* [1985] Imm AR 110.
3   *RM (Kwok On Tong: HC 395 para 320) India* [2006] UKAIT 00039 at [10].

5.106   However there is no duty on the immigration judge to raise points not taken by the SSHD.[1] If a judge lacks material evidence for determining whether a part of the Rules only recently identified as relevant is satisfied, or where a faulty decision-making process has led to inadequate evidence being before him, then the appeal should be allowed for want of accordance with the law,[2] making a direction that the application be re-considered in the light of any favourable findings and leaving other aspects of the case to be assessed afresh[3] (as already stated, new-style appeals under the relevant provisions of NIAA 2002 operate under narrower grounds of appeal). A person who seeks to show that he qualifies under a different part of the Rules than that under which he applied must appreciate that he is opening up the range of his appeal in all respects.[4] A person who qualifies under a different aspect of the Rules at the date of decision than that under which he applied may succeed on appeal (at least so long as it is within the same immigration route):[5]

'they are entitled to rely upon that change as constituting a "matter" which was "relevant to the substance of the decision" and which had arisen "after the date of the decision".'

1   Pill LJ in *Secretary of State for the Home Department v FV (Italy)* [2012] EWCA Civ 1199 at [35](f).
2   *CP (s 86(3) and (5), wrong immigration rule) Dominica* [2006] UKAIT 00040 at [22]–[23].
3   *RM (Kwok On Tong: HC 395 para 320) India* [2006] UKAIT 00039 at [11]; *JF (para 320 refusal, substantive rule?) Bangladesh* [2008] UKAIT 00008 at [10].
4   *TB (student application, variation of course, effect) Jamaica* [2006] UKAIT 00034 at [31].
5   *YZ and LX (effect of s 85(4), 2002 Act) China* [2005] UKAIT 00157 at [17].

5.107   Where the Immigration Rules change between the date of decision and the date of hearing, it is the Rules in force at the latter date which are the relevant ones, absent some transitional provision to the contrary:[1]

'in the absence of any statement to the contrary, the most natural reading of the Rules is that they apply to decisions taken by the SSHD until such time as she promulgates new rules, after which she will decide according to the new rules. The same applies to decisions by tribunals and the court'

This accords with the principle that the tribunal's powers to fully review matters of both fact and law in the course of an appeal[2] effectively gives it a role akin to that of primary decision maker.[3]

1   Aikens LJ in *YM (Uganda) v Secretary of State for the Home Department* [2014] EWCA Civ 1292 at [39]; Bean LJ in *ZZ (Tanzania) v Secretary of State for the Home Department* [2014] EWCA Civ 1404 at [20].
2   Rix LJ in *Ascioglu v Secretary of State for the Home Department* [2012] EWCA Civ 1183 at [81] onwards.

3   Lloyd LJ in *DS (Afghanistan) v Secretary of State for the Home Department* [2011] EWCA
     Civ 305 at [71], citing *R (Razgar) v Secretary of State for the Home Department* [2004]
     UKHL 27 at [15].

The general refusal reasons on appeal; statutory presumptions

5.108   Immigration applications may be refused not only because of a failure
to meet the relevant substantive requirements of an Immigration Rule, but
additionally because, under Pt 9 of the Rules, some aspect of an applicant's
conduct or immigration history counts against them. Once again, the different
scope of appeals under the saved and relevant provisions of NIAA 2002 is likely
to significantly alter the course of legal argument in cases where the general
refusal reasons are in play. In new-style appeals, the relevance of the general
refusal reasons will presumably be to show that the public interest points in
favour of an interference with private and family life being found proportionate.
A person refused under the general refusal reasons who has an appeal on
human rights grounds (which ousts his access to administrative review) might
use it as a vehicle for demonstrating his honesty even if uncertain as to whether
or not he can persuade the FTT of his human rights claim's ultimate merits.
The principles that follow have all been articulated in the old-style appeals
system where discretions are reviewable on appeal and where there is a 'not in
accordance with the law' ground of appeal. If the decision letter inferentially
raises issues of the general refusal reasons, the judge may consider them on
appeal.[1] Where factors are known to a decision maker which might have led to
the invocation of the discretionary grounds for refusal, but where the decision
letter does not take the point, the judge is entitled to presume that they are
not relevant: if facts that might be relevant to a discretionary refusal become
apparent only at a hearing, then it may be appropriate to allow the appeal on
the grounds that a discretion is now available to be exercised which, through
no fault of the respondent, so far has not been considered.[2] An appeal flowing
from an application refused only on general refusal reason grounds cannot be
allowed without considering whether the substantive requirements of the rule
are satisfied.[3]

1   *MO (long residence rule – public interest proviso) Ghana* [2007] UKAIT 00014 at [5].
2   *RM (Kwok On Tong: HC395 para 320) India* [2006] UKAIT 00039 at [15]–[18]; *NA
     (Cambridge College of Learning) Pakistan* [2009] UKAIT 00031 at [169]; *RM (Kwok On
     Tong: HC395 para 320) India* [2006] UKAIT 00039.
3   *JF (para 320 refusal, substantive rule?) Bangladesh* [2008] UKAIT 00008, headnote.

5.109   Once facts giving rise to a statutory presumption are established, such
as those of dangerousness and serious criminality under NIAA 2002, s 72 (or
the statutory presumptions as to the public interest in NIAA 2002, s 117), the
judge should consider the issue whether or not it was raised by the SSHD,[1]
subject to considerations of fairness.[2] Whilst a decision which addresses only
an element of the appellant's immigration, human rights or asylum claim
adversely to him may well be determinative of an appeal's outcome, there is

something to be said for dealing with all of the major issues raised, for if the case goes further a failure to have a first-instance view on some part of it may hinder its subsequent final disposal.[3]

1   Stanley Burnton LJ in *Secretary of State for the Home Department v TB (Jamaica)* [2008] EWCA Civ 977 at [29]; Sullivan LJ in *AQ (Somalia) v Secretary of State for the Home Department* [2011] EWCA Civ 695 at [27]–[29].
2   *Mugwagwa (s 72 – applying statutory presumptions) Zimbabwe* [2011] UKUT 00338 (IAC), headnote at (3) and [33].
3   *KF (removal directions and statelessness) Iran* [2005] UKIAT 00109 at [18].

Asylum appeals

5.110   The original decision maker should do his utmost in an asylum case to perform his role in the overall process with the anxious scrutiny that the task demands, and a casual approach to status determination has been deplored by the tribunal;[1] but nevertheless the judge must consider whether the immigration decision breaches the relevant international obligations, and so unless there is a serious procedural irregularity which requires a case to be reconsidered by the SSHD, an asylum appeal should be determined on its merits;[2] procedural failings by the respondent should not lead to the substantive success of an asylum appeal.[3] Under the old-style appeals regime, there is no absolute requirement for an asylum claim to be made to the SSHD before being considered on appeal (contrast the new-style regime under which the consent of the SSHD is required to new matters being raised on appeal)[4] and no obligation to adjourn an appeal for a person to be interviewed before his appeal is considered,[5] though there will be cases where it is appropriate for the SSHD to make 'the necessary administrative and procedural arrangements' to take the role of primary decision maker.[6]

1   *Horvath* (17338, 4 December 1998).
2   Collins J in *AH (HC 395, para 340, cooperation) (Algeria)* [2000] UKIAT 00008, aka *Ali Haddad v Secretary of State* [2000] INLR 117.
3   *Nori* [2002] UKIAT 01887; *Ercan Aldogan* [2002] UKIAT 05120 at [10], cited in *C v Secretary of State for the Home Department (Yugoslavia)* [2003] UKIAT 00007.
4   See **4.13** and **4.14** above.
5   *Haque (s 86(2) – adjournment not required) Bangladesh* [2011] UKUT 00481(IAC) at [27]–[28] – though cf *Dirisu, R (on the application of) v Immigration Appeal Tribunal* [2001] EWHC Admin 970 at **5.54**, fn 2 above.
6   Sullivan LJ in *AS (Afghanistan) v Secretary of State for the Home Department* [2009] EWCA Civ 1076 at [107], discussed by Richards LJ in *Chichvarkin, R (on the application of) v Secretary of State for the Home Department* [2011] EWCA Civ 91 at [42].

Wrongful performance of statutory duties and application of policies

5.111   In old-style appeals under the NIA 2002 saved provisions, a failure to consider a statutory duty, such as that to safeguard and promote child welfare under BCIA 2009, s 55, does not necessarily prevent the tribunal from proceeding to determine an appeal: 'What matters is the substance of the attention given to the "overall wellbeing" ... of the child';[1] and 'Where the appeal can be fairly determined on the merits by the judge, it is inappropriate to allow it without substantive consideration simply for a decision to be made in accordance with the law.'[2] However:

'Where an immigration decision is flawed for failure to have regard to an applicable policy outside the Immigration Rules, then immigration judges of both Tribunals have no appellate function to review the merits of the exercise of discretion or a judgment that is required to be made. Except in most unusual circumstances the most that can be done is for the appellate decision to record that the decision-making process is flawed and incomplete and so the application or decision in question remains outstanding and not yet properly determined'[3]

1   Pill LJ in *AJ (India) v Secretary of State for the Home Department* [2011] EWCA Civ 1191 at [22]–[24], passage cited at [43](b).
2   *T (BCIA 2009, s 55 – entry clearance) Jamaica* [2011] UKUT 00483 (IAC), headnote at (iv).
3   *T* (above) at [25], citing *AG (policies; executive discretions; tribunal's powers) Kosovo* [2007] UKAIT 00082 at [51].

5.112   Some policies may be absolute, in which case the tribunal may allow an appeal outright if it finds that on a proper approach to the policy and facts the appellant's case is unanswerable:[1]

'where a policy is expressed in absolute terms, a claimant may be entitled to succeed substantively ... [ie where] (1) the claimant proves the precise terms of the policy, which (2) creates a presumption, on the facts of his case, in favour of granting leave, and (3) there is either nothing at all to displace the presumption, or nothing that, under the terms of the policy, falls for consideration. If all those factors apply to the case, the appeal should be allowed, with a direction as indicated.'

1   *AG (policies; executive discretions; tribunal's powers) Kosovo* [2007] UKAIT 00082 at [48]–[50]; *IA (applying policies) Mauritius* [2006] UKAIT 00082.

5.113   Where the decision maker fails to appreciate that he holds a discretion (which may arise in the context of guidance intended to operate in tandem with the Rules),[1] the consequences will depend on whether it arose within or outside the Immigration Rules. As stated by the tribunal in *UKUS*:[2]

'There are thus four possible situations where the Tribunal is considering an appeal arising from the exercise of a discretionary power:

(i)   the decision maker has failed to make a lawful decision in the purported exercise of the discretionary power vested in him and a lawful decision is required;

(ii)   the decision maker has lawfully exercised his discretion and the Tribunal has no jurisdiction to intervene;

(iii) the decision maker has lawfully exercised his discretion and the Tribunal upholds the exercise of his discretion;

(iv) the decision maker has lawfully exercised his discretion and the Tribunal reaches its decision exercising its discretion differently.'

In scenario (i), the decision must be allowed for want of accordance with the law, whether or not the discretion arises under the Rules. In the other scenarios, the tribunal may finally determine the appeal: if the discretion arises outside the Rules, then it may not review it, but if it arises inside the Rules, it may reverse or approve its exercise, depending on its own evaluation of the relevant factors in the case.

1   *PS (para 320(11) discretion: care needed) India* [2010] UKUT 440 (IAC) at [14].
2   *UKUS (discretion: when reviewable)* [2012] UKUT 00307(IAC) at [22]–[23].

SECOND APPEALS

5.114 Circumstances may lead to a particular appellant traversing the appeals system more than once, and given the period of time for which many persons remain in the UK even after an initial unsuccessful appeal, there will be cases where their removal substantially later raises different issues as to their human rights.[1] The tribunal in *Devaseelan*[2] gave guidance on this situation, which merits setting out in full:

'38. The second Adjudicator must, however be careful to recognise that the issue before him is not the issue that was before the first Adjudicator. In particular, time has passed; and the situation at the time of the second Adjudicator's determination may be shown to be different from that which obtained previously. Appellants may want to ask the second Adjudicator to consider arguments on issues that were not – or could not be – raised before the first Adjudicator; or evidence that was not – or could not have been – presented to the first Adjudicator.

39. In our view the second Adjudicator should treat such matters in the following way.

(1) The first Adjudicator's determination should always be the starting-point. It is the authoritative assessment of the Appellant's status at the time it was made. In principle issues such as whether the Appellant was properly represented, or whether he gave evidence, are irrelevant to this.

(2) Facts happening since the first Adjudicator's determination can always be taken into account by the second Adjudicator. If those facts lead the second Adjudicator to the conclusion that, at the date of his determination and on the material before him, the appellant makes his case, so be it. The previous decision, on

the material before the first Adjudicator and at that date, is not inconsistent.

(3)   Facts happening before the first Adjudicator's determination but having no relevance to the issues before him can always be taken into account by the second Adjudicator. The first Adjudicator will not have been concerned with such facts, and his determination is not an assessment of them.

40.   We now pass to matters that could have been before the first Adjudicator but were not.

(4)   Facts personal to the Appellant that were not brought to the attention of the first Adjudicator, although they were relevant to the issues before him, should be treated by the second Adjudicator with the greatest circumspection. An Appellant who seeks, in a later appeal, to add to the available facts in an effort to obtain a more favourable outcome is properly regarded with suspicion from the point of view of credibility. (Although considerations of credibility will not be relevant in cases where the existence of the additional fact is beyond dispute.) It must also be borne in mind that the first Adjudicator's determination was made at a time closer to the events alleged and in terms of both fact-finding and general credibility assessment would tend to have the advantage. For this reason, the adduction of such facts should not usually lead to any reconsideration of the conclusions reached by the first Adjudicator.

(5)   Evidence of other facts – for example country evidence may not suffer from the same concerns as to credibility, but should be treated with caution. The reason is different from that in (4). Evidence dating from before the determination of the first Adjudicator might well have been relevant if it had been tendered to him: but it was not, and he made his determination without it. The situation in the Appellant's own country at the time of that determination is very unlikely to be relevant in deciding whether the Appellant's removal at the time of the second Adjudicator's determination would breach his human rights. Those representing the Appellant would be better advised to assemble up-to-date evidence than to rely on material that is (*ex hypothesi*) now rather dated.

41.   The final major category of case is where the Appellant claims that his removal would breach Article 3 for the same reason that he claimed to be a refugee.

(6)   If before the second Adjudicator the Appellant relies on facts that are not materially different from those put to the first Adjudicator, and proposes to support the claim by what is in

essence the same evidence as that available to the Appellant at that time, the second Adjudicator should regard the issues as settled by the first Adjudicator's determination and make his findings in line with that determination rather than allowing the matter to be re-litigated. We draw attention to the phrase "the same evidence as that available to the Appellant" at the time of the first determination. We have chosen this phrase not only in order to accommodate guidelines (4) and (5) above, but also because, in respect of evidence that was available to the Appellant, he must be taken to have made his choices about how it should be presented. An Appellant cannot be expected to present evidence of which he has no knowledge: but if (for example) he chooses not to give oral evidence in his first appeal, that does not mean that the issues or the available evidence in the second appeal are rendered any different by his proposal to give oral evidence (of the same facts) on this occasion.

42. We offer two further comments, which are not less important than what precedes then.

    (7) The force of the reasoning underlying guidelines (4) and (6) is greatly reduced if there is some very good reason why the Appellant's failure to adduce relevant evidence before the first Adjudicator should not be, as it were, held against him. We think such reasons will be rare. There is an increasing tendency to suggest that unfavourable decisions by Adjudicators are brought about by error or incompetence on the part of representatives. New representatives blame old representatives; sometimes representatives blame themselves for prolonging the litigation by their inadequacy (without, of course, offering the public any compensation for the wrong from which they have profited by fees). Immigration practitioners come within the supervision of the Immigration Services Commissioner under part V of the 1999 Act. He has power to register, investigate and cancel the registration of any practitioner, and solicitors and counsel are, in addition, subject to their own professional bodies. An Adjudicator should be very slow to conclude that an appeal before another Adjudicator has been materially affected by a representative's error or incompetence; and such a finding should always be reported (through arrangements made by the Chief Adjudicator) to the Immigration Services Commissioner.

Having said that, we do accept that there will be occasional cases where the circumstances of the first appeal were such that it would be right for the second Adjudicator to look at the matter as if the first determination had never been made. (We think it unlikely that the second Adjudicator would, in such a case, be able to build very meaningfully on the first Adjudicator's determination; but we emphasise that, even in such a case, the first determination stands as the determination of the first appeal.)(8) We do not suggest that, in the foregoing, we have covered every possibility. By covering the major categories into which second appeals fall, we intend to indicate the principles for dealing with such appeals. It will be for the second Adjudicator to decide which of them is or are appropriate in any given case.'

1   Judge LJ in *LD (Algeria)* [2004] EWCA Civ 804 (also cited as *Djebbar*) at [13].
2   *Devaseelan* (also known as *D (Tamils)*) [2002] UKIAT 00702 (starred).

5.115   The *Devaseelan* guidelines are not intended to be inflexible:

'the most important feature of the guidance is that the fundamental obligation of every special adjudicator independently to decide each new application on its own individual merits ... The great value of the guidance is that it invests the decision making process in each individual fresh application with the necessary degree of sensible flexibility and desirable consistency of approach, *without imposing any unacceptable restrictions on the second adjudicator's ability to make the findings which he conscientiously believes to be right.*'[1]

1   Judge LJ in *LD (Algeria)* [2004] EWCA Civ 804 (also cited as *Djebbar*) at [30] and [40]; the emphasis was given by Hooper LJ in the minority in *AA (Somalia) and AH (Iran) v Secretary of State for the Home Department* [2007] EWCA Civ 1040 at [14].

5.116   Unchallenged evidence recorded in an earlier determination, even one that is subsequently identified as a nullity, can be taken into account later, however.[1] The impact of a different credibility finding on a particular witness in his own appeal hearing should be taken into account in a re-assessment of the case of an appellant whose account he had previously supported, but would not of itself demand preference over the earlier determination of the instant appellant's appeal.[2] Inadequate representation at an earlier appeal may be relevant when the case is reevaluated.[3] Beyond the appellant, findings upon the evidence of a material witness made in earlier immigration proceedings form a firm footing upon which later decision makers should make their determinations regarding claims 'that have arisen out of the same factual matrix, such as the same relationship or the same event or series of events', though not simply where there is a 'material overlap of evidence'.[4] The later judge is nevertheless not strictly bound by earlier findings, and it will be easier for a migrant than the SSHD to escape being wholly constrained by them, as they will not have been party to both sets of proceedings.[5] The *Devaseelan* principle applies generally to immigration appeals, not just asylum and human rights cases,[6] and regardless of whether the prior findings are in favour of the asylum seeker or the SSHD.[7] There is no principle of *res judicata* in immigration appeals generally.[8]

1   *EN (abandonment – first decision nullity– Devaseelan applied) Cameroon* [2005] UKAIT 00146 at [41].

2   *S (Sri Lanka)* [2004] UKIAT 00039 at [29] and [36].
3   Carnwath LJ with whom Ward LJ agreed in *AA (Somalia) and AH (Iran)* (above) at [20] and [70]; Judge LJ giving the judgment of the Court of Appeal in *LD (Algeria)* (above) at [37].
4   Carnwath LJ with whom Ward LJ agreed (at [75]) in the Court of Appeal in *AA (Somalia) and AH (Iran)* (above) at [69]. See further Auld LJ in *Ocampo v Secretary of State for the Home Department* [2006] EWCA Civ 1276 at [12]; *AS and AA (effect of previous linked determination) Somalia* [2006] UKAIT 00052 at [61], [67] and [70]–[71]; *TK (consideration of prior determination, directions) Georgia* [2004] UKIAT 00149 at [19]; *BK (Democratic Republic of Congo) v Secretary of State for the Home Department* [2008] EWCA Civ 1322 at [15].
5   Carnwath LJ with whom Ward LJ agreed in *AA (Somalia) and AH (Iran)* (above) at [70].
6   *B v Secretary of State for the Home Department (Pakistan)* [2003] UKIAT 00053 at [15].
7   *Mubu (immigration appeals – res judicata) Zimbabwe* [2012] UKUT 398 (IAC).
8   *Mubu* (above), headnote at (1).

GIVING EFFECT TO DETERMINATION, INCLUDING DIRECTIONS

5.117   Where the FTT allows an appeal under the saved provisions of NIAA 2002 (though not in modern appeals under the relevant provisions), it may give a direction for the purpose of giving effect to its decision.[1] It is for the SSHD to identify the appropriate grant of leave when an appeal is allowed,[2] at least in appeals against removal: a direction to grant settlement may be appropriate in an appeal against refusal of indefinite leave to remain.[3] Normally an application for such a direction should be made at the appeal hearing rather than some time thereafter though a subsequent application may be permitted where the requirement for a direction was not previously appreciated.[4] In entry clearance cases,[5]

> 'A direction should not be made unless the judge is satisfied that the appellant will be able to meet the requirements of any relevant rule in the foreseeable future, but where he or she is so satisfied, then, especially where a child or other vulnerable person is involved, a direction may be appropriate.'

1   NIAA 2002, s 87 (see **4.24** above).
2   Pill LJ in *IT (Sierra Leone) v Secretary of State for the Home Department* [2010] EWCA Civ 787 at [15]; Richards LJ in *Farinloye v Secretary of State for the Home Department* [2010] EWCA Civ 203 at [25]–[27]; Floyd LJ in *Alladin, R (on the application of) v Secretary of State for the Home Department* [2014] EWCA Civ 1334 at [53]; Gibbs J in *R (Islam Shahid) v Secretary of State for the Home Department* [2004] EWHC 2550 (Admin) at [45].
3   Auld LJ in *Boafo, R (on the application of) v Secretary of State for the Home Department* [2002] EWCA Civ 44 at [27]; Pill LJ in *IT (Sierra Leone)* (above) at [11].
4   Pill LJ in *IT (Sierra Leone)* (above) at [16], Lloyd LJ at [22]; Auld LJ in *Boafo* (above) at [27].
5   *SP (allowed appeal: directions) South Africa* [2011] UKUT 00188 (IAC) at [14].

5.118   Where an independent and impartial tribunal has come to a conclusion as to the credibility of an account or the risks faced by an individual, it is not open to the SSHD to deviate from those findings merely because he disagrees with them[1] (indeed, 'an unappealed decision ... is binding on the parties', whether or not directions were made to give effect to the determination[2] unless they are objectively shown to be flawed or irrational, or peripheral, or there is genuine fresh evidence available.[3] As Judge LJ put it in *Danaei*:[4]

'The desirable objective of an independent scrutiny of decisions in this field would be negated if the Secretary of State were entitled to act merely on his own assertions and reassertions about relevant facts contrary to express findings made at an oral hearing by a special adjudicator who had seen and heard the relevant witnesses. That would approach uncomfortably close to decision making by executive or administrative diktat. If therefore the Secretary of State is to set aside or ignore a finding on a factual issue which has been considered and evaluated at an oral hearing by the special adjudicator he should explain why he has done so, and he should not do so unless the relevant factual conclusion could itself be impugned on *Wednesbury* principles, or has been reconsidered in the light of further evidence, or is of limited or negligible significance to the ultimate decision for which he is responsible.'

1   The Master of the Rolls in *R (Evans) v HM Attorney General* [2014] EWCA Civ 254 at [37]–[38]; Simon Brown LJ in *R v Secretary of State for the Home Department, ex parte Danaei* [1997] EWCA Civ 2704.
2   Auld LJ in *Boafo, R (on the application of) v Secretary of State for the Home Department* [2002] EWCA Civ 44 at [26].
3   Simon Brown LJ in *Danaei* (above).
4   *Danaei* (above): see further Moses J in *R (Saribal) v Home Secretary* [2002] EWHC 1542 (Admin), [2002] INLR 596 at [17]; Elias J in *R (Mersin) v Home Secretary* [2000] EWHC Admin 348; Stanley Burnton LJ in *Secretary of State for the Home Department v TB (Jamaica)* [2008] EWCA 977 at [32]–[36].

5.119   The same principle applies where the SSHD seeks to rely on further evidence which was in his possession at the date of the earlier hearing but which he failed to put before the tribunal[1] (though if an appellant makes a later application which is subject to discretionary duties as to its refusal, then it may be that a matter can be raised at that time).[2]

1   *Chomanga (binding effect of unappealed decisions) Zimbabwe* [2011] UKUT 00312 (IAC) at [20]–[21]; Stanley Burnton in *TB (Jamaica)* (above) at [35]; *Mubu (immigration appeals – res judicata) Zimbabwe* [2012] UKUT 398 (IAC); *Daby (forgery, appeal allowed, subsequent applications) Mauritius* [2011] UKUT 485 (IAC) at [10].
2   *Daby* (above) at [11]–[14].

Binding effect of tribunal determinations on later decision making

5.120   The *Danaei* principle is inapplicable where the very nature of the second decision calls for a decision on contemporaneous facts: thus, an officer determining whether to grant entry clearance following a successful appeal against its refusal is charged by the Immigration Rules to consider whether this is appropriate 'in the light of the circumstances existing at the time of the decision'[1] (nor does it apply where a different legal regime governs the issues, as where the criteria for nationality may be more stringent than those governing exclusion from the Refugee Convention,[2] nor where an issue was raised before the tribunal but not the subject of conclusive findings).[3] The entry clearance officer must make a decision on all the relevant evidence including that which was previously available but not provided at the appeal: relevant but non-exhaustive considerations will be whether there has been a significant and material change in circumstances or where a material deception has come to light since the appeal hearing.[4] The following propositions were identified in *Rahman*:[5]

'1.	If following a successful appeal, there is a change of circumstances in relation to the application for entry, that is something which the Entry Clearance Officer is not only entitled to consider, but which he must consider in determining whether or not to issue an entry clearance (that is in a case where there is no direction from the Adjudicator).

2.	The performance of his duty is to be distinguished from any wholly improper attempt made by an Entry Clearance Officer to circumvent an Adjudicator's decision by pursuing further enquiries with a view to denying entry on a different basis.

3.	If in the course of reviewing the up-to-date circumstances in connection with an application, which has been successful on appeal (an Entry Clearance Officer discovers deception), that may constitute circumstances which are sufficient to justify the Entry Clearance Officer taking a different view from the adjudicator, who has acted in ignorance of the deception.

4.	The existence of a right of appeal against the adjudicator's decision does not limit the ECO to that course. ... [the judge goes on to explain that requiring the ECO to appeal appeal may not be appropriate, given the narrow confines of the admissible material in an appeal on fresh evidence grounds based on error of fact].[6]

5.	An applicant may pursue an appeal against a re-refusal decision, and that is an appropriate forum for resolution of a disputed factual question.'

1	Immigration Rules, HC 395, para 27.
2	Stanley Burnton LJ in *Secretary of State for the Home Department v SK (Sri Lanka)* [2012] EWCA Civ 16 at [28]–[33].
3	*Secretary of State for the Home Department v IA (Turkey)* [2010] EWCA Civ 625 at [26]; *Boroumand, R (on the application of) v Secretary of State for the Home Department* [2010] EWHC 225 (Admin) at [50]–[58].
4	*Ara (successful appeal – no entry clearance) Bangladesh* [2011] UKUT 00376 (IAC) at [23], citing the then relevant guidance, at that time in Diplomatic Service Procedures; Auld LJ in *Boafo, R (on the application of) v Secretary of State for the Home Department* [2002] EWCA Civ 44 at [28]. Re deception, see the authority cited at **6.77**, fn 5 below.
5	Newman J in *R (on the application of Rahman)* [2006] EWHC 1755 (Admin) at [25], citing Rose J in *Ex parte Yousuf* [1989] Imm App R 554.
6	Newman J in *R (on the application of Rahman)* (above) at [35]–[40].

5.121 The fact that an appeal on asylum grounds has been allowed does not necessarily mean that leave to remain as a refugee must be granted, if there remain other destinations to which the appellant might be removed which have not been the subject of a positive finding that their removal there would be inconsistent with the Refugee Convention.[1]

1   Stanley Burnton LJ in *Secretary of State for the Home Department v ST (Eritrea)* [2010] EWCA Civ 643 at [58].

DETERMINATION OF REMITTED/TRANSFERRED HEARINGS

5.122 The immigration judiciary will occasionally redetermine appeals remitted from the Upper Tribunal. This may be for re-hearing afresh,[1] or for consideration of the appeal to be continued with some appellate guidance. On a fresh hearing, the traditional view was that there should be no regard to the decision of the previous immigration judge,[2] though it is not necessarily an error of law to read his decision, a judicial office holder's independence presumably ensuring that he approaches the case with an independent state of mind.[3] The last, though unreported, guidelines given by the tribunal[4] state

'(1)   As a general rule it is best practice for an adjudicator hearing an appeal de novo not to read the Determination of a previous adjudicator unless expressly invited to do so, so as to avoid any misunderstanding of what has influenced him. There is no prohibition, however, on reading the Determination.

(2)   If the adjudicator considers it appropriate to read the Determination, he should not do so until he has told the parties of his intention, and invited their comments.

(3)   There will be instances where parties invite him to read the Determination because, for example, the findings of fact have been accepted, and the re-hearing is to consider the conclusions to be drawn from those findings. This invitation should be recorded in his Determination.

(4)   The previous record of proceedings, and not the earlier Determination, can if necessary provide confirmation of what evidence was given at a previous hearing.

(5)   If an Appellant does not attend the de novo hearing, an adjudicator may rely on the evidence given at the previous hearing when forming his independent view of the case, but without reference to an earlier Determination.

(6)   Parties seeking to challenge a Determination on the basis that an adjudicator has read a previous Determination should only do so

where there are clear grounds for challenge, other than the mere fact of reading the Determination. Reading a previous Determination of itself is not a proper ground of appeal.'

If possible a vulnerable witness should be spared the ordeal of giving live evidence a second time.[5]

1   See **6.65** below.
2   *Devaseelan* [2002] UKIAT 00702 (starred) at [29].
3   *SA (clarificatory questions from IJs – best practice) Iran* [2006] UKAIT 00017 at [7]; Collins J in *Aissaoui* [1997] Imm AR 184; see further *Swash v Secretary of State for the Home Department* [2006] EWCA Civ 1093 and **6.80** below.
4   *Gashi* (01/TH/02902, 13 November 2001), cited with approval in *A v Secretary of State for the Home Department (Turkey)* [2003] UKIAT 00061 at [10]–[13].
5   See **6.68**, fn 6 below and see further guidance generally on vulnerable witnesses at **5.190** *et seq* below.

ABANDONMENT OF APPEALS

5.123   The tribunal possesses the power to declare an appeal abandoned where the statute deems it to be so,[1] in which case it is to issue a notice to that effect.[2] Parties to an appeal are under a duty to notify the tribunal if one of the deeming events occurs, ie if the appellant:[3]

● has been granted leave to remain;

● has departed from the UK;

● has a deportation order made against him;

● has been issued with EEA documents such as a registration certificate, residence card, derivative residence card, a document certifying permanent residence or a permanent residence card, including registration certificates issued consequent to the Accession of Croatia (Immigration and Worker Authorisation) Regulations 2013 and accession worker cards under the Accession (Immigration and Worker Authorisation) Regulations 2006 and a worker authorisation registration certificate under the Accession of Croatia (Immigration and Worker Authorisation) Regulations 2013, or has his passport stamped with a family member residence stamp.[4]

1   Tribunal Procedure (First-tier Tribunal) (Immigration and Asylum Chamber) Rules 2014, SI 2014/2604, r 16(1).
2   SI 2014/2604, r 16(2).
3   SI 2014/2604, r 16(1).
4   SI 2014/2604, r 16(4)(d).

5.124   An appellant who wishes to proceed with his appeal notwithstanding its otherwise being deemed abandoned by virtue of a grant of leave to remain, for example because an asylum seeker wishes to establish his entitlement to international protection, must serve a notice within 28 days of notification of the grant of leave or issue of the EEA document.[1] An appeal is not to be treated as abandoned simply on the strength of an undertaking to grant leave to remain.[2] If a power is to be implied to otherwise determine an appeal as abandoned (for example because an individual has absconded and not maintained contact with the tribunal) then the old case law of the tribunal suggests that the question of abandonment is one of fact.[3]

1   Tribunal Procedure (First-tier Tribunal) (Immigration and Asylum Chamber) Rules 2014, SI 2014/2604, r 16(3) (see **3.45** above).
2   *BP (DP3/96, unmarried partners) Macedonia* [2008] UKAIT 00045 at [2].
3   *Kamagate* (12618, 23 October 1995); *Khamis* (13854, 2 September 1996).

WITHDRAWAL OF APPEALS

5.125   The 2014 Rules permit withdrawal of an appeal, on an application made with reasons either orally[1] or in writing[2] following which the tribunal will issue a notice recording the fact.[3] Whereas the FTT has a discretion to proceed with an appeal where an immigration decision is withdrawn, there is no equivalent provision where the appellant wishes to withdraw his appeal.[4] There are no (express) equivalent provisions to those of the 2005 Rules which, where an appellant died before his appeal was determined, a direction might be made that his personal representative continue the proceedings in his place.[5] The tribunal is the arbiter of contested withdrawals, and must decide any question as to whether the impugned event was the result of a deliberate and informed decision: if it upholds such a contention, it will declare the purported withdrawal a nullity leaving the appeal extant.[6]

1   Tribunal Procedure (First-tier Tribunal) (Immigration and Asylum Chamber) Rules 2014, SI 2014/2604, r 17(1)(a).
2   SI 2014/2604, r 17(1)(b).
3   SI 2014/2604, r 17(3).
4   Contrast SI 2014/2604, r 17(1) and (2).
5   Asylum and Immigration Tribunal (Procedure) Rules 2005, SI 2005/230, r 17(2A) as amended by the Asylum and Immigration Tribunal (Procedure) (Amendment) Rules 2006, SI 2006/2788.
6   *AP (withdrawals – nullity assessment) Pakistan* [2007] UKAIT 00022.

Revisiting withdrawal

5.126   Notice of withdrawal brings the appeal to an end (ie the appeal does not enter a state of suspended animation),[1] and, if the withdrawal is later contested, the question will be whether, on the balance of probabilities,[2] the purported withdrawal was itself a nullity,[3] as where it was not the result of a deliberate and informed decision, 'in other words, that the mind of the applicant did not go with his act'.[4] Relevant considerations would be:

- a prompt communication to a representative of an almost immediate change of mind;

- circumstances where the withdrawal was sent only to the respondent, not to the tribunal;

- communication by the representative to the tribunal of a withdrawal when there was no true meeting of minds between him and the appellant;

- withdrawal by a representative on the instructions of a sponsor rather than the appellant;

- erroneous communication of a withdrawal to the tribunal by a representative, through lack of care or simple mistake.[5]

1   *AP (withdrawals – nullity assessment) Pakistan* [2007] UKAIT 00022 at [58].
2   *AP* (above) at [57](f).
3   *AP* (above) at [53], [55].
4   *AP* (above) at [57](e).
5   *AP* (above) at [57](f).

5.127 Allegations of invalid withdrawal will be determined at preliminary hearings set down for this purpose,[1] for which standard directions can be expected by which the present representatives confirm (in writing five days before the hearing) that any allegations made against former representatives have been put to them, with an invitation to respond in writing or by attendance at the hearing, the present representative making it clear that legal privilege is being waived or explaining why that is not appropriate.[2] The FTT will accept notice of an intended withdrawal, a Presidential Guidance Note explains, where satisfied that 'the appellant is doing so freely and understands the consequences of the withdrawal' and will assume that a represented appellant understands and intends the consequences of withdrawal.[3]

1   *AP (withdrawals – nullity assessment) Pakistan* [2007] UKAIT 00022 at [59].
2   *AP* (above) at [60].
3   Presidential Guidance Note No 1 of 2014, para 15.

WITHDRAWAL OF DECISIONS

5.128 An appeal is to be treated as withdrawn where the respondent notifies the FTT and other parties that a decision against which it is brought has been withdrawn ('the power to withdraw arises as a matter of general public law, for the decision maker has the implied power, subject to general principles of public law, to withdraw any decision taken under statute or prerogative, unless such power is excluded')[1] and specifies the reasons, 'save for good reason'.[2] This modifies the previous understanding of immigration appeals, which was that a withdrawal of the decision would terminate the appeals process on the basis that with it disappears the lawful basis for the immigration decision which underlies

245

the appeal.[3] The approach of the UT in *SM (Pakistan)* is of interest here.[4] It is unlikely that the mere wish of the appellant to seek a fee award would constitute good reason.[5] The SSHD may use the power in circumstances including those where further material supplied on the appeal warrants a reconsideration of the claim, or where a new claim has been made which should be examined by him as the primary decision maker;[6] he must not use the withdrawal power as a tactical exercise to avoid having to apply for an adjournment, and he must only use it when genuinely contemplating a change of mind upon reconsidering the case:[7] a decision might be withdrawn if legally unsustainable but not merely where better or stronger refusal reasons are identified – those should be raised in advance of the hearing, and further evidence from an appellant would normally lead at most to an adjournment for its consideration and verification rather than a withdrawal.[8] The FTT will, where the notification of withdrawal is received more than 21 days before the hearing date, notify the appellant and enquire whether there is good reason that the appeal should not be treated as withdrawn; if a response is received, or the time for replying expires without one, then a judge will be asked to decide the issue; if there is insufficient time to consult the appellant beforehand then the question of whether the appeal will be treated as withdrawn will be considered at the hearing.[9] The justification for proceeding with the appeal will be explained in the decision and reasons.[10] The FTT must notify each party in writing of the withdrawal of the respondent's decision and that appeal proceedings are therefore no longer considered pending[11] (and that no written decision will follow).[12] If the SSHD certifies an appeal under NIAA 2002, ss 97–98, on the grounds that the matters therein raise issues regarding national security or the public good (and thereby should be pursued in the SIAC) then he must serve a notice to that effect on the tribunal; it in turn should take no action regarding the matter and must notify the parties that the appeal no longer continues.[13]

1   Richards LJ in *Chichvarkin, R (on the application of) v Secretary of State for the Home Department* [2011] EWCA Civ 91 at [63], approving the Divisional Court decision below (see fn 3).
2   Tribunal Procedure (First-tier Tribunal) (Immigration and Asylum Chamber) Rules 2014, SI 2014/2604, r 17(2).
3   Collins J in *Nori* [2002] UKIAT 01887 at [18]–[19]; Collins J in *Glushkov v Secretary of State for the Home Department* [2008] EWHC 2290 (Admin) at [11]–[17]; Kenneth Parker J in *Chichvarkin, R (on the application of) v Secretary of State for the Home Department* [2010] EWHC 1858 (QB) at [34]–[42], endorsed by Richards LJ in *Chichvarkin, R (on the application of) v Secretary of State for the Home Department* [2011] EWCA Civ 91 at [37].
4   See **6.54**, fn 3 below.
5   Presidential Guidance Note No 1 of 2014, para 16.
6   Richards LJ in *Chichvarkin* (above) at [39].
7   Collins J in *Glushkov* (above) at [18].
8   Standing instructions to POs, in place since January 2014, provided to the Law Society Immigration Sub-Committee in late 2014.
9   Presidential Guidance Note No 1 of 2014, para 17.
10   Presidential Guidance Note No 1 of 2014, para 20.
11   SI 2014/2604, r 17(3).
12   Presidential Guidance Note No 1 of 2014, para 18.
13   SI 2014/2604, r 18.

HEARING IN THE ABSENCE OF A PARTY

5.129   The tribunal has a discretion[1] to hear an appeal in the absence of a party, if satisfied[2] that the party has been given notice of the hearing or that reasonable steps have been taken to notify him,[3] and considers that it is in the interests of justice to proceed.[4] It is difficult to conceive of circumstances in which it would be good advice for any representative to tell a client not to attend a tribunal.[5] The appellant's attendance at his hearing will usually be vital:[6]

'it is obviously impossible to have a just disposal of the appeal if an appellant is unfairly and wrongly deprived of the opportunity of giving evidence. That is particularly the position in a case such as this where inevitably his evidence is going to be crucial ... a balance may, in certain circumstances, have to be drawn between the need for the appellant to be heard in order to be able to put forward his appeal in a proper manner and the need for an appeal to be disposed of in a reasonable time. One can imagine examples where, if he was unfit for a period of years, it would be unreasonable to expect the matter to be deferred.'

1   Tribunal Procedure (First-tier Tribunal) (Immigration and Asylum Chamber) Rules 2014, SI 2014/2604, r 28: '*may* proceed'.
2   See Sedley LJ on the possible duty of enquiry before a tribunal may be satisfied of a matter (see **5.4**, fn 4 above).
3   SI 2014/2604, r 28(a).
4   SI 2014/2604, r 28(b) – see Sedley LJ in *Benkaddouri v Secretary of State for the Home Department* [2003] EWCA Civ 1250 at [13] (see **5.40**, fn 3 above).
5   Wall LJ in *RJ (Jamaica) v Secretary of State for the Home Department* [2008] EWCA Civ 93 at [29]; though cf *RS and SS (exclusion of appellant from hearing) Pakistan* [2008] UKAIT 00012 at [6], where the issues involved do not require a person's attendance.
6   Collins in *R v Secretary of State for the Home Department, ex parte Tahir Iqbal* (CO/2469/97, 25 February 1998).

5.130   It is difficult to see that an asylum appeal could be given the 'anxious scrutiny' it deserves without having the appellant available to give oral evidence,[1] though where an appeal in the UT proceeds on the basis of agreed facts and the appellant is represented, and where the only live witnesses are supporting the appellant's case rather than testifying against him, he would not need to be in attendance for the process to be fair.[2]

1   Hooper LJ giving permission to apply for judicial review in the Court of Appeal in *AM (Cameroon), R (on the application of) v Asylum and Immigration Tribunal* [2007] EWCA Civ 131 at [62].
2   *MOJ (return to Mogadishu)* [2014] UKUT 442 (IAC) at [5]–[7].

COMBINED HEARINGS

5.131   Under its case management powers, the tribunal may—

'(b)   consolidate or hear together two or more sets of proceedings or parts of proceedings raising common issues'[1]

We have discussed above the situation where different family members have appeals arising out of related asylum claims.[2] Another scenario may be if some common question of law or fact arises in them.[3] When regulating the conduct of consolidated appeals, each principal appellant is entitled, even in a combined hearing, to have his case determined on its own merits. A principal appellant's appeal should not fail solely because he and another principal appellant cannot *both* be telling the truth: so before proceeding with a combined hearing (even with the consent of the parties) a judicial decision maker would need to be very confident about being able to perform the mental gymnastics involved in treating case A on its merits in the context of apparently contradictory evidence given in support of case B, and vice versa.[4] Where it is thought that the evidence of a witness on some contested matter may be affected by the evidence given by other witnesses, it is the usual practice to exclude witnesses from the hearing room until they begin giving their evidence. In a combined hearing, where there are two or more appellants, each of whom is to give evidence, the effect of this practice is to exclude the appellant in the course of proceedings in an appeal which is (in part) his appeal, but where credibility is in issue, evidence will be more impressive if later witnesses do not listen to the testimony of earlier ones:[5] indeed, the tribunal may (and usually will) direct witnesses' exclusion from a hearing until they have given evidence.[6]

1   Tribunal Procedure (First-tier Tribunal) (Immigration and Asylum Chamber) Rules 2014, SI 2014/2604, r 4(3)(b).
2   See **5.53** *et seq* above.
3   Indeed this was one scenario envisaged by the predecessor rule, the Asylum and Immigration Tribunal (Procedure) Rules 2005, SI 2005/230, r 20(2).
4   *Tabores and Munoz* (17819, 24 July 1998).
5   *RS and SS (exclusion of appellant from hearing) Pakistan* [2008] UKAIT 00012, headnote.
6   SI 2014/2604, r 27(5).

PUBLIC HEARING

5.132   Hearings before the tribunal must in general be held in public.[1] The first exception to this principle is where an allegation of forgery is made with respect to a document in the proceedings, where disclosure of a matter relating to the forgery's detection is said to be contrary to the public interest:[2] in these cases the matter must be investigated in private, from which point the FTT has a discretion to proceed in private to the extent necessary to prevent disclosure. Beyond this scenario, the FTT may give a direction that a hearing, or part of it, is to be held in private.[3] The tribunal may give a direction excluding from any hearing, or part of it:[4]

'(a)   any person whose conduct the Tribunal considers is disrupting or is likely to disrupt the hearing;

(b)   any person whose presence the Tribunal considers is likely to prevent another person from giving evidence or making submissions freely;

(c) any person who the Tribunal considers should be excluded in order to give effect to a direction under rule 13(2) (withholding a document or information likely to cause serious harm); or

(d) any person where the purpose of the hearing would be defeated by the attendance of that person.'

1   Tribunal Procedure (First-tier Tribunal) (Immigration and Asylum Chamber) Rules 2014, SI 2014/2604, r 27(1).
2   NIAA 2002, s 108.
3   SI 2014/2604, r 27(2).
4   SI 2014/2604, r 27(4).

5.133   It may be of interest to recall that the 2005 Rules included a discretion to exclude any or all members of the public from any hearing or part of a hearing if thought necessary in the interests of public order or national security, to protect the private life of a party or the interests of a minor.[1] There is a heavy burden to be discharged to justify a derogation from the principle of open and accessible court proceedings:[2]

'It is a general principle of our constitutional law that justice is administered by the courts in public, and is therefore open to public scrutiny. The principle is an aspect of the rule of law in a democracy'.

1   Asylum and Immigration Tribunal (Procedure) Rules 2005, SI 2005/230, r 54(3).
2   See Lord Reed in *A v British Broadcasting Corporation (Scotland)* [2014] UKSC 25 at [23].

5.134   Anonymity might be necessary where undue publicity would risk subverting the tribunal process by creating risks on return that were not otherwise present.[1] Directions on anonymity will not normally set any precedent.[2] The Guidance Note on anonymity in the FTT[3] sets out that:

'3.   Once anonymity is granted the Tribunal will remove the appellant's name from all published documents that are in the public domain. The names will remain in full on the judicial cause list.

4.   The power to direct anonymity is derived from article 8 ECHR and such directions should be made where public knowledge of the person or the case might impact on that person's protected rights. An interim anonymity direction is more likely to be appropriate during initial stages of an appeal to enable the parties to prepare their cases without interference or hindrance. At the CMR or at the substantive hearing the Immigration Judge should review the application for anonymity and direct whether the appellant should be granted anonymity. There may well be appeals where no application is made by either party but the court will self direct that anonymity should be granted.

5.   Anonymity directions will often, if not always, be made where the appeal involves:

(i)   a child or vulnerable person

      (ii)   evidence that the appeal concerns personal information about the lives of those under 18 and their welfare may be injured if such details are revealed and their names are known

      (iii)   there is highly personal evidence in the appeal that should remain confidential

      (iv)   there is a claim that the appellant would be at risk of harm and that by publishing their names and details it may cause them harm or put others at real risk of harm

      (v)   publication of the determination may be used subsequently to support a *sur place* claim.'

1   See Lord Reed in *A v British Broadcasting Corporation (Scotland)* (above) at [73].
2   Lord Carnwath in *Secretary of State for Home Department v MN and KY (Scotland)* [2014] UKSC 30 at [50].
3   Presidential Guidance Note No 2 (issued Feb 2011, revised July 2011), 'Anonymity directions in FT(IAC)' (see further **6.49**, fn 6).

USE OF DOCUMENTS AND INFORMATION AND THEIR DISCLOSURE

5.135   There is specific provision[1] for an order to be made prohibiting the disclosure or publication of:

'(a)   specified documents or information relating to the proceedings; or

(b)   any matter likely to lead members of the public to identify any person whom the Tribunal considers should not be identified.'

1   Tribunal Procedure (First-tier Tribunal) (Immigration and Asylum Chamber) Rules 2014, SI 2014/2604, r 13(1).

5.136   The tribunal may give a direction prohibiting the disclosure of a document or information to a person if:[1]

- it is satisfied that such disclosure would be likely to cause that person or some other person serious harm;

- it is satisfied, having regard to the interests of justice, that it is proportionate to give such a direction.

1   Tribunal Procedure (First-tier Tribunal) (Immigration and Asylum Chamber) Rules 2014, SI 2014/2604, r 13(2).

5.137   If a party considers such a direction appropriate, he should exclude such documents from those provided to the other side, provide them to the FTT, and explain the reasons justifying exclusion, so that the FTT can decide whether such material should be disclosed, or whether the direction sought should be issued,[1] and must subsequently conduct proceedings as is appropriate in order to give effect to such direction.[2] Where such direction prevents disclosure to a represented party, the FTT may direct that the documents or information be disclosed to his representative, where satisfied that he will not disclose the material to any other person without the FTT's consent.[3]

1   Tribunal Procedure (First-tier Tribunal) (Immigration and Asylum Chamber) Rules 2014, SI 2014/2604, r 13(3).
2   SI 2014/2604, r 13(4).
3   SI 2014/2604, r 13(5) and (6).

5.138   The FTT may, on the application of a party or on its own initiative, give a direction that certain documents or information must or may be disclosed to it on the basis that it will not further disclose it, either generally or regarding specified persons.[1] Where such application is made, its maker may withhold the relevant material pending its grant or refusal. The tribunal must ensure that information is not disclosed contrary to the interests of national security.[2] The tribunal must conduct proceedings and record its decision and reasons appropriately so as not to undermine the effect of any order or direction given under these powers.[3] There would be no objection to an individual's own asylum interview record being put to him if he gave evidence in the appeal of another family member arising out of the same factual matrix.[4]

1   Tribunal Procedure (First-tier Tribunal) (Immigration and Asylum Chamber) Rules 2014, SI 2014/2604, r 13(7) and (8).
2   SI 2014/2604, r 13(9).
3   SI 2014/2604, r 13(10).
4   Auld LJ in the Court of Appeal in *Ocampo v Secretary of State for the Home Department* [2006] EWCA Civ 1276 at [15].

THE RECORD OF PROCEEDINGS

5.139   Although the rules no longer impose an obligation to do so, the Practice Statement mandates that 'The Tribunal shall keep a proper record of proceedings of any hearing ... and attach that record to the Tribunal's case file.'[1] It should not be perceived as a resource which appellants can call upon in order to try and build a case:[2]

'If an Appellant wishes to say that an Adjudicator had no evidence, written or oral, to the effect set out by the Adjudicator or had no evidence to support inferences which the Adjudicator drew, it is not for the Record of Proceedings to be produced through which an Appellant can then trawl for evidence. It is for the Appellant to produce evidence, perhaps in the form of the advocate's notes in order to show that something was not said or was misrecorded. A Home Office Presenting Officer's notes may be relevant to rebut such a factual contention. The Record of Proceedings is not a primary evidential source for Appellants.'

1   Practice Statements, para 5.1.
2   *HD (prison – record of proceedings) Iran* [2004] UKIAT 00209 at [13].

TRANSFER OF PROCEEDINGS BETWEEN JUDICIAL PERSONNEL

5.140   A Chamber President may, once an immigration judge has embarked on hearing an appeal, decide that it is not practicable for the original tribunal to complete the hearing or without undue delay, and so direct the appeal to be heard by a different constitution.[1] The new tribunal shall have power to deal with the appeal as if it had been commenced before them,[2] and any notice or document given to, or by, the original tribunal, shall be treated as if the present tribunal was its author or recipient.[3]

1   Practice Statements, para 9.1.
2   Practice Statements, para 9.2(b).
3   Practice Statements, para 9.2(a).

TRANSFER OF PROCEEDINGS BETWEEN HEARING CENTRES

5.141   Appeals are heard around the country: at Taylor House in central London, at the regional hearing centres (Feltham, Harmondsworth, Birmingham, Bromley, Surbiton, Nottingham, Havant, Leeds, Manchester, North Shields, Stoke on Trent, Sutton, Walsall and Yarl's Wood), and in Newport in Wales, Belfast in Northern Ireland, and Glasgow in Scotland. Whilst there is no formal provision for the geographical location of a particular hearing, the old case law of the tribunal indicates that appeals should be transferred between hearing centres where there is 'good reason' for such a step to be taken[1] (the considerations identified in the Administrative Court's guidance may be thought relevant in these cases[2]); it may be appropriate to request a later start rather than a transfer between hearing centres if the costs of transport are the sole issue calling for listing at a different hearing centre.[3] Proximity of the parties, representatives and witnesses to a particular hearing centre might well provide an overwhelming case for a transfer.[4]

1   See eg *Ahmad* (12033, 21 April 1995).
2   See **8.60**, fn 2.
3   Sullivan J in *R v Secretary of State for the Home Department, ex parte Akli Semaane* (14 October 1997).
4   *Kaur* (13052, 1 March 1996); *Kaygun* (17213, 29 May 1998).

IRREGULARITIES: CORRECTION OF ORDERS AND DECISIONS

5.142   The FTT has powers under the 2014 Rules, r 31 to correct clerical mistakes, accidental slips or omissions in its decisions; to set aside decisions which dispose of proceedings; as well as to grant permission to appeal to the UT. We address these powers in full in Chapter 6.[1]

1   See **6.22–6.28** below.

GIVING OF DECISION AND REASONS

5.143   The FTT must provide the parties with a notice of its decision (no longer styled 'determination'), with notification of the timing and manner of exercising any appeal rights, as soon as reasonably practicable after making a decision that disposes of the proceedings.[1] It may give its decision orally at a hearing.[2] Under the rules, it might seem that only asylum and humanitarian protection decisions will automatically require written reasons, whereas in other cases the tribunal may provide written reasons or otherwise notify the parties of their right to apply for them.[3] However, in practice,[4]

> 'the Tribunal will continue to reserve the substantive decision in an appeal and issue a notice of decision and statement of reasons as a single document in every case. It will be inappropriate to give an ex tempore decision without giving a full statement of reasons at the same time. This is because the factual questions and other issues in dispute in appeals to the Immigration and Asylum Chamber are usually complex and the parties are entitled to receive a full statement of reasons for the decision.'

1   Tribunal Procedure (First-tier Tribunal) (Immigration and Asylum Chamber) Rules 2014, SI 2014/2604, r 29(2).
2   SI 2014/2604, r 29(1).
3   SI 2014/2604, r 29(3).
4   Presidential Guidance Note No 1 of 2014, para 21.

5.144   In cases disposed of by a decision, where no written reasons have been supplied, a party may make a written application for reasons to the FTT,[1] such as to be received by the FTT within 28 days of the date on which the notice of decision was sent or otherwise provided to the party in question.[2]

1   Tribunal Procedure (First-tier Tribunal) (Immigration and Asylum Chamber) Rules 2014, SI 2014/2604, r 29(4).
2   SI 2014/2604, r 29(5).

The FTT's decision: contents of statement of reasons

5.145   Once an application for written reasons is made, the FTT must send a written statement of reasons to each party as soon as reasonably practicable, subject to the rules on withholding a document or information likely to cause serious harm.[1] It is expected that 14 days will be adequate for preparing the statement of reasons and judges are reminded that delay may be incompatible with the overriding objective of the 2014 Rules.[2] If the outcome of the appeal is intimated at the appeal hearing, the judge should make it clear that this is an indication only, and that the notice of decision and statement of reasons will follow in writing[3] (whilst a judge remains seized of the appeal before giving his decision, notwithstanding such intimation, only exceptionally should a judge differ in his written reasons from any indication of the result given at the hearing, and it is likely to be appropriate to relist the appeal in the event of such a change of heart to hear further representations).[4] A statement of reasons should be proportionate to the issues and avoid unnecessary formality.[5] Reasons should be found in the decision rather than in a subsequent response to an appeal against it.[6] The judge should always identify himself when making a decision, including when an appeal is determined without a hearing.[7]

1 Tribunal Procedure (First-tier Tribunal) (Immigration and Asylum Chamber) Rules 2014, SI 2014/2604, r 29(6): see further **5.135** above.
2 Presidential Guidance Note No 1 of 2014, para 22.
3 Presidential Guidance Note No 1 of 2014, para 23.
4 Harrison J in *R v Special Adjudicator, ex parte Bashir* (CO/4643/98, 6 December 1999); Longmore LJ in *SK (Sri Lanka) v Secretary of State for the Home Department* [2008] EWCA Civ 495 at [21].
5 Presidential Guidance Note No 1 of 2014, para 26.
6 Richards LJ in *Krayem v Secretary of State for the Home Department* [2003] EWCA Civ 649 at [20].
7 *NA (excluded decision; identifying judge) Afghanistan* [2010] UKUT 444 (IAC) at [15].

COSTS

5.146   There is a power to award costs in appeal proceedings:[1]

• in relation to costs wasted by the actions of a representative;[2]

• 'if a person has acted unreasonably in bringing, defending or conducting proceedings'.[3]

This includes the recovery of costs involved in making an application under this rule.[4] An opportunity to make representations must be given before any award is made, which will be listed at a hearing where a costs order is contemplated.[5] The Presidential Guidance Note[6] explains that this power

'carries with it considerable responsibility to ensure that its use is appropriate and that it is used fairly and judiciously. In nearly all instances the existence of the power should act as a restraint on the behaviour of parties and their representatives so that the power itself is rarely exercised.'

1 Tribunals, Courts and Enforcement Act 2007, s 29.
2 Tribunal Procedure (First-tier Tribunal) (Immigration and Asylum Chamber) Rules 2014, SI 2014/2604, r 9(2)(a).
3 SI 2014/2604, r 9(2)(b).
4 Presidential Guidance Note No 1 of 2014, para 28.
5 SI 2014/2604, r 9(6); Presidential Guidance Note No 1 of 2014, para 32.
6 Presidential Guidance Note No 1 of 2014, para 27.

5.147 The fact that a party may have acted wrongly or been misguided in his approach is not to be equated with unreasonable conduct.[1] A breach of directions should not warrant use of this rule before due warning and a reminder has been given; nor should an adjournment required because of inadequate preparation necessarily lead to the exercise of the power:[2]

> 'Not only has the paying party the right to offer an explanation but it should be remembered that representatives have many demands on their time and are subject to a multitude of pressures, which may lead even in well-managed organisations to occasional lapses. The making of an order for wasted or unreasonable costs should be a very rare event.'

1 Presidential Guidance Note No 1 of 2014, para 30.
2 Presidential Guidance Note No 1 of 2014, para 31.

Costs: guidance from the FTT

5.148 In *Canciono*[1] in a rare reported decision of the FTT we find the tribunal giving guidance on costs. It sets out that:

- costs are in the discretion of judges taking account of all relevant considerations;[2]

- in general an award should be made for the full measurable amount of costs relating to the offending act or omission;[3]

- as to wasted costs, the power is available against all legal and other representatives[4] – it does not require misconduct or gross neglect, simple negligence sufficing,[5] and pursuing a hopeless case does not justify the making of an order because an appeal might be pursued despite legal advice;[6] the FTT should eschew proceedings that amount to a disciplinary investigation against the lawyers in question;[7]

- discretion should be resolved via a consideration of the facts of the case in hand rather than via recourse to other decisions;[8]

- in general the principles identified in *Ridehalgh v Horsefield* are to be followed;[9]

- as to the power to award costs for unreasonable conduct, this is available against an appellant or respondent (including an unrepresented appellant, though he must be afforded appropriate latitude)[10] though not a 'Mackenzie' friend) who has acted unreasonably in bringing defending proceedings;[11]

- the making of concessions, whether by either side withdrawing their decision or appeal, is not to be discouraged by use of the rule but belated decision making and the late production of evidence may still attract the Rule's proper use and the Home Office could not satisfactorily explain late action just because of the timing of a PO's involvement or by reference to inadequate resources absent exceptional factors or circumstances;[12]

● in general only the clearest cases should be the subject of an award of costs to avoid the possibility that more time, effort and cost goes into the award than are alleged to have been wasted in the first place;[13]

● the costs regime is only available in relation to appeals brought after 20 October 2014, to avoid what would otherwise be an unjustifiable retrospective effect.[14]

1   *Cancino (costs – First-tier Tribunal – new powers)* [2015] UKFTT 59 (IAC).
2   *Cancino* (above) at [6].
3   *Cancino* (above) at [7].
4   *Cancino* (above) at [10].
5   *Cancino* (above) at [11].
6   *Cancino* (above) at [20].
7   *Cancino* (above) at [21].
8   *Cancino* (above) at [22].
9   [1994] Ch 205; *Cancino* (above) at [13].
10 *Cancino* (above) at [26].
11 *Cancino* (above) at [24].
12 *Cancino* (above) at [25].
13 *Cancino* (above) at [27].
14 *Cancino* (above) at [35].

Costs: the governing test and the procedure

5.149   A three-stage test will generally be appropriate:[1]

1   Has the legal representative of whom complaint is made acted improperly, unreasonably or negligently?

2   If so, did such conduct cause the applicant to incur unnecessary costs?

3   If so, is it in all the circumstances of the case just to order the legal representative to compensate the applicant for the whole or any part of the relevant costs?

1   *Cancino (costs – First-tier Tribunal – new powers)* [2015] UKFTT 59 (IAC) at [19].

5.150   The normal procedure should be for:[1]

● the matter to be raised by the FTT of its own motion or by a party, orally or by subsequent written application (within 28 days of the decision or relevant withdrawal);[2]

● the paying person to be given an opportunity to make representations, which may be based on the 'in principle' views of the FTT, such as a pause in proceedings giving an opportunity for consensual resolution of the issues;

- a costs schedule to be provided, which is desirable though not required under the Rules;

- the FTT to make a decision taking account of the nature, timing and duration of the offending conduct and having regard to fairness, expedition and proportionality.[3]

1 *Cancino (costs – First-tier Tribunal – new powers)* [2015] UKFTT 59 (IAC)at [38].
2 Tribunal Procedure (First-tier Tribunal) (Immigration and Asylum Chamber) Rules 2014, SI 2014/2604, r 9(5).
3 *Cancino* (above) at [39]–[40].

5.151 Costs are to be finalised by summary or detailed assessment, or agreement; detailed assessment is to be dealt with, as indicated in the order, on a standard or indemnity basis.[1]

We deal further with the principles that might be involved in assessing unreasonable conduct in Chapter 8.[2]

1 Tribunal Procedure (First-tier Tribunal) (Immigration and Asylum Chamber) Rules 2014, SI 2014/2604, r 9(7) and (9).
2 See **8.43** *et seq.*

PART 5 – THE DETAINED FAST TRACK

SCOPE OF DETAINED FAST TRACK PROCEDURE RULES

5.152 The fast track appeal process is designed for straightforward asylum claims falling within the Detained Fast Track (DFT) process,[1] ie where:

'it appears that a quick decision is possible and none of the detained fast-track suitability exclusion criteria apply.'

1 Detained Fast Track Processes, version 6.0, para 2.1.

5.153 As outlined below,[1] the tribunal must order that the relevant Parts of the fast track procedures shall cease to apply if it is satisfied that the case cannot justly be decided within the timescales set by the Fast Track Rules (FTRs),[2] and so the criteria for inclusion in the process, and the case law on fairness within the DFT, will be relevant to that consideration. Cases suitable for the DFT include those where:[3]

(a) it appears that no further enquiries by the Home Office or the applicant are necessary in order to obtain clarification, complex legal advice or corroborative evidence;

(b) it appears likely that any such enquiries can be concluded to allow a decision to take place within the normal indicative timescales;

(c)   it appears likely that it will be possible to fulfil and properly consider the claim within normal indicative timescales;

(d)   it appears likely that no translations are required in respect of documents presented by an applicant, or that translations can be obtained to allow a decision within normal indicative timescales; and

(e)   the case is one that is likely to be certified as 'clearly unfounded' under NIAA 2002, s 94.

1   See **5.162** below.
2   Tribunal Procedure (First-tier Tribunal) (Immigration and Asylum Chamber) Rules 2014, SI 2014/2604, Sch 1.
3   DFT Guidance, para 2.2.

5.154   Persons that are unlikely to be suitable are:[1]

(a)   women who are 24 or more weeks pregnant;

(b)   family cases;

(c)   children whose claimed date of birth is accepted by the Home Office;

(d)   those with a disability which cannot be adequately managed within a detained environment;

(e)   those with a physical or mental medical condition which cannot be adequately treated or managed in such an environment;

(f)   those who lack the mental capacity or coherence to understand the asylum process and/or cogently present their claim;

(g)   applicants about whom a competent authority has decided that they are a victim of trafficking or that there are reasonable grounds for regarding them as a potential victim of trafficking; and

(h)   those in respect of whom there is independent evidence of torture.

1   DFT Guidance, para 2.3.

5.155   There is additionally 'an Operational Considerations list, colloquially known as the RAG, Red Amber Green, list of countries', which is not intended to be exhaustive or to be used rigidly, which addresses operational factors relevant to the speed at which a case can be processed, the colours indicating the extent to which senior officials have to be consulted before a case should proceed within the DFT.[1] The process is not suitable for cases which require expert evidence, including where it is required to rebut material produced by the SSHD;[2] nor is it appropriate for cases which cannot 'be reliably established without evidence from sources external to the claimant himself' where further time is legitimately required to obtain that evidence,[3] nor for those which are criticised for a lack of corroborative evidence on a particular point.[4] It must always be recalled that the DFT, whilst lawful, works at the margins of fairness: 'anything quicker would be impossible to justify.'[5]

1   Cited by Ouseley J in *Detention Action v Secretary of State for the Home Department* [2014] EWHC 2245 (Admin) at [63]–[64].
2   Moses LJ in *SH (Afghanistan) v Secretary of State for the Home Department* [2011] EWCA Civ 1284 at [8].
3   Moore-Bick LJ in *JB (Jamaica), R (on the application of) v Secretary of State for the Home Department* [2013] EWCA Civ 666 at [29].
4   Philip Mott QC sitting as a Deputy High Court judge in *RQ (Jordan), R (on the application of) v Secretary of State for the Home Department* [2014] EWHC 559 (Admin) at [29].
5   Collins J in the Administrative Court in *R (Refugee Legal Centre) v Secretary of State for the Home Department* [2004] EWHC 684 (Admin) at [16].

5.156   As of December 2014, the Court of Appeal has found that the detention of asylum seekers in the DFT who are not at risk of absconding whilst their appeals are pending is unlawful, because the detention policy does not meet the required standards of clarity and transparency, and is arguably unjustified.[1]

1   Beatson LJ in *Detention Action, R (on the application of) v Secretary of State for the Home Department* [2014] EWCA Civ 1634 at [70] and [96]–[97].

FAST TRACK: GENERAL CONSIDERATIONS

5.157   Appeals in the fast track operate in a broadly similar fashion to those in the normal tribunal, albeit that they have their own set of Procedure Rules, the FTRs, and important elements of the rules for directions and non-compliance,. substitution and addition of parties, sending, delivery and language of documents, use of documents and information, use of documents and information, receiving evidence and submissions, summoning witnesses, making orders that questions be answered or documents produced, treating appeals as abandoned, finally determined or withdrawn, certification of pending appeals, and the conduct of hearings, are common to both systems.[1] They are applicable to appeals for those continuously detained at Colnbrook House Immigration Removal Centre, Harmondsworth, Middlesex; Harmondsworth Immigration Removal Centre, Harmondsworth, Middlesex; Yarls Wood Immigration Removal Centre, Clapham, Bedfordshire.[2] The relevant appeal form to launch an appeal is IAFT-5 Fast, found on the formfinder page of the justice.gov.uk website. A party does not stop being continuously in detention in a place specified merely because he is transported between specified places of detention; nor where he leaves and returns to such a place of detention for any purpose between the hours of 6 am and 10 pm.[3]

1   FTRs, para 1(4), Table 2.
2   FTRs, para 2(3).
3   FTRs, para 2(2).

FAST TRACK: PROCEDURE AT FIRST INSTANCE

5.158   Although Form IAFT-5 is specific to the DFT, its contents are the same as set out above.[1] A person who wishes to appeal must give a notice of appeal not later than two working days after the day on which he was provided with notice of the immigration decision against which he wishes to appeal.[2] The appeal form may be given to the FTT or the asylum seeker's custodian; in the latter case, the custodian must forward the appeal immediately to the FTT upon its receipt, endorsing it with the date of service.[3] Where a notice of appeal is given outside the time limit, the tribunal must not extend the time for appealing unless it is in the interests of justice to do so,[4] any consideration of late provision of notice of decision, or extension of time, being addressed at the hearing of the appeal.[5] If late notice of appeal is given, where the respondent has notified the tribunal that removal directions are due to take effect within five working days of receipt of that notice, the FTT must, if reasonably practicable, make any decision on extension of time before removal is due, and may do so as a preliminary issue.[6] A refusal to extend time must be provided within one day of being made, and may be given orally at a hearing.[7]

1   See **5.12** *et seq* above
2   FTRs, para 5(1).
3   FTRs, para 4(1) and (2).
4   FTRs, para 5(2).
5   FTRs, para 5(3).
6   FTRs, para 5(4).
7   FTRs, para 5(5) and (6).

5.159   When the tribunal receives a notice of appeal and further documents or information, it shall immediately serve a copy upon the respondent.[1] The respondent must file the documents required by the 2014 Rules not later than two days after the day on which the tribunal provides them with the notice of appeal.[2] The appellant should provide his witness statement, supporting evidence, chronology and skeleton the business day before the hearing, if practicable, or otherwise on the day itself.[3] The tribunal shall fix a hearing date which is not later than three working days after the day on which the respondent files the necessary documents; or if the tribunal is unable to arrange a hearing within that time, as soon as practicable thereafter.[4] The tribunal must serve notice of the date, time and place of the hearing on every party as soon as practicable, and in any event not later than noon on the business day before the hearing.[5] The appeal will be considered at a hearing unless it lapses, is treated as abandoned or is withdrawn or treated as such as under the 2014 Rules,[6] or where the tribunal adjourns the hearing,[7] or all of the parties consent to determination without a hearing.[8] The tribunal is to provide a notice of decision and its reasons in writing two days after the hearing or other conclusion of the appeal.[9] Where its notice of decision is amended under the 2014 Rules, the tribunal must, not later than one day after making the amendment, serve an amended version on every party on whom it served the original.[10]

1   FTRs, para 6.
2   FTRs, para 7(1) (see **5.12** *et seq* above).
3   Practice Directions, para 2.1, 7.5(a) and (b).

4   FTRs, para 8(1) – though it would seem that a Practice Direction extending this to six working days is in prospect (para 8(3)).
5   FTRs, para 8(2).
6   FTRs, para 9(2)(a).
7   FTRs, para 9(2)(b).
8   FTRs, para 9(2)(c).
9   FTRs, para 10(1) and (2).
10 FTRs, para 13.

FAST TRACK: ADJOURNMENT

5.160   The tribunal may only adjourn a hearing where it is satisfied that:

● the appeal could not be justly decided on the hearing date fixed under the FTRs; and

● there is an identifiable future date, not more than ten days later, by which it can be justly determined.[1]

1   FTRs, para 12.

5.161   It can be anticipated that applications will be made much closer to the time of hearing than would be acceptable for appeals generally,[1] and indeed the Practice Directions provide for adjournment applications to be made at the hearing listed.[2]

1   Practice Directions, para 9.1.
2   Practice Directions, para 9.7.

FAST TRACK: TRANSFER OUT OF FAST TRACK PROCEDURE

5.162   The tribunal must order that the relevant Parts of the fast track procedures shall cease to apply if

● all the parties consent;[1]

● if it is satisfied that the case cannot justly be decided within the timescales set by the FTRs.[2]

When making such an order, the tribunal may adjourn any hearing of the appeal or application, and give directions relating to the further conduct of the proceedings.[3]

1   FTRs, para 14(1)(a).
2   FTRs, para 14(1)(b).
3   FTRs, para 14(2).

PART 6 – EVIDENCE

ADMISSIBLE EVIDENCE, CORROBORATION, FOREIGN LAW

5.163   Migrants must establish their case by evidence, and the forms of material upon which they can do so are broader than may be the case in other areas of law:

'The Tribunal may admit evidence whether or not–

(a)   the evidence would be admissible in a civil trial in the United Kingdom.'[1]

1   Tribunal Procedure (First-tier Tribunal) (Immigration and Asylum Chamber) Rules 2014, SI 2014/2604, r 14(2).

5.164   This liberal approach to the reception of evidence means that in tribunal proceedings 'the area of legitimate debate is about relevance and weight, not admissibility';[1] and 'Tribunals do not have a general discretion to refuse to receive relevant evidence on the basis of procedural defects as to how it was obtained.'[2] The need to take a realistic approach in order to secure the interests of justice is shown by the guidance in immigration appeals that, for example, where there are no countervailing factors generating suspicion as to the intentions of the parties,[3]

'Evidence of telephone cards is capable of being corroborative of the contention of the parties that they communicate by telephone, even if such data cannot confirm the particular number the sponsor was calling and the country in question. It is not a requirement that the parties also write or text each other'.

1   Lord Carnwath in *Secretary of State for Home Department v MN and KY (Scotland)* [2014] UKSC 30 at [22].
2   *MB (admissible evidence; interview records) Iran* [2012] UKUT 119 (IAC), headnote at (3).
3   Blake J in *Goudey (subsisting marriage – evidence) Sudan* [2012] UKUT 41 (IAC).

5.165   In asylum appeals:[1]

'where this country's compliance with an international convention is in issue, the decision-maker is ... not constrained by the rules of evidence that have been adopted in civil litigation, and is bound to take into account all material considerations when making its assessment about the future.'

1   Brooke LJ in the Court of Appeal in *Karanakaran v Secretary of State for the Home Department* [2000] Imm AR 271 at [101].

5.166 The general law of procedure is nevertheless relevant to tribunal proceedings.[1] No party or witness may be compelled to give any evidence or produce any document which could not be the trial of a civil claim in the part of the United Kingdom in which the hearing is taking place:[2] this addresses the privilege against self-incrimination, ie the

> 'rule ... that no one is bound to answer any question if the answer ... would ... have a tendency to expose the deponent to any criminal charge, penalty or forfeiture which the judge regards as reasonably likely to be preferred or sued for.'[3]

1   The tribunal in *Kapela* [1998] Imm AR 294.
2   Tribunal Procedure (First-tier Tribunal) (Immigration and Asylum Chamber) Rules 2014, SI 2014/2604, r 15(3).
3   Goddard LJ in *Blunt v Park Lane Hotel Ltd* [1942] 2 KB 253, cited in *Coogan v News Group Newspapers Ltd* [2012] EWCA Civ 48 at [14]–[18].

5.167 Evidence may be given on oath or affirmation, or with neither, at the discretion of the tribunal.[1] The Tribunal may take account of any statements and documents, as well as the evidence of witnesses, and may have regard to written statements by witnesses not available for cross-examination and to documents notwithstanding that their provenance is not explained by direct written or oral evidence[2] (though self-evidently it will be best practice to explain the background to a document's production in order to assist the tribunal). There is no requirement that an asylum claimant's testimony be corroborated before it can be accepted as genuine;[3] material that he prays in aid of his appeal will inevitably be intended to promote his cause, so description of it as 'self-serving' may not add anything of substance to its evaluation.[4] However it is

> 'important ... for independent supporting evidence to be provided where it would ordinarily be [readily] available; that where there is no credible explanation for the failure to produce that supporting evidence it can be a very strong pointer that the account being given is not credible.'[5]

1   Tribunal Procedure (First-tier Tribunal) (Immigration and Asylum Chamber) Rules 2014, SI 2014/2604, r 14(3).
2   *NA (Cambridge College of Learning) Pakistan* [2009] UKAIT 31 at [102], citing *Khawaja* [1983] UKHL 8 at [111] and [125].
3   The Master of the Rolls in *Karakas v Secretary of State for the Home Department* (IATRF 97/1023/4, 10 June 1998); *Kasolo* (13190); UNHCR Handbook, para 196; Directive 2004/83, Art 4(1) and (5); Immigration Rules, HC 395, para 339L.
4   Toulson LJ in *AK (Afghanistan) R (on the application of) v Secretary of State for the Home Department* [2007] EWCA Civ 535 at [29].
5   Thomas LJ in *TK (Burundi) v Secretary of State for the Home Department* [2009] EWCA Civ 40 at [20].

Anonymous evidence; interview records; foreign law

5.168 There is no prohibition on the admission of anonymous evidence: the effect of anonymity will go to the weight to be attached to the material in question and care must always be taken in assessing the weight of such material.[1] Where no representative is present to keep an independent record, the practice of tape recording asylum interviews has been permitted by the Home Office following the decision in *Dirshe*, and a judge may decline to assign weight to an interview record where a recording raises issues as to its reliability, though a failure to record an interview does not prevent its admissibility in a subsequent appeal.[2] Interview records should always be disclosed because:

> 'the affected person must be alerted to the essential elements of the case against him. ... The interview is the vehicle through which this discrete duty of disclosure will, in practice, be typically, though not invariably or exclusively, discharged.'[3]

The meaning of foreign law is to be approached as a question of fact.[4]

1   *CM (EM Country Guidance; disclosure) Zimbabwe CG* [2013] UKUT 59 (IAC) at [17].
2   *MB (admissible evidence; interview records) Iran* [2012] UKUT 119 (IAC) at [2] and [25], and headnote, citing *R (Dirshe) v Secretary of State for the Home Department* [2005] EWCA Civ 421.
3   *Miah (interviewer's comments: disclosure: fairness)* [2014] UKUT 515 (IAC) at [13].
4   Waller LJ in *King v Brandywine Reinsurance Company* [2005] EWCA Civ 235 at [66].

THE BURDEN OF PROOF AND STANDARD OF PROOF

5.169   The burden of proof generally lies on the appellant, who must make his case.[1] In international protection appeals the standard of proof is a low one, essentially whether there is a 'real risk' of the feared persecution or serious harm eventuating[2] and the benefit of the doubt is afforded to an asylum seeker.[3] There may be cases where the shared duty of co-operation in determining an asylum claim[4]

> 'means, in practical terms, that if, for any reason whatsoever, the elements provided by an Applicant for international protection are not complete, up to date or relevant, it is necessary for the Member State concerned to co-operate actively with the Applicant, at that stage of the procedure, so that all the elements needed to substantiate the application may be assembled. A Member State may also be better placed than the Applicant to gain access to certain types of documents.'[5]

1   The general principle in English law is that he who asserts, must prove; see IA 1971, s 3(8) for a specific statutory provision that places the burden of proof on a person asserting British citizenship or any exemption from statutory provisions.
2   Directive 2004/83, Art 2(c) and (e); *R v Secretary of State for the Home Department, ex parte Sivakumaran* [1991] Imm AR 80; *Karanakaran v Secretary of State for the Home Department* [2000] Imm AR 271.
3   UNHCR Handbook, paras 196 and 204; the ECtHR in *RC v Sweden* [2010] ECHR 307 at [50].
4   Directive 2004/83, Art 4(1).
5   The CJEU in *MM v Minister for Justice, Equality and Law Reform, Ireland* (277/11, 22 November 2012) at [64]–[66], discussed in *NA (UT rule 45: Singh v Belgium) Iran* [2014] UKUT 205 (IAC) at [23]–[25]; Fulford LJ in *PJ v Secretary of State for the Home Department* [2014] EWCA Civ 1011 at [32].

5.170 Immigration appeals generally proceed on the same basis as civil proceedings, in that disputed facts are determined on the balance of probabilities. As Lord Hoffman put it in *Re B*:[1]

> 'If a legal rule requires a fact to be proved (a "fact in issue"), a judge or jury must decide whether or not it happened. There is no room for a finding that it might have happened. The law operates a binary system in which the only values are 0 and 1. The fact either happened or it did not. If the tribunal is left in doubt, the doubt is resolved by a rule that one party or the other carries the burden of proof. If the party who bears the burden of proof fails to discharge it, a value of 0 is returned and the fact is treated as not having happened. If he does discharge it, a value of 1 is returned and the fact is treated as having happened.'

1   *In Re B (children)* [2008] UKHL 35 at [2].

5.171 In cases involving the general refusal reasons, the burden of proof rests on the SSHD,[1] which has to be established by suitably convincing evidence, albeit that 'there is only one civil standard of proof and that is proof that the fact in issue more probably occurred than not',[2] which must be borne in mind when earlier statements that 'an allegation of forgery needs to be established to a high degree of proof, by the person making the allegation'[3] are considered. Essentially, as the tribunal put it in *NA*:[4]

> 'for the respondent to satisfy us he has discharged the burden of proof on him on the balance of probabilities he would, in the context of this type of case, need to furnish evidence of sufficient strength and quality and he (and the Tribunal) would need to subject it to a "critical", "anxious" and "heightened' scrutiny.'

1   Lord Fraser in *R v Secretary of State for the Home Department, ex parte Khawaja* [1984] IAC 74 at 97E; *Shen (paper appeals, proving dishonesty)* [2014] UKUT 236 (IAC) at [2].
2   Lord Hoffman, *In Re B (children)* [2008] UKHL 35 at [13], Baroness Hale at [62]–[75].
3   *RP (proof of forgery) Nigeria* [2006] UKAIT 00086 at [14]; see further *JC (Part 9 HC 395 – burden of proof) China* [2007] UKAIT 00027 at [10]–[11].
4   *NA (Cambridge College of Learning) Pakistan* [2009] UKAIT 00031 at [101], cited and followed by the UT in *Khalid (Ealing, West London and Hammersmith College) Pakistan* [2011] UKUT 295 (IAC).

POST-DECISION EVIDENCE: THE SAVED PROVISIONS

5.172 In appeals under NIAA 2002, s 82, and appeals against decisions to refuse refugee leave but to grant some lesser leave, or to downgrade a person's leave, the general rule, as set out in NIAA 2002, s 85(4), is that:

> 'the Tribunal may consider evidence about any matter which it thinks relevant to the substance of the decision, including evidence which concerns a matter arising after the date of the decision.'[1]

Thus,

> 'where an Appellant claims that the decision "is not in accordance with immigration rules", he is entitled to adduce evidence as to the present position, even if it is clear ... that the requirements of the Immigration Rules were not met at the date of the decision itself.'[2]

1   NIAA 2002, s 85(4).
2   *LS (post-decision evidence; direction; appealability) Gambia* [2005] UKAIT 00085 at [9].

5.173   However, this regime is subject to certain exceptions. In appeals against refusal of entry clearance and refusal of certificates of entitlement to the right of abode, under NIAA 2002, s 85A(2), 'the Tribunal may consider only the circumstances appertaining at the time of the decision.'[1] This is the case whatever the ground of appeal: the remedy for a person who is concerned that his human rights might be infringed is a further application, as the relevant guidance states that 'A person who has an appeal pending can make a fresh application for entry clearance in the same or any other category. There is no requirement for a person to withdraw an appeal';[2] and 'Where a change of circumstances is alleged by someone who is outside the jurisdiction, the entry clearance officer will often be best placed to evaluate the effect of this.'[3] In an entry clearance appeal, evidence of subsequent actions which casts light upon the position at the date of the decision is admissible (as where 'later events clarify the question of the parties' intentions towards each other and the genuineness of their relationship as at the date of decision'[4]). In the starred decision of *DR Morocco* it was said that evidence of subsequent events differing from the position at that time, even if predicted or reasonably foreseeable (eg a changed intention to live together; obtaining employment which was predicted or reasonably foreseeable) was not admissible, though that view is not held in the higher courts, where it has been said that 'The Tribunal must have regard to all relevant circumstances when considering the issue of proportionality, and in my view that includes in an appropriate case having regard to likely future events'.[5] Treasury counsel has accepted that there 'may be circumstances in which such an offer may shed light on the circumstances which appertained at the date of the refusal of entry clearance'.[6]

1   NIAA 2002, s 85A(2).
2   Entry Clearance Guidance, 'Appeal procedures: APL01', para 1.20.
3   Lord Phillips in *AS (Somalia) v Secretary of State for the Home Department* [2009] UKHL 32 at [9], though Lord Hope at [19] thought there might be cases where the proportionality of the restriction would have to be considered. See further *SA (ambit of s 85(5) of 2002 Act) Pakistan* [2006] UKAIT 00018.
4   *AH (scope of s 103A reconsideration) Sudan* [2006] UKAIT 00038 at [63].
5   Elias LJ in *AP (India) v Secretary of State for the Home Department* [2015] EWCA Civ 89 at [26].
6   *DR (ECO – post-decision evidence) Morocco* [2005] UKIAT 00038 (starred); contrast *ECO Islamabad v Yousaf* (TH/19930/90) and Glidewell J in *R v IAT, ex parte Kwok on Tong* [1981] Imm AR 214, cited in *DR Morocco* for the possibility that under IAA 1999, s 77(4) foreseeability was relevant; see *SF (Afghanistan) v Entry Clearance Officer* [2011]

EWCA Civ 758 at [14] for the concession; Maurice Kay LJ stated in *Amarteifio v Entry Clearance Officer, Accra* [2006] EWCA Civ 1758 at [11] that 'there is an established practice of permitting evidence of subsequent events if they were reasonably foreseeable at the time, and a period of six months has been established as the customary period with that in mind'.

5.174   This restriction does not capture refusals of EEA family permits:

'Although an EEA family permit under reg 12 of the EEA Regulations is similar in its function to entry clearance, it is not entry clearance and is therefore not caught by the terms of s 85(5). The Immigration Judge was entitled to look at all evidence "relevant to the substance of the decision, including evidence which concerns a matter arising after the date of the decision".'[1]

1   *IS (marriages of convenience) Serbia* [2008] UKAIT 00031 at [25].

POST-DECISION EVIDENCE: THE POINTS-BASED SYSTEM; HISTORIC TIME-LINES

5.175   In appeals against refusal of leave to enter or to refuse to vary leave to remain, involving applications considered under the points-based system, where the grounds of appeal relied upon are the application of the Immigration Rules and exercise of discretions under them, or accordance with the law,[1] the only evidence that may be considered is:

- material provided in support of, and at the time of making, the application to which the immigration decision related;[2]

unless the evidence is provided:[3]

- in relation to other grounds, such as human rights or race discrimination;

- to prove that a document is genuine or valid;

- in relation to a requirement of the Rules, or discretion under them, arising other than in relation to the acquisition of points (for example in relation to discretions arising under the general refusal reasons in Pt 9 of the Rules).

1   NIAA 2002, s 85A(3).
2   NIAA 2002, s 85A(4)(a).
3   NIAA 2002, s 85A(4)(b)–(d).

5.176   As to this last point, the specific rules addressing the viability and credibility of entrepreneur applications have been interpreted as relevant to the acquisition of points, thereby excluding post-application evidence in relation to those questions.[1]

1   *Ahmed (PBS: admissible evidence)* [2014] UKUT 365 (IAC) at [5]–[7].

5.177 Beyond the points-based system, the Rules sometimes specify a historic time-line,[1] and in these circumstances the appeal must focus on whether, as at the date of the hearing, it is established that certain criteria were satisfied at the date of the decision against which the appeal is brought (as with those Rules that require the financial requirements for maintenance to be assessed as at the date of application):[2]

'The effective operation of a points based system requires the points to have been accumulated at the date of the Secretary of State's decision.'

1   Eg Appendix C, para A1.2(a)(i).
2   Sullivan LJ in *AQ (Pakistan) v Secretary of State for the Home Department* [2011] EWCA Civ 833 at [41]; Sedley LJ in *Secretary of State for the Home Department v Pankina* [2010] EWCA Civ 719 at [39].

POST-DECISION EVIDENCE: APPEALS UNDER THE RELEVANT PROVISIONS OF NIAA 2002 AS AMENDED BY IA 2014

5.178 Under NIAA 2002, as amended by IA 2014, post-decision evidence will generally be admissible, there being no distinction between entry clearance and certificate of entitlement cases on the one hand and 'in-country' appeals on the other:[1]

'On an appeal under section 82(1) against a decision the Tribunal may consider any matter which it thinks relevant to the substance of the decision, including a matter arising after the date of the decision.'

1   NIAA 2002, s 85(1), relevant provisions.

5.179 This would not seem to alter the approach in the 'fixed historic time line' cases already identified where a Rule poses criteria focused on the date of application. However:[1]

'the Tribunal must not consider a new matter unless the Secretary of State has given the Tribunal consent to do so.'

1   NIAA 2002, s 85(4), relevant provisions (see **4.13–4.14** above).

5.180 This restriction on admissibility to those matters to which the SSHD consents operates in cases where a 'new matter' is sought to be raised: a new matter is one which is a ground of appeal within s 84 where the SSHD has not previously considered the matter in the context of the refusal appealed, or in a 'one-stop' notice.

POWER TO EXCLUDE EVIDENCE; APPROACH TO LATE EVIDENCE

5.181   Under the 2005 Rules, the immigration judge possessed explicit powers to exclude evidence which was not served in compliance with directions, albeit subject to the overriding objective of fairness;[1] there is no equivalent provision in the 2014 Rules, save for the general rule addressing non-compliance with rules and directions, which mandates a just and proportionate response ranging from waiving the requirement in question to referring the matter to the UT.[2] The very greatest care must be taken before refusing to admit late evidence,[3] with costs sanctions being preferable to exclusion;[4] it would be very difficult to see that the evidence of a material witness could be excluded merely for failure to provide a witness statement.[5] Material that is intentionally reserved until after a hearing is commenced may properly be excluded:[6]

> 'On the point of admissibility of evidence, where the Secretary of State's representative reserves material until a late point in the case it is clearly a matter for the Adjudicator to consider whether such material should or should not be admitted. No contemporaneous complaint appears to have been made about his decision and there was none in the grounds of appeal.'

1   Asylum and Immigration Tribunal (Procedure) Rules 2005, SI 2005/230, rr 51(4) and 4.
2   See **5.68** above.
3   *AK (admission of evidence – time limits) Iran* [2004] UKIAT 00103 at [13].
4   Sir Paul Kennedy in *RJ (Jamaica) v Secretary of State for the Home Department* [2008] EWCA Civ 93 at [26].
5   *A (Somalia)* [2004] UKIAT 00065 at [34]; *MA (rule 51(4), not oral evidence) Somalia* [2007] UKAIT 00079 at [15].
6   *Onovwakpoma* (13464, 4 June 1996).

5.182   A party who advisedly refrains from producing evidence at first instance may be constrained from relying upon it later.[1] The deliberate absence of a party should not prevent his opponent from adducing evidence at the hearing simply because the absent party is thereby unable to make representations on it.[2] It would be understandable if evidence-gathering efforts were concentrated at critical moments of the appeals process, and it would be unrealistic to expect continuous monitoring of potential new evidence in the intervening periods.[3] An appellant against a points-based system decision, who produces 'specified documents' at the hearing, or serves them so soon beforehand as to provide no opportunity for the SSHD to take the reasonable verification steps required by the Rules, should not necessarily be granted an adjournment for checks to be carried out: a judge in such a case may consider the authenticity of the documents in line with the evidence in the case as a whole.[4] As a former President put it:

> 'Apart from circumstances where lateness of the evidence means it is unfair to receive it, issues of fairness go to the weight to be attached to evidence, not admissibility.'[5]

1   Keene LJ in the Court of Appeal in *R v Immigration Appeal Tribunal, ex parte Azkhoshravi* [2001] EWCA Civ 977 at [23].
2   *SA (absence of party – late evidence) Sri Lanka* [2005] UKIAT 00028 at [21].
3   Carnwath LJ giving judgment of the Court of Appeal in *E v Secretary of State for the Home Department* [2004] EWCA Civ 49 at [16].
4   *Butt (para 245AA(b) – 'specified documents' – judicial verification) Pakistan* [2011] UKUT 00353(IAC) at [21]–[29].
5   *MB (admissible evidence, interview records) Iran* [2013] UKUT 119 at [3].

ORAL EVIDENCE

5.183   Oral evidence often assists an immigrant to establish his entitlement to remain in the United Kingdom, but it is not a prerequisite of success. The relevant considerations are set out in the case of *Coskuner*:[1]

'We entirely endorse the view that merely not giving evidence cannot, of itself, be a factor tending to show that a person is not to be believed. It is also, however, and equally clearly, not a factor tending to show that the person is to be believed. If doubts have been raised about the credibility or plausibility of certain evidence, and the facts related by that evidence are not supported by other evidence, the position may be that the fact-finder remains in doubt. The consequence of a fact-finder's doubt is or may be that the burden of proof is not discharged and so the party who has the burden of proof loses his case. The fact-finder does not strictly need to reach any view on credibility at all. It is open to him to reason as follows: "The appellant has stated such and such. Various points have been raised against his story. I consider those points are well made. There has been no further evidence which might persuade me that the original story was the truth. On the evidence before me I decline to make findings of fact in the appellant's favour." If an appellant does not give evidence, he cannot be cross-examined: that may be an advantage to him. But it carries a risk, because he also does not have the opportunity to give oral support to his previous statements. Strictly speaking his story does not require corroboration; but tactically, the position may be that if the appellant does not answer questions or meet points made against him, the adjudicator may not be prepared to accept the evidence. Overall, the adjudicator's task is to decide whether the appellant has made his case. If his conclusion is that the evidence does not discharge the burden of proof that is the end of the matter.'

1   *Coskuner* (16769, 23 July 1998).

5.184   It is advisable for oral evidence to be summarised in a decision:[1]

'Whilst there is of course no general requirement for an adjudicator to set out at length the oral evidence given before him, and in many cases no useful purpose would be served by doing so, nevertheless he ought as a matter of good practice to summarise at least the material parts of the evidence which he has heard so as to enable an informed reader to ascertain the nature and content of that evidence, and also to enable him to be satisfied that the adjudicator has directed his mind properly to the material aspects of the evidence.'

1   *AK (failure to assess witnesses' evidence) Turkey* [2004] UKIAT 00230 at [9].

5.185   The SSHD is free to seek to call an asylum claimant as a witness, although he would not be able to cross-examine him.[1] Care should be taken in eliciting information from persons not called as witnesses, and such enquiries should be confined to matters not in dispute.[2] Demeanour may be thought an unreliable indicator of credibility.[3]

'The great virtue of the English trial is usually said to be the opportunity it gives to the judge to tell from the demeanour of the witness whether or not he is telling the truth. I think that this is overrated. It is the tableau that constitutes the big advantage, the text with illustrations, rather than the demeanour of a particular witness. On that I would adopt in their entirety (this being the highest form of judicial concurrence) the words of MacKenna J: "I question whether the respect given to our findings of fact based on the demeanour of the witnesses is always deserved. I doubt my own ability, and sometimes that of other judges, to discern from a witness's demeanour, or the tone of his voice, whether he is telling the truth. He speaks hesitantly. Is that the mark of a cautious man, whose statements are for that reason to be respected, or is he taking time to fabricate? Is the emphatic witness putting on an act to deceive me, or is he speaking from the fullness of his heart, knowing that he is right? Is he likely to be more truthful if he looks me straight in the face than if he casts his eyes on the ground perhaps from shyness or a natural timidity?"'

1   *Prendi* (01/LS/00060, 8 August 2001) at [4].
2   The legal tribunal in *Yogalingam* (01/TH/02671, 4 January 2002) at [9].
3   Webster J in *R v Secretary of State for the Home Department, ex parte Dhirubhai Gordhanbhai Patel* [1986] Imm AR 208.

WITNESSES BESIDES APPELLANTS

5.186   The fact that a witness is awaiting the outcome of his own immigration application or appeal does not prevent him giving evidence in another person's appeal, given the need to deal with cases comprehensively at the first opportunity,[1] subject to the undesirability of an asylum seeker being questioned in an adversarial process prior to his case being presented in a less hostile interview process.[2] It would be quite wrong to discount evidence because it comes from a friend of the appellant.[3] Witnesses with refugee status or other grants of leave to remain should provide all available information in order to establish the basis upon which their application was granted, and those whose evidence has previously been the subject of evaluation in the immigration courts should put relevant determinations forward.[4] A determination of status by the SSHD will not carry the same weight as one made by a judge upon appeal, being an unreasoned administrative decision[5] – though it should be noted that, from around April 2005, the Home Office policy has been that:[6]

'Consideration minutes must be prepared in cases where leave is being granted ... explaining reasons for granting leave and the period of leave that is to be granted. Human Rights issues, if raised, must also be discussed in this minute.'

1   *S (Sri Lanka)* [2004] UKIAT 00039 at [34].
2   See **5.54**, fn 2 above.
3   Ouseley J in *R (Sri Lanka)* [2004] UKIAT 00056 at [12].
4   *AB (witness corroboration in asylum appeals) Somalia* [2004] UKIAT 00125 at [11]; *TK (consideration of prior determination, directions) Georgia* [2004] UKIAT 00149 at [19].
5   *AC (witness with refugee status – effect) Somalia* [2005] UKAIT 00124 at [14].
6   Home Office policy, 'Implementing substantive decisions', in force from around April 2005, addressing the 'Consideration minute' at para 9.6.

5.187   It might be thought as undesirable to go behind a reasoned finding by the SSHD in such a minute, in all but exceptional circumstances, as it would be to revisit a concession.[1] Findings upon the evidence of a material witness in earlier proceedings should be addressed on *Devaseelan* principles where their cases arise out of the same factual matrix.[2] It is customary for witnesses who have not yet given evidence to wait outside the hearing room.[3] The UT has given specific guidance for cases where a veiled witness gives evidence:[4]

'(1)   Where the face of a party or witness is substantially covered by a veil or other form of attire, it is incumbent on the Tribunal to strike the balance between the rights of the person concerned, the administration of justice and the principle of open justice. The Tribunal will consider options which should, simultaneously, facilitate its task of assessing the strength and quality of the evidence, while respecting as fully as possible the rights and religious beliefs of the person concerned.

(2)   Such measures may include the following:

(a)   A sensitive enquiry about whether the cover can be removed, in whole or in part.

(b)   Where appropriate, a short adjournment to enable the person concerned to reflect and, perhaps, seek guidance or advice.

(c)   The adoption of limited screening of the person and/or minimising the courtroom audience.

This is not designed to operate as an exhaustive list.

(3)   In cases where a Tribunal considers that the maintenance of the cover might impair its ability to properly assess the person's evidence and, therefore, could have adverse consequences for the appellant, the Tribunal must ventilate this concern.

(4)   Issues of religious attire and symbols must be handled by tribunals with tact and sensitivity.'

1   See **5.74** above.
2   See **5.116**, fn 4 above.
3   *RS and SS (exclusion of appellant from hearing) Pakistan* [2008] UKAIT 00012, headnote (see **5.131**, fn 5 above).
4   *AAN (veil) Afghanistan* [2014] UKUT 102 (IAC).

GIVING EVIDENCE BY ELECTRONIC MEANS

5.188   Normally witnesses give evidence in person. Nevertheless there may be cases where the provision of evidence by electronic means is desirable or necessary in the interests of justice. The issues have been extensively discussed in *Nare*:[1]

- Given that the usual model in the common-law system is for direct oral evidence to be given in the courtroom, and that departures from this 'are likely to reduce the quality of evidence, the ability of the parties to test it, and the ability of the judge to assess it, particularly where it has to be assessed against other oral evidence', the procedure should be used only where justified 'in the interest of justice, bearing in mind particularly the rights of other parties to challenge the evidence': a decision to take this route will not be taken lightly, and will be subject to directions, and it is unlikely that it will be permitted if they are not complied with.

- The provision of electronic evidence requires regulation such that it is subject to a measure of formality and supervision, subject to the same or similar constraints under which live evidence is given – so it should normally be given in formal surroundings, subject at the very least to control by appropriate officials, and it should be clear that nothing can be happening 'off camera' (or equivalent) that could cast doubt on the integrity of the evidence.

- It is for the party seeking to call evidence by electronic link to make the arrangements at the distant end, and to pay any expenses, and an adjournment should not be given simply because of delay in making such arrangements.

1   *Nare (evidence by electronic means) Zimbabwe* [2011] UKUT 00443 (IAC) at [17]–[20].

5.189   The *Nare* tribunal goes on to propose the following as 'the minimum requirements':

'a.   A party seeking to call evidence at an oral hearing by electronic link must notify all other parties and the Tribunal at the earliest possible stage, indicating (by way of witness statement) the content of the proposed evidence. (If the evidence is uncontested, an indication of that from the other parties may enable the witness's evidence to be taken wholly in writing.)

b.   An application to call evidence by electronic link must be made in sufficient time before the hearing to allow it to be dealt with properly. The application should be made to the relevant judge (normally the Resident Senior Immigration Judge) at the hearing centre at which the hearing is to take place, and must give (i) the reason why the proposed witness cannot attend the hearing; (ii) an indication of what arrangements have been made provisionally at the distant site; (iii) an undertaking to be responsible for any expenses incurred.

c.   The expectation ought to be that the distant site will be a court or Tribunal hearing centre, and that the giving of the evidence will be subject to on-site supervision by court or Tribunal staff.

d.   If the proposal is to give evidence from abroad, the party seeking permission must be in a position to inform the Tribunal that the relevant foreign government raises no objection to live evidence being given from within its jurisdiction, to a Tribunal or court in the United Kingdom. The vast majority of countries with which immigration appeals (even asylum appeals) are concerned are countries with which the United Kingdom has friendly diplomatic relations, and it is not for an immigration judge to interfere with those relations by not ensuring that enquiries of this sort have been made, and that the outcome was positive. Enquiries of this nature may be addressed to the Foreign and Commonwealth Office (International Legal Matters Unit, Consular Division). If evidence is given from abroad, a British Embassy, High Commission or Commonwealth may be able to provide suitable facilities.

e.   The application must be served on all other parties, in time for them to have a proper opportunity to respond to it.

f.   The decision whether to grant the application is a judicial one. The judge making the decision will take into account the reasons supporting the application, any response from other parties and the content of the proposed evidence, as well as of the overriding objective of the rules. If the application is granted, there may be further specific directions, which must be followed.

g.   If there is a direction for the taking of evidence by electronic link, the Tribunal will nevertheless need to be satisfied that arrangements at the distant end are, and remain, appropriate for the giving of evidence. A video link, if available, is more likely to be suitable than a telephone link. The person presiding over the Tribunal hearing must be able to be satisfied that events at the distant site are, so far as may be, within the observation and control of the Tribunal, and that there is no reason to fear any irregularity.

h.   There will need to be arrangements to ensure that all parties at the hearing, as well as the judge, have equal access to the input from the electronic link. Particular attention needs to be given to the accommodation of any interpreter.

i.   In assessing any challenged evidence, the Tribunal may have to bear in mind any disadvantages arising from the fact that it was given by electronic link, and should be ready to hear and consider submissions on that issue.

j.   Nothing in this guidance is intended to affect the existing arrangements for the hearing of bail applications by video link from secure video conferencing suites. Nor is this guidance intended to affect the arrangements for video linking of one Tribunal room to another for the purposes of hearing submissions by video link.'

VULNERABLE AND SENSITIVE WITNESSES

5.190   Care should be given to the treatment of vulnerable witnesses, whose circumstances are now addressed by specific Practice Directions[1] of general application across the tiers of the tribunal system: it applies to children, vulnerable adults and sensitive witnesses. The Practice Direction shows the increasing awareness of the need to treat such witnesses appropriately:[2]

'Courts are becoming, not before time, much more conscious of the need to help vulnerable witnesses. If a party is unable to put forward his best account through lack of appropriate assistance in the way he gives evidence there would be every likelihood of an Article 6 breach.'

1   Joint Presidential Guidance Note No 2 of 2010, 'Child, vulnerable adult and sensitive appellant guidance'; at Annex B is found the Senior President's Practice Direction of 30 October 2008 for the First-tier and Upper Tribunal on child, vulnerable adult and sensitive witnesses; see *OO (gay men: risk) Algeria CG* [2013] UKUT 63 (IAC) at [2] for a practical application of its use.
2   Toulson LJ refusing permission to appeal to the Court of Appeal in *FS (Iraq) v Secretary of State for the Home Department* EWCA Civ 928.

5.191   A vulnerable adult is defined[1] as:

'a person [who] has attained the age of 18 and –

(a)   he is in residential accommodation,

(b)   he is in sheltered housing,

(c)   he receives domiciliary care,

(d)   he receives any form of health care,

(e)   he is detained in lawful custody,

(f)   he is by virtue of an order of a court under supervision by a person exercising functions for the purposes of Part 1 of the Criminal Justice and Court Services Act 2000 (c. 43),

(g)   he receives a welfare service of a prescribed description,

(h)   he receives any service or participates in any activity provided specifically for persons who fall within subsection (9),

(i)   payments are made to him (or to another on his behalf) in pursuance of arrangements under section 57 of the Health and Social Care Act 2001 (c. 15), or

(j)   he requires assistance in the conduct of his own affairs.'

1   See the Safeguarding Vulnerable Groups Act 2006, s 59.

5.192   A sensitive witness[1] is:

'an adult witness where the quality of evidence given by the witness is likely to be diminished by reason of fear or distress on the part of the witness in connection with giving evidence in the case'.

1   See Senior President's Practice Direction (above), para 1(c).

5.193   The consequences of the identification of such a witness vary: the judge must decide upon the extent of the witness's vulnerability, the effect on the quality of his evidence, and the ultimate weight to be afforded his evidence.[1] Relevant factors to be taken into account are:[2]

●   mental health problems;

●   social or learning difficulties;

●   religious beliefs and practices, sexual orientation, ethnic social and cultural background;

●   domestic and employment circumstances;

●   physical disability or impairment that may affect the giving of evidence.

1   Joint Presidential Guidance Note No 2 of 2010, para 3.
2   Joint Presidential Guidance Note No 2 of 2010, para 2.

5.194   Such individuals should be called as witnesses only where the tribunal determines that the evidence is necessary to a fair hearing and that their welfare would not be prejudiced by participation,[1] such decision being made by reference to all available evidence and the submissions of the parties;[2] as to these, it may be appropriate for the tribunal to invite input from interested persons, such as a child's parents.[3] It may be appropriate for the tribunal to direct that the evidence should be given by telephone, video link or other means, or to direct that a person be appointed for the purpose of the hearing who has the appropriate skills or experience in facilitating the giving of evidence by a child, vulnerable adult or sensitive witness.[4] A single gender tribunal may be appropriate in some cases.[5]

1   Joint Presidential Guidance Note No 2 of 2010, Annex B: Senior President's Practice Direction, para 2.
2   Senior President's Practice Direction, para 3.
3   Senior President's Practice Direction, para 4.

4 Senior President's Practice Direction, para 7.
5 Joint Presidential Guidance Note No 2 of 2010, para 5.3(i); *AD (fresh evidence) Algeria* [2004] UKIAT 00155 at [29].

5.195   It is desirable for these issues to be addressed at the case management stage:[1] primary responsibility for raising vulnerability lies with the representative, but he may not always identify the issue himself.[2] The parties should be encouraged to agree disputed issues, to achieve maximum focus and minimise potential trauma.[3] It may be appropriate to bar the public, or family members, from the hearing room.[4] In general questions should be open-ended where possible, and any aggressive or improper questioning should be curtailed.[5] The judge should bear in mind that such individuals may not be used to answering questions or to having their views listened to, may be more inclined to volunteer speculative answers, and may be easily influenced by others: contradictory answers may show a lack of understanding of the questions.[6] The decision should show whether a witness falls within the Practice Direction and what impact this had on the procedure and consideration; and allowance should be made[7]

> 'for possible different degrees of understanding by witnesses and appellant compared to those who are not vulnerable ... Where there were clear discrepancies in the oral evidence, consider the extent to which the age, vulnerability or sensitivity of the witness was an element of that discrepancy or lack of clarity.'

1 Joint Presidential Guidance Note No 2 of 2010, para 4.
2 Joint Presidential Guidance Note No 2 of 2010, para 5.
3 Joint Presidential Guidance Note No 2 of 2010, para 9.
4 Joint Presidential Guidance Note No 2 of 2010, para 10.
5 Joint Presidential Guidance Note No 2 of 2010, para 10.2.
6 Joint Presidential Guidance Note No 2 of 2010, para 10.2.
7 Joint Presidential Guidance Note No 2 of 2010, paras 14–15.

CHILDREN AS WITNESSES AND APPELLANTS

5.196   Beyond vulnerable and sensitive witnesses, children also fall within the scope of the Practice Direction, including appellants whose age is disputed.[1] Child appellants should be identified upon entering the tribunal system, and if they are pursuing an asylum claim then the FTT should identify and record any responsible adult involved with their case (a role which a legal representative is forbidden from taking), who should attend any hearing (there is no provision in the FTT for the appointment of a guardian, intermediary or facilitator).[2] It will only rarely be appropriate for a child aged under 12 to give contentious evidence:[3]

> 'Although there can be no hard and fast rule, we would be very concerned if children below the age of 12 were expected to give contentious evidence in an asylum or other immigration appeal, without the express consent and support of their parent or guardian or appropriate adult. We acknowledge

the fact that children younger than this age have given evidence before the criminal courts, but in these cases there have been extensive arrangements to support the child before, during and after the testimony in question. Such arrangements are outside the resources and the procedures adopted by the First-tier or Upper Tribunal and very careful consideration would need to be given to the child's best interests and welfare before a Tribunal judge of his or her own motion asked such for an appellant to go into the witness box.'

1   Joint Presidential Guidance Note No 2 of 2010, para 5.2(v).
2   Joint Presidential Guidance Note No 2 of 2010, para 5.
3   *ST (child asylum seekers) Sri Lanka* [2013] UKUT 292 (IAC) at [36].

5.197   Under BCIA 2009, s 55, the SSHD must make arrangements ensuring that immigration, asylum and nationality functions are discharged having regard to the need to safeguard and promote the welfare of children who are in the United Kingdom. Thus the best interests of the child should receive central attention. This principle requires regard to be had to the rights proclaimed throughout the Convention on the Rights of the Child (CRC) in the context of being a member of an especially vulnerable group[1] taking into account the other three foundational principles of the CRC: non-discrimination (Art 2), the child's inherent right to life, and the obligation to ensure to the maximum extent possible the survival and development of the child, taking this notion in its broadest sense as a holistic concept, embracing the child's physical, mental, spiritual, moral, psychological and social development (Art 6) and the participatory rights enshrined in Art 12:[2]

> '2.   ... the child shall in particular be provided the opportunity to be heard in any judicial and administrative proceedings affecting the child, either directly, or through a representative or an appropriate body, in a manner consistent with the procedural rules of national law.'

1   See eg the UNCRC's General Comment No 14 (2013) on 'The right of the child to have his or her best interests taken as a primary consideration', paras 75–76.
2   See the discussion by Baroness Hale in *ZH (Tanzania) v Secretary of State for the Home Department* [2011] UKSC 4 at [34]–[37].

5.198   Article 12 finds its domestic expression in Home Office policy guidance:[1]

'Children should be consulted and the wishes and feelings of children taken into account wherever practicable when decisions affecting them are made, even though it will not always be possible to reach decisions with which the child will agree'

1   UKBA statutory guidance cited in *AJ (India) v Secretary of State for the Home Department* [2011] EWCA Civ 1191 at [16].

Children and their best interests

5.199   It may be necessary, or desirable, for a child to be separately represented in some cases (and it should not automatically be assumed that his interests are the same as those of his parents).[1] The SSHD has various policies designed to give effect to the s 55 duty, including procedural duties in asylum claims, in which context 'case owners may need to be proactive in their pursuit and consideration of objective factors and information relating to the child's claim'.[2] On appeal, it will normally be for the child's representatives to put forward relevant information regarding the assessment of best interests: rarely, it may be necessary for the tribunal to take in an inquisitorial function to ensure that it is appropriately armed to answer the question[3] ('the Tribunal encourages either party to provide independent assessments from teachers, doctors, social workers, or other child-centred professionals'[4]):

> 'Being adequately informed and conducting a scrupulous analysis are elementary prerequisites to the inter-related tasks of identifying the child's best interests and then balancing them with other material considerations. This balancing exercise is the central feature of cases of the present type. It cannot realistically or sensibly be undertaken unless and until the scales are properly prepared.'[5]

1   Baroness Hale in *ZH (Tanzania) v Secretary of State for the Home Department* [2011] UKSC 4 at [35]; Lady Hale in *EM (Lebanon)v Secretary of State For The Home Department* [2008] UKHL 64.
2   Home Office Guidance, 'Processing an Asylum Application from a Child', para 16.1.
3   Laws LJ in *SS (Nigeria) v SSHD* [2013] EWCA Civ 550 at [34]–[35]; McCombe LJ in *CW (Jamaica) v Secretary of State for the Home Department* [2013] EWCA Civ 915 at [22]–[29].
4   *RS (immigration and family court proceedings) India* [2012] UKUT 218 (IAC) at [38].
5   *JO (s 55 duty) Nigeria* [2014] UKUT 00517 (IAC) at [11].

5.200   Even though the many principles surrounding the consideration of the case of a child do not have the full force of law, nevertheless the 'immigration judge must of course show himself aware of the child's age and be sensitive of it.'[1]

1   Laws LJ in *MD (Guinea) v Secretary of State for the Home Department* [2009] EWCA Civ 733 at [12].

ASSERTIONS

5.201   Assertion is not evidence: 'findings have to be made on evidence'[1] and 'it is the judicial function to determine litigious disputes on the basis of the evidence presented by the parties.'[2] The SSHD should produce the evidence that underlies any assertions made in a decision letter – both the 2014 Rules[3] and the long-standing approach[4] of the tribunal require this:

> 'The Tribunal has commented in other cases about the unfortunate practice of making statements of fact in the letters of refusal or grounds of appeal which cannot be evidentially supported. It is our task to consider the facts of the appellant's case as established and to set those facts into whatever framework can be objectively established.'

A failure to provide the best evidence available to a party (as where they hold an original document but decline to produce it without good reason) may well count against the acceptance of secondary evidence that they put forward.[5]

1   *RP (proof of forgery) Nigeria* [2006] UKAIT 00086 at [17]. See also eg the Master of the Rolls in *Coleen Properties Ltd v Minister of Housing and Local Government* [1971] EWCA Civ 11: 'the mere *ipse dixit* of the Local Council is not sufficient. There must be some evidence to support their assertion.'
2   *NA (UT r 45: Singh v Belgium) Iran* [2014] UKUT 205 (IAC) at [14].
3   Tribunal Procedure (First-tier Tribunal) (Immigration and Asylum Chamber) Rules 2014, SI 2014/2604, rr 23(1)(e) and 24(1)(d).
4   *Gebretensae* (14794, 27 March 1997).
5   See eg *R v Governor of Pentonville Prison, ex parte Osman* [1991] WLR 277 at 308, cited by Nicol J in *Arowolo v Department for Work and Pensions* [2013] EWHC 1671 (Admin) at [18].

DOCUMENTARY EVIDENCE: DOCUMENTS PARTICULAR TO THE APPELLANT AND ALLEGATIONS OF FORGERY

5.202   Where the SSHD asserts that an item of evidence is forged, the burden of proof is upon him to establish the proposition by convincing evidence,[1] and mere assertions will not suffice to discharge that burden bearing in mind that even the most sensitive evidence regarding the means by which forgeries are detected can be put forward in private, via the procedure established by NIAA 2002, s 108.[2]

1   *RP (proof of forgery) Nigeria* [2006] UKAIT 00086 at [14] onwards; *EB (fresh evidence, fraud, directions) Ghana* [2005] UKAIT 00131 at [14]; see Lord Hoffman in *In Re B (children)* [2008] UKHL 35 at [13], Baroness Hale at [62]–[75] for discussion of the operation of the civil standard in these cases.
2   NIAA 2002, s 108; *RP* (above) at [15]–[17].

5.203   Detailed guidance has been given in *OA Nigeria* as to how that procedure should operate:[1]

- Judges should bear in mind that whilst any invitation to depart from open justice must be scrutinised with care, nevertheless there is an important public interest in having informants and the respondent's methods of detection protected, including ensuring that the sources of information do not dry up.

- The application must be heard in private, absent the appellant and his representative, though they should be invited to make submissions, necessarily of some generality, before being invited to withdraw.

- The PO should explain which documents are under suspicion, the basis for this suspicion, and the reasons why the public interest would be damaged by disclosure of the intelligence in question, during the private element of the hearing; the judge should not assume that an expert on forgery has any further expertise unless it is evidenced.

- The judge should explain the outcome of his deliberations on disclosure upon the hearing resuming.

- The judge should explain his reasoning for taking this route in his written decision, as much as he feels properly able without undermining the rationale for the process.

- If the s 108 application is refused, then the hearing should proceed in public, though the issue of forgery will remain to be determined based on the evidence as a whole, unless the allegation is withdrawn, for example where the PO does not want to have the under lying evidence disclosed.

1   *OA (alleged forgery, s 108 procedure) Nigeria* [2007] UKIAT 00096 at [30]–[38].

5.204   Whether or not a document is a forgery, however (outside of cases involving the general refusal reasons), is seldom the central question in the appellate enquiry.[1] The tribunal gave guidance in the case of *Tanveer Ahmed*:[2]

'1.   In asylum and human rights cases it is for an individual claimant to show that a document on which he seeks to rely can be relied on.

2.   The decision maker should consider whether a document is one on which reliance should properly be placed after looking at all the evidence in the round.

3.   Only very rarely will there be the need to make an allegation of forgery, or evidence strong enough to support it. The allegation should not be made without such evidence. Failure to establish the allegation on the balance of probabilities to the higher civil standard does not show that a document is reliable. The decision maker still needs to apply principles 1 and 2.'

1   *OA (alleged forgery, s 108 procedure) Nigeria* [2007] UKIAT 00096 at [35].
2   Now reported as *A v Secretary of State for the Home Department (Pakistan)* [2002] UKIAT 00439 (starred). Thus the concession that the burden of proof was on the respondent, made in *R v IAT, ex parte Shen* [2000] INLR 389, went too far.

5.205   The principle does not apply where the documents are essentially self-proving or are positively demonstrated to be authentic by reference to material, including expert evidence, that is independent of the appellant himself.[1] Nor does it apply to witness statement evidence of a factual nature, as opposed to documents.[2]

1   Laws LJ in *R v Immigration Appeal Tribunal, ex parte Davila-Puga* [2001] EWCA Civ 931.
2   His Honour Judge Anthony Thornton QC in *T v Secretary of State for Home Department* [2012] EWHC 988 (Admin) at [99].

Dealing with disputed documents

5.206   Where an apparently genuine document is said to be a forgery, there will inevitably be an evidential burden on the SSHD to undermine its authenticity;[1] and it should be made clear, given 'that there are two different kinds of inauthenticity: forgery of the document itself, and the making of false entries on a genuine document', which is actually alleged.[2] It is necessary to give proper, intelligible and adequate reasons for arriving at a conclusion that a document is unreliable.[3] Regardless of questions such as burden of proof, it would be to put the cart before the horse if suspicions regarding documents were employed to cast doubt on the general credibility of an appellant;[4] nor should documents be rejected *solely* due to concerns about an appellant's account[5] (although that principle should not be applied mechanistically, the real question being whether the evidence has been considered in the round)[6] – indeed, if 'the only issue is the appellant's status, and the documents relied on, if genuine, are conclusive of status, it can only rarely be helpful or relevant to test out the appellant's veracity or dependability in other ways'.[7] The fact that a document is a poor copy does not compel a conclusion that it is not to be relied on.[9] It may well be that oral evidence of a witness is to be preferred over documentary evidence provided by the respondent.[10] Under the modern Immigration Rules,

> 'the scheme ... is not about forgery. Documents are to be rejected if there are reasons to doubt their genuineness and it is not possible to verify that they are in fact genuine.'

A judge in these cases will need to make an assessment of the genuineness of documents, where the SSHD has not been given an opportunity to do because of their late submission, in the context of the evidence as a whole.[11]

1   Latham LJ in the Court of Appeal in *Mungu v Secretary of State* [2003] EWCA Civ 36 at [16]–[18].
2   Sedley LJ in *SA (Kuwait) v Secretary of State for the Home Department* [2009] EWCA Civ 1157 at [15].
3   *MT (credibility assessment flawed – Virjon B applied) Syria* [2004 UKIAT 00307 at [8].
4   Sullivan J in *R v Immigration Appeal Tribunal, ex parte Gomez-Salinas* [2001] EWHC Admin 287.
5   *MT* (above) at [7].
6   *GB (evidence not probative is irrelevant) Zimbabwe* [2005] UKAIT 00153 at [39]; Auld LJ in *MS (Iran) v Secretary of State for the Home Department* [2007] EWCA Civ 271 at [35].
7   Sedley LJ in *SA (Kuwait)* (above) at [14].
8   *GB* (above) at [38]–[40].
9   *O (Turkey)* [2003] UKIAT 00006 at [5].
10 *FZ (fingerprint evidence) Afghanistan* [2004] UKIAT 00304 at [8]–[9].
11 *Butt (para 245AA(b) – 'specified documents' – judicial verification) Pakistan* [2011] UKUT 00353 (IAC) at [27], and [21]–[29] generally.

EVIDENCE OF CRIMINALITY

5.207   In cases raising issues of a person's deportation being conducive to the public good, there is no bar on the admission of evidence from criminal proceedings (including victim impact statements) that did not result in a conviction, given that criminal and immigration proceedings have different purposes and the general rule that evidence may be admissible in immigration appeals notwithstanding that it would not be admitted in a court of law:[1]

'The only issue for the Crown Court was whether, on the criminal standard of proof, the prosecution had overcome the burden of proving that the claimant murdered F. The ultimate issue for the Secretary of State is whether it is conducive to the public good to deport the claimant.'[2]

Such evidence must be weighed in the balance, with any flaws in its cogency being duly evaluated:[3]

'whilst I see that this evidence inevitably loses considerable weight by being anonymous and (in part) hearsay, thereby preventing any direct challenge to the relevant witnesses, I cannot say that this evidence must inevitably be given no weight by the tribunal – or that to admit the evidence at all will inevitably deny the claimant a fair hearing.'

1   Hickinbottom J in *V, R (on the application of) v Asylum and Immigration Tribunal* [2009] EWHC 1902 (Admin) at [41].
2   Hickinbottom J in *V* (above) at [36]; *Bah (EO (Turkey) – liability to deport) Sierra Leone* [2012] UKUT 196 (IAC) at [48]–[49].
3   Hickinbottom J in *V* (above) at [46].

5.208   The greater the difficulty in assessing the reliability of such evidence, the less the weight that can properly be given to it;[1] it is likely to gain in weight where supported by other relevant material which is consistent with a complainant's narrative.[2] The standard of proof remains the balance of probabilities taking account of the importance of the issues that must be established:[3]

'Any specific acts that have already occurred in the past must be proven by the Secretary of State, and proven to the civil standard of a balance of probability. The civil standard is flexible according to the nature of the allegations made, see House of Lords in *Re B* [2008] UKHL 35, and a Tribunal judge should be astute to ensure that proof of a proposition is not degraded into speculation of the possibility of its accuracy. ... where the Secretary of State seeks to exercise the power to make a deportation decision against a person who is not a British citizen or otherwise exempt under the Immigration Acts, she must first identify the factual basis for the exercise of the power in the decision letter or amplified reasons for the decision; second, where the factual basis is contested she must satisfy the Tribunal of the factual basis on the balance of probabilities. Third, any material relevant to meet that standard may be received by the Tribunal whether it is hearsay or a summary of information held by others, if it is supplied in time and in accordance with case management directions but the weight to be attached to such material will depend on its nature, the circumstances in which it was collected or recorded, the susceptibility of the informant or original informant to error, and the extent to which the appellant is able to comment or rebut it.'

1   *Bah (EO (Turkey) – liability to deport) Sierra Leone* [2012] UKUT 196 (IAC) at [54].
2   *Farquharson (removal – proof of conduct) Jamaica* [2013] UKUT 146 (IAC) at [89].
3   *Bah* (above) at [63] and [65].

5.209   It is critical that timely disclosure be made of the relevant materials, which should be supported by a police witness statement that puts them into context and is transparent as to the means that they were accumulated:

> 'conduct based on intelligence and crime reports can be relied on in immigration appeals provided that there is some decree of transparency about how the material is accumulated and what it consists of. If intelligence is so sensitive that a sufficient gist of it cannot be disclosed, then it should not be raised in the appeal. Mere assertion will not be enough.'[1]

The same principles for assessing evidence apply in removal cases as to deportation ones.[2]

1   *Farquharson (removal – proof of conduct) Jamaica* [2013] UKUT 146 (IAC) at [89]–[93].
2   *Farquharson* (above), headnote at (1).

SPECIFIC DUTIES OF INVESTIGATION IN ASYLUM CLAIMS

5.210   There will be occasions where it is appropriate for the respondent to make further enquiries in asylum cases, where rejecting them without checking their authenticity would fall short of the careful and rigorous investigation expected of national authorities in order to protect the individuals concerned from torture, harm or inhuman or degrading treatment under ECHR, Art 3, for example when a simple process of enquiry would resolve conclusively whether documents are authentic and reliable,[1] as where the documentation comes from an unimpeachable source.[2] In other cases, it might be unfeasible or disproportionate to initiate such enquiries, because of the risk of endangering persons in the country of origin, or the difficulty in making covert enquiries in a foreign country without the permission of the authorities there.[3] In a case where the duty of enquiry arises,[4]

> 'the consequence of a decision that the national authorities are in breach of their obligations to undertake a proper process of verification is that the Secretary of State is unable thereafter to mount an argument challenging the authenticity of the relevant documents unless and until the breach is rectified by a proper enquiry. It follows that if a decision of the Secretary of State is overturned on appeal on this basis, absent a suitable investigation it will not be open to her to suggest that the document or documents are forged or otherwise are not authentic.'

1   *Singh v Belgium* (33210/11, 2 October 2102, Second Section of the European Court of Human Rights).
2   *MJ v Secretary of State for the Home Department* [2013] UKUT 00253 at [50].

3   Fulford LJ in *PJ v Secretary of State for the Home Department* [2014] EWCA Civ 1011 at [29].
4   Fulford LJ in *PJ* (above) at [31].

EXPERT EVIDENCE

Instructing experts

5.211   The instruction of experts is regulated by Practice Direction.[1] A party who instructs an expert must provide clear and precise instructions, together with all relevant information concerning the nature of the appellant's case, including his immigration history, the refusal reasons leading to the appeal, and copies of any relevant previous reports.[2] It is the duty of an expert to help the tribunal on matters within his own expertise; this duty is paramount and overrides any obligation to the person from whom he has received instructions or by whom he is paid.[3] Expert evidence should be the independent product of the expert uninfluenced by the pressures of litigation, assisting the tribunal by providing objective, unbiased opinion on matters within the author's expertise, and should not assume the role of an advocate.[4] The expert should:

- consider all material facts, including those which might detract from his opinion;[5]

- make it clear when a question or issue falls outside his expertise; and

- state when he is unable to reach a definite opinion, for example because of insufficient information.[6]

1   Practice Directions, section 10.
2   Practice Directions, para 10.1.
3   Practice Directions, para 10.2.
4   Practice Directions, para 10.3; Collins J in *Slimani* (01/TH/00092, 21 December 2000, starred) citing *National Justice Compania Naviera SA v Prudential Assurance Co Ltd (The Ikarian Reefer)* [1993] 2 Lloyds Rep 68 at 81–82, Cresswell J; *SR (Iraqi Arab Christian: relocation to KRG) Iraq CG* [2009] UKAIT 00038 at [86].
5   Practice Directions, para 10.5.
6   Practice Directions, para 10.6.

5.212   If, after producing a report, an expert changes his view on any material matter, that change of view should be communicated to the parties without delay, and when appropriate to the tribunal.[1] An expert's report should be addressed to the tribunal and not to those instructing him.[2]

1   Practice Directions, para 10.7.
2   Practice Directions, para 10.8.

5.213   Additionally an expert's report must:[1]

(a)   give details of the expert's qualifications;

(b)   give details of any literature or other material which the expert has relied on in making the report;

(c)   contain a statement setting out the substance of all facts and instructions given to the expert which are material to the opinions expressed in the report or upon which those opinions are based;

(d)   make clear which of the facts stated in the report are within the expert's own knowledge;

(e)   say who carried out any examination, measurement or other procedure which the expert has used for the report, give the qualifications of that person, and say whether or not the procedure has been carried out under the expert's supervision;

(f)   where there is a range of opinion on the matters dealt with in the report–

        (i)   summarise the range of opinion, so far as reasonably practicable, and

        (ii)   give reasons for the expert's own opinion;

(g)   contain a summary of the conclusions reached;

(h)   if the expert is not able to give an opinion without qualification, state the qualification; and

(j)   contain a statement that the expert understands his duty to the tribunal, and has complied and will continue to comply with that duty.

1   Practice Directions, para 10.9.

5.214   A suitable Statement of Truth would take the following form:

'I confirm that insofar as the facts stated in my report are within my own knowledge I have made clear which they are and I believe them to be true, and that the opinions I have expressed represent my true and complete professional opinion.'[1]

1   Practice Directions, paras 10.10–10.11.

5.215   Whilst the instructions to the expert are not protected by privilege, cross-examination of the expert on the contents of the instructions will only be allowed if the tribunal permits it (or where the party who gave the instructions consents to it). In determining whether this is appropriate, the tribunal must be satisfied that there are reasonable grounds to consider that the statement in the report or the substance of the instructions is inaccurate or incomplete, and if so satisfied, it should allow cross-examination where this is in the interests of justice.[1]

1   Practice Directions, para 10.12.

General principles relating to expert evidence

5.216   Persons with expertise relevant to the business of the tribunal frequently provide reports in support of appeals. Whether such persons are strictly speaking 'experts' matters less in informal proceedings than the weight that their evidence deserves;[1] their expertise may be relevant to the assessment of objective risk or to the credibility of an account.[2] The author should not trespass on the arena of the judicial decision maker:[3]

> 'Insofar as he or she has reason to comment on an individual case, his or her remarks should normally be confined to assessing whether what is said to have happened to a particular individual or individuals correlates or not with the general evidence about persons similarly situated.'

1   The tribunal in *Kapela* [1998] Imm AR 294.
2   Buxton LJ in *H v Secretary of State for the Home Department* [2006] EWCA Civ 803 at [15]; Keith J granting judicial review in *R (Ucar) v Immigration Appeal Tribunal* [2003] EWHC 1330 Admin at [8].
3   *GG (non-state actors: Acero-Garces disapproved) (Colombia)* [2000] UKIAT 00007 at [10].

5.217   Whilst the ultimate assessment of an appeal is for the immigration judge who hears it, an expert's uncontradicted testimony should carry considerable force.[1] Where an expert goes beyond the admissible ambit of his expertise, 'it is the judge's task to separate the inadmissible chaff from the admissible wheat and to evaluate the latter.'[2] Close regard must be had to the precise qualifications and extent of expertise of language analysts, and guidelines from the tribunal should not be unduly proscriptive as to the weight to be given to their reports.[3]

1   May LJ in the Court of Appeal in *Gurpreet Singh v Secretary of State for the Home Department* [2001] EWCA Civ 516.
2   Sedley LJ in *AA (Saudi Arabia) v Secretary of State for the Home Department* [2009] EWCA Civ 1241 at [11].
3   Lord Carnwath in *Secretary of State for Home Department v MN and KY (Scotland)* [2014] UKSC 30.

Assessment of country expert evidence

5.218   Numerous factors have been attributed weight in the assessment of expert materials. Particularly important will be:

> 'the authority and reputation of the author, the seriousness of the investigation by means of which they were compiled, the consistency of their conclusions and their corroboration by other sources.'[1]

Relevant considerations include whether the author of the report was available for cross-examination[2] (though the Court of Appeal has warned against too much weight being attached to this),[3] and whether his perspective seems partisan.[4]

1   *HC and RC (trafficked women) China CG* [2009] UKAIT 00027, citing *NA v United Kingdom* [2008] ECHR 616; Lord Carnwath in *Secretary of State for Home Department v MN and KY (Scotland)* [2014] UKSC 30 at [48].
2   *Kapela* [1998] Imm AR 294.
3   Buxton LJ in *Tarlochan Singh v Secretary of State for the Home Department* (IATRF 1999/0055/4, 5 July 1999).
4   *Kapela* (above).

Medical evidence; the Istanbul Protocol

5.219   Medical and psychiatric reports deserve careful and specific consideration, with proper, adequate and intelligible reasons being given for findings upon them;[1] it would be wrong to treat them as speculative or conjectural simply because they inevitably amount to a professional's opinion.[2] However, the variable quality of reports means that not all deserve the same degree of attention, and it is the quality of the report and the standing of its author that are the final benchmark of their force.[3] Reports that follow the approach of the Istanbul Protocol will be especially impressive.[4] That instrument sets out, under the heading 'D. Examination and Evaluation following specific forms of Torture':

'187. ... For each lesion and for the overall pattern of lesions, the physician should indicate the degree of consistency between it and the attribution

(a)   Not consistent: the lesion could not have been caused by the trauma described;

(b)   Consistent with: the lesion could have been caused by the trauma described, but it is non-specific and there are many other possible causes;

(c)   Highly consistent: the lesion could have been caused by the trauma described, and there are few other possible causes;

(d)   Typical of: this is an appearance that is usually found with this type of trauma, but there are other possible causes;

(e)   Diagnostic of: this appearance could not have been caused in anyway other than that described.

188. Ultimately, it is the overall evaluation of all lesions and not the consistency of each lesion with a particular form of torture that is important in assessing the torture story'

Account should be taken of the extent to which a report follows established methods and criteria, and whether it is based on an in-depth or superficial interview process.[5]

1   *AK (failure to assess witnesses' evidence) Turkey* [2004] UKIAT 00230 at [14]–[15].
2   Sedley LJ in *Miao v Secretary of State for the Home Department* [2006] EWCA Civ 75 at [17].

3   Elias J in the Administrative Court in *R v Special Adjudicator, ex parte Singh* [2001] EWHC
    Admin 184; *HE (DRC – credibility and psychiatric reports) Democratic Republic of Congo*
    [2004] UKIAT 00321 at [16]; *KV (scarring – medical evidence)* [2014] UKUT 230 (IAC) at
    [316]; though cf the ECtHR in *RC v Sweden* (41827/07, 9 March 2010) [2010] ECHR 307.
4   Potter LJ in *SA v Secretary of State for the Home Department* [2006] EWCA Civ 1302 at
    [29]: the Istanbul Protocol: Manual on the Effective Investigation and Documentation of
    Torture and Other Cruel, Inhuman or Degrading Treatment or Punishment was submitted to
    the United Nations High Commissioner for Human Rights on 9 August 1999.
5   *SP (risk, suicide, PTSD, IFA, medical facilities) Kosovo CG* [2003] UKIAT 00017 at [16](b).

Role of medical evidence

5.220   Medical evidence has its limitations: the medical profession quite
properly takes the evidence of its patients at face value[1] and it may be that
psychiatric symptoms such as depression have a cause other than that given in
the patient's account,[2] and credibility is ultimately a question for the judicial
decision maker,[3] though this does not prevent an expert giving his opinion as
to the plausibility of a claim in the light of his findings.[4] One role for a medical
report is 'to corroborate and/or lend weight to the account of the asylum seeker
by a clear statement as to the consistency of old scars found with the history
given'.[5]

1   *HE (DRC – credibility and psychiatric reports) Democratic Republic of Congo* [2004]
    UKIAT 00321 at [17].
2   *HE* (above) at [18]–[19]; *Appellant AE and Appellant FE* [2002] UKIAT 05237.
3   *JL (medical reports – credibility) China* [2013] UKUT 145 (IAC), headnote at (3); *HH
    (Ethiopia)* [2007] EWCA Civ 306 at [17]–[18]); *KV (scarring – medical evidence)* [2014]
    UKUT 230 (IAC), headnote at (6); Davis LJ in *IY (Turkey) v Secretary of State for the Home
    Department* [2012] EWCA Civ 1560 at [47].
4   *SR (Iraqi Arab Christian: relocation to KRG) Iraq CG* [2009] UKAIT 00038 at [86];
    Neuberger LJ in the Court of Appeal in *HK v Secretary of State for the Home Department*
    [2006] EWCA Civ 1037 at [44]; *JL* (above), headnote at (4).
5   Potter LJ in *SA v Secretary of State for the Home Department* [2006] EWCA Civ 1302 at [27].

5.221   It may be that an expert's conclusion that an individual suffers from
PTSD is effectively decisive of his claim to have suffered torture, abuse or
mistreatment; or it may be that the evidence as a whole may require the
appellant's account to be rejected, notwithstanding a supportive medical
report;[1] equally:

> 'In the context of a holistic assessment, where for example a claimant has
> given a strongly consistent and plausible account of his claim to have been
> tortured, but the medical evidence points against this, a decision maker
> might properly conclude that the claimant has nevertheless made out his
> claim to the lower standard.'[2]

1   Davis LJ in *IY (Turkey) v Secretary of State for the Home Department* [2012] EWCA Civ
    1560 at [47].
2   *KV (scarring – medical evidence)* [2014] UKUT 230 (IAC) at [295].

5.222 'Good and objective'[1] reasons need to be provided before finding that an appellant has connived to mislead an expert:[2]

'to say that it is not the duty of a doctor to disbelieve the account given by a patient may be correct but takes one absolutely nowhere. It is plain that a psychiatrist does exercise his critical facilities and experience in deciding whether he is being spun a yarn or not, and all of us sitting in these courts in different jurisdictions from time to time have heard psychiatrists saying that they do believe an account or that they do not believe an account.'

1   Sedley LJ in *Y (Sri Lanka) v Secretary of State for the Home Department* [2009] EWCA Civ 362 at [12].
2   Moses J in *Minani, R (on the application of) v Immigration Appeal Tribunal* [2004] EWHC 582 (Admin) at [26].

Medical reports and their consideration

5.223 It is important that a medical expert's report:

● shows that the author has read all relevant evidence including adverse assessments of the credibility of the patient's account by decision makers, resisting any temptation to conduct a running commentary on the approach of a judge;[1]

● explains the extent to which his belief in an account is based on medical indicia independent of the patient's word;[2] and

● addresses the possibility of self-infliction of scars by the appellant or by proxy where there is some presenting feature that enlivens this possibility – though this possibility should not be considered unless an appellant has had the opportunity to deal with such an suggestion.[3]

1   *JL (medical reports – credibility) China* [2013] UKUT 145 (IAC), headnote at (1); *KV (scarring – medical evidence)* [2014] UKUT 230 (IAC) at [308].
2   *JL* (above), headnote at (2).
3   *KV* (above), headnote at (3) and [299]–[300].

5.224 The absence of evidence of torture is not necessarily inconsistent with an account of ill-treatment in the past:[1] 'some methods of torture do not produce scarring and the absence of scarring does not mean that the torture did not take place, merely that there is nothing physical to document.'[2] A report should not be discounted simply because of findings on the other evidence in the case, as that would be to put the cart before the horse:[3]

'where there is medical evidence corroborative of an appellant's account of torture or mistreatment, it should be considered as part of the whole package of evidence going to the question of credibility and not simply treated as an "add-on" or separate exercise for subsequent assessment only after a decision on credibility has been reached on the basis of the content of the appellant's evidence or his performance as a witness.'

1   The Committee against Torture in *Bouabdallah Ltaief v Tunisia*, Communication No 189/2001, UN Doc CAT/C/31/D/189/2001 (2003), para 10.5; Smith LJ in *Reka v Secretary of State for the Home Department* [2006] EWCA Civ 552 at [35].
2   Home Office Policy Instructions, 'Medical foundation cases'.
3   Potter LJ in *SA v Secretary of State for the Home Department* [2006] EWCA Civ 1302 at [32]; see also Forbes J in the Administrative Court in *R v Special Adjudicator, ex parte Beqaraj* [2002] EWHC 1469 (Admin) and Hooper J in *R v Immigration Appellate Authority and Secretary of State for the Home Department, ex parte Gautam* [2003] EWHC 1160 (Admin).

5.225   Nevertheless a fact finder has to start his deliberations somewhere: a judge may have evaluated the evidence as a whole notwithstanding that he mentions the medical evidence only at a particular point in his decision.[1] Some institutions, such as the Medical Foundation and the Helen Bamber Foundation, are recognised as producing reports of particular value and are thus the subject of a specific Home Office policy which recognises the desirability of deferring consideration of an asylum claim pending receipt of their report, where it would be material to the outcome of an asylum claim ('the [Home Office caseworker] should normally suspend the substantive decision if they are not minded to grant any leave' pending receipt of such report[2]).

1   *HH (medical evidence; effect of Mibanga) Ethiopia* [2005] UKAIT 00164 at [21], approved by Rix LJ in *S v Secretary of State for the Home Department* [2006] EWCA Civ 1153 at [23] and [32].
2   Asylum Policy Instruction Medico-Legal Reports from the Helen Bamber Foundation and the Medical Foundation Medico-Legal Report Service (version 3.0, 17 January 2014) at para 2.4; see further the Home Office Policy Instructions, 'Medical foundation cases'; see also *T (Turkey)* [2004] UKIAT 00052 at [12].

Chapter 6

Onward appeals to the Upper Tribunal, Court of Appeal and the Supreme Court

PART 1 – GENERAL PRINCIPLES

INTRODUCTION

6.1   This chapter addresses the procedures by which appeals move beyond the FTT, initially both by review (though this process appears to be used very sparingly) and on appeal to the UT, and thence onwards to the higher courts. We deal with proceedings in the Court of Appeal in some detail as immigration appeals have developed their own distinctive jurisprudence there, and have numerous distinct procedures; we briefly address appeals to the Supreme Court, given that the processes there are largely generic. We mention some differences in procedures between the Court of Session and Court of Appeal of Northern Ireland where these arise from the Upper Tribunal Rules,[1] but in general we do not address those specialist jurisdictions, which have their own procedures.

1   The Tribunal Procedure (Upper Tribunal) Rules 2008, SI 2008/2698.

6.2   The old Immigration Appeal Tribunal was from its inception intended to bring a measure of harmony and to 'give authoritative guidance ... on the exercise of ... discretion',[1] and the UT has inherited its role. The UT sits principally at its headquarters at Field House, off Chancery Lane,[2] though it occasionally holds proceedings at Hatton Cross, Birmingham, Leeds, Glasgow and occasionally in Manchester, Newport and Belfast.[3] Judges of the UT (formerly senior immigration judges) sitting in the UT, will be identified in their written judicial decisions as 'Upper Tribunal Judge X'; in court they should be addressed as 'Sir' or 'Madam' as the case may be, and in correspondence it will usually be appropriate to use the salutation 'Dear Judge'.[4] Those wishing to engage the UT's jurisdiction should consider carefully whether their challenge to the FTT's decision is motivated by a point of principle or other clear error, rather than being 'a simple quarrel with the Judge's assessment of the various pieces of evidence':[5]

'different tribunals, without illegality or irrationality, may reach different conclusions on the same case ... The mere fact that one tribunal has reached what may seem an unusually generous view of the facts of a particular case does not mean that it has made an error of law'[6]

Under the saved provisions of NIAA 2002, the UT has recognised that it possesses a wide jurisdiction to apply principles of public law.[7]

1   *Report of the Committee on Immigration Appeals* 1967 (Cmnd 3387: 'the Wilson Report') summarised by the tribunal in *Khan* (18129; 19 March 1999).
2   Field House, 15–25 Breams Building, London, EC4A 1DZ.
3   These being the hearing centres as at October 1999, as recorded by Hooper J in the High Court in *R v Secretary of State for the Home Department, ex parte Thakar Singh* (CO/1364/99, 5 October 1999). The tribunal now has video conferencing facilities available for hearings where representatives are unable to attend the London headquarters (see **8.33**, fn 2): see eg *Chen* [2002] UKIAT 00726. The speech by the Hon Mr Justice Blake, President of the UT to the Upper Tribunal Immigration Judiciary, 'The Arrival of the Upper Tribunal Immigration and Asylum Chamber' (11 February 2010) indicates that the UT would continue to visit the regions in the future.
4   Joint Presidential Guidance Note 2011 No 3, 'Judicial titles in UTIAC and FtTIAC (2011)'.
5   The President McCloskey J in *MR (permission to appeal: tribunal's approach)* [2015] UKUT 29 (IAC) at [5].
6   Carnwath LJ in *Mukarkar v Secretary of State for the Home Department* [2006] EWCA Civ 1045 at [40]; at [41] he stressed that the government's representatives, as well as lawyers acting for migrants, should exercise restraint in launching appeals, even where a decision seemed inconsistent with government policy. See further Presidential Guidance Note 2011 No 1, para 13(a).
7   Speech by the Hon Mr Justice Blake, President of UTIAC to the Upper Tribunal Immigration Judiciary, 'The Arrival of the Upper Tribunal Immigration and Asylum Chamber' (11 February 2010) – though the narrowing of the grounds of appeal under the amended NIAA 2002 via the reforms of IA 2014 may end this era. See generally Chapter 4.

Key legal provisions governing the UT

6.3   It must be remembered that the Immigration and Asylum Chamber now takes its place as one part of a larger system[1] and it is beyond our scope to exhaustively describe the processes of the UT beyond the UT. Rather we concentrate on those rules which will frequently be relevant to representatives appearing in the UT. No doubt decisions of the tribunal and courts made with reference to predecessors of the Rules will have to be read in the light of the wording of the present set; but they may very well retain a relevance in predicting the response of the immigration judiciary to matters of practice and procedure before them, and so we cite them in this chapter. We occasionally cite older unreported determinations from the pre-reporting era where they express a point that chimes with our experience of current thinking and where they are not inconsistent with more recent statements of principle.

1   Thus joining the Administrative Appeals Chamber, the Tax and Chancery Chamber, and the Lands Chamber.

6.4   The procedures of the UT are regulated by the Tribunal Procedure (Upper Tribunal) Rules 2008, combined with Practice Directions and Practice Statements;[1] fast track cases have their own rules[2] and it must always be recalled that appeals against FTT decisions, being brought to the UT initially via the FTT, will be governed by the 2014 Rules.[3]

- TCEA 2007, ss 9–14;

- the Tribunal Procedure (Upper Tribunal) Rules 2008, SI 2008/2698;

- Presidential Guidance Note 2011 No 1: Permission to appeal to UTIAC (amended September 2013 and July 2014);

- Practice Statement of the Immigration and Asylum Chambers of the First-tier and Upper Tribunal on or after 13 November 2014 ('Practice Statement');

- Practice Direction of the Immigration and Asylum Chambers of the First-tier and Upper Tribunal on or after 13 November 2014 ('Practice Direction').

There is a useful 'Guide for unrepresented claimants in Upper Tribunal Immigration and Asylum Chamber', which is in itself a good introductory guide to the UT's processes.[4]

1   Tribunal Procedure (Upper Tribunal) Rules 2008, SI 2008/2698; made by the Senior President of Tribunals for the Immigration and Asylum Chamber of the First-tier Tribunal and the Upper Tribunal.
2   As to fast track procedure cases, see the Fast Track Rules forming the Schedule to the Tribunal Procedure (First-tier Tribunal) (Immigration and Asylum Chamber) Rules 2014, SI 2014/2604, which entered force on 4 April 2005.
3   SI 2014/2604.
4   Presidential Guidance Note 2013 No 3.

DECISIONS WHICH MAY BE CHALLENGED BY APPEAL OR REVIEW

6.5   Appeal lies to the UT on a point of law arising from decisions other than excluded ones, by way of permission granted by the FTT or the UT;[1] thus there is no challenge to:

- *'any procedural, ancillary or preliminary decision* made in relation to an appeal against a decision under section 40A of the British Nationality Act 1981, section 82, 83 or 83A of the Nationality, Immigration and Asylum Act 2002 6, or regulation 26 of the Immigration (European Economic Area) Regulations 2006';[2]

- the FTIAC's own review of its decision, or refusal to do so;[3]

- the FTIAC's own refusals to refer a matter to the UT;[4]

- a decision of the FTT that has been set aside.[5]

1   TCEA 2007, s 11(3)–(4).
2   The Appeals (Excluded Decisions) Order 2009, SI 2009/275 (as made under TCEA 2007, ss 11(5)(f) and 13(8)(f)). See *Abiyat (rights of appeal) Iran* [2011] UKUT 314 (IAC) at [11]–[12] and [24], for the relationship between the order and the interpretation of appeal rights, including the necessity for appeal rights under the unified tribunal system to be interpreted to preserve the same breadth of appeal rights as previously extant.
3   TCEA 2007, s 11(5)(d)(i)–(iii).
4   TCEA 2007, s 11(5)(d)(iv).
5   Under TCEA 2007, s 9: s 11(5)(e).

6.6   Those excluded decisions may only be attacked by way of judicial review rather than statutory appeal. Excluded decisions include those on the extension of time or the existence of an appealable immigration decision where this is dealt with under the distinct preliminary issue procedure in the FTT.[1] However, where the FTT has admitted an appeal into its remit, and then issued a decision upon it, even one terminating proceedings due to jurisdiction or timeliness, a right of appeal lies to the UT[2] (and it is important that misleading information to the contrary is not given by way of guidance in a notice of decision).[3] Other appealable decisions are:

• Under the saved provisions of NIAA 2002 (ie the pre-2014 Act system), there is an express right of appeal conferred regarding the making of directions, which are treated as part of the FTT's decision for the purposes of onwards appeal to the UT.[4]

• There is no apparent barrier to appealing against a decision to remit the case for rehearing: such a decision is clearly not ancillary and cannot be properly described as either procedural or preliminary.[5]

1   Now found within the Tribunal Procedure (First-tier Tribunal) (Immigration and Asylum Chamber) Rules 2014, SI 2014/2604, r 20 and Practice Statement, para 3 for the FTT and UT, its predecessor under the 2005 Rules, r 9 is discussed in *Abiyat (rights of appeal) Iran* [2011] UKUT 314 (IAC); see further *NA (excluded decision; identifying judge) Afghanistan* [2010] UKUT 444 (IAC) at [16]–[23]; see Dyson LJ in *MK (Iran), R (on the application of) v Asylum and Immigration Tribunal* [2007] EWCA Civ 554 for a practical example of a judicial review of a refusal to extend time.
2   Richards LJ in *JH (Zimbabwe) v Secretary of State for the Home Department* [2009] EWCA Civ 78 at [9]; *Abiyat* (above); *Ved (appealable decisions; permission applications; Basnet) Tanzania* [2014] UKUT 150 (IAC); Practice Statement, para 3.4; for decisions regarding the pre-FTT/UT system, see *MM (out of time appeals) Burundi* [2004] UKIAT 00182 (starred); *SA (s 82(2)(d): interpretation and effect) Pakistan* [2007] UKAIT 00083; *ST (s 92(4)(a): meaning of 'has made') Turkey* [2007] UKAIT 00085; *SB (family visit appeal: brother-in-law?) Pakistan* [2008] UKAIT 00053; Collins J in the Administrative Court in *R (Secretary of State for the Home Department) v Immigration Appeal Tribunal* [2004] EWHC 3161 (Admin); *Gremesty v Secretary of State for the Home Department* [2001] INLR 132.
3   *Ved* (above) at [17].
4   NIAA 2002, s 87(4).
5   Contrast *R (Secretary of State for the Home Department) v Immigration Appeal Tribunal* [2001] EWHC Admin 261 (the '*Zengin*' judicial review); NIAA 2002, s 103(3) explicitly provided that the remittal of an appeal to an adjudicator was not the determination of the appeal for the purposes of an appeal from the IAT; see also IAA 1999, Sch 4, para 23.

6.7   Examples of non-appealable decisions are:

● fee awards, being an ancillary decision;[1]

● refusal to issue a witness summons;[2]

● decisions in relation to costs;[3]

● a refusal to make a recommendation for leave to remain outside of the Rules.[4]

There may also be the exceptional prospect of challenging a denial of fair hearing by judicial review, notwithstanding that the statutory appellate mechanisms have upheld a decision.[5]

1   Sharp LJ in *Singh v Secretary of State for the Home Department* [2014] EWCA Civ 438.
2   *B v Suffolk County Council* [2010] UKUT 413 (AAC) at [27].
3   Presidential Guidance Note No 1 of 2014, para 33.
4   Such recommendations were relatively common before the entry into force of HRA 1998. See *R v Immigration Appeal Tribunal, ex parte Chavrimootoo* [1995] Imm AR 267; the Court of Appeal in *Khatib-Shahidi v Immigration Appeal Tribunal* (C/2000/0342, 20 July 2000); *Gillegao* [1990] Imm AR 17.
5   *AM (Cameroon) R (on the application of) v Asylum and Immigration Tribunal* [2007] EWCA Civ 131, Rix LJ at [128] for discussion of those 'very rare cases' relating to jurisdiction or 'procedural irregularity of such a kind as to constitute a denial of the applicant's right to a fair hearing'; see further Hickinbottom J in *V, R (on the application of) v Asylum and Immigration Tribunal* [2009] EWHC 1902 (Admin) at [52]–[60].

DETERMINING JURISDICTION

6.8   The FTT and UT have jurisdiction to determine their own jurisdiction;[1] a decision wrongly made at an earlier stage cannot confer jurisdiction on those who later consider the question[2] and a tribunal may raise the question of jurisdiction itself.[3] A decision made in the absence of a jurisdictional objection will be a precarious one (as Sedley LJ put it, being made with constitutive but not adjudicative jurisdiction), but may still stand absent some future challenge, particularly once the time limit for appeal has passed.[4]

1   *MM (out of time appeals) Burundi* [2004] UKIAT 00182 referring to *B (Zimbabwe)* [2004] UKIAT 00076; Farwell LJ in *R v Shoreditch Assessment Committee, ex parte Morgan* [1910] 2 KB 859 at 880.
2   Patten LJ in *Virk v Secretary of State for the Home Department* [2013] EWCA Civ 652 at [20]–[24]; *Nirula, R (on the application of) v Secretary of State for the Home Department* [2012] EWCA Civ 1436; [2008] UKUT 1 (AAC) (CAF/1913/2008) at [25]–[26], citing CAF/1133/2007 and Stanley Burnton J in the Administrative Court of the Queen's Bench Division of the High Court in a group of cases relating to the application of time limits in the Pensions Appeal Tribunal (PAT) in the case of *R (on the application of the Secretary of State for Defence) v PAT (Lockyer-Evans, interested parties)* [2007] EWHC 1177 (Admin).
3   Longmore LJ in *Nirula* (above) at [31].
4   Sedley LJ in *Anwar v Secretary of State for the Home Department* [2010] EWCA Civ 1275 at [19]–[23]; Longmore LJ in *Nirula* (above) at [32].

MATERIALITY

6.9   Appeals against decisions of the FTT must identify an error of law,[1] and for such an error to lead to a viable challenge, they will usually need to be material to the outcome of the appeal,[2] albeit permission 'should only be refused on the basis that the error was immaterial, if it is a plain case that the error could have made no difference to the outcome'.[3] Once an error of law is identified, in determining whether the decision can nevertheless stand, the question will be whether the decision maker would have inevitably reached the same conclusion absent the error:

> 'it is a high burden, falling upon the [respondent], to persuade anyone that the [judge below] would have been bound to have reached the same conclusion, notwithstanding an error of law, in relation to the approach to and conclusions about an important piece of factual evidence .... the question for us is whether the error of law was material in the sense that the [judge below] must have reached the same conclusion'.[4]

1   TCEA 2007, s 11(1). This is essentially the same jurisdiction as was extant under the review and reconsideration provisions of NIAA 2002, s 103. Before 9 June 2003, the jurisdiction was a wider one under which a party could appeal if 'dissatisfied' with a determination: Laws LJ in *Subesh v Secretary of State for the Home Department* [2004] EWCA Civ 56 interpreted this, on factual issues, as connoting a case where the appellate court felt itself *required* to make a different decision.
2   Brooke LJ for the Court of Appeal in *R (Iran) v Secretary of State for the Home Department* [2005] EWCA Civ 982 at [10]; Laws LJ in *CA v Secretary of State for the Home Department* [2004] EWCA Civ 1165 at [14]. TCEA 2007, s 12(2)(a), addressing proceedings on appeal to the UT, states that the UT 'may (but need not) set aside the decision of the First-tier Tribunal'.
3   Presidential Guidance Note 2011 No 1, para 16. See also, on materiality, the approach on judicial review, **8.138**, fn 8 below.
4   *Detamu v Secretary of State for the Home Department* [2006] EWCA Civ 604, Moses LJ at [14] and [18]; See further Neuberger LJ in the Court of Appeal in *HK v Secretary of State for the Home Department* [2006] EWCA Civ 1037 at [45] and Lord Neuberger of Abbotsbury in the Court of Appeal in *SS (Iran) v Secretary of State for the Home Department* [2008] EWCA Civ 310 at [23]; Sir Stanley Burnton in *ML (Nigeria) v Secretary of State for the Home Department* [2013] EWCA Civ 844 at [16]. For similar principles regarding materiality and judicial review, see **8.138**, fn 8 below.

6.10   It has been said that:[1]

> 'There are two categories of case in which an identified error of law by the FTT or the Upper Tribunal might be said to be immaterial: if it is clear that on the materials before the tribunal any rational tribunal must have come to the same conclusion or if it is clear that, despite its failure to refer to the relevant legal instruments, the tribunal has in fact applied the test which it was supposed to apply according to those instruments.'

1   Sales LJ in *Secretary of State for the Home Department v AJ (Angola)* [2014] EWCA Civ 1636 at [49].

THE *ROBINSON* DUTY TO IDENTIFY OBVIOUS POINTS OF CONVENTION LAW

6.11 The tribunal is under the *Robinson* duty to identify points in favour of an appellant in fundamental rights cases notwithstanding that they were not raised below,[1] both when granting permission to appeal and at a full hearing:[2]

> 'it is the duty of the appellate authorities to apply their knowledge of Convention jurisprudence to the facts as established by them when they determine whether it would be a breach of the Convention to refuse an asylum-seeker leave to enter as a refugee, and that they are not limited in their consideration of the facts by the arguments actually advanced by the asylum seeker or his representative.'

1 Lord Woolf MR in *R v Secretary of State for the Home Department and Immigration Appeal Tribunal, ex parte Robinson* [1997] Imm AR 568 at [37].
2 *AM (Serbia) v Secretary of State for the Home Department* [2007] EWCA Civ 16.

6.12 However, the duty does not arise regarding an abstruse point, nor in relation to purely procedural matters,[1] but only where an 'obvious point of Convention law favourable to the asylum-seeker ... does not appear in the decision ... which has a strong prospect of success'.[2] The principle extends to issues arising under the ECHR[3] and by analogy must extend to points of international protection law beyond the Refugee Convention, those being aspects of European Union law.[4] New material, as opposed to legal arguments, should normally be pursued via the further representations procedure rather than on appeal.[5] The *Robinson* approach would not normally extend to issues such as the construction of Home Office policies.[6] Although the principle generally arises in favour of asylum seekers, a question going to an integral part of the refugee assessment, such as exclusion (or the statutory presumptions as to criminality),[7] can also be taken on appeal by the SSHD, where it is clearly available on the facts already found below,[8] though there is probably no duty to permit unpleaded human rights points to be taken in the government's favour.[9] Beyond asylum, it may well be inappropriate to permit reliance on previously available points that were not set out in the original pleadings.[10]

1 Simon Brown LJ in *Taore v Secretary of State for the Home Department* [1998] Imm AR 450; Tucker J in *R v Immigration Appeal Tribunal, ex parte Mohamed* (CO/4494/99, 24 October 2000); Kay J in *R v Secretary of State for the Home Department and Immigration Appeal Tribunal, ex parte Bogou* (CO/2972/99, 15 February 2000).
2 Lord Woolf MR in *Robinson* [1997] Imm AR 568 at [39].
3 *AM (Serbia) v Secretary of State for the Home Department* [2007] EWCA Civ 16 at [29]; *Xhejo* (01/TH/00625, 12 July 2001) at [6]; *VM (FGM, risks, Mungiki,Kikuyu/Gikuyu) Kenya CG* [2008] UKAIT 00049 at [44]; Carnwath LJ in the Court of Appeal in *EM (Lebanon) v Secretary of State for the Home Department* [2006] EWCA Civ 1531 at [43].
4 Given the principle of effectiveness under European Union law, see eg the Consolidated Treaty of the European Union, Art 19(1); see the President McCloskey J in *Nixon (permission to appeal: grounds)* [2014] UKUT 368 (IAC) at [7].

5   Immigration Rules, HC 395, para 353. See *R (Iran) v Secretary of State for the Home Department* [2005] EWCA Civ 982 at [82]–[83]; eg Evans-Lombe J granting permission for judicial review in the Administrative Court in *R (Diaby) v Secretary of State for the Home Department* [2003] EWHC 2605 (Admin) – though cf Patten LJ in *SA (Sri Lanka) v Secretary of State for the Home Department* [2014] EWCA Civ 683 at [12]–[13]. See **6.75**, fn 3 below.
6   *Mugwagwa (s 72 – applying statutory presumptions) Zimbabwe* [2011] UKUT 00338 (IAC), headnote at (2), [32].
7   *HM (policy concessions not Convention recognition) Iraq* [2006] UKAIT 00092; *PD (grounds, implied variation, s 86(3)) Sri Lanka* [2008] UKAIT 00058. Though it might as to statutory provisions, see Elias LJ in the Court of Appeal in *MF (Sri Lanka) v Secretary of State for the Home Department* [2009] EWCA Civ 1505; Sedley LJ in the Court of Appeal in *MJ (Angola) v Secretary of State for the Home Department* [2010] EWCA Civ 557 thought that this might be the case only on an 'exceptional' basis, at [16].
8   The Court of Appeal in *Secretary of State for the Home Department v A (Iraq)* [2005] EWCA Civ 1438.
9   Brooke LJ for the Court of Appeal (Sir Paul Kennedy made a major contribution to the judgment) in *GH (Afghanistan) v Secretary of State for the Home Department* [2005] EWCA Civ 1603 at [15] onwards; Maurice Kay LJ in *Miftari v Secretary of State for the Home Department* [2005] EWCA Civ 481 at [39].
10   Toulson LJ in *EB (Turkey) v Secretary of State for the Home Department* [2008] EWCA Civ 1595 at [9]–[11], referencing a failure to raise the abuse of rights principle in the Home Office refusal letter.

PART 2 – APPEALS AND REVIEW OF FIRST INSTANCE DECISIONS: PRACTICE AND PROCEDURE FOR CHALLENGES VIA THE FTT

PERMISSION TO APPEAL TO THE UT VIA THE FTT: TIME AND PROCEDURE

6.13   A party seeking permission to appeal to the UT must make his application in writing:[1]

- identifying the decision challenged,

- identifying the alleged error(s) of law,[2]

- stating the desired result of the proceedings, and

- whether any extension of time is sought.[3]

1   Tribunal Procedure (First-tier Tribunal) (Immigration and Asylum Chamber) Rules 2014, SI 2014/2604, r 33(1).
2   See **6.106** below.
3   SI 2014/2604, r 33(5).

6.14   Grounds of appeal supporting a permission application should be concise and precise:

'It is axiomatic that every application for permission to appeal to the Upper Tribunal should identify, clearly and with all necessary particulars, the error/s of law for which the moving party contends. This must be effected in terms which are recognisable and comprehensible. A properly compiled application for permission to appeal will convey at once to the Judge concerned the error/s of law said to have been committed. It should not be necessary for the permission Judge to hunt and mine in order to understand the basis and thrust of the application. While in some cases it will be possible for the permission Judge to engage in a degree of interpretation and/or making inferences for this purpose, this should never be assumed by the applicant and cannot operate as a substitute for a properly and thoroughly compiled application. These are elementary requirements and standards … There can be no substitute for properly tailored and carefully crafted grounds of appeal which clearly reflect the unique facts, features and issues pertaining to the individual case.'[1]

---

1   The President McCloskey J in *Nixon (permission to appeal: grounds)* [2014] UKUT 368 (IAC) at [6], [9]

6.15   Permission applications must be made following a party being 'provided with' written reasons by the FTT,[1] and no later thereafter than:

- 14 days where the appellant is in the United Kingdom,[2]

- 28 days where he is outside the United Kingdom,[3] or

- three days in a fast track case.[4]

---

1   Presidential Guidance Note No 1 of 2014, para 4.
2   Tribunal Procedure (First-tier Tribunal) (Immigration and Asylum Chamber) Rules 2014, SI 2014/2604, r 33(2).
3   SI 2014/2604, r 33(3).
4   FTRs, r 11.

6.16   Time runs from the provision of amended reasons where there is such an amendment.[1] If there has been no written statement of reasons for a decision when an application for permission to appeal is made, the FTT will treat the permission application as a request for such reasons, and may then either determine the application or direct that it be treated as an application for correction, set aside or review;[2] a late application for a statement of reasons may only launch a permission application where that is in the interests of justice.[3] The application for permission to appeal to the FTT may be made at any time up to midnight.[4]

---

1   Tribunal Procedure (First-tier Tribunal) (Immigration and Asylum Chamber) Rules 2014, SI 2014/2604, r 33(4).
2   SI 2014/2604, 33(6), r 36.
3   SI 2014/2604, r 33(7).
4   SI 2014/2604, r 11(1); see Blake J in *Semere, R (on the application of) v Asylum and Immigration Tribunal* [2009] EWHC 335 (Admin) at [50].

6.17   The completed IAFT-4 application form is to be sent[1] by post or fax[2] to:

First-tier Tribunal (Immigration and Asylum Chamber)
PO Box 7866
Loughborough
LE11 2XZ
Fax: 01264 347987

An application may also be emailed to IAFT4@hmcts.gsi.gov.uk so long as the file size does not exceed 17MB: an automatic email response from the tribunal's email address will confirm receipt.[3] Applications in fast track cases are to be sent to the IAC hearing centre attached to the detention centre where the appellant is residing: those centres have their own email addresses, IAFT4Harmondsworth@hmcts.gsi.gov.uk or IAFT4Yarlswood@hmcts.gsi. gov.uk.[4]

1   Tribunal Procedure (First-tier Tribunal) (Immigration and Asylum Chamber) Rules 2014, SI 2014/2604, r 12(1) explains that documents to be provided may be delivered, sent by post, document exchange, fax, e-mail, or by any other method, identified by the tribunal.
2   SI 2014/2604, 12(1)(c); and in the UT, see Tribunal Procedure (Upper Tribunal) Rules 2008, SI 2008/2698, r 13(1)(b).
3   Immigration and Asylum (Upper Tribunal) guidance at www.justice.gov.uk/tribunals/ immigration-asylum-upper/appeals#1.
4   Ibid.

6.18   There are no express provisions for deemed service under the 2014 Rules. Where an issue arises as to the timing of a decision's receipt, evidence from a well-administered solicitor's firm is likely to be the most impressive before the tribunal[1] (and there should always be some evidence as to the receipt of the decision where this is relevant to the extension of time).[2] In cases where the SSHD has effected service, it is incumbent on him to be clear as to when a document has been posted.[3]

1   Blake J in the Administrative Court in *Semere, R (on the application of) v Asylum and Immigration Tribunal* [2009] EWHC 335 (Admin) at [41]; see further Presidential Guidance Note 2011 No 1, para 24.
2   *Wang and Chin (extension of time for appealing)* [2013] UKUT 343 (IAC) at [20].
3   *EY (asylum determinations, date of service) Democratic Republic of Congo* [2006] UKAIT 00032 at [11]–[12]: however from 20 October 2014 service is only effected by the SSHD in limited circumstances, limited to asylum cases where the UT refuses permission to appeal (see **6.43**, fn 3 below).

EXTENSION OF TIME

6.19   The time limit for lodging grounds of appeal may be extended, though there is no longer reference to 'special circumstances' as there was under the 2005 Rules: rather consideration will be driven by the overriding objective to deal with cases fairly and justly, in a manner that is proportionate to the importance of the case and resources of the parties whilst ensuring full participation in proceedings and avoiding unnecessary delay.[1] Absent good reason for extending time, the tribunal may not admit the application;[2] an explanation should be advanced sooner rather than later[3] and the tribunal will investigate the merits of extension applications rather than simply making assumptions based on the general desirability of letting applications proceed.[4] Reasons should be given for refusing to extend time.[5] The strength of the grounds is relevant to whether time should be extended: but it cannot be the only factor.[6] Confusion over the procedural complexities of the tribunal may explain delay.[7]

1   See **5.3** above.
2   See overriding objective at the Tribunal Procedure (First-tier Tribunal) (Immigration and Asylum Chamber) Rules 2014, SI 2014/2604, r 2(1)–(2), though there is no rule equivalent to the Asylum and Immigration Tribunal (Procedure) Rules 2005, SI 2005/230, r 24(4), expressly barring admission.
3   *AK (tribunal appeal – out of time) Bulgaria* [2004] UKIAT 00201; Burton J refusing an application for judicial review in the Administrative Court in *Khoobiari, R (on the application of) v Asylum and Immigration Tribunal* [2006] EWHC 2660 (Admin).
4   Contrast *AK* (above) at [24] with Lord Denning in *R v IAT, ex parte Mehta* [1976] Imm AR 38; *Wang and Chin (extension of time for appealing)* [2013] UKUT 343 (IAC) at [20]; *Mohammed (late application-First-tier Tribunal) Somalia* [2013] UKUT 467 (IAC).
5   Davis J in the Administrative Court in *R v Immigration Appeal Tribunal, ex parte Tofik* [2002] EWHC 2889 Admin at [14]; *Wang and Chin* (above) at [20].
6   *AK* (above) at [19].
7   Blake J in the Administrative Court in *Semere, R (on the application of) v Asylum and Immigration Tribunal* [2009] EWHC 335 (Admin) – or where an error by the tribunal misled the applicant, eg *Hammond* [2002] UKIAT 04742.

6.20   A bare assertion of administrative error may not impress the tribunal,[1] and nor will an allegation of routine overwork:[2] the considerations identified in *BO Nigeria* are likely to be a useful checklist.[3] A failure to notice an application having been made late cannot constitute a positive exercise of discretion to extend time:[4] a decision made in the light of this kind of oversight is irregular rather than void, and hence one that is effective unless a party raises an objection to it. If no objection is raised before a final determination of the appellate proceedings is issued, then the disadvantaged party must be taken to have acquiesced in the extension of time, whereas if the matter of time comes alive, then the grant of permission is treated as conditional.[5] If the UT's own permission grant did not identify lateness, then presumably, by analogy with *Boktor and Wanis*, a UT judge later seized of the appeal can raise the point.[6] A judge may take account of the vagaries of the postal system of his own motion where an application appears to have been made in the expectation of timeous delivery.[7]

1   *AK (tribunal appeal – out of time) Bulgaria* [2004] UKIAT 00201 at [26].
2   *EY (asylum determinations, date of service) Democratic Republic of Congo* [2006] UKAIT 00032.
3   *BO (extension of time for appealing) (Nigeria)* [2006] UKAIT 00035 (see **5.28** above).
4   *AK* (above) at [20].

5   *AK* (above) at [23]; *Boktor and Wanis (late application for permission) Egypt* [2011] UKUT
    442 (IAC); Presidential Guidance Note 2011 No 1, para 17.
6   Presidential Guidance Note 2011 No 1, para 29.
7   Presidential Guidance Note 2011 No 1, paras 20 and 22.

CONTENT AND TREATMENT OF THE APPLICATION

6.21   The application should contain all relevant grounds.[1] There is no express
limitation of the grounds considered to those advanced with the application.[2]
These applications will be decided by one FTT judge on a list approved by the
President.[3] The same judge may determine subsequent applications without
danger of bias, depending on the circumstances of the case.[4] If the tribunal
issues two determinations on the same application for permission to appeal,
the latter will be void;[5] various solutions have been judicially discussed where
grounds are overlooked despite having been submitted in timely and valid
fashion[6] (though the first port of call under the 2014 Rules will now be the set
aside and other powers identified below). Considerations addressed below in
relation to the UT's approach to permission applications may well be relevant
at the FTT stage.[7]

1   Tribunal Procedure (First-tier Tribunal) (Immigration and Asylum Chamber) Rules 2014,
    SI 2014/2604, r 33(5)(b).
2   SI 2014/2604, r 33(5)(b) contains no equivalent to the original 2005 Rules, r 26(3), which had
    expressly stated there was no requirement to consider other grounds; though see **6.11** above
    for the *Robinson* principle.
3   Practice Statement, para 2.1(11).
4   Schiemann LJ in *R v Immigration Appeal Tribunal, ex parte Menya* (C/2000/6022, 17 July
    2000) at [13]–[16].
5   Lawrence Collins J in the Administrative Court in *R v Immigration Appeal Tribunal, ex parte
    Kordghahchekilov* [2002] EWHC 1439 (Admin).
6   See *Entry Clearance Officer, Bombay v Patel* [1991] Imm AR 553, following Lord Widgery
    CJ's ruling in *Kensington and Chelsea Rent Tribunal, ex parte Macfarlane* [1974] 1 WLR
    1488; also *R (Ahmed) v Immigration Appeal Tribunal* [2004] EWCA Civ 399; Ouseley J
    in the Administrative Court in *R v Immigration Appeal Tribunal, ex parte Nuredini* [2002]
    EWHC 1582 (Admin) and in *R v Immigration Appeal Tribunal, ex parte Orlenko* [2002]
    EWHC 1960 Admin; *R v Immigration Appeal Tribunal, ex parte Naing and Eyaz* [2003]
    EWHC 771 Admin.
7   See **6.37** *et seq* below.

FTT'S POWERS AND DUTIES AS TO REVIEW

6.22   The FTT has a power to review its own decisions (save for excluded
ones), which it may exercise of its own volition or on a party's application.[1] In
the light of such review it may:[2]

●   correct accidental errors in the decision or in a record of the decision,

●   amend reasons given for the decision,

●   set the decision aside.

1   TCEA 2007, ss 9(1) and 11(5) (see **6.5** above).
2   TCEA 2007, s 9(1) and (2).

6.23   Where setting the matter aside, it must either re-decide the matter concerned, or refer that matter to the UT, which will then re-decide the matter itself, making any decision that could have been made by the FTT,[1] and whichever tribunal reconsiders the matter, it may make any necessary findings.[2] Once the decision is reviewed, there may be further review of the remade decision only with respect to accidental errors therein.[3] There may only be one review of a decision, and once a decision is made not to review, then it may not be re-visited.[4] The FTT may review a decision upon receipt of a permission application, considering this option before considering permission.[5] A decision may only be reviewed where there is an error of law within it.[6] The tribunal must notify the parties in writing of the review's outcome and of any consequent right of appeal.[7] Where a decision is taken without giving an opportunity to every party to make representations, the notice must state that the disadvantaged party may apply for the decision to be set aside, and the FTT may accordingly treat the review process as incomplete.[8]

1   TCEA 2007, s 9(1) and (4).
2   TCEA 2007, s 9(5)–(7).
3   TCEA 2007, s 9(9).
4   TCEA 2007, s 9(10).
5   TCEA 2007, s 9(10).
6   Tribunal Procedure (First-tier Tribunal) (Immigration and Asylum Chamber) Rules 2014, SI 2014/2604, r 35(1)(b); Practice Statement, para 4.1.
7   SI 2014/2604, r 35(2).
8   SI 2014/2604, r 35(3).

FTT'S POWERS AND DUTIES AS TO SET ASIDE PROCEEDINGS AND MAKE CORRECTIONS FOR IRREGULARITIES

6.24   There is a further, separate, power to set aside a decision which disposes of proceedings, or part of such a decision, and to re-make the whole decision or the defective part,[1] where this is thought to be in the interests of justice and where:

- a document relating to the proceedings was not provided to, or received at an appropriate time by, a party or his representative;

- a document relating to the proceedings was not provided to the tribunal at an appropriate time;

- a party or his representative was not present at a hearing related to the proceedings;

- there has been some other procedural irregularity.[2]

1   Tribunal Procedure (First-tier Tribunal) (Immigration and Asylum Chamber) Rules 2014,
    SI 2014/2604, r 32(1).
2   SI 2014/2604, r 32(2).

6.25   An application for a decision, or part of one, to be set aside, must be
made within a certain number of days of having been sent the decision:

- 28 days where the appellant is outside the United Kingdom, or

- 14 days where the appellant is within the United Kingdom.[1]

1   Tribunal Procedure (First-tier Tribunal) (Immigration and Asylum Chamber) Rules 2014,
    SI 2014/2604, r 32(3).

6.26   In the context of review, the power to set a decision aside and re-
decide it is likely to be adopted only where the error of law:

- deprived a party of a fair hearing or other opportunity to put his case, or

- where there are highly compelling reasons for so doing (which are likely
  to be rare).[1]

1   Practice Statement, para 4.2.

6.27   Authority relating to similar older powers suggested that it should be
exercised where 'there was a risk of serious injustice, because of something
which had gone wrong at the hearing, or some important evidence which had
been overlooked'.[1] This process exists alongside the power of the tribunal to
address essentially clerical and administrative irregularities by way of the
correction of orders and decisions,[2] which may be exercised 'at any time' (and
so is available where the matter is drawn to the FTT's attention in a permission
application).[3] The FTT may suspend the effect of its own decision pending the
determination of a permission application by itself or by the UT, including any
appeal or review of that decision.[4]

1   *E v Secretary of State for the Home Department* [2004] EWCA Civ 49, cited in *Montes and
    Loiza v Secretary of State for the Home Department* [2004] EWCA Civ 404.
2   Tribunal Procedure (First-tier Tribunal) (Immigration and Asylum Chamber) Rules 2014,
    SI 2014/2604, r 31.
3   See, regarding the predecessor rule, *MF (r 60, correction, R1 procedure) Palestinian
    Territories* [2007] UKAIT 00092.
4   SI 2014/2604, r 4(3)(l). However the general suspension on removal whilst an appeal is
    pending is likely to render this provision otiose in immigration appeals: NIAA 2002, ss 78
    and 104.

FTT'S POWERS AND DUTIES AS TO GRANTING
PERMISSION TO APPEAL

6.28   Where the tribunal decides not to review the decision, or decides to
take no action in relation to the decision or part of it, then it must go on to

consider whether permission to appeal should be given.[1] There is a published Guidance Note on relevant considerations.[2] In international protection cases, anxious scrutiny should be given to the decision below,[3] and 'there is room for departure from an inflexible application of common law rules and principles where this is necessary to redress unfairness'.[4] There is no longer an obligation to make the decision within any specified period.[5] The tribunal must send a record of its permission decision to the parties[6] and if the application is refused, notifying them of the right to apply direct to the UT, and the time limit and method for so doing.[7] The tribunal may give permission on limited grounds, but must comply with its obligations to give written reasons and to describe the mode of appeal regarding any grounds which are refused (using Form IA68).[8] The pragmatic suggestion in the President's Guidance is that a limitation on the grounds is often more trouble than it is worth,[9] and it has been said that:

'such a limited grant is unlikely to be as helpful as a general grant, which identifies the ground or grounds that are considered by the judge to have the strongest prospect of success … which can then form the backdrop for the Upper Tribunal's subsequent case management directions'[10]

1   Tribunal Procedure (First-tier Tribunal) (Immigration and Asylum Chamber) Rules 2014, SI 2014/2604, r 34(1) and (2).
2   Presidential Guidance Note 2011 No 1.
3   Presidential Guidance Note 2011 No 1, para 8.
4   *MM (unfairness; E and R) Sudan* [2014] UKUT 105 (IAC) at [25].
5   Contrast the Asylum and Immigration Tribunal (Procedure) Rules 2005, SI 2005/230, r 25(3); though part of the overriding objective under r 2(2)(e) is 'avoiding delay, so far as compatible with proper consideration of the issues'.
6   SI 2014/2604, r 34(3): ie a record, rather than written reasons, unless refusing permission.
7   SI 2014/2604, r 34(4).
8   SI 2014/2604, r 34(5). *Ferrer (limited appeal grounds; Alvi) Philippines* [2012] UKUT 304 (IAC) at [21]–[22] and [30].
9   Presidential Guidance Note 2011 No 1, para 25.
10 *Ferrer (limited appeal grounds; Alvi) Philippines* [2012] UKUT 304 (IAC), headnote at (1).

6.29   The permission grant should clearly identify the judge's reaction to the alleged errors,[1]

'irrespective of whether permission to appeal is granted on all of the grounds advanced or some thereof only, a reasoned decision is always required in respect of each and every ground, which reinforces the necessity of considering all grounds with scrupulous care … nothing of an unduly elaborate, burdensome or analytical nature is expected of the permission Judge. The reasons for granting or refusing permission to appeal, in whole or in part, in any given case will almost invariably be capable of being expressed in a concise and focused manner. In most cases, a couple of carefully constructed sentences will suffice.'

1   The President McCloskey J in *Nixon (permission to appeal: grounds)* [2014] UKUT 368 (IAC) at [8], cited in *MR (permission to appeal: tribunal's approach)* [2015] UKUT 29 (IAC) at [7], with the latter phrase added in *MR* at [7].

6.30   Any limitation on the grounds of appeal should be clear and unambiguous.[1] The structure of the FTT and UT is such that a party wishing to renew an application for permission, having been refused leave on one ground, needs to apply again, direct to the UT.[2] An application for permission to appeal may be treated as an application for a document to be corrected, set aside or reviewed; so too may an application for review, correction or set aside be treated as a permission application.[3] Errors of law on points irrelevant to the substance of the decision in hand are unlikely to justify a permission grant, and the UT is thought better placed to identify those cases which, merits of the individual appeal aside, raise points of general importance.[4]

1   Davis LJ in *Secretary of State for the Home Department v Rodriguez* [2014] EWCA Civ 2 at [80]; *Ferrer (limited appeal grounds; Alvi) Philippines* [2012] UKUT 304 (IAC), headnote at (2).
2   *Ferrer* (above); Tribunal Procedure (First-tier Tribunal) (Immigration and Asylum Chamber) Rules 2014, SI 2014/2604, r 33(1); Tribunal Procedure (Upper Tribunal) Rules 2008, SI 2008/2698, r 21(2).
3   SI 2014/2604, r 36.
4   Presidential Guidance Note 2011 No 1, para 13(c).

FTT POWERS AT THE PERMISSION STAGE: SUMMARY

6.31   From the foregoing it will be seen that the options for an FTT judge considering a first application for permission to appeal are:[1]

- to make an order for correction of 'clerical mistake or other accidental slip or omission' under the 2014 Rules, r 31;

- to review the decision under the 2014 Rules, r 35 if there is an error of law by which a party has been deprived of a fair hearing or other opportunity to put his case, or, rarely, if there are other compelling reasons for the matter being redecided by the FTT;[2]

- to set aside the decision under the 2014 Rules, r 32 where a document went astray, a relevant person was absent from a hearing, or some other procedural irregularity casts doubt over the proceedings;[3]

- to grant permission to appeal to the UT against the decision of the FTT, in whole or in part under the 2014 Rules, r 34.[4]

1   Presidential Guidance Note 2011 No 1, para 33.
2   See **6.22** and **6.23** above.
3   See **6.24** *et seq* above.
4   See **6.28** *et seq* above.

FAST TRACK CASES

6.32   The 2014 Rules apply generally to cases within the fast track unless express provision is made within the FTRs.[1] These apply where the applicant has been in the fast track system continuously (ie detained in the institutions identified in those Rules).[2] The time limit for lodging notice of appeal is shortened in these cases, such that notice of appeal may be given within three days of the decision being provided to the party receiving it.[3] The power to suspend the effect of a decision pending appeal is disapplied by the FTRs[4] and it appears that, consistent with the system under the 2005 Rules, it is not intended that decisions are to be reviewed (as opposed to appealed) within the fast track, though the powers of set aside and correction are available,[5] notice of such amendments being given not later than one working day after their being made.[6]

1   FTRs, para 1.
2   FTRs, para 2(1) and (3) – Colnbrook House, Harmondsworth and Yarl's Wood IRCs.
3   FTRs, para 11.
4   FTRs, Table 2, referencing Tribunal Procedure (First-tier Tribunal) (Immigration and Asylum Chamber) Rules 2014, SI 2014/2604, r 4(3)(l) (see **6.27**, fn 4 above).
5   FTRs, Table 2, referencing SI 2014/2604, r 34(1).
6   FTRs, para 13.

PART 3 – APPEALS AND REVIEW OF FIRST INSTANCE DECISIONS: PRACTICE AND PROCEDURE FOR CHALLENGES IN THE UT

DIRECT APPLICATIONS FOR PERMISSION TO APPEAL TO THE UT: FORM AND CONTENT

6.33   A person may apply to the UT for permission to appeal directly if the application for permission to appeal via the FTT does not succeed.[1] It would be rare, though not impossible, for the UT to entertain a permission application notwithstanding a failure to approach the FTT, though it would be necessary to show highly compelling reasons.[2]

1   Tribunal Procedure (Upper Tribunal) Rules 2008, SI 2008/2698, r 21(2).
2   Given the power to waive procedural requirements in the Tribunal Procedure (Upper Tribunal) Rules 2008, SI 2008/2698, r 7(2), see *Ved (appealable decisions, permission applications, Basnet) Tanzania* [2014] UKUT 150 (IAC) at [22]–[26].

6.34   The application must state:

- the name and address of the appellant,

- his representative (if any),

- an address to receive documents,

- the FTT's full reference number,

- the grounds relied upon,

- an indication of whether a hearing is sought,[1]

- a copy of any written record of the decision, and

- the notice of refusal of permission to appeal below.[2]

1   Tribunal Procedure (Upper Tribunal) Rules 2008, SI 2008/2698, r 21(4).
2   SI 2008/2698, r 21(5).

6.35   There is provision for the application for permission (as opposed to the appeal itself) to be considered at an oral hearing, though as an alternative to a bare paper consideration, not in addition.[1] There is no requirement for any formal notice of appeal, beyond the grounds themselves.[2] The completed IAUT-1 application form should be sent by post or fax to:

Upper Tribunal (Immigration and Asylum Chamber)
IA Field House
15–25 Breams Buildings
London
EC4A 1DZ
Fax: 0870 3240111

1   Unlike some other species of Upper Tribunal appeal outside of the UT where there may be a renewal of permission, see Tribunal Procedure (Upper Tribunal) Rules 2008, SI 2008/2698, r 22(3)(a); see further Presidential Guidance Note 2011 No 1, para 26; Form IAUT-1, Part G, 'Upper Tribunal Immigration and Asylum Chamber Application for permission to appeal from First-tier Tribunal (Immigration and Asylum Chamber)' gives the option. See Laws LJ in *Sengupta v Holmes* [2002] EWCA Civ 1104 at [38] for the centrality of oral argument to the common law.
2   SI 2008/2698, r 23(1A).

DIRECT APPLICATIONS FOR PERMISSION TO APPEAL TO THE UT: TIME LIMITS

6.36   Times are calculated from the date that the FTT permission refusal was sent to the appellant:[1]

- for 'in-country' appeals the time limit is 14 working days;[2]

- for fast track appeals, four working days;[3]

- for 'out of country' appeals, a month from the date that permission was refused, or refused to be admitted.[4]

The application should be made by 5pm on the working day in question,[5] though UT judges will take a sensible approach to modest lateness and 'fax transmissions received after that time … can be the beneficiaries of an extension without any explanation being presented'.[6]

1   Tribunal Procedure (Upper Tribunal) Rules 2008, SI 2008/2698, r 21(3)(aa).
2   SI 2008/2698, r 21(3)(aa)(i).
3   SI 2008/2698, r 21(3)(aa)(ii).
4   SI 2008/2698, r 21(3)(b).
5   SI 2008/2698, r 12(1).
6   Presidential Guidance Note 2011 No 1, para 22: note that FTT Presidential Guidance Note No 1 of 2010, 'Documents sent to the tribunal by fax' remains on the judiciary.gov.uk website and states that a faxed application 'will be treated as served on a particular day if it is completely transmitted before midnight on that day'.

CONSIDERATIONS REGARDING PERMISSION TO APPEAL[1]

6.37   The task of a UT judge considering a permission application is different from the role of a judge of the FTT, because the latter must first decide whether there is any call for the slip rule (for clerical error or other accidental slip or omission or administrative error on the part of the tribunal or its staff) and whether to review the FTT decision (either for correction of accidental errors, amendment of reasons or with a view to setting it aside altogether); whereas the UT judge is confined to the question of permission to appeal.[2] Save in the plainest of cases, the permission decision should only identify the existence of an *arguable* error of law.[3] There may be occasional cases where a decision to remit may nevertheless be made.[4] Fairness strongly indicates that a new point should not be taken when refusing permission.[5] There is no provision for submissions to be made against the grant of permission,[6] though the Home Office might be under a duty, in an appropriate case, to consider representations as to the asserted weakness of its case, albeit that ordinarily the SSHD has no general duty to reconsider the ultimate prospects of success.[7] Under NIAA 2002 prior to the entry into force of TCEA 2007, only an unsuccessful litigant could launch an appeal against a determination with which he was dissatisfied: this reasoning was based on the requirement that an error of law be 'material'.[8] The tribunal has nevertheless long recognised that it should grant permission to appeal to a dissatisfied appellant where his appeal has been allowed, where he might obtain a more beneficial status than that which the decision appealed suggests he is entitled.[9]

1   See also the general duties already identified in relation to the FTT at **6.13** and **6.32** above.
2   Tribunal Procedure (Upper Tribunal) Rules 2008, SI 2008/2698, r 2 (see above at **6.31**, fn 1).
3   Presidential Guidance Note 2011 No 1, paras 12 and 37.
4   Presidential Guidance Note 2011 No 1, para 38.
5   Kay J in *R v Immigration Appeal Tribunal, ex parte Shafiq* (CO/908/98, 25 November 1998).
6   *Sivanesan* (14113, 11 November 1996).
7   *Rechachi, R (on the application of) v Secretary of State for the Home Department* [2006] EWHC 3513 (Admin).
8   *AN (only loser can appeal) Afghanistan* [2005] UKIAT 00097.
9   See eg *Zagol* (00/HX/00964, 8 May 2000) or *Hassan* [2002] UKIAT 00062; *EG and NG (UT r 17: withdrawal; r 24: scope) Ethiopia* [2013] UKUT 143 (IAC) at [47].

6.38   The Upper Tribunal Rules permit an application for permission to appeal even if the FTT dealing with the 'first application' has not admitted the case (eg because of a refusal to extend time)[1] but in such cases should only do so where it considers that this is in the interests of justice.[2] The decision on the grounds should focus on their evaluation rather than description, and whilst it may be acceptable for the UT judge to adopt the reasoning of his FTT predecessor, further reasons will clearly be required where that approach has been challenged in the renewed permission application, and a formulaic approach is undesirable.[3] As the jurisdiction of the UT is engaged only by identification of an error of law, it is essential that the grounds of appeal truly identify one; if the UT was to wrongly entertain appellate proceedings absent such error, an appeal against its decision to the appropriate appellate court would necessarily succeed.[4] When construing the application before it, 'what is required is a fair and reasonable examination of the grounds of appeal to see whether a point of law is identifiable.'[5] The UT does not approach decisions of the FTT on the basis that the latter is a specialist tribunal, because that 'would be to negate the purpose for which the Upper Tribunal has been established … to provide specialist guidance on issues of law arising in the First-tier.'[6]

1   Tribunal Procedure (Upper Tribunal) Rules 2008, SI 2008/2698, r 21(2) and (7); *Ved (appealable decisions, permission applications, Basnet) Tanzania* [2014] UKUT 150 (IAC) at [22].
2   SI 2008/2698, r 21.
3   Presidential Guidance Note 2011 No 1, para 29.
4   Buxton LJ in *Miftari v Secretary of State for the Home Department* [2005] EWCA Civ 481 at [26]–[27].
5   Maurice Kay LJ in *MA (Palestinian Territories) v Secretary of State for the Home Department* [2008] EWCA Civ 304 at [14].
6   Carnwath LJ in *AP (Trinidad and Tobago) v Secretary of State for the Home Department* [2011] EWCA Civ 551 at [46].

6.39   The SSHD should anticipate a robust response to any challenge he seeks to bring on the grounds of insufficient reasoning or on account of a lack of evidence having been before the FTT where his officers have failed to provide documents at first instance as required under the 2014 Rules.[1]

1   *Cvetkovs (visa – no file produced – directions) Latvia* [2011] UKUT 212 (IAC) at [9]–[12].

Permission decisions: materiality and points of public interest

6.40   The recommendation from Lord Woolf MR in *Robinson* that considerations of transparency and consistency called for some indication as to the tribunal's practice in granting leave to appeal was eventually taken up with the ascendancy of Blake J to the tribunal's Presidency,[1] and the publication of Presidential Guidance Note 2011 No 1 which is replete with valuable insights into the relevant considerations.[2] The permission application to the UT is not to be treated as an appeal against the refusal by the FTT; it is desirable that direct applications to the UT specify the extent to which the original grounds are being relied upon.[3] It may be appropriate to grant permission to appeal where a good case is made for reconsideration of an existing precedent or principle, absent a clear-cut answer to the challenge, given that a refusal will extinguish the appeal.[4] Though errors of law must normally be material to warrant a permission grant, this is not always required: 'Whilst the existence of reasonable prospects of success is a relevant criterion to apply to the grant of permission, it is not a precondition for its grant' – though such cases will be rare and the overriding objective to ensure cases are dealt with justly and fairly counts against encouraging an appellant whose appeal is ultimately bound to fail.[5] Nevertheless 'the UT may wish to use the opportunity of the application to review the existing jurisprudence on the topic, to address frequently arising problems or give guidance in a reported case on a novel or important issue.'[6] Permission should only be refused on materiality grounds where there 'is a plain case that the error could have made no difference to the outcome ... Disputes about materiality are best left to the appeal process itself rather than summarily determined by refusal of permission',[7] though 'Where there is no reasonable prospect that any error of law alleged in the grounds of appeal could have made a difference to the outcome, permission to appeal should not normally be granted in the absence of some point of public importance'.[8]

1   Lord Woolf MR in *R v Secretary of State for the Home Department and Immigration Appeal Tribunal, ex parte Robinson* [1997] Imm AR 568 at [41].
2   Presidential Guidance Note 2011 No 1.
3   Presidential Guidance Note 2011 No 1, para 11.
4   Presidential Guidance Note 2011 No 1, para 13(d).
5   Presidential Guidance Note 2011 No 1, para 14.
6   Presidential Guidance Note 2011 No 1, para 15.
7   Presidential Guidance Note 2011 No 1, para 16.
8   Blake J in *Anoliefo (permission to appeal)* [2013] UKUT 345 (IAC) at [16].

LATE APPLICATIONS TO THE UT

6.41   If the application is made out of time, a request for an extension of time and the reasons for it must be provided.[1] The tribunal must only admit the application if it agrees to extend time, there being no specific test for this; however, if the UT is being asked to grant permission to appeal with respect to a case where the application to the FTT was refused for lateness, then an explanation must be provided, and an extension may be granted only if it is in the interests of justice.[2] A grant of permission to appeal which overlooks the lateness of the application falls to be treated as conditional.[3] It will usually be expedient to consider the merits of the grounds as well as making a decision on timeliness, particularly where 'there is only a marginal excess of the strict time limits in the Rules'.[4] Time will presumably be extended in circumstances similar to those where the UT's predecessors operated their discretion in the past.[5] In a case of an application direct to the UT where the application to the FTT was not admitted because it was not in time, there must be an explanation of why the first application was late and the UT can only admit it if it considers that 'it is in the interests of justice for it to do so'. If the question of time was overlooked below, it may be appropriate for the UT judge considering permission to reconstitute himself as the FTT.[6] A lengthy delay (exceeding 28 days) may need to be the subject of an oral permission hearing on notice to the respondent so that he can make submissions on whether letting the appeal go forward would cause active prejudice.[7] There is good reason to think that an out-of-time applicant may apply to the Administrative Court for relief against removal directions pending a determination of his late permission application,[8] though the UT may be able, in such a case, to use its case management power, to 'in an appeal, or an application for permission to appeal, against the decision of another tribunal, suspend the effect of that decision pending the determination of the application for permission to appeal, and any appeal'.[9]

1   Tribunal Procedure (Upper Tribunal) Rules 2008, SI 2008/2698, r 21(6)(a). See **6.19**, fn 2 above.
2   SI 2008/2698, r 21(7).
3   *Samir (FTT permission to appeal: time) Afghanistan* [2013] UKUT 3 (IAC).
4   Presidential Guidance Note 2011 No 1, para 19.
5   See generally **6.36** above.
6   SI 2008/2698, r 21(7); *Samir* (above); *Mohammed (late application – First-tier Tribunal) Somalia* [2013] UKUT 467 (IAC).
7   Presidential Guidance Note 2011 No 1, para 26; *Ogundimu (Art 8 – new rules) Nigeria* [2013] UKUT 00060 (IAC) at [21].
8   By analogy with Pitchford J in *Kagabo, R (on the application of) v Secretary of State for the Home Department* [2009] EWHC 153 (Admin), particularly at [48]–[52], holding that *R (Erdogan) v Secretary of State for the Home Department* [2004] EWCA Civ 1087 bound him for the proposition that NIAA 2002, s 78 did not protect a late appellant from removal from the jurisdiction while awaiting the tribunal's decision whether to extend time. See further **6.136** below.
9   SI 2008/2698, r 5(3)(m).

GRANT OR REFUSAL OF PERMISSION TO APPEAL

6.42   If the UT refuses permission to appeal, it must send written notice to the appellant.[1] If it gives permission to appeal, then it must give notice to all parties, giving reasons for any limitations or conditions.[2] The application for permission stands as the notice of appeal, subject to contrary direction of the tribunal, which will then send the respondent a copy of the application and supporting documents.[3] The appeal may be determined without obtaining further response from the parties if they so consent.[4] There is a special procedure in 'asylum cases' – defined as those 'proceedings before the Upper Tribunal on appeal against a decision in proceedings …in which a person claims that removal from, or a requirement to leave, the United Kingdom would breach' the Refugee Convention.

1   Tribunal Procedure (Upper Tribunal) Rules 2008, SI 2008/2698, rr 21, 22(1).
2   SI 2008/2698, rr 21, 22(2)(a). See **6.28**, fn 9 above on limited permission grants.
3   SI 2008/2698, rr 21, 22(2)(b).
4   SI 2008/2698, rr 21, 22(2)(c).

6.43   That definition appears to require that the appeal proceedings must maintain asylum issues, not merely that the immigration decision succeeded the making of an asylum claim.[1] In such cases, where the UT refuses permission or declines to admit it (thereby marking the moment when appellate remedies are exhausted and the appeal is no longer pending),[2] and where the appeal involves an 'in-country' right of appeal outside of the fast track, notice of refusal should be given to the SSHD as soon as reasonably practicable, who must send it to the appellant within 30 days, notifying the UT that this has been done; absent such notification the UT will send the notice onwards itself, as soon as reasonably practicable.[3] Because such Rules give the SSHD an advantage in having advance notice of the result of proceedings that is unusual in adversarial litigation (albeit one that is now significantly less marked given that it only arises at the exhaustion of appellate remedies stage, not at every instance of asylum appeal determination as under the 2005 Rules), the tribunal has ruled that compliance with the notice requirement is a mandatory one and that such Rules are to be construed against the respondent where issues of interpretation arise.[4] The Court of Appeal has explained that the consequences of any non-compliance with the duty by the SSHD will vary between cases.[5] Where service is effected by the Home Office, it is imperative it operates procedures that clarify the date of posting.[6] A decision on permission may be set aside, because it is a 'decision which disposes of proceedings', where a document went astray, a relevant person was absent from a hearing, or some other procedural irregularity casts doubt over the proceedings.[7] Clerical mistakes or other accidental slips and omissions can be corrected under r 42.[8] It is particularly important that the parties engage properly with observations of the UT made on or following the grant of permission to appeal.[9]

1   Contrast Tribunal Procedure (Upper Tribunal) Rules 2008, SI 2008/2698, r 1(3) and its definition of 'asylum case' with *HH (r 23: meaning and extent) Iraq* [2007] UKAIT 00036 at [14].
2   See **4.35** above.
3   SI 2008/2698, r 22A; see **6.28** *et seq* above for the general position on giving of UT decisions.
4   *RN (r 23(5): respondent's duty) Zimbabwe* [2008] UKAIT 00001 at [19] and [25]; *HH* (above).
5   Jackson LJ in the Court of Appeal in *NB (Guinea) v Secretary of State for the Home Department* [2008] EWCA Civ 1229 at [19].
6   *EY (asylum determinations, date of service) Democratic Republic of Congo* [2006] UKAIT 00032 at [11].
7   SI 2008/2698, r 43; Presidential Guidance Note 2011 No 1, para 35 (see **6.122**, fn 1 below).
8   See **6.123**, fn 2.
9   *Boodhoo (EEA Regs: relevant evidence)* [2013] UKUT 00346 (IAC), headnote at (3).

RESPONSE TO THE NOTICE OF APPEAL AND CROSS APPEALS

6.44   There is provision for a response to the notice of appeal[1] which is to be sent in writing within a month (under the Upper Tribunal Rules,[2] however the UT prefers to receive these within 14 days)[3] of the respondent receiving notice of the grant of permission to appeal. Its provision is optional,[4] a failure to provide the predecessor notice in the era of the AIT being considered relevant, though not conclusive, in establishing an error of law, depending on the facts of the case including the merits of the grounds.[5] The respondent wishing to resurrect arguments that failed below will be wise to give notice of his intentions.[6] A response essentially gives notice about how the respondent intends to respond to the appeal that the appellant has permission to pursue: however, if the respondent wishes to argue that the FTT should have reached a materially different conclusion, then he needs permission to appeal.[7]

1   Tribunal Procedure (Upper Tribunal) Rules 2008, SI 2008/2698, r 24(1A), subject to direction.
2   SI 2008/2698, r 24(2); this will be one month from being sent notice of permission to appeal where the FTT granted permission: rr 23(1A) and 24(2)(a); where the UT has granted permission to appeal, one month from the UT sending notice of appeal: r 24(2)(b); and one day before the hearing in a fast-track case: r 24(2)(aa).
3   See Presidential Guidance Note 2013 No 3, para 4.3.
4   Contrast the Asylum and Immigration Tribunal (Procedure) Rules 2005, SI 2005/230, r 30(1) as amended 'he must file with the Tribunal and serve on the applicant a reply setting out his case if he contends that – (a) there was no error of law' with SI 2008/2698, r 24(1A) 'may provide a response'.
5   *MB (r 30 Procedure Rules) DRC* [2008] UKAIT 00088.
6   *AG (late service of respondent's notice) Eritrea* [2004] UKIAT 00134 at [10].
7   *EG and NG (UT r 17: withdrawal; r 24: scope) Ethiopia* [2013] UKUT 143 (IAC) at [46].

6.45   The response must state:

• the name and address of the respondent and his representative (if any);

• an address to receive documents;

• whether the respondent opposes the appeal;

• the grounds relied upon (including any on which the respondent was unsuccessful below but intends to rely on in these proceedings) and an indication of whether a hearing is sought.[1]

Time for a response may be extended where such is requested.[2] The UT must serve a copy of the response and supporting documents on the appellant.[3]

1   Tribunal Procedure (Upper Tribunal) Rules 2008, SI 2008/2698, r 24(3).
2   SI 2008/2698, r 24(4).
3   SI 2008/2698, r 24(5).

REPLY

6.46   The appellant may provide a reply to the respondent's response (subject to the UT's direction).[1] This must be in writing and must be sent or delivered to the UT so that it is received by the earlier of the following pair of dates: one month after the copy of the response was sent, or five days before the hearing of the appeal.[2] The UT is then to provide it to the respondent.[3]

1   Tribunal Procedure (Upper Tribunal) Rules 2008, SI 2008/2698, r 25(1).
2   SI 2008/2698, r 25(2A). Though as with responses, the UT would sooner have a response within 14 days: see Presidential Guidance Note 2013 No 3, para 4.5.
3   SI 2008/2698, r 25(3).

PART 4 – PROCEEDINGS IN THE UT

CONSTITUTION OF THE UT; LISTING APPEALS

6.47   Where the matter is thought by the Senior President or Chamber President to involve a question of law of special difficulty or an important point of principle or practice, or it is otherwise appropriate, the matter is to be decided by two or three UT judges;[1] other compositions may be one or two UT judge(s) and one other member.[2] When the UT was first established, a limited panel of senior immigration judges was identified to consider permission applications, in order to 'distinguish between First tier and UTIAC considerations; focus on common approaches and standards; and ensure consistency and the engagement of High Court and equivalent judges without a public perception of dissipation of these standards at the outset'.[3] None of this is to prevent procedural and ancillary matters being decided by any UT judge;[4] and aside from these special situations, jurisdiction is to be exercised by a single judge.[5] The senior judge is to preside where more than one judge comprises the panel determining the matter.[6] Permanent judges of the higher courts are members of the UT (and indeed the FTT).[7] Queries regarding case management should be raised with the regional senior immigration judge.[8] When a party receives a hearing notice, he will normally be given the opportunity to assent to a short notice listing should an earlier place in the queue of cases awaiting hearing become available.[9]

1   Practice Statement, para 6.2; the Chamber President can delegate this matter to another UT judge.
2   Practice Statement, para 6.3.
3   Speech by the Hon Mr Justice Blake, President of the UT to the Upper Tribunal Immigration Judiciary, 'The Arrival of the Upper Tribunal Immigration and Asylum Chamber' (11 February 2010); Practice Statement, para 6.3.
4   Practice Statement, para 6.5.
5   Practice Statement, para 6.1.
6   Practice Statement, para 8.2.
7   TCEA 2007, s 6(1). Thus they may reconstitute themselves as the FTT if required, see *Samir (FTT permission to appeal: time) Afghanistan* [2013] UKUT 3 (IAC).
8   Letter from Blake J to Immigration Lawyers Practitioners Association of 16 March 2010.
9   Thus text accompanying the hearing notice allows this option to be ticked: 'I would like this appeal to be considered for a short notice hearing should a place become available. I am content that I will receive a minimum of five working days' notice before the date of the hearing.'

UT: CHARACTER

6.48   Essential features of the tribunal system include its 'accessibility, freedom from technicality, and expertise'.[1] The UT's predecessors were creatures of statute and possessed no inherent powers beyond those necessary to prevent their procedures from abuse.[2] The UT possesses some more muscular features: it is a superior court of record[3] and has the same powers, rights, privileges and authority as the High Court in relation to the attendance and examination of witnesses, production and inspection of documents, and all other matters incidental to its own functions.[4] It presumptively acts within its powers unless the contrary is shown, it may set precedent, and it may punish for contempt:[5]

> 'The powers of referral to the Upper Tribunal which have now been conferred on tribunals in order to aid them in ensuring compliance with their orders may have very serious consequences, including the deprivation of a person's liberty'

and it may regulate its own procedure, subject to TCEA 2007 and other enactments.[6] It inherits the mantle of its predecessors as an expert tribunal entitled to have its decisions reviewed on the basis that, absent indications to the contrary, it is familiar with the procedures and tests applicable in the course of its business;[7] and when the UT reviews decisions of the FTT, it does so on the basis that it is itself the expert tribunal, giving no deference to the expertise of the decision making below (for that would 'negate the purpose for which the Upper Tribunal has been established, which is to provide specialist guidance on issues of law arising in the First-tier'), albeit that it will share 'the anxiety of [any] appellate court not to overturn a judgment at first instance unless it really cannot understand the original judge's thought processes when he/she was making material findings'.[8]

1   Lady Hale in *Gillies v Secretary of State for Work and Pensions* [2006] 1 WLR 781 at [36] *et seq*; Lord Carnwath in *Secretary of State for Home Department v MN and KY (Scotland)* [2014] UKSC 30 at [22] *et seq*.
2   Scott Baker J in *Secretary of State for the Home Department v Immigration Appeal Tribunal* [2001] EWHC Admin 261 (the *'Zengin'* judicial review).
3   TCEA 2007, s 3(1).
4   TCEA 2007, s 25(1).
5   *MD v Secretary of State for Work and Pensions* [2010] UKUT 202 (AAC) at [10]; Laws LJ in the Divisional Court in *Cart, R (on the application of) v Upper Tribunal* [2009] EWHC 3052 (Admin) addressed the meaning of 'superior court of record'; Lord Glennie in *Eba, Re Judicial Review* [2010] ScotCS CSOH_45 at [23]; see further *PA v CMEC* [2009] UKUT 283 (AAC) at [14].
6   Tribunal Procedure (Upper Tribunal) Rules 2008, SI 2008/2698, r 5(1).
7   Baroness Hale in *AH (Sudan) v Secretary of State for the Home Department* [2007] UKHL 49 at [30] (see further **6.156** below).
8   Carnwath LJ in *AP (Trinidad and Tobago) v Secretary of State for the Home Department* [2011] EWCA Civ 551 at [46]–[47].

GENERAL POWERS OF THE UT

6.49   The tribunal has a power to extend any time limit under its own Rules.[1] It has broad powers to seek further information from the parties which are its nearest equivalent to a disclosure jurisdiction, and may 'require a party or another person to provide documents, information, evidence or submissions to the Upper Tribunal or a party'.[2] This power (which might be exercised as an 'unusual and exceptional course')[3] supplements the general duty on the SSHD:

● to avoid knowingly misleading the tribunal;

● to avoid misleading the tribunal regarding material of which the SSHD should be aware[4] (including providing an expert report obtained for the purposes of the instant case);[5]

● to ask for and be informed about any reliable material that might qualify a published assessment.[6]

1   Tribunal Procedure (Upper Tribunal) Rules 2008, SI 2008/2698, r 5(3)(a).
2   SI 2008/2698, r 5(3)(d). This power might not save the occasional need for a case to be better pursued in the Administrative Court because of the 'consequential obligations of voluntary disclosure of relevant material pursuant to judicial review principles' that prevail there, thought desirable in *Limbu, R (on the application of) v Secretary of State for the Home Department* [2008] EWHC 2261 (Admin) at [9]: see *CM (EM Country Guidance, disclosure) Zimbabwe CG* [2013] UKUT 59 (IAC) at [36]. See **8.112** for the general principles on disclosure.
3   *CM* (above) at [51].
4   *CM* (above) at [36]–[52]; Lord Woolf *R v Secretary of State for the Home Department, ex parte Kerrouche No 1* [1997] Imm AR 610; *Cindo, R (on the application of) v Immigration Appeal Tribunal* [2002] EWHC 246 Admin at [10]; see also *MS (risk on return) Kosovo* [2003] UKIAT 00031 (reported as *FZ* [2003] Imm AR 633), citing *McGinley and Egan v United Kingdom* (1998) 27 EHRR 1.
5   Thorpe LJ, whose comments were the subject of specific agreement by Evans LJ, in *R v Secretary of State for the Home Department and Immigration Officer, ex parte Besnik Gashi* [1999] Imm AR 415, citing *Re L (minors) (police investigation)* [1997] AC 1.
6   *CM* (above) at [46].

POWERS REGARDING DISCLOSURE AND ANONYMITY

6.50   The UT may make an order prohibiting the disclosure or publication of:

● specified documents or information relating to the proceedings; or

● any matter likely to lead members of the public to identify any person whom the UT considers should not be identified.[1]

1   Tribunal Procedure (Upper Tribunal) Rules 2008, SI 2008/2698, r 14(1).

6.51   It may also make a direction prohibiting the disclosure of a document or information to a person:

- if this would cause him, or someone else, serious harm,

- where it is proportionate to the interests of justice so to rule.[1]

1   Tribunal Procedure (Upper Tribunal) Rules 2008, SI 2008/2698, r 14(2); this may be done following an application by a party: r 14(3).

6.52   A party may apply for such non-disclosure directions, excluding the relevant document or information from that otherwise supplied to the other party/parties, and providing the underlying material to the UT with his reasoning, so that the UT may determine whether to make the relevant direction;[1] it may direct disclosure if satisfied that this would be in the applying party's interest and that his representative will not disclose it to any other person, directly or indirectly, without the UT's express consent.[2] Unless the UT gives a direction to the contrary, information about mental health cases and the names of any persons concerned in such cases must not be made public.[3] The UT may, on its own initiative or on application, direct that certain documents or information must or may be disclosed to it on the basis that it will not disclose them to other persons, or specified other persons;[4] a party so applying may withhold the relevant material from other parties until the application has been granted or refused.[5] The UT must ensure that information is not disclosed contrary to national security interests where these arise.[6] The UT must ensure that it conducts proceedings and delivers its reasons such as not to undermine any of these orders.[7]

1   Tribunal Procedure (Upper Tribunal) Rules 2008, SI 2008/2698, r 14(3).
2   SI 2008/2698, r 14(5)–(6).
3   SI 2008/2698, r 14(7).
4   SI 2008/2698, r 14(8).
5   SI 2008/2698, r 14(9).
6   SI 2008/2698, r 14(10).
7   SI 2008/2698, r 14(11).

6.53   The UT's Practice Direction on anonymity[1] explains that:

'6.   The starting point for consideration of anonymity orders in UTIAC, as in all courts and tribunals, is open justice. This principle promotes the rule of law and public confidence in the legal system. UTIAC sits in open court with the public and press able to attend and nothing should be done to discourage the publication to the wider public of fair and accurate reports of proceedings that have taken place.

7.   Given the importance of open justice, the general principle is that an anonymity order should only be made by UTIAC to the extent that the law requires it or it is found necessary to do so.

Cases where the law requires anonymity

8. The law requires anonymity to be respected in certain circumstances, whether or not the Tribunal has made an order. These circumstances include:

   a. Section 1 of the Sexual Offences Amendment Act 1992, as amended, requires anonymity for a victim or alleged victim of a sexual offence listed in section 2 of that Act.

   b. Section 97 (2) of the Children Act 1989 requires anonymity for a child subject to family law proceedings and includes a prohibition on the disclosure of any information that might identify the address or school of that child.

   c. Section 49 of the Children and Young Persons Act 1933 prohibits publication of the name, address, school or any other matter likely to identify a person under 18 as being concerned in proceedings before the Youth Courts. A child or young person is concerned in proceedings if they are a victim, witness or defendant.

   d. Another jurisdiction has made an order forbidding disclosure of certain information, for example a temporary restraint on publication under section 4 of the Contempt of Court Act 1981.

Cases where the law permits anonymisation

General

9. UTIAC has power to make an anonymity order or otherwise direct that information be not revealed, where such an order is necessary to protect human rights, whether (for example) the private life of a party subject to the jurisdiction or the life, liberty and bodily integrity of a witness or a person referred to in proceedings. The Tribunal may also make such an order where it is necessary in the interests of the welfare of a child or the interests of justice would otherwise be frustrated.

10. Parties may apply for an anonymity order or UTIAC may consider making one of its own volition. Where anonymity is an issue, the UTIAC judge should deal with the matter as a preliminary issue and decide, first, the extent of any anonymity order made, if any.

11. A decision to make an anonymity order where not required by law may require the weighing of the competing interests of an individual and their rights (for example, under Articles 3 or 8 of the ECHR or their ability to present their case in full without hindrance) against the need for open justice.

12. An anonymity order will not be made because an appellant or witness has engaged in conduct that is considered socially embarrassing

to reveal. In particular, that the fact that someone has committed a criminal offence will not justify the making of an anonymity order, even if it is known that such a person has children who may be more readily identified if the details of the person are known.'

Anonymity might be necessary where undue publicity would risk subverting the tribunal process by creating risks on return that were not otherwise present.[2]

1   UT Presidential Guidance Note 2013 No 1, 'Anonymity orders'. See further **5.132** *et seq* above.
2   Lord Reed in *A v British Broadcasting Corporation (Scotland)* [2014] UKSC 25 at [73].

WITHDRAWAL OF APPEALS

6.54   A party may withdraw his case in writing or orally but under r 17 such notice 'will not take effect unless the UTIAC consents to the withdrawal', unless the matter is simply an application for permission to appeal;[1] and a party who has withdrawn his case may apply to the tribunal for his reinstatement by written application within one month of the notice being received by the tribunal or the date of hearing at which the application was withdrawn.[2] The withdrawal of a decision does not deprive the UT of jurisdiction to continue to entertain the appeal, albeit that, given the general reluctance of courts to entertain academic issues absent some public interest in their determination or an issue of bad faith in the decision making, the desirability of the SSHD being the primary decision maker, and the overriding objectives of the Upper Tribunal Rules, the UT may often choose to make a formal disposal of the appeal, which may include allowing it where it is desirable to award the migrant his costs by way of fee for bringing the appeal.[3] A party contesting the withdrawal of a decision may not seek to pursue the appeal by maintaining that any response he has provided amounts to an application for permission to appeal on his own account.[4] The UT cannot prevent the withdrawal of an underlying immigration decision by the respondent under its r 17 powers, however.[5]

1   Tribunal Procedure (Upper Tribunal) Rules 2008, SI 2008/2698, r 17(1)–(2).
2   SI 2008/2698, r 17(4).
3   *SM (withdrawal of appealed decision: effect) Pakistan* [2014] UKUT 64 (IAC) (see further **5.128** above).
4   *EG and NG (UT r 17: withdrawal; r 24: scope) Ethiopia* [2013] UKUT 143 (IAC) particularly at [16] and [46].
5   *SM (above)* at [23].

EVENTS LEADING TO DEEMED ABANDONMENT

6.55   The Upper Tribunal Rules make provision for abandonment.[1] Parties are to notify the tribunal if they are aware that the appellant:

- has left the United Kingdom,

- has been granted leave to enter or remain here,

- has been the subject of a deportation order, or

- has been issued a document attesting to his possession of EEA rights of free movement.[2]

1   Tribunal Procedure (Upper Tribunal) Rules 2008, SI 2008/2698, r 17A; NIAA 2002, s 104(4), (4A) and (5) (see **4.35** *et seq*).
2   SI 2008/2698, r 17A(1).

6.56   If the appeal is deemed abandoned, the tribunal must notify the parties by way of written notice.[1] Those wishing to pursue their appeals on Refugee Convention or Race Discrimination grounds must serve a notice to such effect within 30 days (if leave was granted by post) or 28 days (if personally or electronically served).[2] These are strict time limits incapable of extension.[3]

1   Tribunal Procedure (Upper Tribunal) Rules 2008, SI 2008/2698, r 17A(2).
2   SI 2008/2698, r 17A(3); NIAA 2002, s 104(4A)–(4C).
3   SI 2008/2698, r 17A(5).

DECISIONS WITHOUT HEARINGS AND ORAL DECISIONS

6.57   Decisions may be made with or without a hearing, though the views of the parties as to the need for a hearing must be considered,[1] and in a party's absence, if he has been notified of the hearing, or reasonable steps have been taken to so notify him, and it is in the interests of justice so to do.[2] A party is otherwise entitled to attend a hearing.[3] Part of a hearing may be held in private if this is considered necessary, the UT having power to direct who should be able to attend which part of proceedings.[4] The UT may direct the exclusion of a person whose conduct is disrupting the hearing or is likely to do so, or who might impede the giving of evidence or making of submissions, or whose presence might prejudice a non-disclosure order or otherwise defeat the hearing's purpose.[5] Proceedings may be the subject of despatch by way of consent order, the tribunal then making appropriate provision as agreed by the parties.[6] Rulings may be given orally albeit that a decision notice must follow in writing giving notice of rights of appeal or review.[7] The UT, having made a decision that finally disposes of all issues in the proceedings, must provide it to each party as soon as reasonably practicable, via a notice stating its decision and identifying any rights of review or appeal and the time and manner for their exercise.[8] Written reasons must support the decision absent the parties' consent to the contrary.[9]

1   Tribunal Procedure (Upper Tribunal) Rules 2008, SI 2008/2698, r 34.
2   SI 2008/2698, r 38.
3   SI 2008/2698, r 35(1).
4   SI 2008/2698, r 37(2)–(3).

5   SI 2008/2698, r 37(4).
6   SI 2008/2698, r 39.
7   SI 2008/2698, r 40(1), 40A.
8   SI 2008/2698, r 40(2).
9   SI 2008/2698, r 40(3).

OBJECTIVES OF THE UT; DUTIES OF PARTIES; CASE MANAGEMENT

6.58   The overriding objective of the Rules governing the UT is to deal with cases 'fairly and justly',[1] rather than 'fairly, quickly and efficiently' (the overriding objective of its predecessor, the Asylum and Immigration Tribunal),[2] giving a clear steer that it is substantive justice rather than speed at which it aims. Rule 2(2) explains that:

'(2)   Dealing with a case fairly and justly includes–

(a)   dealing with the case in ways which are proportionate to the importance of the case, the complexity of the issues, the anticipated costs and the resources of the parties;

(b)   avoiding unnecessary formality and seeking flexibility in the proceedings;

(c)   ensuring, so far as practicable, that the parties are able to participate fully in the proceedings;

(d)   using any special expertise of the Upper Tribunal effectively; and

(e)   avoiding delay, so far as compatible with proper consideration of the issues.'

1   Tribunal Procedure (Upper Tribunal) Rules 2008, SI 2008/2698, r 2(1).
2   Asylum and Immigration Tribunal (Procedure) Rules 2005, SI 2005/230, r 4.

6.59   The parties are under a duty to help the UT achieve its objective, and to co-operate with it generally.[1] The UT may make a direction, on a party's reasoned application (orally at a hearing or in writing) or on its own initiative;[2] written notice must be given to every party and any affected person (unless there is good reason not to do so)[3] and a party dissatisfied with such direction may challenge it 'by applying for another direction which amends, suspends or sets aside the first direction'.[4] There are broad case management powers, which include the power to:

●   extend or shorten the time for complying with any rule, practice direction or direction;[5]

●   permit or require amendment of a document;[6]

- permit or require the provision of documents, information, evidence or submissions from a party or another person;[7]

- require a party to produce a bundle for a hearing;[8]

- suspend the effect of its own decision pending its appeal or review,[9] or that of the FTT pending a decision on a permission application and appeal;[10]

- to require any person, body or other tribunal whose decision is the subject of proceedings to provide reasons, or other information or documents in relation to the decision or any proceedings.[11]

1   Tribunal Procedure (Upper Tribunal) Rules 2008, SI 2008/2698, r 2(4).
2   SI 2008/2698, r 6(1)–(3).
3   SI 2008/2698, r 6(4).
4   SI 2008/2698, r 6(5).
5   SI 2008/2698, r 5(3)(a).
6   SI 2008/2698, r 5(3)(c).
7   SI 2008/2698, r 5(3)(d).
8   SI 2008/2698, r 5(3)(i).
9   SI 2008/2698, r 5(3)(l). The power to stay or suspend decisions that may be the subject of appeal to the UT arises only where another enactment authorises such a step: r 20A(1).
10 SI 2008/2698, r 5(3)(m).
11 SI 2008/2698, r 5(3)(n). This is a broader power than that in the 2014 Rules, which for example only require the provision of an 'unpublished document' referred to in written reasons: r 13(1)(c), or empower a direction requesting 'further details of his case, or any other information which appears to be necessary for the determination of the appeal': r 45(4) (d)(iii).

Adjournment, stay and directions

6.60   The UT may adjourn proceedings when the overriding objective so requires:[1] when considering when proceedings should be stayed behind a lead case, the relevant question is whether the anticipated appellate decision will have a critical impact upon the proceedings in hand.[2] It may well be advisable to permit the respondent's advocate a short adjournment to take instructions on a question of policy in an important case.[3] A direction may be given of its own initiative or on application, which may be in writing or made orally during a hearing.[4] Some of the broader powers of the UT beyond the Immigration and Asylum Chamber, such as the ability to strike out a party's case,[5] or to award costs (save where there has been unreasonable conduct in bringing, defending or conducting proceedings, which we address in detail in Chapters 5 and 8),[6] are not available in the immigration context. Notice of the hearing must be given of at least 14 days unless the case is urgent or exceptional, or where the parties consent.[7] The UT expects its directions to be taken seriously:

'We must expect that the legal profession and UKBA representatives will respond to these directions and be imaginative in sanction if they don't. Although this chamber of the UT may not have the power to strike out

325

cases for non-compliance, there are other measures available in terms of identifying the issues and how they will be determined that may sorely disadvantage defaulting parties whoever they are'.[8]

1 Tribunal Procedure (Upper Tribunal) Rules 2008, SI 2008/2698, r 5(3)(h).
2 Jackson LJ in *AB (Sudan) v Secretary of State for the Home Department* [2013] EWCA Civ 921 at [32].
3 Davis LJ in *Secretary of State for the Home Department v Rodriguez* [2014] EWCA Civ 2 at [56].
4 SI 2008/2698, r 6(1)–(2).
5 SI 2008/2698, r 8(1A), other than where it lacks jurisdiction: r 8(2) applied by r 8(1A).
6 SI 2008/2698, r 10(1)(b) read with the Tribunal Procedure (First-tier Tribunal) (Immigration and Asylum Chamber) Rules 2014, SI 2014/2604, r 9(2). See **8.45** and **8.46** for the principles generally. *Okondu (wasted costs, SRA referrals, Hamid)* (IJR) [2014] UKUT 377 (IAC), citing *Ridehalgh v Horsefield* [1994] EWCA Civ 40 at [11]. See further **5.146** and **5.147** above.
7 SI 2008/2698, r 36(2).
8 Speech by the Hon Mr Justice Blake, President of the UT to the Upper Tribunal Immigration Judiciary, 'The Arrival of the Upper Tribunal Immigration and Asylum Chamber' (11 February 2010).

NON-COMPLIANCE WITH RULES AND DIRECTIONS

6.61   A failure to comply with rules, practice directions or directions, does not itself render the proceedings or any step therein void.[1] The tribunal may take such action as is considered just, including waiving the unfulfilled requirement, or requiring the failure to be remedied,[2] though it will not restrict a party's participation in proceedings.[3] Where there has been a breach of requirements imposed by the FTT including the attendance and examination of witnesses, and the production and inspection of documents, the UT may take action as if the requirement had been imposed by itself.[4]

1 Tribunal Procedure (Upper Tribunal) Rules 2008, SI 2008/2698, r 7(1). See **6.104**, fn 1 below.
2 SI 2008/2698, r 7(2)(d).
3 SI 2008/2698, r 7(2)(a)–(b).
4 TCEA 2007, s 25(2); SI 2008/2698, r 7(3)–(4).

SENDING AND DELIVERY OF DOCUMENTS

6.62   Any document to be provided to the UT must be sent by pre-paid post, document exchange, facsimile, or by such other method as the UT may permit or direct, or may be delivered by hand, to the address specified for the proceedings.[1] Where a party provides a fax number, email address or other details for the electronic transmission of documents to him, that party must accept delivery of documents by that method, unless he informs the UT to the contrary.[2] The UT and parties may, when receiving an electronic copy by fax or email, as soon as practicable, request the sender to provide a hard copy.[3] The UT and the parties may assume that the address provided for a party or his representative is to be used for service until receiving written notification to the contrary.[4] Any document submitted to the UT must be accompanied by an English translation, though in proceedings that are in Wales or have a connection there, a document or translation may be submitted in Welsh.[5]

1   Tribunal Procedure (Upper Tribunal) Rules 2008, SI 2008/2698, r 13(1).
2   SI 2008/2698, r 13(2)–(3).
3   SI 2008/2698, r 13(4).
4   SI 2008/2698, r 13(5).
5   SI 2008/2698, r 13(6)–(7).

VARIATION OF GROUNDS

6.63   The variation of grounds of appeal within the UT is not the subject of express treatment in the Rules; however, given that express provision was thought necessary to prevent additional grounds being relied upon before it otherwise than by consent in judicial review proceedings,[1] variation must be permissible as part of its general powers to 'permit or require a party to amend a document'.[2] Whilst a ground upon which permission to appeal has been refused is not beyond resurrection (or a new ground may arise), as where more mature considerations on the part of legal advisors lead to the formulation of new points or where the tribunal wrongly refused a meritorious ground, it is unlikely that the overriding objective will generally be advanced by permitting grounds to be argued when they lack permission, beyond the *Robinson* duty to take obvious points of law; certainly any approach that permits 'parties to cause delay by raising issues at the last minute and/or pursuing irrelevant or otherwise unmeritorious lines of argument' should be avoided.[3] Guidance on the approach to the late raising of new grounds from the era of reconsideration may be relevant; it will usually be unacceptable to seek to raise a new ground where this would require an appeal to be adjourned in order for the respondent to have an opportunity to consider the point.[4] On the other hand, the overriding objectives of ensuring effective participation in the proceedings and using the UT's expertise may point towards recognising a duty to ensure that a party is not disadvantaged in what are essentially public law proceedings where there is a general interest in decisions being lawful. The tribunal should take care before assuming a ground of appeal has been abandoned.[5]

1   See Tribunal Procedure (Upper Tribunal) Rules 2008, SI 2008/2698, r 32. See *AH (scope of s 103A reconsideration) Sudan* [2006] UKAIT 00038 at [27]–[32].
2   SI 2008/2698, r 5(3)(c).
3   See **6.11**, fn 1 above. See also *AM (Serbia) v Secretary of State for the Home Department* [2007] EWCA Civ 16 at [27]. Cf *Ferrer (limited appeal grounds; Alvi)* [2012] UKUT 00304(IAC) at [27]–[29], considering that *DL-H v Devon Partnership NHS Trust v Secretary of State for Justice* [2010] UKUT 102 (AAC) at [3], cited by Moore-Bick LJ in *Sarkar v Secretary of State for the Home Department* [2014] EWCA Civ 195 at [17], was unlikely to apply in the more adversarial proceedings of the UT.
4   See *AH* (above) at [42]–[45]; Longmore LJ in *A v Secretary of State for the Home Department* [2006] EWCA Civ 149 at [17]; Latham LJ in in *DK (Serbia) v Secretary of State for the Home*

Department [2006] EWCA Civ 1747 at [21]; Toulson LJ in *EB (Turkey) v Secretary of State for the Home Department* [2008] EWCA Civ 1595 at [10].
5   Carnwath LJ in *Dede v Secretary of State for the Home Department* [2006] EWCA Civ 576 at [18].

JURISDICTION REGARDING APPEALS IN THE UT

6.64   TCEA 2007 empowers the UT, where it finds an error of law in the FTT's decision,[1] to set the decision aside if it sees fit, to remit the case to the FTT (whether or not to the same personnel) with directions for its reconsideration, or to re-make the decision itself.[2] In so doing it may make any decision which the FTT could have made, coming to any findings of fact as appropriate along the way.[3]

1   TCEA 2007, s 12(1).
2   TCEA 2007, s 12(2) and (3).
3   TCEA 2007, s 12(4).

ERROR OF LAW HEARINGS IN THE UT

6.65   Parties should presume, when preparing for a hearing in the UT, that unless otherwise directed, the UT will decide whether the FTT erred in law; having done so, it will proceed to re-make the decision, if satisfied that the original should be set aside, by reference to the surviving findings of fact.[1] Where the UT finds that the making of the decision involved an error on a point of law, the matter may be remitted to the FTT,[2] for hearing before a different constitution of the FTT where this is thought appropriate.[3] One Court of Appeal permission grant observed that remission to the same immigration judge was unusual because it was generally recognised that reconsideration by the same judge can sometimes be a source of difficulty and embarrassment.[4] This course of action, rather than remaking the decision in the UT, is to be adopted where:

- the effect of the error has been to deprive a party before the FTT of a fair hearing or other opportunity for that party's case to be put to and considered by the FTT; or

- the nature or extent of any judicial fact finding which is necessary in order for the decision in the appeal to be re-made is such that, having regard to the overriding objective in r 2, it is appropriate to remit the case to the FTT.[5]

1   Practice Direction, para 3.1(a)–(c).
2   TCEA 2007, s 12(2).
3   TCEA 2007, s 12(3). See Rix LJ in *Kizhakudan v Secretary of State for Home Department* [2012] EWCA Civ 566 at [27] *et seq* for the approach once an error of law is identified.
4   *SS (Sri Lanka) v Secretary of State for the Home Department* [2008] EWCA Civ 1558.

5   Practice Statement, para 7.2. Sullivan LJ for the Court in *JD (Congo) v Secretary of State for the Home Department* [2012] EWCA Civ 327 at [36] thought that the judicial policy expressed in the original version of the para 7.2 provision which aimed to keep appeals in the UT for final determination absent 'highly compelling reasons' was eminently sensible.

6.66   Remaking decisions rather than remitting them will nevertheless be the normal approach, even where some degree of further fact finding may be necessary.[1] Remittal should not be adopted only to avoid a future appellant facing the rigours of the 'second appeals' test.[2]

1   Practice Statement, para 7.3.
2   Sullivan LJ for the Court in *JD (Congo) v Secretary of State for the Home Department* [2012] EWCA Civ 327 at [36]–[37].

TRANSFER OF PROCEEDINGS FOLLOWING IDENTIFICATION OF ERROR OF LAW

6.67   Where following identification of an error of law the proceedings are transferred, the UT shall prepare written reasons for finding an error of law to have been committed, which shall be sent to the parties before the next hearing.[1] Those reasons will form part of the final decision.[2] The written reasons can be departed from or varied by the tribunal that makes the final decision only in very exceptional cases;[3] clarification can always be sought from the original constitution of the UT if there is a lack of clarity in its ruling.[4] In the era of reconsideration that preceded the creation of the UT, the Administrative Court thought it hard to imagine a case where the proper challenge to the contents of a reconsideration order was to be made other than by awaiting the final decision of the UT following the decision being remade absent very exceptional circumstances, such as 'a binding authority or a material Country Guidance case [having] been overlooked … a material error based on arguments which had not been deployed [or] … incompetent representation at the first hearing'.[5]

1   Practice Direction, para 3.6.
2   Practice Direction, para 3.7.
3   Practice Direction, para 3.7.
4   The Deputy President in *JA (practice on reconsideration: Wani applied) Ecuador* [2006] UKAIT 00013 at [19].
5   Collins J in *Wani, R (on the application of) v Secretary of State for the Home Department* [2005] EWHC 2815 (Admin) at [18]–[25]; cf Sullivan J in *Salnikov, R (on the application of) v Secretary of State for the Home Department* [2007] EWHC 426 (Admin); Wilson and Carnwath LJJ in *HS (Afghanistan) v Secretary of State for the Home Department* [2009] EWCA Civ 771.

REMAKING OF DECISIONS IN THE UT

6.68   Parties attending for a hearing to establish the question of error of law should assume that the UT will 'generally expect to proceed' to re-make the decision in cases where no further oral evidence is required; any new documentary evidence which it is reasonably practicable to adduce should therefore be filed and served.[1] Thus it is unlikely for an adjournment to be required where there is no need to hear oral evidence (unless there is a need to update the available evidence).[2] Where the UT is minded to proceed to re-decide the case, directions may be given either before, or actually at, the relevant hearing.[3] Thus, once the UT has identified legal errors requiring re-determination of an appeal, it will consider whether it is feasible to re-make the decision by reference to the findings of the FTT and any further evidence which it is reasonably practicable to adduce.[4] There are good reasons for the existing factual findings to be retained where not legally flawed:[5]

> 'If a discrete element of the first determination is faulty, it is that alone which needs to be reconsidered. It seems to me wrong in principle for an entire edifice of reasoning to be dismantled if the defect in it can be remedied by limited intervention, and correspondingly right in principle for the AIT to be cautious and explicit about what it remits for redetermination.'

Indeed Carnwath LJ stated in *HF (Algeria)*:[6]

> 'the appellant should not be subjected without good reason to the stress and uncertainty of a new hearing on an issue on which he has succeeded. Both aspects are relevant to the present case. ... From a human point of view, appearing in front of a tribunal in support of an asylum claim must be a gruelling experience at the best of times. To require it to be repeated on issues which have already been decided is not only wasteful of the tribunal's time and resources, but oppressive and potentially unfair for the applicant.'

1   Practice Direction, paras 3.1(c), 3.2 and 3.3.
2   Practice Direction, para 3.2.
3   Practice Direction, para 3.2.
4   Practice Direction, para 3.1(c). See *AH (scope of s 103A reconsideration) Sudan* [2006] UKAIT 00038 at [26].
5   Sedley LJ in *Mukarkar v Secretary of State for the Home Department* [2006] EWCA Civ 1045 at [44].
6   *HF (Algeria) v Secretary of State for the Home Department* [2007] EWCA Civ 445 at [26]; see also *DK (Serbia) v Secretary of State for the Home Department* [2008] 1 WLR 1246 at [25]; Buxton LJ in *MY (Turkey) v Secretary of State for the Home Department* [2008] EWCA Civ 477; *LS (Uzbekistan) v Secretary of State for the Home Department* [2008] EWCA Civ 909; Carnwath LJ in *HA (Afghanistan) v Secretary of State for the Home Department* [2011] EWCA Civ 1758; and Harrison J in *R (Ghanbarpar) v Immigration Appeal Tribunal* [2005] EWHC 123 (Admin) at [29], citing Symes and Jorro in *Asylum Law and Practice*. Richards LJ in *Rajaratnam v Secretary of State for the Home Department* [2014] EWCA Civ 8 at [18] confirmed the ongoing relevance of these principles in the era of the UT.

6.69   It may be appropriate for the UT to exercise powers in the rules governing the First-tier Tribunal where it is remaking decisions;[1] it will additionally be under the same duties to consider particular statutory presumptions and considerations as is the FTT.[2] Nevertheless findings may be reopened, by agreement between the parties or their acquiescence in a hearing where the judge indicates he is minded to do so.[3] Relevant considerations in ordering a full re-hearing will include:

- the nature and extent of flaws in the decision,

- the likely ambit and extent of any new hearing, and

- whether it is fair and reasonable to expect errors made at the hearing below to be corrected.[4]

1   Lord Carnwath in *Secretary of State for Home Department v MN and KY (Scotland)* [2014] UKSC 30 at [42].
2   See **5.109** above.
3   Richards LJ in *Rajaratnam v Secretary of State for the Home Department* [2014] EWCA Civ 8 at [18]; *NJ (Iran) v Secretary of State for the Home Department* [2008] EWCA Civ 77.
4   Claire Montgomery QC in *Dhar (Alok Kumar), R (on the application of) v Immigration Appeal Tribunal and Secretary of State for the Home Department* [2005] EWHC 2725 (Admin) at [19].

6.70   Defective reasons regarding some aspects of credibility are unlikely to leave much confidence in the rest of the decision.[1] If the UT decides that it cannot proceed without making further findings of fact, there will be an adjournment for relevant evidence to be adduced, so that the case may conclude before the same UT panel; if this is not reasonably practicable, then the case may need to be transferred to another constitution of the UT.[2] Any documents sent to or given by the adjourning tribunal are taken to have been sent by or given to its successor.[3] The UT will apply relevant Practice Directions and principles as would the FTT when determining an appeal substantively,[4] and will be under the same statutory duties, for example to begin its substantive deliberations on an asylum appeal by reference to the statutory provisions addressing criminality, dangerousness and exclusion;[5] it assumes the FTT role as to fee awards.[6] It need not re-determine a ground that was raised inadequately, or abandoned, in the FTT, simply because it has granted permission to appeal on another viable point,[7] though when remaking a decision, it may think it right to consider issues not previously raised below.[8]

1   Carnwath LJ in *NM (Afghanistan) v Secretary of State for the Home Department* [2007] EWCA Civ 214 at [14].
2   Practice Direction, para 3.4.
3   Practice Direction, para 3.5, Practice Statement, paras 9.2–9.3.
4   eg Joint Presidential Guidance Note No 2 of 2010, 'Child, vulnerable and sensitive appellants'.
5   See **4.38** above.
6   Joint Presidential Guidance Note No 4 (2011), 'Fee awards in immigration appeals', para 3.
7   Moore-Bick LJ in *Sarkar v Secretary of State for the Home Department* [2014] EWCA Civ 195 at [13]–[19].
8   *Ferrer (limited appeal grounds; Alvi) Philippines* [2012] UKUT 304 (IAC) at [31]–[32]; Rix LJ in *Kizhakudan v Secretary of State for the Home Department* [2012] EWCA Civ 566 at [30]–[33].

EVIDENCE AND WITNESS SUMMONS

6.71   The UT may give directions as to the issues on which it requires evidence or submissions, the nature of any such material provided and any limitation on the number of witnesses, as to expert evidence, and whether the parties must jointly appoint a single expert to provide such evidence.[1] It may make directions as to the timing of evidence and submissions, and as to whether they are to be provided orally or in writing.[2] Evidence may be admitted notwithstanding that it would not be admissible in a civil trial in the United Kingdom, and whether or not it was available to a previous decision maker.[3] It may exclude otherwise admissible evidence where it is supplied in breach of directions, or where it would be unfair to admit it.[4] The UT may consent to a witness giving, or require any witness to give, evidence on oath, and may administer an oath for that purpose.[5] A witness may be excluded from the hearing until he has given his evidence.[6] A summons may be issued to require a person to attend as a witness, or to order any person to answer any questions or produce any documents in his possession or control.[7]

1 Tribunal Procedure (Upper Tribunal) Rules 2008, SI 2008/2698, r 15(1)(a)–(d). The UT posited joint instruction of expert witnesses in *RB (linguistic evidence Sprakab) Somalia* [2010] UKUT 329 (IAC) at [158]; *HM (Art 15(c)) Iraq CG* [2010] UKUT 331 (IAC) at [52] (iii).
2 SI 2008/2698, r 15(1)(e)–(f).
3 SI 2008/2698, r 15(2)(a) (see **5.172** above).
4 SI 2008/2698, r 15(2)(b).
5 SI 2008/2698, r 15(3).
6 SI 2008/2698, r 37(5).
7 SI 2008/2698, r 16; including by application, r 16(5). For more on witness summons, see **5.73** above.

FRESH EVIDENCE PROCEDURE

6.72 A party wishing to provide documentary evidence should take steps to have it ready for the first hearing in the UT, or demonstrate by good reason why it is not reasonably practicable to provide it in good time.[1] Fresh evidence can be submitted to the UT but must be accompanied by a notice (a 'r 15 notice') indicating its nature and which explains whether it is relevant to:

● the question of establishing an error of law,[2] or

● in connection with the remaking of the decision if an error of law is detected.[3]

Additionally that notice should state:

● whether the evidence is in oral or documentary form and whether it should be considered at the relevant (error of law) hearing,[4] and

● the reasons why it was not submitted sooner.[5]

1 Practice Direction, para 3.3.
2 Practice Direction, para 4.2(a).
3 Practice Direction, para 4.2; Tribunal Procedure (Upper Tribunal) Rules 2008, SI 2008/2698, r 15(2A)(a). If there is a wish to adduce additional oral evidence, then the notice should detail such evidence, explain why it is desirable, and make a time estimate: para 4.5.

4   Practice Direction, para 4.3.
5   Practice Direction, para 4.1.

6.73   The Tribunal must then consider whether there has been unreasonable delay in submitting the evidence.[1] Such evidence must be provided in line with any directions and otherwise as soon as practicable after permission to appeal has been granted.[2] Any such notice should be considered at the time the hearing is adjourned or transferred, if the present constitution is not to finally decide the matter.[3]

1   Tribunal Procedure (Upper Tribunal) Rules 2008, SI 2008/2698, r 15(2A)(b).
2   Practice Direction, para 4.1.
3   Practice Direction, para 4.6.

6.74   An attempt to have further evidence admitted without complying with this procedure will fall on stony ground, it being doubtful that there could be a discretion to admit evidence outside the Rules when there is a clear process within them,[1] not least because of the want of natural justice occasioned by the lack of notice to the other party, even if the evidence is in the public domain.[2] In asylum cases decisions as to the exclusion of evidence will have to be made taking account of the potentially grave consequences for the asylum seeker whose very life may be put at risk by an adverse decision,[3] though bearing in mind that the 'further representations' route is always available.[4] However, it is possible that an application at a hearing could be treated as a notice such as to avoid a failure to consider Convention obligations, with an adjournment being offered to the other side to avoid it being disadvantaged by the surprise.[5]

1   By analogy with Peter Gibson LJ in *Macharia v Immigration Appeal Tribunal* [2000] INLR 267 at [16]; Keene LJ in *R v Immigration Appeal Tribunal, ex parte Azkhosravi* [2001] EWCA Civ 977 at [23]; Pill LJ in *Azkhosravi* [2001] EWCA Civ 977 at [39].
2   Peter Gibson LJ in the Court of Appeal in *Macharia* (above) considered there were too many sources in the public domain to automatically warrant their subsequent adduction.
3   See eg Lord Bridge's often cited comments in *Bugdaycay v Secretary of State for the Home Department* [1987] AC 514 at 531.
4   Immigration Rules, HC 395, para 353B provides for the consideration as to whether further representations amount to a fresh human rights or asylum claim.
5   Peter Gibson LJ in *Macharia* (above) at [18].

ERROR OF LAW AND FRESH EVIDENCE

6.75   When considering challenges against first instance appeal decisions, the UT focuses on the material that was before the immigration judge below[1] – and it is difficult to see that an error of law can be established by reference to evidence that was not before the tribunal below.[2] Presidential Guidance Note 2011 No 1 puts it thus:

'(b) Whilst disregard or misstatement of evidence that was placed before the FtT may amount to an error of law ..., or a failure to act fairly, the submission of further evidence following the hearing to contradict a finding (even if it would have been admissible in the original proceedings) cannot usually be said to be an error of law unless the evidence is submitted to demonstrate unfairness or the decision is based on an entirely false factual hypothesis … or concerns questions of jurisdictional fact.'[3]

1   Laws LJ in *CA v Secretary of State for the Home Department* [2004] EWCA Civ 1165 at [14]–[15]. Blake J in the Administrative Court in *Semere, R (on the application of) v Asylum and Immigration Tribunal* [2009] EWHC 335 (Admin) at [45](ii) indicated that on a question of jurisdictional fact, such as that relevant to proving relevant dates of service, the tribunal was not confined to the evidence below.
2   Brooke LJ for the Court of Appeal in *R (Iran) v Secretary of State for the Home Department* [2005] EWCA Civ 982 at [68].
3   Presidential Guidance Note 2011 No 1, para 13(b).

6.76   For fresh evidence to be admissible towards establishing the existence of an error of law it would have to be related to the alleged error of law in the decision,[1] and even then must pass the *Ladd v Marshall* tests, ie that it could not have been obtained with reasonable diligence sooner, that it probably would have an important influence on the result and that it is apparently credible although not necessarily incontrovertible,[2] subject to exceptional circumstances and the requirement of anxious scrutiny in asylum cases which may require some relaxation of the due diligence limb of the test.[3] Overall, whilst it must be appreciated that 'the efficiency of the whole appeal system would be seriously undermined if parties conceive that they can readily adduce on appeal evidence not placed before the First-tier Tribunal', there is some scope for adducing such evidence, exceptionally in the interests of justice.[4] Further evidence cited in the course of a Country Guidance determination post-dating the impugned decision will not be admissible towards showing an error of law.[5] Evidence can only be said to establish the true situation uncontentiously where it is truly undisputed, or where any dispute with it is 'frivolous, vexatious or abusive'.[6]

1   Brooke LJ for the Court of Appeal in *R (Iran) v Secretary of State for the Home Department* [2005] EWCA Civ 982 at [90](5); *AG (Turkey – CA – fresh evidence)* [2005] UKIAT 00014 at [7] and [15]; *AI (statutory review – evidence) Somalia* [2005] UKIAT 00063 at [3].
5   Lord Denning in *Ladd v Marshall* [1954] 3 All ER 745 (CA); *AG* (above) at [15]; *MA (fresh evidence) Sri Lanka* [2004] UKIAT 00161 (starred).
3   Carnwath LJ giving the judgment of the Court of Appeal in *E v Secretary of State for the Home Department* [2004] EWCA Civ 49 at [82] and [88]; Latham J in *R v Secretary of State for the Home Department, ex parte Aziz* (CO/3762/98, 30 March 1999); Keene LJ in the Court of Appeal in *A v Secretary of State for the Home Department* [2003] EWCA Civ 175, citing *Bugdaycay v Secretary of State for the Home Department* [1987] 1 AC 514 at 531.
4   Davis LJ in *IY (Turkey) v Secretary of State for the Home Department* [2012] EWCA Civ 1560 at [36].
5   Patten LJ in *SA (Sri Lanka) v Secretary of State for the Home Department* [2014] EWCA Civ 683 at [12]–[13].
6   *MA* (above).

6.77   Evidence is admissible at the stage where an error of law is being contended for in certain circumstances:[1]

- where it was itself relevant to proving the existence of an error of law such as an error of fact;[2]

- to show procedural irregularity;[3]

- to show that, once an error of law had been found to exist, the new evidence, which could then become admissible, could lead to a different outcome on the appeal;[4] and

- to adduce cogent evidence of fraud, 'on the principle that fraud unravels everything'.[5]

1   Dunn LJ giving the judgment of the Court of Appeal in *R v Secretary of State for the Environment, ex parte Powis* [1981] 1 WLR 584 at 595G, cited in *E* [2004] EWCA Civ 49 at [71] and [89].
2   See eg *AH (determination without hearing – mistake) Eritrea* [2005] UKIAT 00015 at [17]–[18].
3   *AG (Turkey – CA – fresh evidence)* [2005] UKIAT 00014 at [9].
4   *AI (statutory review – evidence) Somalia* [2005] UKIAT 00063 at [3].
5   *EB (fresh evidence – fraud – directions) Ghana* [2005] UKAIT 00131 at [16]–[17]: see further **6.110**, fn 1.

6.78   Ultimately, where the evidence is credible and sufficiently cogent to be capable of affecting the final decision, the tribunal should be slow to exclude it.[1] Decision makers granting permission should avoid making primary findings of fact on fresh evidence in all but very clear-cut cases, for their role normally requires that either they say in terms that the new facts put forward do not raise any arguable ground, or that they give permission to appeal.[2] Historically there has been suggestion that the tribunal may have been able to consider evidence submitted subsequent to a permission application, but prior to its determination.[3]

1   Keene LJ in the Court of Appeal in *R v Immigration Appeal Tribunal, ex parte Azkhosravi* [2001] EWCA Civ 977.
2   Stanley Burnton J in the Administrative Court giving permission for judicial review in *R v Immigration Appeal Tribunal, ex parte Kanthasamy* [2001] EWHC Admin 478 at [10]–[12].
3   Although speaking in the context of previous Procedure Rules, see Pill LJ in *R v Immigration Appeal Tribunal, ex parte Muhammed Zahid Ali* (FC3 98/5502/4, 2 October 1998).

Making further findings

6.79   Normally a re-hearing in an asylum case will take place in the light of the relevant country evidence and Country Guidance then prevailing, at least absent reprehensible 'conduct, or ignoring of any policy, on the part of the Secretary of State'. It will otherwise be wrong to give a 'windfall' to asylum seekers where determinations below have been shown to be unlawful or otherwise need revisiting in the light of some clarification of the law by permitting them to benefit from more favourable Country Guidance than those now extant.[1] We address redetermination of appeals in the light of historic policy positions in Chapter 8.[2]

1   Davis LJ in *SS (Zimbabwe) v Secretary of State for the Home Department* [2013] EWCA Civ 237 at [47].
2   See **8.119**, fnn 5–6 below.

APPROACH TO ORIGINAL DECISION ON RE-HEARING

6.80   A judge charged with remaking a decision may (and doubtless usually will) read the original determination which may contain relevant information,[1] unless the interests of justice militate against this[2] (and in general they will need to have regard to any preserved findings).[3] Nevertheless 'the judge must be careful not to be influenced by the discredited findings'.[4]

1   Phillips LJ in *Swash v Secretary of State for the Home Department* [2006] EWCA Civ 1093 at [17] and [22]; Pill LJ in the Court of Appeal in *R v Secretary of State for the Home Department* [2006] EWCA Civ 446 at [18].
2   Phillips LJ in *Swash* (above) at [21].
3   See **6.68** above.
4   Phillips LJ in *Swash* (above) at [20].

SUMMARY OF PROCEEDINGS IN THE UT

6.81   It can be seen that the main stages in the UT procedure, from the grant of permission to the hearing should be that:

●   the appellant considers, if granted permission by the FTT, whether there are any grounds on which he has been refused permission that he wishes to pursue, via an application direct to the UT;

●   the appellant and respondent have regard to the terms of the permission grant for any directions relevant to future conduct of the case;

●   the respondent considers whether to file and serve a response under r 31, within one month (though two weeks is preferred by the UT)[1] of the UT sending him the permission grant, or whether there is any aspect of the determination below, not appropriate for a response, against which he should seek permission to appeal, within the time limits identified above;[2]

●   the appellant considers whether to file and serve a reply to any respondent's response under r 32 (within one month, or sooner);[3]

●   the parties consider whether they wish to submit any further evidence, and if doing so should supply a r 15A notice (in line with directions or otherwise as 'soon as is practicable')[4] indicating its nature (ie whether it is oral or documentary, and addressing whether it is necessary for it to be considered in relation to establishing error of law or only in the event the decision must be remade) and why it was not submitted below, as soon as practicable after permission to appeal is granted subject to other directions of the UT;[5]

- any skeleton argument is provided, five working days before the hearing under the generic standard directions or as otherwise directed;[6]

- at the first hearing, the UT will consider whether an error of law has been established;[7]

- if it has not, the appeal will be dismissed, orally at the hearing or subsequently in writing;

- if an error of law has been established, the UT will proceed to remake the decision;

- in general the expectation should be that the decision is remade there and then, subject to the need to make further findings of fact which, if a significant amount of oral evidence is required, is likely to require an adjournment or transfer in the UT or remittal to the FTT, subject to directions having been given prior to the first hearing for the taking of such evidence;[8]

- remittal to the FTT is appropriate where either–

  - there was not a fair hearing below, or one party lost the opportunity to put his case fully to the FTT,[9]

  - the extent of future fact finding demands this, ie a full re-hearing (necessitated because all findings in the decision are contaminated by the error(s) of law identified) is more likely to require remittal than an appeal where there is an extant platform of findings on which to build.[10]

1   See **6.44** and **6.45** above.
2   See **6.36** above.
3   See **6.46** above.
4   Practice Direction, para 4.1.
5   Tribunal Procedure (Upper Tribunal) Rules 2008, SI 2008/2698, r 15(2A); Practice Direction, para 4.2.
6   Practice Direction, para 7.5(a)(iii).
7   TCEA 2007, s 12(1); Practice Direction, para 3.
8   Practice Direction, para 3.
9   *MM (unfairness, E and R) Sudan* [2014] UKUT 105 (IAC) at [27].
10 Practice Statement, para 7.

GIVING OF DECISION; TIME

6.82   The special service provisions for decisions in asylum cases in the UT, similar to those found then elsewhere in the appeals system, were revoked in October 2014.[1] Time has its own basis for calculation in the UT. Acts done by rules or directions must be completed by 5pm on that day.[2] The days in the week following Christmas are excluded from being 'working days'.[3]

1 Tribunal Procedure (Amendment No 3) Rules 2014, 2014/2128, r 15 (20 October 2014).
2 Tribunal Procedure (Upper Tribunal) Rules 2008, SI 2008/2698, r 12(1) (being 27–31 December).
3 SI 2008/2698, r 12(3A).

UNHCR IN THE UT; REPRESENTATION GENERALLY

6.83   The UNHCR may give notice that it wishes to participate in proceedings, in which case its office is to receive all documents to which the parties are entitled.[1] Parties must not be represented by persons prohibited from so doing by IAA 1999, s 84.[2] The UT will presume that the representative below continues to act for the party unless it receives notice to the contrary;[3] any new representative must come on the record by providing the UT with his name and address (a failure to do so does not prevent the UT permitting a new representative from providing assistance at a hearing), and having received such information the UT must pass it on to any other party.[4] A party granted public funding must as soon as practicable notify the tribunal providing a copy of the relevant funding notice, and notify other parties, of the fact.[5] A party receiving notification of a representative taking part in proceedings must provide him with any document that should be provided to his client, and may assume he remains authorised until otherwise notified.[6]

1 Tribunal Procedure (Upper Tribunal) Rules 2008, SI 2008/2698, r 9(5)–(6).
2 SI 2008/2698, r 11(1).
3 SI 2008/2698, r 11(10).
4 SI 2008/2698, r 11(2)–(2A) and (5).
5 SI 2008/2698, r 18.
6 SI 2008/2698, r 11(4).

FAST TRACK CASES

6.84   The UT may direct that a case be removed from the fast track:[1]

● where the parties consent,

● where the appeal or application could not be justly determined within the fast track.[2]

1 Defined as being a case where a person remains detained, the FTT or UT not having directed the contrary, within the places designated as fast track under the FTRs, r 2(3) at the time the original notice of immigration decision generating his appeal was served upon him (see the provisions on interpretation in the Tribunal Procedure (Upper Tribunal) Rules 2008, SI 2008/2698, r 1(3)).
2 SI 2008/2698, r 5(4). See Chapter 5, 'The detained fast track' at **5.152** *et seq* above.

6.85   An application for permission to appeal must be brought within four working days of the date on which notice of the FTT's refusal of permission was sent to the appellant.[1] Notice of the hearing of at least one day must be provided by the tribunal;[2] such hearing must be no later than five working days after the FTT or UT sent the appellant notice of the grant of permission to appeal (two working days in the event of electronic or personal service),[3] or alternatively, as soon as reasonably practicable.[4]

1   Tribunal Procedure (Upper Tribunal) Rules 2008, SI 2008/2698, r 21(3)(aa)(ii).
2   SI 2008/2698, r 36(2)(aa).
3   SI 2008/2698, r 36A(1).
4   SI 2008/2698, r 36A(2).

Response, reply and timetable

6.86   Any response to the notice of appeal must be lodged two days before the hearing;[1] whereas a reply to a response (which must be in writing) may be provided on the day of the hearing.[2] There is no special procedure for serving notice of decision in fast track cases.[3]

1   Tribunal Procedure (Upper Tribunal) Rules 2008, SI 2008/2698, r 24(2)(aa).
2   SI 2008/2698, r 25(2A)(b).
3   SI 2008/2698, r 22A(1)(c).

6.87   Parties should attend with all available witnesses and evidence, subject to contrary direction, for a UT hearing which will determine whether there is an error of law in the decision of the FTT (so there is no r 15A procedure in these cases; adjournment or transfer will be unusual in such proceedings).[1] These are the expected timings for fast track proceedings in the UT:

- Application for permission to appeal – within four working days of notice of FTT permission refusal.

- Listing of UT hearing – not later than five working days from permission grant being notified.

- Notice of UT hearing – at least one day.

- Response to grounds – not later than two days before the hearing.

- Reply to response – the day of the hearing.

1   Practice Direction, paras 3.8 and 4.7.

PART 5 – THE ROLE OF THE SENIOR IMMIGRATION JUDICIARY

THE TRIBUNAL AND CONSISTENCY

6.88   The tribunal's expertise permits it to play an important part in promoting consistent decision making, this being one dimension of justice

('It is a cardinal principle of good public administration that all persons who are in a similar position shall be treated similarly'[1]), although individual cases will have to be treated on their own facts and the fact that factual conclusions of two decision makers might differ does not itself demonstrate that either has erred in law.[2] The systems of starring and reporting are the chief means by which this objective is promoted.

'In the absence of a starred case the common law doctrine of judicial precedent shall not apply and decisions of the AIT and one constitution of the Chamber do not as a matter of law bind later constitutions. Judges of the FTT are, however, expected to follow the law set out in reported cases, unless persuaded that the decision failed to take into account an applicable legislative provision or a binding decision of a superior court.'[3]

1   Sir John Donaldson MR in *R v Hertfordshire County Council, ex parte Cheung* (transcript, 26 March 1986); Lord Carnwath in *Secretary of State for Home Department v MN and KY (Scotland)* [2014] UKSC 30 at [22].
2   See *FL (r 30: extension of time?) China* [2005] UKAIT 00180 at [46]; Auld LJ in *Independent Assessor v O'Brien* [2004] EWCA Civ 1035 at [123].
3   Upper Tribunal Immigration and Asylum Chamber Guidance Note 2011 No 2, 'Reporting decisions of the Upper Tribunal Immigration and Asylum Chamber'.

6.89   The guidance given is not confined to points of law, as to which rules of precedent may apply, but extends to issues of principle relating to factual, procedural or other matters of common application in a particular specialist field.[1]

1   Lord Carnwath in *Secretary of State for Home Department v MN and KY (Scotland)* [2014] UKSC 30 at [27].

PRECEDENT AND 'STARRING'

6.90   The first concerted effort to introduce a coherent system came under the presidency of Sir Andrew Collins, when the tribunal began the practice of elevating certain determinations to prominence and binding effect by 'starring' them.[1] In such cases, a legal panel, chaired by the President or his Deputy (and sometimes featuring both) sit together, to determine issues upon which authority is divided, or which are of general importance. Thus Practice Direction, para 12.1 states:

'Reported determinations of the Tribunal, the AIT and the IAT which are "starred" shall be treated by the Tribunal as authoritative in respect of the matter to which the "starring" relates, unless inconsistent with other authority that is binding on the Tribunal.'

1   The initiative was first seen in *Haddad* (00/HX/00926, 13 March 2000). A full list is available at the tribunal's website at www.judiciary.gov.uk/tribunal-decisions/immigration-asylum-chamber/. It is not unknown for it to be said that a formally unstarred ruling should be treated as if authoritative: see *Carcabuk and Bla* (00/TH/01426, 18 May 2000) at [2].

6.91 Speaking as supervising Lord Justice in relation to immigration cases, Laws LJ in *Sepet and Bulbul* endorsed the system, stating that adjudicators should consider themselves bound by such decisions and other divisions of the tribunal should depart from them only if satisfied that they were clearly wrong.[1] The tribunal will endeavour to state the law as clear and succinctly as possible.[2] The summary which introduces most reported decisions is not part of the determination.[3]

1   *Sepet and Bulbul v Secretary of State for the Home Department* [2001] EWCA Civ 681.
2   *WK (Art 8 – expulsion cases – review of case-law) Palestinian Territories* [2006] UKAIT 00070 at [18].
3   *JY (effect of following AE) Sudan* [2006] UKAIT 00084 at [17].

REPORTING OF TRIBUNAL DECISIONS

6.92 From May 2003 the era of universal publication of appellate immigration tribunal determinations ended. Henceforth the senior immigration judiciary were to identify those decisions which were 'reportable'.[1] Decisions of the Immigration and Asylum Chambers will bear numbers in the format laid down by the general practice statement dealing with such matters.[2] The decision to report a decision is not perceived (at least by the tribunal) to be one in which the parties have an interest, and will only be one following a hearing or other consideration where the tribunal's jurisdiction was exercised by the Senior President, the Chamber President, or a UT judge.[3] A decision of the tribunal which has not been reported[4] may not be cited in proceedings before the tribunal unless:

• the appellant in the present proceedings, or a member of the appellant's family, was a party to the proceedings in which the previous determination was issued;[5] or

• the tribunal gives permission.[6]

1   Reported decisions can be found in a number of electronic locations including www.bailii. org and there is a searchable set on the Tribunals Service website; though those without the leisure to read each decision at length would do well to become subscribers to the Electronic Information Network (www.ein.org.uk) so as to be able to see the same cases indexed and, these days, headnoted too. A few are reported in the *Immigration and Nationality Law Reports* (published by Jordans) and the official *Immigration Appeal Reports* (published by The Stationery Office). The scheme now has a statutory footing, see NIAA 2002, s 107(3): 'A practice direction may, in particular, require the Tribunal to treat a specified decision of the Tribunal or Upper Tribunal as authoritative in respect of a particular matter', which gives the scheme greater force; see *HGMO (relocation to Khartoum) Sudan CG* [2006] UKAIT 00062.
2   In accordance with the Practice Statement 'Form of decisions and neutral citation: First-tier Tribunal and Upper Tribunal on or after 3 November 2008' (31 October 2008), a determination of the IAC will be numbered in the following way: Upper Tribunal (Immigration and Asylum Chamber): [200n] UKUT 1 (IAC); First-tier Tribunal (Immigration and Asylum Chamber): [200n] UKFTT 1 (IAC).
3   Practice Statement, paras 11.2 and 11.3.

4   Such determinations will be placed on the tribunal's website: Practice Statement, para 11.4.
    Searches on the bailii.org website will retrieve unreported tribunal determinations.
5   Practice Direction, para 11.1(a).
6   Practice Direction, para 11.1(b). *YK (citation of unreported decisions) Serbia and Montenegro*
    [2004] UKIAT 00207 at [18]–[20]; *AO (unreported determinations are not precedents) Japan*
    [2008] UKAIT 00056.

Citing unreported decisions

6.93   An application for permission to cite a decision which has not been
reported must include a full transcript of the decision; identify the proposition
for which the decision is to be cited; certify that the proposition is not found in
any reported decision of the tribunal or of the IAT and has not been superseded
by a decision of a higher authority.[1] A party citing a decision of the IAT
bearing a neutral citation number prior to 2003 (including all series of 'bracket
numbers') must be in a position to certify that the matter or proposition for
which the decision is cited has not been the subject of more recent, reported,
decisions of the AIT, IAT or the tribunal.[2] The tribunal will not shut out viable
arguments, but these should only rarely need to be advanced by reference to
an unreported determination.[3] A pattern in recent FTT decisions is capable of
assisting in determining a Country Guidance case, as the evidence therein has
some degree of cogency, having been tried and tested forensically.[4]

1   Practice Direction, para 11.2; this also applies to decisions of the AIT, IAT and adjudicators:
    Practice Direction, para 11.4.
2   Practice Direction, para 11.5. The tribunal's website is the only official source of the
    determinations of the tribunal: Practice Statement, para 11.6.
3   Practice Direction, para 11.3.
4   Maurice Kay LJ in *MP (Sri Lanka) v Secretary of State for the Home Department* [2014]
    EWCA Civ 829 at [28]–[29].

Reporting criteria

6.94   From 15 February 2010 the criteria for reporting are that a case:

- has general significance and utility in the development of UT case law;

- is sufficiently well reasoned and is consistent with binding statutory
  provisions or precedent of the senior courts.

6.95   Additionally such decisions can be expected to exhibit at least one of
these features:[1]

- consideration of previous decisions on the issue(s) with sufficient
  argument on them;

- an assessment of facts of a kind that others ought to be aware of, or some
  other compelling reason;

- guidance likely to be of general assistance;

- consideration of a novel point of law, construction, procedure or practice, or development of previous decisions in the same area;

- some other compelling reason for reporting.

1   'Criteria for reporting', 15 February 2010, annexed to letter from Blake J to Immigration Lawyers Practitioners Association of 16 March 2010.

6.96   Abroad it has been said that the publication of tribunal decisions is generally desirable as asylum seekers are entitled to see the law that will apply to determination of their status, and to be able to predict the tribunal's responses to recurring factual issues; in addition, this best serves the principle of equal treatment.[1] Non-publication may give rise to issues of equality of arms if one party's advocates have better access to unreported decisions.[2]

1   Geoghegan J in the Supreme Court of Ireland in *Atanasov v Refugee Appeals Tribunal* [2006] IESC 53.
2   See Refugee Status Appeals Authority of New Zealand in *Refugee Appeal Nos 76627 and 766299* (A Mackey (Chairperson) and RPG Haines QC, 7 July 2009) at [26]–[27] and [30].

THE ROLE OF THE TRIBUNAL IN GIVING COUNTRY GUIDANCE

6.97   A reported decision bearing the letters 'CG' shall be treated as an authoritative finding on the Country Guidance[1] issue identified in the decision (including by the higher courts),[2] based upon the evidence before the determining division of the UT:[3]

'They are one of the ways that a specialist Tribunal with judges with experience of the protection risks in various parts of the world and expert in the application of legal principles to a frequently shapeless and changing mass of country information, give effect to the over-riding objectives'[4]

1   See Lord Woolf MR in *Manzeke v Secretary of State for the Home Department* [1997] Imm AR 524 at [24]–[26] for one of the earliest discussions of the Country Guidance concept.
2   Stanley Burnton LJ in *SG (Iraq) v Secretary of State for the Home Department* [2012] EWCA Civ 940 at [49].
3   Practice Direction, para 12.2.
4   *HM (Art 15(c)) Iraq CG* [2012] UKUT 409 (IAC) at [19].

6.98   Unless it has been expressly superseded or replaced by any later 'CG' decision, or is inconsistent with other authority that is binding on the tribunal, such a Country Guidance case is authoritative in any subsequent appeal, so far as that appeal relates to the Country Guidance issue in question, and depends upon the same or similar evidence.[1] If Country Guidance is overturned for legal error, cases that have materially relied upon it will be infected by the identified errors.[2] Lists of current CG cases,[3] and pending ones,[4] will be maintained on the tribunal website, and representatives will be expected to be conversant with their contents.[5]

1   Practice Direction, para 12.2.
2   *OM (AA(1) wrong in law) Zimbabwe CG* [2006] UKAIT 00077 at [12].
3   https://tribunalsdecisions.service.gov.uk/utiac.
4   www.judiciary.gov.uk/wp-content/uploads/2014/06/pending-cg-cases-may2014.pdf.
5   Practice Direction, para 12.3.

Applying Country Guidance cases

6.99   Because of the principle that like cases should be treated in like manner, any failure to follow a clear, apparently applicable Country Guidance case or to show why it does not apply to the case in question is likely to be regarded as grounds for appeal on a point of law[1] in most cases,[2] even if the authority in question was not before the immigration judge:[3] 'decision makers and tribunal judges are required to take Country Guidance determinations into account, and to follow them unless very strong grounds supported by cogent evidence, are adduced justifying their not doing so.' [4] Ultimately cases will turn on an objective and fair assessment of their own facts (strictly speaking, the tribunal lays down no precedent on fact)[5] without construing Country Guidance as if it was statute,[6] and justice would be ill-served by pigeon-holing cases rather than determining the appeal based on the evidence presented by the individual asylum seeker.[7]

1   Practice Direction, para 12.4. Sedley LJ in *GM (Burundi) v Secretary of State for the Home Department* [2007] EWCA Civ 18 at [10]; Brooke LJ for the Court of Appeal in *R (Iran) v Secretary of State for the Home Department* [2005] EWCA Civ 982 at [27]. *HGMO (relocation to Khartoum) Sudan CG* [2006] UKAIT 00062 at [142].
2   Keene LJ in *IA (Somalia) v Secretary of State for the Home Department* [2007] EWCA Civ 323 at [13], Rix LJ therein at [20]. *SE (deportation, Malta, 2002, general risk) Eritrea* [2004] UKIAT 00295; *OW (approach to subsequent tribunal decisions) Somalia* [2005] UKIAT 00052 at [3].
3   *BD (application of SK and DK) Croatia CG* [2004] UKIAT 00032 at [68]–[69].
4   Stanley Burnton LJ in *SG (Iraq) v Secretary of State for the Home Department* [2012] EWCA Civ 940 at [47]; see also *MK (AB and DM confirmed) Democratic Republic of Congo CG* [2006] UKAIT 00001 at [14].
5   Lord Hope in *Januzi v Secretary of State for the Home Department* [2006] UKHL 5 at [50].
6   Toulson LJ in the Court of Appeal in *OD (Ivory Coast) v Secretary of State for the Home Department* [2008] EWCA Civ 1299 at [11].
7   Munby J in the Administrative Court in *R (Martin) v Secretary of State for the Home Department* [2006] EWHC 799 (Admin) at [17].

Preparing and deciding Country Guidance cases

6.100   Those preparing cases marked as possible Country Guidance should consider whether expert witnesses should be available to give oral evidence.[1] The SSHD should not seek to withdraw his own decision so as to prevent a case demarcated for Country Guidance proceeding;[2] and, equally, it is undesirable for those representing asylum seekers to frustrate the system by making a late assessment that the case no longer meets public funding criteria: this consideration means that 'in highly unusual circumstances … a case [might] proceed without claimant representation'.[3] The UT has emphasised that steps should be taken to ensure asylum seekers can be represented at public expense in such proceedings, because 'their importance in saving costs in future cases, quite apart from their general importance, makes the grant of representation in the public interest highly desirable irrespective of the view formally taken of the appellant's/claimant's chances of establishing his or her need for international protection',[4] and the Court of Appeal has made it clear that a case should proceed with the asylum seeker unrepresented only where all alternative possibilities have been exhausted, including considering whether an *amicus curiae* could be appointed or whether the UNHCR might feel able to participate, because of the overall importance of securing proper argument on its behalf.[5] High standards of procedural fairness are required in the treatment of expert and other sources of evidence.[6] The UT should be as clear and concise as possible when giving such decisions, and should isolate the issues on which the relevant guidance is being given;[7] any headnote should fully and accurately reflect the guidance therein.[8] Such cases should be listed and determined with an open mind: abroad, the Canadian Board was once found to have been biased in its conduct of a test case intended to give guidance regarding the treatment of Hungarian Roma cases.[9]

1   *VH (call witnesses) Moldova* [2004] UKIAT 00325 at [40].
2   *MA (operational guidance – prison conditions – significance) Sudan* [2005] UKAIT 00149 at [28]. Under the Upper Tribunal Rules, the UT has to consent to a withdrawal (see **6.54**, fn 1 above).
3   *HM (Art 15(c)) Iraq CG* [2012] UKUT 409 (IAC) at [19].
4   *HM* (above) at [15].
5   Richards LJ in *HM (Iraq) v Secretary of State for the Home Department* [2011] EWCA Civ 1536 at [39]–[47]. None of these possibilities proved fruitful following remittal to the UT, see *HM* (fn 3 above) at [11]–[13].
6   Maurice Kay LJ in *PO (Nigeria) v Secretary of State for the Home Department* [2011] EWCA Civ 132 at [12]–[29].
7   Carnwath LJ in *PO (Nigeria)* (above) at [50]–[54].
8   Carnwath LJ in *PO (Nigeria)* (above) at [55]–[56], Maurice Kay LJ at [35]–[37].
9   Evans JA in the Federal Court of Appeal of Canada in *Kozak v Canada (Minister of Citizenship and Immigration)* 2006 FCA 124 at [60]–[61].

Effect of appeals and challenges in relation to Country Guidance

6.101   Once Country Guidance has been given it is binding and it 'remains authoritative unless and until it is set aside on appeal or replaced by a subsequent Country Guidance decision',[1] and its effect is not stayed by subsequent developments such as an onwards appeal against it.[2] It may be necessary for removals to be suspended pending the giving of relevant Country Guidance, depending on the circumstances, including the strength and nature of the claimant's case, the state of the objective evidence, and the issues arising in the pending country guidance case;[3] adjournment of an appeal should be considered with similar considerations in mind.[4] The authoritative position was set down in *SG (Iraq)*:[5]

- As to evidence that was before the UT in the Country Guidance case, it is unlikely that a stay will be appropriate unless the reasons given for the grant of permission against its decision 'cast substantial doubt on the reliability of the findings of the Tribunal'.

- As to material that was not before the UT therein, there must be 'a clear and coherent body of evidence that the findings of the Tribunal were in error'.

1   Stanley Burnton LJ in *SG (Iraq) v Secretary of State for the Home Department* [2012] EWCA Civ 940 at [67].
2   Stanley Burnton LJ in *SG (Iraq)* (above) at [53].
3   Elizabeth Laing QC sitting as a deputy High Court judge in *R (Nasire) v Secretary of State for the Home Department* [2010] EWHC 3359 (Admin) at [92]; Mr CMG Ockelton sitting as a deputy High Court judge in *R (Qader) v Secretary of State for the Home Department* [2011] EWHC 1765 (Admin); for a decision in favour of deferral, see Collins J in the Administrative Court in *R (Lutete) v Secretary of State for the Home Department* [2007] EWHC 2331 (Admin) at [14].
4   See *OM (AA(1) wrong in law) Zimbabwe CG* [2006] UKAIT 00077.
5   Stanley Burnton LJ in *SG (Iraq)* (above) at [69]–[71].

6.102   Challenges should be through the direct route of assault on the decision in question via the express identification of fresh material evidence;[1] the Administrative Court is not an ideal venue to mount a challenge.[2] When a challenge is brought in the Court of Appeal against Country Guidance, it must be subjected to rigorous scrutiny, asking whether the underlying evidence was properly evaluated after full argument.[3] Guidelines should be applied except where the particular facts of a case make them inapplicable (ie 'country guidance is not to be applied inflexibly');[4] or where there is evidence that circumstances have changed in a material way;[5] or where there is significant new evidence which shows that the views originally expressed require revision or refinement, even without any material change in circumstances.[6] The relevant Guidance Note states that:

> 'If there is credible fresh evidence relevant to the issue that has not been considered in the Country Guidance Case or if a subsequent case includes further issues that have not been considered in the CG case, the judge will reach the appropriate conclusion on the evidence, taking into account the conclusion in the CG case so far as it remains relevant.'[7]

1   *MY (Country Guidance cases – no fresh evidence) Eritrea* [2005] UKAIT 00158; *OM (AA(1) wrong in law) Zimbabwe CG* [2006] UKAIT 00077 at [12].
2   Buxton LJ in the Court of Appeal in *Kapoor v Secretary of State for the Home Department* [2007] EWCA Civ 770 at [12]; Richards LJ in *Ariaya v Secretary of State for the Home Department* [2006] EWCA Civ 48 at [52].
3   Maurice Kay LJ in *KS (Burma) v Secretary of State for the Home Department* [2013] EWCA Civ 67 at [20].
4   Davis LJ in *SS (Zimbabwe) v Secretary of State for the Home Department* [2013] EWCA Civ 237 at [24]; Maurice Kay LJ in *KS (Burma)* (above) at [19].
5   Though see Elias LJ in *TM (Zimbabwe) v Secretary of State for the Home Department* [2010] EWCA Civ 916 at [8] for the proposition that even in 'a rapidly changing political landscape we must assume that the guidance still holds good'.

6   *NM (lone women – Ashraf) Somalia CG* [2005] UKIAT 00076 at [140].
7   Upper Tribunal Immigration and Asylum Chamber Guidance Note No 2 of 2011, 'Reporting decisions of the Upper Tribunal Immigration and Asylum Chamber', para 11.

6.103   There is a higher duty to give reasons in 'guideline' cases than in run-of-the-mill decisions.[1] Knowledge of such cases can be presumed (absent some patent misunderstanding), and they need not be rehearsed in detail in a decision.[2] Before a case is promulgated and designated as a Country Guidance case it is considered by the relevant country convener and the Reporting Committee and advice may be tendered to the determining judges.[3] Challenges to CG decisions to the Court of Appeal will be listed for oral hearing before one or more Lord/Lady Justices as soon as is practicable rather than awaiting a decision on the papers in the normal run of appeals.[4]

1   Laws LJ in *S v Secretary of State for the Home Department* [2002] EWCA Civ 539 at [29]; the Lord Chief Justice in the Court of Appeal in *P and M v Secretary of State for the Home Department* [2004] EWCA Civ 1640 at [24]; *AS and AA (effect of previous linked determination) Somalia* [2006] UKAIT 00052 at [65].
2   Pill LJ in the Court of Appeal in *BA (Pakistan) v Secretary of State for the Home Department* [2009] EWCA Civ 1072 at [29].
3   Upper Tribunal Immigration and Asylum Chamber Guidance Note No 2 of 2011, 'Reporting decisions of the Upper Tribunal Immigration and Asylum Chamber', para 11, an approach upheld as lawful in *MOJ (return to Mogadishu) CG* [2014] UKUT 442 (IAC) at [8]–[22].
4   Maurice Kay LJ in *SG (Iraq) v Secretary of State for the Home Department* [2012] EWCA Civ 940 at [77].

CONSEQUENCES OF PROCEDURAL IRREGULARITIES

6.104   Lord Woolf MR sitting in the Court of Appeal in *Jeyeanthan*[1] set out the three stages by which the consequences of a failure to comply with formalities should be considered under the common law:

- First, it must be considered whether the document employed by the delinquent party 'substantially complies' with the requisite procedures (so a failure to make a declaration of truth might have the effect that there was no substantial compliance with the rule).

- Secondly, it must be asked whether the failure is capable of waiver.

- Thirdly, the consequences of non-compliance should be analysed and if those consequences transpire to be purely technical, and cause no prejudice, then little weight need be attached to the irregularity.

1   Lord Woolf MR in *R v Secretary of State for the Home Department, ex parte Jeyeanthan* [1999] EWCA Civ 3010, addressing a failure to sign the form seeking permission to appeal.

6.105   This decision preceded the current regime under which the UT has express and extensive powers to condone irregularities. Now the UT has such a wide discretion that it is difficult to envisage a future need for *Jeyeanthan* principles to apply on a free-standing basis, though they may be relevant to the exercise of the r 7 discretion.[1] In pre-*Jeyeanthan* times, where the SSHD served notice of appeal against only one of multiple co-respondents in a consolidated determination, the tribunal has held that there was no valid appeal in respect of the other,[2] though the question would have to be judged in the light of the grounds of appeal as well as the content of the notice itself;[3] a failure to name all the appellants below may well mean that there is no application in respect of some of them before the tribunal, albeit that the proceedings that some are involved with may well be taken to settle the immigration situation of the others too.[4]

1   Eg the Tribunal Procedure (Upper Tribunal) Rules 2008, SI 2008/2698, rr 7(1) and 43(2)(d) (see **6.61** above).
2   *Kani and Obengi* (11814, 31 January 1995); *Caballero* [1986] Imm AR 409.
3   *Shirwa and Ali* (11818, 7 February 1995).
4   *TD (para 297(i)(e): 'Sole Responsibility') Yemen* [2006] UKAIT 00049.

PART 6 – ERRORS OF LAW

COMMON ERRORS OF LAW

6.106   The most common errors of law likely to be found in decisions of the FTT will be those defects set out in the landmark case of *R (Iran)*:[1]

'(i)   Making perverse or irrational findings on a matter or matters that were material to the outcome ('material matters');

(ii)   Failing to give reasons or any adequate reasons for findings on material matters;

(iii)   Failing to take into account and/or resolve conflicts of fact or opinion on material matters;

(iv)   Giving weight to immaterial matters;

(v)   Making a material misdirection of law on any material matter;

(vi)   Committing or permitting a procedural or other irregularity capable of making a material difference to the outcome or the fairness of the proceedings;

(vii)   Making a mistake as to a material fact which could be established by objective and uncontentious[2] evidence, where the appellant and/or his advisers were not responsible for the mistake, and where unfairness resulted from the fact that a mistake was made'[3]

1   *R (Iran) v Secretary of State for the Home Department* [2005] EWCA Civ 982 at [9]; see further *Begum v London Borough of Tower Hamlets* [2003] UKHL 4. See a fuller litany of errors of law in the immigration context at **8.134**.

2　*MA (fresh evidence) Sri Lanka* [2004] UKIAT 00161 (starred) at [52]–[53].
3　Carnwath LJ for the Court in *E v Secretary of State for the Home Department* [2004] EWCA Civ 49 at [66]; see an even crisper summary by Sir John Dyson SCJ *in MA (Somalia) v Secretary of State for the Home Department* [2010] UKSC 49 at [44].

6.107　Challenges that do not truly identify flaws of this nature are likely to be rejected as unprincipled disagreement with a decision:

'Terms such as "erred" or "erred in law" or "was wrong in law" or "misdirected itself in law" are unacceptable unless accompanied by a clear specification of the error/s of law alleged and suitable brief particulars.'[1]

Irrationality for these purposes might alternatively be described as an 'error of reasoning which robs the decision of logic'[2] for all that it represents a high hurdle to surmount:[3] in an asylum case the requirement of 'anxious scrutiny', ensuring every aspect of the case is adequately evaluated, will intensify the review of factual findings.[4] A decision will be unlawful if unsupported by evidence.[5] A decision on proportionality under the ECHR will only be unlawful if it is flawed by these standards.[6] It 'has become a generally safe working rule that the substantive grounds for intervention are identical' in judicial review claims and statutory appeals.[7]

1　See *Nixon (permission to appeal: grounds)* [2014] UKUT 368 (IAC) at [10] and above at **6.2**, fn 5.
2　Sedley J (as he then was) in *Balchin, R (on the application of) v Parliamentary Commissioner for Administration* [1996] EWHC Admin 152.
3　Brooke LJ for the Court of Appeal in *R (Iran) v Secretary of State for the Home Department* [2005] EWCA Civ 982 at [11]–[12]; Keene and Maurice Kay LJJ in *Miftari v Secretary of State for the Home Department* [2005] EWCA Civ 481 at [36] and [38]; the President McCloskey J in *Nixon (permission to appeal: grounds)* [2014] UKUT 368 (IAC) at [12]; *Alexander Machinery (Dudley) Ltd v Crabtree* (1974) ICR 120. See further McKeown J in the Federal Court of Canada in *Dhillon v Canada (Minister for Citizenship and Immigration)* [2001] FCT 1194 at [17].
4　See **6.117**, fn 5 below; see further **8.140**, fnn 6 and 7 below.
5　Brooke LJ in the Court of Appeal in *R (Iran)* (above) at [90].
6　Brooke LJ in the Court of Appeal in *R (Iran)* (above) at [20].
7　Carnwath LJ for the Court of Appeal in *E v Secretary of State for the Home Department* [2004] EWCA Civ 49 at [48].

Weight, materiality and referencing authority

6.108　Any error must be *material* in order to render the decision unlawful.[1] A doubt as to whether an error is a material one must be resolved in favour of the individual complaining of the error;[2] once some findings have been identified as unlawful, a decision may only be upheld where the tribunal is 'tolerably confident that the tribunal's decision would have been the same on the basis of the reasons which have survived its scrutiny'.[3] The weight to be given to particular aspects of the evidence is for the first instance judge to decide, and a complaint based on findings being against the weight of the evidence is unlikely to involve an error of law:[4] 'the question of evidential weight is quintessentially a matter for the tribunal.'[5] Identifying alternative approaches to credibility that might have been taken below will not make good a contention of error of law.[6] There is no obligation upon a tribunal or lower court to refer to any particular authority so long as relevant principles contained in binding authorities are duly applied.[7] Where an error of fact is transplanted from a decision of the SSHD into a decision of a tribunal it may be appropriate to treat the latter's decision as vitiated.[8]

1   Brooke LJ in the Court of Appeal in *R (Iran) v Secretary of State for the Home Department* [2005] EWCA Civ 982 at [15]–[16]; *GB (evidence not probative is irrelevant) Zimbabwe* [2005] UKAIT 00153 at [49]. See further **6.40** above.
2   Sir Stanley Burnton in *ML (Nigeria) v Secretary of State for the Home Department* [2013] EWCA Civ 844 at [16].
3   Neuberger LJ in *HK v Secretary of State for the Home Department* [2006] EWCA Civ 1037 at [45].
4   Lord Hoffman in *Tesco Stores Ltd v Secretary of State for the Environment* [1995] 1 WLR 759 at [13] and [17]; Jackson LJ in *J1 v Secretary of State for the Home Department* [2013] EWCA Civ 279 at [88]; the Master of the Rolls in *Gurung, R (on the application of) v Secretary of State for the Home Department* [2013] EWCA Civ 8 at [35].
5   Hickinbottom J in *V, R (on the application of) v Asylum and Immigration Tribunal* [2009] EWHC 1902 (Admin) at [31]; Underhill LJ in *AN (Afghanistan) v Secretary of State for the Home Department* [2013] EWCA Civ 1189 at [17].
6   *MM (DRC – plausibility) Democratic Republic of Congo* [2005] UKIAT 00019 at [21]–[22].
7   Wilson LJ in *OH (Serbia) v Secretary of State for the Home Department* [2008] EWCA Civ 694 at [13].
8   Rix LJ in *TN (Bangladesh) v Secretary of State for the Home Department* [2009] EWCA Civ 519 at [22]–[27].

Bias, case management, fairness and decisions made in ignorance of decisive facts

6.109   If an allegation is made of judicial misconduct amounting to bias, it must go beyond a vague general assertion, and show something of significance which the party claiming disadvantage was willing and able to support, showing that there was the prospect of evidence being obtained for the appeal.[1] Challenges to case management decisions, being questions of judgment rather than discretion, require the identification of some error of principle within them[2] – adjournment decisions may be challenged on grounds of public law error or lack of fairness, and usually turn on whether the party whose application was refused was thereby deprived of a fair hearing.[3] Where issues of fairness arise, on appeal the question is whether the procedure below was right or wrong, and is not to be approached via the prism of rationality:[4]

'Whether fairness is required and what is involved in order to achieve fairness is for the decision of the courts as a matter of law. The issue is not one for the discretion of the decision-maker. The test is not whether no reasonable body would have thought it proper to dispense with a fair hearing. The *Wednesbury* reserve has no place in relation to procedural propriety'

1 *YB (allegations against adjudicator: Presidential Note) Jamaica* [2005] UKIAT 00029.
2 *K (Côte d'Ivoire)* [2004] UKIAT 00061; *WT (adjournment, fresh evidence) Ethiopia* [2004] UKIAT 00176. Sedley LJ in the Court of Appeal in *Benkaddouri v Secretary of State for the Home Department* [2003] EWCA Civ 1250 at [13].
3 *Nwaigwe (adjournment: fairness)* [2014] UKUT 00418 (IAC), headnote and [7].
4 Sedley LJ in in *AK (Iran) v Secretary of State for the Home Department* [2008] EWCA Civ 941 at [26]; Moses LJ in *SH (Afghanistan) v Secretary of State for the Home Department* [2011] EWCA Civ 1284 at [13]–[14]; Simon Brown LJ in *R v Secretary of State for the Home Department, ex-parte the Kingdom of Belgium* (CO/236/2000, 15 February 2000) endorsing a passage in De Smith, Woolf and Jowell, *Principles of Judicial Review* (5th edition) at 406–407.

6.110 Where the tribunal below has proceeded in ignorance of a potentially decisive fact, its decision may be set aside on appeal.[1] A fundamental mistake of fact induced by forgery or fraud may provide grounds for challenge, but a rational case must be put forward going beyond mere assertion.[2] A decision taken in defiance of basic standards of fairness and morality may be treated as a nullity.[3]

1 Carnwath LJ in *E v Secretary of State for the Home Department* [2004] EWCA Civ 49 at [66]. See also Carnwath LJ, agreeing with the lead judgment of May LJ, in *Khan v Secretary of State for the Home Department* [2003] EWCA Civ 530; Buxton LJ in the Court of Appeal in *Secretary of State for the Home Department v Cabo Verde* [2004] EWCA Civ 1726 at [19]. Brooke LJ for the Court of Appeal in *R (Iran) v Secretary of State for the Home Department* [2005] EWCA Civ 982 at [29] lists eight examples of the kind of matter that could constitute an error of fact in this sense.
2 Sullivan J in the Administrative Court in *Salnikov, R (on the application of) v Secretary of State for the Home Department* [2007] EWHC 426 (Admin) at [11]; Stanley Burnton J in the Administrative Court in *Dube, R (on the application of) v Secretary of State for the Home Department* [2006] EWHC 2975 (Admin) at [11].
3 Sedley LJ in *Anwar v Secretary of State for the Home Department* [2010] EWCA Civ 1275 at [25].

REVIEWING FINDINGS OF FACT

6.111 When reviewing findings, less deference need be afforded an inference from facts found than to findings of primary fact,[1] a sparing approach being apt regardless of the identity of the party challenging the decision;[2] findings on country evidence are also more susceptible to challenge than those on oral evidence.[3] The tribunal's greatest disinclination to interfere with factual findings is where the challenge is to the approach to credibility of a judge who has heard oral evidence, for then the decision maker below has a very significant advantage over an appellate judge,[4] though less so where the case turns on the acceptance of events abroad, where the reasoning is based on plausibility rather than other features of the evidence.[5]

1 See the Earl of Halsbury, Lord Chancellor, in *Montgomerie & Co Ltd v Wallace-James* [1904] AC 73; Lord MacMillan in *Jones v Great Western Railway Co* (1930) 47 TLR 39 at 45, HL; *Rowland v Environment Agency* [2003] EWCA Civ 1885.

2   Laws LJ in *Arshad v Secretary of State for the Home Department* [2001] EWCA Civ 587 at [20]–[22].
3   Tuckey LJ in *Sarker v Secretary of State for the Home Department* (C/1999/0227, 8 November 2000); Jowitt J in *R v Immigration Appeal Tribunal, ex parte Balendran* [1998] Imm AR 162.
4   Simon Brown J in *R v Immigration Appeal Tribunal, ex parte Begum and Khatun* [1988] Imm AR 199, though given the judicial warnings given against over-reliance on demeanour, see eg **5.193**, fn 1 above, one may wonder whether too much is sometimes made of this advantage.
5   Neuberger LJ in *HK v Secretary of State for the Home Department* [2006] EWCA Civ 1037 at [29]; Keene LJ in *Y v Secretary of State for the Home Department* [2006] EWCA Civ 1223 at [25].

Findings flawed by lack of evidence, wrongful approach or misunderstanding

6.112   Undue elevation of a factor which might properly be attributed weight into a mandatory requirement of credibility may render a finding of fact unsustainable.[1] There is authority that errors of fact, if they amount to a basic misunderstanding of the asylum case brought, may vitiate a decision altogether.[2]

1   The tribunal in *Faustino* (13020, 1 March 1996) warned against the elevation of a factor, amongst other factors which affects weight, into something bordering upon the mandatory. Munby J in the Administrative Court in *Choudhrey v Immigration Appeal Tribunal* [2001] EWHC Admin 613 at [32].
2   Kirby J in the High Court of Australia in *Dranichnikov v Minister for Immigration and Multicultural Affairs* [2003] HCA 26 at [88]; Moses LJ in *ML (Nigeria) v Secretary of State for the Home Department* [2013] EWCA Civ 844 at [10]: 'factual errors, if they are significant to the conclusion, can constitute errors of law.'

DELAYS IN ISSUING DECISIONS

6.113   Given the dangers in determining an individual's credibility based on oral evidence heard some time earlier, a practice developed in the tribunal whereby 'any period in excess of three months between the date of hearing and the date of promulgation would be unacceptable'.[1] This was never an inflexible rule, however, and its invocation would depend upon the length of the delay and the circumstances of the case,[2] always remembering that the prime focus of an appeal is whether there is an error of law, not merely whether there is delay.[3] The Court of Appeal expressly considered the 'three month' rule in *Sambisavam*, indicating that it was not to be viewed as an inflexible rule but as a presumption, given the twin policy reasons for avoiding such delays: ie that they would affect the recollection of the decision maker, and undermine the confidence of the litigants in the decision. The principle would not bite where credibility was hopelessly damaged by factors which were not determined by oral evidence, or where the appeal failed for other reasons. The tribunal can check the file to see whether the delay was due to administrative reasons alone.[4] A reviewing court will be readier to infer evidence has been overlooked where there has been a delay.[5] At one time there was a Guidance Note to immigration adjudicators in relation to part-heard hearings, saying that care should be taken where there was a three-month delay between listings, and that it might be desirable to re-hear evidence or read out the tribunal's record of proceedings, in order to safely determine the appeal.[6] Presidential Guidance Note No 1 of 2014 states that:[7]

> 'A period of 14 days, (2 working days in respect of Fast Track appeals), for preparing the statement of reasons should be adequate and judges are expected to have their decisions and statements of reasons completed within this period.'

1   See the memorandum circulated around tribunal chairpersons cited in *Waiganjo* (R 15717, 24 November 1997).
2   Elias J refusing judicial review in *R (Ghorbani) v Secretary of State for the Home Department and Immigration Appeal Tribunal* [2004] EWHC 510 (Admin), citing the Privy Council in *Cobham v Frett* [2001] 1 WLR 1775. One of the fuller considerations of the issues is to be found in the decision of the tribunal in *Gorniak* (15119, 9 June 1997).
3   Mummery LJ in the Court of Appeal in the employment context in *Bangs v Connex South Eastern Ltd* [2005] EWCA Civil 1442 at [42]–[43].
4   Potter LJ in *Sambisavam v Secretary of State for the Home Department* [2000] Imm AR 85.
5   Elias J refusing judicial review in *R (Ghorbani) v Secretary of State for the Home Department and Immigration Appeal Tribunal* [2004] EWHC 510 (Admin) at [11].
6   Guidance Note 2 (May 2002) – which at the time of writing no longer appears on the online list of Guidance Notes for the former AIT that are now relevant to FTT.
7   Para 22.

KEY ATTRIBUTES OF DECISIONS

6.114   Under the 2014 Rules, the written outcome of an appeal is given by way of decision and reasons:[1] thus judicial decisions are no longer styled 'determinations', and we seek to follow that description in this book. Appellants should concentrate on matters of substance rather than form[2] and it is very important that decisions are read as a whole in a common sense way,[3] and with an eye to making sense of their contents,[4] though always having regard to the fundamental issues at stake in asylum cases.[5] Good decision-making is demonstrated more by quality of reasoning rather than length.[6] The four critical elements of a decision are that the judge should:

● direct himself as to the relevant law;

● identify the important facts or factual issues and, where these are disputed, state his findings on them;[7]

● state the overall conclusion which he draws from his factual findings and from the material before him as to whether the appellant has a valid claim; and

- explain his reasons for his conclusions sufficiently that the parties can see that relevant matters have been considered, and why the case has been so decided.[8]

1   Tribunal Procedure (First-tier Tribunal) (Immigration and Asylum Chamber) Rules 2014, SI 2014/2604, r 29.
2   Munby J in the Administrative Court in *R v Special Adjudicator, ex parte Gashi* [2002] EWHC 227 Admin at [21].
3   Sullivan J in the Administrative Court in *R v Immigration Appeal Tribunal, ex parte Puspalatha* [2001] EWHC Admin 333; Munby J in the Administrative Court in *Choudhrey v Immigration Appeal Tribunal* [2001] EWHC Admin 613; Sullivan J in *R v Immigration Appeal Tribunal and Secretary of State for the Home Department, ex parte Bahcaci* [2003] EWHC 1178 Admin. See also the observations of the majority of the High Court in *Minister for Immigration and Ethnic Affairs v Wu Shan Liang* (1996) 185 CLR 259 at 271–272, in the judicial review context but of analogous relevance, citing *Collector of Customs v Pozzolanic* (1993) 43 FCR 280.
4   Neuberger LJ in the Court of Appeal in *N v Secretary of State for the Home Department* [2006] EWCA Civ 1166 at [19] and [27].
5   Lord Neuberger of Abbotsbury in *SS (Iran) v Secretary of State for the Home Department* [2008] EWCA Civ 310 at [12].
6   *Slimani* (01/TH/00092, 21 December 2000, starred).
7   Schiemann J in *Mohd Amin* (1992) Imm AR 367 once stated that it was a requirement of a determination that it showed what evidence had been accepted, rejected, found doubtful, and considered irrelevant, though later decisions emphasised that the central obligation was to deal with material evidence: see eg *Rai* (00/TH/00048, 17 February 2000) at [8]; *Slimani* (01/TH/00092, 21 December 2000, starred) at [10].
8   Toulson LJ in *OD (Ivory Coast) v Secretary of State for the Home Department* [2008] EWCA Civ 1299 at [12].

6.115   Although the tribunal is not a court of grammar and will not overturn a decision due to errors that are plainly typographical,[1] carelessness may raise doubts as to whether the facts of the case were truly in the judge's mind, making his decision unsafe.[2] A decision and reasons should adequately record the material evidence presented to the immigration judge;[3] and do so in a coherent manner.[4] In order to ensure consistency in the formatting of determinations, the member of the tribunal who is preparing the determination shall state in the heading whether the appeal is being determined with or without a hearing; number sequentially each paragraph of the determination; and sign and date the determination at the end of the document or employ such electronic methods as the Senior or Chamber President may approve for signifying that the determination is finalised.[5] A party who takes part in proceedings after a determination has been promulgated with missing pages may waive the possibility of arguing the decision to be a nullity.[6]

1   *SA (clarificatory questions from IJs – best practice) Iran* [2006] UKAIT 00017; Sir Paul Kennedy in the Court of Appeal in *HB (Albania) v Secretary of State for the Home Department* [2007] EWCA Civ 569; Moses LJ in the Court of Appeal in *Detamu v Secretary of State for the Home Department* [2006] EWCA Civ 604 at [18].
2   Keene LJ in the Court of Appeal in *R (Ahmed) v Secretary of State for the Home Department and Immigration Appeal Tribunal* [2004] EWCA Civ 552 at [12]; Moses LJ in *ML (Nigeria) v Secretary of State for the Home Department* [2013] EWCA Civ 844 at [10].
3   *Shafiq* (10255, 2 September 1993); *Esquivel* (17731, 17 July 1998).

4   Sedley LJ in the Court of Appeal in *Jasim v Secretary of State for the Home Department* [2006] EWCA Civ 342.
5   Practice Statement, para 10.
6   The tribunal in *W v Secretary of State for the Home Department (Ethiopia)* [2004] UKIAT 00074 at [21].

REASONS

6.116   The wealth of judicial guidance on the duty to give reasons pays homage to the frequency with which their sufficiency is challenged. In short, the authorities recognise that reasons must be given for both the determination of the appeal and the material findings of fact upon which that decision is based and they must be provided in sufficient detail to 'enable the reader to know what conclusion the decision maker has reached on the principal controversial issues.'[1]

'The overriding test must always be: is the Tribunal providing both parties with the material which will enable them to know that the Tribunal has made no error of law in reaching its findings of fact? ... A party appearing before a Tribunal is entitled to know, either expressly stated by it or inferentially stated, what it is to which the Tribunal is addressing its mind. In some cases it may be perfectly obvious without any expressed reference to it by the Tribunal; in other cases it may not. Secondly, the appellant is entitled to know the basis of fact upon which the conclusion has been reached.'[2]

1   Lord Bridge in *Save Britain's Heritage v No 1 Poultry Ltd* [1991] 1 WLR 153. There is a full survey of the then extant authorities in *R v Immigration Appeal Tribunal, ex parte Dhaliwal* [1994] Imm AR 387.
2   Lord Lane in *Mahmud Khan* [1982] Imm AR 134; *Khan (Mahmud)* [1983] 2 WLR 759.

6.117   Inadequate reasoning is not a ground for allowing an appeal if on analysis the approach is justified;[1] sometimes express reasons will not be required, if the reasoning can be readily inferred, either because of the general thrust of the decision ('reasons need not be extensive if the decision as a whole makes sense, having regard to the material accepted by the judge'),[2] or where the argument raised is clearly without merit.[3] Reasons should be found in the decision, not in responses to subsequent challenges thereto.[4] The requirement to give anxious scrutiny to asylum claims means that the reasoning in their determination must be especially clear, showing that every factor that might tell in an asylum seeker's favour has been taken into account.[5] The need to engage with the issues becomes greater as the complexity of the material increases, particularly when there is expert evidence present.[6] Adopting the reasons of the SSHD will not be objectionable where they deal with the whole scope of the material relied upon on appeal, although the need for independent reasons will increase with the addition of material on appeal.[7] Clear reasons need to be given for adverse credibility findings,[8] albeit that it may be possible to accept the credibility of an account without giving much by way of reasons.[9]

1   *R v Immigration Appeal Tribunal, ex parte Dhaliwal* [1994] Imm AR 387, Judge J citing Phillips J's judgment in *Hope v Secretary of State for the Environment* [1975] as it was itself summarised by Lord Bridge in *Save Britain's Heritage v No 1 Poultry Ltd* [1991] 1 WLR 153.
2   *Shizad (sufficiency of reasons: set aside)* [2013] UKUT 85 (IAC) at [10].
3   Gibbs J in *R v Special Adjudicator and the Secretary of State for the Home Department, ex parte Kurecaj* [2001] EWHC Admin 1199.
4   Richards J in *Krayem v Secretary of State for the Home Department* [2003] EWCA Civ 649 at [20]; Rix LJ in *Kizhakudan v Secretary of State for Home Department* [2012] EWCA Civ 566 at [26].
5   *R v Secretary of State for the Home Department, ex parte Bugdaycay (Musisi)* [1987] Imm AR 250; Carnwath LJ in the Court of Appeal in *YH (R on the application) v Secretary of State for the Home Department* [2010] EWCA Civ 116 at [24]; Moses LJ in *ML (Nigeria) v Secretary of State for the Home Department* [2013] EWCA Civ 844 at [1]; Kirby J in the High Court of Australia in *Minister for Immigration and Multicultural Affairs v Ibrahim* [2000] HCA 55 at [196].
6   Henry LJ in *Flannery v Halifax Estate Agencies Ltd* [2000] 1 WLR 377 at 381.
7   *BT (former solicitors' alleged misconduct) Nepal* [2004] UKIAT 00311; Stanley Burnton J in the Administrative Court in *R v Immigration Appeal Tribunal, ex parte Zazoun* [2002] EWHC 434 (Admin) at [11].
8   Moses LJ in *Detamu v Secretary of State for the Home Department* [2006] EWCA Civ 604 at [19]; Collins J in *R v Secretary of State for the Home Department, ex parte Chugtai* [1995] Imm AR 559; Toulson LJ in Court of Appeal in *JK (Democratic Republic of Congo) v Secretary of State for the Home Department* [2007] EWCA Civ 831 at [31]; *MK (duty to give reasons) Pakistan* [2013] UKUT 641 (IAC), headnote at (1)–(2).
9   Buxton LJ in *RH (Ghana) v Secretary of State for the Home Department* [2007] EWCA Civ 640 at [14]; Toulson LJ in *JK (Democratic Republic of Congo)* (above) at [31]; Buxton LJ in *Tarlochan Singh v Secretary of State for the Home Department* (IATRF 1999/0055/4, 5 July 1999).

Considerations in 'reasons' challenges

6.118   A deficient decision should not be saved by the amplification of reasoning that does not bear the weight afforded it.[1] If it is 'unclear' from a decision whether an error has been made, that is normally taken as an indication of materially defective reasoning, which itself may be a ground for intervention.[2] There may be cases where it is appropriate to give the opportunity to the judge criticised for a lack of reasons an opportunity to provide them, 'except perhaps where there is a danger of ex post facto rationalisation of the decision that has been made',[3] though this is less likely to be appropriate in fundamental rights cases where anxious scrutiny of the original decision is required.[4] It is important to differentiate between the 'largely procedural nature of an "inadequate reasons" challenge and a substantive challenge that the reasons given display an error of law or other public law flaw.'[5]

1   Sedley LJ in *Anya v University of Oxford* [2001] EWCA Civ 405.
2   Buxton LJ in *AA (Uganda) v Secretary of State for the Home Department* [2008] EWCA Civ 579.
3   McCombe LJ in *CW (Jamaica) v Secretary of State for the Home Department* [2013] EWCA Civ 915 at [31].
4   Stanley Burnton J in *Nash v Chelsea College of Art and Design* [2001] EWHC Admin 538 at [35]–[36].
5   Beatson LJ in *Haleemudeen v Secretary of State for the Home Department* [2014] EWCA Civ 558 at [33].

DRAFTING GROUNDS OF APPEAL, INCLUDING CHALLENGES TO CONDUCT OF THE HEARING

6.119   It is imperative that the author of grounds of appeal liaises with the advocate who appeared below. Grounds of appeal do not prove themselves, and any criticism that is made of the conduct of an immigration judge should be fully evidenced by way of witness statement;[1] a Presidential Note once explained that an allegation, to be arguable, should be both detailed and particularised, in the sense of being confirmed by a person who witnessed the hearing[2] (and evidence should be 'collected while memories are fresh'[3]); it may, rarely, be appropriate for the permission consideration to be adjourned, for any further evidence of the allegation to be provided.[4] It is important that a judge is alert throughout proceedings, though where it is alleged that standards have fallen short of this, 'cogent evidence of the actual or apparent behaviour in question', such as falling asleep, is required:[5] whilst it is always desirable that such conduct be challenged in the forum below, 'it is unrealistic not to recognise the difficulty, even for legal representatives, in raising with the ... tribunal a complaint about the behaviour of a ... member who, if the complaint is not upheld, may yet be part of the ... tribunal deciding the case.'[6] It may be that comment will be sought from the judge whose conduct has been criticised, it being made clear that any response from them may be disclosed to both sides.[7] Grounds should be as succinct as possible.[8] Allegations against former representatives will need to be supported by independent evidence and may require waiver of legal professional privilege so the former adviser can respond to the point.[9] The separation of the roles of advocate and witness are such that it may well be inappropriate for the advocate who appeared below, and now wishes to give evidence of what transpired there, to represent on appeal:[10]

'(iii)   Those compiling applications for permission to appeal must be alert to the important distinction between legal submissions and arguments (on the one hand) and evidence (on the other). This distinction must not be blurred.

(iv)   Where it is decided that a witness statement of the kind which materialised in the present case must be made, the legal representative concerned should, as a general rule, not present the appeal before the Upper Tribunal. The roles of advocate and witness are distinct, separated by a bright luminous line. An advocate must never assume the role of witness. This conflict may be avoided if, for example, the facts bearing on the judicial aberration in question are undisputed. Otherwise, the appellate advocacy function must be relinquished to another representative.'

1   The tribunal in *Aftab Ahmed* (00/TH/00230, 1 March 2000); *WN (Surendran, credibility, new evidence) Democratic Republic of Congo* [2004] UKIAT 00213 at [25]; Presidential Guidance Note 2011 No 1, para 27.
2   *YB (allegations against adjudicator: Presidential Note) Jamaica* [2005] UKIAT 00029 cited the President's Note to vice-presidents of 23 November 2004.

3   Headnote to *Azia (proof of misconduct by judge) Iraq (Rev 1)* [2012] UKUT 96 (IAC).
4   Presidential Guidance Note 2011 No 1, para 27.
5   *KD (inattentive judges) Afghanistan* [2010] UKUT 261 (IAC).
6   *KD* (above) at [15], citing *Stansbury v Datapulse plc* [2004] ICR 523, CA.
7   *HA (conduct of hearing: evidence required) Somalia* [2009] UKAIT 00018 at [3]–[4];
    Presidential Guidance Note 2011 No 1, para 27.
8   See eg Burton J in *R v Immigration Appeal Tribunal, ex parte Malik* [2001] EWHC Admin
    356.
9   Presidential Guidance Note 2011 No 1, para 28.
10 *BW (witness statements by advocates) Afghanistan* [2014] UKUT 00568 (IAC).

PART 7 – CHALLENGING THE UT

APPLICATION FOR PERMISSION TO APPEAL TO THE COURT OF APPEAL: PROCEDURE

6.120   Permission is required to bring a statutory appeal, from the appropriate appellate court (ie the Court of Appeal in England and Wales, the Court of Appeal in Northern Ireland and the Court of Session in Scotland)[1] if it has not been granted by the UT.[2] We concentrate on the procedures in the Court of Appeal. An application to the UT for permission to appeal to the Court of Appeal must be made by filing with the tribunal a written application in a statutory appeal[3] (there are special procedures for judicial review appeals which we address in Chapter 8).[4] The application notice must identify:

* the decision to which it relates,

* any alleged errors of law, and

* state the result sought on the appeal.[5]

1   TCEA 2007, s 13(12).
2   TCEA 2007, s 13(3).
3   Tribunal Procedure (Upper Tribunal) Rules 2008, SI 2008/2698, r 44(1).
4   See **8.47** and **8.81**.
5   SI 2008/2698, r 44(7).

6.121   Before seeking to call on the jurisdiction of the appropriate appellate court, the SSHD should consider carefully whether the policy of streamlining litigation is best served by challenging a decision which goes against the grain of government policy;[1] all advisors should think long and hard before challenging the decision of both a senior immigration judge and a Lord Justice of Appeal where there is a closely reasoned decision at first instance[2] and it should be recalled that the quality of the tribunal has improved under the Presidency of High Court judges.[3]

1   Carnwath LJ in the Court of Appeal in *Mukarkar v Secretary of State for the Home Department*
    [2006] EWCA Civ 1045 at [40].

2   Brooke LJ in the Court of Appeal refusing permission to appeal in *Salemi v Secretary of State for the Home Department* [2006] EWCA Civ 264 at [13]; *Dareshoorian v Secretary of State for the Home Department* [2006] EWCA Civ 85.
3   Brooke LJ for the Court of Appeal in *R (Iran) v Secretary of State for the Home Department* [2005] EWCA Civ 982 at [92]–[93].

SET ASIDE, CLERICAL AND ADMINISTRATIVE SLIPS AND OMISSIONS

6.122   The tribunal may set aside a decision which disposes of proceedings, or part of it, and re-make the same (which might include a decision on a permission application);[1] this may take place on a party's written application.[2] Such action may be required where the interests of justice so demand and where one of these circumstances applies:

(a)   a document relating to the proceedings was not sent to, or was not received at an appropriate time by, a party or a party's representative;

(b)   a document relating to the proceedings was not sent to the UT at an appropriate time;

(c)   a party, or a party's representative, was not present at a hearing related to the proceedings; or

(d)   there has been some other procedural irregularity in the proceedings.[3]

1   Tribunal Procedure (Upper Tribunal) Rules 2008, SI 2008/2698, r 43(1); Presidential Guidance Note 2011 No 1, para 35.
2   SI 2008/2698, r 43(3).
3   SI 2008/2698, r 43(2).

6.123   A written application must be sent or delivered such that it is received by the tribunal no later than:

●   12 days after service by the tribunal (or the SSHD) where the appellant is in the United Kingdom; or

●   within 38 days where he is outside the country.[1]

The UT may also at any time correct clerical mistakes or other accidental slips and omissions, which it may notify by sending the amended decision.[2]

1   Tribunal Procedure (Upper Tribunal) Rules 2008, SI 2008/2698, r 43(3).
2   SI 2008/2698, r 42(1).

THE UT'S POWERS OF REVIEW

6.124   The UT may review its own decisions,[1] other than excluded ones (most relevantly, decisions on permission to appeal to itself against the FTT, its own decisions on review or to set aside its own decisions),[2] either on its own initiative or on application.[3] In so doing it may:

- correct accidental errors in the decision;

- amend the reasons given; or

- set the decision aside, in this last scenario then remaking the decision itself and making appropriate findings of fact along the way.[4]

1   TCEA 2007, s 10(1).
2   TCEA 2007, s 10(1), defined in s 13(8).
3   TCEA 2007, s 10(2).
4   TCEA 2007, s 10(4)–(6).

6.125   Once the decision is reviewed, there may be further review of the remade decision only with respect to accidental errors therein;[1] and there may be only a single review of a decision, the conclusion on so doing not being capable of being revisited.[2] Having received an application for permission to appeal, the UT may review the decision, but only where:

- a legislative provision or binding authority was overlooked which could have had a material effect on the decision, or

- where, since the decision, a court has made a decision that is binding on the UT.[3]

The outcome of the review must be notified to the parties, and a failure to inform them of their right to make representations means that the notice must offer them the right to apply for set aside again.[4]

1   TCEA 2007, s 10(7).
2   TCEA 2007, s 10(8).
3   Tribunal Procedure (Upper Tribunal) Rules 2008, SI 2008/2698, r 45(1). The result must be notified: r 46(2).
4   SI 2008/2698, r 46(2) and (3).

APPLICATION TO THE UT FOR PERMISSION TO APPEAL AGAINST ITS OWN DECISION

6.126   Where no review is carried out, or no action is taken after a review, the UT must go on to consider whether to give permission to appeal in relation to a decision, or part of it.[1] It must send a record of its decision to the parties as soon as practicable.[2] If the tribunal refuses permission to appeal, it must send its reasons with its decision, and a notification of the ensuing right of appeal;[3] permission may be granted on limited grounds, in which case appeal rights must again be signified.[4] There is power to correct any clerical mistake or other accidental slip or omission in a decision or record of decision by sending notification of the amended decision or record to all parties, and making any necessary amendment to any information published in relation to the matter.[5] The UT should identify which court is the appropriate appellate one before making its decision on permission.[6]

1   Tribunal Procedure (Upper Tribunal) Rules 2008, SI 2008/2698, r 45(2).
2   SI 2008/2698, r 45(3).
3   SI 2008/2698, r 45(4).
4   SI 2008/2698, r 45(5).
5   SI 2008/2698, r 42.
6   TCEA 2007, s 13(11) and (12).

UT POWERS AT THE PERMISSION STAGE: SUMMARY

6.127   From the foregoing it will be seen that the options for a UT judge considering an application for permission to appeal are:[1]

- to make an order for correction of 'clerical mistake or other accidental slip or omission' under SI 2008/2698, r 42;

- to review the decision under SI 2008/2698, rr 45(1) and 46 if the UT has overlooked legislative provisions and precedents that could have had a material effect on its decision;[2]

- to set aside the decision under SI 2008/2698, r 43 where a document went astray, a relevant person was absent from a hearing, or some other procedural irregularity casts doubt over the proceedings;[3]

- to grant permission to appeal to the Court of Appeal against the decision of the UT, in whole or in part: SI 2008/2698, r 45(2)–(5).[4]

1   See **6.123**, fn 2 above.
2   See **6.124** and **6.125** above.
3   See **6.122** and **6.123** above.
4   See **6.126** above.

TIME LIMIT FOR COURT OF APPEAL APPLICATION

6.128   A written application must be sent or delivered such that it is received by the tribunal within a certain number of days after the impugned decision has been served by the tribunal (or by the SSHD):

- 12 working days where the appellant is in the United Kingdom,

- seven working days if the individual is in detention,[1]

- 38 days where the individual is outside the country.[2]

1   Tribunal Procedure (Upper Tribunal) Rules 2008, SI 2008/2698, r 44(3B)(a).
2   SI 2008/2698, r 44(3B)(b).

6.129 The time limit for cases where the migrant is at liberty, in detention, or abroad, are respectively reduced to ten, five, or ten working days where notice of decision is delivered in person or electronically.[1] Late applications must be accompanied by explanations and a request for extension.[2] Applications must identify the decision to which they relate, identify errors of law, and state the result sought.[3]

1 Tribunal Procedure (Upper Tribunal) Rules 2008, SI 2008/2698, r 44(3C).
2 SI 2008/2698, r 44(6).
3 SI 2008/2698, r 44(7).

CHALLENGES TO THE UT MADE TO THE COURT OF APPEAL DIRECTLY

6.130 Any party may appeal to the appropriate appellate court[1] 'on any point of law arising from a decision made by the Upper Tribunal other than an excluded decision'.[2] Excluded decisions are those in relation to:

- national security certificates,

- exercise of the powers of review and set aside,

- decisions that have been set aside themselves, and

- matters designated by order of the Lord Chancellor.[3]

1 TCEA 2007, s 13(12).
2 TCEA 2007, s 13(1) and (2).
3 TCEA 2007, s 13(8)(a) and (d)–(f).

6.131 Appeals require the grant of permission.[1] Appeals may be brought only where the UT has refused permission.[2] A notice of appeal must be filed with the Court of Appeal following a grant of permission to appeal by the tribunal, and where this is overlooked, specific principles have been laid down, recognising the desirability of permitting such appeals to proceed, and that delay due to legal representatives should not impact on an asylum seeker;[3] similarly a body of law grew out of the need to address the fact that the Asylum and Immigration Tribunal was unable to extend time for such applications, though the UT's powers so to do should obviate the need for recourse to such authorities.[4] The Court of Appeal will not hold it against applicants if they are prejudiced by the tribunal sending out the wrong form.[5] The appellant's notice must be accompanied by the fee or fee remission certificate.[6] The grounds of appeal should be as concise as possible and identify relevant errors of law in the decision below: 'The reasons why the decision under appeal is wrong or unjust must not be included in the grounds of appeal and must be confined to the skeleton argument.'[7] Any missing documents should be identified and may be provided subsequently.[8]

1   TCEA 2007, s 13(3).
2   TCEA 2007, s 13(5); CPR, r 52.3(2)(b).
3   *BR (Iran) v Secretary of State for the Home Department* [2007] EWCA Civ 198 at [23].
4   See the Court of Appeal in *Ozdemir v Secretary of State for the Home Department* [2003] EWCA Civ 167; *Yacoubou v Secretary of State for the Home Department* [2005] EWCA Civ 1051. Now see the Tribunal Procedure (Upper Tribunal) Rules 2008, SI 2008/2698, r 44(6).
5   Lloyd LJ giving permission to appeal to the Court of Appeal in *Omed Abdulrahman v Secretary of State for the Home Department* [2005] EWCA Civ 1650 at [8].
6   CPR PD 52C, para 3(1).
7   CPR PD 52C, para 5(2).
8   CPR PD 52C, para 6.

Filing notice of appeal

6.132   Documents are to be filed at this address:

Civil Appeals Office Registry
Room E307
Royal Courts of Justice
Strand
London
WC2A 2LL

6.133   Three copies of the appellant's notice are to be provided and one copy of each of the following:

(a)   the sealed order or tribunal decision being appealed;

(b)   any order granting or refusing permission to appeal, together with a copy of the judge's or tribunal's reasons for granting or refusing permission to appeal;

(c)   any witness statements or affidavits relied on in support of any application included in the appellant's notice;

(d)   in cases where the decision of the lower court was itself made on appeal, the first order, the reasons given by the judge who made it, and the appellant's notice of appeal against that order;

(e)   the original decision which was the subject of the application to the lower court;

(f)   the order allocating the case to a track (if any);

(g)   the appellant's skeleton argument in support of the appeal;

(h)   the approved transcript of the judgment.[1]

1   CPR PD 52C, para 3(3).

6.134   Where there are multiple applicants, they should be the subject of separate fee-paid applications unless the parties were already the subject of single proceedings, or where the proceedings have been formally consolidated.[1] The notice may be amended, with the court's permission, before a permission hearing, normally without a hearing.[2] Regional advisors should bear in mind the possibility of a video link hearing for a permission application.[3]

1   Moore-Bick LJ in *Rasheed v Secretary of State for the Home Department* [2014] EWCA Civ 1493 at [11].
2   CPR PD 52C, para 30(1) and (2).
3   *Dareshoorian v Secretary of State for the Home Department* [2006] EWCA Civ 85.

FILING A NOTICE OF APPEAL AND LATE APPEALS

6.135   In immigration appeals the appellant's notice must be filed at the Court of Appeal within 21 days of the decision below[1] together with a spare copy for each respondent which is to be sealed by the court and returned for service upon them[2] (together with the supporting evidence)[3] and upon the UT.[4] An application to extend time may be made, before or after the time limit has expired,[5] within the appellant's notice, stating the reason for the delay and the steps taken prior to the application being made;[6] the respondent has the right to oppose that application and to be heard at any hearing of the issue, having been served with a copy of any supporting evidence and providing the court with written objections to an extension of time within seven days of being served with the appellant's notice (risking costs if he unreasonably opposes the application).[7] An application for an extension of time will normally be determined without a hearing unless the court directs otherwise.[8]

1   CPR, r 52.4(2)(b).
2   CPR PD 52C, para 3(4).
3   CPR PD 52C, para 7.2.
4   CPR, r 52.4(3). The UT may then be requested by the Court of Appeal to send copies of the documents that were before it when it considered the appeal; CPR PD 52C, para 28(1)(a).
5   CPR, rr 52.6, 3.1(2)(a).
6   CPR PD 52C, para 4(1)–(2).
7   CPR PD 52C, para 4(3).
8   CPR PD 52C, para 4(3)(c).

Extension of time

6.136   The need to honour Convention obligations, and the undesirability of holding the error of a representative against an asylum seeker, call for special consideration when the question of an extension of time is considered,[1] though nevertheless representatives should ensure they have adequate systems in place to trigger timely actions.[2] The government can be expected to speedily decide as to the necessity for onwards appeal,[3] and, being competently represented, cannot expect to be indulged if applying late, particularly given the need for the SSHD to set an example in this field.[4] The existence of strongly arguable points of principle might nevertheless justify an extension of time.[5] Immigration appeals operate to stay the decision challenged,[6] and, regarding out-of-time appeals, the Court has an inherent jurisdiction to protect its proceedings from being set at naught and might, in an exceptional case (where satisfied by strong evidence that a significant injustice has probably occurred, recognising that with each passing day it becomes less likely that the jurisdiction will be exercised), require the SSHD to refrain from an appellant's removal from the jurisdiction while it considers the application before it.[7]

1   *BR (Iran) v Secretary of State for the Home Department* [2007] EWCA Civ 198 at [17]–[18], see also *MJ (Sudan) v Secretary of State for the Home Department* [2007] EWCA Civ 530; *IM (Turkey) v Secretary of State for the Home Department* [2007] EWCA Civ 505.
2   Brooke LJ dismissing an application for permission to appeal to the Court of Appeal in *R (RG) v Secretary of State for the Home Department* [2006] EWCA Civ 396.
3   Toulson LJ in *EB (Turkey) v Secretary of State for the Home Department* [2008] EWCA Civ 1595 at [13].
4   Moses LJ in *OO (Cameroon) v Secretary of State for the Home Department* [2009] EWCA Civ 383.
5   Davis LJ in *Secretary of State for the Home Department v Rodriguez* [2014] EWCA Civ 2 at [63].
6   CPR 52, r 52.7(b); NIAA 2002, s 78(1).
7   Brooke LJ in *YD (Turkey) v Secretary of State for Home Department* [2006] EWCA Civ 52 at [24]–[25], [41]. See **8.47**, fnn 12 and 13 below.

SECOND APPEALS TEST

6.137   There is one very significant limitation on the circumstances in which permission to appeal will be given, being the 'second appeals' criteria, introduced to provide 'certainty, reasonable expense and proportionality',[1] by which:

'The Court of Appeal will not give permission unless it considers that–

(a)   the appeal would raise an important point of principle or practice; or

(b)   there is some other compelling reason for the Court of Appeal to hear it.'[2]

1   1997 Bowman Review of the Business of the Court of Appeal (Civil Division), cited in *PR (Sri Lanka) v Secretary of State for the Home Department* [2011] EWCA Civ 988 and *Tanfern Ltd v Cameron-MacDonald* [2000] 1 WLR 131.
2   TCEA 2007, s 13(6); Appeals from the Upper Tribunal to the Court of Appeal Order 2008, SI 2008/2834; and CPR, r 52.13(2). See also **8.82** below.

6.138   This is in stark comparison to the test generally prevailing outside second appeals, which looks to whether the court considers that the appeal would have a real prospect of success or there is some other compelling reason why the appeal should be heard.[1] Where the 'important point of principle or practice' limb is relied upon, it is necessary to distinguish between (a) establishing a principle or practice, and (b) applying it correctly; only the former justifies a second appeal.[2] As to compelling reasons, these will normally be legal ones, although exceptionally it is possible that political or emotional ones will add weight to these; that the case raises asylum issues is alone not enough,[3] though the extremity of consequences for the individual in combination with a strong argument that there has been an error of law may suffice,[4] and the fact that there has only been one tier of consideration, because the UT has remade the decision particularly where it heard an appeal afresh rather than preserving first tier findings, may be a relevant factor.[5]

1   CPR, r 52.3(6).
2   Dyson LJ in *Uphill v BRB (Residuary) Ltd* [2005] EWCA Civ 60 at [18].
3   *PR (Sri Lanka) v Secretary of State for the Home Department* [2011] EWCA Civ 988 at [36] and [41]; *MT for Judicial Review of a Decision of the Upper Tribunal (Immigration and Asylum Chamber)* [2013] ScotCS CSOH_93.
4   Sullivan LJ for the Court in *JD (Congo) v Secretary of State for the Home Department* [2012] EWCA Civ 327 at [22], [26] and [27]; *MS (Sri Lanka) v Secretary of State for the Home Department* [2012] EWCA Civ 1548 at [17]; *OA (Nigeria) v Secretary of State for the Home Department* [2011] EWCA Civ 688; see Maurice Kay LJ in *MS (Sri Lanka)* (above) at [17] for an asylum case where the severity of consequences plus the fact that the appellant had succeeded in the FTT was sufficient.
5   *PR (Sri Lanka)* (above) at [53]; Sullivan LJ for the Court in *JD (Congo)* (above) at [14], [23], [30] and [31].

6.139   In a 'compelling reason' case it is unlikely that the court will give permission unless the prospects of success are considered to be very high[1] (unless procedural failing renders the proceedings unfair)[2] – for example where the judge on the first appeal made a decision which is perverse or otherwise plainly wrong or the decision is clearly inconsistent with subsequent authority of which the appellant had been unaware.[3] A case involving the best interests of a child may more easily meet the 'compelling' criteria, so long as a real and material error of law is established.[4] Application of the second appeals test involves a judgment by the court, considering all the circumstances, and past *dicta* on its operation should not be treated as if set in stone.[5] The qualifications or experience of the decision maker in the UT, save in those very rare cases where it is contended that the statutory criteria for appointment as a deputy judge of the UT were not met, are not relevant to the test.[6] The fact that an unsuccessful party will subsequently face the second appeals test is not a reason for remitting an appeal to the FTT rather than finally determining it in the UT.[7] A challenge to country guidance might constitute a compelling reason.[8] The factor elevating the case to the second appeal threshold should be clearly identified and concisely expressed.[9]

1   Dyson LJ in *Uphill v BRB (Residuary) Ltd* [2005] EWCA Civ 60 at [24](1).
2   Dyson LJ in *Uphill v BRB (Residuary) Ltd* (above) at [24](3); Lord Jones in *YHY (China) (AP), Re Judicial Review* [2014] ScotCS CSOH_11 at [19]–[29].
3   Dyson LJ in *Uphill v BRB (Residuary) Ltd* (above) at [24](1) and (2).
4   Sullivan LJ for the Court in *JD (Congo) v Secretary of State for the Home Department* [2012] EWCA Civ 327 at [14], citing *Re B (residence: second appeal)* [2009] 2 FLR 632 [2009] EWCA Civ 545 at [14]; *MD (India) v Secretary of State for the Home Department* [2012] EWCA Civ 340; *AA, R (on the application of) v Upper Tribunal* [2012] EWHC 1784

(Admin); cf *SS (Sri Lanka) v Secretary of State for the Home Department* [2012] EWCA Civ
945 at [14]–[16].
5   Sullivan LJ for the Court in *JD (Congo)* (above) at [13], citing *Cramp v Hastings Borough
Council* [2005] 4 All ER 1014; Lord Boyd of Duncansby in *MT for Judicial Review of a
Decision of the Upper Tribunal (Immigration And Asylum Chamber)* [2013] ScotCS
CSOH_93 at [36]. See Lord Glennie in *PW, Re Judicial Review* [2014] ScotCS CSOH_64 for
a practical example of the test's evaluation.
6   Sullivan LJ for the Court in *JD (Congo)* (above) at [36]–[37].
7   Sullivan LJ for the Court in *JD (Congo)* (above) at [39]–[40].
8   *AHC (AP), Re Judicial Review* [2012] ScotCS CSOH_147.
9   CPR PD 52C, para 5A(1); Ouseley J in *Khan, R (on the application of) v Secretary of State
for the Home Department* [2011] EWHC 2763 (Admin).

SKELETON ARGUMENT

6.140   The skeleton argument should accompany the notice of appeal (the
Practice Direction pre-October 2012 required a skeleton argument to be filed
within 14 days of filing the notice of appeal: now, though, appellants should
appreciate that failing to serve a contemporaneous skeleton argument puts
them at risk of sanctions)[1] and be served on the respondent.[2] Its purpose is to
assist the court by setting out as concisely as practicable a party's arguments[3]
(and so it should not exceed 25 pages, excluding front and backsheets, on A4
paper in not less than 12 point font and 1.5 line spacing).[4] Beyond achieving
concision, it should:

- aim to define and confine the areas of controversy, via numbered
  paragraphs;

- be cross-referenced to any relevant document in the bundle;

- be self-contained; and

- avoid extensive quotations.[5]

1   CPR PD 52C, para 3(3)(g).
2   CPR PD 52C, para 7.1A.
3   CPR PD 52A, para 5.1(1).
4   CPR PD 52C, para 31(1).
5   CPR PD 52A, para 5.1(2); if the skeleton argument fails to effectively present the party's case,
it faces a real risk of not recovering its costs, see eg *Inplayer Ltd v Thorogood* [2014] EWCA
Civ 1511 at [52]–[57].

6.141   There is a distinct difference between the role of the skeleton
argument, and grounds of appeal, the latter, properly drafted, being confined to
a short and succinct identification of the asserted errors of law, without going
into the background circumstances and full arguments.[1] All documents relied
on must be identified.[2] When referencing an authority, the skeleton argument
should state the proposition of law the authority demonstrates, and it should not
cite multiple authorities to support a given proposition without justification.[3]
A skeleton that fails to meet these standards or is provided late risks not being

allowed as a cost on assessment (any statement of costs must show the skeleton cost separately).[4]

1   Moore-Bick LJ in *Rasheed v Secretary of State for the Home Department* [2014] EWCA Civ 1493 at [12].
2   CPR PD 52A, para 5.1(3).
3   CPR PD 52A, para 5.1(4).
4   CPR PD 52A, para 5.1(5), 5.3; CPR PD 52C, para 31(4).

6.142   It may be necessary to provide a list of persons who feature in the case or glossaries of technical terms; a chronology of relevant events will be necessary in most appeals.[1] The same skeleton may be used for the full hearing as for the permission application.[2] The respondent, where legally represented, must provide a skeleton argument if attending to address the court, within 42 days of notification of the listing window.[3] A supplementary skeleton argument may be filed 'only where strictly necessary and only with the permission of the court'; it must be lodged as soon as practicable requesting permission for its admission, with an explanation for its necessity and its timing; only exceptionally may one be provided within seven days of the hearing.[4]

1   CPR PD 52A, para 5.2.
2   CPR PD 52C, para 31(2).
3   CPR PD 52C, paras 13 and 21, Timetable Part 1 'Listing window notification to lodging bundle'.
4   CPR PD 52C, para 32.

ORAL RENEWAL OF PERMISSION APPLICATIONS

6.143   Where permission is refused, the person seeking permission may request the decision to be reconsidered at a hearing.[1] Appeals against Country Guidance determinations will be listed for hearing without a paper consideration.[2] The notice of appeal may be amended only with permission.[3] If the appeal court refuses an application for permission to appeal and considers that the matter is totally without merit, it must record the fact and consider whether it is appropriate to make a civil restraint order.[4]

1   CPR, r 52.3(4).
2   See **6.103**, fn 4.
3   CPR, r 52.8.
4   CPR, r 52.10(5) and (6).

GENERAL CONSIDERATIONS IN THE COURT OF APPEAL

6.144   Where two or more appeals are pending in the same or related proceedings, the parties must seek directions as to whether they should be heard together or consecutively by the same judges.[1] In such cases, the parties must attempt to agree a single appeal bundle or set of bundles for all the appeals and seek directions if they are unable to do so.[2] The court may direct that the hearing of an appeal be expedited, and will deal with requests for expedition without a hearing, which must be made by letter (or email) setting out succinctly the grounds on which expedition is sought, marked for the immediate attention of the court and copied to the other parties to the appeal.[3] In cases of extreme urgency, the Civil Appeals Office must be informed as soon as possible, via the Royal Courts of Justice switchboard on 020 7947 6000, asking for a member of the security staff to contact the duty judge.[4] An expedited hearing will be listed at the convenience of the court and not according to the availability of counsel.[5] After the grant of permission, an appeal notice may be amended only with the court's permission, a matter which will normally be addressed at the hearing unless that would cause unnecessary expense or delay, in which case a request should be made for the application to amend to be heard in advance.[6] Advocates must consider this affects the time estimate already provided, seeking to agree a new estimate within seven days of service of the application to amend.[7]

1   CPR PD 52C, para 25(1).
2   CPR PD 52C, para 25(2).
3   CPR PD 52C, para 26(1) and (2).
4   CPR PD 52C, para 26(3).
5   CPR PD 52C, para 26(4).
6   CPR PD 52C, para 30(3).
7   CPR PD 52C, para 30(4).

ERRONEOUS EXERCISE OF JURISDICTION BY TRIBUNAL WHERE NO ERROR OF LAW IN FTT DECISION

6.145   The UT would be wrong to entertain an appeal where the grounds of appeal do not properly identify any error of law[1] (where it is shown to have done so, the original decision should be reinstated)[2] albeit that it is important not to leave a decision flawed by legal error where on a fair reading of the grounds the relevant points can be isolated,[3] though the SSHD is under a duty to ensure that those who draft the Home Office's grounds of appeal are able to identify errors of law.[4] Jurisdiction could not be conferred by concession in such a case.[5]

1   Buxton LJ in the Court of Appeal in *Secretary of State for the Home Department v Abbas* [2005] EWCA Civ 992 citing Lord Phillips of Worth Maltravers MR in *B v Secretary of State for the Home Department* [2005] EWCA Civ 61 at [18]. See further **6.44**, fn 4 above.
2   Brooke LJ in the Court of Appeal in *Mlauzi v Secretary of State for the Home Department* [2005] EWCA Civ 128 at [42].
3   *ZT v Secretary of State for the Home Department* [2005] EWCA 1421 at [10]; Buxton LJ in *Jasarevic v Secretary of State for the Home Department* [2005] EWCA Civ 1784 at [12].
4   Lord Phillips giving the judgment of the Court of Appeal in *B* (above) at [10].
5   Hooper LJ in *Hussain v Secretary of State for the Home Department* [2006] EWCA Civ 382 at [13].

BUNDLES FOR THE HEARING

6.146 As the UT will be requested to produce an appeal bundle comprising 'copies of the documents which were before the relevant tribunal when it considered the appeal', there may be no requirement for an appellant to himself file an additional one,[1] though he should ensure that he provides items (a)–(e) and (g) of the documents that should accompany their application notice.[2] Within 21 days of the date of the listing window notification, the respondent should consider whether he is content with the proposed bundle, supplying a revised index if he has amendments to propose and if the parties cannot agree bundle content, a supplementary bundle must be produced by those proposing the inclusion of controversial material;[3] the bundles are to be filed no later than 42 days before the appeal hearing.[4] Any such bundle must be in chronological order, indexed and paginated.[5] Subject to any court order, the bundle should include:[6]

(a)   a copy of the appellant's notice;

(b)   a copy of any respondent's notice;

(c)   a copy of any appellant's or respondent's skeleton argument;

(d)   a copy of the order under appeal;

(e)   a copy of the order of the lower court granting or refusing permission to appeal together with a copy of the judge's reasons, if any, for granting or refusing permission;

(f)   a copy of any order allocating the case to a track;

(g)   the approved transcript of the judgment of the lower court.

1   CPR PD 52C, para 28(1); similar requirements were discussed by Brooke LJ in the Court of Appeal in *T v Secretary of State for the Home Department* [2006] EWCA Civ 483.
2   CPR PD 52C, para 28(1)(c) (see **6.133**, fn 1 above).
3   CPR PD 52C, para 21, Timetable Part 1 'Listing window notification to lodging bundle'.
4   CPR PD 52C, para 21, Timetable Part 2 'Steps to be taken once hearing date fixed: lodging bundles, supplemental skeletons and bundles of authorities'.
5   CPR PD 52C, para 27(1).
6   CPR PD 52C, para 27(2).

6.147 Realistically, given that the bundle produced by the court tends just to contain the material decisions and determinations in the case, it may be necessary to file a Bundle B addressing evidence particular to the appellant and a Bundle C with more general evidence. Where relevant to the grounds of appeal, it is apt to consider including the following documents:[1]

(a)   statements of case;

(b)   application notices;

(c)   other orders made in the case;

(d)   a chronology of relevant events;

(e)   witness statements made in support of any application made in the appellant's notice;

(f)   other witness statements;

(g)   other documents which the appellant or respondent consider relevant to the appeal.

Original documents should not be supplied but should be brought to the hearing if required.[2] Bundles will be destroyed at the conclusion of proceedings without further notification.[3]

1   CPR PD 52C, para 27(3).
2   CPR PD 52C, para 27(4).
3   CPR PD 52C, para 27(5).

RESPONDENT'S NOTICE

6.148   A respondent must file and serve a respondent's notice, if seeking the decision below to be upheld for reasons different from or additional to those within it.[1] Permission to appeal must be requested if required in such circumstances[2] and any other application required may be included therein, the parties informing the court as to whether this issue should be listed with the appeal itself or requires advance consideration, bearing in mind any impact on the time estimate.[3] It must be filed within 14 days from service of the appellant's notice where the UT granted permission, or otherwise 14 days from learning of the permission grant from the Court of Appeal,[4] and served on the appellant as soon as practicable, and in any event not later than seven days, after filing;[5] two additional copies must be provided for the court and one copy each for the appellant and any other respondents.[6] Application may be made for an extension of time if required, in the notice itself.[7] A skeleton argument must be provided to the court and to every other party within 14 days of filing.[8] Beyond the respondent, any person may apply permission to file evidence or make representations, so long as he makes a prompt application to do so.[9]

1   CPR, r 52.5(2); CPR PD 52C, para 8.
2   CPR PD 52C, para 11.
3   CPR, r 52.5(3).
4   CPR, r 52.5(4) and (5).
5   CPR, r 52.5(6).
6   CPR PD 52C, para 10.
7   CPR PD 52C, para 12.
8   CPR PD 52C, para 9.
9   CPR, r 52.12A.

NOTICE OF HEARING AND TIMETABLE

6.149   Parties will receive a letter notifying them of the window within which the appeal is likely to be heard: they should note the date of such letter as it will set in train a timetable for future actions.[1] Accordingly:

- seven days thereafter, the appellant must serve a proposed bundle index;[2]

- 14 days thereafter, the appeal questionnaire must be filed and served on every respondent[3] (who should indicate any disagreement with the contents within seven days);[4]

- 21 days thereafter, the appellant must serve on every respondent an appeal skeleton (without bundle cross references); also the respondent must confirm agreement with the proposed bundle contents and provide a revised index in the event of disagreement, the parties between them providing a supplemental bundle containing any non-agreed material;[5]

- 42 days thereafter, the respondent must lodge and serve his skeleton argument, presuming no respondent's notice has been provided.[6]

1   CPR PD 52C, paras 1 and 21.
2   CPR PD 52C, para 21, Timetable Part 1 'Listing window notification to lodging bundle'.
3   CPR PD 52C, para 21, Timetable Part 1 'Listing window notification to lodging bundle' and para 23.
4   CPR PD 52C, para 24.
5   CPR PD 52C, para 21, Timetable Part 1 'Listing window notification to lodging bundle' and para 27.
6   CPR PD 52C, para 21, Timetable Part 1 'Listing window notification to lodging bundle' and para 13.

6.150   Other material deadlines for filing and service are:

- respondent's notice – within 14 days of receipt of the appellant's notice where the UT granted permission, or within 14 days of the court's own permission grant, or notification that the permission application will be listed with the appeal to follow;[1]

- a skeleton argument from the respondent where a respondent's notice has been provided, 14 days after the latter's filing;[2]

- a time estimate from a respondent who dissents from the appellant's estimate, seven days after service of the appellant's appeal questionnaire.[3]

1   CPR PD 52C, para 21, Timetable Part 1 'Listing window notification to lodging bundle' and para 8.
2   CPR PD 52C, para 21, Timetable Part 1 'Listing window notification to lodging bundle' and para 9.
3   CPR PD 52C, para 21, Timetable Part 1 'Listing window notification to lodging bundle' and para 24.

6.151   Once the appeal is listed, the remaining timetable is calculated by reference to the hearing date:[1]

- no later than 42 days before, appeals bundles are to be lodged;

- no later than 14 days before, the appellant must lodge and serve any replacement skeleton argument;

- no later than seven days before, the respondent must lodge and serve any replacement skeleton argument;

- no later than seven days before, the authorities bundles must be lodged;

- no later than seven days before, any other materials must be lodged.

1   CPR PD 52C, para 21, Timetable Part 2 'Steps to be taken once hearing date fixed: lodging bundles, supplemental skeletons and bundles of authorities'.

THE AUTHORITIES BUNDLE

6.152   The relevant authorities should be filed by the appellant's advocate following consultation with any opposing advocate,[1] providing the most authoritative report of any authority as identified in the relevant Practice Direction, side-lined to show relevant passages.[2] Copies should be in portrait rather than landscape format, not reduced in size,[3] and should be confined to support of disputed propositions;[4] there should not be more than ten authorities unless the issues in the appeal justify more extensive citation.[5] The bundle should certify that these requirements have been given attention and complied with by the relevant advocates.[6]

1   CPR PD 52C, para 29(1).
2   CPR PD 52C, para 29(2).
3   CPR PD 52C, para 29(3).
4   CPR PD 52C, para 29(4)(a).
5   CPR PD 52C, para 29(4)(b).
6   CPR PD 52C, para 29(5).

THE HEARING

6.153   The appeal will be limited to a review of the decision of the lower court unless the court considers it necessary to hold a re-hearing;[1] the Court of Appeal may draw any inference of fact it considers justified on the evidence.[2] Oral evidence or evidence not relied upon below will not normally be received,[3] and permission will be required to rely on any matter not within the appeal notice.[4] An appeal will be allowed where the decision below was wrong or unjust because of a serious procedural or other irregularity in the proceedings.[5] The Court of Appeal will usually remit an appeal, error of law having been established, unless 'the appeal in question would in any event be bound to succeed, [or] it would be unjust in all the circumstances to remit.'[6]

1   CPR, r 52.11(1)(b).
2   CPR, r 52.11(4).
3   CPR, r 52.11(2).
4   CPR, r 52.11(5).
5   CPR, r 52.11(3)(b).
6   Davis LJ in *SS (Zimbabwe) v Secretary of State for the Home Department* [2013] EWCA Civ 237 at [48].

APPELLATE POWERS OF THE COURT OF APPEAL

6.154   Where the Court of Appeal finds that the making of the decision involved legal error, it may set aside the decision, and then remit the matter to the UT or FTT, or re-make the decision itself,[1] and it has a power to make factual findings if required:[2] however, in its appellate role it will as a general rule do so only if there are clear findings of fact by the tribunal which are undisputed and which as a matter of law admit of only one answer to the appeal.[3] When remitting an appeal it may order that the persons involved are different to those who previously heard the matter.[4] The UT, upon receiving the appeal back, may further remit the matter back to the FTT for determination consistent with the directions of the Court of Appeal, with directions that the matter be heard by persons other than the original judge(s) and with further directions of its own if required.[5] The court will take account of the expertise of the UT in considering whether it has made a material error of law.[6] In determining whether there is an error of law present, the court will focus on the law as it was to be applied at the time of the decision of the UT, not on the law as it has subsequently developed; however, in remaking the appeal it will apply the principles in force at the date of its own decision.[7] The court may entertain appeals on points of law not argued below ('If justice both requires a new point of law to be entertained and permits this to be done without unfairness, the court can and should entertain it unless forbidden to do so by statute'[8]), although it will be 'extremely reluctant to exercise its discretion in favour of doing so if this involves finding further facts'.[9]

1   TCEA 2007, s 14(1) and (2).
2   TCEA 2007, s 14(4).
3   Sullivan LJ in *KR (Nepal) v Secretary of State for the Home Department* [2010] EWCA Civ 1619 at [12]; *Hayat v Secretary of State for the Home Department* [2012] EWCA Civ 1054 at [30](e).
4   TCEA 2007, s 14(3).
5   TCEA 2007, s 14(5) and (6).
6   See **6.48** above.
7   Aikens LJ in *YM (Uganda) v Secretary of State for the Home Department* [2014] EWCA Civ 1292 at [36]–[39].
8   Sedley LJ in *Miskovic v Secretary of State for Work and Pensions* [2011] EWCA Civ 16 at [124], finding as did the other judges alongside him that there was no jurisdictional bar to a new ground under TCEA 2007.
9   *Miskovic* (above), Elias LJ at [69].

6.155   The court may refuse to hear argument on a point not included in a duly filed skeleton argument.[1] The court has all the powers of the tribunal below,[2] and may affirm, set aside or vary any order or judgment made or given, refer any claim or issue for determination, order a new trial or hearing, make orders for the payment of interest, or make a costs order,[3] in relation to the whole of, or part of, the matter before it.[4] The court may strike out the whole or part of an appeal notice, set aside permission to appeal in whole or in part, or impose or vary conditions upon which an appeal may be brought, but only where there is a compelling reason for doing so.[5] A party present at a hearing where permission was given may not subsequently apply for permission to be set aside or for conditions to be imposed.[6] It may well not be appropriate for a challenge to the lawfulness of Country Guidance that have now been superseded to proceed, when a more expedient process would be for the SSHD to withdraw the original decision and reconsider the matter.[7] The court might accept evidence from the well of the court, exceptionally and in the interests of justice, if this is appropriate.[8] Whilst normally the Court of Appeal will confine itself to the arguments before the court below,[9]

> 'justice is best served by a power in appellate courts or tribunals to entertain new points of law, but with a concomitant power not to do so if it would either be unfair to another party or would place the court itself in an untenable position.'

1   CPR PD 52C, para 31(3).
2   CPR, r 52.10(1).
3   CPR, r 52.10(2).
4   CPR, r 52.10(4).
5   CPR, r 52.9(2).
6   CPR, r 52.9(3).
7   Richards LJ refusing permission to appeal in *HS (Zimbabwe) v Secretary of State for the Home Department* [2009] EWCA Civ 308.
8   See for example *TN (Bangladesh) v Secretary of State for the Home Department* [2009] EWCA Civ 519 at [18].
9   Sedley LJ in *Miskovic v Secretary of State for Work and Pensions* [2011] EWCA Civ 16 at [112].

THE UT AS AN EXPERT TRIBUNAL

6.156   Whilst the UT can be presumed to have applied the law correctly unless the contrary is shown,[1] the higher courts owe it no deference on questions of statutory construction[2] and 'while the special role given by Parliament to an expert tribunal must be respected, so must the constitutional responsibility of the Court of Appeal for the correct application of the law';[3] there is no principle that the worse the apparent error is, the less ready an appellate court should be to find that it has occurred.[4] These principles do not apply when the UT examines decisions of the FTT.[5] Where the FTT and UT have differed as to the outcome of an appeal, the court will need to make up its own mind as to which of them was nearest the mark, albeit according the usual respect to the UT.[6]

1   Baroness Hale in *AH (Sudan) v Secretary of State for the Home Department* [2007] UKHL 49 at [30]; *MP v Secretary of State for the Home Department* [2014] EWCA Civ 829 at [19]; *D v Secretary of State for the Home Department* [2012] EWCA Civ 39 at [21]–[22]; Munby J in the Administrative Court in *R v Immigration Appeal Tribunal, ex parte Sarkisian* [2001] EWHC Admin 486, citing Lord Hoffmann in *Piglowska v Piglowski* [1999] 1 WLR 1360 at 1372G; Sir John Dyson SCJ in *MA (Somalia) v Secretary of State for the Home Department* [2010] UKSC 49 at [45]–[46].
2   Blake J in *Etame, R (on the application of) v Secretary of State for the Home Department* [2008] EWHC 1140 (Admin) at [35].

3   Carnwath LJ in *AA (Uganda) v Secretary of State for the Home Deparment* [2008] EWCA Civ 579 at [50].
4   Sedley LJ in *ECO Mumbai v NH (India)* [2007] EWCA Civ 1330 at [28]; Carnwath LJ in *AA (Uganda)* (above) at [42]–[46] and in *SK (Sierra Leone) v Secretary of State for the Home Department* [2008] EWCA Civ 853 at [17].
5   Carnwath LJ in *AP (Trinidad and Tobago) v Secretary of State for the Home Department* [2011] EWCA Civ 551 at [46].
6   Carnwath LJ in *AP (Trinidad and Tobago)* (above) at [25]–[26].

DISPOSAL OF THE APPEAL WITHOUT A HEARING

6.157   An appellant who does not wish to pursue an application or appeal may request the appeal court to dismiss the application or the appeal. If such a request is granted it will usually be subject to an order that the appellant pays the costs,[1] subject to obtaining a letter signed by the respondent to the contrary.[2] Where a settlement has been reached disposing of the application or appeal, the parties may make a joint request to the court for the application or appeal to be dismissed by consent.[3] Although normally the court will not make an order allowing an appeal unless satisfied that the decision of the lower court was wrong or unjust because of a serious procedural or other irregularity, it may set aside or vary the order of the lower court by consent and without determining the merits of the appeal if it is satisfied that there are good and sufficient reasons for so doing; a request by all parties setting out the relevant history of the proceedings and the matters relied on as justifying the order, accompanied by a draft order, may be made.[4] Where one of the parties is a child or protected party, any disposal of an application or the appeal requires the court's approval; a draft order signed by the parties' solicitors should be sent to the appeal court, together with an opinion from the advocate acting on behalf of the child or protected party and, in the case of a protected party, any relevant documents prepared for the Court of Protection.[5]

1   CPR PD 52A, para 6.1.
2   CPR PD 52A, para 6.2.
3   CPR PD 52A, para 6.3.
4   CPR PD 52A, para 6.4.
5   CPR PD 52A, para 6.5.

RECOVERING COSTS

6.158   The court may make an order that the recoverable costs of an appeal will be limited,[1] having regard to the means of both parties, all the circumstances of the case, and the need to facilitate access to justice,[2] though such an order may not be appropriate where the appeal raises an issue of principle or practice upon which substantial sums may turn.[3] An application must be made as soon as practicable and will be determined without a hearing unless the court orders otherwise.[4] When the Court of Appeal allows an appeal and remits the case to the UT based on the agreement of the parties as expressed in a consent order, it is implicitly accepting and acting upon an error of law which is the sole justification for its jurisdiction to do so, notwithstanding that the statement of reasons may indicate that the error of law is merely 'arguable' and that the SSHD consents to the order for 'purely pragmatic reasons', and so the respondent to the appeal will ordinarily be liable for costs absent rare features or complexities, whether or not the SSHD had encouraged or acquiesced in the particular errors motivating the remittal.[5] We deal with costs more generally at **8.127** below. The court's power to 'make an order that the recoverable costs of an appeal will be limited to the extent which the court specifies'[6] does not 'contemplate an order in favour of just one party, win or lose' (ie it rules out one-way costs shifting); both parties should give prompt consideration to whether they are able and willing to apply for an order so as to maintain a 'no costs' or 'low costs' regime upon appeal:[7]

> 'It would be helpful if the literature provided by HMCTS to appellants and respondents drew attention to the court's power under rule 52.9A and the need to make any application under that rule as soon as practicable.'[8]

1   CPR, r 52.9A(1).
2   CPR, r 52.9A(2).
3   CPR, r 52.9A(3).
4   CPR, r 52.9A(4).
5   Maurice Kay LJ in *AL (Albania) v Secretary of State for the Home Department* [2012] EWCA Civ 710 at [11] and [19]–[23].
6   CPR, r 52.9A(1).
7   Jackson LJ in *JE v Secretary of State for the Home Department* [2014] EWCA Civ 192 at [5]–[10].
8   Jackson LJ in *JE* (above) at [15].

PART 8 – APPEALS TO THE SUPREME COURT

6.159   An appeal lies to the Supreme Court from any order or judgment of the Court of Appeal in England and Wales in civil proceedings, and from any order or judgment of a court in Scotland if an appeal lay from that court to the House of Lords at or immediately before the commencement of the Constitutional Reform Act 2005, s 40.[1] The court has power to determine any question necessary for the purposes of doing justice in an appeal to it;[2] appeal lies with the permission of the Court of Appeal or the Supreme Court.[3] An application for permission to appeal must be filed within 28 days from the date of the order or decision of the court below.[4] Provided the Registrar and the other parties have been notified in writing, an application by an appellant for public funding or legal aid suspends the commencement of proceedings and the time limit is extended until 28 days after the determination of the application for public funding or legal aid (including any appeals against a refusal of funding).[5]

1   Constitutional Reform Act 2005. s 40(2) and (3).
2   Constitutional Reform Act 2005, s 40(5).
3   Constitutional Reform Act 2005, s 40(6).
4   Supreme Court Rules 2009, SI 2009/1603, r 11(1).
5   UKSC Practice Direction 8, para 8.12.3.

6.160   Judgments made from 13 April 2015 can be the subject of a 'leapfrog' appeal from the High Court to the Supreme Court where there is a point of law of general public importance in relation to a matter of national importance, or where the result of the proceedings is so significant that a hearing by the Supreme Court is justified, or where the judge is satisfied that the benefits of earlier consideration by the Supreme Court outweigh the benefits of consideration by the Court of Appeal.[1] There is a similar provision for leapfrogging from the UT to the Supreme Court on those same grounds, though one that has not yet been brought into effect. Such certificates may be made only following the application of a party. This power will be available to the tribunal regarding a point of law of general public importance which relates wholly or mainly to the construction of an enactment or statutory instrument, and has been fully argued in the proceedings and fully considered in the judgment of the UT, or a point of law in respect of which the UT is bound by a decision of the relevant appellate court or the Supreme Court in previous proceedings which fully considered the issue. The grant of such a certificate permits a party to make an application direct to the Supreme Court within one month for permission to appeal.[2]

1   Criminal Justice and Courts Act 2015, s 63.
2   Criminal Justice and Courts Act 2015, s 64.

Chapter 7

Appeals to the Special Immigration Appeals Commission

THE GENESIS OF THE SPECIAL IMMIGRATION APPEALS COMMISSION

7.1   In *Chahal v United Kingdom*,[1] the ECtHR in November 1996, as well as finding that deportation of the applicant to India would violate his Art 3 rights, held that the UK had violated his rights under ECHR, Arts 5(4) (right to challenge lawfulness of detention before a court) and 13 (right to effective domestic remedy), in relation to Art 3, as a result of the lack of full independent scrutiny of the decisions to deport him and detain him, notwithstanding the alleged 'national security' interests that were at issue. Mr Chahal was an Indian citizen who, after visiting the Punjab in 1984, where he was detained and tortured by the police, became a leading figure among British Sikhs supporting an independent Sikh homeland. In 1990 the SSHD decided to deport him in the interests of national security and the need to combat terrorism, and he was detained under immigration powers.[2] Mr Chahal's application for asylum was refused and, because the decision to deport him concerned national security, he had no right of appeal to an adjudicator.[3] Instead his case was examined by an advisory panel in 1991, who reported to the SSHD, but Mr Chahal was allowed no representation and was not told of the evidence against him. The advisory panel – the 'three wise men' – was chaired by a Court of Appeal judge and included a former President of the IAT. A deportation order was signed and Mr Chahal's application for judicial review failed as, in the absence of evidence of the risk posed to national security, the court was unable to assess whether the SSHD's decision to refuse asylum was irrational. So he applied to the ECtHR.[4] The court held, unanimously, that there had been violations of Art 5(4) owing to the refusal to allow Mr Chahal recourse to domestic appeal procedures, as it should be possible to find a method of protecting confidential information without denying access to the court system – the panel could not be considered as a 'court' within the meaning of Art 5(4); and, also unanimously, that there had been a breach of Art 13, under which Mr Chahal had the right to an independent examination of his claim of the risk of Art 3 violating ill treatment if deported to India. Similarly, in *Shingara*[5] the ECJ, in June 1997, expressed concerns about the 'three wise men' advisory panel procedure.

The government's response to the criticism of the international courts was SIACA 1997 setting up the SIAC to deal with immigration appeals in cases where national security interests are involved.

1   *Chahal v United Kingdom* (1996) 23 EHRR 413.
2   Contained in IA 1971, Sch 3, para 2: see *Asylum Law and Practice* (2nd edition, Bloomsbury Professional), Ch 13.
3   See IA 1971, s 15(1)(a) and (3) and see also AIAA 1993, s 8(3)(a) and Sch 2, para 6: see **2.1** and **2.4** above.
4   Via the then European Commission on Human Rights (see (1994) 18 EHRR CD193 for the Commission's admissibility decision and (1995) 20 EHRR CD19 for the Commission's substantive opinion), as to which see eg *Asylum Law and Practice* (above), para 11.5, fn 4.
5   *R v Secretary of State for the Home Department, ex parte Shingara* [1997] 3 CMLR 703.

THE SIAC

7.2   The SIAC was established on 3 August 1998 and is constituted by three members, appointed by the Lord Chancellor,[1] with one acting as Chairman.[2] At least one of the members must hold or have held high judicial office within the meaning of the Constitutional Reform Act 2005, Pt 3 (High Court/Court of Session level or above[3]), or is or has been a member of the Judicial Committee of the Privy Council, and another must be or have been a judge of the FTT or of the UT assigned to the Immigration and Asylum Chamber.[4] The third member is likely to have had experience in dealing with security matters.[5] On occasion it has been necessary for such members to be recused from sitting on cases where there is a risk that their personal knowledge of witnesses or of officials from a relevant country may give an appearance of bias – the basic test being that set out by Lord Hope in *Porter v McGill*:[6] 'The question is whether the fair-minded and informed observer, having considered the facts, would conclude that there was a real possibility that the Tribunal was biased'.[7] Like the UT, the SIAC is a superior court of record[8] and accordingly it has power to punish for contempt.[9] In *Cart* in the Divisional Court,[10] Laws LJ concluded that the SIAC is in principle amenable to judicial review for any excess of jurisdiction but explained how limited in practice this could ever be: a final determination of an appeal by SIAC is subject to appeal to the Court of Appeal (see below) and so, as judicial review is a discretionary remedy of last resort, it will not be deployed to assault SIAC's appealable determinations. Nor will it go to interlocutory decisions on the way to such a determination, 'at least without some gross and florid error'.[11] As regards bail, Laws LJ continued:

> 'the court will not allow judicial review to be used as a surrogate means of appeal where statute has not provided for any appeal at all. In a sensitive area where the tribunal is called on to make fine judgments on issues touching national security, I would anticipate that attempts to condemn the refusal (or grant) of bail as violating the *Wednesbury* principle will be doomed to failure. A sharp-edged error of law will have to be shown.'[12]

1   SIACA 1997, s 1 and Sch 1, paras 1 and 5 (in force from 3 August 1998: Special Immigration Appeals Commission Act 1997 (Commencement No 2) Order 1998, SI 1998/1892, art 2).

2   SIACA 1997, s 1 and Sch 1, para 2.

3   See the Constitutional Reform Act 2005, s 60(2)(a).

4   SIACA 1997, Sch 1, para 5 (as amended by the Constitutional Reform Act 2005, s 145 and Sch 17, from 1 October 2009: Constitutional Reform Act 2005 (Commencement No 11) Order 2009, SI 2009/1604; and by A&I(TC)A 2004, s 26(7), Sch 2, from 4 April 2005: Asylum and Immigration (Treatment of Claimants, etc) Act 2004 (Commencement No 5 and Transitional Provisions) Order 2005, SI 2005/565; and from 15 February 2010 by the Transfer of Functions of the Asylum and Immigration Tribunal Order 2010, SI 2010/21, arts 1 and 5(1), Sch 1, paras 14 and 16).

5   See Hansard HC, 6th Series, Vol 301, col 1038, 26 November 1997. See also *Rehman v Secretary of State for the Home Department* [1999] INLR 517 at 530D/E per the SIAC.

6   *Porter v McGill* [2001] UKHL 67 at [103].

7   See *J1 v Secretary of State for the Home Department (deportation – recusal application – granted)* [2014] UKSIAC 98/2010 (25 February 2014) and *J1 v Secretary of State for the Home Department (deportation – recusal application – granted)* [2014] UKSIAC 98/2010 (28 February 2014) regarding two separate 'third members'. See also *Ekaterina Zatuliveter v Secretary of State for the Home Department (deportation – the hearing of an application by the appellant – refused)* [2011] UKSIAC 103/2010 (29 September 2011).

8   SIACA 1997, s 1(3) (as inserted by the Anti-terrorism, Crime and Security Act 2001, ss 35 and 127(2) from 14 December 2007).

9   See eg per Laws LJ in *Cart v Upper Tribunal; R (C) and (U) v Special Immigration Appeals Commission* [2009] EWHC 3052 (Admin) at [75]. For an example of the SIAC using its power to imprison an appellant for contempt, owing to his refusal to identify himself or to cooperate with establishing his identity, see *B (Algeria) v Secretary of State for the Home Department* [2011] EWCA Civ 828; aff'd [2013] UKSC 4 (see **7.41** below).

10 *Cart* (above), per Laws LJ at [72]–[73] and [82]–[86].

11 *Cart* (above) at [85].

12 *Cart* (above) at [85]. In the event, the claimants C and U were successful in their challenges, on ECHR, Art 5(4) grounds, to SIAC's refusals of bail and so the *Cart* case proceeded to the Court of Appeal ([2010] EWCA Civ 859) and then to the Supreme Court ([2011] UKSC 28) without their or SIAC's further involvement.

7.3   However, in *R (SSHD)*[1] the Divisional Court permitted the SSHD to proceed with judicial reviews of the SIAC's preliminary decisions in respect to the extent to which the SSHD had to provide disclosure of closed material to special advocates appointed to represent the interests of the appellants (see **7.25** and **7.28–7.30** below regarding special advocates and closed material) in review cases (see **7.10** below) because otherwise there could be no effective appeal in relation to the issue of principle involved which would affect all such review cases.

1   *R (Secretary of State for the Home Department) v Special Immigration Appeals Commission* [2015] EWHC 681 (Admin).

RIGHTS OF APPEAL IN IMMIGRATION AND ASYLUM CASES TO THE SIAC UNDER SIACA 1997

7.4   Under NIAA 2002, s 97, the SSHD may prevent a person from appealing against a decision, on any grounds, to the FTT under NIAA 2002, s 82(1) (or prior to 6 April 2015 under saved s 83(2) or 83A(2)) by certifying that the decision was taken by himself or in accordance with his directions on the grounds that the person's exclusion or removal from the UK is in the interests of national security or in the interests of the relationship between the UK and another country.[1] Furthermore, the SSHD can also preclude an appeal to the FTT, under NIAA 2002, s 82(1) (or prior to 6 April 2015 under saved s 83(2) or 83A(2)) by certifying that the decision is or was taken wholly or partly in reliance on information which in his opinion should not be made public in the interests of national security, in the interests of the relationship between the UK and another country or otherwise in the public interest.[2] NIAA 2002, s 99 specifically provides that where a certificate is issued under s 97 in respect of a pending appeal, the appeal shall lapse.[3] In all cases, the reference to the SSHD certifying is to the SSHD acting in person.[4] For 'interests of national security' and 'the relationship between the UK and another country', see *Rehman*[5] and *Lord Carlile's case*[6] (see further below).

1   NIAA 2002, s 97(1) and (2) (as amended by IANA 2006, Sch 1 from 31 August 2006: Immigration, Asylum and Nationality Act 2006 (Commencement No 2) Order 2006, SI 2006/2226; and most recently by IA 2014, Sch 9(4) from 20 October 2014 to delete references to ss 83(2) and 83A(2): see **7.5**, fnn 1 and 2 below). Note that such a certificate prevents an appeal being 'brought or continued'.
2   NIAA 2002, s 97(3) (as amended as above). Again, such a certificate prevents an appeal being 'brought or continued' (see fn 1 above).
3   See above regarding a s 97 certificate preventing an appeal being 'brought or continued'.
4   NIAA 2002, s 97(4).
5   *Rehman v Secretary of State for the Home Department* [2001] UKHL 47.
6   *R (Lord Carlile of Berriew) v Secretary of State for the Home Department* [2014] UKSC 60.

SIAC'S JURISDICTION UNDER SIACA 1997, S 2

7.5   The SIAC's appellate jurisdiction, under SIACA 1997, s 2[1] is to hear and determine appeals under NIAA 2002, s 82(1), or under saved NIAA 2002, s 83(2) or 83A(2),[2] in those cases where a right of appeal to the FTT is precluded by the SSHD having issued a certificate under NIAA 2002, s 97 on national security related grounds,[3] or where a pending appeal to the FTT under NIAA 2002, s 82(1), 83(2) or 83A(2) lapses under NIAA 2002, s 99 by virtue of a certificate under NIAA 2002, s 97.[4] In the latter case – where a person has already given notice of appeal to the FTT but that appeal lapses owing to a certificate being issued under NIAA 2002, s 97 – the person must again give notice of appeal, this time to the SIAC and within the stipulated time limit from the date on which he is served with notice that his appeal to the FTT has lapsed[5] (see below as regards procedure). In either scenario, a person may bring an appeal to the SIAC against an immigration decision while he is in the UK only if he would be able to bring or continue the appeal while he was in the UK if it were an appeal to the FTT under saved NIAA 2002, s 82(1).[6] The following provisions of IA 1971 and NIAA 2002, with any necessary modifications, apply to an appeal to the SIAC against an immigration decision as they apply in relation to an appeal under saved NIAA 2002, s 82 to the FTT:[7]

(a) IA 1971, ss 3C and 3D (continuation of leave pending appeal);

(b) NIAA, s 78 (no removal while appeal pending);

(c) NIAA, s 79 (deportation order: appeal);

(ca) NIAA, s 78A (restriction on removal of children and their parents);

(d) NIAA 2002, s 82(3) (variation or revocation of leave to enter or remain: appeal) (with transitional effect only[8]);

(e) NIAA 2002, s 84 (grounds of appeal);

(f) NIAA 2002, s 85 (matters to be considered);

(g) NIAA 2002, s 86 (determination of appeal);

(h) NIAA 2002, s 87 (successful appeal: direction);

(i) NIAA 2002, s 96 (earlier right of appeal);

(j) NIAA 2002, s 104 (pending appeal);

(k) NIAA 2002, s 105 (notice of immigration decision);[9] and

(l) NIAA 2002, s 110 (grants).

1   SIACA 1997, s 2 (as substituted by NIAA 2002, s 114(3) and Sch 7, para 20, from 1 April 2003: Nationality, Immigration and Asylum Act 2002 (Commencement No 4) Order 2003, SI 2003/754, art 2(1) and Sch 1; and as amended by IANA 2006, s 14, Sch 1, para 14, from 31 August 2006: Immigration, Asylum and Nationality Act 2006 (Commencement No 2) Order 2006, SI 2006/2226; and as to be further amended by IA 2014, Sch 9(4), para 26(2) so as to delete the references to NIAA 2002, s 83(2) or 83A(2): see fn 2 below). Note that provisions in IAA 1999, s 70 preventing appeals to adjudicators for national security reasons (see **2.19** above) continued to have effect after the commencement of NIAA 2002 (SI 2003/754, art 3(1), (2) and 4(1)(b)(iv) and Sch 2, para 6(4)) and in such cases the appeal would be under SIACA 1997, s 2 (as unamended by NIAA 2002) and remained pending on and after 1 April 2003 in accordance with SIACA 1997, s 7A (as unamended by NIAA 2002: SI 2003/754, art 3(1), (2) and 4(1)(b)(iii) and Sch 2, para 5).

2   NIAA 2002, ss 83 and 83A are 'saved provisions' as to which see Chapter 3. The amending provisions in IA 2014, Sch 9(4), para 26(2) (see fn 1 above) will, when appointed, delete the references in SIACA 1997, s 2 to NIAA 2002, ss 83 and 83A in keeping with the deletion of these sections in NIAA 2002, Pt 5 as amended by IA 2014 (see Chapter 4). Note however that as of 6 April 2015, IA 2014, Sch 9(4), para 26(2) has not yet been brought into force: see the Immigration Act 2014 (Commencement No 3, Transitional and Saving Provisions) Order 2014, SI 2014/2771, art 2(e) which explicitly excludes para 26(2), (3) and (5) from the provisions of IA 2014, Sch 9, Pt 4 otherwise brought into force on 20 October 2014.

3   SIACA 1997, s 2(1)(a) (as substituted and amended as per fnn 1 and 2 above).

4   SIACA 1997, s 2(1)(b) (as substituted and amended as per fnn 1 and 2 above).

5   See the Special Immigration Appeals Commission (Procedure) Rules 2003, SI 2003/1034, rr 7 and 8(3) and (4).

6   SIACA 1997, s 2(5) (as substituted as per fn 1 above). 'Immigration decision' has the same meaning given by saved NIAA 2002, s 82(2) (see Chapter 3): SIACA 1997, s 2(6) (sub-ss (5) and (6) as to be amended and repealed respectively by IA 2014, Sch 9(4), para 26(2), so

as to omit references to 'immigration decision', as per fnn 1 and 2 above). For immigration decisions against which an appeal will lie in non-asylum cases whilst the appellant can remain in the UK, see saved NIAA 2002, s 92(2). Note that subject to clearly unfounded certification an appeal will lie against an immigration decision whilst the appellant remains in the UK if the appellant has made an asylum claim or a human rights claim while in the UK: saved NIAA 2002, s 92(4)(a) (see Chapter 3).

7   SIACA 1997, s 2(2) (as substituted and amended as per fn 1 above). Note that the provisions at (d), (h) and (l) in the list are saved provisions of NIAA 2002 that have otherwise been repealed, and the references to them in SIACA 1997, s 2(2) are set to be omitted by IA 2014, Sch 9(4), para 26 (see fnn 1 and 2 above). Other provisions in the list are either 'amended' or saved provisions of NIAA 2002 and so which applies will depend on whether or not the appellant is subject to the 'relevant' or to the saved provisions in accordance with the Immigration Act 2014 (Commencement No 3, Transitional and Saving Provisions) Order 2014, SI 2014/2771. The provision at (ca) in the list is itself added by IA 2014, Sch 9(1), para 2.

8   NIAA 2002, s 82(3) ceased to have effect from 31 August 2006 except in relation to decisions made before that date: IANA 2006, s 11 and SI 2006/2226.

9   See the Immigration (Notices) Regulations 2003, SI 2003/658.

7.6   Similarly, the following provisions of NIAA 2002, with any necessary modifications, apply to an appeal on asylum grounds only to the SIAC as they apply in relation to an appeal under saved NIAA 2002, s 83(2) or 83A(2) to the FTT:[1]

(a)   NIAA 2002, s 85(4) (matters to be considered);[2]

(b)   NIAA 2002, s 86 (determination of appeal);

(c)   NIAA 2002, s 87 (successful appeal: direction); and

(d)   NIAA 2002, s 110 (grants).

It is specifically provided for in SIACA 1997, s 2(4) that an appeal to the SIAC against the rejection of a claim for asylum shall be treated as abandoned if the appellant leaves the UK.[3]

1   SIACA 1997, s 2(3) (as substituted and amended as per **7.5**, fn 1 above). This provision is set to be repealed by IA 2014, Sch 9(4), para 26(2) (see **7.5**, fnn 1 and 2 above).

2   Note that the saved provisions of sub-ss (1)–(3) and (5) of s 85 are irrelevant to appeals under ss 83 and 83A.

3   SIACA 1997, s 2(4) (as substituted as per **7.5**, fn 1 above and as set to be repealed by IA 2014, Sch 9(4), para 26: see **7.5**, fn 2 above). Note that, by contrast, appeals on asylum grounds to the FTT under saved NIAA 2002, ss 83 or 83A are not treated as abandoned if the appellant leaves the UK (because saved NIAA 2002, s 104(4) only applies to appeals under saved s 82(1)).

APPEALS TO THE SIAC AGAINST DEPORTATION DECISIONS

7.7   In particular, where the SSHD certifies under NIAA 2002, s 97A(1) that a decision to make a deportation order in respect of a person was taken on the grounds that his removal from the UK would be in the interests of national security,[1] or where the SSHD certifies, under NIAA 2002, s 97A(1A), in the case of a person subject to 'automatic deportation' under UKBA 2007, s 32(5), that the person's removal from the UK would be in the interests of national security,[2] then no right of appeal will lie to the FTT (because the SSHD shall be taken to have certified the decision to make the deportation order under s 97[3]) and the 'normal' provision as to whether a suspensive right of appeal lies to the SIAC, in SIACA 1997, s 2(5) (see **7.5**, fn 6 above), does not apply.[4] Rather the following provisions apply:[5]

- The person, while in the UK may not bring or continue an appeal under SIACA 1997, s 2 against the decision to make the deportation order, or against any refusal to revoke the deportation order, unless he has made a human rights claim while in the UK: NIAA 2002, s 97A(2A).

- However sub-s (2A) does not allow the person while in the UK to bring or continue an appeal if the SSHD certifies that removal of the person to the country or territory to which the person is proposed to be removed, and despite the appeals process not having been begun or not having been exhausted, would not be unlawful under HRA 1998, s 6:[6] NIAA 2002, s 97A(2B).

- The grounds upon which a certificate may be given under sub-s (2B) include (in particular) that the person would not, before the appeals process is exhausted, face a real risk of serious irreversible harm (as to which, see **4.28** above) if removed to the country or territory to which the person is proposed to be removed; and or that the whole or part of any human rights claim made by the person is clearly unfounded: NIAA 2002, s 97A(2C).

- However, if a certificate in respect of a person is given under sub-s (2B), the person may apply to the SIAC to set aside the certificate: NIAA 2002, s 97A(2F).

- If a person makes an application under sub-s (2F) then the SIAC, in determining whether the certificate should be set aside, must apply the principles that would be applied in judicial review proceedings: NIAA 2002, s 97A(2G), meaning that it will not apply a merits review, as it would on a statutory appeal, but the more limited judicial review as explained in Chapter 8.

- The SIAC's determination of a review under sub-s (2F) is final: NIAA 2002, s 97A(2H), meaning that no appeal lies under SIACA 1997, s 7 to the Court of Appeal (or other appeal court: see **7.60** below). On its face this provision would also preclude a judicial review challenge, in the High Court, on *Cart* principles.[7]

- The SIAC may direct that a person who has made and not withdrawn an application under sub-s (2F) is not to be removed from the UK at a time when the review has not been finally determined by the Commission:

NIAA 2002, s 97A(2J). To this extent the person has a suspensive remedy against deportation on national security grounds.

1   NIAA 2002, s 97A inserted by the IANA 2006, s 7(1), from 31 August 2006: Immigration, Asylum and Nationality Act 2006 (Commencement No 2) Order 2006, SI 2006/2226 and most recently amended by IA 2014, Sch 9(4), para 43 from 20 October 2014 subject to savings and transitional provisions as specified in the Immigration Act 2014 (Commencement No 3, Transitional and Saving Provisions) Order 2014, SI 2014/2771, art 9. Note that where the SSHD so certifies in an asylum case he is relying on Art 33(2) of the Refugee Convention which excludes from the benefit of non-refoulement 'a refugee whom there are reasonable grounds for regarding as a danger to the security of the country in which he is ... .' See *Asylum Law and Practice* (2nd edition, Bloomsbury Professional), para 9.9.
2   NIAA 2002, s 97A(1A) inserted by the Crime and Courts Act 2013, s 54(2) and the Crime and Courts Act 2013 (Commencement No 1 and Transitional and Saving Provision) Order 2013, SI 2013/1042 from 25 June 2013.
3   NIAA 2002, s 97A(2)(b). For s 97, see **7.4** above.
4   NIAA 2002, s 97A(2)(c). Furthermore, NIAA 2002, s 79 – which prevents a deportation order being made whist an appeal against a decision to deport could be brought or is pending – does not apply: NIAA 2002, s 97A(2)(a).
5   These are the provisions of NIAA 2002, s 97A that are in effect from 6 April 2015, with sub-ss (2D), (2E) and (3) all repealed by IA 2014, Sch 9(4), para 43(b) (see fn 1 above). NIAA 2002, s 97A(3) provided for a discrete right of appeal to the SIAC against a certificate issued by the SSHD under s 97A(2D) which, in turn, provided that NIAA 2002, s 97A(2A) (see text above) does not allow the person while in the UK to bring an appeal on a non-human-rights ground, or to continue an appeal so far as brought on non-human-rights grounds, if the SSHD certifies that removal of the person to the country or territory to which the person is proposed to be removed, and despite the appeals process, so far as relating to appeal on non-human-rights grounds, not having been begun or not having been exhausted, would not breach the UK's obligations under the ECHR. NIAA 2002, s 97A(2E) explained that 'non-human-rights ground' means any ground other than the ground that removal of the person from the UK in consequence of the decision to make the deportation order would be unlawful under HRA 1998, s 6 as being incompatible with a person's Convention rights.
6   Amendment by IA 2014, Sch 9(4), para 43(a) changed this wording from previously stating that removal '... would not breach the UK's obligations under the Human Rights Convention'.
7   See *Cart v Upper Tribunal; R (C) and (U) v Special Immigration Appeals Commission* [2009] EWHC 3052 (Admin); [2010] EWCA Civ 859; [2011] UKSC 28; and see **7.2** above.

7.8   Further provision is made in NIAA 2002, s 97A to the effect that provisions in SIACA 2007, ss 5 and 6 (as to which see below) apply to reviews under sub-s (2F) as they apply to appeals under SIACA 1997, ss 2 and 2B[1] (NIAA 2002, s 97A(2K)) and that any exercise of power to make rules under SIACA 2007, s 5 in relation to reviews under sub-s (2F) is to be with a view to securing that proceedings on such reviews are handled expeditiously (NIAA 2002, s 97A(2L)). Finally it is provided that the SSHD may repeal s 97A by order (NIAA 2002, s 97A(4)). See further **7.10** below regarding SIACA 1997, s 2E and SIAC's review of 'certain deportation decisions'. There appear to be no published decisions of SIAC, so far, deciding applications made under NIAA 2002, s 97A(2F) against certificates made under s 97A(2B).

1   SIACA 2007, s 2B (as inserted by NIAA 2002, s 4(2) from 1 April 2003: Nationality, Immigration and Asylum Act 2002 (Commencement No 4) Order 2003, SI 2003/754, with transitional limitations relating to pending appeals) provides that a person may appeal to the SIAC against a decision to make an order under the British Nationality Act 1981, s 40

(deprivation of citizenship) if he is not entitled to appeal to the FTT under s 40A(1) of that Act because of a certificate under s 40A(2) (the SSHD certifies that the decision was taken wholly or partly in reliance on information which in his opinion should not be made public: (a) in the interests of national security, (b) in the interests of the relationship between the UK and another country, or (c) otherwise in the public interest).

RIGHTS OF APPEAL TO THE SIAC AGAINST EEA DECISIONS

7.9 Under EEA Regs 2006, reg 28 an appeal lies to the SIAC in circumstances that 'mirror' those in NIAA 2002, ss 97 and 99 and SIACA 1997, s 2 (see above). Accordingly an appeal lies to the SIAC[1] where the SSHD certifies that the EEA decision[2] was taken by himself or in accordance with his directions, identifying the person to whom the decision relates, on the grounds that the person's exclusion or removal from the UK is in the interests of national security or in the interests of the relationship between the UK and another country.[3] Similarly so where the SSHD certifies that the EEA decision was taken wholly or partly in reliance on information which in his opinion should not be made public in the interests of national security, in the interests of the relationship between the UK and another country or otherwise in the public interest.[4] In all cases, the reference to the SSHD certifying is to the SSHD acting in person.[5] Where such a certificate is issued in respect of a pending appeal to the FTT or UT, the appeal shall lapse[6] and an appeal lies instead to the SIAC.[7] The SIACA 1997 applies to appeals under the EAA Regs as it applies to appeals against immigration decisions to which SIACA 1997, s 2(2) applies (see above).[8] Under EEA Regs 2006, reg 28A,[9] NIAA 2002, s 97A (see above) applies to an appeal against an EEA decision, with appropriate modifications, where the SSHD has certified under reg 28 that the EEA decision was taken in the interests of national security;[10] and where s 97A so applies it has effect as if the references in that section to a deportation order were to an EEA decision. The effect of the modifications[11] is such that the provisions of NIAA 2002, s 97A can apply to any EEA decision (rather than just to deportation decisions).

1   EEA Regs 2006, reg 28(1).
2   For 'EEA decisions' see **1.12** above.
3   EEA Regs 2006, reg 28(2) and (3).
4   EEA Regs 2006, reg 28(4).
5   EEA Regs 2006, reg 28(5).
6   EEA Regs 2006, reg 28(6).
7   EEA Regs 2006, reg 28(7).
8   EEA Regs 2006, reg 28(8). But para (i) of SIACA 1997, s 2(2) – applying NIAA 2002, s 96 (earlier right of appeal) – does not apply to EEA appeals to the SIAC: reg 28(8). Note that reg 28(8) still refers to appeals against an immigration decision.
9   EEA Regs 2006, reg 28A was inserted by Immigration (European Economic Area) (Amendment) (No 2) Regulations 2013, SI 2013/3032, Sch 1, para 24 from 1 January 2014.
10   EEA Regs 2006, reg 28A(1).
11   In EEA Regs 2006, reg 28A(2).

JUDICIAL REVIEW JURISDICTION OF THE SIAC

7.10   Under SIACA 1997, ss 2C, 2D and 2E, SIAC has a judicial review jurisdiction in respect to certain decisions as follows:

- SIACA 1997, s 2C (as added by the Justice and Security Act 2013, s 15 from 25 June 2013[1]): where the SSHD makes any direction about the exclusion of a non-EEA national from the UK, which is–

    (a)   made by the SSHD wholly or partly on the ground that such exclusion is conducive to the public good,

    (b)   is not subject to a right of appeal,[2] and

    (c)   is certified by the SSHD as a direction that was made wholly or partly in reliance on information which, in the opinion of the SSHD, should not be made public in the interests of national security, in the interests of the relationship between the UK and another country, or otherwise in the public interest,[3]

    the non-EEA national to whom the exclusion direction relates may apply to the SIAC to set aside the direction.[4] In determining whether the direction should be set aside, the SIAC must apply the principles which would be applied in judicial review proceedings[5] and if the Commission decides that the direction should be set aside, it may make any such order, or give any such relief, as may be made or given in judicial review proceedings.[6]

- SIACA 1997, s 2D (as added by the Justice and Security Act 2013, s 15 from 25 June 2013) has similar effect in respect to certain naturalisation and citizenship decisions.[7]

- SIACA 1997, s 2E (as added by IA 2014, s 18 from 6 April 2015[8]): where a relevant deportation decision has been certified under NIAA 2002, ss 97 or 97A(1)[9] (see **7.4–7.8** above), the person to whom the decision relates may apply to the SIAC to set aside the decision.[10] In determining whether the decision should be set aside, the SIAC must apply the principles which would be applied in judicial review proceedings[11] and if the Commission decides that the decision should be set aside, it may make any such order, or give any such relief, as may be made or given in judicial review proceedings.[12] A 'relevant deportation decision' means a decision of the SSHD about the deportation of a person from the UK, if and to the extent that–

    (a)   the decision is not subject to a right of appeal, or

    (b)   the decision (being subject to a right of appeal) gives rise to issues which may not be raised on such an appeal.[13]

---

1   Subject to transitional and savings provisions specified *inter alia* in the Justice and Security Act 2013 (Commencement, Transitional and Saving Provisions) Order 2013, SI 2013/1482,

art 4 which purports to provide that where the SSHD made any direction or decision of a kind falling within SIACA 1997, s 2C, before 25 June 2013, the SSHD may certify under s 2C(1)(c) on or after 25 June 2013, any such direction or decision with the effect that the certificate terminates any judicial review proceedings, or proceedings on appeal from such proceedings, which relate to the direction or decision to which the certificate relates, whether the proceedings began before, on or after 25 June 2013. See however *R (Ignaoua) v Secretary of State for the Home Department* [2013] EWCA Civ 1498 and see **7.12** below.

2   An exclusion direction was not an 'immigration decision' under saved NIAA 2002, s 82(2) and so no right of appeal would arise under saved s 82(1). Nor would a right of appeal arise against such an exclusion direction under 'new' (as amended by IA 2014, s 15) NIAA 2002, s 82(1). Accordingly the remedy for the non-EEA national would have to be by way of judicial review, normally – without the certification under SIACA 1997, s 2C(1)(c) – in the Administrative Court or in the UT.

3   SIACA 1997, s 2C(1). A 'non-EEA national' means any person who is not a national of an EEA state and references to the SSHD are to the SSHD acting in person: s 2C(5).

4   SIACA 1997, s 2C(2).

5   SIACA 1997, s 2C(3).

6   SIACA 1997, s 2C(4).

7   SI 2013/1482, art 4 similarly purports (see fn 1 above) to enable the SSHD to certify such decisions that he made prior to 25 June 2013 so as to put a stop to on-going judicial review proceedings in the High Court or Court of Appeal. See also *R (AHK) v Secretary of State for the Home Department* [2014] EWCA Civ 151.

8   By the Immigration Act 2014 (Commencement No 4, Transitional and Saving Provisions and Amendment) Order 2015, SI 2015/371, art 4(a).

9   SIACA 1997, s 2E(1).

10   SIACA 1997, s 2E(2).

11   SIACA 1997, s 2E(3).

12   SIACA 1997, s 2E(4).

13   SIACA 1997, s 2E(5).

7.11   See further **7.12** below regarding s 2C. As regards s 2E, it has the effect of replacing the rights of appeal, with merits review, under SIACA 1997, s 2 and NIAA 2002, s 97A(3) (pre-repeal: see **7.7**, fn 5 above) in national security deportation cases with a more limited judicial review jurisdiction on an application to the SIAC in such cases.[1]

1   See *R (Secretary of State for the Home Department) v Special Immigration Appeals Commission* [2015] EWHC 681 (Admin) concerning the consequences of the more limited jurisdiction on review, rather than on appeal, in respect to the duties of disclosure on the SSHD.

PRACTICAL APPLICATION OF SIAC JUDICIAL REVIEW JURISDICTION

7.12   The additions of ss 2C and 2D were brought by the Justice and Security Act 2013, s 15 in order that the SIAC, and its procedures, could be used in judicial review cases relating to exclusion, and certain nationality matters, where the SSHD is seeking to rely on material that he does not wish to be made public (as above).[1] As noted above (see **7.10**, fn 1) the commencement order for the 2013 Act, s 15 purported to provide a power for the SSHD to, in effect, put a stop to *on-going* judicial review proceedings, whether in the

High Court or on appeal, when he issues a certificate under SIACA 1997, s 2C or 2D following commencement on 25 June 2013. In *Ignaoua*,[2] however – where the SSHD had issued, on 16 July 2013, a certificate under SIACA 1997, s 2C(1)(c) in an exclusion case that was already pending on a judicial review challenge in the High Court – the Court of Appeal held that the empowering provisions in the 2013 Act were insufficiently specific and express to allow for a statutory provision to empower the SSHD, who was the defendant to judicial review proceedings, to terminate those proceedings automatically and without the intervention of the court, whatever stage they had reached, and that accordingly the relevant provision in art 4(3) of the commencement order (see **7.10**, fn 1 above) was *ultra vires* the 2013 Act and so had no effect. Nonetheless, when *Ignaoua* was remitted to the Administrative Court, for reconsideration alongside two nationality cases effected by s 2D (above), the SSHD successfully applied for a stay of those judicial review proceedings for the claimants to pursue their remedies under ss 2C and 2D in the SIAC.[3] The court considered that the balance of advantage, in fairness and in the effective administration of justice, lay in staying the proceedings:

- First, a specific statutory provision had been made enabling this type of case to go to the SIAC, rather than to stay in the Administrative Court, and the subject-matter was very much within the SIAC's remit.

- Secondly, the expectation of the Court of Appeal[4] pointed to the suitability of the SIAC route as an alternative remedy and hence to the application of the principle that judicial review in the Administrative Court (always a discretionary remedy) should not be pursued instead.

- Thirdly, there were advantages to the SIAC route in the SIAC's experience and expertise in establishing whether material should be protected or not, and in handling the material if it should.

- Fourthly, it was difficult to see what disadvantages there were to the SIAC dealing with the claims. They would continue to be presided over by a High Court judge. Sections 2C and 2D made it clear that judicial review principles would apply. There was no reason to suppose that cases would proceed more quickly in the Administrative Court than in the SIAC, or that a transfer of existing cases would put them back in a SIAC queue. Although the claimants had asserted that they should be allowed to invoke the common law procedure of public interest immunity before in effect having their cases transferred, there was no value in that: what was important was that the SSHD had to justify withholding material from the claimant on the basis of the asserted harm which its disclosure would cause.

---

1   For problems that arise on judicial reviews in the Administrative Court in cases where the SSHD seeks to keep material relied upon 'secret' from the claimant and the public by way of making public interest immunity certificates, see eg the line of cases in *R (AHK)/MH v Secretary of State for the Home Department* [2009] EWCA Civ 287; [2012] EWHC 1117 (Admin); [2013] EWHC 1426 (Admin); [2014] EWCA Civ 151. See also in this broad

context *R (Malik) v Manchester Crown Court* [2008] EWHC 1362 (Admin). See also, as relevant to the on-going proceedings in the SIAC in respect to both *AHK* and *R (Ignaoua) v Secretary of State for the Home Department* [2013] EWCA Civ 1498, *R (Secretary of State for the Home Department) v Special Immigration Appeals Commission* [2015] EWHC 681 (Admin).

2   *Ignaoua* (above).
3   *R (Ignaoua) v Secretary of State for the Home Department* [2014] EWHC 1382 (Admin). See also *R (AHK) v Secretary of State for the Home Department* [2014] EWCA Civ 151.
4   In *Ignaoua* (above) and even more so in *AHK* (fn 3 above).

PROCEDURE BEFORE THE SIAC

7.13   Procedure before the SIAC is governed principally by provisions within the SIACA 1997 and by the Special Immigration Appeals Commission (Procedure) Rules 2003[1] ('the 2003 Rules') as provided for by SIACA 1997, ss 5 and 8 (and the Anti-terrorism, Crime and Security Act 2001, ss 24(3) and 27(5)[2]). SIACA 1997, s 5 provides *inter alia* that Rules made under it:

- shall provide that an appellant has the right to be legally represented in any proceedings before the SIAC on an appeal under s 2 or 2B, subject to any power conferred on the Commission by such rules;[3]

- may do anything which may be done by Tribunal Procedure Rules;[4]

- may make provision enabling proceedings before the SIAC to take place without the appellant being given full particulars of the reasons for the decision which is the subject of the appeal;[5]

- may make provision enabling the SIAC to hold proceedings in the absence of any person, including the appellant and any legal representative appointed by him;[6]

- may make provision about the functions in proceedings before the SIAC of persons appointed under s 6 (see below regarding 'special advocates');[7] and

- may make provision enabling the SIAC to give the appellant a summary of any evidence taken in his absence.[8]

1   SI 2003/1034, commenced 1 April 2003. By r 55 the previous 1998 Rules (the Special Immigration Appeals Commission (Procedure) Rules 1998, SI 1998/1881) were revoked with transitional provisions provided for by r 56. The 2003 Rules have been amended by SIAC (Procedure) (Amendment) Rules in 2007 (the Special Immigration Appeals Commission (Procedure) (Amendment) Rules 2007, SI 2007/1285 and the Special Immigration Appeals Commission (Procedure) (Amendment No 2) Rules 2007, SI 2007/3370) and 2013 (the Special Immigration Appeals Commission (Procedure) (Amendment) Rules 2013, SI 2013/2995) and most recently from 12 April 2015 by the Special Immigration Appeals Commission (Procedure) (Amendment) Rules 2015, SI 2015/867.
2   Note that both ss 24 and 27 of the 2001 Act have subsequently been repealed.
3   SIACA 1997, s 5(2).
4   SIACA 1997, s 5(2A) as added by NIAA 2002, Sch 7, para 23(b).
5   SIACA 1997, s 5(3)(a).

6   SIACA 1997, s 5(3)(b).
7   SIACA 1997, s 5(3)(c).
8   SIACA 1997, s 5(3)(d).

7.14   It is also required that, in making rules under s 5 the Lord Chancellor shall have regard, in particular, to:

(a)   the need to secure that decisions which are the subject of appeals are properly reviewed, and

(b)   the need to secure that information is not disclosed contrary to the public interest.[1]

1   SIACA 1997, s 5(6).

7.15   SIACA 1997, s 6A[1] provides that ss 5 and 6 (as to s 6, see **7.25** below) apply in relation to reviews under s 2C, 2D or 2E (see **7.10** above) as they apply in relation to appeals under s 2 or 2B.[2] SIACA 1997, s 8 provides for the Lord Chancellor to make rules regulating and prescribing the procedure to be followed on applications to the SIAC for leave to appeal from its decisions, under s 7, to the appropriate appeal court (see **7.60** below).

1   SIACA 1997, s 6A added by the Justice and Security Act 2013 from 25 June 2013 and amended by IA 2014.
2   As to appeals under s 2B, see **7.8**, fn 1 above.

GENERAL DUTY OF THE SIAC

7.16   The 2003 Rules[1] apply to appeals to the SIAC, applications to the SIAC for review under SIACA 1997, s 2C, 2D or 2E, applications to the SIAC for leave to appeal to the Court of Appeal, the Court of Session or the Court of Appeal in Northern Ireland, as well as to applications to the SIAC for bail.[2] It is specifically provided, in r 4 under the heading 'General duty of the Commission', that when exercising its functions, the SIAC shall secure that information is not disclosed contrary to the interests of national security, the international relations of the UK, the detection and prevention of crime, or in any other circumstances where disclosure is likely to harm the public interest.[3] Where the Rules require information not to be disclosed contrary to the public interest, that requirement is to be interpreted in accordance with the above[4] and that subject to these requirements the SIAC must satisfy itself that the material available to it enables it properly to determine proceedings.[5] In *W (Algeria)*[6] the Court of Appeal considered that there could be no doubt that r 4 (and r 38) provided for an outcome where an appellant was not to be told the essence of the closed material (see further **7.28–7.30** below regarding 'closed material') if that would be contrary to the interests of national security and that in passing both the SIACA 1997 and in approving the Rules,[7] Parliament had clearly confronted the fact that the right to a fair trial was being curtailed by the powers and procedures being approved. In *IR v UK*[8] the ECtHR rejected, as inadmissible, the applicants' complaints that their exclusion from the UK and the proceedings before SIAC violated their rights under Art 8 and/or Art 13 (right to effective domestic remedy) of the ECHR.

1   See **7.13**, fn 1 above.
2   2003 Rules, r 3.
3   2003 Rules, r 4(1).
4   2003 Rules, r 4(2).
5   2003 Rules, r 4(3).
6   *W (Algeria) v Secretary of State for the Home Department* [2010] EWCA Civ 898; reversed [2012] UKSC 8 (see **7.38** below).
7   SIACA 1997, ss 5(8) and (9) and 8(3) and (4) provide that the power to make rules under these sections shall be exercisable by statutory instrument and that no rules shall be made under these sections unless a draft of them has been laid before and approved by resolution of each House of Parliament.
8   *IR v United Kingdom* (2014) 58 EHRR SE14.

SIAC PRACTICE NOTE

7.17   The Chairman of the SIAC[1] has issued a 'Practice Note for Proceedings before SIAC' dated 30 April 2014 and applicable from 21 May 2014[2] under his delegated power[3] to make directions under r 39 of the Rules.[4] The Practice Note provides that procedures and practices laid down in it are to be followed in all cases, save where there is a direction otherwise. It continues by stating that 'Variation can be sought, but only for good reason, turning on the facts or circumstances of the specific case.'

1   Who in practice is a High Court Judge (see **7.2** above) and is currently Irwin J.
2   Available at www.judiciary.gov.uk/publications/practice-note-for-proceedings-before-siac/.
3   2003 Rules, r 5(1) provides for certain powers of the SIAC under the Rules to be exercised by the chairman or any other member of the Commission who holds, or has held, high judicial office or who is or was a tribunal judge (see **7.2** above).
4   Regarding directions under r 39, see **7.24** below.

BRINGING AN APPEAL OR AN APPLICATION FOR REVIEW BEFORE THE SIAC

7.18   An appeal to the SIAC under SIACA 1997, s 2 (or s 2B in a nationality case) or under, now repealed, NIAA 2002, s 97A(3) (see **7.7–7.8** above) must be made by giving notice of appeal in accordance with the 2003 Rules.[1] An application to the SIAC for a review under SIACA 1997, ss 2C, 2D or 2E must be made by giving notice of an application in accordance with the 2003 Rules.[2] In either case the notice must be given by filing it with the SIAC[3] unless the appellant[4] is in detention under the Immigration Acts[5] in which case the notice can, as an alternative, be served on the person having custody of him.[6] The notice of appeal must set out the grounds for the appeal and give reasons in support of those grounds.[7] In this regard it can be seen that the grounds need to develop the challenge to the SSHD's decision in greater detail than is the case with appeals to the FTT.[8] The notice of application for review must:

(a) specify, by reference to the principles which would be applied in an application for judicial review, the grounds for applying for a review;

(b) give reasons in support of those grounds; and

(c) specify the order or relief sought.[9]

1   2003 Rules, r 7(1).
2   2003 Rules, r 7(1A).
3   2003 Rules, r 7(2). The person must at the same time serve a copy of the notice and any accompanying documents on the SSHD: r 7(4).
4   The term 'appellant' applies equally to a person appealing to the SIAC and to a person applying for a review to the SIAC: 2003 Rules, r 2(1) 'interpretation'.
5   Meaning under powers of detention contained in IA 1971, Sch 2 (in respect to persons seeking entry to the UK or those having been refused entry; illegal entrants; crews of ships and aircraft; or persons subject to removal decisions under IAA 1999, s 10 or saved IANA 2006, s 47) or Sch 3 (in respect to persons facing deportation) or NIAA 2002, s 62 (powers of the SSHD to detain in specified circumstances) or UKBA 2007, s 36 (in respect of persons facing 'automatic deportation' having served a period of imprisonment).
6   2003 Rules, r 7(3). In this event the person having custody must endorse on the notice the date on which it was served on him and forward it to the SIAC: r 7(5)(a), and the SIAC must then serve a copy of the notice and any accompanying documents on the SSHD: r 7(5)(b).
7   2003 Rules, r 9(1).
8   Contrast the Tribunal Procedure (First-tier Tribunal) (Immigration and Asylum Chamber) Rules 2014, SI 2014/2604, r 19(4)(a) which merely requires the notice of appeal to the FTT must set out the grounds of appeal.
9   2003 Rules, r 9(1A).

7.19   In either case the notice must state the name and address of the appellant and of any representative,[1] must be signed and dated by the appellant or his representative[2] and must be accompanied by a copy of the notice of direction or decision against which he is appealing, or in respect of which he is applying for a review, and any other document which was served on him containing the reasons for that direction or decision,[3] eg the refusal letter. Note that there is no fee payable for bringing an appeal or an application for a review before the SIAC. The appellant may vary the grounds of appeal or application for review only with the leave of the SIAC.[4] The appellant must file any proposed variation of the grounds with the SIAC and serve a copy on the SSHD.[5]

1   2003 Rules, r 9(2).
2   2003 Rules, r 9(3). If the representative signs the notice he must also certify in the notice that it has been completed in accordance with the appellant's instructions: r 9(4).
3   2003 Rules, r 9(5) (as substituted from 12 April 2015 by the Special Immigration Appeals Commission (Procedure) (Amendment) Rules 2015, SI 2015/867, r 5: see **7.13**, fn 1 above).
4   2003 Rules, r 11(1). In respect to appeals, this is subject to NIAA 2002, s 85(2) (as applied by SIACA 1997, s 2(2): see **7.5** above), which provides, as in effect applied, that if an appellant makes a statement of additional grounds on appealing, the SIAC shall consider any matter raised in that statement which constitutes a ground of appeal against the decision appealed against.
5   2003 Rules, r 11(2).

TIME LIMITS FOR APPEALING OR FOR APPLYING FOR A REVIEW

7.20   An appellant,[1] who is in detention under the Immigration Acts[2] when he is served with notice of a decision that he wishes to challenge by way of appeal or review, must give his notice of appeal or review not later than five days after he is served with notice of the decision.[3] Otherwise, if he is in the UK but not detained under the Immigration Acts, he must give his notice of appeal or review not later than ten days after he is served with notice of the decision.[4] In both cases this means 'business days'[5] (thereby excluding Saturdays, Sundays, bank holidays, Christmas Day, Good Friday and the period 27–31 December[6]) and excludes the day on which the period begins[7] and so excludes the day of receipt of the notice of decision. A notice of decision that was sent by post or through a document exchange from and to a place within the UK is deemed to be served, and thus received, on the second day after it was sent unless the contrary is proved.[8] If the notice of decision was served personally on the appellant, by being left with him, or was served by fax or by email, it is deemed to be served, and thus received, on the day on which it was sent or delivered or left with the appellant, again unless the contrary is proved.[9] An appellant who is outside the UK when the notice of decision is served on him must give his notice of appeal or review not later than 28 days after he is served with the notice of decision,[10] which, if it is sent by post to him, is deemed to be served, and thus received, on the 28th day after it was sent unless the contrary is proved.[11] Where an appellant is in the UK when he is served with notice of the decision against which he wishes to appeal, but he may not appeal against the decision while remaining in the UK by reason of SIACA 1997, s 2(5) (see **7.5** above), he must give his notice of appeal not later than 28 days after his departure from the UK.[12] The 28-day period for appealing does not exclude 'non-business days' but where the period would otherwise end on a non-business day, the act is done – the appeal or application is given – if done on the next business day.[13]

1   Being a person who is either appealing or applying for a review to the SIAC (see **7.18**, fn 4 above).
2   See **7.18**, fn 5 above. The point being that a person detained under immigration powers is facing removal (a cell with three walls: as distinct from persons who are serving a prison sentence or are remanded in custody) and hence the shorter time limit for appealing or seeking a review.
3   2003 Rules, r 8(1)(a). In respect of applications for review, r 8(4A) (as added by the Special Immigration Appeals Commission (Procedure) (Amendment) Rules 2013, SI 2013/2995, r 10(d) from 28 November 2013) provides that the date from which the time limit for giving a notice of application for review begins is the latter of either the date on which the person is served with a notice of certification under SIACA 1997, ss 2C(1)(a) (exclusion cases) or 2D(1)(b) (nationality cases) (see **7.10** above) or the date on which para (4A) came into force (being 28 November 2013): see *R (Ignaoua) v Secretary of State for the Home Department* [2013] EWCA Civ 1498 where one of the issues was that procedure rules had not yet been brought into effect to address applications for review in the SIAC under the new provisions in SIACA 1997, ss 2C and 2D (see **7.12** above). Note that r 8(4A) has not yet been amended so as to also refer to applications for review under SIACA 1997, s 2E.

4   2003 Rules, r 8(1)(b)(i). See regarding applications for review in fn 3 above.
5   2003 Rules, r 51(1)(b) – where the period is ten days or less, excluding any day which is not
     a business day.
6   2003 Rules, r 51(3).
7   2003 Rules, r 51(1)(a).
8   2003 Rules, r 49(5)(a).
9   2003 Rules, r 49(1), (2) and (5)(c).
10   2003 Rules, r 8(1)(b)(ii).
11   2003 Rules, r 49(5)(b). Note however that in the more unlikely event that the notice of
     decision is served personally or by email or by fax, it is deemed served on the day it was sent
     or delivered or left with him: see fn 9 above.
12   2003 Rules, r 8(2).
13   2003 Rules, r 51(2).

7.21   Where an appellant's pending appeal under NIAA 2002, s 82, 83 or
83A, before the FTT (or, on further appeal before the UT) lapses by virtue
of a certificate being issued by the SSHD under NIAA 2002, s 97 (see **7.4**
above), the appellant must give notice of appeal to the SIAC against the
original decision that was the subject of the appeal before the tribunal within
the following time periods after he is served notice that his previous appeal has
lapsed:[1]

- not later than five business days if he is in detention under the Immigration
  Acts;[2]

- not later than ten business days if he is in the UK, but not so detained;[3]

- and not later than 28 days if he is outside of the UK.[4]

1   2003 Rules, r 8(3) and (4). *T6 v Secretary of State for the Home Department* [2011] UKSIAC
     95/2010 is an example of a case where the appellant had appealed to the tribunal but, prior to
     substantive hearing, the SSHD issued a certificate under NIAA 2002, s 97 so that his appeal
     lapsed and he had to appeal again, this time to the SIAC.
2   2003 Rules, r 8(4)(a).
3   2003 Rules, r 8(4)(b)(i).
4   2003 Rules, r 8(4)(b)(ii).

EXTENSION OF TIME FOR APPEALING OR FOR
APPLYING FOR REVIEW

7.22   In all cases the SIAC may extend the time limits for appealing or
applying for a review if it is satisfied that by reason of special circumstances it
would be unjust not to do so.[1] In *E2*[2] it was conceded by the appellant, with the
approval of the SIAC, that it is for the appellant to demonstrate that by reason
of special circumstances it would be unjust not to extend the statutory time
limit for giving notice of appeal and that it is for him to prove, to the balance of
probabilities standard, any necessary facts to enable him to demonstrate this,
for example that he did not in fact receive notice of the decision as at the date
on which it was deemed to have been received by him (see **7.20** above). In *H2*[3]

Irwin J cited approvingly from the determination in *Ogundimu*[4] where Blake J stated that:

> 'Factors relevant to the exercise of discretion to extend time … will include, but are not limited to (1) the length of any delay; (2) the reasons for the delay; (3) the merits of the appeal; and (4) the degree of prejudice to the respondent if the application is granted. The merits of the appeal cannot be decisive (see the reasons given in *Boktor and Wanis* [2011] UKUT 00442 (IAC)).'

1   2003 Rules, r 8(5).
2   *E2 v Secretary of State for the Home Department* [2012] UKSIAC 117/2012 (2 August 2012) at [10].
3   *H2 v Secretary of State for the Home Department* [2013] UKSIAC 120/2012 (25 July 2013).
4   *Ogundimu* [2013] UKUT 00060 (IAC). See generally regarding the principles to be applied to applications to extend time for appealing, *R (Hysaj) v Secretary of State for the Home Department* [2014] EWCA Civ 1633 and *SS (Congo) v Secretary of State for the Home Department* [2015] EWCA Civ 387.

7.23   In *L1*,[1] a deprivation of nationality case, the Court of Appeal held that the fact that the SSHD had deliberately delayed in serving her decision, to deprive the appellant of British nationality, until after he had left the UK on a trip abroad, was a factor that meant that the SIAC had erred in not extending time for his appealing to it. McCombe LJ criticised the SIAC for apparently having been prepared to take the national security issues, raised by the SSHD in support of her tactic, as militating against there being any appeal at all, whereas in his judgment the security case, although of course highly material on the appeal itself, was nothing to the point on whether the appellant should be denied a right of appeal.[2]

1   *L1 v Secretary of State for the Home Department* [2013] EWCA Civ 906.
2   *L1* (above) at [42].

PROCEDURES AND DIRECTIONS ONCE A NOTICE OF APPEAL OR APPLICATION FOR REVIEW IS FILED

7.24   The SIAC must, unless it orders otherwise, fix a directions hearing as soon as reasonably practicable after notice of appeal or notice of application for review is filed, at which the parties and their representatives, and any special advocate (see below), may be present.[1] The parties are the appellant and the SSHD.[2] The UK representative of the UNHCR may give written notice to the SIAC that he wishes to be treated as a party to proceedings and, where he does so, he is treated as a party from the date of that notice.[3] Any restrictions imposed in relation to the appellant, as to disclosure of material, attendance at hearings, notifications of orders, directions or determinations and communication from the special advocate (as to which see below), also apply to the UNHCR's UK representative.[4] The Chairman's Practice Note (see **7.17** above) sets out, in some detail, standard directions with time frames for the parties completing the required actions.[5] In summary, the most important initial steps (and see below regarding disclosure duties) are as follows:

● Where the SSHD intends to oppose an appeal (here as distinct from an application for review[6]), he must file with the SIAC–

(a) a statement of the evidence on which he relies in opposition to the appeal; and

(b) any exculpatory material of which he is aware.[7]

The exculpatory material is particular to proceedings before the SIAC because, where the SSHD's case is in part that an appellant is a danger to national security, the burden is on him to establish this (see further below). Unless the SSHD objects to the statement being disclosed to the appellant or his representative, he must serve a copy of the statement of evidence on the appellant at the same time as filing it.[8] Where the SSHD does so object then the special procedures relating to 'closed material' (as to which see below) apply.[9] In any event, where a special advocate has been appointed (see below), the SSHD must serve on him a copy of the statement and material as per (a) and (b) above.[10]

● Where the SSHD intends to oppose an application for review, he must file with the SIAC a statement of the evidence on which he relies in opposition to the application for review and material relevant to the issues in the application for review;[11] and unless the SSHD objects to the statement and material, or to part thereof, being disclosed to the appellant or his representative, he must serve a copy of the statement and material, or as much of the statement and material as he does not object to disclosing to the appellant or his representative, on the appellant at the same time as filing it.[12] Where the SSHD does object to the statement and material, or to part thereof, being disclosed to the appellant or his representative, then the special procedures relating to 'closed material' (as to which see below) apply in respect of the statement and material, or the part thereof which the SSHD objects to disclosing to the appellant or his representative.[13] Where a special advocate is appointed, the SSHD must serve on him a full copy of the statement and material.[14]

● The Chairman's Practice Note requires that within 21 days of service of the notice of appeal or notice for review, the SSHD is to serve on the appellant (in the case of open material and documents), and on the special advocate (in the case of open and closed material and documents):

1 an open synopsis of the issues arising, in the form of a Scott schedule;[15]

2 a closed synopsis of the issues arising, in the form of a Scott schedule;

3   a gist or summary of the submissions to the SSHD or other minister who took the relevant decision,[16] in both open redacted form and in closed un-redacted form;

4   copies of all relevant decision letters; and

5   draft directions, including a proposed timetable to progress the case in a proper manner.[17]

- The Practice Note continues with the stipulation that not later than 14 days following receipt of items (1) to (5) above, the appellant, and where appropriate the special advocate, are to serve and file:

1   agreed draft directions, if agreement has been reached;

2   proposed alternative directions, to the extent that agreement has not been reached; and

3   submissions on the summary or summaries of issues, in the Scott schedule.[18]

Then, not later than seven days following the service and filing of this material, the parties must jointly apply for a directions hearing before SIAC.[19] Not later than seven days before the first directions hearing, the SSHD and/or the special advocate must indicate in writing whether or not there is a need for a closed session at the directions hearing (as to which see below), and if so, why. This indication is to be given, wherever possible, openly to the appellant, even if requiring amplification in a 'closed form' (ie not provided to the appellant). This is because a 'closed hearing' without notice to the appellant would, for obvious reasons, be highly undesirable.[20]

- According to the Chairman's Practice Note, the first objective of the directions hearing is to identify the issues arising in the case, in open and (where necessary) closed hearings, so as to inform the order for directions, the timetable in the case and the discharge by the SSHD of the obligations of disclosure. It is the responsibility of all parties to give active assistance in identifying the issues which arise.[21] The 2003 Rules, rr 9A and 39 provide the SIAC with wide ranging powers to give directions[22] in respect of such matters as to the order in which, and the time within which, the documents are to be filed and served;[23] as to the dates of hearings;[24] for particular matters to be dealt with as a preliminary issue or for a pre-hearing review to be held;[25] to specify the manner in which any evidence is to be given and the witnesses, if any, to be heard;[26] to provide for a hearing to be conducted or evidence given or representations made by video link or by other electronic means;[27] and to make provision to secure the anonymity of the appellant or a witness.[28] For the consequences of a failure to comply with directions, see **7.41** below.

1   2003 Rules, r 9A(1).

2   2003 Rules, r 32(1). See **7.18**, fn 4 above regarding the meaning of 'appellant'. Rule 33 provides for representation of the parties with the stipulation that an appellant's representative must not be prohibited from providing immigration services by IAA 1999, s 84 (see **5.94** above).

3   2003 Rules, rr 2(1) and 32(2).

4   2003 Rules, r 32(3).

5   See 2003 Rules, rr 9A(2) and (3) and 39 and see the Chairman's Practice Note as referred to in **7.17** above.

6   2003 Rules, r 10(A1). See in this regard *R (Secretary of State for the Home Department) v Special Immigration Appeals Commission* [2015] EWHC 681 (Admin).

7   2003 Rules, r 10(1).

8   2003 Rules, r 10(2).

9   2003 Rules, r 10(3).

10   2003 Rules, r 10(4).

11   2003 Rules, r 10B(1).

12   2003 Rules, r 10B(2).

13   2003 Rules, r 10B(3).

14   2003 Rules, r 10B(4).

15   A 'Scott schedule' is in the form of a table, with numbering and columns, intended to identify precisely the questions that a judge has to decide. A 'Google' search on the term 'Scott schedule' should suffice.

16   In many SIAC cases the SSHD will have reached his decision following advice from the Security Services in the form of a submission as to why the appellant poses a risk to national security or as to why it is not in the public interest to disclose material relied upon for the decision. See further **7.27** below.

17   See Chairman's Practice Note for proceedings before SIAC, para 1. The note at para 1(5) goes on to stipulate requirements that the draft directions must address. Prior to the Practice Note being issued on 30 April 2014, the Court of Appeal in *L1 v Secretary of State for the Home Department* [2013] EWCA Civ 906 agreed (not disputed by the SSHD) that the SIAC had erred in adopting a truncated *ad hoc* procedure.

18   See Chairman's Practice Note for proceedings before SIAC, para 4.

19   Ibid, para 5.

20   Ibid, para 6.

21   Ibid, para 7.

22   Directions under r 39 may be given orally or in writing and can be given in the absence of the parties: r 39(3) and (6).

23   2003 Rules, rr 9A(2) and 39(5) and see the Practice Note as referred to above and in respect of disclosure and closed material, below. In addition to disclosed evidence, the documents to be served can include witness statements, written submissions and skeleton arguments on behalf of the parties and the special advocate.

24   2003 Rules, r 9A(3) – that is any hearing relating to bail, under r 38 in relation to closed matters and the substantive hearing of the appeal or the application for review.

25   2003 Rules, r 39(5)(d).

26   2003 Rules, r 39(5)(f).

27   2003 Rules, r 39(5)(g).

28   2003 Rules, r 39(5)(h). See **7.46–7.47** below regarding hearings in private.

SPECIAL ADVOCATES

7.25   The fundamental point of the SIAC is that it deals with appeals and judicial reviews in cases where the SSHD has determined and certified that his decision under challenge relies wholly or in part on material that cannot be made public for national security related reasons (see more fully in **7.4** above) and that accordingly this material cannot safely be disclosed to the appellant or to his representatives.[1] Thus it is that under SIACA 1997, s 6, provision is made for the appointment of a person to represent the appellant's interests – the so called 'special advocate' – in any proceedings before the SIAC from which the appellant and any legal representative of his are excluded.[2] The special advocate is appointed by the relevant law officer – in relation to proceedings before the SIAC in England and Wales, that is the Attorney General; in Scotland, the Lord Advocate; and in Northern Ireland, the Advocate General for Northern Ireland.[3] It is expressly provided that the special advocate shall not be responsible to the person whose interests he is appointed to represent.[4] Upon being served with a copy of a notice of appeal or application for review, the SSHD must give notice of the proceedings to the relevant law officer,[5] unless the SSHD does not intend to oppose the appeal or application[6] or does not intend to object to the disclosure of any material to the appellant (see further below),[7] or a special advocate has already been appointed[8] (perhaps in previous or linked proceedings). The relevant law officer may (sic) then appoint a special advocate,[9] and where any proceedings are pending before the SIAC but no special advocate has been appointed, the appellant or the SSHD may at any time request the relevant law officer to appoint one.[10] The Chairman's Practice Note (see **7.17** above) envisages that in each case, and so effectively in every case, at least one special advocate will be required from the outset of proceedings.[11]

1   See **7.1–7.12** above.
2   SIACA 1997, s 6(1).
3   SIACA 1997, s 6(1) and (2). Sub-s (3) sets out the necessary legal qualifications for a special advocate.
4   SIACA 1997, s 6(4).
5   2003 Rules, r 34(1).
6   2003 Rules, r 34(2)(a)(i).
7   2003 Rules, r 34(2)(a)(ii).
8   2003 Rules, r 34(2)(b).
9   2003 Rules, r 34(3).
10   2003 Rules, r 34(4).
11   See Chairman's Practice Note for proceedings before SIAC, para 3. Indeed it is unclear what would be the purpose of proceedings being in the SIAC at all – rather than in the tribunal or the High Court – if there was no need for a special advocate.

FUNCTIONS OF A SPECIAL ADVOCATE

7.26   The functions of a special advocate are to represent the interests of the appellant by making submissions at any hearings from which the appellant and his representatives are excluded, by adducing evidence and cross-examining witnesses at any such hearings and by making written submissions to the SIAC.[1] The special advocate may communicate with the appellant or his representative at any time before the SSHD serves material on him which he objects to being disclosed to the appellant.[2] However, after the SSHD serves such material on the special advocate, he must not communicate with any person about any matter connected with the proceedings, other than with the SIAC, the SSHD, the relevant law officer (or any person acting for him) and any other person, except for the appellant or his representative, with whom it is necessary for administrative purposes for him to communicate about matters not connected with the substance of the proceedings.[3] The special advocate may request directions from the SIAC authorising him to communicate with the appellant or his representative or with any other person[4] in which case the SIAC must notify the SSHD of the request and the SSHD must, within a period specified by the SIAC, file with the Commission and serve on the special advocate notice of any objection which he has to the proposed communication, or to the form in which it is proposed to be made.[5] The SSHD has indicated that his office's 'best endeavours' will be used to respond within 24 hours to purely procedural type requests from the special advocate to communicate with the appellant's representatives.[6] The Chairman's Practice Note provides that where the SSHD has no objection to a proposed communication (whether on an administrative matter or otherwise) from a special advocate to the appellant's representative, the SSHD shall promptly make the communication to the representative, copied to the Special Advocates Support Office (SASO),[7] indicating that the communication is being made at the request of the special advocate and without need for authorisation or direction of the SIAC.[8]

1   2003 Rules, r 35.
2   2003 Rules, r 36(1).
3   2003 Rules, r 36(2) and (3). This does not prohibit the appellant from communicating with the special advocate after the SSHD has served the relevant material on him, but the appellant may only communicate with the special advocate through a legal representative in writing and the special advocate must not reply to the communication other than in accordance with directions of the SIAC, except that he may without such directions send a written acknowledgment of receipt to the appellant's legal representative: r 36(6).
4   2003 Rules, r 36(4).
5   2003 Rules, r 36(5).
6   See Chairman's Practice Note for proceedings before SIAC, para 22 citing from a letter dated 31 December 2012. The Practice Note continues by stating that if in a given case a response is not forthcoming within one working day, then the Commission will consider a written application for specific directions on the matter.
7   Part of the Government Legal Department (formerly the Treasury Solicitor's office).
8   Chairman's Practice Note for proceedings before SIAC, para 23.

DISCLOSURE DUTIES

7.27   Carrying on from **7.24** above and the SSHD's duties under 2003 Rules, rr 10 and 10B to file and serve a statement of the evidence on which he relies *and* any exculpatory material of which he is aware:[1]

- the Chairman's Practice Note confirms that it is important for the SSHD to serve *both* before the appellant serves his statement of evidence under r 10A (see below). The Chairman notes that there are good reasons why that obligation is imposed, both for speed and economy, and for fairness. The obligation arises in respect of any material which adversely affects the case of the SSHD or would lend support to the position of the appellant.[2] In particular the SSHD is taken to *'be aware'* of any material relevant to the decision(s) taken which he has actually considered, and of material which is or has been in the possession or control of:

– the Home Office;

– the Security Service (MI5) and the Secret Intelligence Service (MI6) and or the Government Communications Headquarters (GCHQ) – including material arising from port stops, police arrests and interviews ensuing from either; and

– the Foreign and Commonwealth Office (FCO), in relation at least to the issue of safety on return.[3]

• The Chairman emphasises the need for full and fair disclosure of exculpatory material under rr 10 and 10B (in respect to review applications[4]) particularly in the context where the appellant may be in ignorance of most or all of the key allegations against him, because they are made within the closed procedure (see below).[5] Of particular importance it is noted that the SSHD has an obligation to disclose exculpatory material, whether under the relevant rules or otherwise, even if it was obtained in circumstances – such as torture or arising from an abuse of process – which would lead the SSHD to decline to rely on it, if it were favourable to his case against the appellant.[6] See in this respect *A*[7] in which the House of Lords held that evidence of a suspect or witness which had been obtained by torture may not lawfully be admitted *against a party* to proceedings in a UK court, irrespective of where, by whom or on whose authority the torture had been inflicted and that accordingly, although the SIAC might admit a wide range of material which was inadmissible in judicial proceedings, it could not admit such evidence (see further below regarding evidence).

• Where the appellant wishes to rely on evidence in support of his appeal (here as distinct from an application for review[8]), he must file with the SIAC and serve on the SSHD and on any special advocate a statement of that evidence.[9] On receiving the appellant's statement, the SSHD must make a reasonable search for further exculpatory material; notify the appellant of the extent of that search, subject to concerns over disclosure (below); file any exculpatory material with the SIAC; and file with the SIAC a statement of any further evidence he wishes to rely on[10] and must serve copies of any such materials and statements on any special advocate and, subject to disclosure concerns (below), on the appellant.[11] The Chairman notes that this obligation on the SSHD is to respond to any matters raised in the statement served by the appellant and observes that this duty in turn depends on the appellant's obligation to set out his full case in written evidence in a timely fashion, so as to avoid duplication of effort and delay. The SIAC will consider limiting the issues in a case if that duty is not observed.[12] The SSHD is to confirm in writing that the relevant disclosure obligations have been fulfilled.[13] Specific direction as to disclosure may be sought from the SIAC if the circumstances of the case require it.[14]

- Where the SSHD considers that the disclosure of particular information (as above) would be contrary to the public interest, he must omit that information from the notification to be served on the appellant and serve a copy of the notification, including that information, on the special advocate.[15] Both the appellant and any special advocate may apply to the SIAC for a direction requiring the SSHD to file further information about his case or other information[16] and must indicate why the information sought is necessary for the determination of the appeal.[17] If the SIAC considers that the sought for information is necessary for the determination of the appeal and that it may be provided without disproportionate cost, time or effort, it will make an appropriate direction[18] and the SSHD must then file and serve the information,[19] unless the SSHD objects to disclosure of such information, in which case the 'closed material' procedure will apply (see below).[20]

- The above duties, in respect to filing material or statements of evidence, continue until the appeal has been determined and where material or a statement to which those duties extend comes to a party's attention before the appeal has been determined, he must immediately file it with the SIAC and serve it on the other party and on any special advocate, subject to the SSHD's public interest objections as above.[21]

1   See **7.24**, fnn 6–14 above.
2   See Chairman's Practice Note for proceedings before SIAC, para 8.
3   Ibid, para 9.
4   Ibid, para 11: r 10B sets out the obligations of the SSHD for disclosure arising in a review; the SIAC's duty under r 4(3) – subject to the interests of national security, the SIAC must satisfy itself that the material available to it enables it properly to determine proceedings (see **7.16** above) – arises in review proceedings just as in an appeal. In the absence of particular circumstances being placed before the Commission, the evidence on which the SSHD relies in opposition to the application for review must include all the material placed before the minister or official who took the decision(s) challenged, in addition to any other material relied on. See however *R (Secretary of State for the Home Department) v Special Immigration Appeals Commission* [2015] EWHC 681 (Admin) for the SSHD's challenge to the SIAC's position on the same level of duty of disclosure in review proceedings (see **7.30**).
5   See Chairman's Practice Note for proceedings before SIAC, para 10.
6   Ibid, para 12.
7   *A v Secretary of State for the Home Department (No 2)* [2005] UKHL 71.
8   2003 Rules, r 10A(A1).
9   2003 Rules, r 10A(1).
10   2003 Rules, r 10A(2). The factors relevant in deciding the reasonableness of a search include: the number of documents involved; the nature and complexity of the proceedings; whether the documents are in the control of the SSHD; the ease and expense of retrieval of any particular document; and the significance of any document which is likely to be located during the search: r 10A(3). See further below regarding disclosure duties.

11 2003 Rules, r 10A(8).
12 See Chairman's Practice Note for proceedings before SIAC, paras 10 and 15.
13 Ibid, para 14.
14 Ibid, para 13.
15 2003 Rules, r 10A(4).
16 2003 Rules, r 10A(5).
17 2003 Rules, r 10A(6).
18 2003 Rules, r 10A(7).
19 2003 Rules, r 10A(8).
20 2003 Rules, r 10A(9).
21 2003 Rules, r 10A(10) and (11).

CLOSED MATERIAL

7.28   Returning to the theme of the particular purpose of the SIAC and the role of the special advocate, 'closed material' means material which the SSHD would otherwise be required to disclose to the appellant under r 10, 10A or 10B (see **7.24** and **7.27** above) but which the SSHD objects to disclosing to the appellant or his representative.[1] The SSHD may only rely upon closed material if a special advocate has been appointed to represent the interests of the appellant,[2] in which case the SSHD must file with the SIAC and serve on the special advocate a copy of the closed material, if he has not already done so, along with a statement of his reasons for objecting to its disclosure.[3] At the same time the SSHD, to the extent that it is possible to do so without disclosing information contrary to the public interest, must file and serve a statement of the material in a form which can be served on the appellant.[4] Where the SSHD serves on the special advocate any closed material which he has redacted on grounds other than those of legal professional privilege, he must file the material with the SIAC in an un-redacted form, together with an explanation of the redactions, and the SIAC must give a direction to the SSHD as to what he may redact.[5] The Chairman's Practice Note provides that the special advocate should be permitted to inspect (but not hold or copy) the un-redacted text, unless:

(a)   the redacted text is subject to legal professional privilege;

(b)   the redacted text relates to a separate subject matter with no impact on the issues in the case before SIAC; or

(c)   there is a specific sensitivity arising from national security, or otherwise within the terms of r 4(1) (see **7.16** above).

1   2003 Rules, r 37(1).
2   2003 Rules, r 37(2).
3   2003 Rules, r 37(3)(a) and (b).
4   2003 Rules, r 37(3)(c) and (4).
5   2003 Rules, r 37(4A).

7.29   In such cases, the SSHD should annotate the document, indicating which of these reasons is relied upon, and where redaction is on grounds (b) or (c) the SIAC may be requested to review the redacted material.[1] The SSHD may, with the leave of the SIAC or the agreement of the special advocate, at any time amend or supplement the closed material that has been filed.[2] Where the SSHD serves on the appellant any statement or material which he has redacted on grounds other than those of legal professional privilege, he must notify the appellant that the statement or material has been redacted and on what grounds it has been redacted and file the statement or material with the SIAC in an unredacted form, together with an explanation of the redactions.[3]

1 See Chairman's Practice Note for proceedings before SIAC, para 17.
2 2003 Rules, r 37(5).
3 2003 Rules, r 38A.

7.30 In *R (SSHD)*,[1] the Divisional Court held, on the SSHD's challenge to the SIAC's preliminary decisions on 'closed disclosure' to the special advocates in review challenges under SIACA 1997, ss 2C and 2D (see **7.10** above), that whilst it is not sufficient for closed disclosure to be limited to the summary prepared for the SSHD, or his official, plus any other documents not before the summary writer but taken into account by the official or SSHD, on the other hand, if SIAC intended to require the SSHD to disclose everything that the report or summary writer might have been able to access in the preparation of advice for officials or the minister, then this was in error. The correct approach requires disclosure of such material as was used by the author of any relevant assessment to found or justify the facts or conclusions expressed; or if subsequently re-analysed, disclosure should be of such material as is considered sufficient to justify those facts and conclusions, and which was in existence at the date of decision.

1 *R (Secretary of State for the Home Department) v Special Immigration Appeals Commission* [2015] EWHC 681 (Admin) at [38].

RULE 38 HEARINGS

7.31 Where the SSHD has filed his statement of his reasons for objecting to the disclosure of the 'closed material' (above)[1] and or where the SSHD has objected to any proposed communication between the special advocate and the appellant (see **7.26** above),[2] the SIAC must decide whether to uphold the objection.[3] The SIAC must fix a hearing – the 'r 38 hearing' – for the SSHD and the special advocate to make oral representations unless:[4]

- the special advocate gives notice to the SIAC that he does not challenge the objection – the special advocate must give such notice within 14 days of being served with notice of the objection;[5]

- the SIAC has previously considered an objection by the SSHD relating to the same or substantially the same communication or material, and is satisfied that it would be just to uphold the objection without a hearing; or

• the SSHD and the special advocate consent to the SIAC deciding the issue without an oral hearing.

1 That is under the 2003 Rules, r 37(3)(b) (see **7.28** above).
2 That is under the 2003 Rules, r 36(5)(b) (see **7.26** above).
3 2003 Rules, r 38(1).
4 2003 Rules, r 38(2).
5 2003 Rules, r 38(3).

7.32 Where the Commission fixes a r 38 hearing:[1]

• the special advocate may file and serve a reply to the SSHD's objection;

• the SSHD may file and serve a response to the special advocate's reply;

• together they must file a schedule identifying the issues which cannot be agreed between them, which must list the items or issues in dispute, give brief reasons for their contentions on each, and set out any proposals for the SIAC to resolve the issues in dispute. This should be in the form of a Scott Schedule, following discussion and containing the competing submissions in respect of material where agreement has not been reached, to be filed with the SIAC not less than seven days before the r 38 hearing.[2]

1 2003 Rules, r 38(4).
2 See Chairman's Practice Note for proceedings before SIAC, para 18.

7.33 The Chairman's Practice Note enjoins the SSHD and the special advocate to co-operate so as to ensure that there is good opportunity for discussion to narrow issues before the r 38 hearing and to ensure proper and timely disclosure so as to avoid adjournments or extensions of time limits, unless there is a compelling reason for such adjournment or extension.[1] Inherently, a r 38 hearing takes place in the absence of the appellant and his representative.[2] However, throughout the proceedings the SSHD and the special advocate have a duty, both before a particular step has been taken, and afterwards, to inform the appellant's representatives of the nature and purpose of any closed steps in the proceedings (including written submissions, oral hearings, rulings, and decisions) in so far as this is possible consistently with r 4(1) (see **7.16** above). In particular, at the end of any closed hearing and/or following any closed ruling or decision, the SSHD and special advocates shall consider, and if possible agree, what may be said to the appellant's representatives by the SIAC in relation to that hearing, ruling or decision.[3]

1 See Chairman's Practice Note for proceedings before SIAC, para 16. In particular, the Chairman notes that transcripts of closed hearings can only be prepared by security-cleared personnel under secure conditions and that as this is expensive and needs advance planning, particularly if there is a need for overnight transcription, then, in any case in which overnight transcription is to be sought, a specific application must be made with good reason, at least 21 days before the relevant hearing: para 21.
2 2003 Rules, r 38(5).
3 See Chairman's Practice Note for proceedings before SIAC, para 20.

7.34   On a r 38 hearing the SIAC may uphold or overrule the SSHD's objection;[1] but it must uphold a 'closed material' objection where it considers that the disclosure of the material would be contrary to the public interest.[2] Where the SIAC upholds the SSHD's 'closed material' objection it must consider whether to direct the SSHD to serve a summary of the closed material on the appellant and, if so, it must approve any such summary to secure that it does not contain any information or other material the disclosure of which would be contrary to the public interest.[3] Where the SIAC overrules the SSHD's 'closed material' objection, or where it directs him to serve a summary of the closed material on the appellant (as above), then, nevertheless, the SSHD is still not required to serve that material or summary on the appellant. However if he does not do so, the SIAC may hold a further hearing, at which the SSHD and the special advocate may make representations, and:[4]

- if the SIAC considers that the material or anything that is required to be summarised might adversely affect the SSHD's case or support the appellant's case, it may direct that the SSHD shall not rely on such points in his case, or shall make such concessions or take such other steps, as the SIAC may specify; or

- in any other case, the SIAC may direct that the SSHD shall not rely in the proceedings on that material or on that which is required to be summarised.

1   2003 Rules, r 38(6).
2   2003 Rules, r 38(7).
3   2003 Rules, r 38(8).
4   2003 Rules, r 38(9).

7.35   In effect, therefore, if the SIAC disagrees with the SSHD over the need to not disclose material to the appellant, but the SSHD is nonetheless adamant that he will not disclose it, then the SSHD cannot rely on that material to the advantage of his case against that of the appellant and may have to make appropriate concessions to the appellant's case.

THE USE OF CLOSED MATERIAL

7.36   In *MT (Algeria)*,[1] the Court of Appeal held that the SIAC had been entitled to use closed material. Although there was no doubt that a domestic court or tribunal had to engage in rigorous scrutiny of an ECHR, Art 3 case, the presence throughout of the appellant, or the giving to him of all of the evidence, was not a necessary component of that rigorous scrutiny. The presence and participation of the appellant was a very important element in the process of reaching the right answer, but its absence did not in itself disqualify what otherwise was rigorous scrutiny. Furthermore, in creating the SIAC and its procedures, Parliament had squarely confronted what it was doing and accepted the political cost and so it was not open to the court to interfere with the statutory scheme. This was affirmed on appeal to the House of Lords in *RB (Algeria)*:[2] where safety on return was in issue, it was not likely to be critically important for the special advocate representing the interests of the appellant to obtain input from him in relation to the evidence which the receiving state (here Algeria) wished to remain closed. The appellant would usually be aware of the information personal to him that bore on the question of whether he would be safe on his return. The use of closed material in relation to the issue of safety on return would not necessarily render the process unfair or in breach of the principles of legality and the appellants had not been denied a fair trial by reason of the use of closed material. In *LI*,[3] on remittal from the Court of Appeal (see **7.22–7.23** above), the appellant submitted that the SIAC should not receive evidence in a closed material procedure; in riposte the SSHD submitted that in the absence of closed material the SIAC would have to assume that the national security case was compelling, especially where the good faith of the SSHD in taking the decision was not in issue, in the sense that there was no suggestion that the decision was taken for an ulterior motive, and that it would be very hard for the SIAC to conclude against the SSHD if the SIAC had deprived itself of the opportunity to see information upon which he acted. The SIAC ruled in favour of the SSHD and stated that:[4]

'We see clear advantages to both sides in the capacity of the Commission to examine the closed material. It is often assumed, when submissions are made that closed material procedures should not be engaged, that closed material only favours the Secretary of State. That is not the experience of those who have conducted closed proceedings.'

1   *MT (Algeria) v Secretary of State for the Home Department* [2007] EWCA Civ 808.
2   *RB (Algeria) v Secretary of State for the Home Department* [2009] UKHL 10.
3   *LI v Secretary of State for the Home Department* [2013] UKSIAC 100/2010 (18 December 2013).
4   *LI* (above) at [9].

'AN IRREDUCIBLE MINIMUM OF DISCLOSURE'?

7.37   In *IR (Sri Lanka)*[1] the Court of Appeal upheld the SIAC's rejection of the submission that, in national security deportation and exclusion cases, appellants were entitled to a standard of procedural fairness which embraced disclosure at the irreducible minimum level required in ECHR, Arts 5(4) and 6 (rights to challenge lawfulness of detention and to fair trial respectively) and held that their entitlement was solely that contained in the 2003 (Procedure) Rules. The need for some form of adversarial proceedings was satisfied by the proceedings in the SIAC and, to the extent that the proceedings were closed, the use of special advocates reduced the risk of unfairness.[2] In respect to EEA decisions and appeals to SIAC (see **7.9** above), in *ZZ (France)*[3] the ECJ gave a preliminary ruling that in the context of a decision taken under the Citizens Directive,[4] Art 27 (restrictions on the right of entry, etc), the essence of the grounds on which the decision was based had always to be disclosed to the individual concerned and that this was a minimum requirement which could not yield to the demands of national security. The position was, however, different in respect of the related evidence, which could be withheld for reasons of national security. The SIAC had to ensure that the individual was informed of the essence of the grounds in a manner that took account of the necessary confidentiality of the evidence. It had to protect the confidentiality of evidence which, if disclosed, would be contrary to national security.[5] However, in *D2*,[6] a non-EEA case, the SIAC held that there was no irreducible, minimum obligations of disclosure arising, derived either from Strasbourg authority or from the application of *ZZ (France)*, and that there was no obligation here to disclose the 'essence of the grounds' relied on against the appellant, if to do so would infringe the Commission's obligations under the 2003 Rules, r 4(1) (see **7.16** above).[7] Irwin J emphasised, nonetheless, that the SIAC will, as a matter of law and as a matter of established practice, disclose as much information as possible, provided that r 4(1) is not infringed; and that where the information is not disclosed, every effort will be made by redaction, the provision of summaries and gists, and by any other means, to ensure that the appellant is able properly to present his case; and that the SIAC will be astute to consider what inferences may or may not fairly be drawn, in the light of what can and what cannot be disclosed.[8]

1   *IR (Sri Lanka) v Secretary of State for the Home Department* [2011] EWCA Civ 704. See also *R (BB (Algeria)) v Special Immigration Appeals Commission* [2012] EWCA Civ 1499.
2   The Court of Appeal considered *inter alia* the Strasbourg Court's judgment in *Al-Nashif v Bulgaria* (2003) 36 EHRR 37 in which complaints of violations of Arts 5(4), 8 and 13 (right to effective remedy) were upheld where domestic statutory provisions denied challenges by way of judicial review or appeal to detention and deportation on national security grounds. See also *A v United Kingdom* (2009) 49 EHRR 29 and *Secretary of State for the Home Department v AF (No 3)* [2009] UKHL 28.
3   *ZZ (France) v Secretary of State for the Home Department* (C-300/11) [2013] QB 1136.
4   European Union Council Directive of 29 April 2004 on the right of citizens of the Union and their family members to move and reside freely within the territory of the Member States (2004/38/EC): see **1.7**. See especially Arts 27, 30 and 31; see also the Charter of Fundamental Rights of the European Union, Art 47.
5   See also *ZZ (France) v Secretary of State for the Home Department* [2014] EWCA Civ 7.
6   *D2 v Secretary of State for the Home Department* [2014] UKSIAC 116/2012 (15 April 2014).
7   The SIAC also rejected the appellant's submission that any additional obligations of disclosure arose by reference to the Data Protection Act 1998.
8   *D2* (above) at [67].

W (ALGERIA) AND ABSOLUTE AND IRREVERSIBLE NON-DISCLOSURE ORDERS

7.38   Just as there can be evidence upon which the SSHD wishes to rely but which he wishes to keep secret from the appellant for reasons that can include the interests of the relationship between the UK and another country (see **7.4** above), there can be evidence upon which an appellant wishes to rely that he would wish to keep secret from the authorities of that other country – eg evidence from a person in that country, going to safety on return issues, but who would be too afraid to give it were there any risk at all that it would ever come to the attention of those authorities. In *W (Algeria)*[1] the Supreme Court, reversing the Court of Appeal,[2] ruled that it was open, under strict conditions, for the SIAC to make an absolute and irreversible *ex parte* order[3] in favour of an appellant before it, prohibiting the SSHD from ever disclosing to any third party (especially the authorities of a foreign state) the identity and evidence of a witness from whom the appellant proposed to adduce evidence in circumstances where that witness would not give evidence unless absolutely sure that his identity and evidence would under no circumstances be passed on to anyone other than the SSHD and the SIAC itself. However, the court considered that this approach was 'the lesser of two evils'[4] and therefore the power to make such guarantees was to be most sparingly exercised. The SIAC should first require the fullest disclosure from the appellant of:

(a)   the proposed evidence;

(b)   the particular circumstances in which the witness claimed to fear reprisals; and

(c)   how the appellant came to hear about the proposed evidence and what steps had been taken to encourage the witness to give evidence in the usual way, namely with the protection of anonymity orders and private hearings (as to which see below).

Furthermore, if it turned out that the information was important to national security issues, it should be open to the SSHD to try to persuade the SIAC to seek from the witness a waiver of confidentiality.[5]

---

1   *W (Algeria) v Secretary of State for the Home Department* [2012] UKSC 8.

2   See *W (Algeria) v Secretary of State for the Home Department* [2010] EWCA Civ 898 in which the Court of Appeal had held there was no irreducible minimum of information that had to be provided to appellants in proceedings before the SIAC about the risk they posed to national security (see **7.37** above) and that appellants were not entitled to any procedural protection akin to the 'closed material' procedure available to the SSHD's witnesses.

3   It was common ground that the 2003 Rules, rr 4 (see **7.16** above), 39 (directions: see above) and 43 (hearings in private, see below) are wide enough to give SIAC the *jurisdiction* to make such an order.

4   The imperative need to maximise the SIAC's chances of arriving at the correct decision on any ECHR, Art 3 challenge to removal by an appellant versus the SSHD's case that the giving of the guarantees contended for could never be appropriate because he might then find himself in possession of information which (whether or not appreciated by the SIAC, the appellant or even the witness himself) might in one way or another suggest the existence of a terrorist threat abroad or some other risk to national security, but because of the SIAC's order, the SSHD would be unable to alert the foreign state to the risk, thereby gravely imperilling future diplomatic relations and causing deep embarrassment if the risk were then to eventuate.

5   For practical consideration see the SIAC determinations in *J1 v Secretary of State for the Home Department (deportation – appellant's application for an absolute and irrevocable confidentiality order – refused)* [2014] UKSIAC 98/2010 (14 January 2014); and then *J1 v Secretary of State for the Home Department (deportation – W (Algeria) application – granted)* [2014] UKSIAC 98/2010 (8 May 2014).

PROCEDURE IN RELATION TO EX PARTE ORDERS

7.39   A special procedure applies in the event that the SIAC proposes to serve on the appellant notice of any order or direction made or given in the absence of the SSHD[1] – of potential particular relevance where it is proposed to make an *ex parte 'W (Algeria)* order'.[2] Prior to serving any such document on the appellant, the SIAC must first serve notice on the SSHD, and on any special advocate, of its intention to do so[3] and the SSHD may, within five days of the service of such a notice, apply to the SIAC to amend the proposed order or direction if he considers that his compliance with the order or direction, or that the notification to the appellant of any matter contained in the order or direction, would cause information to be disclosed contrary to the public interest.[4] The SSHD must serve a copy of such an application on the special advocate[5] and the SIAC must give the special advocate and the SSHD an opportunity to make representations, in effect as to what should or should not be stated in or required by the order or direction, and may then determine the SSHD's application with or without a hearing.[6] The SIAC must not serve the document containing the order or direction on the appellant before the time limit for the SSHD to make an objection has expired or, where an objection has been made, before it has been determined.[7] Inherently, any hearing of any such representations would likely be 'closed' to the appellant and the public.

1   2003 Rules, r 48(1)(a).
2   In *J1 v Secretary of State for the Home Department (deportation – appellant's application for an absolute and irrevocable confidentiality order – refused)* [2014] UKSIAC 98/2010 (14 January 2014) (see **7.38** above), Irwin J noted at [31], as a 'striking matter', that the SSHD had 'indicated clearly that she will not attend, and will not be represented, at any hearing where evidence from the Appellant is given subject to the conditions sought'.
3   2003 Rules, r 48(2).
4   2003 Rules, r 48(3).
5   2003 Rules, r 48(4).
6   2003 Rules, r 48(5).
7   2003 Rules, r 48(6).

WITHDRAWAL OF APPEALS OR APPLICATIONS FOR REVIEW; ABANDONMENT OF APPEALS

7.40   An appellant may withdraw an appeal or an application for review orally, at a hearing, or at any time, by filing written notice with the SIAC.[1] An appeal or an application for review shall be treated as withdrawn if the SSHD notifies the SIAC that the decision, to which the appeal or application for review relates, has been withdrawn.[2] If an appeal or an application for review is withdrawn or treated as withdrawn, the SIAC must serve on the parties and on any special advocate a notice that the appeal or application has been recorded as having been withdrawn.[3] Furthermore an appeal against an 'immigration decision'[4] lodged by an appellant whilst in the UK, is treated as abandoned if the appellant is granted leave to remain in the UK;[5] and an appeal against either an immigration decision or against rejection of an asylum claim is treated as abandoned if the appellant leaves the UK.[6] 'Leaves the UK' has been held to mean physically leaving UK territory or territorial waters, regardless of any intention to return; a day trip to France will suffice to cause a pending appeal to be treated as abandoned.[7] In *E*[8] the claimant unsuccessfully sought to challenge, on human rights' grounds, the SSHD's decision that, by leaving the UK, he was to be treated as having abandoned his appeal to SIAC against the cancellation of his indefinite leave to remain in the UK. An appeal against an immigration decision refusing leave to enter, refusing a certificate of entitlement, varying or refusing to vary leave or revoking indefinite leave, is treated as finally determined if a deportation order is made against the appellant.[9]

1   2003 Rules, r 11A(1).
2   2003 Rules, r 11A(2). See also Chapter 5 in this regard and see *R (Chichvarkin) v Secretary of State for the Home Department* [2011] EWCA Civ 91.
3   2003 Rules, r 11A(3).
4   That is a decision listed in saved NIAA 2002, s 82(2) – the appeal would be under saved s 82(1) but for the certification under s 97: see SIACA 1997, s 2(1) and see **7.4** and **7.5** above.
5   Saved NIAA 2002, s 104(4A) as applied by SIACA 1997, s 2(2) (see **7.5** above).
6   As regards an immigration decision: saved NIAA 2002, s 104(4) as applied by SIACA 1997, s 2(2); and as regards rejection of an asylum claim: SIACA 1997, s 2(4) (see **7.6** above).
7   See *Dupovac v Secretary of State for the Home Department* [2000] Imm AR 265, CA; and see *R (MM (Ghana)) v Secretary of State for the Home Department* [2012] EWCA Civ 827.
8   *R (E) v Secretary of State for the Home Department* [2014] EWHC 1030 (Admin).
9   Saved NIAA 2002, s 104(5) as applied by SIACA 1997, s 2(2) (see **7.7** above). The immigration decisions are those listed in (a), (c), (d), (e) and (f) of saved NIAA 2002, s 82(2).

'STRIKING OUT' AND FAILURE TO COMPLY WITH DIRECTIONS

7.41   Under the 2003 Rules, the SIAC may strike out a notice of appeal, a notice of application for review or a reply by the SSHD (see **7.24** above), if it appears to the SIAC that it discloses no reasonable grounds for bringing or defending the appeal or for seeking or opposing the application for review, as the case may be.[1] The SIAC may also strike out a notice of appeal or a notice of application for review if it appears to the SIAC that it is an abuse of the SIAC's process.[2] Furthermore, where a party or the special advocate fails to comply with a direction (see **7.24** above), the SIAC may serve on him a notice which states the respect in which he has failed to comply with the direction, a time limit for complying with the direction, and a warning that the SIAC may either proceed to determine the appeal or application for review on the material available to it if the party or special advocate fails to comply with the direction within the time specified, or strike out the notice of appeal or notice of application for review or the SSHD's reply, as the case may be.[3] And where a party or a special advocate still fails to comply with the direction, the SIAC may proceed accordingly.[4] However, where the SIAC has struck out a notice of appeal, etc, it may subsequently reinstate the notice or reply if it is satisfied that circumstances outside the control of the appellant or the SSHD made it impracticable for the party to comply with the direction.[5] This last provision, relating to reinstating an appeal, etc, was added to the 2003 Rules in 2013[6] following the judgment in *R1*[7] in which the SIAC had struck out the appellant's appeal following his having absconded from his bail conditions and his having failed to comply with a consequent SIAC direction, as served on his representatives, to surrender immediately to the police or an immigration officer and to notify SIAC of his intentions regarding the appeal. Once the appellant was apprehended he then sought to set aside the striking out order. Having rejected the appellant's submissions that the striking out order was invalid, Irwin J went on to consider whether the SIAC had any inherent power to reinstate the appeal but concluded that it did not – he stated his view, however, that it would on balance be desirable for an explicit power of reinstatement to be provided for in the Rules.[8] In *B*[9] the appellant refused to identify himself or to cooperate in such a way as to establish his true identity (he was known to be Algerian) and he was committed, by the SIAC, to prison for four months for contempt owing to this refusal.[10] The SSHD applied to the SIAC for his appeal to be struck out as an abuse of the SIAC's process and, in the alternative, for the appellant's failure to comply with directions in respect of identifying himself properly. It had previously been established that the appellant was a risk to national security and the remaining issue on appeal was risk on return to Algeria. Safe removal to Algeria depended on 'diplomatic assurances' being given by the Algerian authorities[11] and since, in the absence of identification, no such assurances could be obtained, the SIAC considered that the appellant would succeed on his appeal owing to his own continuing contempt and abuse of process. In these circumstances, and notwithstanding accepted mental health issues, the SIAC concluded that the proportionate and fair step was to strike out the appeal.[12]

1   2003 Rules, r 11B(a).
2   2003 Rules, r 11B(b).
3   2003 Rules, r 40(1).
4   2003 Rules, r 40(2).
5   2003 Rules, r 40(3).
6   2003 Rules, r 40(3) was added by the Special Immigration Appeals Commission (Procedure) (Amendment) Rules 2013, SI 2013/2995, r 29(c) from 28 November 2013 (see **7.13**, fn 1 above).
7   *R1 v Secretary of State for the Home Department (deportation – application to re-instate appeal – refused)* [2013] UKSIAC 105/2012 (10 July 2013).
8   See *R1* (above) at [28].
9   *B v Secretary of State for the Home Department (deportation: application to strike out)* [2014] UKSIAC SC092005 (1 July 2014).
10   SIAC's committal order was upheld by the Court of Appeal and the Supreme Court: see *B (Algeria) v Secretary of State for the Home Department* [2011] EWCA Civ 828; aff'd [2013] UKSC 4 (see **7.2**, fn 9 above).
11   Regarding such assurances and the proper approach to them, see *RB (Algeria) v Secretary of State for the Home Department* [2009] UKHL 10 at [23]–[29], [107], [120]–[122],

[158], [182]–[183], [192] and [237]; see further in *Asylum Law and Practice* (2nd edition, Bloomsbury Professional), para 11.45.
12   See *B* (above) at [7]–[38]. But see for now, *B v Secretary of State for the Home Department* [2015] EWCA Civ 445.

NOTIFICATION OF HEARING AND ADJOURNMENTS

7.42   Unless the SIAC orders otherwise (eg in relation to a 'closed' r 38 hearing: see **7.31** *et seq* above), it must serve notice of the date, time and place fixed for any hearing on every party, whether or not entitled to attend that hearing, and on the special advocate, if one has been appointed.[1] The SIAC may adjourn the hearing of any proceedings.[2] Whether or not to adjourn is a matter for the SIAC's discretion, acting in the interests of justice and applying the principle of 'fairness'[3] and, as with any court, the following factors are likely to be relevant:

(a)   the importance of proceedings and their likely adverse consequences to the party seeking the adjournment;

(b)   the risk of the party being prejudiced in the conduct of the proceedings if the application were refused;

(c)   the risk of prejudice or other disadvantage to the other party if the adjournment were granted;

(d)   the convenience of the court;

(e)   the interests of justice generally in the efficient despatch of court business;

(f)   the desirability of not delaying future litigants by adjourning; and

(g)   the extent to which the party applying for the adjournment had been responsible for creating the difficulty which had led to the application.[4]

1   2003 Rules, r 41.
2   2003 Rules, r 42.
3   See per Moses LJ in *SH (Afghanistan) v Secretary of State for the Home Department* [2011] EWCA Civ 1284.
4   See per Simon Brown LJ in *R v Kingston upon Thames Justices, ex parte Martin* [1994] Imm AR 172.

7.43   In *EI*[1] the appellant, having recently changed solicitors and funding from private to legal aid, applied for an adjournment of the substantive hearing. On the evidence presented, the SIAC considered that the appellant had had opportunity to change representation and seek legal aid at a much earlier stage and so was substantially responsible for his own predicament. The SIAC noted the problems involved for the SSHD's security service witness who 'is required to immerse him or herself in the detail of the case for many weeks before the hearing'[2] and concluded that it was not in the interests of justice to adjourn the substantive hearing.

1   *El v Secretary of State for the Home Department (refusal of entry – application for adjournment – refused)* [2011] UKSIAC 93/2010 (23 March 2011).
2   See *El* (above) at [8].

HEARING OF APPEALS AND APPLICATIONS FOR REVIEW; HEARING TWO OR MORE PROCEEDINGS TOGETHER

7.44   Under the 2003 Rules, every appeal and every application for review must be determined at a hearing before the SIAC except where:

- the appeal is treated as abandoned or is withdrawn by the appellant (see **7.40** above);[1]

- the application for review is withdrawn by the appellant;[2]

- the SSHD consents to the appeal being allowed or to the granting of the order or the relief sought in the application for review;[3] or

- the appellant is outside the UK or it is impracticable to give him notice of a hearing and, in either case, he is unrepresented.[4]

1   Treated as abandoned where NIAA 2002, s 104(4A) or (4B) – as applied by SIACA 1997, s 2(2) – or SIACA 1997, s 2(4) apply (see **7.5–7.6** above): 2003 Rules, r 12(a) as amended, from 12 April 2015, by the Special Immigration Appeals Commission (Procedure) (Amendment) Rules 2015, SI 2015/867, r 8.
2   2003 Rules, r 12(aa).
3   2003 Rules, r 12(b).
4   2003 Rules, r 12(c).

7.45   Where two or more appeals which relate to decisions or action taken in respect of the *same person* are pending at the same time, the SIAC must so far as is reasonably practicable hear the appeals together, unless to do so would cause unreasonable delay to any of the appeals.[1] Otherwise, where two or more appeals or applications are pending at the same time, the SIAC may direct them to be heard together if:

- some common question of law or fact arises in each of them;

- they relate to decisions or action taken in respect of persons who are members of the same family; or

- for some other reason it is desirable for the proceedings to be heard together.[2]

The SIAC must give all the parties, who would be entitled to attend the hearing of the proceedings, an opportunity to make representations before hearing proceedings together as above.[3]

1   2003 Rules, r 46(3).
2   2003 Rules, r 46(1).
3   2003 Rules, r 46(2).

HEARINGS IN PRIVATE

7.46   The general principle that justice must be seen to be done and that court proceeding are open to the public applies to the SIAC in the normal way. However, if the SIAC considers it necessary for the appellant and his representative to be excluded from a hearing or part of a hearing in order to secure that information is not disclosed contrary to the public interest (as to which see generally above), it must direct accordingly and conduct the hearing, or that part of it from which the appellant and his representative are excluded, in private.[1] Furthermore, the SIAC may conduct a hearing or part of a hearing in private for any other good reason.[2] In *BB*[3] the SIAC postulated that the very fact that parts of its proceedings must be held in 'closed sessions' militated against the use of 'non-closed' private hearings:

> 'There are specific boundaries within which the Commission is properly required to act in the absence of the public and the appellant and his representative. Otherwise it should conduct its proceedings in open. Indeed, the distinction in the Rules between open and closed material, and private and other hearings, emphasises to our minds that a power which might have to be exercised in a court which lacked those distinctions and procedures should be exercised very sparingly indeed by the Commission. It might be deployable for example if there was material which an appellant for very good reason wished to prevent entering the public domain, or perhaps where sensitive information had been disclosed inadvertently, as a way of reducing the damage to the relevant public interest.'[4]

1   2003 Rules, r 43(1).
2   2003 Rules, r 43(2).
3   *BB v Secretary of State for the Home Department* (SC/39/2005, 14 November 2006).
4   *BB* (above) at [22]. In *Naseer v Secretary of State for the Home Department* [2010] UKSIAC 77/2009 (18 May 2010) some of the closed material was inadvertently disclosed to the appellants' representatives and the SIAC held a private hearing pursuant to the 2003 Rules, r 43(2).

7.47   Nonetheless in a number of cases the SIAC has held parts of the hearings in private where it has accepted that particular sensitive evidence is to be given. For example, in the case of an asserted Russian spy working for a British Member of Parliament, the SIAC heard some of the evidence from the MP in private and, furthermore, invited the appellant to give evidence, as to any approaches that may have been made to her by Russian intelligence services, in a private session, so as to avoid any possible repercussions for her or her family in Russia.[1] Similarly in *T6* the appellant, an Algerian businessman who asserted that he would be at risk from the personal hostility of the Algerian President, gave much of his evidence – his own and that of his witnesses – in private sessions.[2]

1   See *Ekaterina Zatuliveter v Secretary of State for the Home Department (deportation – substantive – allowed)* [2011] UKSIAC 103/2010 (29 November 2011) at [2], [43], [61](i):

note that the appellant consistently denied any involvement with, and any approach to her by, the Russian intelligence services and the SIAC were sure that she was not a Russian agent.

2 See *T6 v Secretary of State for the Home Department (deportation – substantive – dismissed)* [2011] UKSIAC 95/2010 (18 February 2011) at [11].

GIVING OF EVIDENCE BEFORE THE SIAC

7.48 The SIAC may receive evidence in documentary or any other form.[1] The evidence of witnesses may be given orally before the SIAC and/or in writing, in which case it is to be given in such a manner and at such time as the SIAC directs (see **7.24** above).[2] An appellant is entitled to the services of an interpreter for bringing his appeal or application for review, when giving evidence and in such other circumstances as the SIAC considers necessary.[3] Every party shall be entitled to adduce evidence and to cross-examine witnesses during any part of a hearing from which he and his representative are not excluded[4] and the special advocate shall also be entitled to adduce evidence and to cross-examine witnesses.[5] However, no person can be compelled to give evidence or produce a document which he could not be compelled to give or produce on the trial of a civil claim in the part of the UK in which the proceedings before the SIAC are taking place.[6] Subject to that, the SIAC may, by issuing a summons, require any person in the UK to attend as a witness at the hearing of any proceedings before the SIAC and, at the hearing, to answer any questions or produce any documents in his custody or under his control which relate to any matter in issue in the proceedings.[7]

1 2003 Rules, r 44(2).
2 2003 Rules, r 44(1). The SIAC may require a witness to give evidence on oath: r 44(6).
3 2003 Rules, r 43A.
4 2003 Rules, r 44(5).
5 2003 Rules, r 44(5A).
6 2003 Rules, r 44(4). See in this regard **5.166** above, and the privilege against self-incrimination as explained by Goddard LJ in *Blunt v Park Lane Hotel Ltd* [1942] 2 KB 253, 257, cited in *Coogan v News Group Newspapers Ltd* [2012] EWCA Civ 48 at [14]–[18].
7 2003 Rules, r 45(1). No person shall be required to attend a hearing in compliance with a summons issued under para (1) unless the summons is served on him and the necessary expenses of his attendance are paid or tendered to him: r 45(2); and where a summons is issued at the request of a party, that party must pay or tender the expenses of the witness: r 45(3).

EVIDENCE OBTAINED BY TORTURE

7.49 Just as with the tribunal, the SIAC may receive evidence that would not be admissible in a court of law.[1] However, of particular relevance to SIAC proceedings, where it is the SSHD who bears the burden of establishing the national security grounds upon which he asserts that an appellant's deportation is conducive to the public good (see further **7.50–7.52** below), it is an absolute rule that evidence of a suspect or witness which has been obtained by torture, may not lawfully be admitted against a party to proceedings in any UK court, irrespective of where, by whom or on whose authority the torture had been inflicted and that accordingly, although the SIAC might admit a wide range of material which was inadmissible in judicial proceedings, it could not admit such evidence.[2] Accordingly, in *A*[3] the House of Lords held that the SIAC should refuse to admit evidence if it concluded that it was obtained by torture, but (by a majority of 4 to 3[4]) not merely if it was unable to conclude that there was not a real risk that the evidence had been obtained by torture. Thus the SIAC should not admit the evidence if it concluded on a balance of probabilities that it was obtained by torture, but if, on the other hand, the SIAC was left in doubt as to whether the evidence was obtained by torture, then it should admit it, but it had to bear its doubt in mind when evaluating the evidence.[5] The minority[6] considered that the SIAC should refuse to admit the evidence if it was unable to conclude that there was not a real risk that it had been obtained by torture. If it was in doubt whether the evidence had been procured by torture, then, per the minority, the SIAC should exclude the evidence. In *Al-Sirri*,[7] the tribunal, having concluded that certain evidence, relating to convictions in Egypt, had probably been obtained by torture, ascribed 'little weight' to it. On appeal, the SSHD took the position that it was open to a judicial tribunal in this country to give at least marginal weight to such evidence. Sedley LJ was unequivocal in his rejection of this submission:

'there was only one principled way in which to deal with the Egyptian convictions once the probability of torture was established, and that was to accord them no evidential weight at all. The reluctance of the Home Secretary to accept this principle is a matter of concern, and the failure of the AIT to respect it was in my judgment a serious error of law.'[8]

1 2003 Rules, r 44(3). See further and in detail Chapter 5 regarding evidence.
2 See *A v Secretary of State for the Home Department* [2005] UKHL 71.
3 *A* (above).
4 Lords Hope, Rodger, Carswell and Brown.
5 The majority considered that this approach was consistent with the International Convention against Torture and other Cruel Inhuman or Degrading Treatment or Punishment 1984, Art 15, which provides that a statement could not be used as evidence if it was 'established' to have been made as a result of torture; it did not say that the statement had to be excluded if there was an unrebutted suspicion of torture.
6 Lords Bingham, Nicholls and Hoffmann.
7 *Al-Sirri v Secretary of State for the Home Department* [2009] EWCA Civ 222, per Sedley LJ at [40]–[44].
8 *Al-Sirri* (above) at [44]. Longmore LJ at [80] specifically agreed. This point was not questioned on appeal to the Supreme Court: [2012] UKSC 54.

CONSIDERATION OF APPEALS AND APPLICATIONS FOR REVIEW BY THE SIAC

7.50   In many, if not most, appeals before the SIAC there will be two fundamental issues for consideration and determination:

(a)   whether the SSHD can demonstrate that an appellant's deportation, removal or exclusion from the UK is conducive to the public good on national security, or related, grounds (see **7.4** above),[1] the burden here being on the SSHD; and

(b)   whether the appellant can be deported, removed or excluded from the UK compatibly with the Refugee Convention and without violation of his human rights, the burden here being on the appellant in the normal way.

1   See NIAA 2002, s 97(1) and (2) – the decision was taken by the SSHD in the interests of national security or in the interests of the relationship between the UK and another country.

7.51   In some appeals only one of these issues will be live, for example in *Zatuliveter*[1] only (a) was in issue; in *T6*[2] only (b). In applications for review of exclusion decisions under SIACA 1997, s 2C a modified version of issue (a) above will always be central (see **7.10** above);[3] and issue (b), if live at all, could only be on the ground that, if the national security, etc case is not made out, then exclusion would breach Art 8 rights.

1   *Ekaterina Zatuliveter v Secretary of State for the Home Department* [2011] UKSIAC 103/2010 (29 November 2011).
2   *T6 v Secretary of State for the Home Department* [2011] UKSIAC 95/2010 (18 February 2011): there was no need to make a decision to deport on national security grounds because the appellant was an overstayer subject to a removal decision under IAA 1999, s 10 (see **1.11** above); the reason why the appeal came before the SIAC was because the SSHD certified it under NIAA 2002, s 97(3)(b) and (c) on the grounds that that the decision to refuse T6 asylum was taken wholly or partly in reliance on information which in the SSHD's opinion should not be made public in the interests of the relationship between the UK and another country nor otherwise in the public interest.
3   Direction that exclusion is conducive to the public good and is certified by the SSHD as a direction that was made wholly or partly in reliance on information which, in the opinion of the SSHD, should not be made public in the interests of national security, in the interests of the relationship between the UK and another country, or otherwise in the public interest.

NATIONAL SECURITY AND INTERNATIONAL RELATIONS CONSIDERATIONS

7.52   As regards (a) in **7.50** above, in *Rehman*[1] the House of Lords held that the SSHD has a very wide discretion in terms of determining whether an immigration decision to remove or exclude a person is in the interests of national security. The interests of national security are not limited to measures protecting against direct threats to the UK or its citizens, but can extend to measures directed against international terrorist activities. Decisions as to whether something is or is not in the interests of national security are for the SSHD and can only be interfered with by the courts if the view taken by the SSHD is one that could not be reasonably entertained. The SSHD was entitled to have regard to all the information available to him relating to the actual and potential activities of an individual and in making his decision no particular standard of proof was required. It was necessary that there be material upon which he could reasonably and proportionately determine that it was a real possibility that activities which were harmful to national security might occur but there was no necessity that he be satisfied that such material was proved. There was no need to ascertain degrees of probability when concluding whether deportation was in the interests of the public good. The House of Lords also held that the then three listed matters (in IA 1971, s 15(3): see **2.1** above) – namely that the deportation is conducive to the public good as being in the interests of national security or of the relations between the UK and any other country or for other reasons of a political nature – all overlapped and the SSHD did not have to 'pin his colours to one mast and be bound by his choice'.[2] Nonetheless, as explained by Lord Hoffman,[3] this does not mean that the whole decision on whether deportation would be in the interests of national security is surrendered to the SSHD so as to 'defeat the purpose for which the Commission was set up'. The SIAC serves at least three important functions which were shown to be necessary by the decision in *Chahal*:[4]

- First, the factual basis for the SSHD's opinion that deportation would be in the interests of national security must be established by evidence and it is therefore open to the SIAC to say that there was no factual basis for the SSHD's opinion, eg that the appellant was actively supporting terrorism in the UK or abroad or that the appellant is a spy (*Zatuliveter*[5]). In this respect, although the SIAC's ability to differ from the SSHD's evaluation may be limited by considerations inherent in an appellate process, it is not so limited by the principle of the separation of powers. The effect of the latter principle is only, subject to the next point, to prevent the SIAC from saying that although the SSHD's opinion that the appellant was actively supporting terrorism abroad had a proper factual basis, it does not accept that this was contrary to the interests of the UK's national security.

- Secondly, the SIAC may reject the SSHD's opinion on the ground that it was 'one which no reasonable minister advising the Crown could in the circumstances reasonably have held', ie that it was irrational.

- Thirdly, an appeal to the SIAC may turn upon issues which at no point lie within the exclusive province of the executive and the best and most obvious example of this is where Art 3 human rights are in issue (see below).

1   *Rehman v Secretary of State for the Home Department* [2001] UKHL 47, especially per Lord Slynn at [17], [22], [26], per Lord Steyn at [31] and per Lord Hoffmann at [37], [49], [50], [52], [53], [57]–[58], [62]. See also *A v Secretary of State for the Home Department* [2004] UKHL 56, per Lord Bingham at [29], [37]–[38] and per Lord Rodger at [175]–[178]. And see also *R (Lord Carlile of Berriew) v Secretary of State for the Home Department* [2014] UKSC 60, especially per Lord Sumption.
2   See *Rehman* (above), per Lord Slynn at [17]; see also per Lord Hoffmann at [59], [60]. Compare now the grounds for certification in NIAA 2002, s 97(2) (the first two of the

previous matters only, with 'relations' changed to 'relationship') and 97(3) (the first two matters plus a variation of the third into 'otherwise in the public interest') (see **7.4** above).

3   *Rehman* (above) at [54].
4   *Chahal v United Kingdom* (1996) 23 EHRR 413 (see **7.1** above).
5   *Ekaterina Zatuliveter v Secretary of State for the Home Department* [2011] UKSIAC 103/2010 (29 November 2011) (see **7.47**, fn 1 above).

ASYLUM AND HUMAN RIGHTS ISSUES

7.53   As regards (b) in **7.50** above, the first point to note is that where national security is in issue and the SIAC finds in the SSHD's favour on this issue – and obviously the SIAC's practice is to consider this first: see, for example, *Abu Qatada's case*[1] – then this is likely by itself to defeat an asylum claim under the Refugee Convention because, aside from any Art 1F exclusion issues that may arise,[2] under Art 33(2), the removal of a refugee, of whom there are reasonable grounds for regarding as a danger to the security of the country in which he claims, or has obtained, asylum, is not contrary to the Refugee Convention:[3] see again *Abu Qatada's case*.[4] Furthermore, where national security considerations apply in relation to an appeal on 'asylum grounds',[5] the SSHD is also likely to have issued a certificate under IANA 2006, s 55 – in addition to the certificate under NIAA 2002, s 97 (causing the appeal to be brought before the SIAC rather than the FTT) – stating that the appellant is not entitled to the protection of the Refugee Convention, Art 33(1) because Art 1F applies to him (whether or not he would otherwise be entitled to protection) or Art 33(2) applies to him on grounds of national security (whether or not he would otherwise be entitled to protection).[6] In which case the SIAC must begin its substantive deliberations on the asylum appeal by considering those statements in the SSHD's certificate[7] and if it agrees with those statements it must dismiss the appeal on its asylum grounds before going on to consider any other aspect of the case.[8] Note that, aside from national security issues, in an appropriate case the SSHD may also have issued a certificate under NIAA 2002, s 72, in relation to a 'serious criminal'.[9] In which case the SIAC must begin its substantive deliberation on the asylum appeal by considering the certificate and, having given the appellant an opportunity for rebuttal, if it agrees that the presumptions, as to serious criminality and danger to the community, apply,[10] it must dismiss the appeal in so far as it relies on refugee asylum grounds.[11]

1   *Abu Qatada v Secretary of State for the Home Department* [2007] UKSIAC 15/2005 (26 February 2007). See also the series of cases involving Algerian appellants, most recently *BB, G, PP, U, W, Y, Z v Secretary of State for the Home Department (deportation – substantive – remitted appeal)* [2013] UKSIAC 39/2005 (25 January 2013).
2   See *Asylum Law and Practice* (2nd edition, Bloomsbury Professional), Ch 8. See for a particular example of exclusion under Art 1F(c) in these circumstances, *Abu Qatada* (above) at [93]–[106].
3   See *Asylum Law and Practice* (above), Ch 9.
4   *Abu Qatada* (above) at [107]–[110].
5   See **2.4** above.

6   IANA 2006, s 55(1). See also **1.2** and **4.38** above regarding IANA 2006, s 55 – 'refugee convention: certification' – and appeals to the FTT.
7   IANA 2006, s 55(3).
8   IANA 2006, s 55(4).
9   NIAA 2002, s 72(9)(b). See **1.2** and **4.38** above regarding NIAA 2002, s 72 – 'serious criminal' – and appeals to the FTT.
10 NIAA 2002, s 72(2)–(6) and see *EN (Serbia) v Secretary of State for the Home Department* [2009] EWCA Civ 630 (see further **4.38** above).
11 NIAA 2002, s 72(9) and (10).

ART 8 CONSIDERATIONS

7.54   Similarly, Art 8 considerations, including those relating to the best interests of any children (as required to be taken account of by BCIA 2009, s 55), will not avail an appellant found to be a risk to national security. See in this regard per Mitting J in *E1*:[1]

'If the Secretary of State's case is right, then there will be compelling reasons to put the interests of the children and of the family a distant second to the need to protect national security; if the Secretary of State's case is not right, then their interests will call, inevitably, for the revocation of the decision, even if there might be other reasons for upholding it.'

1   *E1 v Secretary of State for the Home Department (refusal of entry – application for adjournment – refused)* [2011] UKSIAC 93/2010 (23 March 2011) at [21]. See also *G v Secretary of State for the Home Department* [2007] UKSIAC 2/2005 (08 February 2007) at [19].

ART 3 CONSIDERATIONS

7.55   Article 3 however, owing to the absolute nature of the right not to be subjected to torture or inhuman or degrading treatment or punishment,[1] will protect even those found to be a risk to national security. Returning to Lord Hoffman's third important function of the SIAC (see **7.52** above), the restraint necessary when the SIAC is considering whether the SSHD has correctly decided that an appellant is a threat to national security, is not necessary in determining whether the rights of an appellant under Art 3 are likely to be infringed by removal:

'The European jurisprudence makes it clear that whether deportation is in the interests of national security is irrelevant to rights under article 3. If there is a danger of torture, the Government must find some other way of dealing with a threat to national security. Whether a sufficient risk exists is a question of evaluation and prediction based on evidence. In answering such a question, the executive enjoys no constitutional prerogative.'[2]

1   See especially *Chahal v United Kingdom* (1997) 23 EHRR 413 and *Saadi v Italy* (2009) 49 EHRR 30.
2   *Rehman v Secretary of State for the Home Department* [2001] UKHL 47 at [54].

7.56   Accordingly the focus of the SIAC's consideration of safety of return issues will be on whether there is a real risk of a violation of the appellant's Art 3 rights on arrival back in the country of return.[1] In some cases a real risk of a 'flagrant' denial of the appellant's Arts 5 and 6 rights – rights to 'liberty' and to a fair trial – will also be in issue, as these are relevant to 'foreign' cases (ie where the issue is what will happen when the appellant is sent back to his 'home' country on removal from the UK[2]) where the real risk is of such a 'flagrant' breach as to constitute, in effect, a nullification or denial of the essence of the right.[3]

1   See in this regard *Soering v United Kingdom* (1989) 11 EHRR 439; *Cruz Varas v Sweden* (1992) 14 EHRR 1; *Saadi v Italy* (2009) 49 EHRR 30; and see further in *Asylum Law and Practice* (2nd edition, Bloomsbury Professional), para 11.31.
2   See *R (Ullah) v Special Adjudicator; Do v Immigration Appeal Tribunal* [2004] UKHL 26, per Lord Bingham at [7]–[9] for the distinction between 'domestic' and 'foreign' cases as relevant to human rights and immigration issues.
3   See especially *RB (Algeria) v Secretary of State for the Home Department* [2009] UKHL 10 and *Brown (aka Bajinja) v Government of Rwanda and Secretary of State for the Home Department* [2009] EWHC 770 (Admin); and see *Asylum Law and Practice* (2nd edition, Bloomsbury Professional), paras 11.64 and 11.65.

ASSURANCES AND MONITORING

7.57   In practice, the SIAC's answer to whether there is, or is not, a real risk of breaches of Art 3, and/or 'flagrant breaches' of Arts 5 and 6 rights, on return, has often turned on whether there are in place sufficiently reliable 'assurances', from the government of the country of proposed return, that the individual appellant's rights in these regards will not be breached if he is removed there. Such assurances have played a particularly important part in cases involving Algerian appellants over the last several years.[1] In *Naseer*[2] the SIAC held that confidential assurances from the Pakistan authorities were an insufficient safeguard against a real risk of Art 3 violation. In *J1*[3] the SIAC held that although there was a real risk that the appellant would suffer ill-treatment contrary to Art 3 if he were returned to Ethiopia in the absence of assurances, it found that the Ethiopian government could be trusted to comply with assurances given by it in a memorandum of understanding. However, there was only one organisation in Ethiopia which existed to monitor human rights and the SIAC found that it had not yet developed proper capacity for monitoring and therefore could not be trusted to report deliberate breaches by the Ethiopian authorities.[4] The SIAC nevertheless upheld the decision to deport the appellant on the basis that the SSHD had undertaken not to deport him before the necessary work had been done to develop the Ethiopian organisation's monitoring capacity and had undertaken to give removal directions five days before the date of deportation, to allow the appellant sufficient time to commence judicial review proceedings if he contended that the necessary work had not yet been done. On appeal, the Court of Appeal in *J1*[5] held that the SIAC had erred in law by effectively delegating the monitoring issue to the SSHD; rather the SIAC was obliged to determine that issue on the basis of the current evidence,[6] and that as currently the monitoring capacity was insufficient, the SIAC ought therefore to have held that deportation of the appellant to Ethiopia would constitute a breach of Art 3.

1   See **7.41** above. See *RB (Algeria) v Secretary of State for the Home Department* [2009] UKHL 10 at [23]–[29], [107], [120]–[122], [158], [182]–[183], [192] and [237]; see further in *Asylum Law and Practice* (2nd edition, Bloomsbury Professional), para 11.45. See most recently from the SIAC on Algeria, *BB, G, PP, U, W, Y, Z v Secretary of State for the Home Department (deportation – substantive – remitted appeal)* [2013] UKSIAC 39/2005 (25 January 2013).

2   *Naseer v Secretary of State for the Home Department* [2010] UKSIAC 77/2009 (18 May 2010) at [35]–[37].

3   *J1 v Secretary of State for the Home Department (deportation – substantive (safety on return) – dismissed)* [2011] UKSIAC 98/2010 (11 July 2011).

4   See *RB (Algeria)* (above) regarding the importance of adequate monitoring in order to render assurances reliable.

5   *J1 v Secretary of State for the Home Department* [2013] EWCA Civ 279.

6   See *R v Secretary of State for the Home Department, ex parte Ravichandran* [1996] Imm AR 97.

GIVING OF DETERMINATION: 'OPEN', 'CLOSED' AND 'CONFIDENTIAL' JUDGMENTS

7.58   When the SIAC determines any proceedings it must record its decision and the reasons for it[1] and must, within a reasonable time, serve on the parties a written determination – known as the 'open judgment' – containing its decision and, if and to the extent that it is possible to do so without disclosing information contrary to the public interest, the reasons for it.[2] However, prior to serving the determination on the appellant, the SIAC must first serve notice on the SSHD, and on any special advocate, of its intention to do so[3] and the SSHD may, within five days of the service of such a notice, apply to the SIAC to amend the proposed determination (or 'open judgment') if he considers that the notification to the appellant of any matter contained in it would cause information to be disclosed contrary to the public interest.[4] The SSHD must serve a copy of such an application on the special advocate[5] and the SIAC must give the special advocate and the SSHD an opportunity to make representations, as to what should or should not be in the 'open judgment', and may determine the application with or without a hearing.[6] The SIAC must not serve the determination on the appellant before the time limit for the SSHD to make an objection has expired or, where an objection has been made, before it has been determined.[7] Whether or not following on from any objections made by the SSHD, where the 'open judgment' does not include the full reasons for its decision, the SIAC must also serve on the SSHD and the special advocate a separate determination – the 'closed judgment' – including those reasons.[8] Where the SIAC serves a separate 'closed' judgment or determination, the special advocate may apply to the SIAC to amend both that determination, the 'closed judgment', and the 'open judgment' on the grounds that the 'closed judgment' contains material the disclosure of which would not be contrary to the public interest.[9] The special advocate must serve a copy of such an application on the SSHD[10] and the SIAC must give the special advocate and the SSHD an opportunity to make representations, as to what should be in the closed and what should be in the open judgments, and may determine the application with or without a hearing.[11] Accordingly the SSHD has an opportunity to object to material being included in the 'open judgment' and to make representations as to why it should be put in the 'closed judgment' and the special advocate has an opportunity to object to material being included in the 'closed judgment' and to make representations as to why it should be put in the 'open judgment'. Inherently, any hearings of any such representations, in either case, would likely be 'closed' to the appellant and the public. The SIAC's 'open judgments' are published on its own website[12] as well as on BAILII.[13] On occasion, the SIAC may also issue a confidential judgment' to the parties and to the special advocate, particularly where it has heard part of the evidence in private (see **7.46–7.47** above) and although this confidential judgment may also be served on specified bodies, it will not be published. For example, in *T6*[14] the confidential judgment was made available to the Administrative and Divisional Courts, to the UN Commissioner for Human Rights and to reputable human rights organisations such as Amnesty International and Human Rights Watch, subject to redaction of the identity of the witness who gave evidence in private. The Foreign and Commonwealth Office was entitled to supply a copy of the open, but not the confidential, judgment to the Ministry of Justice in Algeria.

1   2003 Rules, r 47(1) and (2).
2   2003 Rules, r 47(3). Note that the Rules do not refer to 'open' or 'closed judgments', rather this taxonomy has developed autonomously with a tendency to refer in practice to a 'judgment' rather than, as per the Rules, to a 'determination'; perhaps this is because the authors have been High Court judges.
3   2003 Rules, r 48(1)(b) and (2).
4   2003 Rules, r 48(3).
5   2003 Rules, r 48(4).
6   2003 Rules, r 48(5).
7   2003 Rules, r 48(6).
8   2003 Rules, r 47(4).
9   2003 Rules, r 47(5): see fn 2 above re open and closed judgments.
10   2003 Rules, r 47(6).
11   2003 Rules, r 47(7).
12   www.gov.uk/appeal-to-the-special-immigration-appeals-commission#previous-decisions.
13   www.bailii.org.
14   *T6 v Secretary of State for the Home Department* [2011] UKSIAC 95/2010 at [11]. See also *Naseer v Secretary of State for the Home Department* [2010] UKSIAC 77/2009 (18 May 2010) at [44].

ERRORS OF PROCEDURE AND CORRECTING ORDERS AND DETERMINATIONS

7.59   Where in any proceedings, before they have been determined by the SIAC, there has been an error of procedure, such as a failure to comply with a rule, then, subject to the 2003 (Procedure) Rules, the error does not invalidate any step taken in the proceedings unless the SIAC so orders and the SIAC may make an order or take any other step that it considers appropriate to remedy the error.[1] Furthermore, the SIAC may at any time amend an order or determination to correct a clerical error or other accidental slip or omission.[2] Where an order or determination is so amended, the SIAC must serve – subject to the procedure of giving advance notice to the SSHD[3] – the amended order or determination on every person on whom the original order or determination was served;[4] and the time within which a party may apply for permission to appeal against an amended determination runs from the date on which the party is served with the amended determination.[5]

1   2003 Rules, r 53.
2   2003 Rules, r 54(1).
3   See 2003 Rules, r 48 and see **7.39** and **7.58** above.
4   2003 Rules, r 54(2)(a).
5   2003 Rules, r 54(2)(b).

APPEALS FROM SIAC TO THE APPROPRIATE APPEAL COURT

7.60   Where the SIAC has made a final determination of an appeal, any party to the appeal may bring a further appeal to the appropriate appeal court on any question of law material to that determination.[1] Where the SIAC has made a final determination of a review (under SIACA 1997, ss 2C or 2D: see **7.10** above), any party to the review may bring an appeal against that determination to the appropriate appeal court.[2] In either case an appeal may be brought only with the leave of the SIAC or, if such leave is refused, with the leave of the appropriate appeal court.[3] Accordingly, an application for leave to appeal must be made, in the first instance, by filing with the SIAC an application in writing.[4] The time limits are, for the appellant, not later than five days after he is served with the SIAC's determination, meaning the 'open judgment', if he is in detention under the Immigration Acts[5] and otherwise not later than ten days after he is so served;[6] and for the SSHD, not later than ten days after he is served with the SIAC's 'open judgment' determination.[7] The SIAC may accept an application filed after the expiry of the relevant time period, as above, if it is satisfied that, by reason of special circumstances, it would be unjust not to do so.[8] The application must state the grounds of appeal, be signed by the applicant or his representative and be dated[9] and the applicant must serve a copy of the application notice on every other party.[10] The SIAC may decide an application for leave to appeal without a hearing unless it considers that there are special circumstances which make a hearing necessary or desirable.[11] An application for permission to appeal may be heard and determined by a single member of the SIAC, in practice by the Chairman.[12] Where the SIAC refuses permission, or leave, to appeal, an application may be made directly to the appropriate appeal court:[13] meaning, in relation to a determination made by the SIAC in England and Wales, the Court of Appeal; in relation to a determination made by the SIAC in Scotland, the Court of Session; and in relation to a determination made by the SIAC in Northern Ireland, the Court of Appeal in Northern Ireland.[14] Procedural issues pertaining to appeals, and to applications for permission to appeal, to the Court of Appeal in England and Wales are governed by CPR, Pt 52 and are addressed in Chapter 6. Of specific relevance here, the Practice Direction provides that the appellant's notice must be filed at the Court of Appeal within 21 days of the date on which the SIAC's decision, granting or refusing permission to appeal to the Court of Appeal, is given.[15] In *L1*,[16] Laws LJ considered the extent to which the Court of Appeal should examine the SIAC's 'closed judgment' on an application for permission and held that:[17]

> 'the court enjoys a discretion, which in my judgment should only be exercised in favour of examining SIAC's closed reasons on a permission application where it is not possible otherwise to do accurate justice. Where the court is confident on the basis of the open reasons alone that the right course is to refuse permission, it will generally not be necessary to look at the closed judgment; so also where the point is one of law, practice or procedure which does not depend on findings of fact which, it may be, are to be found in the closed judgment. But if the court concludes there is more than a fanciful possibility that the issue of permission to appeal may turn on the closed reasons, it should examine them.'

Where the court does intend to consider the closed judgment, the special advocate should be given an opportunity to make representations as to the effect of the closed judgment.[18]

1   SIACA 1997, s 7(1).
2   SIACA 1997, s 7(1A) as added by the Justice and Security Act 2013, from 25 June 2013 (see **7.12** above). Note that the provision in IA 2014, Sch 9(4), para 26(5) that amends SIACA 1997, s 7(1A) so as to add a reference to SIACA 1997, s 2E has not yet been brought into force despite the bringing into force of s 2E itself (see **7.10** above). Such an appeal is not explicitly limited to being on a question of law material to the determination. This is in conformity with the general approach to appeals to the Court of Appeal from the High Court in judicial review cases (see further Chapter 8).
3   SIACA 1997, s 7(2). There is no additional hurdle, akin to the 'second appeals test' for a grant of permission to appeal on a material question of law from a final determination of the SIAC to the appropriate appeal court.
4   2003 Rules, r 27(1). See **7.13–7.15** above regarding SIACA 1997, s 8 and specific provision for making rules prescribing and regulating the procedure to be followed on applications, to the SIAC, for leave to appeal under SIACA 1997, s 7.
5   2003 Rules, r 27(2)(a). See **7.18**, fn 5 above regarding detention under the Immigration Acts.
6   2003 Rules, r 27(2)(b). For the counting of days and the meaning of service, see **7.20** above.
7   2003 Rules, r 27(2A).
8   2003 Rules, r 27(2B). See further **7.22–7.23** above regarding extending the time limit for appealing when by reason of special circumstances, it would be unjust not to do so.
9   2003 Rules, r 27(3).
10 2003 Rules, r 27(4).
11 2003 Rules, r 27(5).
12 SIACA 1997, s 8(2) (see fn 4 above) and the 2003 Rules, r 5(1)(d) (see **7.17**, fn 3 above).

13 See SIACA 1997, s 7(2) and fn 3 above.
14 SIACA 1997, s 7(3).
15 CPR PD 52D, para 17.1(2).
16 *Ll v Secretary of State for the Home Department* [2013] EWCA Civ 906.
17 *Ll* (above) at [3].
18 *Ll* (above) at [4].

HEARING IN THE COURT OF APPEAL

7.61   The general rule is that any hearing in the Court of Appeal is held in public[1] but it is specifically provided for that a hearing, or any part of it, may be held in private if it involves matters relating to national security.[2] In *Rehman* in the Court of Appeal,[3] counsel was specially appointed at the request of the court in case there was a need to conduct part of the proceedings in a closed session and Lord Woolf MR explained[4] that, if it was necessary in the interests of justice for the court to hear submissions in the absence of the appellant (actually the respondent on this appeal) and his counsel, then under the inherent jurisdiction of the court, counsel instructed by the Government Legal Department, with the agreement of the Attorney General, would be able to perform a similar role to that of a special advocate, although without the advantage of any statutory backing for this being done. He noted that a court will only hear submissions on a substantive appeal in the absence of a party in the most extreme circumstances, but that considerations of national security can create situations where this is necessary.

1 CPR, r 39.2(1).
2 CPR, r 39.2(3)(b).
3 *Rehman v Secretary of State for the Home Department* [2000] EWCA Civ 168.
4 *Rehman* (above) at [31].

JURISDICTION OF THE COURT OF APPEAL

7.62   In terms of challenging the SIAC's conclusions, even on the risk on return issue (see (b) in **7.50** above), on an appeal restricted to a question of law, only general public law grounds such as irrationality, in the sense that no reasonable tribunal, properly directed, could have reached the decision that was reached, or materially inadequate reasoning, will suffice[1]. So held the House of Lords in *RB (Algeria)*[2] in rejecting the submission that compatibility with the ECHR was itself a question of law, so that on each appeal the Court of Appeal had an unrestricted jurisdiction to review the conclusion reached by the SIAC. Rather, the questions of whether an appellant is at real risk of being subjected to Art 3 prohibited mistreatment if returned to his country of origin and whether assurances obviate that risk, are questions of fact, to be decided in the light of all the evidence, and the role of the Court of Appeal is, expressly, a secondary, reviewing, function limited by statute to questions of law.[3]

1   See further in *R (Iran) v Secretary of State for the Home Department* [2005] EWCA Civ 982 at [9].
2   *RB (Algeria) v Secretary of State for the Home Department* [2009] UKHL 10.
3   See *RB (Algeria)* (above), per Lord Phillips at [62]–[73]; see also per Lord Hoffmann at [184]–[191], per Lord Hope at [212]–[217] and per Lord Brown at [253] and [254].

Chapter 8

Judicial review

8.1 This chapter addresses judicial review in the context of immigration cases. There are numerous textbooks of unimpeachable authority that address the theory and practice of judicial review in the Administrative Court and we do not propose recreating here what is well presented elsewhere. Neither is it our objective to lay out a detailed explanation of the substantive law of immigration, asylum, European Union law or unlawful detention and human rights in the migration context: these matters too are all treated expertly in specialist texts.[1] We begin by discussing the distribution of competence for judicial review between the UT and the Administrative Court, then address the procedures within each system, and conclude with a discussion of procedures and the law relating to public law remedies that are common to both jurisdictions.

1 See **1.1**.

DISTRIBUTION OF COMPETENCE: UT AND ADMINISTRATIVE COURT

Jurisdiction of UT and Administrative Court

8.2 In immigration, as in other areas, applications for judicial review have long been issued in the Queen's Bench Division of the High Court, in recent years within the Administrative Court. Consistently with the developing expertise of the Upper Tribunal and the public policy position that judicial review should be devolved to the relevant specialist jurisdiction, many classes of challenge are now to be brought in the UT. In general the UT will have the power to determine a judicial review claim if certain conditions are established,[1] namely that the claim seeks no orders or relief other than:

- a mandatory order, a prohibiting order, a quashing order, a declaration, or an injunction,[2]

- damages, restitution or the recovery of a sum due in relation to the claim and interest thereon,[3]

and additionally that it:

- does not question anything done by the Crown Court,[4] and

431

8.3   *Judicial review*

- relates to a class of application designated for transfer following Directions made under the Constitutional Reform Act 2005, Sch 2.[5]

1   TCEA 2007, s 18(1)–(3).
2   TCEA 2007, ss 15(1), 18(1).
3   TCEA Act 2007, s 18(4).
4   TCEA Act 2007, s 18(5).
5   TCEA Act 2007, s 18(6).

8.3   From 17 October 2011, a specific category of judicial review challenge was moved to the jurisdiction of the UT by virtue of a Direction under the Constitutional Reform Act 2005:

- those in relation to refusals to recognise further representations as amounting to fresh asylum or human rights claims including where there was a failure to make such a decision, or

- to make removal directions associated with those representations' failure.[1]

1   Direction given in accordance with the Constitutional Reform Act 2005, Sch 2, Pt 1 and the Tribunals, Courts and Enforcement Act 2007, s 18. The Direction of Lord Thomas, Lord Chief Justice, of 24 October 2013 confirmed that this class of judicial review continued to fall within the UT jurisdiction, if issued before the 21 August direction. A claim challenging a legacy decision was not one that involved further submissions advanced as a human rights or asylum claim: Davis LJ in *UZ (Pakistan) v Secretary of State for the Home Department* [2014] EWCA Civ 1319.

8.4   However, from 1 November 2013 (including claims issued and permission renewal requests in the Administrative Court from 9 September 2013), a much broader range of judicial reviews are to be initiated in the UT as designated by Practice Directions,[1] namely all those questioning:

- decisions made pursuant to the Immigration Acts,

- decisions made pursuant to instruments made under them, and

- decisions made outside the Rules, and decisions of the FTT made where there is no appeal to the UT.

1   Made under the Tribunals, Courts and Enforcement Act 2007, s 18(6).

8.5   However there are exceptions to this general rule which require an application to nevertheless be brought in the Administrative Court, namely, challenges to:

- the *vires* of statute, statutory instrument or Immigration Rule,

- the compatibility of such provisions with HRA 1998,

- decisions of the SIAC,

- decisions of the UT,

- the lawfulness of detention (though an application will not necessarily amount to such a challenge merely because it challenges a decision in relation to bail),

- decisions as to inclusion on the register of licensed sponsors, or any authorisation of such sponsors;

- decisions determining entitlement to British nationality or citizenship,

- decisions determining entitlement to welfare support (ie under or by virtue of IAA 1999, s 4 or Pt VI, or by virtue of NIAA 2002, Pts II or III (other support and assistance)).[1]

1 Lord Chief Justice's Direction regarding the transfer of immigration and asylum Judicial Review cases to the Upper Tribunal (Immigration and Asylum Chamber).

8.6 Additionally, age dispute cases, whilst not specified as automatically amenable to transfer to the UT, are very likely to be despatched there (because of the greater expertise and fact-finding powers of the UT, though this will not be possible where decisions under the immigration or nationality legislation are challenged at the same time as a local authority decision on age, which is a reason why the SSHD should not necessarily be joined as a party in such cases; normally the Administrative Court will determine permission before transfer, subject to it being inappropriate to give directions for subsequent conduct of the case or to direct a rolled-up hearing.[1]

1 *R (FZ) v Croydon LBC* [2011] EWCA Civ 59 at [31] (see **8.8**, fn 9 below), as discussed in *R (ota JS) and R (ota YK) v Birmingham City Council* (AAJR) [2011] UKUT 00505 (IAC) at [10]–[12].

8.7 Where a claim has been lodged in the wrong jurisdiction, the UT will be unable to entertain it, and will have to transfer the matter to the Administrative Court:[1]

'A judge considering an application for permission made to the Upper Tribunal must transfer the application to the Administrative Court if the application is not within the Lord Chief Justice's direction. In such a case, the High Court may, nevertheless decide that the application should be transferred to the Tribunal on a discretionary basis'.[2]

1 TCEA 2007, s 18(3). The High Court may similarly transfer cases to the UT, as discussed below.
2 UT JR Practice Statement, para 2.1 and in the unnumbered paragraph headed 'No jurisdiction'.

8.8 Lodging in the wrong court might have costs implications[1] though it is not understood that sanctions have been levied in cases of innocent error. Additional grounds that would bring a power or duty to transfer a matter to the High Court require permission,[2] including where the matter has previously been transferred to the UT.[3] Following transfer 'any steps taken, permission (or leave) given or orders made by the tribunal in relation to the application are to be treated as taken, given or made by the High Court'.[4] The UT has 'strike out' powers under the Upper Tribunal Rules[5] where it lacks jurisdiction once a claim has been issued,[6] which may be used in tandem with its case management power to transfer proceedings to another court or tribunal which has relevant jurisdiction because of a change of circumstances since the proceedings were started or because that is considered to be a more appropriate forum.[7] The UT must notify parties of transfers to its jurisdiction and give appropriate directions for the application's future conduct.[8] The High Court has similar powers to transfer a matter to the UT, albeit that it may not do so where the application questions a decision made under the Immigration Acts or the British Nationality Act 1981 or instruments made under them[9] and any steps, permissions or orders made by the High Court in relation to the application are from then onwards to be treated as taken, given or made by the UT,[10] which thereafter has the function of deciding the matter even if it does not fall within the directed class of cases.[11] Lodging a judicial review in the Administrative Court only because of an unmeritorious unlawful detention claim annexed to a challenge to removal might constitute an abuse of process;[12] and the fact that detention or other collateral issues are raised is not necessarily a reason to allow the related removal decisions to be determined in the Administrative Court.[13]

1   Tribunal Procedure (Upper Tribunal) Rules 2008, SI 2008/2698, r 10(3)(d).
2   SI 2008/2698, r 33A(2); these transfer powers arise only in England and Wales: r 33(1).
3   SI 2008/2698, r 33A(3).
4   TCEA 2007, s 18(9)(b).
5   SI 2008/2698.
6   SI 2008/2698, r 8(2).
7   SI 2008/2698, r 5(3)(k).
8   SI 2008/2698, r 27(1). In so doing provisions of SI 2008/2698, Pt 4 addressing judicial review in the UT may be disapplied. The UT JR Practice Directions, para 2.3 make it clear that 'In the case of proceedings transferred to the Tribunal by a court, the Tribunal will expect the applicant to have complied with all relevant Practice Directions of that court that applied up to the point of transfer.'
9   Seniors Courts Act 1981, s 31A including any decisions made under 'other provision of law for the time being in force which determines British citizenship, British overseas territories citizenship, the status of a British National (Overseas) or British Overseas citizenship': s 31A(7). There are similar powers in Northern Ireland proceedings under the Judicature (Northern Ireland) Act 1978.
10   Seniors Courts Act 1981, s 31A(3)(c).
11   Seniors Courts Act 1981, s 31A(4).
12   *Ashraf v Secretary of State for the Home Department* [2013] EWHC 4028 (Admin).
13   Green J in *Khan, R (on the application of) v Secretary of State for the Home Department* [2014] EWHC 2494 (Admin) at [70](xiii).

JUDICIAL REVIEW IN THE UT

Governing legal instruments; legal representation

8.9   The principal legal materials governing judicial review in the UT are:

• TCEA 2007,

- the Upper Tribunal (Procedure) Rules 2008,[1]

- the Practice Direction of 17 October 2011 (amended on 1 November 2013),[2]

- the Practice Statement relating to claims lodged on or after 1 November 2013.[3]

1 Tribunal Procedure (Upper Tribunal) Rules 2008, SI 2008/2698.
2 Practice Directions regarding Immigration Judicial Review in the Immigration and Asylum Chamber of the Upper Tribunal (Lord Justice Carnwath Senior President of Tribunals, 17 October 2011; amended by Sir Jeremy Sullivan (Senior President of Tribunals, 1 November 2013) ('UT JR Practice Directions').
3 Practice Statement regarding Immigration Judicial Review in the Immigration and Asylum Chamber of the Upper Tribunal on or after 1 November 2013 (Lord Justice Carnwath Senior President of Tribunals, 17 October 2011; amended by Sir Jeremy Sullivan (Senior President of Tribunals, 1 November 2013) ('UT JR Practice Statement') – this replaced the Practice Statement: Fresh Claim Judicial Reviews in the Immigration and Asylum Chamber of the Upper Tribunal on or after 29 April 2013.

8.10 The UT's own Rules are different and separate from the Civil Procedure Rules (CPR) and 'it is generally right to be wary of reading concepts from the CPR into them.'[1] A person may only be represented by a person authorised to conduct litigation in the High Court under the Legal Services Act 2007, and rights of audience are restricted to those authorised to appear in the High Court:[2] OISC firms are not permitted to so act, according to their regulating body.[3]

1 *R, R (on the application of) v FTT (HESC) and Hertfordshire CC* [2013] UKUT 294 (AAC) at [30].
2 Tribunal Procedure (Upper Tribunal) Rules 2008, SI 2008/2698, r 11(5A)–(5B).
3 Practice note on the use of the Public Access Scheme by OISC regulated advisers, which states at para 6 that 'No OISC adviser should seek to use either the PAS [Public Access Scheme] or LAS [Licensed Access Scheme] to instruct a barrister to undertake work before the High Court as to do so is contrary to the Legal Services Act 2007', read with IAA 1999, s 84.

Jurisdiction of the UT

8.11 The judicial review jurisdiction of the UT arises from TCEA 2007, which empowers it to grant relief by way of:

- mandatory order,

- prohibiting order,

- quashing order,

- declarations, and

- injunctions.[1]

1 TCEA 2007, s 15(1) (mandamus, prohibition and certiorari in Northern Ireland: s 18(6)).

8.12 The relief granted has the same effect as the corresponding relief granted by the High Court, and is similarly enforceable,[1] and the UT grants such orders on the same basis as would the High Court,[2] ie asking whether 'it would be just and convenient for the declaration to be made or the injunction to be granted' bearing in mind:

'(a) the nature of the matters in respect of which relief may be granted by mandatory, prohibiting or quashing orders;

(b) the nature of the persons and bodies against whom relief may be granted by such orders; and

(c) all the circumstances of the case.'[3]

1 TCEA 2007, s 15(3).
2 TCEA 2007, s 15(4) (see **8.53**, fn3).
3 TCEA 2007, s 15(5), with reference to the Senior Courts Act 1981, s 31(2).

8.13 Where the challenged decision is quashed, the UT may remit the matter to the original decision-maker to reconsider the matter in line with its findings: though where the impugned decision is of the FTT, it may substitute its own decision on the issue in question where there was an error of law absent which the decision could be made only one way,[1] at which point the decision takes effect as if it had been that of the inferior tribunal.[2]

1 TCEA 2007, s 17(1)–(2).
2 TCEA 2007, s 17(3). See *R (on the application of Mamour) v Secretary of State for the Home Department* (FCJR) [2013] UKUT 86 (IAC) for the difficulties in the UT going further than quashing a decision absent circumstances where there was only one rational response to the application.

Powers of the UT

8.14 Where a money award is made, it may be enforced as in the High Court.[1] Permission[2] is required to bring a claim for relief and will be granted only where the applicant has sufficient interest in the matter;[3] permission refusals may be appealed to the Court of Appeal which may then determine the matter substantively.[4] Either permission or relief on the substantive judicial review may be refused:

'where the tribunal considers–

(a) that there has been undue delay in making the application, and

(b) that granting the relief sought on the application would be likely to cause substantial hardship to, or substantially prejudice the rights of, any person or would be detrimental to good administration.'[5]

1   TCEA 2007, s 16(7).
2   TCEA 2007, s 16(2). 'Leave' is required in Northern Ireland.
3   TCEA 2007, s 16(3).
4   TCEA 2007, s 18(8).
5   TCEA 2007, s 16(4), (5).

Forms

8.15   In practice, judicial reviews are launched in the UT via a judicial review claim form, T480,[1] which is accompanied by supporting Guidance notes on its completion.[2] Applications are generally lodged in person at Field House or one of the regional centres of the tribunal.[3] Claims should be issued as soon as possible; if further documents are required, then they should follow the claim rather than delay it.[4] The applicant must serve a statement confirming that the respondent and any interested party have been provided with a copy of the application within nine days of issuing.[5] If an order is sought for interim relief, judgment on a contested issue such as stay, disclosure or directions, Form T484 should be used.[6] Information as to any change of representation is to be provided via Form T486.[7]

1   T480 UT Judicial Review Claim Form; UT JR Practice Directions, para 3.1.
2   T481 Guidance Notes on Completing the UT Judicial Review Claim Form; UT JR Practice Statement, para 2.1.
3   Field House, 15–25 Breams Buildings, London, EC4A 1DZ. The regional centres are Birmingham, Civil Justice Centre, Priory Courts, 5th Floor, 33 Bull Street, Birmingham, B4 6DS; Cardiff Civil Justice Centre, 2 Park Street, Cardiff, CF10 1ET; Leeds Combined Court, 1 Oxford Row, Leeds, LS1 3BG; and Manchester Civil Justice Centre, 1 Bridge Street West, Manchester, M60 9DJ.
4   T481 Guidance Notes.
5   Tribunal Procedure (Upper Tribunal) Rules 2008, SI 2008/2698, r 28A(2); T485 Statement under Upper Tribunal Rule 28A(2)(b).
6   T484 Application Notice.
7   T486 Notice of Change of Solicitor.

8.16   Thus the key forms in the UT[1] are:

- T480 (claim form),

- T481 (guidance notes on completing T480),

- T482 (UT acknowledgment of service),

- T483 (UT application for urgent consideration),

- T484 (application notice: for seeking orders),

- T485 (statement of service of claim on respondent and other interested parties),

- T486 (notice of change of solicitor).

1   Found at www.justice.gov.uk/tribunals/immigration-asylum-upper/application-for-judicial-review.

Fees

8.17 Fees may be charged:

- on an application for permission,

- if permission is granted, and

- if any further applications are made during the claim,

similarly to those levied in the Administrative Court; they are set out in an order, and can thus be varied by that instrument's amendment.[1] As of January 2014 it is:

- £140 to issue a claim,

- £350 for an oral permission renewal,

- £700 for a full hearing,

- £80 for applications on notice,

- £45 for consent orders and other applications, and

- £40 for a witness summons.

Requests for copy documents from the tribunal will be £5 for up to ten pages, and 50p a page thereafter.[2]

1 Upper Tribunal (Immigration and Asylum Chamber) (Judicial Review) (England and Wales) Fees Order 2011, SI 2011/2344, Sch 1.
2 Ibid.

8.18 The UT must not accept an application unless it is accompanied by the required fee, or an undertaking (in urgent cases) is given to pay the fee.[1] Fees are not payable if the applicant receives certain benefits, or if his income is below a specified threshold.[2] Failure to pay the required fee after the grant of permission will lead to the automatic striking out of the claim.

1 Tribunal Procedure (Upper Tribunal) Rules 2008, SI 2008/2698, rr 28A(1), 8(1)(b).
2 The Upper Tribunal (Immigration and Asylum Chamber) (Judicial Review) (England and Wales) Fees Order 2011, SI 2011/2344, regs 2–3.

Filing the application in the UT

8.19 The parties in judicial reviews in the UT are styled 'applicant' and 'respondent' rather than 'claimant' and 'defendant' as would be the case in the Administrative Court.[1] Applications must be made in writing.[2] The application must state:

- the name and address of the applicant, the respondent and any other person whom the applicant considers to be an interested party (ie a person likely to be directly affected by the application, such as the SSHD who will have been the respondent in FTT or UT proceedings where the tribunal's decision is now challenged);

- the name and address of the applicant's representative (if any);

- an address where documents for the applicant may be sent or delivered;

- details of the decision challenged (including the date, the full reference and the identity of the decision maker);

- that the application is for permission to bring judicial review proceedings;

- the outcome that the applicant is seeking; and

- the facts and grounds on which the applicant relies.[3]

1   Tribunal Procedure (Upper Tribunal) Rules 2008, SI 2008/2698, r 28(4)(a).
2   SI 2008/2698, r 28(1).
3   SI 2008/2698, r 28(4).

8.20   The claim form should be accompanied by

- a copy of any written record of the decision in the applicant's possession or control;

- copies of any other relevant documents;[1]

- any written evidence on which it is intended to rely, which may be relied upon as evidence where accompanied by a statement of truth;

- copies of any relevant statutory material;

- a list of essential documents for advance reading;[2] and

- two copies of a paginated and indexed bundle containing all the documents.[3]

We discuss the necessary and advisable supporting documents to support a judicial review application in more detail below, at **8.63**.

1   Tribunal Procedure (Upper Tribunal) Rules 2008, SI 2008/2698, r 28(6).
2   UT JR Practice Directions, paras 4.1(a) and 4.2.
3   UT JR Practice Directions, para 5.1.

Time limits for bringing application in the UT

8.21   Applications

'must be made promptly and, unless any other enactment specifies a shorter time limit, must be sent or delivered to the Upper Tribunal so that it is received no later than 3 months after the date of the decision, action or omission to which the application relates.'[1]

There is a shorter time limit of one month for challenging a decision of the FTT.[2] Late applications must be supported by a reasoned request for an extension of time, and the application may be admitted only where time is duly extended;[3] satisfactory reasons must be provided with factual assertions supported by evidence, and the UT may have regard to any relevant time limits for statutory appeals.[4] Relevant factors might be a delay in obtaining public funding,[5] the importance of the issue in question,[6] and the pursuit of alternative remedies. The nature of any prejudice to the SSHD caused by delay in an immigration case is much less direct and immediate than it might be to a respondent in a planning case, albeit that prejudice to good administration could nevertheless be a relevant consideration.[7] It may be thought better to issue a timely application for judicial review than to pursue the Pre Action Protocol, because a claim can be barred altogether if time is not extended, whereas a failure to comply with the Protocol, whilst reprehensible, is unlikely to lead to anything worse than a failure to recover costs, or other procedural sanction.

1   Tribunal Procedure (Upper Tribunal) Rules 2008, SI 2008/2698, r 28(2).
2   SI 2008/2698, r 28(3).
3   SI 2008/2698, r 28(7); a decision on time and permission will be considered at the same time: UT JR Practice Statement, para 2.3.
4   UT JR Practice Statement, para 2.4. See by analogy Ouseley J in *Khan, R (on the application of) v Secretary of State for the Home Department* [2011] EWHC 2763 (Admin) regarding judicial review of refusals of permission to appeal to the UT at [5]. See further the considerations identified at **8.56** below.
5   Pill LJ in the Court of Appeal in *Sacker (Helen) v HM Coroner for the County of West Yorkshire* [2003] EWCA Civ 217.
6   Taylor J in the High Court in *R v Secretary of State for the Home Department, ex parte Ruddock* [1987] 1 WLR 1482, at 1485.
7   *WO, Re Judicial Review* [2012] ScotCS CSOH_88 at [47].

Acknowledgment of Service

8.22   Those sent or provided with a copy of the application for judicial review, as defendant or interested party, must provide an Acknowledgment of Service if wishing to participate in the proceedings, within 21 days, to the tribunal[1] and applicant.[2] It must be in writing and state whether they support or oppose the application for permission, their grounds for so doing, and any other submission or information which they consider may assist the UT, including the name and address of any other person not named in the application as a respondent or interested party whom the person providing the acknowledgment considers might participate.[3] Those sent or provided with the application not providing an Acknowledgment of Service may not take part in the permission application, unless allowed to do so by the UT, though if permission is granted they may thereafter participate.[4] The application for permission will not be decided unless the time for lodging an Acknowledgment of Service has expired, unless the respondent requests urgent consideration of the application, or an application for interim relief has been refused and the judge considers it

appropriate to deal with permission simultaneously.[5] We deal with failures to
file an Acknowledgment of Service below, amongst procedures common to the
UT and Administrative Court.[6] We address general considerations regarding
the Acknowledgment of Service further below.[7]

1   Tribunal Procedure (Upper Tribunal) Rules 2008, SI 2008/2698, r 29(1).
2   SI 2008/2698, r 29(1).
3   SI 2008/2698, r 29(2).
4   SI 2008/2698, r 29(3).
5   UT JR Practice Statement, para 2.2.
6   See **8.120** below.
7   See **8.120** *et seq* below.

Urgent procedure in the UT (including challenges to removal directions/interim relief)

8.23   There is a particular form specified where matters require urgent
consideration.[1] The UT may only consider such an application where the
underlying judicial review application has been issued, otherwise the matter
must be brought in the Administrative Court.[2] Details should be provided as to:

●   the need for urgency,

●   the timescale sought for the consideration of the application (eg 'within
     72 hours'), and

●   the date by which the substantive hearing should take place (eg 'within
     six weeks').[3]

1   T483 Application for Urgent Consideration.
2   See Tribunal Procedure (Upper Tribunal) Rules 2008, SI 2008/2698, rr 34 and 40; UT JR
     Practice Statement, para 3.1.
3   UT JR Practice Direction, para 11.1; see also **8.104** and **8.105** below.

8.24   Where an interim injunction is sought, the applicant must also provide:

●   the draft order and the relevant grounds (which must be served by fax
     and post on the respondent and any interested parties, advising them of
     the application and their entitlement to make representations).[1]

1   UT JR Practice Direction, paras 11.2, 12.2.

8.25   The application must be accompanied by the representative's
statement:

●   explaining the need for urgency,

●   when the challenged decision came to the claimant's notice, and

●   certifying that there is nothing in the application that is not in their
     opinion properly arguable.[1]

1   UT Practice Statement, para 3.2.

8.26   Both the claim form (T480) and the request for urgent consideration (T483) must be served by fax and post on the respondent and interested parties, advising them of the application and that they may make representations; any order must be similarly provided.[1] An urgent application lodged after 9.30am and before 4.15pm on a working day will be considered by a judge of the UT that day.[2]

1   UT JR Practice Direction, para 12.1, Practice Statement, para 3.2.
2   UT JR Practice Statement, para 3.3.

8.27   The tribunal will consider the application within the time requested and may make such order as it considers appropriate.[1] If the tribunal specifies that a hearing shall take place within a specified time, the representatives of the parties must liaise with the tribunal and each other to fix a hearing of the application within that time (it may take place on the very day that it is arranged, though it is understood that it is only where there are removal directions in force that a challenge to them will be so treated).[2] Special arrangements have been made for applications lodged at centres outside London for urgent applications made before permission is granted to be considered by judges at those centres before the case is transferred to Field House.[3] An urgent application for a stay on removal will be considered on the papers by a judge of the UT, unless the judge adjourns the application for an oral hearing at which both sides can makes submissions.[4] An application for an injunction requiring the respondent to return a person who has been previously removed from the United Kingdom may only be made after an oral hearing of which the respondent has notice.[5] Where a judge considers an urgent application on the papers, and concludes that further information is needed from the respondent, the judge may telephone the Home Office and seek the further information, keeping a note of any information supplied.[6]

1   UT JR Practice Direction, para 13.1.
2   UT JR Practice Direction, para 13.2.
3   UT JR Practice Direction, para 3.4.
4   UT JR Practice Direction, para 3.5.
5   UT JR Practice Direction, para 3.6 (see **8.125** below).
6   UT JR Practice Direction, para 3.7.

8.28   Where the application challenges removal, there are certain additional requirements[1] (which do not prevent a person bringing an application following his removal).[2] Any such applications should make plain that this aspect of the Practice Direction is in play[3] and provide a copy of the removal directions, underlying decisions, and any other document served with those directions including a factual summary by the SSHD, as well as a detailed statement of the applicant's grounds for making the application;[4] and any inability to so comply should be explained.[5] The Immigration Factual Summary (Form ICD.2599) should be in plain English and should include:

●   a chronology of the case history,

- information as to whether any appeal rights have been previously exercised,

- past applications for judicial review.[6]

1 UT JR Practice Direction, para 14.1.
2 UT JR Practice Direction, para 14.2.
3 UT JR Practice Direction, para 15.1(a).
4 UT JR Practice Direction, para 15.1(b).
5 UT JR Practice Direction, para 15.2.
6 Enforcement Instructions and Guidance (EIG), Ch 60, section 18.

8.29 The issued application form and accompanying documents must be provided 'immediately upon issue' to the address specified by the Secretary of State.[1] Unreasoned non-compliance with these requirements will lead to the staff of the tribunal referring the matter to a judge for speedy consideration, notifying the parties of this action.[2]

1 UT JR Practice Direction, para 15.3.
2 UT JR Practice Direction, para 16.1.

8.30 Where an urgent application is granted, the judge should forthwith draw up a reasoned order which is sent to both parties;[1] if it is refused, short written reasons should be supplied, together with any material information obtained from the SSHD.[2] An urgent application that is refused on the papers may be renewed orally to a judge of the UT upon application being made promptly to the tribunal and notice given to the respondent: such applications will be listed as soon as practicable in all the circumstances of the case.[3] A refusal of an oral urgent application is final at UT level, though may be appealed to the Court of Appeal.[4] The provisions of the Practice Statement addressing decisions on renewed applications, as to summary reasons, permission to the Court of Appeal and any stay related to such application, costs, and disposal, apply similarly to urgent applications.[5]

1 UT JR Practice Direction, para 3.8.
2 UT JR Practice Direction, para 3.9.
3 UT JR Practice Direction, para 3.10.
4 UT JR Practice Direction, para 3.11 (see **8.81**, fn 4 below).
5 UT JR Practice Direction, para 3.12, cross referring to paras 2.14–2.16 (see **8.34**, fnn 4 and 5 below).

Decision on permission

8.31 The UT must provide its decision in relation to the permission application and its reasons for any refusal of the application, or any limitations or conditions on permission being granted, to the applicant, respondent, or interested parties.[1] Brief written reasons must be given.[2] Permission applications 'generally, in the first instance' will be considered without a hearing;[3] the paper consideration may be adjourned to an oral hearing if required.[4] Where the application is refused without a hearing, an applicant may apply for that decision's reconsideration at an oral hearing[5] such that the UT receives a renewal application within nine days of the refusal having been sent by the UT,[6] unless the UT records in that decision that it considers the application to be totally without merit (a person in receipt of such an order must appreciate that an injunction will now be essential to prevent removal):[7] which is a finding that should be reserved for the 'truly hopeless' case.[8] When refusing an application, the judge may additionally:

- make an appropriate order regarding the costs of the Acknowledgment of Service,

- normally curtail the period for renewal from the nine days provided in the Rules to seven days, and

- state that renewal of the application shall not bar removal.[9]

A permission hearing must be the subject of at least two days' notice to the parties.[10]

1   Tribunal Procedure (Upper Tribunal) Rules 2008, SI 2008/2698, r 30(1).
2   UT JR Practice Statement, para 2.8.
3   UT JR Practice Directions, para 6.1; SI 2008/2698, r 30(4)(c).
4   UT JR Practice Statement, para 2.6(iii).
5   SI 2008/2698, r 30(3)–(4); UT JR Practice Direction, para 17.1.
6   SI 2008/2698, r 30(5).
7   SI 2008/2698, r 30(4A); UT JR Practice Statement, paras 2.9 and 2.7(iii). Collins J in *R, Santur (on the application of) v Secretary of State for the Home Department* [2007] EWHC 741.
8   Collins J in *Santur* at [23]
9   UT JR Practice Statement, para 2.7.
10   SI 2008/2698, r 36(2)(a).

Renewal hearings, and appeal against permission refusal

8.32   An application for a renewed application for permission by way of oral hearing is to be made by a renewal notice (there appears to be no set form), which must explain:

- the basis for renewal,

- the grounds thereof, and

- any response to the permission refusal.[1]

1   UT JR Practice Statement, para 2.10.

8.33   A renewal hearing will be listed promptly at Field House, London, with at least two days' notice to the applicant and to any party serving an Acknowledgment of Service.[1] Legal representatives wishing to make arrangements by video link should notify the tribunal in good time, giving details of their proposal, having particular regard to the requirements of the CPR,[2] relevant considerations being that significant savings can be achieved by way of cost and time, though the governing question must be whether its use will be likely to be beneficial to the efficient, fair and economic disposal of the litigation, bearing in mind that it is usually preferable to take witness evidence remotely than in person.[3] Field House will be styled the 'local site' and the location(s) elsewhere will be the remote site(s), and before seeking a direction to progress use of this facility, the applicant, who will be responsible for costs subject to contrary order, should notify the listing officer, diary manager or other appropriate court officer of the intention to seek it, and should enquire as to the availability of court equipment for the day or days of the proposed video conferencing event, and make appropriate arrangements for the use of documents and witness handling.[4] A renewed permission application will be assigned a time estimate of 45 minutes subject to an application which:

- explains why a longer hearing is necessary,

- explains what steps have been taken to minimise the time taken, and

- gives a realistic revised time estimate.[5]

1   UT JR Practice Statement, para 2.11.
2   UT JR Practice Statement, para 2.12.
3   *Nare (evidence by electronic means) Zimbabwe* [2011] UKUT 00443 (IAC).
4   CPR PD 32, Annex 3.
5   UT JR Practice Statement, para 2.13.

8.34   Skeleton arguments may be provided to assist the UT in permission hearings, and should do so not less than seven days prior to the hearing date, otherwise confirming in writing that they are relying only on documents previously filed and served.[1] Bundles will normally be destroyed absent specific request to the contrary.[2] If permission is refused at a hearing, then the judge so doing will:

- deliver a judgment giving the decision with summary reasons for the refusal of the application or any part of it (and arrange for subsequent delivery of written reasons, which will constitute disposal of the proceedings);[3]

- consider any application made at that hearing for permission to appeal to the appropriate appellate court (see **8.47** below for onwards appeals generally) and rule on the issue, whether or not an application is made: this decision on permission is deemed to be made as if on an application by a party, so triggering the subsequent appellate jurisdiction);[4] or

- adjourn the hearing for a short time to give the party concerned more time to make his own application (determining whether a stay on removal is appropriate in the meantime); and

- consider any costs orders made arising from the application.[5]

1   Standard Directions as of Autumn 2014: they may be provided by email to utiac.londonjr.
    skeletonarguments@hmcts.gsi.gov.uk and if an electronic version is provided, then no paper
    copy needs to be supplied.
2   Standard Directions as of Autumn 2014: after a substantive hearing an opportunity will be
    given for the parties to collect bundles, although they will be destroyed two working days
    after the final decision of the UT has been given.
3   UT JR Practice Statement, para 2.10.
4   UT JR Practice Statement, para 2.16; Tribunal Procedure (Upper Tribunal) Rules 2008,
    SI 2008/2698, rr 40(1)(a) and 44(4)(c); TCEA 2007, s 13(4). This addresses the difficulty
    identified in *NB (Algeria)* [2012] EWCA Civ 1050 that no application to the Court of Appeal
    was otherwise possible until receipt of written reasons significantly after the permission
    refusal.
5   UT JR Practice Statement, para 2.14.

8.35   As a hearing must be held in immigration judicial review proceedings
before making a decision which disposes of proceedings,[1] a party will always
have the opportunity to apply for permission to appeal at that hearing, and the
question of permission should be considered whether it is raised or not.[2] The
time limit for appeal to the appropriate appellate court is seven days where the
permission refusal states the application is totally without merit.[3]

1   Tribunal Procedure (Upper Tribunal) Rules 2008, SI 2008/2698, r 34(3).
2   SI 2008/2698, r 44(4A)–(4B).
3   SI 2008/2698, r 44(4C).

Post grant of permission steps: procedure to the hearing

8.36   A person who receives notice of a permission grant must provide
detailed grounds for contesting the application (or supporting it, on additional
grounds),[1] to be sent or delivered such that they are received not more than
35 days after the UT sent notice of the permission grant.[2] No grounds beyond
those upon which permission was granted may be relied upon without the
UT's permission.[3] A post-permission application to vary grounds must be
made prior to the substantive hearing via 'written notice to the tribunal and
to any other person served with the application, not later than seven working
days before that hearing'.[4] If there is a possibility of settlement then the UT
administration should be informed so the case may be removed from the
warned list; a case will be treated as withdrawn only once a consent order
is signed by both parties, addressing costs as well as other issues, and duly
filed, and if it is agreed that it should succeed, then an agreed order should
be lodged for the UT's consideration.[5] Parties and, with the UT's permission,
other persons, may submit evidence (though not at the permission application),
make representations at hearings that they are entitled to attend, and make
written representations in relation to a decision to be made without a hearing.[6]
The Rules for holding hearings, their listing, attendance thereat, public and
private hearings, and determination of a matter in a party's absence, are the
same for substantive judicial review matters as they are for statutory appeals.[7]
The permission of the UT is required for a party to withdraw his 'case'.[8] The

parties have been encouraged to communicate with the UT electronically where possible.[9] The standard form signed by advocates upon arriving at hearing rooms will require the details of their client and their professional address or source of instructions, in contrast to immigration appeals where forms appropriate to the regulatory scheme focus on the advocate's location in the structure set up under IAA 1999.

1   Tribunal Procedure (Upper Tribunal) Rules 2008, SI 2008/2698, r 31(1); cf *Kumar, R (on the application of) v Secretary of State for the Home Department (acknowledgement of service; Tribunal arrangements)* (IJR) [2014] UKUT 104 (IAC) at [11].
2   SI 2008/2698, r 31(2).
3   SI 2008/2698, r 32.
4   UT JR Practice Direction, para 7.1; see further UT JR Practice Statement, para 2.15.
5   Standard Directions as of Autumn 2014.
6   SI 2008/2698, r 33.
7   See Chapter 6.
8   See Chapter 6 at **6.54** *et seq* above.
9   *Muwonge, R (on the application of) v Secretary of State for the Home Department (consent orders: costs: guidance)* (IJR) [2014] UKUT 514 (IAC) at [17](viii).

Skeleton arguments for full hearings in the UT

8.37   Skeleton arguments should be provided by the applicant 21 days before the substantive hearing, and 14 days before by the respondent[1] and should contain:[2]

(a)   a time estimate for the complete hearing, including the giving of the decision by the tribunal;

(b)   a list of issues;

(c)   a list of the legal points to be taken (together with any relevant authorities with page references to the passages relied on;

(d)   a chronology of events (with page references to the bundle of documents);

(e)   a list of essential documents for the advance reading of the tribunal (with page references to the passages relied on if different from that served with the application), a time estimate for that reading, and a list of persons referred to therein.

1   UT JR Practice Direction, paras 8.1, 8.2; see email address at **8.34**, fn 1 above; see **6.140** above for further guidance on how a skeleton argument might impress its audience.
2   UT JR Practice Direction, para 8.3.

Trial bundle

8.38   The trial bundle for the hearing, including agreed additions from the respondent, should be supplied at the same time as the applicant's skeleton argument.[1] The bundle must include those documents required by the respondent and any other person who is expected to make representations at the hearing.[2] Careful attention should be given to providing relevant correspondence, orders, and further evidence for which permission has been given, within the bundle. Normally counsel will take responsibility for filing and serving an agreed bundle of legal authorities.

1   UT JR Practice Direction, para 9.1.
2   UT JR Practice Direction, para 9.2.

Applications for stay and other orders

8.39   Applications for orders including stays are to be made on Form T484.[1] That form gives space to state briefly:

• the nature of the order sought,

• the reason for it,

• the material facts relied on,

• any relevant rule or statutory provision.

1   Available on the UT website www.justice.gov.uk/tribunals/immigration-asylum-upper/application-for-judicial-review.

8.40   At Part B the evidence relied upon is identified, which may take the form of:

• an attached witness statement/affidavit, or

• the statement of case already supplied to launch the judicial review,

or may otherwise:

• be set out in Part C on the form's reverse side.

8.41   Additionally the addresses of solicitors for the applicant and respondent should be provided. When considering when proceedings should be stayed behind a lead case, the relevant question is whether the anticipated appellate decision will have a critical impact upon the proceedings in hand.[1]

1   Jackson LJ in *AB (Sudan) v Secretary of State for the Home Department* [2013] EWCA Civ 921 at [32].

Orders and consent orders

8.42   Where there is agreement as to the terms of the final order, the applicant should file two copies signed by all parties setting out its terms, together with a short statement of the matters relied on as justifying the proposed agreed order and copies of any authorities or statutory provisions relied on;[1] the UT will consider these documents and make the order if satisfied that it is appropriate,[2] and will otherwise list the matter for final hearing, to rule on the final order after argument.[3] The UT must hold a hearing before making a decision disposing of proceedings,[4] subject to limited powers to strike out a case, consent to withdrawal under the Upper Tribunal Rules, r 17, determine a permission application, or make a consent order.[5] All parties should proactively take all necessary and appropriate steps to resolve proceedings within three weeks of the time that a draft consent order is first tabled, unless there are good and sustainable reasons to the contrary.[6] Where the UT is presented with an unexecuted consent order, each side should provide an explanation, within four weeks of the date of receipt of the draft order, and if the case is listed for hearing, not less than five clear working days before the hearing; any further alteration in the explanations should be provided not later than two clear days before the hearing.[7] A breach of these strictures should be explained in writing and might have costs explanations.[8]

1 UT JR Practice Direction, para 10.1.
2 UT JR Practice Direction, para 10.2.
3 UT JR Practice Direction, para 10.3.
4 Tribunal Procedure (Upper Tribunal) Rules 2008, SI 2008/2698, r 34(3).
5 SI 2008/2698, r 40(1A)–(1B); r 39 permits disposal of proceedings where the UT considers this appropriate.
6 *Muwonge, R (on the application of) v Secretary of State for the Home Department (consent orders: costs: guidance)* (IJR) [2014] UKUT 514 (IAC) at [17](iii).
7 *Muwonge* (above) at [17](v)–(vi).
8 *Muwonge* (above) at [17](vii), (ix).

Costs procedures and principles in the UT

8.43   There is a discretion to determine the costs of and incidental to proceedings in the UT, which has full power to determine who should pay costs (so far the UT has embraced the principle of cost-shifting, without considering whether the overriding objectives are truly served by the risk of parties being liable for one another's costs, in contrast to the approach taken in the Administrative Appeals Chamber),[1] including a power to disallow costs or order a representative to pay wasted costs.[2]

1 *LR, R (on the application of) v FTT (HESC) and Hertfordshire CC* [2013] UKUT 294 (AAC) at [31]–[36].
2 TCEA 2007, s 29(1)–(3). All representatives conducting proceedings are so liable, not just legal representatives: s 29(6).

8.44   Wasted costs are defined as:

● any costs incurred by a party due to improper, unreasonable or negligent act or omission on a representative's part or that of their employee which the tribunal considers it is reasonable to expect them to pay.[1]

'Improper' conduct signals:

- a significant breach of a substantial duty imposed by a relevant code of professional conduct or which would be thought improper by a consensus of professional opinion.

'Unreasonable conduct' is that which is:

- vexatious, designed to harass the other side rather than advance the case's resolution.

'Negligent' conduct equates to:

- a failure to act with the competence reasonably to be expected of ordinary members of the profession.[2]

1   TCEA 2007, s 29(5).
2   See *Okondu (wasted costs, SRA referrals, Hamid)* (IJR) [2014] UKUT 377 (IAC) citing *Ridehalgh v Horsefield* [1994] EWCA Civ 40 at [7].

8.45   Wasted costs may be awarded against either side to proceedings, regardless of whether they win or lose: relevant considerations will be a lack of frankness including making a claim which is inconsistent with evidence held by the representatives and conduct in breach of the overriding duty to the court,[1] and the conduct of the firm in the instant, and related, cases.[2] The UT may make costs orders on its own motion:[3] a party seeking costs should provide a written application to the UT and to the person against whom the order is sought, with a schedule sufficient to provide for summary assessment[4] within one month of the decision finally disposing of all issues or of a notice that withdrawal has ended the proceedings.[5]

1   See candour, at **8.117** and **8.118** below; see further Hickinbottom J in *Singh, R (on the application of) v Secretary of State for the Home Department* [2013] EWHC 2873 (Admin) at [27].
2   *Okondu (wasted costs, SRA referrals, Hamid)* (IJR) [2014] UKUT 377 (IAC) citing *Ridehalgh v Horsefield* [1994] EWCA Civ 40; *Okondu* at [37]–[39].
3   Tribunal Procedure (Upper Tribunal) Rules 2008, SI 2008/2698, r 10(4); indeed it may have an inherent power to make costs orders, too: see *Okondu* (above) at [16].
4   SI 2008/2698, r 10(5)(a).
5   SI 2008/2698, r 10(6).

8.46   An opportunity must be given to the paying party to make representations as to whether they should pay, and the UT must consider the financial means of any individual in respect of whom an order is sought.[1] An order may be made by summary assessment, or following agreement or absent agreement, an assessment of the whole or part of the costs and expenses claimed, with provision for application to the High Court for detailed assessment thereafter.[2] A party may be ordered to pay a sum on account before detailed assessment.[3] Where a judge of the UT makes an order that the applicant is to pay a sum to the respondent in respect of the Acknowledgment of Service or the costs of resisting an urgent application,[4] and there has been no prior opportunity on the paying party to make representations or to have an inquiry into that party's means, the order takes effect as a provisional order subject to representations to be made in writing within ten working days of the order, which becomes absolute if no such representations are received within the time specified.[5] Any such representations are to be referred promptly to the judge making the order or to such other judge as is available for determination.[6] A party may not avoid costs simply by seeking to withdraw their application as the UT has a continuing jurisdiction to dispose of the matter until its final order is made.[7] We deal with the general principles governing the award of costs, common to both the UT and the courts, below.[8]

1   Tribunal Procedure (Upper Tribunal) Rules 2008, SI 2008/2698, r 10(7).
2   SI 2008/2698, r 10(8)–(9).
3   SI 2008/2698, r 10(10).
4   SI 2008/2698, r 10(3)(a).
5   UT JR Practice Statement, para 4.1.
6   UT JR Practice Statement, para 4.2.
7   *Okondu (wasted costs, SRA referrals, Hamid)* (IJR) [2014] UKUT 377 (IAC) at [35].
8   See **8.127** *et seq* below.

Onwards appeals from the UT

8.47   There is a right of appeal against decisions of the UT, which arises from any point of law save for excluded decisions,[1] which is exercisable with permission (leave in Northern Ireland) from either the UT or the appropriate appellate court:[2] appeal may be brought directly only after a permission refusal by the UT,[3] which should specify the relevant appellate court thereafter.[4] The procedure and time limits for applications to appeal to the Court of Appeal generally are set out above.[5] As a hearing must be held in immigration judicial review proceedings before making a decision which disposes of proceedings,[6] a party will always have the opportunity to apply for permission to appeal at that hearing, and the question of permission should be considered whether it is raised or not.[7] There is no equivalent procedure to that within CPR, r 52.15(3) allowing for a grant of judicial review by the Court of Appeal rather than a grant of permission to appeal.[8] Appeal lies against permission refusals as well as against the outcome of full hearings,[9] though where a claim is designated to be 'totally without merit', there will be no prospect of an oral renewal in the Court of Appeal.[10] It may be necessary, where awaiting a transcript of the judgment, which should be requested at the oral refusal hearing on an expedited basis, to lodge interim grounds pending an understanding of the full reasoning of the judge, as the finalised decision is likely to be more accurate than any note of the judgment taken at the hearing (though an agreed note might be obtained in an appropriate case); and proceedings, and the provision of a skeleton argument, might be stayed in the meantime. The UT will always consider the question of permission to the Court of Appeal when refusing permission.[11] Even though there may be a period during which the Court of Appeal lacks jurisdiction pending a permission refusal by the UT, it may nevertheless grant a stay against removal as part of its 'inherent jurisdiction to protect its proceedings from being set at naught';[12] there should be no presumption as to stay absent making a formal application specifically seeking such relief.[13] A refusal of interim relief should be renewed to an oral hearing rather than being the subject of an appeal to the Court of Appeal.[14] Judicial review appeals do not need to pass the 'second appeals' gateway because the provisions of TCEA 2007 that allow for the imposition of those criteria only bite on statutory appeals from the UT.[15]

1 TCEA 2007, s 13(1). See **6.130**, fn 3 above.
2 TCEA 2007, s 13(3)–(4).
3 TCEA 2007, s 13(5).
4 TCEA 2007, s 13(11)–(13): the Court of Appeal, the Court of Session or the Court of Appeal of Northern Ireland.
5 See **6.128** and **6.129** above.
6 Tribunal Procedure (Upper Tribunal) Rules 2008, SI 2008/2698, r 34(3).
7 SI 2008/2698, r 44(4A)–(4B).
8 Identified in *NB (Algeria)* [2012] EWCA Civ 1050 at [23]–[24], the Master of the Rolls suggesting that it might be proper if unorthodox in such cases for the Lord or Lady Justice to constitute themselves as a full court in order to grant permission for judicial review.
9 CPR, r 52.15A(1).
10 CPR, r 52.15A(2).
11 UT JR Practice Statement, para 2.14; see **8.34**, fn 5 above.
12 *NB (Algeria)* [2012] EWCA Civ 1050 at [28]–[30].
13 *Pharis, R (on the application of) v Secretary of State for the Home Department* [2004] EWCA Civ 654. See **6.136** above.
14 See **8.93**, fn 7 below.
15 TCEA 2007, s 13(4), (6) and (7).

General powers, case management; sanctions for breach of the Upper Tribunal Rules and service

8.48   In general the UT's powers and procedures for case management, the giving of directions, and sanctions for breach of the Procedure Rules or Directions are available in judicial review proceedings as they are in statutory appeals.[1] Under the Upper Tribunal Rules, unlike the CPR, there is no general rule or practice whereby parties may, unless specifically prohibited, extend time limits in the Rules by agreement, without recourse to the UT, though the views of the parties will be a relevant consideration when the UT considers its general power to 'extend or shorten the time for complying with any rule, practice direction or direction.'[2] Additionally the UT has 'the same powers, rights, privileges and authority as the High Court'[3] regarding:

'(a)   the attendance and examination of witnesses,

(b)   the production and inspection of documents, and

(c)   all other matters incidental to the Upper Tribunal's functions.'

1   See **6.49–6.53** and **6.58–6.61** above.

2   *Kumar, R (on the application of) v Secretary of State for the Home Department (acknowledgement of service, tribunal arrangements)* (IJR) [2014] UKUT 104 (IAC) at [10], referring to r 5(3)(a).
3   TCEA 2007, s 25; discussed in *Okondu (wasted costs, SRA referrals, Hamid)* (IJR) [2014] UKUT 377 (IAC) at [15]–[16].

Provisions particular to proceedings in the Court of Session or Northern Ireland

8.49   There are certain provisions which are particular to proceedings in the Court of Session or Northern Ireland (though in general there should be no material difference between the principles that govern the tribunals, which have a national jurisdiction).[1] Judicial review in Scotland is sought via a petition to the Court of Session in Edinburgh, and there is no permission stage; if an applicant is granted a first order by which the application is accepted, he may serve his petition on the office of the Advocate General, and removal will normally be deferred subject to the usual exceptions set out in the Home Office judicial review policy for particular classes of removal discussed below.[2] Where an application is made to the supervisory jurisdiction of the Court of Session, it must transfer the case to the UT where the application seeks no more than an exercise of its supervisory jurisdiction and is within an act of sederunt class; it has a discretion to transfer where the claim is not within an act of sederunt class and is not a devolved Scottish matter.[3] Where the Court of Session transfers proceedings to the UT, the UT must thereafter provide any decision on summary dismissal of all or part of the application, or limitations and conditions on the application's subsequent progress, to the parties.[4] Where the application is summarily dismissed without a hearing, an applicant may apply for that decision's reconsideration at an oral hearing.[5] The UT must notify parties of transfers to its jurisdiction and give appropriate directions for the claim's future conduct: provisions of the Upper Tribunal Rules, Pt 4 addressing judicial review in the UT may be disapplied, and if the Court of Session did not make a first order specifying the required intimation, service and advertisement of the petition, then the UT must state its requirements, and whether it will consider summary dismissal of the proceedings.[6] Judicial review in Northern Ireland is pursued by means of an application to the High Court of Justice and applications are to be brought to the attention of the Crown Solicitor's Office via the litigation team at Festival Court in Glasgow, who act on the Home Office's behalf in these cases and who can provide advice on how to proceed.[7]

1   Lord Kerr in *Secretary of State for Home Department v MN and KY (Scotland)* [2014] UKSC 30 at [7].
2   EIG, section 16.
3   TCEA 2007, s 20.
4   Tribunal Procedure (Upper Tribunal) Rules 2008, SI 2008/2698, r 30(2).
5   SI 2008/2698, r 30(3)–(4).
6   SI 2008/2698, r 27(3).
7   EIG, section 17.

JUDICIAL REVIEW IN THE ADMINISTRATIVE COURT

Governing legal instruments

8.50   The principal legal materials governing judicial review in the Administrative Court are:

- the Senior Courts Acts 1981,

- TCEA 2007,

- the CPR, particularly Part 54,

- the Practice Direction to Part 54 of the CPR (CPR PD 54).

There is also a document on the www.justice.gov.uk website entitled 'Administrative Court guidance on applying for judicial review' which provides useful insights into the process.

Jurisdiction of the Administrative Court

8.51   The Administrative Court will be the appropriate forum for those judicial reviews which challenge:

- the *vires* of statute, statutory instrument or Immigration Rule,

- the compatibility of provisions with HRA 1998,

- decisions of the SIAC,

- the lawfulness of detention,

- decisions determining entitlement to British nationality or citizenship,

- decisions regarding welfare support.[1]

1   See **8.5**, fn1 above. The identified welfare support challenges arise under or by virtue of IAA 1999, s 4 or Pt VI, or by virtue of NIAA 2002, Pts II or III (other support and assistance).

8.52   The various orders available stem from the Senior Courts Act 1981 which provides for the making of:

- mandatory, prohibiting or quashing orders,

- declarations,

- injunctions.

8.53   The latter two remedies may be granted where it is just and convenient to do so having regard to the nature of the relief sought and taking account of the nature of the person or body against whom it is made and all the circumstances of the case.[1] There is a similar requirement to remit an application to the competent decision maker whose decision has been quashed as under the UT's jurisdiction, and a similar inhibition against substituting its own decision for that of a court or tribunal absent clarity that discretion could have been lawfully exercised in only one direction.[2] The court will grant declarations and injunctions with regard to the nature of the case brought and the relief which would be appropriate, bearing in mind the nature of the persons and bodies against whom relief may be granted by such orders and all the circumstances of the case such as the conduct of the applicant, including whether it would be just and convenient for the declaration to be made or the injunction to be granted.[3]

1   Senior Courts Act 1981, s 31.
2   Senior Courts Act 1981, s 31(5)-(6) (see **8.13**, fnn 1 and 2 above); CPR, r 54.19. In such cases the substituted decision will take effect as it were that of the impugned decision maker, unless the court directs otherwise: Senior Courts Act 1981, s 31(5b). See *R (on the application of Sultana) v Secretary of State for the Home Department* (IJR) [2015] UKUT 226 (IAC).
3   Taylor LJ in *Nichol v Gateshead Metropolitan Borough Council* (1988) 87 LGR 435.

8.54   Where the judicial review involves a human rights claim, there are specific provisions[1] by which a claimant:

- identifies the relevant Convention right,

- details the nature of the claimed infringement,

- specifies the relief sought,

- identifies any allegation of a declaration of incompatibility in accordance with HRA 1998, s 4 (in which case the allegedly offending provision should be identified and the nature of infringement explained),

- identifies any damages sought in respect of a judicial act conducted in good faith.

1   Practice Direction 16 on 'Statements of case'.

8.55   There are specific provisions governing intervenors, who must apply at the earliest reasonable opportunity, identifying the relevant claim they wish to join and explaining their reasons for intervening, the form of participation they have in mind, and explaining any prospective order as to costs that they intend to seek; the court may determine an application to intervene by the parties' consent without a hearing, and may make case management directions and give a conditional permission to intervene.[1]

1   CPR PD 54, para 17.

Time limits for bringing claim in the Administrative Court

8.56   Claims for judicial review must be brought expeditiously: under the Senior Courts Act 1981, where there is adjudged to have been 'undue delay' in making an application for judicial review, the court may refuse to grant either permission or substantive relief if it considers that the granting of the relief sought would be likely to cause substantial hardship to, or substantially prejudice the rights of, any person or would be detrimental to good administration.[1] As the CPR puts it,[2] claims must be brought:

'(a)   promptly; and

(b)   in any event not later than 3 months after the grounds to make the claim first arose.'

1   Senior Courts Act 1981, s 31(6).
2   CPR, r 54.5(1).

8.57   The time limit may not be extended by agreement.[1] We address factors relevant to the extension of time above.[2] It is from the original decision, and not any response to a Pre Action Protocol letter, that time runs.[3] The clock does not start to run in relation to non-appealable decisions if the subject has not been effectively notified of the decision.[4] The court's decision at the permission stage that the claimant's time for applying for judicial review should not be extended cannot be reopened at the substantive hearing.[5] The defendant will in those circumstances be limited to relying upon the provisions of the Senior Courts Act 1981 at the substantive hearing, which requires demonstrating, not only undue delay, but also the detriments already mentioned.[6] Under European law, time for bringing proceedings generally runs from the date the claimant knew or ought to have known of his ability to challenge a decision, and a requirement to bring proceedings 'promptly' other than within three months has been held unlawful for being contrary to the European Union law principles of certainty and effectiveness.[7]

1   CPR, r 54.5(1)–(2).
2   See **8.21**, fn 4 above.
3   Introduction to Pre Action Protocol: 'This Protocol … does not affect the time limit specified by Rule 54.5(1) of the Civil Procedure Rules'.
4   The 1971 Act, s 4(1) provides that powers to refuse or vary leave to remain shall be exercised by notice in writing given to the person affected; thus the Secretary of State has to be able to prove that notice of such a decision was communicated to the person concerned, in order for it to be effective; see *Syed (curtailment of leave – notice) India* [2013] UKUT 144 (IAC), headnote at (3). If the decision is susceptible to administrative review (see Chapter 9 addressing eligible decisions), then receipt is deemed to have taken place within specified time limits 'unless the contrary is shown': Immigration Rules, HC 395, para 34R.
5   Lord Slynn in *R v Criminal Injuries Compensation Board, ex parte A* [1999] 1 AC 330.
6   Senior Courts Act 1981, s 31(6).
7   eg *R (Buglife) v Medway Council* [2011] EWHC 746 (Admin) at [61]–[63]; *R(U & Partners (East Anglia) Ltd) v Broad Authority and Environment Agency* [2011] EWHC 1824 (Admin) [2011] JPL 1583 at [37]–[47] (in the context of public procurement and Environmental Impact Assessment challenges).

Forms

8.58   The claim form (Form N461) must contain the information specified within it, including details of interested parties and any remedy or interim remedy claimed. It must be served on the defendant and any interested party within seven days of its issue)[1] (unless the court directs that an interested party need not be served).[2] The parties are to effect service on any respondent or interested party, with a Certificate of Service in Form N215 being provided to the Administrative Court Office within seven days of so doing.[3]

1   CPR, r 54.7.
2   CPR, r 54.7(b).
3   CPR PD 54, para 7.6.1. Service on the Immigration Tribunals is via the Official Correspondence Unit, PO Box 6987, Leicester, LE1 6ZX or fax number 0116 249 4240; service on the SSHD and other emanations of the Crown is via the Government Legal Department. See Administrative Court Guidance on Applying for Judicial Review, para 7.11.

Fees

8.59   Fees are payable as follows:

- £140 payable when the application is lodged,

- £350 for an oral permission renewal,

- £700 is payable if the claim is to be pursued where permission is granted in order to proceed to the full hearing,

- £155 for an application on notice,

- £50 for an application by consent or without notice,

- £10 for copy documents of less than ten pages, and 50p a page thereafter.

Cheques should be made payable to HMCTS.[1] A person wishing to apply for fee remission, for example because in receipt of benefits, may do so using the relevant form.[2]

1   Civil Proceedings Fees (Amendment) Order 2014, SI 2014/874.
2   Form EX160 (Application for a Fee Remission) which is to be lodged with the claim form.

Filing the claim in the Administrative Court

8.60   Claims should be filed on an Administrative Court claim form (N461) and sent to the appropriate Administrative Court Office in 'the region with which the claimant has the closest connection',[1] depending on relevant circumstances such as the parties' reasoned preference, the location of the defendant and the claimant's legal representative, ease and cost of travel to any hearing bearing in mind the possibility of videolink, media interest, the time in which the proceedings should be determined, the volume of claims issued at, and the capacity, resources and workload of the court at which it is issued, its similarity to another outstanding claim, or the possibility of devolution issues being live:[2] these arrangements are intended to facilitate access to justice by enabling cases to be administered and determined in the

8.61 *Judicial review*

most appropriate location and to provide flexibility in relation to where claims are to be administered enabling claims to be transferred to different venues.[3] There are procedures for urgent applications to be made regionally in office hours (though this will not necessarily determine the future venue);[4] out of hours applications must be made via the London telephone number.[5] Cases may later be assigned to another venue.[6] Judicial reviews in relation to Tribunal decisions made in Scotland should be brought in the Court of Session.[7]

1   CPR PD 54D, para 5.2.
2   CPR PD 54D, para 5.2(1)–(10).
3   CPR PD 54D, para 1.2, subject to the claim falling into an excepted class, in which case there will be a transfer of proceedings to London. The various relevant addresses are presently: Room C315, Royal Courts of Justice, Strand, London, WC2A 2LL; Civil Justice Centre, Priory Courts, 5th Floor, 33 Bull Street, Birmingham, B4 6DS; Cardiff Civil Justice Centre, 2 Park Street, Cardiff, CF10 1ET; Leeds Combined Court, 1 Oxford Row, Leeds, West Yorkshire LS1 3BG; Manchester Civil Justice Centre, 1 Bridge Street West, Manchester, M60 9DJ.
4   CPR PD 54D, para 5.3.
5   CPR PD 54D, para 4.1: 'Any urgent application to the Administrative Court during the hours when the court is closed, must be made to the duty out of hours High Court judge by telephoning 020 7947 6000.'
6   CPR PD 54D, para 5.1 *et seq.*
7   Brooke LJ in *Majead, R (on the application of) v Secretary of State for the Home Department* [2003] EWCA Civ 615 at [19].

8.61   The claim form must include or be accompanied by:

- a detailed statement of the claimant's grounds for bringing the claim for judicial review,

- a statement of the facts relied on,

- any application to extend the time limit for filing the claim form,

- together with written evidence supporting this,

- any application for directions,

- a copy of any order that the claimant seeks to have quashed,

- where the claim for judicial review relates to a decision of a court or tribunal, an approved copy of the reasons for reaching that decision,

- copies of any documents and statutory material on which the claimant proposes to rely (two copies of the entire bundle are required for the court, plus a copy to be stamped for service on each defendant/interested party),[1] and

- a list of essential documents for advance reading by the court (with page references to relevant passages – the essential reading list should be minimal, equating to the documents that the advocate would actually take the judge to in court).[2]

1   CPR PD 54A, para 5.9.
2   CPR PD 54A, paras 5.6–5.7.

8.62   Where it is not possible to file all the above documents, the claimant must indicate which documents have not been filed and the reasons why they are not currently available.[1] There is a useful guide available online at the www.justice.gov.uk website to assist with filling out the form.[2] Filing absent compliance with the relevant CPR requirements will normally lead to the application's rejection and return for due compliance before issuing, unless a decision is sought from the court in exceptional circumstances (defined as a case where a decision is sought within 14 days of lodging – though if such urgency emanates only from a need to beat the time limit for lodging, the court will still return the application and expect its return with an appropriate request for extension of time).[3]

1   CPR-PD 54A, para 5.8.
2   Guidance Notes on Completing the Judicial Review Claim Form.
3   Administrative Court Guidance on Applying for Judicial Review, at 'NB' to para 7.9.

8.63   Checklist of issues to cover when filing the claim:

●   Full details provided for claimant (N461, Section 1).

●   Full details provided for relevant defendant and interested party (other parties to court proceedings will be such: for example, the SSHD will be an interested party in any challenge to decisions of the FTT or UT) (N461, Section 2).

●   Details of the decision to be judicially reviewed – date and description of the decision(s) in question (N461, Section 3).

●   Permission related questions – indicate if CPR PD 54 on challenging removal is in play (N461, Section 4); whether any other applications are being made, eg a request for disclosure; confirm whether public funding legal aid certificate is in place; whether urgent consideration is sought (in which case N463 is additionally required); confirm Pre Action Protocol has been complied with, providing reasons if not; confirm the claim is being issued in region with which the claimant has the closest connection.

●   Whilst the claim form provides for a detailed statement of grounds and at Section 8 for the statement of facts relied on, many who draft pleadings will provide both in a single document, which can be incorporated by a reference to it in the claim form (N461, Sections 5, 9).

●   Immigration cases do not involve the Aarhus Convention, which addresses to access to information and public participation in decision-making and access to justice in environmental matters (N461, Section 6).

●   Details of remedy sought, ie (a) a mandatory order (eg that the defendant take a particular step, eg reconsider a case); (b) a prohibiting order (eg that the defendant desist from a step, eg removal); (c) a quashing order (eg that the refusal letter of a particular date be quashed); or (d) an injunction (ie that pending the claim being heard, a particular step should be suspended, eg removal directions) (N461, Section 7).

● Other applications (eg for further information, for a particular form of listing) are made using another form, Form PF244 (N461, Section 8).

● The claim form should be verified by a statement of truth, which is particularly important where assertions of fact are being made in an accompanying statement of grounds. The inapplicable words should be struck out depending on whether or not the claimant is represented.

● A witness statement from the instructing solicitor or claimant drawing the relevant facts together, where the documents do not otherwise offer a full account of the material circumstances: 'It is self evident that where the Applicant's case relies on alleged facts which are not documented in the papers – such as conversations or dates of receipt of documents or verbal assurances or promises allegedly given, or facts which have previously been disputed by the Respondent – these will have to be fully addressed in a carefully composed witness statement.'[1]

● Supporting documents – whilst the objective is to provide all relevant documents from the outset of the claim, bear in mind that at the permission stage it may only be necessary to provide certain documents providing relevant and sufficient, but not excessive, detail of the claim, and if there are documents that are not presently available but which it is intended to use to support the claim, these should be identified together with their date of anticipated availability, and the reasons for their present non-availability should be provided (N461, Section 10).

1   McCloskey J in *R (on the application of Bilal Mahmood) v Secretary of State for the Home Department (continuing duty to reassess)* (IJR) [2014] UKUT 439 (IAC) at [20].

Acknowledgment of Service

8.64   The defendant must lodge an Acknowledgment of Service if he wishes to take part in the judicial review proceedings.[1] It must be filed within 21 days of the service of the claim form, on the claimant and any other person named in the form. This time may not be extended by agreement (though in practice the defendant will write seeking agreement before notifying the court of any failure to produce an Acknowledgment of Service in time: see **8.120** below). It should, where the claim is being contested, set out a summary of the reasons for so doing, identify any person considered by the person filing it to be an interested party, and may include an application for directions.[2] The Acknowledgment of Service will contain the summary grounds of defence. Should permission for judicial review be granted, there will be an opportunity for the defendant to file full ('detailed') grounds of defence. Failure to file an Acknowledgment of Service prevents further participation in the permission application without the court's agreement, although a defendant may nevertheless take part in the full hearing, should permission be granted, so long as detailed grounds are provided.[3] The defendant may ask for an order that the claim is clearly without merit, or he may request expedition of the case. Where an Acknowledgment of Service is filed and served with such a request, and raises new and unexpected points, or alternatively it is provided together with a new or updated refusal letter which changes the backdrop to the case, it may be procedurally unfair for the court to acquiesce to a speedy determination without giving an adequate opportunity to the claimant to amend his grounds. There is no barrier to supplying a reply to the Acknowledgment of Service, albeit that the CPR does not envisage such a document. However the court prefers to receive minimal documentation, so it will only be if the summary grounds of defence are thought misleading or otherwise deficient that it would be advisable to supply any further submission. If important new information has come to light on the claimant's side, this may require the submission of amended grounds for judicial review: there is no objection to varying grounds before an order is made on permission. In removal cases where the process is expedited, the Home Office caseworker will instruct the Government Legal Department to lodge the Acknowledgment of Service more speedily than the normal 21 days.[4] We address general considerations regarding the Acknowledgment of Service further below.[5]

1   CPR, r 54.8.
2   CPR, r 54.8(4),
3   Under CPR, rr 54.14 and 54.9(1)(b). The failing may be relevant to costs: CPR, r 54.9(2).
4   Enforcement Instructions at EIG, section 9.1.
5   See **8.120** *et seq* below.

Urgent procedure in the Administrative Court

8.65   There are specific procedures in the Administrative Court for urgent measures, of which interim relief is of particular importance. Bail may also be available albeit that this is not strictly a matter arising as interim relief but rather under the court's inherent jurisdiction;[1] seeking bail from the FTT may be the more appropriate remedy for most cases. In these cases, not only a Form N461 but also an N463 Application for Urgent Consideration must be supplied, which requires the provision of:

● the reasons for urgency,

● a proposed timetable for consideration of the application for interim relief,

● the substantive grounds for relief,

● a date for the substantive hearing if permission is granted,

● if required, an application for abridgement of time for the Acknowledgment of Service,

- the interim relief sought, and

- a draft order.[2]

1   *R v Secretary of State for the Home Department, ex parte Sezek* [2002] 1 WLR 348.
2   Form N463. See further the Practice Statement (Administrative Court: Listing and Interim Relief) [2002] 1 WLR 810 at 811–812 by Scott Baker J (see also **8.104** and **8.105** below).

8.66   There is a specific Practice Direction addressing urgent removals[1] to be read in conjunction with the SSHD's Enforcement Instructions and Guidance at Chapter 60.[2] It applies where a person has received removal directions and been notified that this procedure applies, and makes a pre-removal application for judicial review.[3] The Practice Direction does not prevent post-removal applications for judicial review.[4]

1   CPR PD 54A, para 18.1 relating to pre-removal challenges to judicial review once a migrant has received removal directions. It explains that cases are dealt with by the Judicial Review Unit (JRU) (Enforcement), the Third Country Unit (TCU) (Third country removals) and the Criminal Casework Directorate (CCD). Claimants' representatives will probably be dealing with the Local Immigration Team (LIT) who liaise with these specialist units, and with the Home Office's Operational Support and Certification Unit (OSCU).
2   Chapter 60, 'Judicial reviews and injunctions'.
3   CPR PD 54A, para 18.1.
4   Ibid.

8.67   A person whose application for judicial review is made in the face of removal directions must:

- make clear on the claim form that the Practice Direction applies,

- provide a copy of the removal directions and the underlying decision,

- provide any factual summary from the Home Office, or explain why this information is not available, and

- immediately upon issue of the claim, send copies of the issued claim form and accompanying documents to the address specified.[1]

1   CPR PD 54A, para 18.2 (see **8.28**, fn 6 above for details of the factual summary). The claim may be sent electronically to UKVIPAP@homeoffice.gsi.gov.uk or by post to the Judicial Review Unit, UK Visa and Immigration, Lunar House, 40 Wellesley Rd, Croydon, CR9 2BY.

8.68   A non-compliant claim will be referred to a judge as soon as practicable, the Administrative Court notifying the parties that it has done so.[1] The refusal of permission in these cases may additionally include an indication that the claim is considered to be totally without merit.[2] When renewing an application, it is necessary for the lawyers to certify that they have considered that indication and that they are nevertheless satisfied that the claim being advanced is one that can properly be made.[3]

1   CPR PD 54A, para 18.3.

2　CPR PD 54A, para 18.4. See **8.31**, fn 7 for further discussion of 'totally without merit' indications.

3　The President of the Queens Bench Division in *Awuku, R (on the application of) v Secretary of State for the Home Department* [2012] EWHC 3298 (Admin) at [2]–[3].

Decisions on permission

8.69　　When giving permission for judicial review, the court may give directions and/or order a stay of the proceedings.[1] A case involving an important point of principle can be referred to the Divisional Court.[2] The court will serve the order giving or refusing permission on the parties.[3] Sometimes the court adjourns the paper application into open court on notice to the defendant for argument, as where the grounds for permission are borderline, complex or involve issues of public importance. Under the CPR a grant of permission decision may not be set aside on the application of the defendant or another party[4] albeit that the court has an inherent jurisdiction to do so in an appropriate case, permitting the revision of a mistaken order, such as permission due to an inadvertent oversight of a seemingly conclusive statutory provision or legal authority, or where a decision was procured by fraud.[5]

1　CPR, r 54.10.
2　CPR, r 54.10(2)(b).
3　CPR, r 54.11. This may include directions which must be given careful attention.
4　CPR, r 54.13.
5　Davis J in *R (Wilkinson) v Chief Constable of W Yorkshire* [2002] EWHC 2352 Admin at [43], approved in *AA, R (on the application of) v Upper Tribunal* [2012] EWHC 1784 (Admin).

Renewal hearings

8.70　　If permission is refused, it is necessary to request a reconsideration at a hearing where the application may be renewed orally.[1] Any such request must be made within seven days after service of the reasons.[2] Notice will be given of the permission hearing of at least two days (the court no longer necessarily liaises with counsel as to their availability for such hearings). Normally these hearings are listed with a minimal time marking, for example 30 minutes, and the court should be advised if this is not thought sufficient.[3] An oral renewal hearing will usually find the defendant represented by Treasury counsel, who may be the person who drafted the summary grounds of defence (although these are often drafted in house by the Government Legal Department), though it is not compulsory for them to be represented (for which reason they will normally receive costs for doing so).[4]

1　CPR, r 54.12(3).
2　CPR, r 54.12(4).
3　Administrative Court Guidance on Applying for Judicial Review, para 11.4.
4　CPR PD 54A, paras 8.5–8.6; Auld LJ in *Mount Cook Land Ltd v Westminster City Council* [2003] EWCA Civ 1346 at [72].

Post grant of permission steps: procedure to the hearing

8.71   Where permission is granted, the statement of case may be amended
with the court's permission or if all parties agree.[1] Once permission is
granted, the defendant must file and serve detailed grounds of defence, and
any written evidence, within 35 days of service of the permission grant.[2]
If the claimant wishes to rely on further grounds than those on which
permission was granted, the court's leave to do so must be separately
sought.[3] Permission may be given to argue an issue at the substantive hearing
notwithstanding its earlier refusal if there is a real justification for so doing,
because of a change of circumstances, new evidence, or a change in the law.[4]
A substantive judicial review claim may be determined without a hearing
where the parties agree.[5] Where an advocate's details have been placed on
the court record, the parties will be contacted by the relevant Administrative
Court List Office in order to seek to agree a date for the hearing, with a range
of dates being offered which they may respond to within 48 hours, subject
to which the hearing will be fixed without further notice.[6] Discontinuance is
governed by CPR, Pt 38 and renders the claimant liable for the costs incurred
by the other parties up to the point proceedings have reached; Form N279
should be filed, though a defendant may object within 28 days of being
served with notice.[7]

1   CPR, r 17.1. The implication of this express provision is that, pre permission, there is no
     objection to raising grounds that were not in the claim as lodged, subject to giving the
     defendant an opportunity to address them.
2   CPR, r 54.14(1); CPR PD 54A, para 14.
3   CPR, r 54.15; notice must be given: CPR-PD 54.15.
4   See eg the Lord Chief Justice in *Smith (Trevor) v Parole Board* [2003] EWCA Civ 1014 at
     [16].
5   CPR, r 54.18; consent orders should be filed with a fee of £50.00: Administrative Court
     Guidance on Applying for Judicial Review, para 16.1.
6   Administrative Court Guidance on Applying for Judicial Review, para 13.3.
7   CPR, r 38; Administrative Court Guidance on Applying for Judicial Review, para 17.

Skeleton arguments for full hearings in the Administrative Court

8.72   A skeleton argument must be filed by the claimant not less than 21
working days (ie around four calendar weeks) before the hearing (or warned
date);[1] the respondent must produce one 14 days before those dates.[2] There are
standard requirements, such as:

● a chronology,

● time estimate for the hearing including delivery of judgment and for the
   pre-reading,

● a list of issues,

● a list of the legal points to be taken with relevant passages from the authorities identified, and

● a list of persons referred to therein.[3]

1 CPR PD 54A, para 15.1.
2 CPR PD 54A, para 15.2.
3 CPR PD 54A, para 15.3.

Trial bundle

8.73 It is the claimant's responsibility to produce the trial bundle, to be filed and served with the skeleton argument.[1] It is to be an agreed bundle, with the claimant taking responsibility for adding materials sought for inclusion by the defendant and any other party.[2] Careful attention should be given to providing relevant correspondence, orders, and further evidence for which permission has been given, within the bundle. Normally counsel will take responsibility for filing and serving an agreed bundle of legal authorities.

1 CPR PD 54A, para 16.1.
2 CPR PD 54A, para 16.2.

Applications for adjournment, stay and other orders

8.74 Any adjournment of a hearing should be agreed if possible, and otherwise Form PF244 must be used to apply for an order, backed by evidence.[1] Other orders should also be sought using Form PF244.[2] It may be appropriate for applications for judicial review to be stayed because of other proceedings in the Administrative Court or the Court of Appeal, particularly where the same or similar arguments have been pursued and are at a more advanced stage than the instant claim (the test being whether the other litigation is likely to have a critical impact on the present proceedings).[3] Additionally it will be necessary to draft a consent order if the matter is agreed, or, absent agreement, a draft order for the court to consider endorsing. The form provides for the provision of a draft order, and asks for certain details:

● how the application should be dealt with, ie with or without a hearing,

● a time estimate, and

● the information in support of the application.

1 Administrative Court Guidance on Applying for Judicial Review, paras 13.4–13.5 (see **8.41**, fn 1 above).
2 Administrative Court Guidance on Applying for Judicial Review, para 14.1 – there is also Form AC001, which may be used when applying for an adjournment.
3 Jackson LJ in *AB (Sudan) v Secretary of State for the Home Department* [2013] EWCA Civ 921 at [32].

Orders and consent orders

8.75   Where the parties are agreed on a particular course of action that determines or withdraws proceedings, or provides for an interim order, then a draft order may be lodged with the court by consent. This is addressed by a Practice Direction[1] which explains that the parties should lodge with the Administrative Court Office:

- a document (with one copy thereof) signed by the parties,

- setting out the terms of the proposed agreed order, and

- accompanied by a short statement explaining the justification for the order, supported by the relevant authorities and statutory provisions.

1   Practice Direction (Administrative Court: Uncontested proceedings) Queen's Bench Division (Collins J, 17 July 2008, *The Times*).

8.76   The Administrative Court Office provides this document to a Master or Deputy Master who will make the order if satisfied that it is right to do so, without the need for attendance by the parties or their representatives.[1] Additionally the relevant form giving Notice of Discontinuance should be completed where proceedings are to be withdrawn.[2] The preparation of final orders determining proceedings is addressed in the CPR: if the parties agree about the terms then the claimant should file two copies of that order signed by all the parties together with a short statement of the matters relied on as justifying the proposed agreed order and copies of any authorities or statutory provisions relied on; the court will endorse this if it considers that is appropriate, and otherwise set a hearing date.[3] Where the agreement relates to an order for costs only, the parties need only file a document signed by all the parties setting out the terms of the proposed order.[4] In general, final orders will have to address:

- whether permission was granted or refused (eg in rolled-up hearings, where not determined by a separate order),

- whether the substantive application (where permission was given) was granted or dismissed,

- the treatment of costs, which may be agreed or set down for assessment pursuant to written submissions, including provision that the claimant's publicly funded legal costs are to be subject to a detailed assessment under the Access to Justice Act 1999, and

- terms as to any decision on permission to appeal if sought at this point, possibly by exchange of written submissions.

When these documents are finalised, they do not require signature by the solicitors, as they are not consent orders, and so can be settled by counsel.

1   Practice Direction (Administrative Court: Uncontested proceedings) Queen's Bench Division (Collins J, 17 July 2008, *The Times*).
2   Form N279 Notice of Discontinuance.
3   CPR PD 52A, paras 17.1–17.3.
4   CPR PD 52A, para 17.4.

Costs procedures in the Administrative Court

8.77   Where the court orders a party to pay costs to another party, it will generally either make a summary assessment of the costs, or order detailed assessment of the costs by a costs officer.[1] A party should comply with an order for costs within 14 days of their determination or from such other date as the court may specify.[2] Where the court makes a costs order against a legally represented party, and the party is not present when the order is made, his legal representative must notify him in writing of the order within seven days of the legal representative receiving notice.[3] Where the court makes an order which does not mention costs, the general rule is that no party is entitled to costs in relation to it, and orders are deemed to include an order for the applicant's costs in the case where permission to appeal, for judicial review, or any other order or direction sought by a party on an application without notice. Where proceedings are transferred from one court to another, the court to which they are transferred may deal with all the costs, including the costs before the transfer.[4] The court hearing an appeal may, unless it dismisses the appeal, make orders about the costs of the proceedings giving rise to the appeal as well as the costs of the appeal.[5] A party intending to claim costs must itemise them by way of a written statement in the form of a schedule.[6]

1   CPR, r 44.6(1).
2   CPR, r 44.7.
3   CPR, r 44.8.
4   CPR, r 44.10.
5   CPR, r 44.10(5).
6   CPR PD 44, para 9.5.

8.78   Disputes as to costs alone should not be pursued by way of permission renewals:

- the judge refusing permission should include in the refusal a decision whether to award costs in principle and an indication of the amount which he proposes to assess summarily,

- the claimant should be given 14 days to respond in writing and should serve a copy on the defendant,

- the defendant should have seven days to reply in writing,

- thereafter, the decision is made by the judge on the papers.[1]

1   Ouseley J in *Loucif, R (on the application of) v Secretary of State for Home Department* [2011] EWHC 3640 (Admin) at [6], citing Carnwath LJ in *Ewing v Office of the Deputy Prime Minister* [2005] EWCA Civ 1583.

General powers, case management; sanctions for breach of CPR and service

8.79   The court has broad case management powers which permit:

- extension or shortening of time limits (including extending time after the event),

- adjourning or bringing forwards a hearing,

- requiring a party or their representative to attend court,

- holding a hearing by telephone or other means,

- directing part of a claim or counterclaim to be dealt with by separate proceedings,

- staying the whole or part of any proceedings or consolidate them,

- trying two or more claims on the same occasion or separately trying any issue,

- deciding the order in which issues are to be tried,

- excluding an issue from consideration,

- dismissing or giving judgment on a claim after a decision on a preliminary issue,

- ordering the filing and exchanging of costs budgets, and

- taking any other step or make any other order for the purpose of managing the case and furthering the overriding object.[1]

1   CPR, r 3.1.

8.80   Failure to comply with the provisions of the CPR may bring sanctions, and in considering an application for relief from such a sanction the court will consider all the circumstances including the need to conduct litigation efficiently and at proportionate cost and to enforce compliance with the CPR; applications for relief therefrom must be backed by evidence.[1] The public interest in maintaining a fair system of immigration control requires the administration of tough time limits and, for example, a late judicial review appeal to the Court of Appeal would not necessarily be permitted to run.[2] Dates of service and deemed service are calculated in accordance with the general CPR provisions, with the consequence that first class post or Document Exchange (DX) will be treated as served the second business day after it was posted or collected for delivery provided that day is a business day; or if not, the next business day after that (so Wednesday posting gives Friday service; Thursday and Friday posting bring Monday service); faxes are served the second business day after transmission.[3]

1   CPR, r 3.9; *Secretary of State for the Home Department v SS (Congo)* [2015] EWCA Civ 387 at [93].

2   Brooke LJ in *Awan, R (on the application of) v Immigration Appeal Tribunal* [2004] EWCA
    Civ 922.
3   CPR, Pt 6; CPR, rr 6.14 and 6.26 address deemed service; see the useful summary in the
    Guide to Applying for Judicial Review, para 7.12.

Onwards appeals from the Administrative Court

8.81   The appropriate appellate court[1] (we concentrate in this book on
the Court of Appeal) has jurisdiction to hear and determine appeals from any
judgment or order of the High Court.[2] Judicial review appeals receive specific
treatment in the CPR.[3] A person refused permission may apply to the Court
of Appeal for permission to appeal[4] within seven days of the High Court's
refusal.[5] Where the permission refusal is recorded as totally without merit,[6]
then the application will be determined on the papers without an oral hearing.[7]
The Court of Appeal may give permission for judicial review rather than
permission to appeal, in which case the matter will proceed in the High Court
unless the contrary is ordered.[8] A refusal of interim relief should be renewed
to an oral hearing rather being the subject of an appeal to the Court of Appeal.[9]
On an appeal from the Administrative Court, the task of the court is essentially
the same as it was for the judge below, namely, to review the SSHD's decision
on public law grounds.[10] Judicial review appeals from the Administrative Court
do not need to pass the 'second appeals' gateway because they are not 'second
appeals' in that the High Court has entertained judicial review proceedings in
a supervisory, not an appellate, capacity.[11] Thus the relevant test is whether:

'(a)   the court considers that the appeal would have a real prospect of
       success; or

(b)   there is some other compelling reason why the appeal should be heard.'[12]

1   See **8.47** above.
2   Senior Courts Act 1981, s 16(1): including on costs; see *Bahta, R (on the application of) v
    Secretary of State for the Home Department* [2011] EWCA Civ 895.
3   CPR, r 52.15.
4   CPR, r 52.15(1).
5   CPR, r 52.15(2).
6   CPR, r 23.12.
7   CPR, r 52.15(1A).
8   CPR, r 52.15(4).
9   See **8.93**, fn 7 below.
10 Ward LJ in *TM, R (on the application of) v Secretary of State for the Home Department*
    [2012] EWCA Civ 9 at [19].
11 Senior Courts Act 1981, s 16; CPR, r 52.13.
12 CPR, r 52.3(6).

Judicial review of permission refusals by the UT ('Cart' Judicial Reviews)

8.82   Where the UT refuses permission to appeal against a decision of the
FTT,[1] its own decision is amenable to judicial review, albeit that the pressures

on the courts are such that the adoption of the second-tier appeals criteria has been accepted judicially as a rational and proportionate restriction upon the availability of judicial review of the refusal by the UT of permission to appeal to itself.[2] The procedure is now governed by the CPR[3] and applies both to judicial review of a decision by the UT to refuse permission against an FTT decision and to one relating to the underlying FTT decision.[4] Any other application beyond these must be the subject of a separate claim.[5] The application with the following supporting documents:

- the grounds of appeal (bearing in mind that 'an important point of principle or practice has to be capable of being expressed very shortly, with supporting references so far as necessary, to demonstrate that that issue is a correct formulation of an issue which does arise in practice in the case'[6])

- resultant UT refusal,

- prior FTT permission refusal, and

- any other essential documents,

must be made no later than 16 days after the date on which notice of the UT's decision was sent to the applicant).[7] The claim form must be served no later than seven days from the date of issue.[8] Express reference to the fact the claim is brought under this provision is required.[9] The UT and any other defendant wishing to participate in proceedings must file and serve an Acknowledgment of Service within 21 days of service of the claim form upon them,[10] and if wishing for a hearing must make such a request within 14 days of the permission grant being served.[11]

1   See **6.137** *et seq* above.
2   *Cart v Upper Tribunal* (Rev 1) [2011] UKSC 28.
3   CPR, r 54.7A addressing judicial review of decisions of the UT.
4   CPR, r 54.7A(1).
5   CPR, r 54.7A(2).
6   Ouseley J in *Khan, R (on the application of) v Secretary of State for the Home Department* [2011] EWHC 2763 (Admin) at [6].
7   CPR, r 54.7A(3)–(4).
8   CPR, r 54.7A(5).
9   CPR PD 54A, para 19.1.
10   CPR, r 54.7A(6).
11   CPR PD 54A, para 19.2.

8.83   Permission will be given only if the court considers:

'(a)   that there is an arguable case, which has a reasonable prospect of success, that both the decision of the Upper Tribunal refusing permission to appeal and the decision of the First Tier Tribunal against which permission to appeal was sought are wrong in law; and

(b)   that either –

(i)   the claim raises an important point of principle or practice; or

(ii) there is some other compelling reason to hear it.'[1]

1   CPR, r 54.7A(7). See **6.137** *et seq* above.

8.84   The second appeals criteria are to be considered at the permission stage, and do not limit the approach of the court at the substantive hearing, even though this may involve treating a view as to arguability as if it were final;[1] and the higher 'second appeals' threshold must apply to each ground of a '*Cart*' challenge, considered separately.[2] If permission for judicial review is refused on the papers, there is no provision for renewal at an oral hearing;[3] if granted, then the court will quash the UT's permission refusal subject to receiving a request by the UT or an interested party for an oral hearing of the substantive application within 14 days from service of the permission decision.[4] An appeal nevertheless lies to the Court of Appeal against the refusal of permission[5] albeit that there will be no right of oral renewal against the decision on the papers.[6]

1   Charles J in *R (HS) v Upper Tribunal* [2012] EWHC 3126 (Admin) at [30]–[41]; Blair J in *Thangarasa, R (on the application of) v Upper Tribunal (Immigration and Asylum Chamber)* [2013] EWHC 3415 (Admin) at [10]–[11]; Wyn Williams J in *Khatoon v Entry Clearance Officer Islamabad* [2013] EWHC 972 (Admin) at [4]–[6].
2   Philippa Whipple QC sitting as a Deputy High Court judge in *Decker, R (on the application of) v Secretary of State for the Home Department* [2014] EWHC 354 (Admin) at [102].
3   CPR, r 54.7A(8).
4   CPR, r 54.7A(9).
5   CPR, r 52.15(1A) – see **8.81**, fn 2 above for the statutory basis for judicial review appeals.
6   CPR, r 52.15(1A); Davis LJ in *Parekh, R (on the application of) v Upper Tribunal (Immigration Asylum Chamber)* [2013] EWCA Civ 679 at [13]–[18]; Gloster LJ in *GR (Albania) v Secretary of State for the Home Department* [2013] EWCA Civ 1286.

8.85   Summary of the procedure in a '*Cart*' Judicial Review:

• Claimant drafts grounds addressing the second appeal criteria.

• Claimant lodges judicial review within 16 days of the impugned determination being sent to claimant.

• Claimant serves claim on defendant and interested party (ie the respondent to the appeal) within seven days of issue.

• Defendant serves Acknowledgment of Service within 21 days.

• Administrative Court judge makes decision on papers (there is no right of oral renewal).

• If claim is refused, possible appeal to Court of Appeal (there is no right of oral renewal).

• If claim is granted, usually the permission refusal will be quashed leaving the case outstanding before the UT, subject to the UT or interested party wishing there to be a substantive hearing of the judicial review application in the Administrative Court.

MATTERS COMMON TO JUDICIAL REVIEW IN THE UT AND ADMINISTRATIVE COURT

Pre Action Protocol letter

8.86   An application for judicial review should be heralded by a Pre Action Protocol letter that sets out the applicant's case in full and gives the respondent an opportunity to respond. The procedure does not apply in Scotland or in urgent cases of imminent removal, however; nor where the defendant lacks the legal power to revisit its decision, as where it is a tribunal.[1] The full Protocol (which represents a code of good practice which is generally to be followed before issuing a judicial review,[2] on pain of case management or cost sanctions[3]) and specimen Pre Action and Reply letters, are set out online.[4] Alternative dispute resolution should be attempted if possible.[5] Interested parties should be identified.[6] Defendants should usually respond within 14 days, providing an interim response if unable to do so, requesting any further information and proposing a reasonable deadline for the extension of time, which will not bind the applicant if he thinks it unreasonable, but may nevertheless support an argument that the claim was premature if unreasonably rejected.[7] The reply, which should be sent to the claimant and to all interested parties, should be clear and unambiguous in explaining whether the claim is being conceded in full, part or not at all, and where appropriate, should contain a new decision (or give a clear timescale for one), clearly identifying what aspects of the claim are being conceded or not, providing a fuller explanation for the decision if appropriate, addressing any points of dispute (or explaining why they cannot be addressed), enclosing any relevant documentation requested by the claimant (or explaining why this is not being done) and confirming the defendant's stance on any application for an interim remedy.[8]

1   Protocol, Introduction and para 6.
2   Protocol, para 5.
3   Protocol, para 7.
4   www.justice.gov.uk/courts/procedure-rules/civil/protocol/prot_jrv.
5   Protocol, para 3.1 onwards.
6   Protocol, para 11.
7   Protocol, para 14.
8   Protocol, paras 15–17.

8.87   The address for serving the Pre Action Protocol letter is:

Judicial Review Unit,
UK Immigration and Visas,
Lunar House,
40 Wellesley Rd,
Croydon
CR9 2BY

It is now possible to issue the Pre Action Protocol letter by email to ukbapap@ ukba.gsi.gov.uk.

8.88   The letter should contain:

- the title, first and last name and the address of the claimant;

- his reference details with the defendant (specifically in an immigration case, the relevant reference numbers for the Home Office, port, ie immigration service, tribunal and NASS);

- the details of the matter being challenged;

- the date and details of the decision, or act or omission being challenged;

- a brief summary of the facts and why it is contented to be wrong;

- the details of the action that the defendant is expected to take having received and digested the latter;

- the details of the legal advisers, if any, dealing with this claim and their reference for this matter;

- the details of any interested parties and confirmation that they have been sent a copy of the letter;

- the details of any information sought, including any request for a fuller explanation of the reasons for the decision that is being challenged;

- the details of any documentation or policy in respect of which the disclosure is sought, explaining the relevance of any such request;

- details of any statutory duty to disclose;

- the address for reply and service of court documents, and the proposed reply date.

Alternative remedy

8.89   There is a duty on putative litigants to consider the possibility of alternative remedies,[1] whether these are rights of appeal or of complaint. In *Dong*,[2] Treacy J referred to the importance of relief for damages for maladministration under HRA 1998 being proportionate requiring justification of non-recourse to internal complaint procedures or to an ombudsman,[3] even where these avenues became apparent only upon receipt of the grounds of defence: this applied to the relief sought at a substantive hearing as well as at the permission stage. Recourse to an ombudsman might not be appropriate where court proceedings might produce a quicker, fairer and more reasonable and effective outcome.[4] There is in general[5] no requirement that a complainant receive a declaration of unlawful interference with his human rights, bearing in mind the public interest in minimising the unnecessary expenditure of judicial time and resources, so long as just satisfaction was being offered by way of apology, admission of wrongdoing, and the offer of compensation. Proceedings should be stayed rather than dismissed pending utilisation of the complaints process.[6]

1   Lord Woolf in *Cowl v Plymouth City Council* [2001] EWCA Civ 1935 at [27].
2   *Dong v Secretary of State for the Home Department* [2010] EWHC 1015, citing [79]–[81] of *Anufrijeva, R (on the application of) v Secretary of State for the Home Department* [2003] UKHL 36; see further *Anyasinti, R (on the application of) v Secretary of State for the Home Department* [2010] EWHC 1676 (Admin).
3   *Dong v Secretary of State for the Home Department* [2010] EWHC 1015.
4   *McIntyre, R (on the application of) v Gentoo Group Ltd* [2010] EWHC 5 (Admin) at [112].
5   The President of the QBD for the Court of Appeal in *MD (China), R (on the application of) v Secretary of State for the Home Department* [2011] EWCA Civ 453 at [13].
6   *Dong v Secretary of State for the Home Department* [2010] EWHC 1015.

8.90   Where there is a right of appeal, this should generally be pursued, and where a statutory appeal is available the court will exercise its discretion in all but exceptional cases (absent 'special or exceptional factors')[1] by declining to entertain an application for judicial review;[2] however reliance on an out-of-country appeal should not be expected where fundamental rights such as asylum are in play: 'If their fears are well-founded, the fact that they can appeal after they have been returned to the country where they fear persecution is scant consolation.'[3] It will not be appropriate to affirmatively exercise discretion where legal arguments could reasonably have been expected to have been made within an appeal process in the past, particularly where their determination would not be conclusive of the appeal in question.[4] Where there is a debate as to whether there is a right of appeal to the FTT, normally an attempt should be made to bring such an appeal, whereby the FTT may determine its own jurisdiction.[5] An imminent appeal hearing will constitute an alternative remedy whether or not permission for judicial review has been granted, particularly where it constitutes a more effective remedy.[6]

1   McCloskey J in *R (on the application of Bilal Mahmood) v Secretary of State for the Home Department* (continuing duty to reassess) (IJR) [2014] UKUT 439 (IAC) at [11].
2   See *R v IRC, ex parte Preston* [1985] AC 835; *R v Chief Constable of the Merseyside Police, ex parte Calveley* [1986] 1 QB 424; *R v Home Secretary, ex parte Swati* [1986] 1 WLR 477; *R (Sivasubramanian) v Wandsworth County Court* [2003] 2 WLR 475.
3   Lord Phillips MR giving the judgment of the court and permitting judicial review of decisions regarding clearly unfounded cases in *ZL v Secretary of State for the Home Department and Lord Chancellor's Department* [2003] EWCA Civ 25 at [54].
4   *AO (Iraq) v Secretary of State for the Home Department* [2010] EWCA Civ 1637.
5   See Mr Ockelton sitting as a Deputy High Court judge in *Merriman-Johnson, R (on the application of) v Secretary of State for the Home Department* [2010] EWHC 1598 (Admin).
6   *Poyraz, R (on the application of) v Secretary of State for the Home Department* (IJR) (not applicable) [2014] UKUT 151 (IAC) at [27]–[29].

8.91   In *Lim*,[1] Sedley LJ discussed the relative availability of 'out-of-country' appeal and 'in-country' pre-removal judicial review in relation to a student who had breached the terms of his leave to remain by excessive working and was subjected to administrative removal (against which the right of appeal would be available only after leaving the country).[2] He concluded that to permit (in-country) judicial review of an immigration decision which carried only an out-of-country appeal right would defeat the policy of the legislation ('there has been a clear legislative choice by Parliament to make the out of country right of appeal the only available route of appeal in cases where it has been concluded that there has been a sufficiently serious breach of conditions or that deceit has been used in seeking leave to remain which justifies using removal power rather than simply curtailing leave (which triggers an in-country right of appeal)'),[3] even where this might have harsh consequences for the individual,[4] where there was a dispute as to whether the conditions of leave had in truth been breached. However, if the issue was more fundamental, going to, for example, whether the subject of removal directions was in fact a British citizen, or involved a dispute as to the identity of the person facing removal, then judicial review would be available on an 'in-country' basis;[5] issues of public importance will not necessarily change this analysis.[6]

1   *Lim, R (on the application of) v Secretary of State for the Home Department* [2007] EWCA Civ 773, approved in *RK (Nepal) v Secretary of State for the Home Department* [2009] EWCA Civ 359; see further *Yu, R (on the application of) v Secretary of State for the Home Department* [2008] EWHC 3072 (Admin).
2   The right of appeal under NIAA 2002, s 82 is only available out of country if no human rights claim has been made pre-decision such as to trigger the 'in-country' protection of s 92(4)(a); see Lady Scott in *KA (AP), Re Judicial Review* [2013] ScotCS CSOH_184 particularly at [26] *et seq.*
3   Helen Mountfield QC sitting as a Deputy High Court judge in *Ali, R (on the application of) v Secretary of State for the Home Department* [2014] EWHC 3967 (Admin) at [18].
4   Green J in *Khan, R (on the application of) v Secretary of State for the Home Department* [2014] EWHC 2494 (Admin) at [70](x).
5   *Lim* (above) at [19].
6   Green J in *Khan* (above) at [70](xi), citing *Jan, R (on the application of) v Secretary of State for the Home Department (s 10 removal)* (IJR) [2014] UKUT 265 (IAC) at [42].

8.92   There will not normally be a sustainable challenge to the choice of enforcement action taken, notwithstanding that the ultimate selection may seriously disadvantage a migrant,[1] at least where the process investigated the existence of any mitigating circumstances that might have called into play the exercise of discretion[2] bearing in mind that, in a deceit case, the 'evidence of deception should be clear and unambiguous in order to initiate action under section 10'[3] (however, if the choice of enforcement action is 'to prevent the exposure of a shameful decision', or is otherwise an abuse of power,[4] judicial review will be available).[5] There may be cases where it is appropriate to stay the proceedings pending the result of an out-of-country appeal, as where that approach preserves a damages a claim.[6] The *Lim* line of authority, predicated as it is on the availability of an out-of-country right of appeal, applies only to those cases subject to the 'saved provisions' of NIAA 2002.[7] Judicial review may be brought of proceedings that presently remain within the appeals system because of unfairness, though this will only be possible in exceptional cases.[8]

1   *Jan, R (on the application of) v Secretary of State for the Home Department (s 10 removal)*
    (IJR) [2014] UKUT 265 (IAC) at [24]–[30], joining with Coulson J in *R (Zahid) v Secretary
    of State for the Home* Department [2013] EWHC 4290 (Admin) and Green J in *Khan, R
    (on the application of) v Secretary of State for the Home Department* [2014] EWHC 2494
    (Admin) at [67] in disapproving *Thapa v Secretary of State for the Home Department* [2014]
    EWHC 659 (Admin); Lord Jones in *MDMH (Bangladesh) v Secretary of State for the Home
    Department* [2014] ScotCS CSOH_143 at [36]–[37].
2   *Jan* (above) at [29].
3   Helen Mountfield QC sitting as a Deputy High Court judge in *Ali, R (on the application of) v
    Secretary of State for the Home Department* [2014] EWHC 3967 (Admin) at [21].
4   Helen Mountfield QC sitting as a Deputy High Court judge in *Ali* (above) at [63]; Green J in
    Khan (above) at [70](ix).
5   Sedley LJ in *Anwar v Secretary of State for the Home Department* [2010] EWCA Civ 1275
    at [32].
6   Lang J in *Benjamin, R (on the application of) v Secretary of State for the Home Department*
    [2014] EWHC 1396 at [10]–[11].
7   See Chapter 3.
8   See **6.28**, fn 4 (above). See also *R (on the application of AM (Cameroon) v Asylum and
    Immigration Tribunal* [2007] EWCA Civ 131.

Urgent procedures and interim relief

8.93   We have dealt above with the distinct urgent procedures in both
the UT and Administrative Court. However, there are general principles
too that are relevant, as well as an important Home Office policy (EIG,
Ch 60) that explains the notice requirements as perceived by the SSHD:
policies, of course, must be followed.[1] Access to the court is a fundamental
constitutional right: as Lord Millett put it in *Cullen*, 'Access to legal advice
and the independence and integrity of the legal profession are cornerstones
of a free society under the rule of law'.[2] Thus Home Office policy has
consistently reminded its staff enforcing removals that 'It is important to
satisfy yourself that the person concerned has had the opportunity to lodge a
claim with the courts (particularly in section 94 NSA or third country cases
where there is no statutory in-country right of appeal)';[3] and a failure to
give adequate notice has been judicially deplored.[4] There can be a lack of
access to the court notwithstanding compliance with the terms of the Home
Office policy, as where there is no indication of any need for urgent removal
without an opportunity being given to seek legal advice first.[5] Preventing the
removal of a migrant who has properly sought the court's protection is self-
evidently a proper reason for the grant of an injunction.[6] Where interim relief
is refused, the appropriate course of action is to renew the application to the
Administrative Court, to avoid the Court of Appeal having to take the role
of a first instance court without the benefit of a judgment below and without
the parties below having had the advantage of being able to appeal such a
decision;[7] in such cases it is necessary to show an error of law on the part of
the judge below, and there was a high duty of candour on a party so applying
to reveal all relevant facts and legal principles to the appellate judge.[8]

1   See the authorities cited at **8.134**, fnn 8–10 below.

2 Lord Millett in *Cullen v Chief Constable of the Royal Ulster Constabulary* [2003] UKHL 39 at [50]. The common law principle of access to the court was set out by Laws J in the High Court in *Witham, R (on the application of) v Lord Chancellor* [1997] EWHC Admin 237. See further Silber J in *Medical Justice, R (on the application of) v Secretary of State for the Home Department (Rev 1)* [2010] EWHC 1925 (Admin) at [43], which included, at [60], the need for a genuine opportunity to find a legal advisor with the ability and capacity to take the matter forward within a reasonable period; upheld in *Medical Justice, R (on the application of) v Secretary of State for the Home Department* [2011] EWCA Civ 1710, see particularly [19]; see further per Lord Steyn with whom Lords Hoffman, Millett and Scott of Foscote agreed in *R (Anufrijeva) v Secretary of State for the Home Department* [2004] 1 AC 604 at 621 at [26] for the ineffectiveness of decisions that are inadequately communicated to their subject.

3 EIG, Ch 60.

4 *R (on the application of Karas) v Secretary of State for the Home Department* [2006] EWHC 747 (Admin).

5 Clive Lewis QC sitting as a Deputy High Court judge in *Shaw, R (on the application of) v Secretary of State for the Home Department* [2013] EWHC 42 (Admin) at [37]–[39].

6 eg *R v Secretary of State for the Home Department, ex parte Muboyayi* [1992] QB 244, Lord Donaldson at 255H–256A, and Taylor LJ at 269B.

7 Stanley Burnton LJ in *MD (Afghanistan) v Secretary of State for the Home Department* [2012] EWCA Civ 194 at [21].

8 See *Madan v Secretary of State for the Home Department* [2007] EWCA Civ 770 for the appropriate procedure where the matter was appealed to the Court of Appeal; and see further **8.104** and **8.105** below.

Interim relief: the test

8.94   Whether interim relief should be given is a question which centres on considerations of justice and convenience.[1] The key principles are as expressed in *American Cyanimid*:[2]

> 'unless the material available to the court at the hearing of the application for the interlocutory injunction fails to disclose that the Plaintiff has any real prospect of succeeding in his claim for a permanent injunction at the trial, the court should go on to consider whether the balance of convenience lies in favour of granting or refusing the interlocutory relief that is sought. As to that, the governing principle is that the court should first consider whether if the Plaintiff were to succeed at the trial in establishing his right to a permanent injunction he would be adequately compensated by an award of damages'

1 Senior Courts Act 1981, s 37(1)–(2).
2 *American Cyanimid Co v Ethicon Ltd* [1975] AC 396.

8.95   As discussed in *Factortame*,[1] once this question is answered, the next consideration is the balance of convenience, which posits the question as to whether the claimant would be adequately compensated, for example by damages, if his action succeeded only following a lengthy period of illegal interference with his interests. An adequate remedy in damages normally precludes the granting of an injunction. If the claimant is not so precluded then the court will consider the position of the defendant. If the defendant can be adequately compensated by the cross undertaking in damages that means there will be no reason not to grant the injunction on that ground. If damages are not an adequate remedy to either party, then when considering the balance of convenience, the court must consider all the circumstances of the case. Again in *Factortame*, Lord Goff emphasised that where the validity of a law was actually challenged, the relevant question was whether the action was so firmly based as to justify suspending its effect.[2] The basic principle is that the court should take whichever course seems likely to cause the least irremediable prejudice to one party or the other.[3]

1   *R v Secretary of State for Transport, ex parte Factortame Ltd (No. 1)* [1989] UKHL 1.
2   See eg Lord Bridge in *Factortame Ltd* (above).
3   Lord Hoffmann delivering the opinion of the Privy Council in *National Commercial Bank Jamaica Ltd v Olint Corpn Ltd* [2009] UKPC 16 at [16] and [17]. See Sales J in *Awad (R on the application of) v Secretary of State for the Home Department* (3 November 2009) [2009] EWHC (Admin) 3463 and Lang J in *R (on the application of South London College) v Secretary of State for the Home Department* [2015] EWHC 1184 (Admin) for the practical application of the test.

Home Office policy on urgent removal cases

8.96   Under the urgent removals procedure set out in EIG, Ch 60, removal directions will be suspended upon receipt of a claim form with detailed grounds, or one that explains why detailed grounds are not available where the court accepts these are good reasons, or where judicial review is granted, or where the matter has not been considered prior to the scheduled departure time.[1] Where no claim form can be filed because the court is not open outside working hours, there is a discretion in the Home Office to defer removal subject to receiving detailed grounds (and on an undertaking to lodge at the first opportunity) subject to consideration of whether:

● there has been less than three months since a previous judicial review application or statutory appeal has been concluded on the same or similar issues,

● where the issues now raised could reasonably have been raised in a previous judicial review application or statutory appeal within the last three months,

● where a stay on removal relating to the current judicial review has already been refused and not successfully renewed, or

● where the individual is being removed by special arrangements (including by charter flight).[2]

1   EIG, section 4.1.
2   EIG, sections 4.2 and 6.

8.97   Those same grounds apply generally in determining whether there should be an automatic deferral of the removal upon receipt of a permission application (there should nevertheless be a discretionary consideration of deferral).[1] A mere threat of judicial review will not bring a deferral of removal of itself, albeit that it must nevertheless be evaluated in case it discloses circumstances where there has been no effective opportunity to access relief.[2] Where permission is refused, with a finding that the claim is without merit or that it should not impede removal, a departure will be enforced; in other cases usually removal will await the oral renewal hearing.[3] It may be necessary to accept informal confirmation of the suspension of removal directions from a legal representative, and both the staff overseeing removal and any escorting agency must act on any reasonable belief that an injunction may have been granted.[4] Absent some other point of contact, the result of an urgent application or order should be sent to the UK Border Agency's Command and Control Unit.[5]

1   EIG, section 6.
2   EIG, sections 4, 5.
3   EIG, section 12.
4   EIG, section 14.
5   EIG, section 14.2; fax number 0161 261 1640.

8.98   Where removal directions are deferred behind a lead case, removal can proceed if that challenge ultimately fails, where this determines all issues raised by the removee; an opportunity should be given to persons whose claims have been so stayed to amend their grounds if necessary before the removal process is resumed, and from that point notice of 72 hours must be given of removal.[1] If permission for judicial review is granted, all enforcement action must be suspended.[2] In the event of removal in the face of an injunction, the court should be informed and steps should be taken, via the legal representatives here or via escorts or other means, to secure the removee's return, and the relevant Director General of the Home Office should be informed with a view to explaining the incident to the Home Secretary.[3]

1   EIG, section 7.1. Fourteen days for so doing should be given if there is no court order in different terms.
2   EIG, section 10.
3   EIG, section 14.3–14.4.

8.99   Notice of removal will normally be given to the subject of removal directions[1] though where there is a risk to safety or significant risk of disruption then limited notice may be given.[2] The policy[3] explains that:

'Unless an exception applies, there are three rules to consider when calculating the notice period:

(i)   A minimum of 72 hours must be allowed between giving notice of removal and the removal itself.

(ii) This 72-hour notification period must always include at least two working days.

(iii) The last 24 hours before removal must include a working day unless the notice period already includes three working days.'

1   EIG, section 2. Using Form IS151D or IS92.
2   EIG, section 2. Using Form IS151G.
3   EIG, section 2. The policy gives numerous examples of its practical operation: thus removals scheduled for Mondays and Tuesdays (the latter before 5pm) will need notification preceding the prior weekend, and weekend removals must be notified the previous Wednesday or earlier.

8.100   In third country and non-suspensive appeal cases, there will have normally been no prior opportunity for 'legal redress',[1] and so under the Ch 60 policy a minimum of five working days' notice should be given, unless the case is one where special notice procedures operate.[2] Where a threat of judicial review is made in a charter flight case, the terms of the threat must be referred to the relevant Home Office department (OSCU)[3] who will write back if it decides removal remains appropriate, explaining that removal would proceed absent an injunction forestalling it. There are special notice provisions for charter flights (a flight number prefixed PVT indicates a charter flight; the Government Legal Department has agreed to give the Immigration Lawyers Practitioners Association the same notice of charter flight removals as is received by the Administrative Court)[4] by which five working days' notice of removal is always given, but a claimant seeking judicial review is usually required to obtain an express injunction.[5] Precise details of a charter flight may sometimes be withheld.[6]

1   In both kinds of case a certificate is made that ousts the right of 'in-country' appeal, in third country cases under A&I(TC)A 2004, Sch 3, in non-suspensive appeal cases via a clearly unfounded certificate under NIAA 2002, s 92.
2   EIG, section 2.3: so seven calendar days, and eight to nine days where no notice can be given on the weekend before a weekend of removal.
3   EIG, section 2.4.
4   EIG, section 5.1.
5   At the Administrative Court Users Group meeting of 27 June 2012.
6   EIG, section 2.4.

8.101   There is a series of exceptions to the standard notification procedures:[1]

• port cases where removal takes place within seven days of the refusal of leave to enter;[2]

• country and non-suspensive appeal family cases of Ensured Return;[3]

• failed or deferred removal cases,[4] where there has been an ineffective attempt at removal due to the behaviour of a removee, mechanical or other frustration of the flight, in which case, where standard notice was previously given, and the new removal directions are within ten days of the ineffectual ones, it may not be necessary to give standard notification this time around;

• cases where a removal was deferred because of the bringing of a judicial review challenge which has now failed, given the refusal of permission by a judge who has additionally made a finding of 'no merit' or a note that 'renewal should not be a bar to removal'.[5]

1   EIG, section 3.
2   EIG, section 3.1.1.
3   EIG, section 3.1.2.
4   EIG, section 3.2.
5   EIG, section 3.1.3.

8.102   Short notice following a failed or deferred removal should not, however, be given once that ten-day period has passed, or where there has been a significant change of circumstances, such as a change of destination of removal 'to a different country' or of the route of removal, or the receipt and refusal of further submissions has intervened. There is specific treatment of 'change of route' cases: the removal of a port-of-call will not trigger a re-run of time, but the addition of a port-of-call will do so, unless it is one of a specific list of safe countries.[1] Whatever notification is given of removal, in the case of a failed asylum seeker it will have to be sufficient to permit him to challenge the removal directions' implied resolution of any remaining question of safety that was left undetermined at his appeal hearing for want of information as to the arrangements for his return, giving the precise airport or landing strip details if that is required.[2]

1   EIG, section 3.2.
2   Hooper LJ in *AG v Secretary of State for the Home Department* [2006] EWCA Civ 1342 at [30]; Sedley LJ giving the judgment of the Court of Appeal in *HH (Somalia) v Secretary of State for the Home Department* [2010] EWCA Civ 426 at [51].

Children: special notice provisions

8.103   Where a child and his relevant carer or parent faces return under the Immigration Acts, they may not be removed within 28 days from the day when their appeal rights are exhausted (ie when they can no longer bring a future appeal, and have no extant appeal pending), albeit that steps to secure their removal by making removal directions, a deportation order, or other interim or preparatory action, are permitted.[1] Before a family return (one involving a child and his parent or other carer) is made, the SSHD must consult the Independent Family Returns Panel on how best to safeguard and promote the child's welfare in so doing, including regarding the suitability of any detention in pre-departure accommodation.[2] There are special procedures for 'Family cases' involving the notions of Assisted Return, Required Return and Ensured Return.[3] A Family Return Conference will permit options to be discussed, including the availability of any legal challenges or further submissions

481

regarding departure. After this there will be a two-week period of reflection before removal directions are set. Normally ('in almost all cases') the family will then be given the option to make a Required Return, without removal directions, at which they may 'check-in', having lived at home right up to the departure. If these measures fail or are not appropriate, then the usual notification periods identified above will run. Where there has been non-compliance or disruption by the family leading to a previous failed return, a Limited Notice Removal is possible under which removal follows notice of between 72 hours and 21 days.[4]

1   NIAA 2002, s 78A as inserted by IA 2014, s 2, in force from 28 July 2014.
2   BCIA 2009, s 54 as inserted by IA 2014, s 3, in force from 28 July 2014.
3   EIG, section 2.2.
4   EIG, section 2.2.

Critical considerations in an injunction application against removal directions

8.104   Whether or not an injunction against removal directions is sought in the UT or the Administrative Court, there are certain minimum standards as to the provision of information to which representatives must adhere. These are the criteria identified in *Madan*:[1]

'(i)   CPR PD 54.18 makes provision for the hearing of judicial review applications in the Administrative Court against removal from the jurisdiction. Such applications must be made promptly on the intimation of a deportation decision, and not await the actual fixing of removal arrangements.

(ii)   The detailed statement required by PD 18.2(c) must include a statement of all previous applications made in respect of the applicant's immigration status, and indicate how the present state of the case differs from previous applications.

(iii)   Counsel or solicitors attending ex parte before the judge in the Administrative Court are under professional obligations (a) to draw the judge's attention to any matter adverse to their clients' case, including in particular any previous adverse decisions; and (b) to take a full note of the judge's judgment or reasons, which should then be submitted to the judge for approval. ...

(vi)   The Treasury Solicitor should be promptly informed of the intention to apply for injunctive relief, in case he is able to and wishes to attend.

(viii) Counsel will remember that where the application is made ex parte there is a particular obligation to draw the court's attention to relevant authority, including in particular Country Guidance cases.'

1   *R (Madan) v Secretary of State for the Home Department* [2007] 1 WLR 2891; [2007] EWCA Civ 770.

8.105   A failure to implement these measures, and to provide an adequate and reasoned explanation for the need for urgency and when such need was first appreciated, may result in the convening of a *Hamid* hearing.[1] Under that procedure:

- the responsible solicitor and his senior partner will be required to attend the hearing, the firm being identified when the matter is listed;

- a judge may refuse to consider the application for interim relief;

- a referral to the appropriate regulatory body may be made.

Manifestly inappropriate requests for urgent consideration may result in wasted costs orders.[2]

1   This being the procedure set out as to be used in the future by the President of the QBD in *Hamid, R (on the application of) v Secretary of State for the Home Department* [2012] EWHC 3070 (Admin); see the President of the QBD in *Butt, R (on the application of) v Secretary of State for the Home Department* [2014] EWHC 264 (Admin), dealing with cases where unjustifiably late applications for judicial review sought to use the emergency procedures.
2   Administrative Court Guidance on Applying for Judicial Review, para 8.5.

Notice provisions under the IA 2014 appeals regime

8.106   The new single decision procedure makes a migrant removable as a consequence of having no leave rather than requiring a separate decision to be made.[1] The Ch 60 policy sets out a different approach in these cases.[2] Removal directions will no longer be served on the individual, only on the carrier; the single decision notice will give the country of removal and will specify the period of non-removability running from the end of his leave, normally seven days from notice of the decision, unless he is detained, in which case 72 hours' notice is given; however, once three months has passed since notice of liability to removal was given, he will be given a further period to access legal advice prior to removal.[3] It would thus appear that minimal notice of removal will be given, and the question will arise whether this procedure truly gives its subjects an opportunity to access the court.[4] The Pre Action Protocol will not apply in these cases once a person is detained for removal.[5]

1   See Chapter 3.
2   EIG, Ch 60, section 19.
3   Letter from The Rt Hon Theresa May MP, Home Secretary, to The Rt Hon Keith Vaz MP, 25 March 2015, re removal and deportation.
4   See **8.93**, fn 2 above.
5   EIG, Ch 60, section 19.

Expedition of judicial review claims

8.107   The Administrative Court or tribunal may order expedition of judicial review proceedings. The SSHD has indicated that suitable cases will include those where:

- the claimant is in detention,

- the claimant is from a family within the family return process,

- the claim appears to be clearly without merit or to be an abuse of process,

- the claim involves the issue of public safety or a risk of self-harm,

- the decision-making process has previously been subject to accelerated timescales (such as non-suspensive appeal or Detained Fast Track appeal processes), or

- removal involves an enforcement operation such as a special charter flight, or a third country or criminal casework directorate matter.

8.108   In these the target for delivering the Acknowledgment of Service is seven days. Normally the court or tribunal will make a decision within two weeks in an expedited case.[1] When a case is referred to a specialist unit for consideration for expedition, the Home Office file should be made available as a matter of priority (claimant lawyers may wish to consider whether these materials might be the subject of an application for disclosure).[2]

1   EIG, section 11.
2   EIG, section 11.2.

Evidence in judicial review proceedings

8.109   Written evidence may be relied upon only where served under the CPR, under the direction of the court, or where the court has given permission.[1] Where there is a factual dispute in a judicial review application, then in the absence of cross-examination, the facts in the defendant's evidence are normally assumed to be correct, unless there is documentary evidence to the contrary. A claimant wishing to dispute such a factual contention should apply to cross-examine the maker of the witness statement on which the defendant relies.[2] Nevertheless, assertions unsupported by evidence, particularly where made in counsel's drafting, may be rejected;[3] and the defendant must put forward a proper evidential basis for denying facts asserted by a claimant.[4] If a substantial dispute of fact arises in the Administrative Court, it may be appropriate for either party to apply for an order under CPR, r 8.1(3) for the claim to continue as if the claimant had not used the procedure under CPR, Pt 8, which is that generally appropriate for judicial reviews (ie for it to be treated instead as a Pt 7 claim), and for appropriate directions. Where such steps were not taken, it might be appropriate for the claimant's witness statement evidence to be afforded a measure of generosity, if unchallenged by way of cross-examination, albeit that it could be measured against the other written evidence in the case, such as contemporaneous records by immigration officials.[5]

1   CPR, r 54.16(2).
2   Silber J in *R (McVey) v Secretary of State for Health* [2010] EWHC Admin 437, applied in
     the immigration context in *Westech College, R (on the application of) v Secretary of State for
     the Home Department* [2011] EWHC 1484 (Admin).
3   Sullivan J in the Administrative Court in *S v Secretary of State for the Home Department*
     [2006] EWHC 1111 (Admin) at [97]–[98].
4   Green J in *Kadyamarunga v Secretary of State for the Home Department* [2014] EWHC 301
     (Admin) at [19].
5   Sales J in *Hussein, R (on the application of) v Secretary of State for the Home Department*
     [2009] EWHC 2506 (Admin) at [7]–[10].

Fresh decisions, fresh evidence and academic challenges

8.110   If a new decision has been made or where the claimant has achieved
what his application for judicial review originally sought by way of a
suspension of removal or other relief, then the claim may become academic.
It is critical that the court is appraised of any developments to such effect.[1] A
failure to challenge a further decision which answers the material challenge
previously brought may render a claim unarguable.[2] Occasionally the
question may have to be asked: 'Is it right that issues raising important points
of principle which are in dispute between the defendant and those whose
position in this country is regulated by the defendant ... should not be resolved
because they are continuously kicked into touch by individual decisions made
after proceedings are instituted?'[3] Where the challenge raises an important
point of principle that would affect other applicants, it may nevertheless be
entertained,[4] as where 'there is good reason in the public interest for doing so',
so long as a large number of similar cases exist or are anticipated, and provided
that the instant decision will not be fact-sensitive.[5] The court may proceed
to determine a challenge to a further decision than that originally assaulted
by way of permitting an amendment of grounds, as where a new decision
responds to evidence filed in the proceedings and the subsequent decision is
to the same effect as an earlier one, accepting undertakings to pay further fees
as appropriate – though proceedings should not necessarily be stayed to await
a future decision.[6] It is important that the issues for determination are clearly
identified and that a claimant does not start one challenge and then seek to
argue an entirely different one, unpleaded and unsupported by evidence.[7]
Considering material that was not before the primary decision maker may well
deprive the court of the advantage of the view of the body that Parliament has
identified as the primary decision maker and endangers the court straying into
a merits review, which is not its function even when conducting an intensive
review of the compatibility of an administrative decision with fundamental
rights[8] outside of cases where the primary decision maker was under a
continuing duty to assess the compatibility of his decision with HRA 1998 or
other relevant instruments.[9]

1   Stanley Burnton J in the Administrative Court in *Tshikangu v London Borough of Newham*
     [2001] EWHC Admin 92 at [23].

2   See eg Green J in *Hafeez, R (on the application of) v Secretary of State for the Home Department* [2014] EWHC 1342 at [34]–[37].
3   Beatson J in *Omar, R (on the application of) v Secretary of State for the Home Department* [2012] EWHC 3448 at [45].
4   Laws LJ in *AA (Afghanistan) v Secretary of State for the Home Department* [2006] EWCA Civ 1550; see Simon Brown LJ in *R v Secretary of State for the Home Department, ex parte Al Abi* (5 February 1997, 1997/WL/1105932, 1998 COD 103) cited by Ouseley J in *Rathakrishnan, R (on the application of) v Secretary of State for the Home Department* [2011] EWHC 1406 (Admin).
5   Silber J at [32]–[36] of *Zoolife International Ltd v Secretary of State for Environment, Food and Rural Affairs* [2007] EWHC 2995, approved by Singh J in *K v Entry Clearance Officer Tashkent* [2012] EWHC 2875, adopting the approach of Lord Slynn of Hadley *in R v Secretary of State for the Home Department, ex parte Salem* [1999] 1 AC 450; see further *SM (withdrawal of appealed decision: effect) (Pakistan)* [2014] UKUT 64 (IAC) at [54]–[59].
6   Ouseley J in *Rathakrishnan* (above); HHJ Pelling sitting as a Deputy High Court judge in *Bhatti, R (on the application of) v Bury MBC* [2013] EWHC 3093 (Admin) at [17]; Dr Storey in *R (on the application of Natalia Heritage) v Secretary of State for the Home Department and First-tier Tribunal IJR* [2014] UKUT 441(IAC) at [12]–[15].
7   Mitting J in *Khan, R (on the application of) v Secretary of State for the Home Department* [2012] EWHC 707 (Admin) at [16]–17], Ouseley J in *Rathakrishnan* (above).
8   Beatson LJ in *A, R (on the application of) v Kent Constabulary* [2013] EWCA Civ 1706, particularly at [84]; though cf Sales J in *Princely, R (on the application of) v Secretary of State for the Home Department* [2009] EWHC 3095 (Admin).
9   Beatson LJ in *A* (above) at [77]–[78], [91].

8.111   Any new decision should not be produced so late as to disadvantage a claimant, and it will be important to examine the motivation behind it, as to permit poor quality original decision making to be routinely rectified 'might be thought to be the very opposite of the respondent's ongoing commitment to improvement to the quality of decisions made by her officials';[1] and it is undesirable to admit a supplementary justification (as opposed to a genuinely new decision) where 'the alleged true reasons were in fact second thoughts designed to remedy an otherwise fatal error exposed by the judicial review proceedings.'[2] An applicant who receives a new, lawful decision after initiating proceedings with regard to an unlawful one should have a little time to consider the latter's ramifications and can expect to receive his costs up to this time.[3] In the UT, permission is required to withdraw a decision in judicial review proceedings.[4]

1   Dr Storey in *R (on the application of Natalia Heritage) v Secretary of State for the Home Department and First-tier Tribunal IJR* [2014] UKUT 441(IAC) at [12]–[13]; Beatson J in *Omar, R (on the application of) v Secretary of State for the Home Department* [2012] EWHC 3448 at [46]; Lord Tyre in the Court of Session, Outer House, in *AS, Re Judicial Review* [2013] ScotCS CSOH_82 at [11]; *Kerr, R (on the application of) v Secretary of State for the Home Department (IJR)* [2014] UKUT 493 (IAC) at [15].
2   Hutchison LJ in *Ermakov, R (on the application of) v Westminster* [1995] EWCA Civ 42; *Kerr* (above) at [17].
3   *Kerr* (above) at [15].
4   *SM (withdrawal of appealed decision: effect) Pakistan* [2014] UKUT 64 (IAC) at [18].

Disclosure

8.112   Under the CPR, disclosure is not required unless the court orders it.[1]
CPR, Pt 31 sets out detailed procedures for disclosure in the Administrative
Court, by which the existence of a document is revealed by disclosure and
the party receiving such information has a right to inspect it, subject to it
no longer being in the disclosing party's control or there being a right or
duty to withhold it;[2] there is then a timetable for the agreement or order of
disclosure, and under standard disclosure a party must reveal the documents
on which he relies, plus those which adversely affect his own case or that of
another party, or support another party's case.[3] The UT's Rules empower it
to 'require a party or another person to provide documents, information [or]
evidence'.[4] Whatever disclosure regime prevails, there is nevertheless a high
duty on public authorities to disclose all relevant material ('to cooperate and
to make candid disclosure')[5] as, at least once permission is granted, they
are under a duty of candour to lay before the court all the relevant facts and
reasoning underlying the decision under challenge:[6] judicial review being a
'process which falls to be conducted with all the cards face upwards on the
table and [where] the vast majority of the cards will start in the authority's
hands.'[7]

1   CPR PD 54A, para 16.
2   See Richards LJ in *FI, R (on the application of) v Secretary of State for the Home Department*
    [2014] EWCA Civ 1272 at [72]–[75] for a discussion of relevant considerations as to redaction
    of disclosed documents.
3   Tribunal Procedure (Upper Tribunal) Rules 2008, SI 2008/2698, r 5(3)(d).
4   SI 2008/2698, r 5(3)(d).
5   Lord Walker in the Privy Council in *Belize Alliance of Conservation Non-Governmental
    Organisations v Department of the Environment (Belize)* [2004] UKPC 6 at [86].
6   *Tweed v Parades Commission for Northern Ireland* [2007] 1 AC 650. The Treasury Solicitor's
    January 2010 Guidance on 'Discharging the duty of candour and disclosure in judicial review
    proceedings' emphasises that its objective is 'not … to win the litigation at all costs but to
    assist the court in reaching the correct result and thereby to improve standards in public
    administration'.
7   Sir John Donaldson MR in *R v Lancashire County Court, ex parte Huddelston* [1986] 2 All
    ER 941.

8.113   Where the court has not been given a true and comprehensive account,
but has had to tease the truth out of late discovery, it may be appropriate to
draw inferences against the defendant;[1] the SSHD takes a substantial risk in
failing to put sufficient evidence before a court to explain a decision-making
process.[2] The test is whether disclosure is 'necessary in order to resolve the
matter fairly and justly'.[3] Vague assertions that data protection obligations
justify the restriction of disclosure may contravene the right to an effective
remedy.[4] The Contempt of Court Act 1981, s 11 sets out that:

'In any case where a court (having power to do so) allows a name or other
matter to be withheld from the public in proceedings before the court, the
court may give such directions prohibiting the publication of that name

or matter in connection with the proceedings as appear to the court to be necessary for the purpose for which it was so withheld.'

It may be necessary to use these powers to avoid the judicial process being subverted by the creation of risks that were not otherwise extant.[5] The UT has powers of disclosure, and to limit its extent, having regard to the interests of justice and the risk of serious harm to individuals.[6]

1 See eg Laws LJ in the Court of Appeal in *Secretary of State for Foreign and Commonwealth Affairs v Quark Fishing Ltd* [2002] EWCA Civ 1409 at [50] citing *Padfield* [1968] AC 997, per Lord Upjohn at 1061G–1062A.
2 Sales J in *Das, R (on the application of) v Secretary of State for the Home Department* [2013] EWHC 682 (Admin) at [21] citing *Belize Alliance of Conservation Non-Governmental Organisations v Department of the Environment* [2004] UKPC 6; [2004] Env LR 761 at [86], per Lord Walker of Gestingthorpe; *R (Quark Fishing Ltd) v Secretary of State for Foreign and Commonwealth Affairs* [2002] EWCA Civ 1409 at [50], per Laws LJ; and *I v Secretary of State for the Home Department* [2010] EWCA Civ 727, [50]–[55].
3 *Tweed v Parades Commission for Northern Ireland* [2007] 1 AC 650.
4 ECtHR, First Section, in *A L v Austria*, 7788/11 [2012] ECHR 828 at [60]–[61].
5 See generally *A v British Broadcasting Corporation (Scotland)* [2014] UKSC 25; these issues are addressed in more detail at **5.132** *et seq* above.
6 See further **6.49** above.

Consent orders

8.114   Consent orders customarily include standard opening provisions stating that they are a *draft* document initially, leaving space for the judge's details to be added when he authorises the agreement of the parties, and should introduce the scenario by a single paragraph which:

- refers to what papers have been read by the endorsing judge,

- states whether he heard orally from the parties,

- states the premise of the order, eg 'upon the Defendant undertaking to reconsider the claim'.

8.115   The document should then list the actions that are necessary for the order to address, for example:

- any adjournment/vacation of a hearing;

- any stay/withdrawal of the proceedings;

- identifying the event which triggers the next action for the court to take, by deadline or application of a party;

- the timetable for exchange of further decisions, amended grounds and further detailed defence;

- treatment of costs (eg it may be agreed that one party is at fault for late action/inaction and that therefore costs should be borne by that party regardless of the outcome of the overall proceedings);

- if the judicial review is withdrawn, an order for final assessment of the claimant's costs, or an order that costs be assessed by a judge on the papers by written submissions if not agreed;

- where the claim continues, some general provision for the case to return back to the court on application of a party on notice, for example of 48 hours, to the other side;

- appropriate closing details identifying the lawyers with conduct of the case, their address, telephone, email and fax contact details, and their reference numbers for these proceedings.

8.116 Parties should take care to ensure that such orders accurately reflect their intentions (addressing issues such as whether or not any further claim by an applicant is to be made in person).[1] A consent order would only be construed as agreeing to exclude a statutory right of appeal if the clearest words to such effect were used.[2] Where a judge has given permission for judicial review in trenchant terms, the defendant would do well to consider whether it is truly appropriate and proportionate to continue to defend the case, rather than conceding it.[3]

1   *P, R (on the application of) v Secretary of State for the Home Department* (IJR) [2014] UKUT 294 (IAC).
2   Pill LJ in *Bahta, R (on the application of) v Secretary of State for the Home Department* [2011] EWCA Civ 895.
3   Coulson J in *Tshiteya, R (on the application of) v Secretary of State for the Home Department* [2010] EWHC 238 (Admin) at [51].

Conduct of the applicant/claimant and his advisors

8.117 Judicial review, being a discretionary remedy, is normally available only to those who approach the court with clean hands: the court may be expected to respond appropriately (albeit proportionately) with respect to claimants who do not do so.[1] This is not necessarily to say that a claimant must be of impeccable behaviour: a fugitive from justice such as an absconder may have 'gone to ground', but if not in breach of any order of the court may nevertheless seek to vindicate his fundamental rights.[2] There is a duty of candour on an applicant, which includes keeping the court appraised of all the facts, including developments as the case proceeds.[3] Unduly late challenges, particularly to removal, may entitle their receipt with some scepticism.[4] A failure to respect the duty of candour may lead to consequences including:[5]

(a)   a refusal to grant permission,

(b)   a conclusion that the process of the Upper Tribunal has been misused,

(c)   adverse costs implications, which may extend to the practitioners concerned,

(d)   the convening of a '*Hamid*' hearing.[6]

1   Sedley LJ in *Sonmez v Secretary of State for the Home Department* [2009] EWCA Civ 582 at [24].
2   *MR, Re Judicial Review* [2012] ScotCS CSOH_185.
3   McCloskey J in *R (on the application of Bilal Mahmood) v Secretary of State for the home Department (continuing duty to reassess)* (IJR) [2014] UKUT 439 (IAC) at [15]; Collins J in *R (I) v Secretary of State for the Home Department* [2007] EWHC 3103 (Admin) at [8].
4   Stanley Burnton LJ in *MD (Afghanistan) v Secretary of State for the Home Department* [2012] EWCA Civ 194 at [13].
5   McCloskey J in *Bilal Mahmood* (above) at [24].
6   *R (Hamid) v Secretary of State for the Home Department* [2012] EWCH Civ 3070 (Admin).

8.118   It is especially important that a claimant and his legal team keeps the court or tribunal abreast of developments in his case, including ones that may render the ongoing challenge no longer viable.[1] A failure to act with appropriate candour, where it breaches the overriding duty to the court and threatens the due administration of justice, may lead to both a wasted costs order and to referral of the delinquent representatives to the appropriate regulatory body.[2] As Green J put it in *Okundu*:

'It is improper for any practitioner to advance arguments which they know to be false or which they know, or should know, are inconsistent with their own evidence, including medical or other expert evidence. It is also incumbent upon practitioners to ensure that the Tribunal is provided with a fair and comprehensive account of all relevant facts, whether those facts are in favour or against the legal representative's client. It will not be treated as an acceptable explanation for an alleged failure to say that this was inconsistent with the representative's duty to the client; that would be an abnegation of the representative's duty to the court and to the due administration of justice. It will also not be acceptable to say that as of the date of the service of the application the representative was not in possession of all relevant facts because of time constraints. The Tribunal accepts that time pressures might mean that applications that are less than perfect or comprehensive or complete might in actual fact reflect the very best that can be done in urgent circumstances. However, this does not excuse a failure, following service of the application, to complete the fact finding and verification exercise, and then seek to amend the application accordingly so as to ensure that the Tribunal is fully informed of the relevant facts and matters.'

1   McCloskey J in *R (on the application of Bilal Mahmood) v Secretary of State for the home Department (continuing duty to reassess)* (IJR) [2014] UKUT 439 (IAC) at [26].
2   *Okondu (wasted costs; SRA referrals; Hamid)* (IJR) [2014] UKUT 377 (IAC) at [50]–[51].

Disposal of proceedings

8.119   Once an error of law is detected in judicial review proceedings, the challenged decision will be unsafe, and must be re-made (although where the decision was that of an inferior tribunal, the reviewing court or tribunal may re-make the decision itself if it sees fit).[1] It is only if there is no real chance of a different decision (ie where the decision would inevitably have been the same) that a matter would be dismissed outright rather than being remitted back to the decision maker.[2] In an extreme case, the court may hold that the unfairness was so obvious, and the remedy so plain, that there was only one way in which the original decision maker could reasonably exercise their discretion;[3] or there may be conspicuous unfairness, by way of serious errors of administration, such as to amount to an abuse of power, which requires that the court mark the ensuing illegality appropriately.[4] Whilst there is no general principle that a decision recognised as unlawful should be made by reference to the policies or circumstances prevailing at the original date of decision,[5] upon reconsideration, it may be necessary that the SSHD exercises his discretion such as to rectify any injustice arising from illegality in the original decision making: which may require that the application be reconsidered against the legal framework then extant, and not in relation to the modern provisions.[6] This is the case whether or not the case involves conspicuous unfairness.[7]

1   See **8.13**, fn 1 above.
2   See eg *R (Smith) v North East Derbyshire PCT* [2006] 1 WLR 3315 citing *R v Chief Constable of Thames Valley Police, ex parte Cotton* [1990] IRLR 344 at 352; *Simplex G E (Holdings) Ltd v Secretary of State for the Environment* (1989) 57 P & CR 306 at 327; *R v Secretary of State for Environment, ex parte Brent London Borough Council* [1982] 1 QB 593 at 646.
3   See eg *Rashid, R (on the application of) v Secretary of State for the Home Department* [2005] EWCA Civ 744, as explained by Carnwath LJ in *R (S) v Secretary of State for the Home Office Department* [2007] EWCA Civ 546 at [46]; Plender J in *Hailemariam, R (on the application of) v Secretary of State for the Home Department* [2009] EWHC 468 (Admin) at [8].
4   See the authorities cited and conclusion in *S, R (on the application of) v Secretary of State for the Home Department* [2009] EWCA Civ 142. Failings must be those of the Secretary of State: Maurice Kay LJ in *MM (Zimbabwe) v Secretary of State for the Home Department* [2012] EWCA Civ 135 at [12], Hughes LJ at [18].
5   Ouseley J in *Elmi, R (on the application of) v Secretary of State for the Home Department* [2010] EWHC 2775 (Admin) at [38].
6   Stephen Morris QC sitting as a Deputy High Court judge in *Mohammed, R (on the application of) v Secretary of State for the Home Department* [2012] EWHC 3091 (Admin) at [110]–[122] following a detailed citation of authorities: Pill and Dyson LJ of *Rashid*, Carnwath and Moore-Bick LJJ in *R (S) v Secretary of State for the Home Department* [2007] EWCA Civ 546; *Nadarajah v Secretary of State for the Home Department* [2005] EWCA Civ 1363; *MM (Zimbabwe)* (above); *AA (Afghanistan) v Secretary of State for the Home Department* [2007] EWCA Civ 12; *R (on the application of S, H and Q) v Secretary of State for the Home Department* [2009] EWCA Civ 334; and *SL (Vietnam) v Secretary of State for the Home Department* [2010] EWCA Civ 225.
7   Sir Stephen Silber in *Safi, R (on the application of) v Secretary of State for the Home Department* [2015] EWHC 95 (Admin) at [50]–[52].

Acknowledgments of Service and failure to provide

8.120   The Acknowledgment of Service is an important document:

'The objects of the obligation on a defendant to file an acknowledgment of service setting out where appropriate his case are: 1) to assist claimants with a speedy and relatively inexpensive determination by the court of the arguability of their claim; and 2) to prompt defendants – public authorities – to give early consideration to and, where appropriate, to fulfil their public duties'[1]

It also gives an early opportunity to identify knock-out points, procedural bars, or information relevant to expedition, all of which should be possible without incurring significant expense.[2] There is thus a heavy procedural obligation to file one, giving a clear history and brief reasons for the decision promptly to assist the court.[3] Notwithstanding the introduction of specific measures such as basing some Home Office staff at the Government Legal Department to ensure earlier instructions can be given where possible, and the identification of recurring issues which can be the subject of standard summary responses,[4] operational difficulties have led to the SSHD being unable to file Acknowledgments of Service, which has led to similar guidance being issued in the UT[5] and the Administrative Court.[6] Hickinbottom J ruled in *Singh* that the SSHD should aim to provide the Acknowledgment of Service within the 21-day timescale envisaged by the CPR and otherwise within a reasonable period of time, and that there were few cases sufficiently complex to take 42 days, and certainly very few which needed more than six weeks: only a 'very compelling reason' could justify an extension of time in the latter category.[7]

1   Auld LJ in *R (on the application of Mount Cook Land Ltd) v Westminster City Council* [2003] EWCA Civ 1346 at [71].
2   *R (on the application of Ewing) v Office of the Deputy Prime Minister* [2006] 1 WLR 1260 at [43].
3   Hickinbottom J in *Singh, R (on the application of) v Secretary of State for the Home Department* [2013] EWHC 2873 (Admin) at [5]–[6].
4   Set out in *Kumar, R (on the application of) v Secretary of State for the Home Department (acknowledgement of service; Tribunal arrangements)* (IJR) [2014] UKUT 104 (IAC) at [15].
5   *Kumar, R (on the application of) v Secretary of State for the Home Department (acknowledgement of service; Tribunal arrangements)* (IJR) [2014] UKUT 104 (IAC).
6   *Singh, R (on the application of) v Secretary of State for the Home Department* [2013] EWHC 2873 (Admin).
7   Hickinbottom J in *Singh* at [22]–[23].

8.121   First applications for an extension of time do not require detailed evidence or grounds in support,[1] but subsequent ones require a full (and fee-paid) explanation for the delay and a firm promise as to when the CPR will be complied with (avoiding 'barely aspirational' representations), and will be rigorously scrutinised by the court on the understanding that an application that does not show compelling reasons will be rejected.[2] Where a compromise between the parties might settle the action, the summary grounds could be short, explaining their belief in such an outcome and giving a realistic date for a consent order to be lodged.[3] A failure to provide a good reason for delay on a second or subsequent application would be met with cost sanctions, and possibly severe sanctions where the time and effort of the parties were wasted in consequence.[4] Where the defendant is concentrating his submissions principally on matters of law, the public interest in maintaining the court's rules might not defeat the defendant's application to be heard.[5]

1   Hickinbottom J in *Singh* at [24].
2   Hickinbottom J in *Singh* at [25], [29].
3   Hickinbottom J in *Singh* at [26].
4   Hickinbottom J in *Singh* at [27].
5   His Honour Judge Robert Owen sitting as a judge of the High Court in *Khan, R (on the application of) v Secretary of State for the Home Department* [2014] EWHC 2719; Andrew Thomas QC sitting as a Deputy High Court Judge in *RA (Nigeria), R (on the application of) v Secretary of State for the Home Department* [2014] EWHC 4073.

8.122   The UT has followed the lead of the Administrative Court in these cases,[1] indicating that, from January 2014, it would not be considered discourteous, where no application to the *Singh* standard could be made, if the SSHD simply let the time limit expire without explaining himself further.[2] Henceforth parties could expect that the UT would consider the judicial review application at any time from the expiry of six weeks from its lodging; by then the SSHD would be expected to have filed and served either a copy of a written response to the applicant's pre-action letter or written confirmation that none would be forthcoming, provision of which would not absolve him from providing an Acknowledgment of Service and summary grounds if wishing to participate in proceedings, unless there are particular reasons why a specific direction for an Acknowledgment of Service should be made (eg where it would appear that an important factual allegation by the applicant, eg as to his possession of extant leave at a relevant time, could be confirmed or denied speedily).[3] Absent provision of an Acknowledgment of Service, the SSHD would be vulnerable to costs in relation to an unsuccessful judicial review application, where it was refused on the papers and it is considered that it would have been recorded as totally without merit had the summary grounds been previously available; and whatever the ultimate fate of the judicial review, he would normally be vulnerable for the applicant's costs up to the filing of the detailed grounds.[4] Any application to file the Acknowledgment of Service after 42 days would have to show 'compelling reasons' and be made on at least 72 hours' notice to the applicant, so that the UT could be aware of his views on the issue.[5] These arrangements will be kept under review.[6] It would be wrong for the difficulties faced by the SSHD to interfere with the judicial process in achieving fair results for claimants.[7]

1   *Kumar, R (on the application of) v Secretary of State for the Home Department (acknowledgement of service; Tribunal arrangements) (IJR)* [2014] UKUT 104 (IAC) at [18], [30].
2   *Kumar* (above) at [31].
3   *Kumar* (above), headnote at [5]–[7], determination at [54].
4   *Kumar* (above), headnote at [8]–[9].
5   *Kumar* (above) at [44].
6   Ibid.
7   Green J in *Kadyamarunga v Secretary of State for the Home Department* [2014] EWHC 301 (Admin) at [20]–[22].

Damages

8.123   A claim for damages against a public authority, whether brought by way of an application for judicial review or by private law action, must identify an infringement of a private law right – so possible actions might be for false imprisonment, assault or battery, malicious prosecution or malicious process. As was said in *ID v Home Office*, 'there is on the face of it nothing in the slightest bit peculiar about an individual bringing a private law claim for damages against an executive official who has unlawfully infringed his private rights.'[1] There is an extensive jurisprudence on the liability for the SSHD to pay damages for false imprisonment arising from immigration detention.[2] Two different forms of liability for misfeasance in public office have been identified: the first is targeted malice by a public officer, conduct specifically intended to injure a person or persons. The second is where a public officer acts in circumstances where he knows that he has no power to do the act complained of and that it will probably injure the plaintiff (or where he is reckless as to the issue). Common to both forms, however, is the requirement of proving that the misfeasance in question has caused damage and that the public officer was at least reckless as to whether such damage would be caused or not.[3] English law does not presently recognise any cause of action against a public authority for harm done to individuals, even foreseeably, by unlawful acts of public administration (for example, victims of serious delays in granting indefinite leave to remain because the applications had been put on hold pursuant to a priority policy which was subsequently held to be unlawful):[4]

'Mere delay or the making in good faith of mistakes, or the taking in good faith but on an erroneous or incomplete factual basis of decisions adverse to the Claimant, cannot, of themselves, constitute misfeasance.'[5]

1   *ID v Home Office* [2005] EWCA Civ 38.
2   See eg Dunlop and Denholm, *Detention under the Immigration Acts: Law and Practice* (Oxford University Press) and Dubinsky with Arnott and Mackenzie, *Foreign National Prisoners: Law and Practice* (Legal Action Group).
3   Lord Steyn in *Three Rivers DC v Governor and Company of the Bank of England (No 3)* [2003] 2 AC 1.
4   *Home Office v Mohammed* [2011] EWCA Civ 351.
5   *AB v Home Office* [2012] EWHC 226 (QB) at [129].

8.124   HRA 1998, s 8 authorises the payment of compensation where this is necessary to afford just satisfaction, taking into account the principles applied by the ECtHR in relation to the award of compensation under ECHR, Art 41. There are three pre-conditions to an award of just satisfaction: (1) that the court should have found a violation; (2) that the domestic law of the Member State should allow only partial reparation to be made; and (3) that it should be necessary to afford just satisfaction to the injured party.[1] In *Greenfield*, Lord Bingham found, based on the principles applied by the European Court (inevitably these focus on ECHR, Art 6, the focus of consideration therein) that a substantive breach of the right was more likely to lead to damages, albeit noting that in Strasbourg it was routine for the mere finding of a violation to be held to be just satisfaction: however in the appropriate case, where there was a causal connection between the violation found and the loss for which an applicant claimed compensation, heads of loss could be claimed, for example loss of earnings, and 'prolonged uncertainty and anxiety' could be relevant to a 'second head of general or non-pecuniary damage'. In general regard should be had to the level of award in Strasbourg rather than to domestic principles.[2] Relevant considerations are whether there has been a serious and foreseeable impact on the right in question, and if the complaint is that there has been culpable delay in the administrative processes necessary to protect Art 8 rights, substantial prejudice is required; the applicant should, insofar as possible, be placed in the same position as if his Convention rights had not been infringed, relevant considerations being pecuniary loss, the complainant's own responsibility for what has occurred, and the character and conduct of the parties. Factors such as annoyance and a sense of frustration must reach a certain intensity before damages are appropriate: subject to giving a primary role to the Strasbourg approach to quantum, the levels of damages awarded in respect of torts as reflected in the guidelines issued by the Judicial Studies Board and by Criminal Injuries Compensation Board and Ombudsmen awards might provide some rough guidance where there was a relevant comparator. Claims based on maladministration should receive only modest damages.[3]

1   Lord Bingham in the House of Lords in *Greenfield, R (on the application of) v Secretary of State for the Home Department* [2005] UKHL 14 at [12]–[17].
2   Lord Bingham in *Greenfield* at [19].
3   The Lord Chief Justice giving the judgment of the Court of Appeal in *Anufrijeva v London Borough of Southwark* [2003] EWCA Civ 1406.

Returning a removee to the United Kingdom

8.125   Amongst the remedies that might be granted on a judicial review application is the restoration of the claimant to the United Kingdom: a wrongful expulsion decision, for example one breaching Convention rights as where a claim is wrongly identified as clearly unfounded,[1] is unlawful, and so there is an inherent power to order return in line with the general power to correct legal wrongs,[2] albeit that the discretion is a wide one.[3] Relevant considerations in making such orders include:

- whether the removee sought to assert an in-country right of appeal prior to removal where one was available, or an out-of-country one thereafter;[4]

- the failings of legal advisors;[5]

- removal via a decision that was lawful, in that it had not been successfully appealed or otherwise challenged[6] (conversely, an illegal decision, particularly where removal breached an undertaking, will count in favour of ordering return);[7]

- an ability to effectively pursue an out-of-country right of appeal[8] (though bearing in mind the general disadvantages of that limited remedy, which might themselves carry the day for an applicant);[9]

- risks to fundamental rights abroad;[10]

- concerns as to the impact of return and possible re-expulsion in the future on a person's mental health;[11]

- procedural failings of the SSHD which diminished access to the court and his conduct of the litigation in hand;[12]

- having received a conviction for a serious offence; and[13]

- removal following breaches of guidance, unlawful detention, and a lingering perception of unfairness in the asylum process where the pursuit of an asylum claim from abroad would present very substantial difficulties.[14]

1   Scott Baker J in *R (Ahmadi) v Secretary of State for the Home Department* [2002] EWHC 1897 (Admin) particularly at [57]–[58]; Laws LJ in *R (AK (Sri Lanka)) v Secretary of State for the Home Department* [2009] EWCA Civ 447 at [28]; Ouseley J in *R (Ahmed) v Secretary of State for the Home Department* [2009] EWHC 2676 (Admin) at [7].
2   Dyson LJ in *Hilali, R (on the application of) v Secretary of State for the Home Department* [2008] EWHC 2892 (Admin) at [38].
3   Richards LJ in *YZ (China), R (on the application of) v Secretary of State for the Home Department* [2012] EWCA Civ 1022 at [49].
4   Jackson LJ in *R (CM (Jamaica)) v Secretary of State for the Home Department* [2010] EWCA Civ 160 at [28]–[30]; Blake J in *R (Lewis) v Secretary of State for the Home Department* [2010] EWHC 1749 (Admin) at [38](ii).
5   Blake J in *R (Lewis) v Secretary of State for the Home Department* [2010] EWHC 1749 (Admin) at [38](iv).
6   Jackson LJ in *CM (Jamaica)* (above) at [31]; Blake J in *Lewis* (above) at [38](iii); Collins J in *R (Luthra) v Secretary of State for the Home Department* [2011] EWHC 3629 (Admin) at [33]–[35]; Richards LJ in *YZ (China)* (above) at [49].
7   Crane J in *Changuizi, R (on the application of) v Secretary of State for the Home Department* [2002] EWHC 2569 (Admin) at [72].
8   Jackson LJ in *CM (Jamaica)* (above) at [33]–[36]; Crane J in *Changuizi* (above) at [74]; Blake J in *Lewis* (above) at [38](v)–(vi); Ouseley J in *R (Ahmed) v Secretary of State for the Home Department* [2009] EWHC 2676 (Admin) at [11]–[12]; Richards LJ in *YZ (China)* (above) at [54].
9   Ouseley J in *Ahmed* (above) at [10].
10 Nicol J in *R (D) v Secretary of State for the Home Department* [2010] EWHC 2110 (Admin).
11 Crane J in *Changuizi* (above) at [73]–[74].
12 Cranston J in *M, R (on the application of) v Secretary of State for the Home Department* [2011] EWHC 3667 (Admin) at [26]–[27].
13 Richards LJ in *YZ (China)* (above) at [56].
14 Gilbart J in *H, R (on the application of) v Secretary of State for the Home Department* [2015] EWHC 377 (Admin).

8.126   Where a case is made out for the SSHD to use his best endeavours to return the claimant to the United Kingdom, it may be appropriate for him to give an equivalent undertaking so to do.[1] A mistaken decision which failed to identify 'reasonable grounds' for suspecting a person of having been trafficked may justify an order of return.[2]

1 Crane J in *Changuizi, R (on the application of) v Secretary of State for the Home Department* [2002] EWHC 2569 (Admin) at [71].
2 Aikens LJ in *Atamewan, R (on the application of) v Secretary of State for the Home Department* [2013] EWHC 2727 (Admin).

Costs

8.127 Whilst, generally speaking, the unsuccessful party will be ordered to pay the costs of the winning one,[1] the 'fundamental rule is that there are no rules ... and a practice, however widespread and longstanding, must never be allowed to harden into a rule'.[2] The costs assessor must 'have regard to all the circumstances'[3] including conduct before and during the proceedings, compliance with the Pre Action Protocol procedure, the reasonableness and manner of raising, pursuing or contesting particular points, and whether there was any exaggeration of a claim by a successful claimant.[4] Costs are reviewed on the standard or indemnity basis, generally the former unless expressly stated:[5] both analyses will investigate whether costs were reasonably or necessarily incurred, and are proportionate (taking account of the money value of the claim, the value of any non-monetary relief in issue in the proceedings, the complexity of the litigation, any additional work generated by the conduct of the paying party; and any wider factors involved in the proceedings, such as reputation or public importance);[6] but on the latter approach will resolve any doubts as to the reasonableness of the bill in favour of the receiving part:[7] neither approach permits the recovery of costs unreasonably incurred.[8] Relevant factors include:

'(a) the conduct of all the parties, including in particular –

    (i) conduct before, as well as during, the proceedings; and

    (ii) the efforts made, if any, before and during the proceedings in order to try to resolve the dispute;

(b) the amount or value of any money or property involved;

(c) the importance of the matter to all the parties;

(d) the particular complexity of the matter or the difficulty or novelty of the questions raised;

(e) the skill, effort, specialised knowledge and responsibility involved;

(f) the time spent on the case;

(g) the place where and the circumstances in which work or any part of it was done; and

(h) the receiving party's last approved or agreed budget.'[9]

1　CPR, r 44.3(2): 'The unsuccessful party will be ordered to pay the costs of the successful party.'
2　Lord Lloyd of Berwick in *Bolton MDC v Secretary of State for the Environment* [1995] 1 WLR 1176 at 1178.
3　CPR, r 43.3(2)(b).
4　CPR, r 44.3(5).
5　CPR, r 44.3(4).
6　CPR, r 44.3(2), (5).
7　CPR, r 44.3(5).
8　CPR, r 44.3(1).
9　CPR, r 44.4(3).

8.128　Where cases are resolved at a contested trial, the court will be in a strong position to resolve questions of costs in line with the substantive ruling. However, many applications settle by consent. In *Boxall*,[1] Scott Baker J had held that, in the absence of good reason to make any other order, the fall-back position following disposal of proceedings by consent should be to make no order as to costs, unless an alternative order was obviously required bearing in mind the proportionality of such an enquiry and the importance of not discouraging settlement by defendants. In his seminal recommendations Jackson LJ[2] adopted the Bar Council's proposal that, where a claimant has complied with the pre-action protocol, the normal order should be that the defendant pays the claimant's costs. In *Bahta*[3] the Court of Appeal found that a culture in which settlement brings no order as to costs where a public body is the defendant (at one time thought justified because of a perception that costs orders would only transfer funds between public bodies) was no longer acceptable. Whilst costs were not to be awarded because of any perception of a lack of adequate remuneration for publicly funded lawyers, nevertheless parties should recover the costs to which the result of the case entitled them, bearing in mind factors such as the need to maintain a pool of commercially viable legal aid lawyers. An assertion that a claim was being settled for 'pragmatic' reasons (rather than because the grounds for judicial review were accepted as made out by the defendant) would not impress the court unless there was a clear explanation of its underlying basis.[4]

1　*Boxall v Waltham Forest LBC* (2001) 4 CCL Rep 258 at [22].
2　Review of Civil Litigation Costs: Final Report, dated December 2009 ('the Jackson Report').
3　*Bahta v Secretary of State for the Home Department* [2011] EWCA Civ 895.
4　See generally *Bahta* (above) at [61]–[63].

8.129　In *M v Croydon*[1] the court gave a clear ruling as to the modern costs position in judicial review proceedings, stating that it was 'hard to see why a claimant, who, after complying with any relevant Protocol and issuing proceedings, is accorded by consent all the relief he seeks, should not recover his costs from the defendant, at least in the absence of some good reason to the contrary', whether the success followed a trial or an agreement reflected by consent order.[2] Lord Philips has emphasised that 'There is no general principle that protects a local authority that has acted reasonably in the course of its duties from liability for costs in public law proceedings.'[3] Where the claimant does not obtain all the relief he seeks, then the court may be willing to nevertheless adjudicate upon costs where it can decide the question, forming a 'tolerably clear view without much effort';[4] this should not discourage settlement so much as encourage government defendants to concentrate their minds at the pre action stage. Relevant considerations in departing from this presumption would be the lateness of a Pre Action Protocol letter or a failure to fully set out the case therein, a success occasioned by post-issue additions to the evidence, or pursuing the proceedings in an unreasonable manner, or a change in the law which removed the ground from beneath the defendant's feet.[5] There is a real difference between three scenarios: where the settlement represents wholesale or partial victory for an applicant (in the latter case the court will award costs only where the answer to questions such as how reasonable the claimant was in pursuing the unsuccessful claim, how important it was compared with the successful claim, and how much the costs were increased as a result of the claimant pursuing the unsuccessful claim, is 'tolerably clear'), and that where the compromise is due to some factor wholly external to the claim itself (in which case there is a powerful argument for a 'no costs' order unless it can be seen who would probably have won had the matter gone to trial, because this may 'strongly support the contention that the party who would have won did better out of the settlement, and therefore did win').[6] Parties should ensure that the volume of work involved in preparing submissions on costs, and the material the judge is asked to consider, are themselves proportionate to the amount at stake.[7] It would be quite wrong for the SSHD to expect an unrepresented claimant to pay costs when the latter was receiving by consent essentially what he had sought on the judicial review application,[8] and where the SSHD sought to argue for this course (which should be a rare course of action), the claimed justification should be set out in the Acknowledgement of Service.[9]

1   *M v London Borough of Croydon* [2012] EWCA Civ 595. See further Jackson LJ in *TH (Iran), R (on the application of) v East Sussex County Council* [2013] EWCA Civ 1027 at [17]. The principles therein should be treated as settled, see eg Maurice Kay LJ in *KR, R (on the application of) v Secretary of State for the Home Department* [2012] EWCA Civ 1555 at [1].
2   The Master of the Rolls in *M v London Borough of Croydon* (above) at [49].
3   Lord Philips for the Supreme Court in *T (Children), Re* [2012] UKSC 36 at [32].
4   The Master of the Rolls in *M v London Borough of Croydon* (above) at [49]–[51]; see Jackson LJ in *Naureen, R (on the application of) v Salford City Council* [2012] EWCA Civ 1795 for an example of a case where the victor, had the matter gone to trial, was unclear.
5   The Master of the Rolls in *M v London Borough of Croydon* (above) at [56]–[57]. Though see Maurice Kay LJ in *KR* (above) at [12] on cases where it is clear that the defendant would have dug their heels in regardless of the Pre Action Protocol process.
6   The Master of the Rolls in *M v London Borough of Croydon* (above) at [60], [62]–[63].
7   Stanley Burnton LJ in *M v London Borough of Croydon* (above) at [77].
8   *Muwonge, R (on the application of) v Secretary of State for the Home Department (consent orders: costs: guidance)* (IJR) [2014] UKUT 514 (IAC) at [17](i).
9   *Muwonge* (above) at [17](ii).

8.130 Where claims settle, the onus is on the parties to reach agreement on costs wherever possible through reasoned negotiation, mindful of the overriding CPR objective to deal with cases expeditiously, fairly and proportionately having regard to judicial resources and the sums at stake, and having recourse to the court only after so focussing their dispute.[1] A party claiming costs should file and serve submissions within 14 days of the consent order settling the claim, and a resisting party should reply within 14 days; any response submissions should be sent within seven days thereafter.[2] The submissions (of a normal print size, not to exceed two A4 pages without explanation) should:

- confirm that the parties have used reasonable endeavours to negotiate a costs settlement;

- identify what issues or reasons prevented the parties agreeing costs liability;

- state the approximate amount of costs likely to be involved in the case;

- clearly identify the extent to which the parties complied with the pre action protocol;

- state the relief the claimant –

  (i)   sought in the claim form and

  (ii) obtained;

- address specifically how the claim and the basis of its settlement fit the principles in *M v Croydon*, including the significance and effect of any action or offer by the defendant in relation to the claim.[3]

1   Administrative Court Guidance entitled 'How the parties should assist the court when applications for costs are made following settlement of claims for judicial review', promulgated in December 2013 and applicable to all consent orders submitted for approval by the court after 13 January 2014: approved in *Muwonge, R (on the application of) v Secretary of State for the Home Department (consent orders: costs: guidance)* (IJR) [2014] UKUT 514 (IAC) at [19].
2   Administrative Court Guidance (above) at [9]–[11].
3   Administrative Court Guidance (above) at [12].

8.131 Costs are to be assessed on the information available at the date of the costs assessment, not merely on that available at the time the judicial review proceedings were launched.[1] The ability of publicly funded lawyers to recover their funds is an important one which underlies access to justice, as Lord Hope put in *JFS*:[2]

'It is one thing for solicitors who do a substantial amount of publicly funded work, and who have to fund the substantial overheads that sustaining a legal practice involves, to take the risk of being paid at lower rates if a publicly funded case turns out to be unsuccessful. It is quite another for them to be unable to recover remuneration at *inter partes* rates in the event that their case is successful. If that were to become the practice, their businesses would very soon become financially unsustainable. The system of public funding would be gravely disadvantaged in its turn, as it depends upon there being a pool of reputable solicitors who are willing to undertake this work.'

1   Pill LJ in *Bahta v Secretary of State for the Home Department* [2011] EWCA Civ 895 at [58].
2   Lord Hope DPSC in *In re appeals by Governing Body of JFS* [2009] UKSC 1 at [25].

8.132   Decisions on costs are appealable to the Court of Appeal[1] and whilst that court is reluctant to entertain appeals raising issues of costs alone, it will do so where necessary, as where 'the first instance judge departs either from rationality or the correct principles'.[2]

1   See **8.81**, fn 2 above; *M v London Borough of Croydon* 2012] EWCA Civ 595 at [44].
2   Tomlinson LJ granting permission to appeal in *R (SN by his litigation friend Ron Breijer) v London Borough of Croydon* [2014] EWCA Civ 1672 at [7].

SUBSTANTIVE PRINCIPLES OF JUDICIAL REVIEW RELEVANT TO IMMIGRATION

8.133   As already indicated, it is no part of the authors' objective to replicate the existing literature on the ambit of judicial review. Nevertheless it is useful to briefly rehearse the main kinds of challenge brought and the main principles that animate judicial review in so far as relevant in the immigration context.

Grounds for judicial review

8.134   Eligible public law challenges that arise include those alleging:

(a)   Illegality – a failure to follow the law, be it a misunderstanding of legal powers (eg trying to issue removal directions under IAA 1999, s 10 in its 'saved' form against a person who is not an overstayer, leave breacher or maker of false representations); or failing to correctly implement a statutory duty (eg failing to properly consider BCIA 2009, s 55 regarding the duty to safeguard and promote the welfare of minors); or misapplying a test in the Immigration Rules such as the definition of fresh claims for asylum (eg asking whether a claim is 'convincing' rather than whether there is a real chance of its success); or of human rights law (eg failing to take account of third party human rights).

(b)   Failing to take account of a relevant statutory duty – in such a case:

'it was sufficient if the substance of the duty was discharged and that the decision maker did not have to refer explicitly to the statute or the guidance.'[1]

(c)   Public law error in the standard of decision making, of which the crispest summary comes from Brooke LJ in *R (Iran)*:[2]

'(i)   Making perverse or irrational findings on a matter or matters that were material to the outcome ("material matters");

(ii)   Failing to give reasons or any adequate reasons for findings on material matters;

(iii)   Failing to take into account and/or resolve conflicts of fact or opinion on material matters;

(iv)   Giving weight to immaterial matters;

(v)   Making a material misdirection of law on any material matter;

(vi)   Committing or permitting a procedural or other irregularity capable of making a material difference to the outcome or the fairness of the proceedings;

(vii)   Making a mistake as to a material fact which could be established by objective and uncontentious evidence, where the appellant and/or his advisers were not responsible for the mistake, and where unfairness resulted from the fact that a mistake was made.'

(d)   As to irrationality, the first of the public law errors identified in *R (Iran)*, this essentially requires an applicant to demonstrate that the decision maker, whilst not failing to take account of relevant considerations or overlooking evidence, nevertheless acted irrationally in his judgment based on the material before him; it overlaps with perversity, which itself involves 'a very high hurdle' and is found in decisions which are 'irrational or unreasonable in the *Wednesbury* sense (even if there was no wilful or conscious departure from the rational)';[3] it may also be said that 'A decision will be irrational where it is based upon 'an error of reasoning which robs the decision of logic".[4]

(e)   Adopting a strict policy that prevents relevant circumstances from being taken into account[5] – failing to apply policy flexibly where fairness and good sense require a departure from it in order to do justice in the particular circumstances of the case.[6]

(f)   Failing to follow policies – because policies should be followed by those who articulate them (and bearing in mind that 'policy statements should be interpreted objectively in accordance with the language used, read as always in its proper context'):[7]

●   'A public body's promise or practice as to future conduct may only be denied … in circumstances where to do so is the public body's legal duty, or is otherwise … a proportionate response (of which the court is the judge, or the last judge) having regard to a legitimate aim pursued by the public body in the public interest. The principle that good administration requires public authorities to be held to their promises would be undermined if the law did not insist that any failure or refusal to comply is objectively justified as a proportionate measure in the circumstances';[8] thus there will be cases which 'require the Court to establish a balance between the importance of preserving the defendant's right to exercise her discretionary powers in the field of immigration control and the desirability of requiring her to adhere to the statements or practice announced'.[9]

- 'The promulgation of the policy normally creates a legitimate expectation that it will be applied to those falling within its scope unless there is good reason for making an exception. So much is trite law. It is also trite law that the existence of the policy does not excuse the decision-maker from due consideration of cases falling outside it.'[10]

- Re the Immigration Directorate Instructions issued by the SSHD: 'In public law terms, policies, or guides, of this kind have the status of a material consideration in cases where they are engaged. Accordingly, a decision maker's failure to have regard to this kind of instrument may operate to vitiate the decision under challenge. Similarly, where a decision maker purports to have regard to the guidance but misconstrues or misapplies it. This kind of instrument can also, in principle, engender a substantive legitimate expectation to which the law will give effect. Our final observation concerning IDIs is that provided their terms are consistent with the provisions of the Immigration Rules to which they relate, they may, potentially, fulfil a further role, namely that of illuminating the rationale and policy underpinning the relevant Rules.'[11]

(g) Failing to lawfully exercise discretionary powers of waiver and/or further enquiry conferred under the Immigration Rules, as where documents are in the wrong format or otherwise incomplete, under the evidential flexibility proviso[12] – though 'Modern Parliamentary legislation tends to be detailed and complex and normally expressly prescribes the processes, procedures and evidence to be followed and taken into account when statutory decisions are made. That being the case, there may be less scope for courts to read into modern statutes implied procedural obligations than in relation to statutes of greater antiquity.'[13]

(h) Breaches of substantive legitimate expectations, for example where the SSHD resiles from a promise made to an individual in the course of dealing with his case – any such promise must be 'clear, unambiguous and devoid of relevant qualification'[14] and will usually need to be read in the broader context of the relevant provisions of immigration law to avoid offending fundamental principles such as equality before the law and legal certainty, and should not be given effect where the official's statement was inconsistent with his statutory or public duties.[15]

(i)   Failure to consult where there is a legitimate expectation of such consultation, usually arising from an interest which is held to be sufficient to found such an expectation, or from some promise or practice of consultation.[16]

(j)   Substantive unfairness caused, for example, by bureaucratic obstacles and the unyielding application of the Rules in hard cases (as can arise under the points-based system, where procedural restrictions on the admission of evidence might be judged unfair such that a failure under the Rules might lead to a different outcome when matters are re-assessed against the yardstick of proportionality in relation to interferences with family and private life).[17] A statutory or policy-based scheme may have to be supplemented by the common law principle of fairness, eg where there is 'a thoroughly unreasonable and disproportionate, inflexible, application of a policy, without the slightest regard for the facts of the case, or indeed elementary common sense and humanity. Such an approach diminishes, rather than encourages, respect for the policy in question';[18] though it should be recalled that in general 'fairness ... is essentially procedural' and recalling the principle expressed, albeit there in an appellate context, that 'the jurisdiction of this Tribunal to determine that a decision is not in accordance with the law because of a lack of fairness, is not to be degraded to a general judicial power to depart from the Rules where the judge thinks such a course appropriate or to turn a mandatory factor into a discretionary one.'[19]

(k)   Procedural unfairness – 'there is a public law duty on the Secretary of State to act fairly'.[20] There is a presumption that administrative powers conferred by statute will be exercised in a manner which is fair in all the circumstances;[21] where there is unfairness 'It is sufficient if an Applicant can establish that there is a real, as opposed to a purely minimal, possibility that the outcome would have been different';[22] as Lord Bingham once wrote: 'While cases may no doubt arise in which it can properly be said that denying the subject of a decision an adequate opportunity to put his case is not in all the circumstances unfair, I would expect these cases of be of great rarity.'[23]

For example:

●   illegal entrants must, as a matter of fairness, be given an opportunity to be heard before such an adverse decision is taken against them;[24]

●   'The decision-maker's duty to have regard to relevant considerations may require him to 'hear the other side' and thereby take into account the affected person's views about the subject-matter';[25]

●   'Fairness requires the Secretary of State to give an applicant an opportunity to address grounds for refusal, of which he did not know and could not have known, failing which the resulting decision may be set aside on appeal as contrary to law'[26] (and, in a nationality case, which in an exceptional case might require an interview 'unless the applicant knows the areas of concern which could result in the application being refused in many cases, and especially this case, it will be impossible for him to make out his case. The result could be grossly unfair'[27]) – albeit that account must be taken of 'the highly modulated and fact-sensitive way in which the general public law duty of fairness operates', bearing in mind the fair balance to be struck between the public interest in having a particular regime operating in a simple way and the interests of a particular individual who may be detrimentally affected by it,[28] albeit that there is a duty to take account of events of which the SSHD is aware and/or for which he is responsible[29] such as withdrawal of a sponsor licence;[30]

- an appropriate adult should be present during the age assessment process in order for the procedure to comply with the *Merton* standards of good practice;[31]

- interviews may be essential in some cases for the migrant to understand the case against him, and may be required where European Union law rights are in play as where spouses are alleged to be parties to a marriage of convenience.[32]

(l)   Failure to make adequate enquiries before a decision is made – ie 'did the Secretary of State ask himself the right question and take reasonable steps to acquaint himself with the relevant information to enable him to answer it correctly?'[33] The duty is higher where the duty to safeguard and promote child welfare is in play.[34]

(m)   Making decisions which are inconsistent, contrary to 'the well-established principle of administrative law, that 'persons should be uniformly treated unless there is some valid reason to treat them differently''[35] – being a principle that 'is one of the building blocks of democracy and necessarily permeates any democratic constitution ... treating like cases alike and unlike cases differently is a general axiom of rational behaviour.'[36]

(n)   Making a subsequent decision which is contrary to independent judicial findings on those same issues.[37]

(o)   Operating a policy which, applied according to its terms, exposes individuals to a significant or serious risk of a breach of Art 3,[38] causing a deterioration in a person's health, and thereafter failing to procure, to the extent possible, an improvement in a person's medical condition where state conduct has demonstrably caused damage.[39]

(p)   Failing to obtain the appropriate legislative endorsement of a policy or requirement which has the character of an immigration rule by laying it before Parliament[40] – 'The key requirement is that the Immigration Rules should include all those provisions which set out criteria which are or may be determinative of an application for leave to enter or remain'.[41]

(q)   Unlawful detention[42] – most commonly arising because:

- The power to detain has lapsed because removal is no longer reasonably imminent: 'First, the power can only be exercised during the period necessary, in all the circumstances of the particular case, to effect removal. Secondly, if it becomes clear that removal is not going to be possible within a reasonable time, further detention is not authorised. Thirdly, the person seeking to exercise the power of detention must take all reasonable steps within his power to ensure the removal within a reasonable time.'[43] It is for the court itself to determine the answer to whether removal can occur within a reasonable period,[44] and the assessment is to be made as of the date of the decision in question and not with the benefit of hindsight.[45]

- A relevant policy has not been lawfully applied in circumstances that bear materially on the decision to detain.[46]

(r)   Unlawful delays in decision making – decisions must be made within a reasonable time[47] albeit absent some specific obligation or detriment, it may be that the delay must be established as 'manifestly unreasonable';[48] the failure to answer correspondence, to identify any realistic timetable for decision making,[49] or to alleviate detriments caused by the delay, may signal administrative unlawfulness.[50] There are stronger duties on the SSHD in some fields of immigration, for example:

- European Union law (the Immigration (European Economic Area) Regulations 2006 require timely decisions in certain cases; the Common European Asylum System encourages swift decision making);[51]

- where children are the subject of the decision in question ('There should also be recognition that children cannot put on hold their growth or personal development until a potentially lengthy application process is resolved. Every effort must therefore be made to achieve timely decisions for them');[52]

- when there is a vested right in play, for example where an appeal has been allowed and so there is no scope for the further exercise of discretion in the decision making process.[53]

1   Floyd LJ in *Alladin v Secretary of State for the Home Department* [2014] EWCA Civ 1334 at [50]–[51]; *R (Asefa) v Secretary of State for the Home Department* [2012] EWHC 56 (Admin) at [46].
2   Brooke LJ in *R (Iran) v Secretary of State for the Home Department* [2005] EWCA Civ 982 at [9].
3   Brooke LJ in *Iran* (above) at [11] citing *Miftari v Secretary of State for the Home Department* [2005] EWCA Civ 481 citing *Associated Provincial Picture Houses Ltd v Wednesbury Corporation* (1948) 1 KB 223.
4   Sedley J in *R v Parliamentary Commissioner for Administration, ex parte Balchin* [1998] 1PLR 1. See further *Pham* at **8.140**, fn 6 below.

5 Lord Browne Wilkinson in *R v Home Secretary, ex parte Venables* [1998] 1 AC 407, at 496H.
6 Sedley LJ in *Pankina v Secretary of State for the Home Department* [2011] QB 376 at [28];
   and Lang J in *Poloko Huri v Secretary of State for the Home Department* [2014] EWHC 254
   (Admin) at [50].
7 Lord Reed JSC for the Supreme Court in *Tesco Stores Ltd v Dundee City Council* [2012]
   UKSC 13 at [18]–[19]; Dingemans J in *T, R (on the application of) v Secretary of State for
   the Home Department* [2014] EWHC 2453 (Admin) at [22].
8 Laws LJ in *Abdi and Nadarajah v Secretary of State for the Home Department* [2005] EWCA
   Civ 1363 at [68].
9 Sir George Newman in *HSMP Forum Ltd v Secretary of State for the Home Department*
   [2008] EWHC 664 (Admin) at [49].
10 Carnwath LJ in *R (Rudi) v Secretary of State for the Home Department* [2007] EWCA Civ
    1326 at [28].
11 McCloskey J in *Sultana (rules: waiver/further enquiry, discretion)* [2014] UKUT 540 (IAC)
    at [30].
12 McCloskey J in *Sultana* (above) at [23]–[26] referencing Immigration Rules, r 245AA and
    Immigration Directorate Instruction (July 2014) 'Family members under Appendix FM and
    Appendix Armed Forces of the Immigration Rules', Ch 3 'Evidential flexibility'.
13 *Plantagenet Alliance Ltd, R (on the application of) v Secretary of State for Justice* [2014]
    EWHC 1662 (QB) at [89].
14 Bingham LJ in *R v Inland Revenue Commissioners, ex parte MFK Underwriting Agents Ltd*
    [1990] 1 WLR 1545; *Badger Trust, R (on the application of) v Secretary of State for the
    Environment, Food and Rural Affairs* [2014] EWCA Civ 1405 at [24]–[26]; McCloskey J in
    Mehmood (legitimate expectation) [2014] UKUT 469 (IAC).
15 McCloskey J in *Mehmood* (above) at [19]–[20] citing *R v North and East Devon Health
    Authority, ex parte Coughlan* [2001] QB 213 at [86] and *R v Secretary of State for Education,
    ex parte Begbie* [2000] 1 WLR 1115.
16 Lord Reed in *Moseley, R (on the application of) v London Borough of Haringey* [2014] UKSC
    56 at [35]; see *Plantagenet Alliance Ltd* (above) at [97]–[98].
17 See *Alam (s 85A; commencement; Art 8) Bangladesh* [2011] UKUT 424 (IAC) at [15]–[17];
    Ferrer (limited appeal grounds; Alvi) Philippines [2012] UKUT 304 (IAC) at [57], [64]–[68];
    Philipson (ILR – not PBS: evidence) [2012] UKUT 00039 (IAC) at [19]–[23].
18 Sullivan J in *R (Forrester) v Secretary of State for the Home Department* [2008] EWHC
    2307 at [16]; see fairness generally, as addressed in *Plantagenet Alliance Ltd* (above) at
    [84]–[93].
19 *Fiaz (cancellation of leave to remain – fairness* [2012] UKUT 57 (IAC) at [34].
20 *Jan, R (on the application of) v Secretary of State for the Home Department (s 10 removal)*
    IJR [2014] UKUT 265 (IAC) at [38] citing *Kabaghe (appeal from outside UK – fairness)
    Malawi* [2011] UKUT 473 (IAC).
21 Lord Mustill in *R v Secretary of State for the Home Department, ex parte Doody* [1994] 1 AC
    531 at 560D–G.
22 *MM (unfairness; E & R) Sudan* [2014] UKUT 105 (IAC) distilling the principles in *R v Chief
    Constable of Thames Valley Police, ex parte Cotton* [1990] IRLR 344 and citing, in particular,
    Simon Brown J in the judgment appealed in *Cotton*.
23 *MM* (above) citing Bingham LJ in *Cotton* (above).
24 *R (Uluyol) v An Immigration Officer* (CO/1960/00), per Gage J.
25 *R (Khatun) v Newham London Borough Council* [2005] QB 37 at [27], per Laws LJ.
26 *Naved (student – fairness – notice of points)* [2012] UKUT 14(IAC) at [15]–[19].
27 Lord Woolf MR in the Court of Appeal in *R v Secretary of State for the Home Department,
    ex parte Fayed* [1998] 1 WLR 763, at 773F–774A; Sales J in *Thamby, R (on the application
    of) v Secretary of State for the Home Department* [2011] EWHC 1763 (Admin) at [67]–
    [68].
28 Briggs LJ in *EK (Ivory Coast) v Secretary of State for the Home Department* [2014] EWCA
    Civ 1517 at [39]–[40].
29 *Patel (revocation of sponsor licence – fairness) India* [2011] UKUT 00211 (IAC); *Thakur
    (PBS decision – common law fairness) Bangladesh* [2011] UKUT 00151 (IAC).

30   *Thakur (PBS decision – common law fairness) Bangladesh* [2011] UKUT 151 (IAC) at [12]–[19]; *Patel (revocation of sponsor licence – fairness) India* [2011] UKUT 211 (IAC) at [19]–[34]; and *Naved (student: fairness: notice of points)* [2012] UKUT 14 (IAC) at [14]–[16].
31   Lang J in *AAM v Secretary of State for the Home Department* [2012] EWHC 2567 (QB); *B, R (on the application of) v London Borough of Merton* [2003] EWHC 1689 (Admin).
32   *Miah (interviewer's comments: disclosure: fairness)* [2014] UKUT 515 (IAC) at [13].
33   Lord Diplock in *Secretary of State for Education and Science v Tameside MBC* [1977] AC 1014 at 1065B; *Plantagenet Alliance Ltd* (above) at [99]–[100].
34   *JO (s 55 duty) Nigeria* [2014] UKUT 00517 (IAC) at [10]–[11].
35   Carnwath LJ for the majority in *AA (Somalia) v Secretary of State for the Home Department* [2007] EWCA Civ 1040 at [66].
36   *Matadeen v Pointu* [1998] 1 AC 98 PC (per Lord Hoffmann), referencing Prof Jeffrey Jowell QC, *Is Equality a Constitutional Principle?* [1994] Current Legal Problems 1, 12–14 and De Smith, Woolf and Jowell, *Judicial Review of Administrative Action*, paras 13-036–13-045.
37   See **5.117** above.
38   *R (Munjaz) v Mersey Care NHS Trust* [2005] UKHL 58, [2006] 2 AC 148, Lord Bingham at [29], Lord Hope at [80]–[81].
39   Mitting J in *Thompson, R (on the application of) v Secretary of State for the Home Department* [2008] EWHC 107 (Admin) at [6] and [10]; in the detention context, see eg Singh J in *HA (Nigeria), R (on the application of) v Secretary of State for the Home Department* [2012] EWHC 979 (Admin) at [173]–[181].
40   *R (Alvi) v Secretary of State for the Home Department* [2012] 1 WLR 2208: Lord Hope at [41], [54], Lord Dyson at [94], [97], Lord Clarke at [120], Lord Dyson at [45] and [46] of *R (Munir) v Secretary of State for the Home Department* [2012] 1 WLR 2192.
41   Lord Dyson in *Alvi* (above) at [97].
42   Haddon-Cave J gave a good summary of the general principles in *R (on the application of Ahmed Yakoub Mesbah Belkasim) v Secretary of State for the Home Department* [2012] EWHC 3109 (Admin) at [102]–[106].
43   Woolf J in *R v Governor of Durham Prison, ex parte Hardial Singh* [1984] 1 WLR 704; Lord Justice Dyson (as he then was) in *R (I) v Secretary of State for the Home Department* [2002] EWCA Civ 888 at [46].
44   See eg *R (A) v Secretary of State for the Home Department* [2007] EWCA Civ 804, per Toulson LJ at [62] and per Keene LJ at [74]; and *Kambadzi v Secretary of State for the Home Department* [2011] UKSC 23.
45   *Hussein v Secretary of State for the Home Department* [2009] EWHC 2506.
46   Lord Hope in *Kambadzi* (above) at [36], [41]; Baroness Hale at [69].
47   Carnwath LJ in *R (S) v Secretary of State for the Home Department* [2007] EWCA Civ 546 at [51].
48   Collins J in *R (FH) v Secretary of State for the Home Department* [2007] EWHC 1571 at [30].
49   Simon J in the Administrative Court in *Obienna, R (on the application of) v Secretary of State for the Home Department* [2008] EWHC 1476 (Admin).
50   Blake J in *Tekle v Secretary of State for the Home Department* [2008] EWHC 3064 (Admin) at [41]–[47] citing Underhill J in *R (Ghaleb) v Secretary of State for the Home Department* [2008] EWHC 2685 (Admin).
51   eg Immigration (European Economic Area) Regulations 2006, SI 2006/1003 at reg 17(1)–(3) regarding the issue of residence documents; Council Directive 2005/85/EC of 1 December 2005 on minimum standards on procedures in Member States for granting and withdrawing refugee status, at recital 11, Art 10(d); see also the EU Charter of Fundamental Rights, 2000/C 364/01, Art 41.
52   BCIA 2009, s 55; in the context of minor asylum seekers, Council Directive 2003/9/EC at Art 18(1); *ZH (Tanzania) v Secretary of State for the Home Department* [2011] UKSC 4; *Every Child Matters – Change for Children* (Statutory guidance to the UK Border Agency on making arrangements to safeguard and promote the welfare of children issued under BCIA 2009, s 55; November 2009), paras 2.7, 2.20.

53   Lord Denning in *R v Secretary of State for the Home Department, ex parte Phansopkar* [1976] 1 QB 606; Collins J in *R (FH) v Secretary of State for the Home Department* [2007] EWHC 1571 at [24]; *R v Secretary of State for the Home Department, ex parte Mersin* [2000] INLR 511.

8.135   Before a challenge to any particular procedure can be sustained, it is essential that a reasoned case has been put to the SSHD as to why an individual should be the subject of special consideration.[1] It might well be an impermissible fetter of discretion to decline to consider representations based on sufficiently compelling or exceptional factors not anticipated by the relevant policy framework.[2] As a matter of general principle, the mere failure to expressly explain why one of a selection of options was chosen as the basis for proceeding will not be unlawful, absent some express case for contrary treatment having been put.[3] There is a discretion in the SSHD to consider whether an individual has been failed by his legal representatives[4] (indeed Lord Bridge in *Al-Mehdawi* recognised that discretion might provide a solution referring to the old power that the SSHD then possessed under IA 1971, s 21 to rectify any injustice by referring the matter back to the appellate authority): 'there is no general principle of law which fixes a party with the procedural errors of his or her representative' albeit that, outside of the asylum context where anxious scrutiny holds sway, the acts of a representative may be imputed to his client depending on the circumstances.[5]

1   *P, R (on the application of) v Secretary of State for the Home Department* (IJR) [2014] UKUT 294 (IAC) at [12].
2   Blake J in *Aa, Wa and Ck, R (on the application of) v Secretary of State for Foreign and Commonwealth Affairs* [2008] EWHC 2227 (Admin); Carnwath LJ in *R (Rudi) v Secretary of State for the Home Department* [2007] EWCA Civ 1326 at [28].
3   *Jan, R (on the application of) v Secretary of State for the Home Department (s 10 removal)* (IJR) [2014] UKUT 265 (IAC) at [24].
4   *R v Secretary of State for the Home Department, ex parte Syed Mohammed Kazmi* [1995] Imm AR 73, cited in *LD (Algeria) v Secretary of State for Home Department* [2004] EWCA Civ 804 at [34]; see further Bingham LJ in *Khan v Secretary of State for the Home Department* [1987] Imm AR 543 and Elias J in *R v Immigration Appeal Tribunal, ex parte Ganidagli* [2001] EWHC Admin 70.
5   *R (on the application of FP (Iran)) v Secretary of State for the Home Department* [2007] EWCA Civ 13 at [42]–[46]; *R v Secretary of State for the Home Department, ex parte Al-Mehdawi* [1990] 1 AC 87; Collins J in *AFP Nori, R (on the application of) v Secretary of State for the Home Department* [2011] EWHC 1604 (Admin) at [48]; *MM (unfairness; E and R) Sudan* [2014] UKUT 105 (IAC) at [25].

8.136   A policy which cannot be operated lawfully, or which gives rise to an unacceptable risk of unlawful decision making, cannot itself be lawful: the risks arising from an inherently unfair system cannot be addressed only by the prospect of judicial review in individual cases.[1] In these cases:

'we adopt Professor Craig's summary of the three factors which the court will weigh: the individual interest at issue, the benefits to be derived from added procedural safeguards, and the costs to the administration of compliance.'

1   Wyn Williams J in *Suppiah, R (on the application of) v Secretary of State for the Home Department* [2011] EWHC 2 (Admin) at [137]; *R (Refugee Legal Centre) v Secretary of State for the Home Department* [2004] EWCA Civ 1481 at [6]–[7], passage cited is at [8].

8.137   Where the claim challenges the operation of a system, the court has a wide discretion as to remedy and may think it right to make no order other than a declaration of unlawfulness: the Court of Appeal would be unlikely to interfere with the ruling on remedy of a judge who had heard a large amount of evidence in this kind of case.[1] Statutory instruments might be struck down in certain circumstances, as where:[2]

> 'they were found to be partial and unequal in their operation as between different classes; if they were manifestly unjust; if they disclosed bad faith; if they involved such oppressive or gratuitous interference with the rights of those subject to them as could find no justification in the minds of reasonable men, the Court might well say, Parliament never intended to give authority to make such rules; they are unreasonable and ultra vires.'

An Immigration Rule can be challenged at common law for being 'unreasonable' in this sense, too.[3]

1   Longmore LJ in *Detention Action, R (on the application of) v Secretary of State for the Home Department* [2014] EWCA Civ 1270 at [9].
2   Lord Russell of Killowen CJ in *Kruse v Johnson* [1898] 2 QB 91 at 99–100.
3   Aikens LJ in *MM, R (on the application of) v Secretary of State for the Home Department* [2014] EWCA Civ 985 at [96].

General considerations regarding judicial review

8.138   It is axiomatic that an applicant should be given a fair and proper opportunity, at a stage when a possible adverse decision is no more than provisional (at least where there is no remedy by way of appeal available), to deal with important points adverse to his case which may weigh against them.[1] There may be circumstances in which judicial review proceedings may properly be commenced to ensure that domestic remedies are exhausted before venturing to Strasbourg, or to see if, without accepting the merits of the points raised, the Secretary of State might grant some form of leave to remain to avoid such proceedings; but any such process should make its true purpose clear at the earliest appropriate opportunity.[2] Judicial review is an effective remedy for the purposes of European Union law for challenging the rejection of the asylum claims of minors granted less than one year of discretionary leave to remain.[3] Judges will seek consistency so far as possible in a field of such importance as asylum where cases raise common issues such as the safety of a particular third country.[4] A deficient decision should not be saved by the amplification of reasoning that does not bear the weight afforded it,[5] bearing in mind that 'Self deception runs deep in the human psyche; the truth can become refracted, even in the case of honest witnesses, through the prism of self justification';[6] and 'It matters that the Secretary of State approaches decisions lawfully, asking herself the legally relevant questions, having regard to legally relevant considerations and giving legally adequate reasons.'[7] Once a relevant public law error is established, judicial review should be granted, so long as there is a 'real prospect that the Secretary of State might, if directed to retake the decisions according to the guidance, come to a different decision. Put another way, have the [claimants] demonstrated that the error of law on which they rely ... is a material one?'[8]

1   The President of the QBD in *FZ, R (on the application of) v London Borough of Croydon* [2011] EWCA Civ 59 at [21].
2   Ouseley J in *Leitao, R (on the application of) v Secretary of State for the Home Department* [2008] EWHC 1553 (Admin).
3   Maurice Kay LJ in *TN (Afghanistan) v Secretary of State for the Home Department* [2013] EWCA Civ 1609 at [80].
4   Holman J in the Administrative Court in *Malik, R (on the application of) v Secretary of State for the Home Department* [2008] EWHC 888 (Admin) at [14].
5   Sedley LJ in *Anya v University of Oxford* [2001] EWCA Civ 405; Davis LJ in *Andukwa, R (on the application of) v Secretary of State for Justice* [2014] EWHC 3988 (QB) at [80] citing *Hereford Waste Watchers Ltd v Herefordshire Council* [2005] EWHC 191 (Admin); Lord Tyre in the Court of Session, Outer House, in *AS, Re Judicial Review* [2013] ScotCS CSOH_82 at [11].
6   Elias J in *Hereford Waste Watchers Ltd* (above) at [48].
7   Michael Fordham QC sitting as a Deputy High Court judge in *R (on the application of) Ganesabalan v Secretary of State for the Home Department* [2014] EWHC 2712 (Admin) at [44].
8   Floyd LJ in *R (Alladin) v Secretary of State for the Home Department* [2014] EWCA Civ 1334 at [58]; see *Dong, R (on the application of) v Secretary of State for the Home Department* [2014] EWHC 3100 (Admin) at [24]; Keene LJ in *IA (Somalia) v Secretary of State for the Home Department* [2007] EWCA Civ 323 at [15]. See also, on materiality, the approach on statutory appeals, **6.9** and **6.10** above.

8.139   Under the Criminal Justice and Courts Act 2015, s 84 (in force for the High Court from 13 April 2015, but not at the time of writing in force for the UT),[1] the Senior Courts Act 1981, s 31 is amended such that permission for, or relief following, a judicial review application may be refused if it appears to the relevant court or tribunal 'to be highly likely that the outcome for the applicant would not have been substantially different if the conduct complained of had not occurred', unless it is nevertheless appropriate to grant relief for reasons of exceptional public interest in which case the court or tribunal should certify that this condition is satisfied.

1   The Criminal Justice and Courts Act 2015 (Commencement No 1, Saving and Transitional Provisions) Order 2015, SI 2015/778.

Intensity of review – Convention and fundamental rights

8.140   Where a claim turns on whether a decision interferes with a Convention right and if so, whether the interference is proportionate, the court's approach differs from the traditional grounds of judicial review in that it must conduct a high-intensity review of the decision, making its own assessment of the relevant factors and their appropriate weight,[1] albeit that the reviewing judge should not simply substitute his own views for those of other public authorities on all matters of policy, judgment and discretion.[2] The process may require the giving of live evidence and cross examination.[3] Where the primary decision maker has not properly considered all relevant circumstances, his views are bound to carry less weight, making it more likely that the court has to strike the balance for itself, albeit giving due weight to the judgments made by the primary decision maker on such matters as he did consider.[4] A public authority will not have infringed Convention rights simply because the procedure adopted or reasoning given is flawed: 'Ultimately, it is for the court to decide whether or not the Convention rights have been breached.'[5] It is now recognised that the context of the case will determine the intensity of review (which will often incorporate principles of proportionality), whether the legal basis of challenge is the law of the European Union or under ECHR, or arises under the common law. Thus the more fundamental the interest in question to the individual, the more strict the standard by which it will be examined:[6]

> 'the cogency of the justification required for interfering with a right will be proportionate to its perceived importance and the extent of the interference ... the common law no longer insists on a single, uniform standard of rationality review based on the virtually unattainable test stated in *Wednesbury*.'[7]

1 Beatson LJ in *A, R (on the application of) v Kent Constabulary* [2013] EWCA Civ 1706 at [36]; *R (Daly) v Secretary of State for the Home Department* [2001] 2 AC 532 at [27].
2 Lord Reed at [131] of *Axa General Insurance Ltd v HM Advocate* [2011] UKSC 46.
3 Beatson LJ in *A* (above) at [79].
4 *Belfast City Council v Miss Behavin' Ltd* [2007] UKHL 19.
5 Lady Hale in *R (Quila) v Secretary of State for the Home Department* [2011] UKSC 45 at [61]; Lord Bingham in *R (SB) v Denbigh High School* [2006] UKHL 15 at [29], Lord Hoffmann at [68]; see discussion in immigration context at [50]–[59] of *Khairdin, R (on the application of) v Secretary of State for the Home Department* (NIA 2002: Part 5A) (IJR) [2014] UKUT 566 (IAC).
6 *Pham v Secretary of State for the Home Department* [2015] UKSC 19 following *Kennedy v Charity Commission* [2014] UKSC 20.
7 Lord Sumption in *Pham* (above) at [106] and [109].

8.141 When reviewing the SSHD's decision as to whether further representations constitute a fresh asylum or human rights claim, the court's supervisory role is fulfilled by a *Wednesbury* approach, albeit tempered by the demands of anxious scrutiny and bearing in mind that the SSHD must predict the response of a hypothetical immigration judge to the case.[1] Where the challenge is to certification on 'clearly unfounded' grounds,[2] 'the reviewing court must ask itself essentially the questions which would have to be answered by an [immigration judge]';[3] and 'If on at least one legitimate view of the facts or the law the claim may succeed, the claim will not be clearly unfounded':[4] 'If any reasonable doubt exists as to whether the claim may succeed then it is not clearly unfounded.'[5] A further reason for intensive review in a clearly unfounded case is that 'in making a certification decision the Home Secretary acts as judge in his own cause, because to certify a claim when rejecting it is to render an appeal against the rejection extremely difficult to pursue ... [which calls] for close judicial scrutiny.'[6] Disputes as to the primary facts make it more likely that a claim is not clearly unfounded.[7] There is not a great difference between the tests for judicial review of 'clearly unfounded' certificates as opposed to decisions on purported fresh asylum claims.[8] In general, 'Asylum decisions are of such moment that only the highest standards of fairness will suffice'.[9]

1   HC 395 at r 353; Buxton LJ in *WM (DRC) v Secretary of State for the Home Department* [2006] EWCA Civ 1495 at [11], [16]–[19]; Laws LJ in *TK v Secretary of State for the Home Department* [2009] EWCA Civ 1550 at [9] approved and clarified as the correct test by Maurice Kay LJ in *MN (Tanzania), R (on the application of) v Secretary of State for the Home Department* [2011] EWCA Civ 193 at [15]; the difference between the approaches to r 353 and clearly unfounded certificates may be marginal: Beatson J in *Toufighy, R (on the application of) v Secretary of State for the Home Department* [2012] EWHC 3004 (Admin); see Carnwath LJ in *R (YH) v Secretary of State for the Home Department* [2010] EWCA Civ 116 at [22]–[24] for discussion of the 'anxious scrutiny' principle.
2   Both under NIAA 2002, s 94 and A&I(TC)A 2004, Sch 3.
3   Lord Bingham in *Razgar v Secretary of State for the Home Department* [2004] AC 368 at [17]; Carnwath LJ in *YH* (above) at [18]–[21].
4   Lord Phillips in *R (L) v Secretary of State for the Home Department* [2003] EWCA Civ 25 at [58]; which is also essentially the test endorsed by Lord Hodge in *FNG, Petitioner* [2008] CSOH 22 and cited by Lord Hope in *ZT (Kosovo) v Secretary of State for the Home Department* [2009] UKHL 6 at [53]–[54].
5   Lord Phillips in *ZT (Kosovo)* (above) at [23]; see further *ZL v Secretary of State for the Home Department and Lord Chancellor's Department* [2003] EWCA Civ 25 at [57].
6   Sedley LJ in *QY (China) (R on the application of) v Secretary of State for the Home Department* [2009] EWCA Civ 680.
7   Carnwath LJ in *YH* (above) at [19].
8   Laws LJ in *AK (Sri Lanka), R (on the application of) v Secretary of State for the Home Department* [2009] EWCA Civ 447 at [33]–[34]; Lord Brown in *Z T (Kosovo)* (above) at [67], [72], Lord Neuberger at [81], though cf Lord Carswell at [62], Lord Hope at [27]; Maurice Kay LJ in *MN (Tanzania)* (above) at [16].
9   *R v Secretary of State, ex parte Thirukumar* [1989] Imm AR 402, at 414, per Bingham LJ.

Intensity of review: age assessment, sponsor licences, nationality and the general refusal reasons

8.142   Where the age of a child is to be assessed on a judicial review application, the court should evaluate the evidence for itself, rather than gauging the matter only through the lens of public law ('the question whether a person is a "child" is a different kind of question. There is a right or a wrong answer'[1]), though there may be cases where the question should, because of some procedural failing, be remitted to the local authority.[2] The court makes its decision without placing a burden of proof on either party and on the standard of the balance of probabilities.[3] In challenges to the suspension or withdrawal of sponsor licences, the court will take account of the fact that the SSHD has an expertise that includes an understanding of the policy guidelines and their application, and that the Home Office will police the grant of a high level of responsibility to a sponsor carefully,[4] albeit that the usual public law challenges, including principles of fairness which may extend beyond the safeguards mentioned in Home Office policy,[5] are nevertheless available.[6] Where a nationality decision involves the exercise of some discretion, the review will be on conventional public law grounds, but where a person's entitlement to British citizenship is a question of right, it will be for the courts to determine the question, making the appropriate declaration following a trial on the evidence if his claim is disputed ('the court will itself resolve any issues of fact as well as any issues of law'): whether the adverse decision is made by the SSHD or the Passport Office.[7] Questions involving the general refusal reasons must normally be determined by the court itself, these being essentially matters of precedent fact upon which the burden of proof lies on the SSHD[8] bearing in mind that 'an allegation of forgery needs to be established to a high degree of proof, by the person making the allegation'.[9] As the tribunal put it in *NA*:[10]

'for the respondent to satisfy us he has discharged the burden of proof on him on the balance of probabilities he would, in the context of this type of case, need to furnish evidence of sufficient strength and quality and he (and the Tribunal) would need to subject it to a "critical", "anxious" and "heightened" scrutiny.'

1   Baroness Hale in *R (A and M) v Croydon and Lambert Borough Councils* [2009] UKSC 8 at [27], Lord Hope at [51]; the Master of the Rolls in *R (K) v Birmingham City Council* [2012] EWCA Civ 1432 at [50]–[52].
2   Beatson J in *MWA, R (on the application of) v Secretary of State for the Home Department* [2011] EWHC 3488 (Admin) at [5].
3   Pitchford LJ in *R (C J) v Cardiff County Council)* [2011] EWCA Civ 1590 at [22]–[23].
4   eg McGowan J in *London St Andrews College v Secretary of State for the Home Department* [2014] EWHC 4328 (Admin) at [18].
5   Wyn Williams J in *New London College Ltd, R (on the application of) v Secretary of State for the Home Department* [2011] EWHC 856 (Admin) at [60].
6   Wyn Williams J in *New London College Ltd* (above) at [93]–[94].
7   Keene LJ in *Harrison v Secretary of State for the Home Department* [2003] EWCA Civ 432 at [31]–[34].
8   Lord Fraser in *R v Secretary of State for the Home Department, ex parte Khawaja* [1984] IAC 74 at 97E; Slade J in *Palisetty v Secretary of State for the Home Department* [2014] EWHC 2473 (QB) at [9]–[13]; Jay J in *Giri, R (on the application of) v Secretary of State for the Home Department* [2014] EWHC 1832 (Admin) at [28].
9   *RP (proof of forgery) Nigeria* [2006] UKAIT 00086 at [14]; see further *JC (Part 9 HC 395 – burden of proof) China* [2007] UKAIT 00027 at [10]–[11]; *A v Secretary of State for the Home Department* [2010] EWCA Civ 773, Rix LJ at [76]; *Ozhogina and Tarasova (deception within para 320(7B) – nannies) Russia/Russian Federation* [2011] UKUT 197 (IAC); *Shen (paper appeals; proving dishonesty)* [2014] UKUT 236 (IAC); *Ahmed (general grounds of refusal – material non-disclosure) Pakistan* [2011] UKUT 351 (IAC).

10   *NA (Cambridge College of Learning) Pakistan* [2009] UKAIT 00031 at [101] cited and followed by the UT in *Khalid (Ealing, West London and Hammersmith College) Pakistan* [2011] UKUT 295 (IAC): these cases recognised that following Lord Hoffman in *Re B (children)* [2008] UKHL 35 at [13] there was but a single standard of proof in civil proceedings albeit that the cogency of the evidence required to discharge it might vary with the issues at stake.

Chapter 9

Administrative review and post-decision representations

9.1 There are a number of routes by which reconsideration of a decision may be sought. These are:

- Out-of-country cases–

    - an application for administrative review against a refusal of entry clearance in a points-based system case, where the applicant is outside the United Kingdom;

    - lodging an appeal against refusal of entry clearance, as this will automatically (subject only to occasional resource constraints) result in a review of the decision by an Entry Clearance Manager;

    - a Pre Action Protocol letter threatening judicial review proceedings.

- 'In country' cases–

    - an application for administrative review under the Immigration Rules at Appendix AR;

    - an application for reconsideration made under the Home Office policy 'Reconsideration requests';

    - a Pre Action Protocol letter threatening judicial review proceedings;

    - discretionary reconsideration.

OUT-OF-COUNTRY CASES: ENTRY CLEARANCE AND ADMINISTRATIVE REVIEW

9.2 For some years administrative review out of country was available only for those applicants who have applied for entry clearance to come to the UK and remain abroad, and applied to work or study in the UK under Tiers 1, 2, 4 or 5 of the points-based system. The governing material comprised relatively informal policy material and the form itself, the relevant documents being the application form 'Administrative review request notice'

517

and its associated Guidance Notes (March 2009), the online guidance 'Ask for a visa administrative review' and the Policy Document 'Administrative review under the points-based system' (1 April 2008). By the time this book is published it will have become historic and so we do not deal with it in any further detail.

9.3   As from 6 April 2015,[1] administrative review becomes more generally available in entry clearance cases and arises under the Immigration Rules rather than under policy documents. Appendix AR includes specific provisions headed 'Administrative review overseas'. Eligible decisions[2] are entry clearance decisions made *under the Rules* (excluding short-term students under Part 3 of the Rules and visitors) or where human rights applications and claims are made relying on the Rules for family members of HM Forces, or under Part 8 of the Rules or Appendix FM for family members more generally, or where asylum is sought, or where the application relies on the Turkish Association Agreement.[3] In these scenarios 'the appropriate remedy is an appeal under section 82 of the Nationality, Immigration and Asylum Act 2002 rather than an application for administrative review'.[4] Applications must be made whilst the applicant remains abroad.[5] Notice of a decision on an administrative review application is deemed to have been received, unless the contrary is shown, on the 28th day after it was posted.[6]

1   See implementation provisions of HC 1025.
2   Immigration Rules, HC 395, Appendix AR, para AR5.1.
3   Immigration Rules, HC 395, Appendix AR, para AR5.2(a), (b).
4   Immigration Rules, HC 395, Appendix AR, para AR5.2(a).
5   Immigration Rules, HC 395, para 34Q(c).
6   Immigration Rules, HC 395, para 34R(4)(b).

OUT-OF-COUNTRY CASES: ENTRY CLEARANCE MANAGER REVIEW

9.4   There is a general practice by which grounds of appeal submitted against adverse decisions that carry the right of appeal are reviewed by Entry Clearance Managers. The procedure is set out in the guidance note 'ECM appeal review'.[1] This explains:

'An ECM review is required for all decisions refused with a full right of appeal (FRA). The ECM must assess whether the appellant has satisfactorily addressed the reasons for refusal. If the appellant has successfully addressed all the points of refusal the decision should be overturned and a visa issued. If the ECM concludes the appellant has failed to address the reasons for refusal a written statement detailing why the decision is being upheld must be provided.'

1   APL07; version accessed published 10 October 2011.

9.5   The Entry Clearance Manager is to review not only the decision but also the supporting documentation,[1] though only that relevant to the date of decision: where new evidence is supplied on the appeal that might lead to a future application's success, the review should identify this.[2] Where the decision is overturned the entry clearance post should write to the applicant within ten working days requesting that he provides his passport for endorsement of the appropriate visa.[3] Where refusal is maintained, clear reasons must be given, not standard paragraphs of pro forma text.[4] The process is not always satisfactory: the independent inspector wrote in one report that it was 'disappointing to find poor quality decision-making in 144 cases where an ECM review had supposedly been carried out'.[5] The 2014 Rules require that, when defending a decision against which an appeal is lodged, the respondent provides a statement of whether he opposes the appellant's case and his grounds for so doing.[6]

1   APL07, para 3.
2   APL07, paras 3, 5.1.
3   APL07, para 3.
4   APL07, para 3.
5   John Vine CBE QPM Independent Chief Inspector of the UK Border Agency, *Entry Clearance Decision-Making: A Global Review* (December 2010–June 2011), noting this represented a third of all cases in the survey.
6   Tribunal Procedure (First-tier Tribunal) (Immigration and Asylum Chamber) Rules 2014, SI 2014/2604, r 23.

ADMINISTRATIVE REVIEW UNDER THE IMMIGRATION RULES

9.6   Relevant materials for understanding this form of review are:

● Immigration Rules, paras 34M–34Y;

● Immigration Rules, Appendix AR;

● Administrative Review Statement of Intent;

● Policy Document 'Administrative Review, Version 1.0' (valid from 28 November 2014);

● the online guidance;

● the form.[1]

1   Available at https://eforms.homeoffice.gov.uk/test/UKVI_Admin_Review_Guidance.ofml.

9.7   One important feature of the remedy is that it benefits from the statutory extension of leave provided for under IA 1971, in that an 'in time' application for further leave to remain will enjoy an extension of leave, not only during the currency of the application pending a decision upon it, but additionally for such time as an administrative review of the decision on the application for variation could be sought, or is pending.[1] There is a fee of £80 for the service: it is the same whether the application is made in relation to a single decision, or 'two (or more) decisions relating to applications or claims made by a main applicant and a dependant (or dependants) of that person'.[2] No further fee is payable where the original reasons are amended and a further application for review is made.[3] The fee will be refunded if the application succeeds.[4] The fee may be waived or reduced at the discretion of the Secretary of State.[5] According to the Home Office's statement of intent, some 60% of appeals against 'in-country' points-based refusals succeeded because of caseworking error.[6] Given the significantly lower rate of correcting entry clearance decisions cited above in a Freedom of Information request, there may be concerns as to the efficacy of administrative review as opposed to independent judicial scrutiny of individual decisions.

1   IA 1971, s 3C(2)(d).
2   Immigration and Nationality (Cost Recovery Fees) Regulations 2014, SI 2014/581, Sch 6, para 3.
3   SI 2014/581, Sch 6, para 3(3).
4   SI 2014/581, Sch 6, para 3(4).
5   SI 2014/581, Sch 6, para 3(5).
6   Statement of Intent, para 15.

ADMINISTRATIVE REVIEW FROM WITHIN THE UNITED KINGDOM UNDER THE IMMIGRATION RULES

9.8   There is a detailed procedure for administrative review within the United Kingdom under the Immigration Rules. Any decision eligible for such review (save for grants of leave)[1] must be accompanied by a statement of reasons for the decision to which it relates, together with information on the means and time limits for applying.[2] An application may only be made on a dependant's behalf where he was a dependent on the application leading to the decision challenged, or a dependent upon the application leading to the leave now being cancelled.[3] The notice is deemed to have been received 'unless the contrary is shown' on the second working day after the day on which it was posted.[4] Only one application may be made for administrative review unless the result of the refusal is an upholding of the original decision combined with the provision of different or additional reasons for refusal.[5] The application must be made under the provisions set out in the Rules: this requires the submission of an application online (the application is only 'made' online if the relevant online process is 'completed')[6] or by post (there is no provision for applications by fax),[7] in either case paying the specified fee, filling in mandatory sections of the form and providing any mandatory documents (if the form is completed online then documents may be submitted online or must otherwise follow by post within seven working days of the form's submission),[8] and using (and signing and sending to specified address)[9] the appropriate form in a postal application,[10] albeit with allowance being made for an application being made on an out-of-date form within 21 days of its introduction.[11] The time limit for making an application is:[12]

- non-detained cases – no more than 14 calendar days after receipt of notice of the eligible decision;

- detained cases (in Immigration Act detention) – no more than seven calendar days receipt of notice of the eligible decision;

- overseas applicants – no more than 28 calendar days after receipt of notice of the eligible decision;

- in cases where administrative review arises in relation to a grant of leave – no more than 14 calendar days after receipt of notice of the biometric document stating the conditions and length of leave.

1   Immigration Rules, HC 395, para 34L(2).
2   Immigration Rules, HC 395, para 34L(1).
3   Immigration Rules, HC 395, para 34S.
4   Immigration Rules, HC 395, para 34R(4).
5   Immigration Rules, HC 395, para 34N), read with Appendix AR, para AR2.2(d).
6   Immigration Rules, HC 395, para 34U(2).
7   Letter of 16 October 2014 from the Home Office Legal Strategy Team to the Immigration Law Practitioners' Association (ILPA), para 5.
8   Immigration Rules, HC 395, para 34U(3)(c).
9   Immigration Rules, HC 395, para 34V(2)(d), (f).
10   Immigration Rules, HC 395, para 34Y.
11   Immigration Rules, HC 395, para 34O, read with rr 34U (online applications) and 34V (postal ones).
12   Immigration Rules, HC 395, para 34R(1).

9.9   Where the right to administrative review arises because of the addition of reasons to an earlier refusal, time runs as if the new administrative review was itself the eligible decision (ie the same time periods as just specified run again).[1] There is scope for the Secretary of State to accept an application out of time if satisfied that it would be 'unjust not to waive the time limit and the application was made as soon as reasonably practicable';[2] this may include the situation where an application is resubmitted late having been previously rejected as invalid.[3] An application will be invalid if not made in accordance with the requirements of the Rules.[4]

1   Immigration Rules, HC 395, para 34R(2).
2   Immigration Rules, HC 395, para 34R(3).
3   Letter of 16 October 2014 from the Home Office Legal Strategy Team to the ILPA, para 7.
4   Immigration Rules, HC 395, para 34M, referencing rr 34N–34S.

9.10   There are deeming provisions addressing when an application is made:[1]

- on the marked day of posting, if sent by post;

9.11 *Administrative review and post-decision representations*

- on the date of delivery, if sent by courier;

- on the date it is submitted if made online.

1   Immigration Rules, HC 395, para 34W.

9.11   The application must be made whilst the applicant is in the United Kingdom regarding decisions in relation to 'in-country' applications and those decisions made on a person's arrival here.[1] If the applicant requests his passport's return for the purposes of travel abroad pending the application's resolution, in relation to those review applications that can only be made 'in-country', then it will be treated as withdrawn.[2] Those applications that can only be made from within the country will also be treated as withdrawn if the applicant goes abroad.[3] The application may also be withdrawn by expressly writing to the Home Office at the address provided for this purpose online.[4]

1   Immigration Rules, HC 395, para 34Q(a), (b).
2   Immigration Rules, HC 395, para 34X(1).
3   Immigration Rules, HC 395, para 34X(2).
4   Immigration Rules, HC 395, para 34X(3).

9.12   Administrative review under the Rules is available in relation to an *eligible decision* for *case working error*.[1] Eligible decisions have been brought into the scope of the process in stages: thus on 28 October 2014 the first tranche of cases were brought in (Tier 4 migrants and their dependent family members),[2] with further classes of application introduced on 2 March 2015 (Tier 1, Tier 2 and Tier 5 migrants)[3] and then from 6 April 2015:

- all applications for leave to remain, save for visitors and those involving a patent human rights application under the routes of long residence, private life, partner and child of Armed Forces, family members under Appendix FM (domestic violence and bereavement aside) and Part 8 of the Rules (points-based system cases aside), and asylum;

- all applications for leave to remain made under the Turkish Association Agreement.[4]

1   Immigration Rules, HC 395, Appendix AR, paras 2.1 and 3.1.
2   Via Immigration Act 2014 (Commencement No 3, Transitional and Saving Provisions) Order 2014, SI 2014/2771.
3   Via Immigration Act 2014 (Commencement No 4, Transitional and Saving Provisions and Amendment) Order 2015, SI 2015/371.
4   Immigration Rules, HC 395, Appendix AR, para 3.2.

9.13   There will be no consideration of any entitlement to leave to remain on any other basis and administrative review is not to be construed as the marking of an application for leave, nor the variation of one, nor the making of a protection or human rights claim.[1] An otherwise eligible decision becomes ineligible for administrative review where an applicant has been given notice of liability to removal in the preceding six months.[2]

1   Immigration Rules, HC 395, Appendix AR, para 2.6; Statement of Intent, para 4.
2   Immigration Rules, HC 395, Appendix AR, para 3.4.

9.14   Review may be sought of both refusals of leave, and of the conditions and length of leave actually granted.[1] The grounds for review are where the original decision maker:

(a)   was incorrect to refuse an application on the basis of the general refusal reasons as to misrepresentation and overstaying, or to cancel leave to enter which was in force;[2]

(b)   was incorrect to refuse an application on the basis that the date of application was beyond a time limit in the Rules;

(c)   applied the Immigration Rules incorrectly;

(d)   failed to apply the SSHD's relevant published policy and guidance in relation to the application.[3]

1   Immigration Rules, HC 395, Appendix AR, para AR3.3.
2   Immigration Rules, HC 395, Appendix AR, para AR3.3, referencing rr 320(7A) and (7B) and 322(1A).
3   Immigration Rules, HC 395, Appendix AR, para AR2.11.

9.15   These grounds replaced those extant from October 2014 until April 2015 though in general the later set appear to simply represent a more concise expression of the earlier ones, save for the abandonment of a standard of review on credibility issues which was based on unreasonableness rather than correctness.[1] Additionally an error as to the period or conditions of leave is reviewable where it relates to a grant of leave to remain or residence under the Turkish Association Agreement.[2] It is possible to seek administrative review on grounds that will not lead to a different outcome overall, but simply to correct an allegation of fraud, in order to prevent a negative outcome on future applications under the general refusal reasons.[3] Where the decision is made in the control zone (as defined by various instruments), there may be no application until the applicant has left or been removed from that zone.[4]

1   Immigration Rules, HC 395, Appendix AR, para 3.4(g), as in force before 6 October 2015.
2   Immigration Rules, HC 395, Appendix AR, para AR2.12.
3   Immigration Rules, HC 395, Appendix AR, para 2.2(c); letter of 16 October 2014 from the Home Office Legal Strategy Team to ILPA, para 9.
4   Immigration Rules, HC 395, Appendix AR, paras AR1.1 and AR4.3.

9.16   The only evidence that will be considered is that which was before the original decision maker, unless material is submitted to demonstrate the following forms of caseworking error under para AR2.11(a) and (b): [1]

●   where the decision was based on the general refusal reasons or was a cancellation of leave to enter or remain;

●   where the refusal was based on a mistake as to the application being made beyond a permissible time limit in the rules.

Where one of these forms of error is identified by the applicant, the reviewer may contact the applicant or his representative in writing to request relevant evidence, which must then be received within seven working days of the request being made.[2]

1   Immigration Rules, HC 395, Appendix AR, para 2.4.
2   Immigration Rules, HC 395, Appendix AR, para 2.5.

9.17   The outcome of the application may be that:[1]

- the review succeeds and the decision is withdrawn;

- the review fails and the decision remains in force with all reasons maintained;

- the review fails and the decision remains in force with one or more reasons withdrawn;

- the review fails and the decision remains in force with different or additional reasons to those previously specified.

The latter scenario is the only one where there will be a prospect of a further application for administrative review.[2]

1   Immigration Rules, HC 395, Appendix AR, para 2.2.
2   Immigration Rules, HC 395, para 34N(1) and (2), read with Appendix AR, para AR2.2(d).

RECONSIDERATION REQUESTS

9.18   It is open to a migrant dissatisfied with a decision on his case to request a reconsideration. At the time of writing, the relevant Home Office policy is entitled simply 'Reconsiderations'[1] and has been extensively rewritten from earlier incarnations in order to bring it into line with the system of administrative review. The policy explains that it covers requests in relation to:

- immigration decisions for limited or indefinite leave to remain made by postal application, or at a public enquiry office;

- transfers of conditions;

- no time limit applications (ie applications for a passport stamp confirming settlement rights);

- Turkish European Community Association Agreement applications (ECAA).

1   'Reconsiderations, Version 9.0' (valid from 9 April 2015).

9.19   It does not apply to applications for entry clearance, or made in relation to asylum and ECHR, Art 3 or on EEA grounds, nor to decisions in relation to nationality, those made at port, or in relation to curtailment or enforcement decisions, or responding to representations against removal made to a local immigration team, or involving Bulgarian and Romanian nationals. The policy makes it clear that it does not see reconsideration as arising from any legal obligation: in general migrants refused with a right of appeal should exercise that remedy, and those without a right of appeal should seek judicial review or make a further application. The time limit for an application is 14 working days from the deemed date of receipt (described as being two working days from postage unless there is evidence that it was received later), for all decisions made on or after 6 April 2015, unless there are exceptional reasons justifying the delay and the request was made as soon as reasonably practicable. Requests will lapse where the migrant is subsequently granted leave in another category, departs the country where his leave has expired or lapsed, been removed, or unsuccessfully appealed or sought judicial review. Unlike administrative review applications within the Immigration Rules, reconsideration requests do not provide any extension of leave to remain under IA 1971, s 3C, nor, warns the policy, does it prevent removal.

9.20 Under the 'Reconsiderations' policy, the Home Office will normally only reconsider applications, if made in writing and where:

- there is no right of administrative review against the decision;

- the reconsideration request was made on or after 13 November 2012, it relates to a granted application, and the applicant believes the type of leave granted or the expiry date of the leave is incorrect;

- the reconsideration request was made on or after 13 November 2012, it relates to a refused application and the applicant is either–

  – providing new evidence to prove the date of application,

  – providing new evidence that documents submitted with the application are genuine, or

  – identifying relevant material which was not available to the caseworker but was received by the Home Office before the decision date;

- the reconsideration is a legacy request submitted before 13 November 2012, the case has not been resolved one way or another by alternative remedies such as appeal and judicial review, and there are still reasons to reconsider the decision (notably the policy explains that whereas generally reconsiderations focus only on proof of date of application, genuine documents and overlooked material which impact upon the decision outcome and/or any subsequent appeal rights, in a legacy case reconsideration must extend to whether the decision accorded with the relevant Rules, policies, guidance, instructions and statutory duties such as that under BCIA 2009, s 55 to secure child welfare);

- the reconsideration request is about a case affected by the *Alvi* judgment.[1]

1   *R (Alvi) v Secretary of State for the Home Department* [2012] UKSC 33.

9.21   Within the limits of reconsideration, it is necessary for the request to be in writing, explaining why it is incorrect or inconsistent with existing policy, for failing to take account of, or misinterpreting, relevant evidence, law, policy or guidance. Any errors identified during the reconsideration process beyond those raised by the applicant should be addressed by the new decision maker. If following the reconsideration it is determined that the decision was 'wholly or mainly correct' but some deficiencies were spotted requiring the addition of further reasons, or the wrong notification template or inaccurate wording was used, then a supplementary refusal letter should be written and the original date of decision maintained. If reconsideration shows that the application should have been refused for other reasons, then the original decision should be withdrawn and a new notice of decision issued, which will reinstate any statutorily extended leave that the prior decision purported to interrupt. There is an express power to reconsider 'no recourse to public funds' conditions on leave to remain,

> 'if an applicant provided information and evidence which relates to the financial circumstances with their application for leave to remain to support a claim that they are destitute or that there are compelling reasons which relate to the welfare of a child of a parent in receipt of a very low income, but the applicant thinks a casework error has been made in assessing this against the policy on when to allow recourse to public funds.'

9.22   In a case where casework error is established, any further information provided with the reconsideration request will be considered. However, where fresh information is otherwise provided as to the propriety of permitting recourse to public funds and no casework error is alleged, this should be made not via the 'Reconsiderations' policy but via a 'Request for a change of conditions of leave granted on the basis of family or private life'.[1]

1   www.gov.uk/government/uploads/system/uploads/attachment_data/file/286132/change-condition.pdf.

PRE ACTION PROTOCOL LETTERS

9.23   The restricted ambit of reconsideration arising within the 'Reconsiderations' policy does not apply to cases where a Pre Action Protocol letter or letter before claim is written. In these cases the defendant must, under the standard format to the Pre Action Protocol,[1] explain whether the issue in question is conceded in part, or in full, or will be contested. This may in practice provoke a degree of reconsideration in a particular case. We deal further with Pre Action Protocol letters in Chapter 8.[2]

1   At Annex B.
2   See **8.86** *et seq* above.

DISCRETIONARY RECONSIDERATION

9.24   There is a general duty on administrative decision makers to consider exercising their discretion outside the ambit of stated claim.[1] This is recognised in the 'Reconsiderations' policy by phrases such as 'The Home Office will normally only reconsider applications'. Additionally the Civil Service Code[2] explains that there is a duty to take decisions on the merits of the case and not to ignore inconvenient facts or relevant considerations when providing advice or making decisions. This suggests that a serious error, once drawn to the attention of a decision maker, should not go unremedied (particularly given an applicant and the public should not be forced to enter into expensive legal proceedings which are unnecessary). These considerations may in an appropriate and exceptional case require that reconsideration is countenanced outside the terms of the policy. One example is the discretion long recognised by the SSHD to consider whether an individual has been failed by his legal representatives.[3] Another is that the Immigration Rules addressing the points-based system and Appendix FM contain specific procedural (and non-exhaustive) safeguards where an applicant has omitted documents through innocent error, as where some of the documents in a sequence have been omitted, a document is in the wrong format or is a copy and not an original document, or where a document does not contain all of the specified information, in which case the relevant decision maker may contact the applicant or his representative in writing, and request the correct documents, unless its availability would make no decision to the outcome of the application because of other deficiencies.[4] Where this safeguard has been overlooked, a discretionary reconsideration might be appropriate.

1   *British Oxygen Company Ltd v Minister of Technology* [1971] AC 610, per Lord Reid at 625C.
2   Statutory guidance of March 2015.
3   See **8.135**, fn 4 above.
4   Immigration Rules, HC 395, para 245AA and Appendix FM-SE, para D.

Index